ETHICS AND VALUES IN PSYCHOTHERAPY

ETHICS AND VALUES IN PSYCHOTHERAPY

A Guidebook

Edited by

MAX ROSENBAUM

THE FREE PRESS
A Division of Macmillan Publishing Co., Inc.
NEW YORK

Collier Macmillan Publishers
LONDON

THE FREE PRESS
A Division of Macmillan Publishing Co., Inc.
866 Third Avenue, New York, N.Y. 10022

Collier Macmillan Canada, Inc.

Library of Congress Catalog Card Number: 81-67162

Printed in the United States of America

printing number
1 2 3 4 5 6 7 8 9 10

Library of Congress Cataloging in Publication Data
Main entry under title:

Ethics and values in psychotherapy.

   Includes index.
   1. Psychotherapy ethics. I. Rosenbaum, Max
[DNLM: 1. Ethics, Medical. 2. Psychotherapy. WM 62
E83]
RC455.2.E8E835   174'.2   81-67162
ISBN 0-02-927090-1   AACR2

To my father, whose vision of a better life
and better world I shall always cherish

To my wife, Belle, whose honesty, integrity,
and loyalty have been with me through the years

Contents

PART IV   Ethics Beyond Private Practice

Appendixes

Preface

This book was stimulated by many discussions with colleagues, patients, scientists, theologians, editors, and ongoing discussions with my wife and children.

After over three decades of practice, I observed that many things I had taken for granted about the fabric of American society could no longer be taken for granted. The United States is the only country in which the income tax system is based upon the basic honesty of its people. Yet current concerns in business and major industry center on issues such as the morality and honesty of the American public. There is no longer much difference among the concerns of all members of the American society, even if we all have the tendency to lock into separate networks where, for example, lawyers talk to other lawyers, or psychologists talk only to other psychologists, or professional athletes talk to other athletes.

Beyond the horror stories that one hears or observes after many years of practice—the cases where patients simply get poor or inept professional services—there are the more tragic cases of patients who are exposed to venal or malicious behavior from people who represent themselves as trained professionals. Underneath all of this, I observed that many professionals had simply not thought about the larger issues involved in the practice of psychotherapy. This was borne out when I invited friends and colleagues who are considered major figures in the field of psychology or psychiatry to participate in my project. They reacted for the most part with anxiety and confusion. These honorable people, while aware of what they believed to be right or wrong, had great difficulty in setting this down in a form that would enable other professionals to profit from their experiences. The phrase, "It's a great idea. A book that's long overdue," was heard again and again, but the desire to do the job seemed lacking. I could not explain away all of this as writer's block or the burden and pressures of other activities. Many of the contributors to this volume said quite bluntly, "It's the hardest job I ever did." In several cases, prospective contributors gave up the task in despair. I am especially grateful to the contributors for having set forth their experiences and beliefs.

One contributor, president of a major professional society, described to me a variety of practices in which his membership engaged that he could neither understand nor accept. In one instance, members would call up the executive director of the organization and ask, "What's the *in thing* these days?" in order that they might have this *in thing* listed under their areas of expertise or supposed proficiency.

Members of the ministry have occasionally told me that religious ethics is simply the statement of what people know inherently to be true. But those of us who believe in the function of the unconscious realize that this is far too simple a statement. Over two thousand years ago, in *The Bacchae,* Euripides depicted the tragedies that would ensue when people, acting out of good faith, do not balance the hedonistic and the rational.

In a time that has witnessed Auschwitz, it is absurd to accept good faith as the answer to life's problems, especially when we hear daily reports of the barbarism that man has visited upon his fellow man. The idea implied by the line in "Gee, Officer Krupke," in the musical *West Side Story,* "I'm depraved on account of I'm deprived," is an equally insufficient answer. Plato believed that evil was born out of ignorance, which is too simple an answer when we consider the intellectual level of the people who served and conspired with the Nazis. Yet Plato equated truth with goodness and was concerned with those who willfully ignore the truth. In the *Republic* and the *Dialogues,* he is concerned with reason as the force that controls passion.

In the world that Plato described in his *Republic* the rulers must be philosophers. The citizens are divided "into three classes: the common people, the soldiers, and the guardians. The last alone, are to have political power . . . they are to be chosen by the legislator; after that, they will usually succeed by heredity . . . (Russell, 1972, p. 108). "In the main Plato is concerned only with the guardians, who are to be a class apart, like the Jesuits in old Paraguay, the ecclesiastics in the state of the Church until 1870, and the Communist Party in the U.S.S.R. at the present day" (p. 109). "What is a philosopher . . . a philosopher is a lover of wisdom . . . the philosopher is a man who loves the 'vision of truth.'" (p. 120). "The world of the intellect is distinguished from the world of the senses . . ." (p. 124).

Plato, of course, was an antidemocratic philosopher since he believed that the ruling class represented reason and the lower class represented passion, the source of evil. The army stood as guardian between ruling class and lower class. The prophets of Judaism did not accept the Hellenistic view; they wrote and spoke of the passion for righteousness and, indeed, of the wisdom of the heart. Freud believed that reason was the charioteer that controlled passion.

So, after the passage of more time than I thought would be required when I first envisioned this project, with deaths, illnesses, and a variety of other tragedies befalling contributors, this book has come to the reader. The test of a good sermon is reputed to be whether it leaves the listener thinking. Perhaps this is not such a bad model for this book. It is not intended to preach but to stimulate thought and concern so that nothing is taken for granted.

REFERENCE

RUSSELL, B. *A history of Western philosophy*. New York: Simon & Schuster (Touchstone), 1972.

About the Contributors

Milton M. Berger received his M.D. from Middlesex (now Brandeis) University in 1941. He is director of education and training, South Beach Psychiatric Center; clinical associate professor of psychiatry, Downstate Medical Center; chairman and founder, Video Committee, American Psychiatric Association, 1970–1979; and president, American Group Psychotherapy Association, 1960–1962. Dr. Berger is the author of *Working with People Called Patients* and editor of *Videotape Techniques in Psychiatric Training and Treatment.* He is the winner of 12 awards for videotape productions at the International Film and Television Festival of New York.

Morton Berger currently serves as dean of the Ferkauf Graduate School of Yeshiva University and also of the University's School of Professional Psychology, as well as being the university dean of behavioral and social sciences. A former executive secretary to the New York State Board for Psychology, he has also served as chief psychologist for Albany County Mental Health, chief psychologist of the outpatient department of the Veterans Administration Hospital, and a psychologist in private practice. He is a past president of the American Association of State Psychology Boards. Dr. Berger received his Doctorate in psychology from the University of Massachusetts in 1963.

Peter G. Bourne received his M.D. from Emory University in 1962, and in 1969 an M.A. in anthropology from Stanford University, where he also did a residency in psychiatry. He is presently an assistant secretary general with the United Nations Development Programme in charge of the International Drinking Water Supply and Sanitation Decade, and previously served in the White House as special assistant for health issues to President Carter. He is the author of more than 100 articles and 6 books, including *Men, Stress and Vietnam* and *Alcoholism: Progress in Research and Treatment.* He is a member of the faculties of Harvard Medical School and St. George's Medical School, Grenada.

Joseph A. Braun received his Ph.D. in clinical psychology from Fordham University and was trained as psychoanalyst. He is a member of the faculty at the New Jersey Institute for Training in Psychoanalysis and is engaged in private practice.

Fred Brown is professor emeritus of psychiatry (psychology) of the Mount Sinai School of Medicine of CUNY and director emeritus of the division of psychology, department of psychiatry of the Mount Sinai Hospital, New York City. He obtained his doctorate at the Ohio State University under H. H. Goddard, is a recipient of the Carl Murchison Award of the *Journal of Psychology,* and is engaged in the private practice of psychodiagnosis in addition to serving as diagnostic consultant to various agencies.

Gordon F. Derner received his Ph.D. from Columbia University in 1950. He is dean and professor of psychology, Institute of Advanced Psychological Studies, Adelphi University; codirector, Institute of Advanced Psychological Studies-Franklin General Hospital, Biofeedback Laboratory and Clinic; president of the Division of Psychoanalysis, American Psychological Association; and treasurer of the Biofeedback Society of America. Recipient of the Distinguished Professional Award, Division of Psychotherapy, American Psychological Association, 1976; fellow, Royal Society of Health (London); diplomate in clinical psychology, American Board of Professional Psychology, and in clinical hypnosis, American Board of Psychological Hypnosis, his publications include *Handbook of Clinical Psychology* (associate editor); *International Encyclopedia of Psychiatry, Psychology, Psychoanalysis and Neurology* (associate editor); and *Aspects of the Psychology of the Tuberculous.*

James F. Drane received his Ph.D. from the University of Madrid in 1964. During 1976–1977 he studied at the Menninger School of Psychiatry, and presently is visiting research scholar at the Kennedy Institute for Bioethics at Georgetown University. He is professor of philosophy at Edinboro College and on the staff of Warren State Hospital (Pennsylvania). In 1976 he was named to the distinguished teaching chair. Recent books include *Religion and Ethics, The Possibility of God, A New American Reformation,* and *Authority and Institution.*

Nina D. Fieldsteel was born and educated in New York. After graduate work at Columbia University, she had postdoctoral training at Postgraduate Center for Mental Health. At present she is on the faculty of the Postgraduate Center and is a senior supervisor. For five years until 1976 she was coordinator of the Family Therapy program at Postgraduate Center. She was editor of *Group,* the journal of the Eastern Group Psychotherapy Association, for five years.

Stephen G. Flanagan received his Ph.D. in clinical psychology from Syracuse University in 1975. He is currently assistant research psychologist, UCLA School of Medicine, and director of the Clinical Training Team, Developmental Disabilities Services, Camarillo State Hospital. Dr. Flanagan was a contributor to the California Department of Developmental Services' *Standards for Aversive or Restrictive Behavior Intervention Procedures,* and recently published a chapter on behavioral treatment of psychosis in *The Psychiatric Clinics of North America: Symposium on Behavior Therapy.*

Manuel I. Gerton worked toward his Ph.D. in clinical psychology at Ohio University. He interned at the State University of New York Upstate Medical Center in Syracuse and is presently a postdoctoral fellow in clinical psychology at the George Washington University Medical Center in Washington, D.C.

Melvin A. Gravitz, Ph.D., practices clinical psychology in Washington, D.C., where he is also clinical professor of psychiatry and behavioral sciences at the George Washington University School of Medicine. He is a past president of the American Society of Clinical Hypnosis, and he holds specialty diplomas from the American Board of Professional Psychology, American Board of Psychological Hypnosis, and American Board of Forensic Psychology.

Henry Grayson received his Ph.D. from Boston University in 1967 and a post-doctoral certificate in psychotherapy and psychoanalysis from the Postgraduate Center for Mental Health in 1971. He is founder and chairman of the board of directors of the National Institute for the Psychotherapies in New York City. Books include *Three Psychotherapies: A Clinical Comparison* (with C. and G. Loew), *Short Term Approaches to Psychotherapy* and *Changing Approaches to Psychotherapy* (with C. Loew). *Autonomous Intimacy* is in preparation.

Robert Paul Liberman received his M.D. from the Johns Hopkins University School of Medicine in 1963. He is currently professor of psychiatry at UCLA, and chief of the Rehabilitation Medicine Service at Brentwood VA Medical Center (Los Angeles). He is principal investigator of two major research grants, Mental Health Clinical Research Center for the Study of Schizophrenia (funded by NIMH) and the Rehabilitation Research and Training Center (funded by the National Institute for Handicapped Research). He was an NIH Fogarty International Senior Research Fellow during 1975–1976. Two recent publications are *The Handbook of Marital Therapy* (Liberman et al.) and Liberman (ed.), *The Psychiatric Clinics of North America: Symposium on Behavior Therapy.*

Harold I. Lief received his M.D. from New York University College of Medicine in 1942. He is professor of psychiatry in the School of Medicine of the University of Pennsylvania and director of the Marriage Council of Philadelphia. Academic honors include the Gold Medal Award for Distinction and Excellence in Psychiatry presented by the Mt. Airy Foundation of Denver, Colorado; award for Outstanding Contributions to the Field of Human Sexuality presented by the Society for the Scientific Study of Sex; and the annual award of the American Association of Sex Educators, Counselors, and Therapists. He is editor in chief of the text, *Sexual Problems in Medical Practice,* and edited the book *Sex Education in Medicine: A Monograph.*

Joseph E. Mallet is expecting his Ph.D. degree in clinical psychology from the University of Maryland. He is presently an intern at the Veterans Administration Medical Center in Washington, D.C.

Joseph T. Martorano received his M.D. in 1960 from the Downstate Medical Center of the State University of New York. He has been chief consultant in psychiatry for General Motors in New York, and is currently psychiatric consultant to several major pharmaceutical advertising agencies, as well as being in private practice and serving as editor-in-chief of *Psychiatric Practice Management.* Recent publications include *Inner Speech Therapy* (with J. Kildahl).

Paul G. Munyon, Ph.D., has long been involved in social and behavioral science research, including hypnosis. He has a special interest in ideo-motor information processing in altered states.

Max Rosenbaum, who received his Ph.D. from New York University, is the former president of the Association for Group Psychoanalysis and Process and the Eastern Group Psychotherapy Association. Author of *Group Psychotherapy: Theory and Practice, The Intensive Group Experience,* and *Group Psychotherapy and Group Function,* Dr. Rosenbaum is editor of the journal *Group Process,* and is presently clinical professor, postdoctoral program, Adelphi University; consultant, South Beach Psychiatric Center, Manhattan State Psychiatric Center, and Harlem Valley Psychiatric Center; and also maintains an active practice in New York City.

Hyman Spotnitz received his M.D. from the University of Berlin in 1934 and his Med. Sc. D. in neurology in 1939 from Columbia University. He is engaged in the private practice of psychoanalytic psychiatry (individual and group) in New York City. He is the author of numerous published papers on psychotherapy in the severe psychiatric disorders, and of several books. These include *Modern Psychoanalysis of the Schizophrenic Patient* and *Psychotherapy of Preoedipal Conditions.* Dr. Spotnitz is a life fellow of the American Psychiatric Association and American Orthopsychiatric Association, and a fellow of the American Group Psychotherapy Association and the American Association for the Advancement of Science.

Jerome Steiner received his M.D. from the State University of New York, Downstate Medical Center, in 1962, and a Ph.D. in social psychology from Columbia University. He is an assistant professor of clinical psychiatry at Columbia College of Physicians and Surgeons, and an attending psychiatrist at New York State Psychiatric Institute, Columbia-Presbyterian Medical Center, and St. Luke's Hospital, as well as being in private practice. Dr. Steiner has published numerous articles on group therapy, and his elementary textbook in group psychotherapy is scheduled for publication in 1982.

George Stricker received his Ph.D. in clinical psychology from the University of Rochester in 1960. Currently, he is professor of psychology and assistant dean of the Institute of Advanced Psychological Studies at Adelphi University. A diplomate in clinical psychology, he is also on the editorial board of three journals. His published books include *Rorschach Handbook of Clinical and Research Applications, Practical Problems of a Private Psychotherapy Practice,* and *Intimacy.*

Benjamin B. Wolman received his Ph.D. from the University of Warsaw in 1935. Currently professor emeritus, Long Island University, he is editor-in-chief of the *International Encyclopedia of Psychiatry, Psychology, Psychoanalysis and Neurology,* and president of the International Organization for the Study of Group Tensions, as well as having been in private practice since 1939. Dr. Wolman is the recipient of the Dartmouth Medal of the American Library Association and the Distinguished Contribution Award of the American Psychological Association. He has published over 200 papers and 28 books in psychology and related fields, including *The Therapist's Handbook* and *Handbook of Human Sexuality*.

Introduction:
The Issue of Ethics

Max Rosenbaum

Ethics or the ethical problem is essentially the question of what is good and what is evil. Every history of humankind deals with this question. When do we know when an act is good or evil? What code or guide determines good or evil? Some ask whether there is an absolute measure of good and evil that will stand eternally. There are religious beliefs which set up eternal standards of good and evil. An outstanding example is the Ten Commandments of Judaism, believed to have been given to Moses by God at Mount Sinai and believed—at least by adherents of Judaism and Christianity—to be an eternal statement of good and evil.

There are those who approach good and evil in terms of culture, place, and time. For example, a lie given to a sadistic Nazi guard in order to save someone's life is seen as an untruth that served a good purpose. If truth were spoken, an innocent person might be called to die.

I have cited the extremes of the problem of good and evil in order to illustrate the vast range of possibilities when we discuss ethics.

The early philosophers of Greece looked for universal harmony in the environment and saw good and evil as part of the universe. As the philosophers turned more toward a concern with man's behavior, they became concerned with man's desires. Democritus stated that "You can tell the man . . . not by his deeds alone, but also by his desires." Later, the Sophist philosophers became concerned about the independence of the human mind and the individual who must arrive at what is right and wrong without being told what is right and wrong. They were, of course, concerned with human reason.

The major figures in the area of ethics amongst the Greeks that we know today were Socrates, his student Plato, and Aristotle.

Socrates believed that there was a basic principle of right and wrong. He looked for the highest good to use as a measure of the universe. He believed that the highest good is to be found in knowledge. If one knows what is good, one will do it. From this follows Socratic inquiry into one's actions. According to Socrates, "The unexamined life is not worth living."

Plato expanded the Socratic concern with evil and good. He noted

1

the inconsistency of the changing universe. The one constant that Plato noted was the rational aspect of man. Plato saw man as governed by will (spiritual), appetites (desires), and reason. When man lives the best life, reason will govern the spiritual and the desires.

Aristotle saw man as purposive; every act has some end or purpose. What is the highest good, asked Aristotle? Self-realization was his answer, and this could be accomplished best through reason. Later, such Greek philosophers as Epicurus taught that all human life is oriented toward pleasure, but that the rational being will differentiate between short-term physical pleasures that are destructive and pleasures of the mind that are ultimately more gratifying. Here was the Epicurean approach to the good and evil of life. The Stoics believed that ultimate good would come when man acted in harmony with the universe and, in a sense, although they lived at a later time, Greek philosophers returned to pre-Socratic thinking.

With the rise of Christianity, there was a new concern about good and evil being related to the forces of light and darkness. This relates to the early religions of the Middle East.[1] St. Augustine believed that God was good and that when man turned from the goodness of God, evil came to the world. This is related to the early Hebraic commandment, "Behold I have given you a good doctrine, forsake it not." St. Augustine neatly skirted around the problem of evil by stating that since God is good, the world is good, and that evil is merely the absence of good. He was simply saying that when it is dark, there is no light, but that light will come very shortly.

Thomas Aquinas united the Christianity which believed in the goodness and purposefulness of God with the rational observations of Aristotle. According to St. Thomas, when one studies or observes the purpose for which one is created, one will understand the goodness of God. This may be accomplished through reason, faith, or intuition. This will lead you to a stage "where you come to God in heaven." According to Aquinas, the best way to reach God while on earth is to give up one's worldly possessions and enter a monastery or convent. This is the ideal solution according to Aquinas (*cognito dei experimentalis*). In Christian theology it is called "contempt for the world."

After Aquinas, Meister Eckhart was the most prominent Christian theologian. He stressed the purity of God and that man must become one with or "Buried in God."

Throughout medieval theology and its concern with the problems of ethics, stress was placed upon the purity of God and upon the idea that turning away from God must result in evil. The outstanding example would be Adam and Eve and the concept of original sin. As soon as man questioned the purity of God's motives, evil resulted. The proponent of evil was Satan, or the devil.

During the Enlightenment period in eighteenth-century France, Rousseau revived the Christian view of man's life before his fall from grace in the Garden of Eden. Rousseau stressed man's natural goodness in contrast to what others believed to be his inherent depravity. He argued that the evolution of society destroyed the natural, idyllic state of man. In essence, Christian theology did not resolve the problem of good and evil. The religions of the Far East—for example, Buddhism, Shintoism, and other offshoots—established a variety of gods, among them gods of good and evil, which merely circumvented the problem of good and evil without resolving it.

The work of Copernicus and of Descartes, however, and the advent of a new science that attempted to view good and evil in a more reasoned fashion, had brought new factors into the equation. Added to these was the influence of Social Darwinism in the nineteenth century and there were many new points of view introduced. Thomas Hobbes, the seventeenth-century British philosopher, who was one of those who believed in man's innate depravity, was concerned with how people balanced their own self-interests with the interests of the social order. He saw good and evil in terms of authority and government and the need to regulate man's "animal" behavior. He labeled man *homo homini lupus*—a wolf, a vicious and malicious animal with no compassion for his fellows. His concern was with the material basis of the universe. He saw good and evil in terms of their relationship to man; that which pleases the person is good, that which causes pain or displeasure is evil. There is, therefore, no absolute good or evil. It is all contingent, according to Hobbes, on the context in which events or actions take place.

In spite of Descartes' concern with reason and mathematics, he was the completely religious Christian when it came to good and evil. He believed that God was perfect and absolutely good but that man makes mistakes, because God has not given him the capacity always to differentiate good from evil. Therefore, he makes errors because he has not acquired sufficient data and lacks complete understanding of the problem. This is a reconciliation of Descartes' reasoned approach and his deep commitment to religion and God.

Baruch Spinoza was not able to reach the same reconciliation that Descartes had effected. He emphasized the rational quality of man and his desire to preserve himself. Good results when man is able through understanding, to realize his strivings. Evil is the result of being blocked from one's own fulfillment. All of this must be done within an intellectual inquiry or what Spinoza called the "intellectual love of God." None of these theories was acceptable to Spinoza's fellow Sephardic Jews who lived in Amsterdam in the seventeenth century. The elders of the Portugese Synagogue of Amsterdam excommunicated Spinoza for his views, which they considered a threat to Judaism and the Jewish community. Ironically, Spinoza formulated his theories in the library of the rabbinical school adjoining the synagogue where the elders met to excommunicate him. Spinoza remained convinced that the most good comes when man completely understands what he is doing. This is God's desire in Spinoza's depiction of man and God.

John Locke, another seventeenth-century British philosopher, shared the philosophy of Thomas Hobbes to the extent that he believed that being good results in the highest pleasure because one has made a compromise with the society in which one lives. Experience will, to a large measure, determine what is good and evil since good will result in pleasure and evil in pain. Locke perceived mankind as some kind of blackboard which had not been written upon, a "tabula rasa" (a term he popularized in his 1690 "Essay on Human Understanding"). All ideas of good and evil come from the outside world. He did not concern himself with the early Christian preoccupation with God's goodness and purity. Indeed Locke believed that our parents have stressed what is right and wrong, what is good or evil, since the day we were born. We are all so thoroughly indoctrinated that by the time we reach adulthood we believe that we have been born with this capacity to distinguish good from evil.

While Locke believed that God set forth divine laws which when broken will result in sinful behavior, he was far more concerned with the civil laws which determine right and wrong. The society makes the laws and breaches of the laws will be punished. This is another view of good and evil. Locke also believed that people value the opinions of others and want to be thought well of and will therefore act righteously so that others do not criticize them. Finally, Locke stressed that pain and pleasure are part of nature's plan for mankind. Life has been organized, according to Locke, so that we will all attempt to avoid pain and look toward pleasure. Those philosophers who followed Locke's views stressed the "enlightened self-interest" of people—we do good because ultimately it pays off. Thus, the early settlers of the United States joined in a compact because they needed one another. The regulations served to do good and met the community's interests.

Probably the most influential philosopher of the nineteenth century who concerned himself with good and evil, right and wrong, was Immanuel Kant. He struggled with the concepts of duty and morality until the last years of his life. He was deeply concerned with moral law and duty for duty's sake. He followed in the tradition of Rousseau insofar as he believed in man's essential goodness, but he went on to stress the consequences of an act. If an individual acts according to the moral law, the result will be good. If not, the result will be bad or evil.

Kant formulated the term "categorical imperative" as the rule of moral law. He stated that every act should be carried out as if it were or might become a universal law—*"act so that you can will that everybody shall follow the principle of your action."* He believed that moral law resides within us all and that people realize this; otherwise society would be in constant turmoil. He stressed reason in his approach to moral law and believed that if each person acts as if his own acts could become the principle of everyone else's behavior, he will always be able to tell the difference between right and wrong. He also stressed that every person should be viewed "as an end and never as a means." We are not to use people but to serve others as well as ourselves.

It is not the intent of this introduction to cover all of the proponents of differing philosophic views, but to cover what I believe are the major influences.

The most current impact upon the problem of good and evil has been the writings of John Stuart Mill, who wrote in the mid-nineteenth century. He defined good as the question of what will bring the greatest good to the greatest number of people. He believed that goodness could then best be approached as a reasonable solution to the needs of all. He was clearly ahead of his time and was actually egalitarian and believed that women were deprived of their rights. He stated that "unnatural generally means only uncustomary, and everything which is usual appears natural. The subjugation of women to men being a universal custom, any departure from it quite naturally appears unnatural."

Mill would be very much part of the modern, Western tradition that all people are entitled to equal opportunity within their talents or ability. Freud was familiar with the work of Mill and translated his writings into German while still a young man, but differed with Mill in certain areas. The writings of Mill found favor in a technological culture. Indeed, his writing has been called representative of the Utiliarian School. The appeal in this approach is to reason and logic, since selfishness is defined as antigroup and defeats the purpose of what will most help the greatest number.

In the United States, the most influential thinkers are William James and John Dewey. They are representatives of the Pragmatic School and simply define good and evil as related to the group. Good is that act which best serves both individual and group. The stress here is upon the social aspect of behavior. The human being by his conduct is the ultimate measure of morality, of good and evil. The fatal flaw in pragmatism is that it depends upon group consensus. One disruptive individual who decides to sabotage the group decision hampers the ultimate good of all.

For the behavioral scientist, the problem of good and evil is approached through personality theory. The three most influential theories are social learning, cognitive developmental, and psychoanalytic.

Social learning theory is based upon how we learn complex processes of social behavior. Reward and punishment are seen as primary and the stress is upon outside reinforcement. According to social learning theory, the moral person is one who simply conforms to cultural norms and has internalized the standards of society and one's parents. B. F. Skinner (1971), a major learning theorist, relates justice to rewards and punishment. He states, "The issue of fairness is often simply a matter of good husbandry. The question is whether reinforcements are being used wisely" (p. 106).

This is the learning theorist's approach to morality. Conscience is related to reward and punishment. The emphasis is upon behavior that can be observed. The best way to study morality is to observe the reinforcement techniques that have been used—the types of punishment and the models that are or have been used.

Cognitive developmental theory has been largely based upon the work of Jean Piaget, the Swiss psychologist and mathematician (1948). Much of his work on the moral development of the child is to be found in *The Moral Judgment of the Child*. Piaget interviewed young children both extensively and intensively. From this he concluded that there are three major stages in the development of moral judgment.

The first stage he called *moral constraint*, and this would apply to children below the age of seven or eight. At this stage, the child reacts to rules and commands as given from the outside. They are not to be changed since adults give the orders. Justice is equated with adult commands. *Good is obedient.* Bad is to be disobedient. Thus, the parent states, "The baby is good. He does not give me any trouble." At this stage, values are absolute, there is right and wrong, and punishment is the result when one is bad or wrong. The *morality of constraint* has also been called *moral realism.* The child believes that everyone sees things the way he does and all thoughts are perceived as having a physical quality. The ultimate arbiter of morality is the adult (parent) from whom there is no appeal.

The second stage begins at age eight and lasts until age eleven or twelve. As the child begins to play with other children and there is interaction, the direction moves toward reciprocity. The child becomes more independent and becomes concerned about the rightness of punishment. Is it fair or out of keeping with the misdeed?

The third stage is the most mature. It begins at about age eleven or twelve and has been called the stage of *moral relativism* or *autonomous morality.* There is devotion and loyalty to peers, observance of rules and norms. The earlier absolute morality and unquestioning obedience are rejected. Since there is no absolute authority in a peer group, the individual must begin to listen to other points of view and hopefully there is group participation in the rules that are codified. The stress is on the cognitive or, if one looks back at the earlier philosophers, there is stress on reason. Piaget does make note of the cultural and social forces that impinge upon cognitive thinking.

There is no smooth progression in the stages that Piaget describes. While the child may become less self-centered and realistic, his concern for others may not come about until some time has passed. Piaget does stress the importance of grasping the concept before the child can move from one stage to another. An important moving force is the discomfort the child experiences as he observes contradictions. Thus, he attempts to establish a comfortable balance. Again, we are back to the earlier philosophers who wrote of man's effort to establish pleasure or at least to minimize pain.

Psychoanalytic theory stresses that morality is based upon identification with the parents. Conscience is equated with the superego and conscience developes by about five or six years of age with some later modifications, based upon further experiences. Good and evil are the internalized parental rules and the child's response to these arbitrary rules. The superego is punitive and the ego exists to bring some kind of reason into behavior. The *id* functions as the reservoir of untrammeled emotion and passions and drives. Freud stated, "Where the id is, there shall the *ego* be." The *ego,* in current psychoanalytic theory, is adaptational and functions to balance the excessive demands of the superego. The individual, with ego maturation, begins to acquire insight and is less judgmental and more apt to look for the motivations behind another person's behavior.

Freud's theories about the ego resulted in a rather pessimistic view of human behavior since the ego seemed fixed. Later psychoanalytic theorists noted that the ego could continue to develop through adolescence and adulthood with new experiences and exposure to influential figures. It is my belief that there is currently more awareness of Piaget's work and his approach to cognition with an effort to integrate this approach with studies of unconscious emotional forces.

While the presentation until now has been rather cursory, since we are covering untold pages and writings, the effort is to remind the reader that there has been concern with ethics for thousands of years. The question remains as to why most psychotherapists have avoided consideration of ethical issues in psychotherapy. Freud, in his concern that his theories be considered part of science and logical positivism, avoided the area of ethics. He was intrigued by but skeptical about the work of James Jackson Putnam, a Boston based neurologist who was one of the early pioneers in the practice of psychoanalysis in the United States. He was concerned lest psychotherapy become intertwined with theology. Yet Putnam felt that it was impossible to complete intensive psychotherapy with a patient unless morality was explored. Freud's ethic was simple: pursue truth at the cost of the illusion, no matter how comforting that illusion might be. He believed in the pursuit of truth through the method of science. He took for granted what was moral; he had a commitment to the scientific method in preference to the philosophical. In this respect he appears rather naive. To begin with, he himself was exposed to the moral systems of his family. Second, we know today that there are different versions of what the scientific method is. Paradigms in science can be set up that will justify many different approaches to morality. An outstanding example of this view is the brutal experimentation performed by physicians in Nazi Germany under the guise of research.

One philosopher has stressed the psychiatrist's concern with "practical ethics" (Drane, 1978). (See Chapter 1.) The practicing psychotherapist often expresses the belief that decisions have to be made immediately and that there is no time for reflection or consideration of the other possibilities. Drane describes this type of behavior as *situationist* and the term seems very appropriate. The situationist believes that experience will result in the right decision. Ideals and ethics seem irrelevant. This type of person may be following Freud's practice of avoiding the larger moral issue.

The *formalists* (Drane's term, and one that I accept) would be skeptical as to the idea of doing something right because it feels right. This has a touch of early Christian theology and seems to assume that ethics are always there ready to be used. The rightness and wrongness of clinical judgments cannot be decided on the spot since the *situationist* feels free from rules and principles. There is a quality of relativism and an avoidance of reason. There is an avoidance of the uniformity of rules and a belief that feelings will dictate the appropriate choice. There is, then, an avoidance of what past experiences can offer in setting up systematic guidelines. The role of reason in making ethical decisions would be stressed by the formalist—not arbitrary rules. The formalist would state that while feelings and emotions are important, how would the character or temperament of a generally more cheerful psychotherapist influence a clinical decision in contrast with the judgment of a cynical, less optimistic, or more detached psychotherapist. Especially since every new treatment intervention brings to the fore the questions of the patient's rights, patient's consent, and risks or dangers to the patient.

Psychotherapists are not alone. The scandals of Watergate have been felt in all parts of our society. Since Watergate, there has been a heightened awareness of public intrusion into the private life of the individual. Information systems have become more and more complex and sophisticated. The impact was felt in the federal government when the Privacy Act of 1974 was passed by Congress. This was the first effort made by the federal government to put its own house in order and to scrutinize carefully standards for access and use of federal files on individuals. Indeed, the great difficulty that the U.S. Census Bureau is experiencing is the distrust of respondents when they are asked to complete a questionnaire. The distrust is so manifest, especially among minority groups who feel that the data may be used hurtfully, that the entire validity of census data is suspect. We are clearly in the area of trust but, beyond this, we are in the area of concern about the integrity of the census taker. How will the data be used? Hurtfully or to the advantage of the respondent? Again, the question of ethics—good and evil.

While there are differing definitions of what constitutes a scientific approach, there is a responsibility that the clinical practicioner has to be consistent about his behavior. The idea of subjectivity, while attractive, makes every situation a new one and frees us all from defining consistency and inconsistency. The ethical determination of conduct sets up guidelines or principles about the nature of man and what is good and evil. We need not be theologians but we do have to be consistent and confront the moral questions of the work we do.

Polanyi (1958) observed the modern behavioral scientist's desire to protect knowledge from religious dogmatism and its excesses. Modern man began to divorce knowledge from religious belief and began to deny moral beliefs in the process. Polanyi noted that the morality surfaced under a different name. He called this the dynamo-objective coupling of Marxism, the coupling of objective skepticism and moral passion. Thus, scientific assertions become accepted because they satisfy moral passions. Once the passions become excited, they lend further convincing power to the scientific assertions. The circle is complete. If there is criticism of a scientific assertion, the "moral" passion comes forth to rebut the critic. If there are objections or criticisms based on morality, the scientific assertion and finding is brought to the fore.

Polanyi depicts Freud's interpretation of culture as a "moral inversion" where Freud disguised his own moral commitments under the rubric of scientific statements. This happens constantly in the behavioral sciences.

Freud, some fifteen years after the founding of psychoanalysis, believed that he effectively separated sexual morality and the ethic of human relations. He established to his satisfaction that sexuality has nothing to do with good and evil. But he was left with the problem of what constitutes the moral sense. How did it arrive in man? He rather laboriously explained the development of the moral sense—what he called the superego—by defining the complex relationship between the idealized image of the parents and the observing child. But he really avoided the question.

In 1915 he wrote to James Jackson Putnam, the eminent Boston neurologist and one of the early practitioners of psychoanalysis, who believed that psychoanalysis and morality were intertwined:

> When I ask myself why I have always aspired to behave honourably, to spare others and to be kind wherever possible, and why I didn't cease doing so when I realized that in this way one comes to harm and becomes an anvil because other people are brutal and unreliable, then indeed I have no answer. Sensible this certainly was not. In my youth I didn't feel any special ethical aspirations nor does the conclusion that I am better than others give me any recognizable satisfaction. You are perhaps the first person to whom I have boasted in this fashion. So one could cite just my case as a proof for your assertion that such an urge towards the ideal forms a considerable part of our inheritance. If only more of this precious inheritance could be found in other human beings. . . . But as I have said before, I know nothing about this. [P. 308]

Let us now move beyond Freud's letter to Putnam. The reader, it is hoped, will be stimulated by the following pages to begin to formulate or reformulate his code of ethics.

NOTE

1. There is no discussion of Eastern philosophies and ethical systems in this book. The Eastern philosophers maintain that Eastern thought hypothesizes the unity of body, mind, and spirit. Until the twentieth century, most of Western philosophy has been influenced by the body-mind dualism that was stressed so strongly by Descartes and his successors.

   In the late 1950s, volunteers at a neuropsychiatric institute were taught how to control their own brainwaves. This led to biofeedback research. But for hundreds of years there have been yoga approaches to body-mind-spirit unity. These yoga approaches are Hatha Yoga, which emphasizes body discipline; Jnana Yoga—approach of knowledge; Bhakti Yoga—approach of love; Karma Yoga—approach of action; Tantric Yoga—approach of sex; and Raja Yoga—self-analysis. There are many yoga approaches but all of them emphasize meditation.

REFERENCES

Drane, J. F. Making concrete ethical judgments. *Bulletin of the Menninger Clinic*, 1978, **42**(2), 156–159.

Freud, S. Letter to James Putnam, July 8, 1915. In E. L. Freud (ed.), *Letters of Sigmund Freud*, p. 308. New York: Basic Books, 1960.

JONES, E. *The life and work of Sigmund Freud.* 3 vols; vol. 2, pp. 416–418. New York: Basic Books, 1957.

MILL, J. S. *The subjection of women.* London: Longmans, Green, Reader, & Dyer, 1869. Reprinted, Cambridge, Mass.: M.I.T. Press, 1970.

PIAGET, J. *The moral judgment of the child.* New York: Free Press, 1948.

POLANYI, M. *Personal knowledge: Toward a post-critical philosophy.* London: Routledge & Kegan Paul, 1958.

SKINNER, B. F. *Beyond freedom and dignity.* New York: Bantam, 1971.

PART I

ETHICS AND THE PROFESSION OF PSYCHOTHERAPY

Ethics and Psychotherapy: A Philosophical Perspective

James F. Drane

The idea of including a philosophical perspective in a book about psychotherapy may seem strange. Americans are not used to seeing philosophy joined with psychotherapy. And yet the two are intimately related. At the very beginnings of Western philosophy, in fact, there was a concern with psychotherapy. Philosophy could not ignore psychotherapy because philosophical themes are taken from the culture, and Greek culture was intensely interested in the use of the word in the healing process. Although it did not remain at center stage of philosophical reflection, concern about psychotherapy was never completely absent from the history of philosophy.

Homer's epic poem may be understood as a testimony to the power of words to touch men's hearts. There are frequent allusions in both the *Iliad* and the *Odyssey* to uses of words to cure (Lain Entralgo, 1970). Homer spoke of the therapeutic benefits of prayers and charms, but he also referred to what we might call supportive therapy when he spoke of suggestive and cheering speech (*terpnos logos*). Nestor and Patroculus use cheering speech to quiet the souls of their patients (*The Iliad,* 1950).

Because of its impressive effectiveness, philosophers in post-Homeric Greece could not ignore the use of words to cure. Plato took up this theme and attempted a rational explanation of the mysterious effectiveness of the therapeutic word which he referred to as charm (*epode*). He thought that therapeutic effectiveness was related to beauty. The beauty of the word produces wisdom or temperance (*sophrosyne*), a rightful order in the psyche. In Plato the word harmonizes beliefs, feelings, and impulses with knowledge, thought, and value judgments. A new axis is created in the soul by the beautiful word (*logos kalos*) in the form of new beliefs around which the many elements of the self are organized. Plato called this reorganizing and enlightening process *katharsis,* and in working out the details of its effectiveness, he gave us a rigorous, technical, and non-magical theory of psychotherapy (*The Dialogues of Plato,* 1931).

Aristotle also addressed the issue. Effective use of the word to cure was in his time obviously a common experience, and interest in explaining the phenomenon was more than a passing curiosity. Like Plato,

15

Aristotle used the term catharsis to discuss the effectiveness of the therapeutic word. But he defined catharsis as purgation. For Aristotle, words produce change in a person by relieving unconscious and hidden pressures. Besides reordering critical and central beliefs, therapeutic change also occurs by release of pent-up emotion.

According to Aristotle, the words of the tragic poem enter the ears and the mind of the spectator, but have their effect on the humors of the body as well. The therapeutic effect on the body is brought about not by a physical purgative, but by the airy, invisible, and immaterial reality of the poetic word. The word brings about a more balanced, more pleasurable, indeed a healthier state. It effects a reordering of body and soul, the physical, spiritual, and affective dimensions of man. Catharsis for Aristotle was both purgative and purifying.

In effect, Aristotle replied quasi-psychoanalytically to Plato's condemnation of poetry for stirring up the emotions at the expense of the rational parts of the soul. He saw that Plato was in fact espousing repression of the emotions and Aristotle argued for the naturalness and usefulness of the irrational impulses. Excess, he agreed, was harmful, but by the vicarious experiencing of another's emotions, a harmless discharge occurred which brought about a new and healthier measure. But the conclusion of Aristotle's doctrine of catharsis is in effect the same as Plato's: the therapeutic word in either form permits the soul to recover a good order among its parts (*The Basic Works of Aristotle*, 1941).

Aristotle also stressed the role of *kairos*, the notion that the therapeutic word must be spoken at the right time, and *diathesis*, the accommodation of the word to the situation of the hearer. Both Plato and Aristotle insist on a particular relationship between the speaker and hearer of the word (*paraschesis*). And finally a great deal was said by both about *ethos*, the inner being or character of the person who pronounces the therapeutic word.[1] A confluence of all the many above-mentioned elements explains the therapeutic power of the word.

Nothing then is clearer than the fact that philosophy and psychotherapy and the arts were linked (at least since antiquity. Since the Greeks, however, the first two disciplines have grown apart. Psychotherapy in its modern form is more identified with science and medicine. As is the case with most separations, both sides have suffered a loss. Modern clinicians could profit from familiarity with the classic and contemporary philosophical texts on the human condition. And modern philosophers certainly have much to gain from insights into that same condition which have come from the contact of sensitive and intelligent clinicians with human beings in distress. There is evidence that this mutual advantage is beginning to be recognized.

In this century a rapprochement has begun between the two disciplines. Philosophers in the existential and phenomenological movement have rejoined the Greek tradition by explicitly preoccupying themselves with the ancient questions of how human beings become disturbed and how they are cured by talking. The work of Karl Jaspers (1963), for example, a philosopher and psychiatrist, reflects the concerns of both fields. Sartre wrote books on the emotions (1948) and on psychoanalysis (1953). Paul Ricoeur (1970) and Alphonse DeWaelhens (1978) are also examples of philosophers with an interest in psychopathology and psychotherapy. Peter Koestenbaum (1978) and William Richardson (1978), both philosophers, are doing research and actually working in therapy. The long, unnatural, professional separation shows many signs of being overcome.

It is not only philosophers who are concerning themselves with psychotherapy; the traffic runs in the opposite direction as well. The great innovators in psychotherapy of necessity preoccupied themselves with philosophical thought in the form of personality theory which was applied in therapy. Freud is a good example of the psychotherapist/philosopher. Lecan (1978) is another. In the work of the major theoreticians the connection is obvious, but it is verified as well in every serious reflective clinician.

Even those therapists who claim to confine themselves to symptoms relief, in fact, assume a philosophical stance. If philosophy is a concern with reality beyond appearances, there is in all psychotherapy a more substantial level of personal existence assumed to lie beyond the observable. Behaviorists differ from psychoanalysts only as to the depth to which they are willing to pursue this "underlying" reality. Psychological ailments are assumed to have an underlying core and so too the human person. It is impossible for the psychotherapist to avoid being a philosopher in the sense of one who holds explicit beliefs about the nature of man, the nature of illness, and the distinction between appearance and reality.

Psychotherapy is philosophical in yet another way. Associated with a more or less conscious assumption about the nature of human beings is a more or less conscious assumption about the way human beings ought to behave, ought to feel, and ought to live. Speaking in philosophical jargon, where there is an ontology, there is always an ethics. Beliefs about morals follow beliefs about man's nature, and one tries to make the two consistent. Psychotherapists, like philosophers and priests, work with a model of what is desirable and good for human beings, how they should behave toward themselves, others, and society. Altruism, for example, is considered healthier than narcissism, peacefulness better than agression and hostility. Certain forms of psychic organization or character are considered deficient both by standards of normality and morality. The psychotherapist then is a philosopher in the sense of ethicist *malgré lui*.

If the therapist is by profession involved with ontological and ethical beliefs, he is also assumed to be an ethical person. Both Aristotle and Plato called attention to the importance of the character (*ethos*) of the person who pronounces the therapeutic word. And their insight is not lost on training centers for psychotherapists. Where concern about the ethics of candidates is not in evidence, it is either hiding under some other conceptual categories or someone is not doing his job. Directors of psychoanalytic institutes, for example, are rightly concerned with more than intellectual proficiency in their candidates. Many ethical attributes are recognized as essential for functioning as a psychoanalyst. Honesty and concern for others are only the most obvious (Ramzy, 1965).

Ethics, too, in the more traditional sense of evaluation of acts, is never absent even from the most objective and scientific kinds of psychotherapies. There is no way for the therapist to avoid ethical judgments about the patient's life strategies, just as he cannot avoid working with ethical issues which are part of the pathology. The conscience of the patient may be the root of the patient's conflict, and at some point the most neutral analyst sides with sobriety rather than drunkenness, or tolerance rather than prejudice. If ethics is so widely recognized as intimately involved in the hard sciences, it can hardly be ignored in the applied and much more obviously human sciences like psychotherapy (Erikson, 1964; Veatch, 1976).

The ideal of neutrality in "scientific" psychotherapies is real, but it is never absolute. There is a schedule of moral values which the therapist tries to promote in some patients and a strong preference for some values which are closely allied to the therapist's philosophy of life. Karl Menninger (1958) says it most clearly: "What a psychoanalyst believes, what he lives for, what he loves, what he considers to be good and what he considers to be evil, become known to the patient and influence him enormously not as suggestion but as inspiration" (p. 94).

But if philosophy, ethics, and psychotherapy are so closely connected, why has there not been an ongoing awareness of the relationship? Why are books like this one needed to arouse the sensitivity of professional practitioners to this dimension of their work? The answer is not difficult to find.

There are counterpressures in the scientific tradition which tend to "bracket" ethical concerns. Allied with the scientific part of the medical tradition, modern psychotherapy sometimes assumes that science is value free; that is, that it has nothing to do with ethics. The therapist in this understanding treats the patient without reference to ethics or considerations of moral worthiness. Whatever the therapy being administered, it focuses on the patient's needs alone. The psychotherapist may very well have been advised during his training years not to become involved with the ethical, political, philosophical, or religious beliefs of the patient. The implication is that the "business" of psychotherapy, like that of physical medicine, is "nothing but" the relief of suffering. If ethics enters this mindset at all, it is in the form of a gross oversimplification: "Ethical psychotherapy is competent psychotherapy." If only things were that simple!

Still, it must be granted that although the scientific, value-free, amoral stance of the tradition is not altogether accurate, it has nevertheless been very beneficial. It has contributed considerably to the development of an objective perspective in the understanding of mental illness, moving the profession away from superficial moralistic diagnoses and treatments. Prior to the modern period, ill-advised use of ethical categories in the explanation of pathology undoubtedly played a role in the divorce of modern techniques from ethics. Modern psychotherapy was developed so that it could be learned very much as the physician learns his skills, and could then be conducted independently of ethical considerations.

As beneficial as the presupposition of ethical neutrality has been to the profession, it corresponds in fact more to research than to clinical practice. In the day-to-day therapeutic relationship, ethics and values abound both on the side of the therapist and on the side of the patient as well. Ethical concerns, for example, can hardly be ignored when the patient's problem is pedophilia, or when the diagnosis is a character disorder (like Narcissism) with its massive moral deficiencies. But even the more prosaic problems tend to center in what bothers the patient's conscience or interferes with relationships to which he feels an obligation. Work, home, family, and the ethical conflicts associated with them are common themes in clinical practice. Simply stated, it is unrealistic to expect that treatment of such disorders may be carried out by the application of technical principles alone.

Psychotherapy is closely intertwined with ethics, and yet communication between the philosopher/ethicist and the psychotherapist has not been good. The training of the physician/therapist, for example, tends to be very different from that of the philosopher. There is usually a strong science identification in the former which is not always shared by the ethicist. They speak different languages and write in different styles. The clinician tends not to be interested in the "mystical" concern of the philosopher. And to the philosopher, what the clinician wants to discuss under the topic of ethics sounds more like issues of etiquette. This background difference may express itself in an antiscientific or antitechnological bias on the part of the ethicist. But the most serious communication barrier derives from a sense that the writings of ethicists are really instances of mischief making by people who have little or no experience with clinical practice (Callahan, 1975).

Lack of rapport and misapprehensions can sometimes be the result of insecurity. It is easy for an ethicist to stress what he knows (the humanities) and play down or not adequately appreciate what he does not know as well (scientific and technological aspects of clinical practice). It is equally easy for the clinician who has long enjoyed a privileged social position to resent any comment on his behavior from outside sources. Counterpressures, then, to active concern with philosophical ethics on the part of clinicians are real and ongoing.

And yet, since there is no way of avoiding ethics in psychotherapy, the only question is whether the psychotherapist will "do ethics" in a professional way. To do ethics is to engage in a disciplined rational exercise. It means making rationally defensible judgments about morals and values. Given the complexity of clinical practice, doing ethics competently cannot be a matter of following a few norms or the example of a teacher. It requires tough-minded analyses of problems and high-level reflection on psychotherapeutic tradition and principles. In effect, it requires of the therapist a new form of philosophical literacy.

It is my hope that as a result of an identification with both fields, I can provide some assistance to the therapist without adopting either a holier-than-thou or an accusatory attitude. When one professional talks with another, there is no higher station from which one may treat the other condescendingly. A dialogue between ethicists and psychotherapists can only be carried out as an exchange of perspectives. All the philosopher can do is offer to share the symbols and categories of his tradition for whatever benefit they may have for the clinician. Anything more is too much.

My goal, then, has nothing to do with telling someone what to do. Rather, I would like to provide a format or intellectual structure in which the psychotherapist can do his own reflection and come to his own decisions. Ethical choices in situations of conflict are difficult enough in themselves. Often, however, the ethical task is unnecessarily complicated by confusion about the different levels of ethical discourse (Aiken, 1952). In the absence of a methodology which keeps the levels of ethical discourse separate, discussion vacillates among many different levels, thereby compounding confusion. Decisions wind up being made by instinct, because efforts to sort things out more intelligently meet with frustration. Methodology is as important in doing ethics as it is in doing psychotherapy,

Level 1—The Existential: Values and Context

The human being is born into an already established set of meanings and values which we call the cultural world. Even for the child, this world quickly evolves from an amorphous unitary experience into separate objects which have names (meanings) and qualities experienced as pleasurable (values). The smallest child can sense the ethical tone of a parent's voice, and parents appeal to this sensitivity in their attempts to establish guidelines for a safe and healthy life. Besides external object relations, one's own person can be experienced as good or bad. There is no purely physical or value-free reality for the human person except after radical scientific abstraction.

The cultural world, in the sense of the immediate environment in which mature man finds himself, is symbolic; that is, it both bears meaning and is value-laden.[2] And common sense is the term used to refer to the way human beings handle this world, relate to it, use it, and manage to get along in it. Common sense tells us not only what certain things mean, but that certain things are agreeable or disagreeable, healthy or unhealthy, noble or vulgar, beautiful or ugly, just or unjust. For man, then, the world has both a cognitive and a value dimension. It is both something known and something appreciated.

Culture orders both man's meanings and his values. Accepted meanings as well as value judgment become institutionalized within a culture. Parents transmit this reality which precedes every person's birth and persists, usually with only slight modification, throughout his life (unless one happens to live in an age of "future shock"). The world in which the human being comes to be has a culturally enshrined meaning as well as a pre-given ethical structure. It is full of goods and bads, dos and don'ts, which become part of the human person before he is able to form his own mature judgments. One of Freud's many enduring contributions traces the early development of the superego. And continued research into the origins of ethics has pushed superego formation back to the very beginnings of life (Klein, 1957; Guntrip, 1961).

Ethics then, in the philosophical sense of reasoning about the right and wrong of actions, does not begin in the ethereal world of philosophical abstraction, but rather is rooted in man's concrete being in the world. Ethics as a philosophical discipline does not come down from a world of pure forms, but rather comes up from the practical world in which the human person finds himself immersed. The human world is one of values and correspondingly of claims, demands, punishment, approval, obligations, rights, and responsibilities. The discipline called "Ethics" attempts to clarify this world, but it does not create it. Rather, ethics always starts with the buzzing confusion of man's existential condition, and ultimately its theoretical formulations will be verified or falsified in terms of their adequacy or inadequacy for interpreting his lived experience. This is true of ethics generally, as well as of the narrower concerns of professional ethics.

If the human condition is ethical to its core, we can hardly expect psychotherapy not to be so. Ethics in fact permeates every aspect of psychotherapy. It is implicated in the diagnosis, the pathology, the transference, and finally in the goals of treatment.)The context of psychotherapy is interlaced with ethical concerns, and the therapist cannot avoid being immersed in ethics (London, 1964; Rieff, 1959).

Diagnosis involves symbols and meanings organized into a coherent system. This type of high-level understanding is an ethical activity in the sense that it involves the choice of one system of symbols and the rejection of others. Either the psychotherapist devises his own or adopts one of the already developed frameworks for understanding his patient. If clinical experience is meaningful, it is because of the meaningful structures which are used to organize it. But such organizational frameworks are not part of nature. They are chosen. The very concepts and categories by which health is distinguished from illness and normality from abnormality are ethical both in the sense that they are matters of choice and in the sense that the diagnostic model itself incorporates a system of evaluation. One model values adjustment, another productivity, a third the maximization of personal satisfaction (Macklin, 1973).

The theoretical model or conceptual system in light of which clinical experience is sorted out and made meaningful is not a tool which the therapist uses, but becomes part of the therapist's person through identification and commitment. The diagnostic symbol system then tends to order the subjective experience of the therapist as well. But where there is such choice and commitment to basic ideas, there is ethics. Ethics, in the sense of *ethos*, refers to those life-constituting personal choices and commitments to meaning which create a vision of reality and color man's way of responding to it. We will consider this in more detail in the fourth level of ethical discourse.

The sickness diagnosed with the aid of symbols also has an ethical dimension. It is not, as in other branches of medicine, a bacterium or a tumor, but rather ideas, memories, feelings, and sometimes behaviors which either the patient or society considers shameful. Ethical concerns then are often the very sources of anxiety and unhappiness which produce symptoms and bring people to treatment. Try as he may to imitate the mechanic and repair only that part of the mechanism that is functioning badly, the psychotherapist is inevitably pulled into the ethical aspects of a person's pathology.

And the therapist cannot evade the ethical dimension of his work by concentrating exclusively on abstractions like dynamics, structure, or the unconscious. The flesh-and-blood person who is being treated is a philosophical, religious, social, and ethical being, and one has no alternative but to work with the whole complex of this living reality. Especially today, when so many patients suffer from character pathology, superego deficiencies abound. Like it or not, the therapist is up to his neck in ethics and pedagogy. It is a short step from psychological deficiencies to ethical deficiencies in the diagnosis of pathology and the assignment of its etiology (Kohlberg, 1971; Piaget, 1966).

The close connection between ethics and pathology is obvious in situations where the presenting problem is overtly moral or legal—stealing, promiscuity, cruelty to children, exploitation, sexual perversion. If the patient is Catholic, Protestant, Jewish, or of whatever religious persuasion, there is the added dimension of the part played in the problem by the norms and values of a religious tradition. When ethical concerns constitute the overt area of conflict, how can the therapist not be involved? Approaching such problems in an objective and technical way means probing the origins and dynamics of the symptoms as well as examining the functional dimension of a behavior. But it is impossible to keep these approaches separate from the value considerations. The therapist may work toward autonomous value choices by the patient, but there is never a total indifference to the values and behaviors chosen. In fact, therapy in such cases inevitably involves some ethical direction (Abroms, 1978).

The therapeutic relationship is ethical too because the therapist is a person with his own ethical formation rather than a pure *cogito* or a *tabula rasa*. He has a personal history, professional training, religious and philosophical beliefs, cultural formation, and ethnic background, all of which influence the way he determines the good and the right. If the therapist were a priest or a rabbi, his ethical formation might be up front and obvious, but a secular person is not necessarily an ethical neuter. His own ethical formation, interacting with that of his patient, gives a distinctive ethical flavor to the transference and counter-transference patterns.

The therapist's ethics is inevitably transmitted in therapy, and the good therapist is usually aware of this influence. Skillful practitioners are aware of the ethics which informs their practice, and do not confuse it with technical expertise or science. They know that their approval and disapproval count. On one occasion the patient may be gently guided toward better ways. At other times ethical standards are set out explicitly and continuation of treatment is made contingent upon conformity. Paradoxically, the therapist who is aware of his ethics and its operation in therapy is less apt to impose his values. It is the one who is unaware of or denies any ethical component that is most in danger. Ignorance and self-deception easily become the channels of ethical assault (Buhler, 1962).

If ethics permeates both the diagnostic and interpersonal dimensions of therapy, it is even more prominent in therapeutic goal setting. Ethical language, in fact, seems very appropriate for articulating the mutually sought-after alterations in the patient's life. The hysterical patient, for example, looks forward to a gain in self-knowledge; the obsessive patient needs to become more trusting and generous; the antisocial personality must develop a conscience and more sensitivity for other people.

Personality theory itself provides an ethical ideal toward which persons ought to strive, and as such sets out the goal of therapy. One meaning schema proposes the goal of a genital personality, another that of optimal self-actualization. Will to meaning, personal responsibility, creativity, and release of constructive tendencies are other stated ideals. In every instance the personality theory which may have set out to be purely descriptive or even scientific, becomes normative and dictates the goals of therapy.

The giants of psychotherapy all seemed to be aware of the involvement of ethics in treatment. Freud (1949), for example, spoke explicitly of the necessity of superego alteration for effective psychoanalytic therapy, and orthodox analysts work toward "autonomy" and "productivity." In other instances the goals of intended change are expressed in overtly ethical terms. Adler's and Karen Horney's followers, for example, quite openly stress the development of "social responsibility." The success of every modality will be judged to some extent by the patient's increased capacity to develop a personal value system and to act on it. Physical treatment may be considered value free, but even drug and behavioral therapies have their implied values and strong ethical components. Some endorse psychedelic values for patients and society (feeling good), while others abhor drugs and promote more puritanical virtues.[3]

It is one thing to recognize the all-pervasive ethical dimensions of therapy and another to develop a consistent way of handling the ethics. For some persons, training and expertise in medicine and psychology will be considered the equivalent of training in ethics (Veatch, 1976). Rather than moving from recognition of the value aspects of therapy to more reflective considerations of ethical phenomena, there are therapists who consider themselves already competent to make all the ethical judgments they are called upon to face. Somehow their life experience and education suffices to turn them into ethical guides and judges (Drane, 1978). Such persons tend to rely on instinct and intuition. In ethical literature they would be referred to as situationists (Fletcher, 1966).

Others deny any intuition of the right ethical response in therapy, but still see no reason for ethical education. They in fact considered ethics nothing more than a matter of emotion or feeling. If this is the case, what sense does it make to think reflectively about ethics? Argument about ethics is like argument about taste. Saying something is right is considered the equivalent of saying that one likes vanilla. Raised to a more social plane, this view becomes a radical cultural relativism.

Situationists, emotivists, and cultural relativists would discontinue consideration of ethics in psychotherapy at this point. Basically, they avow that all one can do is state one's intuition or feeling. Since each person and each group has its own preferences, and since there is no objective standard, further reflection is pointless. In their crudest forms, these positions are conformist and conservative because there is little basis for challenging the status quo. In fact, taken to their logical extreme, these positions would find therapy itself difficult to defend.

As a professional, the therapist must be ethical in a more reflective way because adherence to rules, norms, and principles is what constitutes him as a professional person. And then, while some of the cases he carries do not warrant much ethical analysis, others force the therapist into ethical considerations. His alternatives are often such that he has no immediate feeling or intuition of the proper course to take. To be an ethical therapist in such circumstances requires recourse to the higher levels of ethical discourse to which we now turn.

Level 2—The Legal: Rules and Norms

Human beings are not only existentially ethical, but are existentially reflective as well. Man is a questioning animal. His drive for reasons can be compared with his drive for sexual satisfaction. Consequently, the human being ordinarily does not remain on the first level of immediate ethical evaluation. Man also inquires into why he feels this is right or that is good. He asks why society endorses certain behaviors and sanctions others. He seeks reasons not only for his own spontaneous evaluations, but for the evaluations of institutions and cultures as well. People try to make sense of ethical feelings and judgments by reference to past experience crystallized in ethical rules. This type of ethical activity requires greater intellectual and personal maturity as it progresses to values in more reasoned propositional forms.

If the first level of ethics is existential in the sense that it concerns the immediate response of a person to the value dimensions of reality, the second level involves a move away from immediacy toward distance, delay, and reflection, but not so far away as to lose contact with the envalued concrete situation. We speak of the certainty and conviction of people with a third-grade education, because they never move away from felt responses which tend to be very persuasive when subjected to neither analysis nor criticism. The second level of ethics asks why a specific behavior is felt to be good or bad, right or wrong, healthy or unhealthy. Why should I be repelled by one action, and applaud another? Should I really feel this way? Are there guidelines by which my feelings about right and wrong can be tested? What are actually the facts in this case?

Reasons and qualifications are asked for and given first in the form of concrete directives called moral rules. Justification for this or that evaluation is made by recourse to directives which prescribe or proscribe certain acts. This attitude is typical of the earliest stages of growth (when there is little understanding on the part of the child of why following mother's rules makes his behavior good), as well as at more mature periods when rules provide a rationale for behavior. Rules and norms are values set down in propositional form and strengthened by a sanction.

Justification may also come in the form of an argument which explains why "X" is good and "Y" is bad. Here, reason enters the ethical project in a more formal way. There is a cognitive dimension to the immediate value judgment, but now this dimension becomes explicit. Now ethics attempts both to specify the structure of the action under consideration with more precision and to argue its justification.[4] Second-level ethical discourse (a) more precisely describes the structure of behaviors; (b) enunciates norms or justifying reasons which cover the case under consideration; and (c) justifies the application of one rule rather than another to a particular circumstance.

Sometimes behavior X or action Y is clear enough and needs little additional attention. In other cases great effort must be expended to find out what is actually happening before judgment is made about what ought to be. In questions of social ethics, for example (war, racial discrimination, distribution of medical resources, and the like), without a clarification of the situation and the proposed action, ethics flounders in gut-responses guaranteed to be bad.

Ethics at this second level is essential for psychotherapy. Before deciding on the evaluation of a particular course in psychotherapy, the objective dimensions of the professional action must be accurately analyzed. Just what are behavior control, confidentiality, patient's rights? What does patient care mean in this circumstance? Given this situation, is the action I propose a benefit to the patient or an intervention on behalf of the staff? Is my attitude toward this patient really kindness or do I act upon some felt need for personal gratification? Am I as therapist acting as an agent of society, or of the patient? Which values are operating in the particular therapy I am delivering? What is the ethical issue in this particular case—patient rights, right to treat, informed consent? If the facts of the situation and the character of the professional behavior are sufficiently clear, then level 2 can concern itself with the development of explanatory reasons or the application of relevant rules.

There are occasions when the rules and justifying reasons are so clear as to require little attention. Kant (1956), for example, assumed the operation of the Ten Commandments in people's lives when he insisted only upon the higher-order principle—"Do your duty." He assumed that people knew the rules and agreed upon what duty entailed.

Today, however, it is difficult to take rules and justifications for granted. Our age is one of moral pluralism in which there are few agreed-upon ethical directives or arguments. Disagreement and moral perplexity rather than agreement and moral clarity are characteristic. Today it is legitimate to ask "Why?" of any norm, and it is imperative that a person be able to defend the reasons for his ethical evaluations. Convincing arguments must be developed to justify a behavior. A "good" justifying reason or argument is coherent, consistent, and convincing. A "bad" one would have none of these qualities.

No one does ethics at this level in a strictly individual way. We all live in society. In fact, it would be more accurate to say that we live in multiple societies. This means in effect that we live in different groups which have distilled their experience and reflection about human behavior into different rules, laws, codes, and commandments. These may be more or less well ordered and explicit, but they are never absent, and they provide standards for what is good and right. These norms require that persons within the community act according to them, and they usually carry some sort of sanction. Their effectiveness in justifying an action depends upon the wisdom they enshrine. Rules validate our judgments and justify our behavior, and these functions take place within the context of social experience. Ten

The Judeo-Christian commandments are examples of ethical rules. They are concrete, specific, direct, and serve both to justify ethical evaluations and to guide practical behavior. An immediate, unreflecting negative response to the sight of a young man mistreating his old father can be validated by referring to the commandment "Honor thy father and thy mother." An attitude of one sort or another toward sexuality can be tested against the rule, "Thou shalt not commit adultery" or "Thou shalt not covet thy neighbor's wife." The rules provide direction for concrete behavior and justification for ways we feel about things. Secular organizations provide their own sets of norms for being a good boy scout, salesman, teacher, or therapist.

The helping professions have ideas about how their members should act. Concrete norms provide specifications of general principles (e.g., "relieve unnecessary pain," "do no harm," "people can be helped") to which the profession is committed. When a person involved in clinical practice attends a lecture or reads an article on ethics, it is more than likely that he is looking for just such rules. Ethics in the mind of a practitioner is often synonymous with rules and norms which guide clinical behavior. Professional ethics is closely identified with the second level of ethical discourse.

Every important philosopher develops an ethics, and every worthwhile ethical system includes rules and rational arguments for and against certain behavior which may be used by a therapist in conducting his practice. Some philosophers would like to downplay this second level in favor of spontaneous and immediate response to the situation in which a person finds himself (Sartre 1956; de Beauvoir 1949). This option, however, is difficult for a professional person. In addition, the question "Why?" is always on the horizon, and articulation of reasons is inevitable for rational man. Experience too tends to speak back telling us that some responses are good and others bad, and this experience inevitably becomes crystallized in rules and codes. The civil law and court judgments also supply guidelines for professional behavior.

But most important are the rules of professional codes which goven the actions, attitudes, and judgments of everyday practice. Besides providing guidance and justification for action, laws and codes are supported by sanctions which produce painful consequences when the roles are violated. They constitute a strong rationale for ethical behavior in psychotherapy.

Codes constitute an important dimension of professional ethics, and their influence on the ethical substance of the helping professions has been and continues to be considerable. The Hippocratic oath, for example, with its origins in the Pythagorean cult and its many subsequent revisions, continues to have its impact on the medical profession. This code created a fraternal spirit among medical practitioners and regulated the conduct of members in their relationship to one another and to their patients. Precise guidelines were laid down in it about sexual conduct, confidentiality, suicide. Specific rules of professional etiquette were established, and standards of decorum were set down.

It would be difficult to exaggerate the ethical impact of this one simple set of professional rules. It contributed more than any other influence to the moral tone of the medical profession and to the strength of the ethical tradition in medicine. And yet it is obvious to everyone that the Hippocratic code cannot meet the ethical requirements of the profession today. Because it was not supported by legal sanctions, heavy religious appeals for personal honor and virtue were made which sound archaic to modern secular practitioners. And neither its specific rules nor its general principles begin to cover the many areas of conflict and concern in contemporary practice.

What is true of the Hippocratic code is true even of the more contemporary sets of rules. Some might say that the professional codes, as they stand, raise more philosophical problems than they solve. Because of their limitations, do they increase or decrease the sensitivity of the practitioner to the ethical dimensions of treatment? Does a code designed to safeguard the needs of a particular profession adequately cover responsibility to patients and to society? What does it mean to uphold or violate the honor of the profession? What is the relationship between duty to the individual patient, the profession, the society? Can a profession devising its own rules of ethical conduct adequately enforce discipline? What is the relationship between the directives of a professional code and the more universal rules of ethical conduct?

And there are problems of ambiguity in professional codes, caused by a lack of concern with system and conceptual clarity. Little or no effort is made to separate out principles with their broad general applicability (see the next section) from rules which specify narrow particular behaviors. These two different forms of ethical discourse with very different ethical functions may be lumped together with "religious" exhortation to live a virtuous life which constitutes still another way of speaking in ethics. The code, in effect, is a grab bag of disparate elements.[6]

The inherent ambiguity of the professional code is compounded by the many different codes under which a particular therapist might function.[7] And different codes frequently establish different standards for the same professional behavior. If we imagine the psychotherapist in the Tarasoff case[8] seeking guidance in professional codes, he would not find clear direction. The old AMA code read, "The physician may not reveal the confidence entrusted to him in the course of medical attendance or any of the deficiencies he may observe in the character of his patients, unless required to do so by law, or unless it becomes necessary to protect the welfare of the individual or of society." Did the welfare of society require breaking confidence? To whom should the confidential material be revealed? If the patient's welfare is paramount, then presumably to the police. But what of the welfare of the victim? And does society's welfare require consideration when violence is only threatened? According to this code, breaking confidentiality would seem to be permissible, but it is legitimate to ask whether its direction is really right.

The new (1980) AMA code reads: "The physician shall respect the right of patients, of colleagues and of other health professionals and shall safeguard the patient's confidences within the constraints of the law."

The safeguarding of confidences in this new formulation of the code is situated in the context of a statement on the rights of patients (and other health professionals). Does this make the requirement of confidence safeguarding a duty which corresponds to a patient's right? If so, what is the status of the patient's right?[9] Certainly it is not absolute because the law is mentioned as a constraining factor. But if the law sets up legitimate constraints on the extent of a patient claim, then presumably the law is expressing the interests of society over that of the individual. The law may constitutionalize the patient's right, but in most cases it attempts to balance an individual interest against a public one. The Tarasoff decision, as a matter of fact, modifies the patient's interest in safeguarding confidentiality by supporting the counterclaim of the victim for revelation and warning rather than confidentiality.

The World Medical Association code, however, is different: "The

codes are different

doctor owes to his patient absolute secrecy of all which has been confided to him or which he knows because of confidence entrusted to him." And similarly, in the Declaration of Geneva: "I will respect the secrets which are confided to me." By these codes there would be a professional obligation not to break confidence. The same therapist, in the same case, adopting a course of action dictated by one code, would be in violation of another to which he may be equally bound.

Because the codes are historical documents, they condense different experience and incorporate different perspectives. Individualism may be the underlying presupposition in one, paternalism in another, egalitarianism in a third. The Hippocratic oath, for example, presupposes a philanthropic model in which the patient is the beneficiary of the great virtues and sacrifices of the physician. It assumes the indebtedness of the patient to the physician who comes across as a hieratic figure. In many instances, underlying perspectives incorporated into a code have more influence than its specific directives or admonitions on the ethics of the profession.

Finally, it is not at all rare that different elements in the same code are in conflict. A specific directive not to reveal confidences may conflict with a proscription against harm. Nothing in the code itself provides for the mediation of such a conflict. In such cases the very legitimacy of some element of the code comes into question. Further reflection is unavoidable. The same questioning and reflection which moves a person from the existential to the legal level of ethics now pushes him beyond the latter. In the next section, we look into the higher-order ethical categories by which even the directives of a professional code are judged.

Before discussing level 3, however, a few comments are in order on contracts, which are being suggested as substitutes for the professional codes (May, 1975). Behavioral therapists especially prefer contracts to codes and call for substitution of individually negotiated personalized terms for each therapeutic encounter. They prefer to use a legal/ commercial model rather than the older professional model for psychotherapy. In it the patient becomes a client/consumer who purchases services under terms negotiated with the supplier. Such an arrangement, it is argued, constitutes an ethical advance because it gives maximum power and dignity to the consumer. Freedom replaces trust as the ethical cornerstone of therapy. The contract which the bourgeoisie popularized in economics, free churchmen employed in religion, and feminists use to define marriage is offered now as the most ethical paradigm for psychotherapy.[10]

The idea of psychotherapy as a contract is not new. In fact, a contractual dimension to the therapeutic relationship has always been recognized (Freud, 1949). The terms of the contract, however, have been implied rather than overtly specified. It is implied that the patient who comes for treatment "contracts" to pay the bill and follow therapeutic directions (Menninger, 1958). That the therapist will work for the patient's improvement, maintain his professional skill, and keep confidence is also implied. A violation of the terms of the implied contract leaves the therapist open to the charge of ethical misconduct or malpractice. What is new, then, is not an insistence upon a contract model, but the substitution of the contract model for the code. Both models have traditionally been used.

Such a substitution does not seem indicated. There is no doubt that certain ethical advances would accompany the switch. More information would be required for the patient to give legal consent to the treatment. But this advance in voluntariness would not offset the loss of professional trust and loyalty promoted by the code. With the contractual arrangement, the client presumably can "shop around" for the best deal, but such increased freedom has little "cash value" when the item is psychiatric services. Seeking relief from tragedies of human existence is different from buying an appliance. Admittedly, there would be more specificity to the obligations assumed by the therapist, but without the functioning of higher-level standards of justice and fairness, how would compliance be evaluated? The contract also cannot supply many of the important ethical elements provided by the code. But whether the specific directives originate in a code or a contract, they require interaction with the higher-level standards discussed next.

Level 3—The Formal: Principles and Virtues

Inquiry into the reasons for this or that ethical response may take the form of a skeptical stance toward moral rules. Is this rule really the basis for right action, or should it be disobeyed in this situation? Serious reservations may also develop about the validity of justifying arguments. Questioning is transcendent in the sense that human beings can move beyond any acquisition by asking yet another question.

Such questioning may emerge subjectively from man's innate capacity for reflective thought. It may also result from a painful objective conflict over what to do in a particular situation—in which rules are in conflict or contradict one another. Sometimes changing conditions may throw a longstanding moral norm into doubt. A suddenly overcrowded world, for example, changed almost everyone's mind about traditional rules against artificial birth prevention.

Questions about the validity of practical rules of morality may be decided by reference to higher-level norms called principles. Principles are ethical values in verbal or propositional form which either have or presume to have universal applicability. If a rule can be shown to violate a higher-level principle like justice, then the rule loses its force. Rules can and should be doubted, but it is not at all commonplace to doubt general principles. Because of their close association with the very fabric of human community and the essential structure of human existence, principles generate greater certainty. It is, for example, much easier to question a particular rule about a just wage than it is to question the validity of the principle of justice.[11]

Principles are enunciations of the prerequisites for a decent human life, regardless of the culture. They represent a high-level distillation of human moral experience in every age, and presume to provide both illumination and direction in the conduct of good life everywhere. Universalizability is an important characteristic of principles, meaning that their mandate remains even if all qualifying objectives and personal pronouns are removed. Principles provide a basis for judging both rules and immediate existential responses. They connect a specialized professional code with the broader human community and give some of its norms real force, though they may weaken others. For all these reasons, principles supply an important, indeed an essential function in ethics.

What are these principles? How many are there? One-word formulation of principles would include life, justice, love, freedom, equality, reasonableness, loyalty, autonomy, truth, care, and beneficence. But it would be difficult to make a definitive list.

Generativity in Erikson's sense of responsibility for the future does not commonly appear on the list of principles, but it should certainly be included. Shared human life is the foundation of ethics, and since life is transgenerational, caring for another generation is basic. Trying to construct the perfect list or to justify every entry would take us too far off course. For our purpose, it is sufficient to show what is meant by a principle, and how principles operate in ethics.

Important as principles are, it is a mistake to identify ethics with principles. Ethics is much more complex than the application of principles to conduct. Principles certainly are related to conduct, but they are more likely to help us determine what is unacceptable (because it is unjust or untruthful) than to provide a positive answer to the question: what shall I do in this situation? It is one thing to subscribe to justice, love, freedom, or respect as ideals, and another thing entirely to know what is the just thing to do, or the loving, respectful, autonomous, truthful response in a particular situation. The relationship of principle to conduct is such that a great deal of freedom intervenes between the principle and the concrete response required by a particular situation. I might fully ascribe to the principle of care or beneficence, but get very little specific direction from that principle for the resolution of my question: what does care require for my patient who is hyperactive or demanding, or about to embark on a homosexual lifestyle?

Because principles are abstract, the person who acts on them requires a considerable amount of creativity. Imagination, intuition, and sensitivity are all required in order to move from principle to concrete behavior. What does justice, love, or care require of me in this situation? Ethical activity, like the ethical self, is one of the supreme acts of human creativity. Only saints carry off the ethical project with a high rate of success. And oddly enough, whatever good they manage to do is experienced by them more as a gift than as a result of their personal efforts.

Principles, however, do play a role in forming the truly ethical therapist. More than rules, principles point toward interiorization. As such, they contribute more directly to the formation of character. Codes and rules establish professional standards and regularities of procedures, but alone they are not enough to constitute the ethical psychotherapist. The ethical psychotherapist must be more than outwardly correct. It is not sufficient that he be a practitioner of good etiquette. The codes, rules, or standards are crucial, but they make up only the outer wall of the complete ethical structure. The inner structure is made up of interiorized principles or virtues. In addition to the guidance they supply and the standards they establish for specific norms, principles, unlike rules, influence character formation and tend to inspire thought and action.

The processes by which principles are interiorized constitutes the core of advanced moral education (Kohlberg, 1969, 1971). Once interiorized, principles become joined with personal attitudes, thereby modifying inherited dispositions and at times readjusting one's views or rules. In this way principles incline the person toward certain consistent behaviors called virtues. Beneficence is close to benevolence, truth obviously linked to honesty, trust to trustworthiness, justice to fairness. The former are principles, the latter virtues or states of character. Kohlberg (1969), Piaget (1966), and Erikson (1964) have all called attention to the interrelationship between the development of ethical character and a schedule of interiorized principles.

Principles, then, are an important ingredient of ethical life. Anyone who takes the ethical task seriously must make an effort to clarify the principles by which he lives. The more the principles are assimilated, the more autonomous and authentic will be a person's ethical behavior. Principles function like anchors and compasses in an inevitably turbulent life. At crossroads and in the midst of forced life choices, when we sense that the next move will have a serious effect on our lives, we can and should have recourse to general principles. Without them, man finds himself not only without criteria for judging rules, but also without personal light and goals. Obviously, they have a crucial role in a professional ethic for psychotherapists.

One thing which strikes us immediately about principles is that they are vague and formal. Rules tend to be specific because they are closer to the concrete situations in which one is called upon to act. Principles are more abstract than rules, and yet they have a certain content. We know something of what truth means although the term is very general. The same is true for freedom and justice. The third level of ethical discourse cannot be confused with the second. Principles do apply to real-life situations, but they do not function as specific directives.

Principles are more stable than rules, and yet there are situations in which they too come into conflict. A conflict between two principles most often stands behind the ethical crises faced by a society and the personal dilemma faced by every person sometime in the course of his life. When the choice is not between a good and an evil, but rather between two goods, or when the realization of one good means the loss of the other, and the choice is such that it will greatly affect the life of the chooser, then we have a tragic situation in ethics.[12]

The best that can be done sometimes in tragic situations is to clarify the dilemma and provide a perspective from which to begin to wrestle with it (see the next section). Our point here is that principles are more stable, formal, abstract, and therefore less arguable than specific rules; and yet, they frequently come into conflict with one another. John Kennedy, who was neither a formal philosopher nor a great ethical thinker, made the astute observation that the tough decisions are not between right and wrong, but between different rights, or different wrongs. And what is true of politics is equally or even more true in psychotherapy.

Since principles are part of ethics in general, they are also part of a professional ethics for psychotherapists. Are there, however, principles which have special force in psychotherapy? Does the role of the therapist or the peculiarity of the therapeutic relationship force certain principles to the fore? After all we have said about principles and universalizability, it sounds contradictory to hear of principles specific to the profession of psychotherapy; yet it is a fact that some principles are more frequently referred to than others in codes for psychotherapists. Whether or not the therapist is a physician, the Hippocratic principles of beneficence and nonmaleficence, for example, will figure prominently in his code, and even more prominently in the profession's tradition of caring behavior and commitment to persons in need. When faced with doubt, conflict, or ambiguity about certain rules, the professional decides by recourse to a principle such as beneficence. He asks what is best for the patient and follows the course of action indicated by this overriding principle.

The peculiarity of beneficence in medical ethics generally and the practice of psychotherapy in particular is its limitation to one's own patient. The professional therapist today, like the ancient physician, is expected to consider the patient's good his first priority and to reflect trust and care in his personal character. But beneficence can and often does conflict with the principle of justice in the sense of fairness to all.

Beneficence is closely linked to the principle of reasonableness or prudence which may be so important in codes governing psychotherapists as to be assumed rather than specifically articulated. To help and care for a patient, the therapist needs to have a thorough understanding of the patient's situation and to exercise prudence in applying means to ends. The professional who does not cultivate the virtue of prudence or pattern his behavior by the principle of reasonableness is incompetent as well as unethical. Reasonableness figures both as a cornerstone of professional ethics and as an implied criterion for judging pathology.

Although the basic principles usually figure in professional oaths and codes in one form or another, some are given much greater prominence than others. There was a time, for example, when equality figured prominently in medical codes. For example, a Chinese code, the *Canon of Medicine*, from the Han Dynasty (200 b.c–200 a.d.), pledged the physician to relieve suffering among all classes. It committed him to a radical equality in which "aristocrat or commoner, poor or rich, aged or young, beautiful or ugly, enemy or friend, native or foreigner, and educated or uneducated are all to be treated equally." Another oath considered to be the work of Maimonides gave the same emphasis to equality. But more modern codes, like the principles of the AMA, following the tradition of the Hippocratic oath, do not mention this principle (Bok, 1977).

Social justice, which is not altogether dissimilar to equality, is another principle which does not receive great attention in professional codes. The principles of medical ethics generally and psychotherapeutic ethics in particular have been primarily individualistic, stressing the relationship of practitioner and patient, and leaving the larger issues of social justice, like allocation of resources, unaddressed. But pressure is being generated from inside and outside the helping professions for more attention to this principle. The ideas of John Rawls (1971) on this topic are commonly considered a good starting place for thinking about this form of justice. Rawls provided criteria by which a particular type of inequity (e.g., in the distribution of psychiatric services) may be judged actually unjust or justified as better than possible alternatives.[13]

Only rarely in history was there any mention of truth in the professional codes, or of the obligation to inform patients truthfully of diagnosis and prognosis. Plato believed that lies told to the patient for his own good, in the professional's judgment, are ethically acceptable, and this belief seems to have been common within the profession. But now there is a concern about loss of trust in helping professions traceable to this habitual "benevolent" untruthfulness, and more attention is being given to the place of truth in professional communications. The requirements of informed consent reinforce the need for truthful communication and demand a more prominent place for this principle in professional ethics.

The principles of autonomy and freedom were historically prominent in codes, but they tended to be limited in their application to the freedom and autonomy of the professional. Awareness of the one-sidedness of these principles has contributed to the formulation of "countercodes," such as the Patient's Bill of Rights. Now, however, contemporary ethical codes of psychiatry and psychoanalysis recognize patient freedom and autonomy in the requirement of free and informed consent. Prudence and reasonableness again are assumed to operate in assessing the level of information and the degree of voluntariness possible in any particular case.

One could actually say that freedom and autonomy are stressed in modern codes. It is the recognized vulnerability of the mental patient and the ease with which coercion might be camouflaged as beneficence that gave rise to more emphasis on respect for patients' rights. The good of the patient (beneficence), however, is often in conflict with the patient's control over his own destiny (freedom). The autonomy of the professional, on the other hand, easily comes into conflict with the requirements of a just distribution of health services. (In fact, some argue that equality or just distribution of services and freedom for the professional are mutually exclusive principles.) The choice of acting in accordance with one principle may mean abandonment of the other.

The operative principles in ethical psychotherapy, however, like the principles of ethics in general, are not the whole of ethics. Because there are many different principles, there is a problem arranging them in hierarchical order. By what principle are the principles themselves ordered? The "many" is always a problem, and one solution is to reduce multiplicity to one key principle. Kant's categorical imperative is one such key principle. But the difficulty is not disposed of so easily. Principles are multiple and they inevitably come into conflict.

One classical example, a version of which may be found in Plato, describes a person who leaves his weapon with a friend who promises to return it upon call. The weapon owner arrives agitated and hostile, demanding the weapon for the express purpose of killing his wife. Truth and fidelity require that the weapon be returned; beneficence demands that it be withheld. The case illustrates a conflict of principles and the situation in which opting for one means a violation of the other. In fact, this particular conflict is not so difficult to resolve because under these circumstances, the principles of beneficence and respect for life would in most people's view take precedence over truth and loyalty.

The more common type of conflict faced by a psychotherapist involves principles related to his professional duty on the one hand and universal principles on the other. Doing good (beneficence), and not doing harm (nonmaleficence) may conflict with a promise made to the patient, or truth, or the patient's freedom. These dilemmas are not as easy to resolve as the dilemma described above. There is no evident way to determine which principles should take precedence over which others. In such painful dilemmas the psychotherapist simply does the best he can.

"Doing one's best," however, means making a decision in light of beliefs about life that constitute the fourth and final level of ethical discourse. It means considering basic personal beliefs and the kind of person the therapist wants to be. Some may question the way a particular therapist resolves such a dilemma. Others may disagree with the direction provided by his basic beliefs. But to do so is to employ a different set of beliefs and a different vision of the good life (ethics at the fourth level). But before we move to this next level, one last consideration of principles is in order.

Existential philosophers have identified one unacceptable solution to ethical dilemmas that involve conflicts of principles. It is *to avoid the issue,* to act as if this conflict is not happening in one's life, or to act in one way rather than another without allowing oneself to be aware of what is actually taking place. Sartre (1956) calls these "non-solutions," or bad faith. They are pseudo-solutions based on pretense. The person who acts in bad faith pretends that no decision is called for, or that the decision is being made by others, or that outside forces make it impossible for him to act otherwise. In contrast, good faith requires a recognition of the ethical dilemma as one's own, and then a conscious effort to come to the best possible decision. Avoiding the decision is itself a decision—the worst one. Making such a decision, however, even for an atheist, involves a "leap of faith" to higher-level ethical phenomena.

We might finish this section by reminding ourselves that each of the different levels of ethical discourse has a degree of autonomy, and yet each is connected to the other up and down the line. Third-level principles are not completely abstract, though they are more so than are rules. Ultimately, they emerge out of a reflection on our human condition in the world, including conditions engendered by the existence of rules and codes. They are linked to human experience and to the lessons human beings have learned about the consequences of human action. Rules are the result of reflection on the task of constructing responses to concrete situations. Principles incorporate a slightly more abstract degree of reflection on the same task. Ultimately, however, the principles themselves have to be grounded and justified, and this enterprise moves us to the fourth and final level of ethical discourse.

The fourth level, philosophical/theological, is in one sense even more abstract, but in another sense it is a reconsideration of primitive, lived experience at the existential level. The ultimate intellectual ground of ethics comes in the form of a philosophy or theology of human existence. Such principles as justice, love, or freedom are justified by rooting them in the structure of human existence. In providing such a justification, an explanation is also provided for man finding himself in an ethical universe in the first place. The first and fourth levels, thus, are closely related.

Level 4—The Philosophical: Visions and Beliefs

If man is the being who can always ask a further question, there is no reason to think that values in the form of ethical principles are excluded from this quest. In more philosophical moments, man asks radical questions. Why love? Why justice? Why freedom? When beneficence? What makes right acts right? What are the essential features of right and wrong acts? What is the meaning of good? Does it make sense to try to be ethical? Is there anything about the human reality which makes ethical striving a necessity for mental health and satisfaction?

All these questions throw ethics into a different mode and announce a new level of ethical discourse. The answers to such questions are a matter either of philosophical theory or religious belief. Closely associated with the way a person feels and acts (first level) are beliefs originating in philosophy or religion, and the deepest convictions anchored in early childhood experience about what is of value (fourth level).

Ethics is about concrete acts and choices, but it is also a matter of theory and beliefs. Man's behavior is linked to his ideas about reality, and he strives to conform his behavior to his reality beliefs. It is typical of man that he forms beliefs about reality and attempts to think through his ethical choices in order to make them consistent with his belief system. Even persons who resist contact with philosophical inquiry are sometimes forced into these more treacherous waters by existential conflicts and dilemmas. This situation frequently arises in clinical practice.

Conflicts force a person to ask not only "what shall I do," but also "what sort of person should I be, what is most valuable to me as a person?" Value considerations eventually move from a focus on actions to a focus on character. Sartre (1946) cites the case of a young man who has to choose either to care for his aged mother or to go abroad to join the resistance; he demonstrates that this conflict is really about the choice of a certain type of self. This kind of dilemma pushes ethics into the arena of self-creation and character choice. Sartre's point is that there is no way of doing ethics and avoiding what we have chosen to call the fourth level of ethical discourse. Ethics is more than concrete situa tions and judgments based on rules and principles. When I choose one principle as dominant for me, or decide that love, freedom, justice, or truth are important for my life, or commit myself to a course of action I think right, I do so in light of a belief about the way human reality is or about the type of person I should be.

Paradoxically, this most abstract level of ethical discourse is simultaneously the farthest removed from the concrete ethical situation with which we began our discussion and the closest to our starting point. Rather than ascending in a straight vertical fashion, the levels of ethics curve downward, so that abstract philosophical beliefs about life and reality connect with immediate feeling responses. Even our perception of values is a function of our way of being which is in turn a function of basic beliefs.

One way of speaking about this level of ethics is to refer to is as "vision" (Hauerwas, 1974). At some point, ethics is about our vision, and an ethical question pushed to its final point represents a search for vision. This vision of life and reality may be expressed either in philosophical or in religious language. In the former we use the categories and concepts of metaphysics or ontology. In the latter we use the language of story or myth.[14]

Ethics, then, is involved in every aspect of life, and for the human being this includes the level of ultimate meaning. It makes sense to ask questions such as: Why be just? Why be ethical? What is real for the human being? What is the reality of my relationship to nature? What is my calling? What is the reality of my personal relations? Who am I? What is my purpose, function, destiny? These questions are not only not nonsensical; they are all closely interrelated. These ultimate questions frequently appear as part of psychiatric pathology, and when a healthy person finds himself in an ethical dilemma in which he must decide in favor of one value over another, then these questions force themselves into consciousness.

The relation between vision and behavior is well known to psychotherapists. Some indeed prefer to understand mental illness as false vision, or as preference for illusion and unreality. Contact with reality requires a true vision of the real. Where vision is sufficiently faulty, not only is reality denied but so too is freedom.[15] Faulty vision creates twisted lives, and psychotherapy (especially an expressive psychotherapy like psychoanalysis) is in part a methodology for vision correction.

If vision, healthy or unhealthy, is diagnostically related to behavior, it is ethically related as well, in the sense of being good or bad. Ethics is first about immediate value choice, then about values in propositional forms of rules and principles, and finally, it is value theory in the sense of vision of what is real, good, and right for man. The vision that a person adopts comes through in the value judgments he makes and in his value preferences. Vision is involved in all the basic ethical factors: intention, disposition, motive, character, the grounding of value, the purpose of life, and value hierarchies. People differ according to their different ethical standards, but more basically, they differ in the different visions according to which they choose to see the world. "Doing ethics," then, is inevitably involved with religious and philosophical beliefs.

Judeo-Christian Vision

The best examples of how vision affects moral lives and ethical choices come from religion. The religious vision, communicated in story or narrative, provides a view of reality as touched by God, and the way in which the believer experiences reality as well as the way he responds to it is constantly checked by referring to a religious narrative. In theory at least, birth, growth, conflict, stress, love, aggression, death—all the basic human experiences—are evaluated and responded to in light of the vision.

The way in which a believer experiences his marriage, responds to his children, suffers disappointment, arranges principles of conduct, and adheres to rules is affected by his belief, or at least such is the challenge associated with the vision. To say this is not to deny the role of the unconscious but to insist that for ethics, especially for religious ethics, the central concern is with the conscious interiorization of a vision.

Religious vision can have a great deal to do with the patient's experience of himself and the world. But this is no less the case with the therapist. Religious belief can function as the ultimate foundation of the therapist's commitment to the relief of suffering. It can be the source of his sensitivity as well as the justification for his respect of the patient's worth and dignity. Specific norms which govern good practice can be rooted in a religious vision—for example, confidentiality and the proscription against sex with patients. The same is true of general principles such as truth, fidelity, freedom, and the like. The major impact, however, is likely to be in the development of inner attitudes and dispositions which substantially influence the way a therapist conducts his practice and resolves his conflicts.

Secular Visions

Religion is not the only source of vision. Historically, philosophy has been either a secular influence or the reflection of a movement toward secularization. The great philosophical systems can be seen as articulations, in less colorful language, of a vision which had formerly been expressed in religious myth. The ethics which corresponds to the great philosophical systems then attempts to communicate a vision of the good which does not depend upon belief in God or commitment to theological categories. Philosophical visions attempt to put good and bad, right and wrong, principles and rules of conduct, and the very purpose of life on a more objective or conceptual footing. Where once there was talk of such concepts as God, sin, and salvation, secular thinkers talk of superego development, categorical imperatives, and the greatest good for the greatest number. In effect, philosophical ethics presumes to provide guidance for those who do not belong to a faith community or who do not share the same religious faith.

Even though philosophical systems provide an alternative to religious valuation, they never completely escape the influence of religion and its language of myth and imagery. Despite their use of linear logic and more objective categories, philosophical ethical systems remain tied to a vision. The classical Greek ethics of Plato and Aristotle rely on an image of man as soul. Utilitarianism is tied to the myth of the English gentleman. Deontology is linked to an enlightenment image of rationality. Existentialism assumes the myth of the solitary hero and Freudianism holds to a mixed biological and humanistic vision of man as a sexual, autonomous, productive individual. The content of secular philosophical theories is communicated without reference to mythology, but a vision of the real and the good is always present. This cannot be expurgated even by the use of metaphysical language. And while faith as a category may not appear in the philosophical system, it too plays a part. Human beings want to think that they know what is right or wrong, and ultimately the source of any certainty about such matters comes from faith in a certain vision of the real. In an ambiguous and complex world, human beings secure their righteousness not so much by the force of logic as by the force of faith. Both religious and secular persons are "religious" in the Tillichian sense of commitment to a vision of what is ultimately real and good (Drane, 1976).

Psychoanalysis

Is there a particular ethical vision peculiar to psychotherapy? Among psychoanalysts, one may guess that a Freudian vision of human reality and human good is more influential than any other. Psychoanalysis is on a level with other great philosophical systems and aspires to provide a vision of the real and the good (Rieff, 1968, 1978). It is more than likely, then, that vision influences the psychoanalyst more than he himself may realize. Those beliefs that are closest to the center of our lives influence us without even being noticed.

The audience to which this book is directed needs no review of

Freudian theory. Suffice it to say that Freud developed a philosophical vision not only of the nature of man but of the nature of ethics as well. Freud's vision (1962) includes details of the origin and development of conscience, guilt, right and wrong, justice, ideals, and the purpose of life. His ethical vision is integrated with a broader vision of the human reality and combines to form a powerful influence on modern man's morality. Obviously, it has an impact on clinical practice.

On the basis of Freud's concept of man's nature, certain behaviors are judged good, others bad; principles such as universal love are downplayed, others such as personal love are highlighted. And there are certain ethical rules or guidelines that follow from his vision, rules such as "Don't be aggressive," or "Don't be harsh toward yourself" (Feuer, 1955).

Utilitarianism

It is altogether possible that a psychotherapist may be influenced by more than one vision or theory of the ultimate basis of right and wrong. If, for example, the psychoanalyst is a physician, his training makes it more than likely that he will also be influenced by a utilitarian vision of the good.

Developed by Jeremy Bentham (1970) and John Stuart Mill (1947), utilitarian theory proposes a standard for determining right and wrong, based on an objective calculation of consequences. The right action is that which produces the best consequences. In this tradition ethics is primarily concerned with ways of determining and then quantifying the consequences of an act.

Utilitarian theory holds to one principle which is the standard by which all other principles and rules are assessed and by which conflicts between principles and rules are settled. "The greatest happiness for the greatest number" is the ordinary articulation of this super principle.

In a situation of choice or conflict, one can determine what ought or ought not to be done by referring to consequences which follow from the alternatives. The right act is that which brings about good consequences or happiness (differently defined by different utilitarian thinkers). In psychotherapy, happiness may be variously considered adjustment, relief of pain, productivity, or sensual satisfaction.

The utilitarian vision is attractive for many reasons. For one thing, it is very liberal. No action is prescribed or proscribed in an a priori manner. Only after identifying and calculating the consequences, can a decision be made about an act's morality. What was once wrong may later become right because of changes in the effects of the act. In addition, the quantifying spirit is well suited for a scientific age. The utilitarian does ethics with means and ends that are familiar to persons who consider themselves scientific.

In the helping professions with urgency pushing toward pragmatism, a modified version of utilitarianism is used as a cornerstone of ethical practice. "What produces the most benefit and the least risk for my patient is the right thing to do" may be considered the therapeutic super principle. Since Hippocrates, the cornerstone of ethical practice has been, "Do what benefits the patient" (positive form), or "Do no harm" (negative form). Assessing the risks and benefits of every intervention then is at the heart of medical and psychotherapeutic practice, such that the ethical therapist is inevitably utilitarian, either exclusively or in conjunction with other visions.

In its classical form, the utilitarian vision is universalistic in the sense that the good and bad consequences are calculated equally for all who are affected by the action. But in medicine and psychotherapy, the good consequences of an intervention for a particular patient is the basis of calculation. What benefits *my* patient is considered good, and indeed the highest good, which may sweep aside considerations of other persons and other values such as truth, freedom, and justice.

The utilitarian vision, then, provides a theoretical foundation for particular judgments, principles, and rules, and it establishes a procedure for conflict resolution as well. But it is open to criticism and indeed roundly criticized, especially when it presumes to be the only theory. Most often it operates conjointly with other visions.

Deontologism   Duty Bound

Contrasted with utilitarianism with its orientation to consequences, is deontology (from the Greek *deon,* meaning duty), which insists upon a basis for right and wrong, independent of consequences. This one term covers a number of different theories about right and wrong, all of which share in denying that right ultimately depends upon the effects of an act. The deontologist believes that certain features of the act itself ground its ethical substance. It is the nature of the act which is the foundation of its rightness and the ultimate reason why it ought to be done.

Kant (1909) provides us with the clearest example of this reasoning:

> The duty of being truthful is unconditional. . . . Although in telling a certain lie I do not actually do anyone a wrong [i.e., do not create bad consequences], I formally but not materially violate the principle of right. . . . To be truthful in all declarations, therefore, is a sacred and absolutely commanding decree of reason, limited by no expediency.
>
> Thus, the definition of a lie as merely an intentional untruthful declara-

tion to another person does not require the additional condition that it must harm another. . . . For a lie always harms another, if not some other particular man, still it harms mankind generally, for it vitiates the source of law itself. [P. 362]

What comes through clearly in Kant's writing is the vision of man as purely rational in the sense of an ideal, neutral, reflective capability. He insists that truth telling is right in itself, and that its right-making characteristics can be recognized by anyone who thinks about the issue calmly. To the question, "Why be ethical," Kant would respond, "Because it is the very nature of man to be ethical." And as to what one must do, he insists that one's duty creates obligation. Deontological theories provide a foundation for principles, but supply very little guidance when principles or duties come into conflict.

Different deontologists hold to different right-making characteristics of acts. An insistence on justice is another example of deontology. Justice, like trust, is held to be a right-making characteristic even if the consequences are not the best. An item-by-item calculation of goods and harms is not required for the deontologist. Unequal distribution of goods is *prima facie* wrong, and fair distribution is *prima facie* right.

Medicine and psychoanalysis are deontological in the sense that certain right-making actions are considered part of the medical and psychoanalytic tradition. Freedom, justice, promise keeping, secret keeping, are included in medical and psychoanalytic codes, and their validity does not depend solely upon calculation of consequences.

In effect then, psychotherapy generally and psychoanalysis in particular presuppose a mixed formalism in the sense of a combination of utilitarianism, deontology, Freudianism, and possibly religious faith. To answer the question, "Why be ethical," one could refer to Freud (1962) or to Erikson (1964), who show the inevitable place of ethics in human life. Rules and principles which establish obligation independently of calculation of consequences are codified by the profession. And in situations of conflict between principles and rules, the professional may use a utilitarian, deontological, or even a religious standard for their resolution.

The psychotherapist does not ordinarily come across references to ethics at this final level because ethical decisions of professional committees are not usually embellished by ethical reasoning. Unlike the situation in law, judgments are not framed by reference to other decisions. And the reasons given for a particular judgment make little reference to formal ethical theories, concepts, or categories. Only those cases which are judged in civil law court have the advantage of an attached set of ethical arguments and legal precedents.

If ethics boards and peer review committees wrote opinions expressing reasons for their judgments, an ethical tradition could be established. If both majority and minority opinion were supported by written argument, future decisions could build on a base and could gradually construct an ethical edifice. Without this procedure, judgments are made without reference to former decisions or to formal ethical categories. But when ethics becomes a serious course of study in psychotherapy training programs, things will begin to change in this regard.

Conclusion

This chapter has attempted to put together the abstract speculation of philosophical ethics with the concrete vicissitudes of clinical psychotherapy. As it is articulated in philosophical literature, ethics easily escapes from the messiness of concrete cases. But the requirements of psychotherapy do not allow such a heady atmosphere. There are individual patients with peculiar histories and the alternatives generated by their situations. Ethical dilemmas of clinical practice are such that they cannot be reflected upon or argued about indefinitely. Action is, in most cases, immediately required.

Speculation and theory, then, must be such that they can be applied to pressing cases. The real everyday problems of people are the starting point of ethics in psychotherapy. And that same source is the testing ground for any psychotherapeutic ethic.

But if the concrete case and the particular patient are the ground of ethics, they cannot be the total picture. Every case has unique characteristics, as well as common aspects. Norms and principles and theories do provide an important perspective from which to view the concrete. General principles and methodology are needed to resolve individual cases. Without these there can be neither continuity, nor consistency, nor systematic progress in professional ethics for psychotherapists.

NOTES

1. One finds reference to these concepts in the *Rhetoric,* among other places (I, 2, 1356, a13, 15, 16; III, 1, 1404, a15). Although in the *Rhetoric,* he is talking of rhetorical discourse rather than poetic, the psychological action of the word was a constant concern of Aristotle, as it was for many Greek thinkers. What he says about rhetoric or the persuasive word applies to an understanding of psychotherapy as much as do his theories about catharsis. Aristotle agrees with Plato that the effectiveness of the word depends upon the reordering of the passions and beliefs of the listener. This may take place by

catharsis in the sense of a persuasive reordering, à la Plato, or by a more turbulent one which follows upon emotional climax, à la Aristotle. In either case the *ethos* or inner being of the therapeutic person must be powerful without being threatening, and able to elicit a deep relationship with the hearer of the word.

2. Using the term "value" can increase rather than dispel confusion. It is used in different ways by different thinkers. In twentieth-century American and continental philosophy, value came to take the place of what Plato talked about under the headings of the good, the right, obligation, virtue, moral judgment, etc. We are using value here in a broad, generic sense to refer to all the phenomena traditionally discussed in ethical treatises: rightness, obligation, duty, virtue, ideals, goals and norms of behavior, those qualities of the thing which make it pleasurable, noble, healthy, just, holy, and finally ethical theory. For our purposes, we are not considering economic and aesthetic values.

3. The proliferation of value words even in the technical therapies reflects their value aspects. The gathering of data on the patient requires attention to what is *relevant*. Diagnostic categories are applied *cautiously* and *carefully* so as to hold out promise of *effective intervention*. The *goals* of therapy must take into consideration the *ideals* of the patient and the *standards* of society. Verbs like *should, ought, prefer, desire,* and *must,* and adjectives like *preferable, desirable, responsible, good, bad, right,* and *wrong* figure prominently in therapy.

4. The act combines with its attending circumstances to provide us with the meaning of the act. Without this context of meaningful circumstances, an act has no meaning and certainly cannot be the object of an ethical evaluation. The movement of a piece of steel through a skull might be interesting and meaningful to the pathologist, but it becomes a meaningful ethical object only when the full context is supplied: "One person has deliberately taken the life of another in the course of a robbery, after shooting up on heroin." Another, different set of circumstances can easily be imagined. The same act by the same person may be committed in defense of one's family against a violent attack by the other person. Ethics as an enterprise cannot neglect a thorough critical assessment of the reality being considered because ethics is both a matter of objective reality and a matter of subjective disposition.

5. Man is never completely rational. It is unrealistic to expect that perfectly rational assessment will be made of the facts of any case. Rational assessments which strive for objectivity are influenced by intuitive factors rooted in deep-seated feelings and grounded in sharply held beliefs. And if the rational assessment which is preliminary to any application of rule has its nonrational facets, so too has the application of the rule itself. Judgment is required as to which rule applies, and to what extent it is applicable. This act of decision strives for the greatest objectivity, but always has its irrational facets.

6. The most recent code with direct importance for the psychotherapist is the Declaration of Hawaii of the World Psychiatric Association. It went through many drafts in an ideological tug of war between psychiatrists from democratic and Marxist regimes. The latter emphasized the psychiatrists' duties

and responsibilities toward society, while the former pushed for the strongest guarantee against societal interference in the doctor-patient relationship. What was finally agreed upon is an important ethical statement, but one full of ambiguity.

7. If the psychotherapist is a physician, he might be bound by a number of other international codes in addition to the Hippocratic oath: the International Code of Medical Ethics, 1949; the Declaration of Geneva, 1949 and 1968; the Declaration of Helsinki, 1964 and 1975; the Declaration of Sidney, 1968; the Declaration of Oslo, 1970; the Declaration of Tokyo, 1975; and the Declaration of Hawaii, 1977. At the national level, he would be bound by the principles of medical ethics of the AMA, 1980, and by the Annotations to the principles of Medical Ethics of the APA, 1973. If a therapist belongs to the American Psychoanalytic Association, he is also bound by their code. And then there is the Patient's Bill of Rights adopted by the American Hospital Association. If he is involved in research, there are any number of additional codes and rules by which professional behavior is evaluated.

8. *Tarasoff* v. *Regents of the University of California,* California Supreme Court (California Reports, 3rd series, 425. Decided July 1, 1976).

9. The very mention of patient's rights is significant. This is the first such recognition in official AMA codes. Placing the confidentiality rule in such a setting seems to provide a different direction to official ethics by putting decisions about disclosure more in the hands of the patient rather than within the province of the physician. But just how much control over disclosure does the patient have? How strong is the patient's right and how strong the corresponding claim on the physician?

10. According to advocates of this alternative, its adoption would mean the abandonment of priestly pretentions on the part of a therapist. Contractualists consider themselves secularizers and demythologizers. Their fundamental values are those of liberalism, individual freedom, and personal autonomy. Whatever rights, duties, or obligations are to bind the therapist would be specified by the contract. Symmetry and mutuality would replace the paternalism and loyalty of the present doctor-patient relationship. Self-interest would take the place of professional virtue, and each party would have easy legal recourse in case of disagreement.

11. A union may disagree with all the laws and rules governing the responsibilities of a worker, and fight for changes under the banner of justice. A revolutionary feminist may object to every traditional norm or rule governing the behavior of a wife and laws governing women in society as well, but she may not object to the basic principle of justice—"Give to every person his or her due." Both the union leader and the feminist attempt to use the principle of justice in order to support their case for a change in concrete norms.

12. The abortion controversy is a good example of such a clash. The right-to-life forces appeal to the principle of life or respect for life to ground their opposition to abortion. The pro-abortion forces appeal to the more personal principle of freedom, which is translated as a positive power on the part of the woman to control her body and its functions. It is not that one side is ethical and the other unethical. In fact, both sides are basing their case on an

established ethical principle that neither side would want to deny. The pro-abortionists do not want to deny the value of biological life or the principle of respect for biological integrity. They would object just as loudly as anyone to acts of mutilation or torture. The pro-lifers, in turn, do not want to forego or to reject the value of individual autonomy. But in a particular situation, both values cannot be realized. Acting according to one principle means violating the other. The abortion controversy repeats the classical conflict of Antigone. Her case involved a clash between the principles of obedience to authority and respect for the dead.

13. Rawls' fairness test is expressed in different formulae: "The higher expectations of those better situated are just if, and only if, they work as part of a scheme which improves the expectations of the least advantaged members of the society." In another version, "The expectations of all those better off at least contribute to the welfare of the more unfortunate. [In other words, if the benefits of the better off were lowered, the worse off would comparably suffer.] An inequality of opportunity must enhance the opportunity of those with lesser opportunity."

14. Some great thinkers use both media of communication. Plato, for example, resorted to myth in the midst of his philosophical search for the real. In the analogy of the cave he gives his vision of reality in mythical form. He tells us what it is to be in the human condition (ontology) and also how a person should behave (ethics). Even in secular philosophies, there is a certain religious quality to the highest and deepest levels of thought. Up against the ultimate questions, argument always gives way to vision and faith.

15. Critics of contemporary culture in both the Christian existentialist and Marxist traditions explain the increase in mental illness today by the erosion of meaningful world views and the substitution of superficial myths for substantial ones. For an elaboration of this theme, see James F. Drane, *The Possibility of God,* (Totowa, N.J.: Littlefield & Adams, 1977).

REFERENCES

ABROMS, G. M. The place of values in psychotherapy. *Journal of Marriage and Family Counseling,* October 1978, **3**(4).

AIKEN, H. D. The levels of moral discourse. *Ethics,* July 1952, **62**(4).

The Basic Works of Aristotle. Ed., with an introduction by R. McKeon. New York: Random House, 1941.

BENTHAM, J. *An introduction to the principles of morals and legislation.* Collected Works of Jeremy Bentham Series, edited by J. H. Burns and H. L. Hart. New York: Humanities Press, 1970.

BOK, S. The tools of bio-ethics. In J. Reese, A. Dyck, and W. Curran (eds.), *Ethics in medicine.* Cambridge: MIT Press, 1977.

BUHLER, C. *Values in psychotherapy.* New York: Free Press, 1962.

CALLAHAN, D. The ethics backlash. *Hastings Center Report,* August 1975, **5**(4).

de BEAUVOIR, S. *The ethics of ambiguity.* New York: Philosophical Library, 1949.

DeWAELHENS, A. *Schizophrenia.* Trans. W. Ver Eecek. Pittsburgh: Duquesne University Press, 1978.

The Dialogues of Plato. Trans., with analysis and introduction by B. Jowett. London: Oxford University Press, 1931.

DRANE, J. F. *The possibility of god.* Totowa, N.J.: Littlefield & Adams, 1976.

DRANE, J. F. *Religion and ethics.* New York: Paulist Press, 1977.

DRANE, J. F. Making concrete ethical judgements. *Bulletin of the Menninger Clinic,* March 1978, **42**(2). (a)

DRANE, J. F. Responsibility of the psychiatrist to society. *Bulletin of the Menninger Clinic,* May 1978, **42**(3). (b)

ERIKSON, E. *Insight and responsibility, Lectures on the ethical implication of psychoanalytic insight.* New York: Norton, 1964.

FEUER, L. S. *Psychoanalysis and ethics.* Springfield, Ill.: C. C. Thomas, 1955.

FLETCHER, J. *Situation ethics: The new morality.* Philadelphia: Westminister Press, 1966.

FREUD, S. *An outline of psychoanalysis.* Authorized trans. by J. Strachey. New York: W. W. Norton, 1949.

FREUD, S. *Civilization and its discontents.* New York: W. W. Norton, 1962.

GUNTRIP, H. *Personality structure and human interaction.* New York: International Universities Press, 1961.

HAUERWAS, S. *Vision and virtue.* Notre Dame, Ind.: Fides, 1974.

The Iliad of Homer. Trans. A. Lang, W. Leaf, and E. Myers. New York: Random House, 1950, Book XV.

JASPERS, K. *General psychopathology.* Trans. J. Hoenig & M. W. Hamilton. Chicago: University of Chicago Press, 1963.

KANT, I. *Critique of practical reason and other works on the theory of ethics.* 6th ed. Trans. by T. K. Abbott. London, Longsman: 1909.

KANT, I. *Critique of practical reason.* Trans., with an introduction by L. W. Beck. New York: Liberal Arts Press, 1956.

KLEIN, M. *Envy and gratitude.* London: Tavistock, 1957.

KOESTENBAUM, P. *The new image of the person: The theory and practice of clinical philosophy.* Westport, Conn.: Greenwood, 1978.

KOHLBERG, L. Moral education in the schools. *School Review,* 1966, **74**(1)

KOHLBERG, L. Stage and sequence: The cognitive development approach to socialization. In D. A. Goslin (ed.), *Handbook for socialization theory and research.* New York: Rand-McNally, 1969.

KOHLBERG, L. From is to ought. In T. Mischel (ed.), *Cognitive development and epistomology.* New York: Academic Press, 1971.

LAIN ENTRALGO, P. *The therapy of the word in classical antiquity.* Trans. I. J. Rather and J. M. Sharp. New Haven: Yale University Press, 1970.

LECAN, J. *The four fundamental concepts of psychoanalysis.* Trans. A. Sheridan. New York: Norton, 1978.

LONDON, P. *The modes and morals of psychotherapy.* New York: Holt, Rinehart & Winston, 1964.

MACKLIN, R. Medical model in psychoanalysis and psychotherapy. *Comparative Psychiatry,* 1973, **14**, 49-70.

MAY, W. Code, covenant, contract or philanthropy. *Hastings Center Report,* December 1975, **5**.

MENNINGER, K. *Theory of psychoanalytic technique.* New York: Basic Books, 1958.

MILL, J. S. *On Liberty.* Crofts Classics Series, edited by Alburey Castell. Northbrook, Ill.: AHM, 1947.

PIAGET, J. *The moral judgment of the child.* Trans. M. Gabain. New York: Free Press, 1966.

RAMZY, I. The place of values in psychoanalysis. *International Journal of Psychoanalysis,* 1965, **46.**

RAWLS, J. *A theory of justice.* Cambridge: Harvard University Press, 1971.

RICHARDSON, W. Toward reading Lecan: Pages from a workbook. *Psychoanalysis and Contemporary Thought,* 1978, **1**(3).

RICOEUR, P. *Freud and philosophy: An essay on interpretation.* Trans. D. Savage. New Haven: Yale University Press, 1970.

RIEFF, P. *The triumph of the therapeutic: Uses of faith after Freud.* New York: Harper & Row, 1968.

RIEFF, P. *Sigmund Freud: The mind of the moralist,* 3rd ed. Chicago: University of Chicago Press, 1978.

SARTRE, J. P. Existentialism and ethics. In B. S. Chazan and J. Soltis (eds.), *Moral education.* New York: Teachers College Press, 1973.

SARTRE, J. P. *L'existentialisme est un humanisme.* Paris: Nagel, 1946.

SARTRE, J. P. *The emotions, Outline of a theory.* Trans. B. Frechtman. New York: Philosophical Library, 1948.

SARTRE, J. P. *Existential psychoanalysis.* Trans., with an introduction by H. E. Barnes. New York: Philosophical Library, 1953.

SARTRE, J. P. *Being and nothingness: An essay on phenomenological ontology.* Trans., and with an introduction by H. E. Barnes. New York: Philosophical Library, 1956.

VEATCH, R. M. *Value-freedom in science and technology.* Missoula, Montana: Scholars Press, 1976.

Ethical Issues in the Training of Psychotherapists

Henry Grayson

Various articles and books have been written to deal with ethical or moral issues and values in the practice of psychotherapy (Buhler, 1962; Dragon, 1974; Franks and Burtle, 1974; Graves, 1976; Szasz, 1965; Van Hoose, 1977), yet there is a dearth of publications which discuss the ethical issues in training. Let us look briefly at those few publications. Barnat (1977) studied the supervisory process and noted that a supervisee's identification with a critical devaluing introject interferes with his or her developing feelings of professional identity. He concluded that by internalizing certain aspects of the supervisory character style, such as spontaneous supervisory metaphors, students experience less potency from the introject. Parker (1976) and Jorgenson (1973) focus on the clinician's need for more adequate ethical training. Sanders (1979) reported one issue brought before the ethics committee of the American Psychological Association regarding supervisory confidentiality. No references which deal with the complexity of ethical issues in the training of psychotherapists were discovered. The purpose of this chapter is to begin to fill some of that void by discussing a number of such issues, raising numerous questions surrounding these issues, and suggesting a few possible alternatives or solutions. I do not purport to possess the answers to so many complex issues, though my bias will undoubtedly come through occasionally. The reader should not consider my bias a *fait accompli,* but should rather use it to stimulate his own thinking and considerations regarding the ethical issue being raised.

For the purposes of this discussion, the training ethical issues are presented in the following general categories: (1) How do we select whom to train? (2) What do we teach? (3) How do we train and what models of ethics do the training institutes and universities themselves set? (4) What are our criteria for certification or graduation?

1. *Whom to train* is one of the foremost ethical issues facing us, both at the university graduate or medical school level and at the independent training institute. What are the criteria used for the selection of candi-

dates? Is selection based solely on traditional academic standards or does it take into account the most current findings as to the qualities found in the most effective therapists? For example, is the candidate's capacity for empathy a consideration? What about the candidate's openness to learning and to new perspectives and new ideas? How "healthy" is the applicant? Is the candidate a rigid or a flexible person? Does he or she have the kind of problems that would interfere with training and with the effective practice of psychotherapy? Would the problems be amenable to therapy—that is, could they realistically be worked out during training? Will the therapist allow his own values to impinge on a patient's freedom? What is the applicants' capacity to be fully "human"? Are those therapists whose intelligence is in the top five percentile the most successful? Will the therapist be effective for patients at all intellectual levels or for only the brighter ones? Implicit in this question is a larger issue: whom do we select to train to work with which populations? Do we select minority group members to work with their own minority groups, or do we select only those minority group members who are culturally similar enough to the young, white, successful middle-class group that when they graduate, they will simply join the abundant ranks of therapists serving this group? Do our training programs even attract minority group members who are enough a part of their own groups to be able to understand and to work effectively with them? And if this selection barrier is surmounted, would the training program itself prepare the minority therapist to work effectively with a variety of minority populations?

An additional problem faces the nonacademic psychotherapy training institutes and independent practitioners who train therapists privately. Do we train people without degrees, and those who are not eligible to be licensed in one of the mental health professions? If we adhere to degree requirement for admission, are we protecting the public from quackery? Or are we also excluding the Anna Freuds, Erik Eriksons, and Asya Kadis from training and potential service to the world? And how can we protect the public and our profession?

While there are no easy answers to these complex questions, it does behoove each training institute to avail itself of the most current findings as to what characteristics are possessed by the more effective therapists for specific populations—and to make such information a part of the selection process. It would be helpful if each training institute or university did in-depth evaluation and research on the relevance of their criteria for selection of students. Even more helpful would be a newsletter reporting all such findings to the various training institutions. We who have been involved in the training of psychotherapists for any length of time have discovered that our training programs have only a certain amount of influence on their trainees. It is indeed a humbling experience, and makes the selection of candidates more importantly an ethical concern. I will always remember Rollo May's belief, as he voiced it many years ago, that good therapists are born, not made.

Closely allied with the issue of selection of candidates is the problem of what to do when we make a mistake in our selection. We discover the candidate is not a healing person, has serious problems that seem unresponsive to therapy and/or training, or is not open to learning and growth. How long do we allow him or her to remain a candidate in training? What interventions do we make to help the candidate and in what spirit do we make them? Do we force the candidate to discontinue his training in our concern for the protection of the public? Some institutes may require the candidate to change therapists, to intensify the therapy, or to change the modality before asking the candidate to withdraw or take a leave of absence. Others may require additional supervision, courses, or a longer time for assimilation. Yet other institutes, or more particularly universities, often feel obliged to continue the candidate in training, regardless of personality factors, as long as the academic standards continue to be met.

If the training program does not take the responsibility for developing clear criteria for discontinuing a student, who will? The responsibility to protect the public cannot be relegated to our legislatures. It must be accepted by the people who know the student's work best, even if it may mean the loss of some income from that student's tuition.

I have known of students in more than one training institute whose gross personality problems or resistance to new learning and growth were obvious to both fellow students and staff, yet they continued in training indefinitely. Is the administrative problem one of economics, political power, passivity, or just a lack of ethical concern?

2. *What to teach?* is a crucial ethical issue in the training of psychotherapists; it raises the ago-old debate regarding the merits of a generalist versus a specialist. One might say that the generalist has difficulty seeing the tree for the forest, while the specialist can't see the forest for the trees.

The medical student receives basic training in all the main specialty areas and then picks a specialty. The student can pick what interests him or her most, and will know better when to refer a patient to another specialist. This practice has only recently begun to find its way into psychotherapy training programs. Instead, schisms have pervaded our field with proponents of the different psychotherapy systems, each claiming *the way,* while pointing fingers of self-righteous condemnation at colleagues who may follow a different messiah. A hierarchical system developed, with psychoanalysts emerging for a time as the high priests. Following the use of behavior therapy in the fifties and the humanistic therapies of the sixties, our consciousness has been broadened to consider other values and potentialities for a changing time. At last, the walls of orthodoxy appear to be crumbling as we realize that, for example, stress may be more effectively reduced in some people by exercise and biofeedback than through depth insight therapy. Yet others may need to work through a characterological change in order to reduce their stress.

I am not suggesting that all specialty training should be abolished in psychotherapy. A particular form of therapy may well fit the personality of one therapist better than another. Compulsive characters will pick certain systems or use them in rigid ways, while more flexible personalities will be creative or perhaps pick more flexible systems for their starting point. What I am proposing is that it is unethical to train practitioners in only one psychotherapy discipline without also providing unbiased introductions to other systems. For a psychoanalyst not to know the merits of treating phobias with behavior therapy or for a behavior therapist not to recognize the role of counter-transference can both be counterproductive for the patient. It is equally important that therapists learn the contraindications of the various therapies, particularly of their own specialty.

While there is much agreement in the field that good therapists in each psychotherapy system are not easily distinguished from one another in terms of their effectiveness, there are also some intrinsic differences—results of the various systems and techniques. Examples are: (1) direct work with the body appears to be particularly effective in breaking through the character armor for many people; (2) phobias and sexual disorders are more responsive to behavioral approaches; (3) affective therapies aid in breaking through schizoid defenses and establishing contact; (4) insight and understanding are useful in many of the so-called neuroses—to list just a few. If a training program neither prepares a therapist to engage in a variety of psychotherapeutic approaches, nor at least provides a deep appreciation for other systems and when to refer to them, the patient and therapist may unnecessarily prolong the treatment and bring undue frustration and feelings of failure to both.

A closely related issue is whether the training is unidimensional or multidimensional. Is the therapist trained to give attention to the body, spirit, and environment of the person, as well as to the mind? For example, a person suffering from depression may come to a therapist; The therapist may see that the patient receives a mood-elevating drug as quickly as possible, even though the patient experiences chronic feelings of helplessness, having projected all feelings of personal power outside him or herself to other people or to pills. The result is that the therapist thereby reinforces the neurosis. Or, one may analyze or render assertiveness training ad infinitum, all to no avail if there is a state of hyperinsulinism or hypoglycemia. Clinical practice has shown that action techniques and body techniques can be as quick and as effective as drugs in certain patients, and can increase the patient's feelings of personal power. Such issues and differential training should be a part of any psychotherapy training. The time for saying, "My way is right and all others are wrong," is past. Now is the time for synergy, if not in practice, at least in knowledge, understanding, and respect.

It is equally important to respect the personality of the therapist and what therapies he or she is most suited to perform. I, for instance, may enjoy the creativity of developing a behavior therapy program, but become bored carrying it out. For any extended behavior therapy, therefore I refer to a colleague who enjoys this kind of work. And while I have a deep appreciation for body work (such as Rolfing, Bioenergetics, the Alexander Technique, etc.), I enjoy doing it mostly in extended time groups and rarely in regular length sessions, preferring to spend most of my time in the talking therapies.

Therapists in training should be objectively introduced to all the therapies available so that they can choose clearly what they wish to practice, know when to refer, and feel comfortable in practicing and in referring. Therapists need also to be made aware of the limitations of each therapy system, and indeed of all of them combined. The limitations presented in training programs are often only those of one's "opponent's" system, not of one's own specialty. I do not intend to present a case against specialization because I believe that it increases another kind of competence, but only if it does not produce tunnel vision as a side effect. A personal anecdote will serve to illustrate. A few years ago, I went to a David Bromberg concert in Central Park with my teenage son and daughter. At first I was impressed by his mastery of the guitar. But then he also played the banjo, the fiddle, and then the mandolin, all with equal skill. It was indeed impressive to see multiple specialization. I was also impressed by his apparently absolute delight in the musicians in his band, who played instruments different from his as well as similar ones. They also enjoyed playing a wide range of music (blues, classical, jazz, folk, latin, and blue grass). I thought then that it would be delightful to see a training program for psychotherapists convey the same spirit of diversity I saw in this musician.

I have already discussed the issue of minority students under the problem of "Whom do we train?" It is, however, such an important ethical issue that it demands further consideration here. Students of all ethnic and social backgrounds learn primarily white, middle-class theories and techniques of psychotherapy, many of which are not directly applicable to the minority populations, and may be particularly irrelevant for minority students who intend to work with those populations. There is great need to bring the indigenous "therapeutic" practices of the minority cultures and economic groups into the training of therapists who may intend to work in those cultures (Stoker, 1971). I am not advocating a purist separation for any cultural group, but rather a full consideration of what the unique needs of each are, and what are the contributions of each. The old missionary philosophy caricatured in "We whites have all the answers for all your problems," is no longer a viable approach. I'm not sure it was ever ethical.

President Carter's Commission on Mental Health has stressed the need to reach unserved populations, not only minority ethnic groups, but also children, adolescents, the aged, the rural, and those with various drug addictions. Largely speaking, training programs train therapists inadequately for these populations. How often have I heard graduates of established training programs minimizing the effect of psychotherapy on people over fifty years of age. People in their fifties and sixties have been some of my most remarkable successes! Courses dealing with these populations and/or experience with them would be a beginning solution.

Among therapists I know, their life style and background largely influence how they work with patients. The more narrow their exposure, the more restrictive and judgmental they are in their interventions with their patients. If they have grown up in families where there is either little or excessive emotional expression, therapists may be prone to inhibit, sedate, or hospitalize too quickly, unless they have had personal exposure to strong and irrational affect and freed themselves from their past; and the reverse may be true as well. The same is true regarding life styles, work attitudes, sexual practices, and monetary values, to list a few. Perhaps psychotherapy training programs should require the student to have a new experience each week, even if it might be for only a few hours. The student then gains exposure to many cultural, social, economic, ethical, religious, geographic, and moral differences, not yet encountered in his own background.

The philosophical and spiritual values implicit in a psychotherapy system deserve in-depth attention in all training programs. In which psychotherapy systems does one have the greatest freedom? Or is the issue of freedom more intrinsic to the practice of a therapist as a person? Is the theory or technique sexist in any way? Do we train the therapist to believe he should have the answers so that he ends his training believing that he has? Or is he more attuned to helping the patients discover their own answers? And perhaps the outcome is related to whether the trainers purported to have the answers for the student.

Do the teachers and supervisors attempt to force the student into their own mold or support him in finding his own way? In so doing, some might question whether this interferes with the trainee becoming a master of the system he is studying. The counter-argument is that mastery of only someone else's system leaves little room for creativity. Would it not be more desirable to inspire creativity instead of conformity in training so that one is in a continual process of creating one's own system? Unfortunately, followers of a psychological disciple often attempt to build shrines to the founder, turning his theory and technique into a fixed system which then becomes the basis of psychotherapy training programs. Disciples tend to forget the spirit of the founder, which was one of creativity, innovation, and inquiry. Perhaps these qualities were of equal significance to the system itself. Thus followers of Freud may become more archaic Freudians, Skinnerian followers more Skinnerian, and Perls disciples more "Gestalty," than either Freud, Skinner, or Perls. Creativity, consequently, is blocked and stagnation and orthodoxy result. Such a spirit can and does easily invade training programs, with teachers and supervisors quoting these authorities as religionists quote the Bible. When this occurs, what unfortunately happens is that the teacher quoting is giving up his own power and creativity merely to affirm what has been, which teaches the student to follow suit. Hence, both regress in search only of other's answers and fail to develop new answers for the present. There is, of course, great wisdom in our fathers' contributions, but they should be used as foundation blocks and inspirational launching pads, not as conclusive or definitive truths.

If training programs were as concerned with the continual creation and evolution of psychotherapy as they are with the teaching of what is already developed, our therapists would be more creative. They could then help patients become more creative as well. A spirit of openness to continual redefinition of psychotherapy is called for in order to foster openness and creativity in the trainee.

A profoundly important related ethical issue is which definition of mental "illness" itself is taught. Training programs range in their philosophical positions from following the APA Diagnostic Manual like a book of statutes, to the radical positions of Thomas Szasz and R. D. Laing. I believe that the central ethical issue is the importance for all positions to be considered continually in training programs along with perpetual creative thinking on the part of faculty and students. Some questions related to this issue emerge for consideration on training. For example, is psychotherapy a process intended to help people adjust to their environments? What if that environment is poisonous? Perhaps people should grow to take responsibility for changing their environment for the better? Is there a universal definition of mental health or is it culturally defined? If it is culturally defined, what does this imply for psychotherapy training and for treatment? Is it desirable to help people adjust better to their culture? Should psychotherapy reflect the culture or be on the creative edge of changing the culture? What is the role of psychotherapy in a culture which rapidly drives people to ulcers and coronaries and other stress-related diseases? Or a culture which does not value both sexes equally? Or a culture which values economics and production above safety and health? Or a culture which is founded on a greater acceptance of violence than of loving sex? Or a culture in which the pursuit of happiness surpasses a transcending meaning or purpose in life? How can the training of psychotherapists be ethical without due consideration to such questions? Does the training program take into consideration the latest research findings and theoretical contributions, even from other disciplines? For example, does the therapy currently include both cerebral hemispheres, or does it function primarily for the left or the right half of the brain? Do we incorporate findings from physiology related to behavior changes of disorders, or do we discount them because they are from another discipline? What about the new physics of relativity and quantum theory? Have we allowed it to permeate our thinking about personality, psychotherapy, and research, or do we continue to think and to function exclusively in the framework of Newtonian physics even though radical new knowledge is available? Does the curriculum give attention to the ethical issues in the practices of psychotherapy? Is it ethical to omit such courses in professional and human ethics from training programs? Is it sufficient to believe that such issues will be adequately covered by supervisors alone?

Is there adequate supervised clinical experience? Some postgraduate training programs may provide ten to twenty patient hours per week under supervision for three to five years. Others, particularly certain predoctoral internships, psychiatric residencies, and social work placements may provide only three or four hours of psychotherapy under supervision a week and that for only a year or two. There are serious questions as to whether this is sufficient to train competent therapists, yet they graduate with the university's blessings to hang up their shingles to practice, often with a false sense of competence and professional adequacy.

3. *How do we train?* There are ethical issues involved in *how* we train as well as in what we teach and whom we select. First, do we train our therapists only in theoretical and technical knowledge, or do we also attend to the personality of the therapist? Perhaps if a training program errs in either direction, something significant has been missed. And second, what models do we convey to our trainees with regard to ethical issues? Let us look at these in reverse order, and at several actual situations which will serve to illustrate the ethical concerns.

A doctoral candidate in clinical psychology at a major university recently was scheduled for the oral defense of her doctoral dissertation. As she entered the examining room, she discovered that one of her examining committee had not read her dissertation at all, another had read it while half asleep at 3:00 A.M., just before coming in. Another responded only to the treatment of the data which was done in comformity with her major advisor. Since her major advisor had not made concessions for one of Dr. ____'s students, he makes difficulty for the advisor's student, requiring her to rewrite several chapters, even though he had agreed earlier to this particular treatment of the subject. He used the student as a pawn to get back at a colleague. Others who had not read or had barely read the dissertation could not take any contrary stand, so they decided not to have the oral defense as scheduled, to let her rewrite for hundreds of precious hours according to Dr. _____'s advice, and to reschedule the oral exam for several months later.

Each of us knows of dozens of episodes like this one, episodes in which a student has been used as a political football. Which of us would subscribe to this kind of model for professional ethics? And yet we rarely wield any influence in such situations to interfere with repeat performances. Is our inactivity ethical?

Another advanced graduate student was applying for an internship at a highly respected clinic. The interview was carried out like an inquisition attempting to break the candidate down. The interviewer threw such comments at the applicant as, "You've not shown me a thing yet, why should I hire you!" "Your previous therapists didn't do you any good. Why don't you apply to Dr. _____'s institute, then, if he thought you turned out so well in therapy with him!" Such contempt and hostility, again, seem to be a displacement of the inverviewer's feelings toward the applicant's previous therapist.

The ethics of power and of those in positions of power can no longer be ignored. How can we expect to produce ethical practitioners if the trainers demonstrate such grossly unethical behaviors. It behooves the universities and institutes to be aware of the nature of the ethics of their faculty and administration and to deal openly and directly with the issues. Too often, the maltreatment of students is merely swept under the carpet, considered the student's projections or paranoid distortions, or excused as the professor's or administrator's eccentricity. I insist that it is unethical for professionals to overlook such behaviors in their colleagues. I do not possess a perfect solution, but if professionals are confronting their colleagues directly and caringly with regard to the maltreatment of students, there is a greater likelihood that ethical considerations will move more into the foreground of thinking.

It is true that students may perceive the behavior of their superiors in exaggerated ways in such stressful situations as interviews and exams. Unfortunately, however, such a recognition aids and abets professionals in shirking their responsibilities as ethical and humane professionals who can treat their students with respect.

I know of one prolific writer and trainer of psychiatrists who will not allow experienced therapists to present cases to him in classes and conferences. Apparently he badgers the younger, inexperienced therapists, and enjoys telling them what they did wrong. An experienced therapist would not defer so easily and would defend himself. Once, an experienced therapist did defend himself, and the senior professional almost decompensated. The ethical issue here is, what is the teacher really teaching through his approach? Is it a theory and technique or is it an attitude toward people which is predominant?

The British learned long ago that the boys who were flagellated the most grew up to become the best flagellators of their younger classmates. So it may be with our professionals. If we use admissions interviews, or oral interviews, or oral examinations like fraternity hazings, we miss both human and professional values, and prepare our students for the wrong thing. We lower ourselves in such instances to the undesirable teaching principle, "Do as I say, not as I do," which rarely works, since much learning takes place through modeling and identification.

Teachers and supervisors can easily fall into the trap of merely imposing their theory, techniques, perceptions of the student's patients on the student therapist. Such a manner of instruction may help the student learn what the teacher or supervisor knows, but it may also help him become rigid, inflexible with his patients, uncreative, and lacking his own identity as a therapist. It is difficult for us to certify "whole" therapists who can help their patients become more "whole" when they have not had trainers who encouraged and supported them in developing all their own resources and style in an ongoing spirit of creativity.

Sex with patients is a clearly stated ethical issue in all professional codes of ethics. Less clearly stated is the issue of sex between teachers or supervisors and students. Opponents contend that sex in such a context sets a model for unethical sexual practices between therapist and patient. Others say that it must necessarily be a transferential, countertransferential, or an acting-out issue. Feminists see it as a sexist issue, since such sexual liasons are usually between female students and male teachers or supervisors.

Those who do not consider sex between faculty and students unethical contend that at graduate or postgraduate levels both parties are adults, and have the right of free choice regarding their sexual behavior. Questions that must be raised, however, are how does such a relationship affect the learning process? Even if a rare individual can proceed into a sexual relationship without transferential and countertransferential issues, one's passion can often blind one's objectivity to such issues until they have caused harm.

I personally know of one former graduate student in clinical psychology whose thesis advisor was also her therapist and her lover. Since I later worked with a couple of her expatients, I was aware that her grossly unresolved conflicts clearly interfered in her therapeutic work. Had there not been such a confusion of roles, the teacher/advisor/therapist might not have had as much pleasure, but the student might have been more successful at resolving her own personal problems and might have become a more competent therapist. It is my contention that it is extremely rare that a student's sexual relationship with a teacher, supervisor, or training therapist does not interfere with the personal and professional growth of the student. The rare exception might be if significant time has elapsed since the professional relationship has ended in order for both parties to have reached a clearer prospective on the real relationship.

We have already discussed what we teach. Now we turn more specifically to the issue of dealing with the personality of the therapist in training and the ethics of how this is done. Broadly considered, it is the issue of whether a training program considers itself responsible for influencing personality factors in the student as well as for supplying information and training in developing skills. At a baseline level, does the training program require personal psychotherapy? Most independent training institutes do, while few universities do at the graduate or resident levels. Since only a portion of the graduates go on past their internships or residencies for formal postgraduate training, one may question the lack of therapy requirements at that level. One may go to graduate or medical school, complete an internship or residency, and be licensed in most states without ever having a day of personal psychotherapy. I have led workshops across the country, that have often had professionals with many years of experience as participants. Those who have had no personal therapy experience are invariably the most rigid personalities with traits that would undoubtedly interfere with their best work with patients. I have often felt that their work could actually harm patients. If the public can be harmed, or even simply not helped adequately, then whether personal therapy is required becomes a moral issue of great significance. Universities have often blamed the institutional bureaucracy for the lack of the therapy requirement. It behooves the leader of such training programs to convince the powers that be of the necessity of such a requirement.

A further difficulty may be that the faculty themselves, particularly in universities, have successfully avoided personal psychotherapy and many have avoided clinical practice. Serious ethical issues are raised over whether these are appropriate people to train clinicians.

Personal psychotherapy is only one way of attending to the personality of the therapist in training. Do the supervisors and teachers attend to how the student's personality might interfere with his work with people, as in further developing those personal qualities which are the student's asset? Are other kinds of structured personal growth experiences, such as group experiences, a psychological autobiography, or psychological tests included in the training?

What happens when the student is discovered to possess personality problems which impede his professional development? Is therapy recommended or required at that time? If he is already in therapy, is he confronted with the issue and the apparent lack of success in working it through in his personal therapy? Are recommendations ever made that the student should consider changing therapists or adding an adjunctive therapy to work out the problem area better? Is the student ever asked to take a leave of absence from training until such problem areas are better worked through so that he can be more responsive to training and/or less injurious to patients?

Is there any focus on helping the student see how he is model for his patients? Is he flexible or rigid? Warm or cold and distant? Empathic or judgmental? Does he model addictions such as cigarettes, coffee, or even work? What values does he live by and demonstrate? How do his values support or block his ability to show acceptance? What are his monetary values? Will he treat anyone for free or at a reduced fee? What are the implications of either decision? What are his religious and/or moral beliefs and how do they effect his interventions and work with patients? What about sexual values? Does his need to please and be liked inhibit him from appropriate confrontations and other interventions?

How can such an important but sensitive issue as the personality of the trainee be dealt with creatively? Some training programs deal with the problem by having meetings of faculty and supervisors in order to assess each student's functioning. Recommendations are then made regarding the student's training and may include recommendations regarding the student's personal therapy. Other programs require periodical written evaluations on each student from faculty and supervisors; a training committee then reads them carefully and discusses each student. Other programs may work through an advisor sytem in which the student's faculty advisor keeps in close contact with the student as well as with the faculty and supervisors. The advisor then makes recommendations to the student directly, and often consults with the training committee. Some programs may include all of the above ways of dealing with the student's personal issues.

Certain pitfalls exist in dealing with the personality of the therapist as well. I have seen numerous faculty members or administrators act out their own transferences and countertransferences toward the students themselves. One common practice is to apply clinical diagnostic labels to the students in a judgmental way. Rarely does anything creative emerge from such an approach, and it is the student who suffers needlessly.

4. *What are our criteria for production or certification?* Important questions are: Does the university or training institute have clearly stated criteria for graduation? Are personality criteria included, or is the fulfillment of academic requirements the sole criterion? If personality criteria are included, are they clear and backed by research and clinical judgment? Continual research regarding the relation of various personality factors to effectiveness as a psychotherapist is a must in order for

one to make responsible and ethical decisions regarding trainees in psychotherapy.

The university or training institute carries the primary responsibility of protecting the public from incompetents or from those whose personality problems could potentially harm people. The states and the professional organizations cannot do it because they do not know the candidates personally. Licensing exams can only do broad screening. The institute which trains the student knows his assets and liabilities, and is therefore in the best position to make a responsible assessment.

It has not been the purpose of this chapter to answer conclusively the ethical issues regarding the training of psychotherapists. That must be done by each individual and each institution; it is hoped that the issues and questions raised here can aid in that never-ending process.

REFERENCES

BARNAT, M. Spontaneous supervisory metaphors in the resolution of trainee anxiety. *Professional Psychology,* August 1977, **8**(3), 307–315.

BUHLER, C. *Values in psychotherapy.* New York: Free Press, 1962.

DRAGON, J. An examination of the role of values in counseling and psychotherapy. *Canadian Counsellor,* October 1974, **8**(4), 272–279.

FRANKS, V., and BURTLE, V. *Women in therapy.* New York: Brunner/Mazel, 1974.

GRAVES, R. L. Values, experience level, and professional setting of training and practicing psychotherapists. *Dissertation Abstracts International,* July 1976, **37**(1-B), 460–461.

JAMES, C. R. The socialization process of psychotherapy training: Self-disclosure, self-concept and conformity of value orientation as mediated by trainer influence. *Dissertation Abstracts International,* January 1974, **34**(7-B), 3498.

JORGENSEN, G. T., and WEGEL, R. Training psychotherapists: Practices regarding ethics, personal growth and locus of responsibility. *Professional Psychology,* February 1973, **4**(1), 23–27.

PARKER, R. S. Ethical and professional considerations concerning high risk groups. *Journal of Clinical Issues in Psychology,* January 1976, **7**(1), 4–19.

RISCHE, H. A validity and reliability study of value systems analysis in counseling and psychotherapy. *Dissertation Abstracts International,* September 1977, **38**(3-A), 1233–1234.

SANDERS, J. Complaints against psychologists adjudicated informally by APA's committee on scientific and professional ethics and conduct. *American Psychologist,* December 1979, **34**(12), 1139–1144.

STOKER, D. Mexicans in the United States. *Pennsylvania Psychiatric Quarterly,* 1971, **6**(3), 30–37.

SZASZ, T. *The ethics of psychoanalysis.* New York: Basic Books, 1965.

VAN HOOSE, W. H. *Ethical and legal issues in counseling and psychotherapy.* San Francisco: Jossey-Bass, 1977.

PART II

ETHICS AND THE
INDIVIDUAL PATIENT

Ethics and the Therapeutic Relationship: Patient Rights and Therapist Responsibilities

Morton Berger

"Patient's Rights," or the matters concerning the recipients of health services as consumers (that is, patients are consumers, just as users of any other goods or services that are offered in the marketplace are consumers), has become a burning issue which is widely debated in the media. Just one example of many that can be offered is that during a recent one-week period, two programs on the subject were aired on the *Today* program. One was a debate between two physicians on the extent to which monetary considerations and economic self-interest dictate decisions on the part of medical practitioners—decisions such as whether to hospitalize a patient, whether to have a patient undergo surgery, or whether to use or order a variety of tests. In a second program, two women patients and a psychologist discussed the sexual relationships which the women had had with their psychiatrists. That such discussions took place is a matter of no great moment, but the example does help to illustrate how routine discussion of therapeutic relationships has become. More and more individuals are making public statements to the effect that the dedication of health practitioners to promoting the welfare of their patients is less than total, to say the least. In such an environment, malpractice suits abound and consumer advocacy groups and organizations are increasingly focusing their attention upon the licensed professions, and on the health professions in particular, with a view toward limiting the degrees of freedom under which the professional practitioner operates. These groups are also interested in creating situations that will increase competition, subjecting the activities of practitioners to closer scrutiny, and overhauling the machinery which provides for accountability of the practitioner to society. The administration of the disciplinary program is taken out of the hands of groups nominated by practitioners themselves and the procedure is increasingly becoming an adversary procedure. It is in this social context that the information in this chapter is being offered. It must be recognized that we live (in the words of an ancient Chinese curse) in "interesting times." These are also peculiar times, characterized on the one hand by an ever-increasing consciousness on the part of the practitioner and the trainers of practitioners of the importance of ethical behavior in the practice of the profession, and of the teaching of such behavior in formal courses. In the field of psychology, for example, all of the recent documents that have been developed to set standards for training in the professional practice areas of psychology have emphasized the importance of courses dealing with issues of professional ethics and professional conduct (Tymchuk et al., 1979). In the field of medicine, provisions for education in these issues are now generally considered an essential part of the medical education program. On the other hand, despite this increased emphasis and increased consciousness, evidence seems to point to the fact that unethical and illegal behavior on the part of health practitioners appears to be on the increase. Instances of professional misconduct in the field of psychological, psychiatric, and psychotherapeutic services in particular are often reported in the media.

It is possible that there has not really been any increase in unethical behavior of practitioners but rather that the spirit of the times is such that this kind of behavior is being brought out into the open much more frequently than it was in the past. The feminist movement, for example, has called attention to the issue of sexual harassment, intimidation, and manipulation of women in various sectors of society.

Whereas in the past the health practitioner was placed on a pedestal and his motives considered above reproach, fewer and fewer instances of inappropriate behavior go unquestioned today. It would be a mistake to conclude that the incidence of unethical behavior in the offering of psychotherapeutic services is greater than in any other area of professional activity. In fact the opposite seems to be the case. If we use the licensed profession of psychology in New York State as an example, we find that psychologists have been licensed for more than two decades, and during that time New York has had the largest number of licensed psychologists of any of the states. It is also a state in which there is a very well-organized system for enforcing statutes and regulations governing professional conduct, under the aegis of the Board of Regents of the State of New York. There is an office of professional conduct which invites complaints by consumers and maintains a staff of investigators to investigate such complaints and to take appropriate disciplinary action. The director of that office, Mr. Robert Asher, in a personal communication, reported to this writer that the number of consumer complaints against licensed psychologists (proportional to the number of practitioners) received over the years is the lowest among the licensed professions in the state. Furthermore, there appear to be generally fewer complaints concerning the receipt of psychotherapeutic services from any of the professions that offer them in New York State, and the majority of complaints that have been received by the office of professional conduct were in regard to the activities of unlicensed practitioners. The office was therefore powerless to act since there is no law in New York State that limits the practice of psychotherapy to licensed practitioners. The number of complaints is, however, on the increase.

In "interesting times" such as these, in an area of practice such as psychotherapy, there is clearly a need for a set of principles to govern patient or client expectancies of the services they will receive. This of course goes along with the need for principles governing ethical conduct in the practice of the mental health professions. Various professional groups have recognized and responded to this need. They are continually updating the principles of professional ethics, as well as attempting to improve the machinery of enforcement. In 1977, the American Psychological Association revised its code of ethical conduct, developed a set of standards for.providers of psychological services, and is in the process of developing additional sets of standards for specialty areas of psychology (1979). The American Psychiatric Association has taken the principles of ethical conduct set forth by the American Medical Association and annotated and adapted them to the practice of psychiatry. The National Association of Social Workers has a similar code of conduct. As might be expected, there are many overlapping principles, and yet the way in which they are elaborated is often quite different from profession to profession.

In addition to the ethics codes of the professional societies, there are licensing laws. Physicians are licensed in all states; psychologists in all but two, and social workers in fifteen. Each of the states which has a licensing law governing the practice of one or more of the mental health professions also has provisions built into that law governing the professional conduct of individuals licensed to practice. In many instances these codes of professional conduct merely refer to the appropriate ethics code of the particular profession. This practice has been viewed by some legal authorities as not legally binding since the particular ethics codes are subject to revision by the society from time to time. One way in which this problem is circumvented is by simply copying the particular code of conduct into the licensing statute or the administrative regulations elaborating that statute. Some state governments have seen fit to develop specific conduct regulations for particular professions. In New York, for example, there is an extensive and detailed code of professional conduct regulations which includes all the licensed professions. There is also a separate code for the health professions, as well as specific conduct regulations for each of the professions. This code was revised by the Board of Regents in 1978 and it has the force of law. As has been pointed out, the purpose of all these codes is to set standards for the practitioner, to guide him in the pursuit of his profession, and to help him avoid those actions which would be deleterious to the consumer. From the various codes, standards, statutes, and regulations, one can abstract a series of principles which might govern the expectations of the consumer of mental health services. These principles were developed by this writer from the perspective of the practicing psychologist, although it is felt that they are equally applicable to the practitioners of other mental health professions. It should also be noted that the writer recognizes the influence of the prevailing conduct norms of the metropolitan New York area which may be very different from those which have prevailed in other parts of this country with regard to some issues. In this chapter, each of the principles or "rights" of client or patient will be followed by a statement of corollary responsibilities of the providers of service which relate to these patients' rights. This will be followed by a general discussion of some of the issues involved, including such things as sources, limitations, and scope of applicability of the particular principle. It should be noted that in some cases there is overlap between some of the principles, since the writer considers it desirable to state certain of the principles separately for the sake of emphasis, even though they might be subsumed under other principles. Nor is the writer proposing that this list is by any means an exhaustive one. It is, however, a representative list of those conditions which the recipient of psychotherapeutic services has a reasonable right to expect to prevail when he or she enters into that process.

1. *The patient has a right to treatment.*

The therapist responsibilities which may be considered corollaries to this right include the following:

   a. To provide treatment (particularly in emergency situations);
   b. Not to terminate therapy once it has been undertaken without preparing the client and without making appropriate provision for continuation of treatment if such is warranted;
   c. To make oneself available to a client in case of an emergency;
   d. Not to deny treatment on the basis of race, creed, color, natural origin, and/or sex;
   e. To provide for a client's immediate treatment needs in the event that the therapist will be unavailable for an extended period (e.g., when on vacation);
   f. To espouse and promote those measures in society which would serve to maximize the availability of psychotherapeutic treatment services to the population.

The right to treatment derives from the most fundamental of human rights, namely those of life, liberty, and the pursuit of happiness. All of the licensed mental health professions have the promotion of human rights and human welfare as their basic goal. The American Medical Association code, for example, states that the principle objective of the medical profession is to render service to humanity. Psychologists are committed to the utilization of knowledge of human behavior for the promotion of human welfare. All of them emphasize respect for the dignity of man. As a consequence, there is a clearly recognized responsibility on the part of providers of service to provide treatment. Despite this recognition, there is no real agreement on just what the scope of the right to treatment is, nor is there agreement as to the scope of the responsibility to provide treatment. For example, the medical ethics principle on the provision of service says that a physician may choose whom he will serve. On the other hand, the American Psychiatric Association elaboration of the code of medical ethics says that a psychiatrist should not be a party to any type of policy that excludes patients on the basis of ethnic origin, race, sex, creed, age, or socioeconomic status. New York and other state laws define professional misconduct as, among other things, refusal to provide professional service to a person because of that person's race, creed, color, or national origin. We must conclude, therefore, that while the patient's right to treatment is not an unlimited one, the therapist's right to choose whom he will serve is being increasingly limited.

The intensely personal nature of the therapeutic relationship has also given rise to the same questions regarding the appropriateness of certain therapist groups (e.g., Chesler, 1972) for serving the needs of certain patient groups. Many feminists have questioned whether a male therapist can possibly relate effectively to the needs of a female client in a nonexploitative manner. Some minority group members have argued that as nonminority group members, therapists can neither identify adequately with the sociocultural realities of being a member of a minority group, nor deal effectively with the impact of the sociocultural forces on the minority patient's psyche.

The right to treatment assumes very special significance when an individual is hospitalized, particularly, if hospitalized involuntarily. The courts have recognized that the continuation of the patient's hospitalization is predicated on the premise that his or her right to treatment is being met. Also implicit in the right to treatment, particularly under conditions of hospitalization or other forms of institutionalization, is the right to refuse treatment. Dr. Morris Chafetz, former director of the National Institute on Alcohol Abuse, pointed out some years ago that we cannot force treatment upon a substance abuser even though we may recognize that his behavior is destructive to himself, his family, and even society in general. He may be hospitalized at the request of others because he is incapable of functioning at the moment, but once he is capable of a rational decision, he is entitled to decide that he does not want treatment. This approach is basic to the functioning of a free society. It can be contrasted with the situation found in a number of Eastern European countries where treatment is forced upon alcohol abusers. It should be pointed out, however, that the results of such mandatory treatment have not been demonstrated to be sufficiently encouraging to warrant such a limitation of individual freedom in the interest of benefit to the individual or society. There are, of course, many instances in which treatment has been mandated for individuals who have broken the law and are judged to be in the need of treatment instead of punishment. An example of this is mandatory treatment for driving while intoxicated. Thomas Szasz (1963) has argued cogently that such an approach is in neither the interest of the individual nor the interest of society. While the Szaszian view has certainly not prevailed thus far in our society, we can see signs of a movement toward the unraveling of issues of punishment and of treatment. We may expect that there will continue to be changes in the ways in which society deals with offenders who show signs of emotional disturbance and individuals who are apparently in need of treatment but who refuse it. Furthermore, an increasing number of students of human behavior tend to favor a social learning model (such as that which underlies Szasz's views on the politics of mental illness) as a fairly valid approach to understanding psychopathology. During the forseeable future, however, the ethical practitioner will continue to be forced to make difficult choices in this area.

The right to choose treatment includes the right to choose one's therapist and to choose not to work with a particular therapist. This, of course, is limited by one's ability to pay and by the aforementioned right of any given therapist to choose not to work with a particular patient. The personal nature of the therapeutic relationship is such that this latter right is a very important one, provided that it does not involve systematic discrimination against a particular group. Nor does the injunction against discrimination prevent the therapist from limiting his practice in certain specific ways, such as limiting the practice to the treatment of children, or of women, based upon the therapist's understanding of his own expertise. This point is emphasized in the proposed American Psychological Association (1979) *Standards for the Providers of Clinical Psychological Services.* Working or not working with a particular patient becomes a crucial issue in institutional settings such as clinics and hospitals in which the patient is most often assigned to a particular therapist. All parties ought to recognize that the wisdom of a particular assignment may be open to question, and the assignment open to review. It is not at all inappropriate for either party to raise the question and to conclude that the particular match is not a good one.

The issue of freedom of choice of therapist is tied significantly to the issue of third party reimbursement. Thus, the laws guaranteeing psychologists or social workers reimbursement rights for delivery of psychotherapeutic services are aptly called "freedom of choice laws." Dörken and Webb (1980) conducted a study of such laws and their effects on the availability of services delivered by psychologists. Their findings indicate that in states where such laws prevail, there tends to be a greater availability of psychological services. The number of psychology practitioners, however, appears to have influenced the passage of such laws, rather than the laws influencing the number of practitioners. The professional societies' tendency to advocate legislation which would grant coverage for their members is most often seen as self-serving. This view ignores the fact that in American society, this form of prepayment for treatment services is the only way in which such services would be available to most people outside of an institutional setting. Also, the consumer usually has little choice regarding the details of the plan under which service is offered since it is negotiated either by his or her employer or by his or her labor union. Under these circumstances, the right to treatment very definitely includes a right to choose one's therapist from among the licensed professional deliverers of such service.

2. *The patient has a right to have a service provided by an individual who is competent to provide that service.*

The responsibilities of the therapist which are corollaries of the above include:

a. To become aware of the expected standards of competence for providers of this service;
b. To gain such competence;
c. To undertake such continuing educational experience as will maintain that competence;
d. To practice only within one's area of competence;
e. To avoid practicing when one's ability to practice is impaired by alcohol, drugs, or physical ailment or disability, or by some psychological incapacity;
f. To make information regarding one's competence and any limitations on that competence immediately available to the client at the outset of therapy;
g. To make certain that any assistants and/or students who are providing services under the authority of the primary practitioner are competent to provide the specific services;
h. To provide regular ongoing supervision of such assistants;
i. To espouse the adoption of standards by professional societies and by governmental agencies that will serve to raise the level of competency of all practitioners in the field of psychotherapy.

The main problem in implementing the above principles and of occupational credentialing is assessing who is competent to do what. Nowhere is this problem more complex and confused than in the delivery of mental health services. Up to this point, we have used the terms psychologist, psychiatrist, social worker, therapist, or deliverer of services essentially as if they were interchangeable when they are not. This chapter is intended to address the broad range of mental health services that might be delivered by a variety of professionals, though the term psychotherapy refers to only one category of such services. Furthermore, psychotherapy itself is a generic term that refers to a wide variety of techniques based upon a wide variety of theoretical orientations.

It has been shown that the empirical investigations of the various techniques vary in both quality and quantity. All these services, however, do have in common the fact that they represent attempts at modifying maladjusted or maladaptive behavior. In a fluid situation such as this, it is difficult to speak definitively about competence. In fact, the number of opinions regarding what constitutes competence in the delivery of mental health services seems almost to exceed the number of available practitioners. The situation has become even more complicated during the past few years with the introduction of large numbers of paraprofessional practitioners. Such individuals tend to operate in a wide variety of institutional treatment settings and to provide all kinds of therapeutic services, often with a minimum of training and/or supervision. Though there has been a great deal of research on the efficacy of such practitioners, as compared with that of more highly trained professionals, the overall findings have not been definitive. This is to some extent due to methodological problems in designing such studies. Despite the lack of clear-cut evidence, many voices (e.g., Hogan, 1979; Buck and Hirschman, 1980) have favored the use of such individuals and the granting of recognition to them as practitioners via licensure in order to reduce the cost of service to the consumer. Since the use of paraprofessionals has become widespread in institutions and clinics which tend to serve individuals with limited financial means (usually at public expense), the effect has been to provide what may well be a double standard of treatment for the "haves" versus the "have nots."

Even among the licensed mental health professions, where there is some agreement regarding the education and training required for entry into the profession, there is a great deal of ambiguity. For social workers, the Master of Social Work degree qualifies the individual to sit for the licensing examination as a social worker. Successful completion entitles the individual to engage in social casework which may or may not be considered psychotherapy, depending on whom one asks. Most people in the field, however, tend to feel that in order for social workers to practice psychotherapy, they should receive advanced postgraduate training.

In psychology, a doctoral degree plus two years of supervised experience is usually the standard for entry into the profession, but psychology is a very broad field and in most states the licensing laws in psychology are generic. This means that they license the general category or title of psychologist or the practice of psychology without specifying a particular area of specialization. Many states have legal provisions which make it unprofessional conduct to practice outside one's area of specialization. The areas of psychological specialization which are usually associated with the delivery of mental health services are clinical psychology, counseling psychology, and school psychology. Psychology is categorized by the rapid development of new knowledge, new techniques, and new applications. As a result, new fields or subfields spring up which are based upon applications of psychological knowledge to specific kinds of problems. An area which in the past would have been considered only an area of research, suddenly becomes an area of application. Behavior modification is an example of a series of techniques, many of which were developed and introduced by psychologists whose training was not in the area of clinical practice. Health psychology represents a new area involving the application of psychological principles and methods to the goal of achieving and maintaining good physical health.

In addition to the foregoing, the situation is complicated by the fact that many individuals trained and licensed as psychologists, whose training was not originally in areas of application, undertook respecialization training subsequent to taking their degrees and even subsequent to licensing. The nature and extent of respecialization training has been exceedingly variable and has led to several attempts on the part of the American Psychological Association to clarify who is entitled to practice in particular specialty areas. The proposed *Standards for Providers of Clinical Psychological Services* (1979), which has been developed by the American Psychological Association, attempts to deal with this problem, as does the report of the task force on specialty criteria of the American Psychological Association entitled, *Characteristics and Criteria for a Specialty* (1980).

Despite the foregoing sources of confusion, the consumer can be offered guidelines with regard to psychological practice. First, anyone offering psychotherapeutic services who has not received a doctorate in clinical psychology, counseling psychology, or school psychology must bear the burden of proof to the consumer, and the world at large, that he or she has completed equivalent coursework and other educational and training experiences in order to practice in these areas. This is stated in the *Standards for Providers of Clinical Psychological Services* and is consistent with the American Psychological Association ethics code, which says that "Psychologists recognize the boundaries of their competence and the limitations of their techniques; and only provide services, use techniques or offer opinions as professionals that meet recognized standards." In many states, there is language in law or regulation which states that practicing beyond one's area of competence constitutes unprofessional conduct which can lead to removal of one's license. The language in New York State law defines unprofessional conduct as "practicing or offering to practice beyond the scope permitted by law or accepting and performing professional responsibilities which the licensee knows, or has reason to know, that he or she is not competent to perform."

There is a clear-cut standard in the medical profession, but there is also ambiguity. The qualifications of a psychiatrist include completion of a medical degree and certification by the specialty board in psychiatry, or at the very least completion of an approved residency in psychiatry. There are many physicians, however, who see the treatment of the emotionally ill and even the practice of psychotherapy as a significant part of their practice. These include general practitioners, practitioners in the fields of family practice and in internal medicine, and in a variety of other fields. In some states, marriage and family counselors are also licensed to practice, in some instances at the doctoral level of training, and in some instances at the master's level.

The common denominator with regard to competency among the various licensed mental health professions is the concept that basic professional training is not in and of itself sufficient training for someone who intends to practice psychotherapy; some form of advanced specialized training and individual supervision over an extended period of time is required. In addition, many groups advocate that the practitioners have undergone personal therapy; this requirement, however, has never been adopted by any legal authority such as in statute or regulation, nor is it embodied in any of the ethics codes of the various professions involved. Finally, in regard to competent practice the ethics codes in both psychiatry and psychology emphasize the importance of basing one's practice upon scientific information which is regularly updated. The psychiatry ethics code warns psychiatrists not to refer patients to treatment programs which are "based only on dogma and authority and not on scientific validation and replication." The proposed *Standards for Providers of Clinical Psychological Services* of the American Psychological Association says that "clinical psychologists [should] maintain current knowledge of scientific and professional development to maintain and enhance their professional competence," and goes on to state that "Professional Clinical Psychologists are encouraged to develop innovative theories and procedures and to support their innovations on an appropriate theoretical and/or empirical basis."

The foregoing represents the situation of the practice of licensed mental health practitioners and paraprofessional assistants. There is also a whole class of nonlicensed practitioners who have received varying amounts of training in so-called psychotherapy institutes. Most of these institutes were originally intended to provide advanced postgraduate training in psychotherapy to licensed practitioners. Since they are neither accredited educational institutions nor under any form of close governmental regulation, they undertook to train individuals who were neither licensed nor students in programs leading to licensure. This is an exceedingly profitable enterprise and has created a large number of nonlicensed practitioners, some of whom are highly skilled psychotherapists. They are currently pressing the legislatures in various states for licensure of psychotherapy (and/or psychoanalysis) as an independent profession.

In the face of the array of confusing information regarding competency, the responsibility of the therapist to provide clients at the outset of treatment with specific information regarding his or her training, licensure status, and competency assumes vital importance. Unlike other areas of practice in which confusion on significant issues is much less likely, the therapist is responsible to clarify for the client his professional training (e.g., a Ph.D. in clinical psychology), his or her licensure status, advanced training or credential status (e.g., diplomate of the American Board of Professional Psychology, or the American Board of Psychiatry and Neurology), completion of special advanced training program (such as a psychoanalytic institute), and also any specific limitations on his or her practice, as advocated by Hare-Mustin et al. (1979).

The ethical responsibility to engage in continuing education in order to maintain high levels of competence is recognized in all the professions. A statutory mandate for continuing education, however, exists in only one-third of the states. The professional associations in medicine and psychology have developed comprehensive programs for providing and accrediting continuing professional education programs, as well as for awarding credit for attending approved programs and for maintaining records of credit received by individual practitioners. Many specialty boards require evidence of such credit for recertification. In the absence of state regulations, the consumer can and should inquire about the provider's status regarding pursuit of continuing education and the therapist should be able to provide such information.

3. *The patient has a right to a reasonable financial arrangement.*

The therapist's responsibilities which are corollaries to the above include the following:

    a. To provide accurate information regarding all costs by the end of the first session;

    b. To arrange for a payment schedule by the end of the first session;

   c. Not to spring unexpected costs upon the client;

   d. Not to split fees;

   e. Not to exploit the client by prolonging treatment unnecessarily or convincing the client to undergo unnecessary treatment or diagnostic procedures;

   f. To assist the client in collecting from third party payers (includes filling out forms in a timely manner, providing complete and accurate information, without requiring payment in advance of providing such information, and cooperating with any reasonable requests of the third party payer);

   g. To make the client aware of contingencies for third party payment;

   h. To take whatever steps are necessary to make oneself eligible for third party reimbursement.

The financial arrangement issue is always a very touchy one. The situation is complicated by the fact that psychotherapy is perhaps the only professional service in which there is a theoretical view which suggests that the payment of the appropriate fee has a beneficial effect on the efficacy of the process. Furthermore, the way in which the client deals with the fee issue is seen under this theoretical view as an indication of the way in which the client relates to the therapeutic process (i.e., the concept of "resistance" in psychoanalytic theory).

On the other hand, it must be pointed out that psychotherapy is an extremely expensive service. It is generally delivered in units of approximately one hour with the per-unit cost currently at approximately $60.00, when provided by a fully trained independent practitioner. The more expensive therapist charges significantly more than that, while students or clinics (usually utilizing less well-trained providers) charge significantly less. Thus, even the cost of an initial consultation session represents a significant outlay for most people. A clearer picture of the economic impact of psychotherapy upon the individual or the family can be readily appreciated when one considers that the annual outlay for psychotherapy for an individual approximates the annual family outlay for an automobile. It has often been noted that the purchase of an automobile usually represents the second most significant purchase a family makes (following that of a home). Given those circumstances, financial considerations cannot be relegated to the status of theoretical constructs in the therapy process. It is not unreasonable for the therapist to quote his hourly fee in the initial phone conversation because the client may find it beyond his means.

It is certainly not inappropriate for the client to request a statement of fee during the initial phone contact. Insurance coverage (depending on the policy) goes a long way toward softening the financial blow to the patient. Most policies will pay from 50 to 80 percent of the cost (though some policies set a dollar limit per session) after a deductible. Patients are often unaware of their own insurance coverage and exploration of this topic has to be undertaken with them by the therapist. The therapist is often aware, merely from the employment information obtained from patient, that there is coverage (since the therapist has previous experience with other employees of the same employer) and is in a position to help the client make appropriate inquiries and obtain the necessary forms. Many practitioners keep a supply of forms provided by those carriers who provide most of the coverage in a particular geographic area. Dörken and Webb (1980) point out that a significant proportion of coverage is provided by relatively few carriers. At the time that insurance coverage is explored, however, it is incumbent upon the therapist to raise and discuss relevant confidentiality issues, which will be discussed later in this chapter. There is general agreement among all the various ethics codes and standards that the issue of fees should be discussed early in the process, generally by the end of the first session. Most ethics codes express the general view that a practitioner ought to contribute a portion of his time to providing services to and for individuals who are not capable of paying the full fee. The ethics code of the National Association for Social Workers (1980) specified the principle that fees should not be unreasonable nor beyond the client's ability to pay. Dörken and Webb (1980) found that for psychologists in 1976, the median amount charged per session varied from one geographic region to another and reflected general economic conditions in the region. Availability of third party reimbursement did not appear to have a significant effect on how much psychologists charge.

The issue of unexpected costs may be pertinent to the practice of psychologists, particularly those who include a battery of psychological tests as a part of the treatment process. Many psychiatrists routinely refer patients for psychological tests. In such cases, the battery of tests which often costs a flat fee equal to approximately three therapy sessions should be discussed with the client at the outset as an anticipated cost of the process. Therapists often don't decide that a test battery is called for until later in the process at which time they attempt to convince a client of the wisdom of such a procedure. In the view of this writer, this approach creates problems and should be avoided when possible.

Fee splitting is a serious problem in the field of psychotherapy, particularly because there are a number of practices which have become rather common and which border on being violations of the fee-splitting prohibition. All the ethics codes and most state professional conduct laws and/or regulations prohibit fee splitting in all professional activity. Fee splitting involves the payment by a professional of money to another professional for that person's referral of a patient. In psychotherapy, three practices which became particularly common in metropolitan areas during the past two decades have created problems in this area. First was the practice adopted by many psychotherapy insitutues or centers of advertising low-cost evaluation and referral services. Subsequent to the evaluation, referral would be made to one or another professional from a list of individuals who were affiliated with the institute or center in some way and who paid the institute or center some fee for that affiliation. This practice was evaluated by the Division of Professional Conduct in New York State and found to be a clear violation of fee-splitting prohibitions. A second practice which has created problems of this kind is that of psychotherapy institutes whose major function is to provide training for student therapists. The service delivery program of such institutes is essentially designed to provide patients for training purposes and services are most often offered at a cost that is lower than the prevailing rates. Under this system, a patient comes to the institute and is assigned to a particular student-therapist for treatment. In many instances the therapy is conducted at the institute's facility. In other instances, however, the therapy is conducted by the student-therapist at his or her office. In either case, the system requires that the institute provide direct supervision for the student-therapist both on an individual basis and through group supervision. In some instances fees are paid by the client directly to the institute. A part of that fee is used to defray the costs of the facilities and the supervision; part is given to the therapist. In addition, the therapist usually takes advanced courses at the institute for which he pays tuition. Many institutes also require that a student-therapist undergo personal psychotherapy at his own expense with a therapist who is affiliated with or a graduate of that particular institute. Fee-splitting violations tend to occur in this situation when the client is seen at the office of the student-therapist to whom the client pays the fee directly. The student-therapist then pays the institute for the supervisory services. In some cases, the supervisory services gradually become nonexistent over a period of a year or two, but the student therapist is expected to pay a portion of his fee for as long as he continues to see that patient, ostensibly on the grounds that the patient was a patient of the institute. This is clearly a fee-splitting violation. Still another practice which has become common is recognized as a kind of fee-splitting violation by the professional conduct regulations in New York State. This is an arrangement whereby an individual practitioner rents space in a facility, and the rental constitutes a percentage of the income or receipts of that practitioner. This kind of activity led to abuses of third party payments through medicaid and such facilities have sometimes been referred to as "Medicaid Mills."

The financial exploitation of a client through influencing him or her to undertake unnecessary diagnostic and therapeutic procedures is one which has aroused a good deal of criticism by consumer groups. In New

York, this gave rise to a specific prohibition when the professional conduct regulations were recodified. A common practice of recommending to individual therapy patients that they also attend group therapy sessions to supplement their therapeutic experience could very well be open to scrutiny on these grounds. Not only, as mentioned above, should the administration of psychological tests be discussed at the outset of therapy, the practice is also open to question on the ground of promoting unneeded services. In this regard, Samuel Messick (1980) has provided a two-pronged approach toward examining the ethics of assessment. His approach stresses the issue of adequacy of a test, which he relates to construct validity and the issue of the appropriateness of the use of a particular test which can be examined by appraisal of the potential social consequences of the testing. The use of construct validity measures as an approach toward justifying assessment procedures has been with us for some time and has demonstrated its utility. The added dimension of the value implications of test interpretation and the social consequences of test use provide the practitioner with a framework for dealing with questions which will arise concerning the appropriateness of assessment procedures in individual cases.

In examining the issue of the length of treatment, one can no longer ignore the consideration of the nature of the insurance reimbursement contract as a factor in the evaluation of the role of treatment in enhancing the patient's overall welfare. More and more practitioners are finding themselves developing therapeutic strategies and timetables to fit reimbursement time limits. The issue of prolonging treatment will be dealt with in connection with the patient's right to a terminable experience.

The availability of third party payments has created still another dimension in the clarification of the relationship between therapist and patient. The importance of establishing just what coverage the particular patient has, early on, has already been stressed.

The responsibility of the therapist to become aware of the contingencies for reimbursement to the patient has also been emphasized. The converse, while obvious, needs to be stated and emphasized. Many therapists have good reason to know in advance that they will not be covered by particular carriers, or they will have good reason to believe that the client will have real difficulty obtaining reimbursement by a particular carrier. Dörkin and Webb's (1980) study revealed among other things that the Blue Cross-Blue Shield insurance policies tended to present a large number of problems as far as reimbursement for services by psychologists was concerned, even in states where freedom of choice laws exist. Despite the situation's ambiguity, the therapist has the responsibility of clarifying it as much as possible so that the client can make an informed choice from the point of view of his or her economic welfare.

This is particularly incumbent upon nonlicensed therapists since all freedom of choice laws require payment only to licensed practitioners. In most instances, payment is limited to physicians and psychologists, though New York social workers recently received some form of coverage.

Unlicensed therapists in particular have the ethical obligation of informing the client that there is no obligation on the part of third party payers to reimburse the patient for their services. These practitioners will hasten to point out that they nevertheless encourage patients to file such claims and discover very frequently that the claims *are* paid!

4. *The patient has a right to a therapist who is committed solely and completely to promoting his or her best interests and personal welfare. Associated with this is the client's right to be provided with the necessary information to enable him or her to make an informed choice regarding therapy.*

The responsibilities of the therapist in connection with this right include the following:

a. To provide the client at the outset with information concerning goals, procedures, and the therapist's theoretical orientation in regard to the therapeutic process;
b. To call attention at the outset to any potential value conflicts between therapist and client;
c. To avoid conflict of interest;
d. To avoid gratifying his or her own needs at the patient's expense;
e. Not to engage in any form of sexual activity with the patient.

The principle of therapist commitment to promoting patient welfare as described above represents the most fundamental right of the patients from which all of the other rights can be derived. On the other hand, when one considers it in isolation, it raises certain specific issues which merit discussion. A good deal of this discussion tends to center on how the best interests of the patient are determined. In a fairly comprehensive discussion of these issues, Hare-Mustin et al. (1979) point out that the responsibility for implementing clients' rights rests on the therapist. They point out that in most instances the client or patient is in a very poor position to ascertain that his or her rights and best interests will be protected. On the other hand, they emphasize that the provision of sufficient information for the patient to make informed choices about entering and continuing therapy is a basic requirement. They state:

> Knowledge of three areas provides the necessary background for such choices:
> 1. The procedures, goals, and possible side effects of therapy;
> 2. The qualifications, policies, and practices of the therapist;
> 3. The available sources of help other than therapy.

The approach which they recommend as the most desirable for accomplishing this goal is that of the formal written contract; this has also been recommended by consumer groups and others (Everstine et al., 1980). They provide examples of such contracts which include the participants, duration (i.e., number of sessions, etc.), as well as goals, fees, and limitations upon the agreement. Many practitioners feel that the issues which would be embodied in the contract ought to be discussed and clarified in an unambiguous way, but that the formal contract is alien to the spirit of the therapeutic relationship. The key question remains, "Just what kinds of details about the therapy ought the therapist to be communicating to the client at the outset?" It has been pointed out with some justification that too detailed an accounting of specific therapeutic technique tends to undermine the efficacy of the therapy itself. As Hare-Mustin and her associates point out (quoting appropriate sources), the therapist needs the freedom to decide how to proceed as far as the details of the treatment are concerned, and spontaneity is often a very important element of the process. Even setting overly specific goals may be considered premature and counterproductive. On the other hand, with the multiplicity of therapeutic forms and approaches in our society it would not be at all uncommon for a particular therapist to have a philosophical orientation toward life and life styles, as well as an action-oriented therapeutic approach based on that philosophical orientation, which might be totally at variance with the orientation of the patient. Clear-cut communication is crucial in such instances so that the therapeutic process does not become a manipulative one in which the goals of the therapist become paramount and those of the patient secondary. London (1964) discusses therapist values and concludes that in insight therapies, as well as action-oriented therapies, there is no way that a truly value-free approach to therapy can be managed. There is in fact a prevailing value system which guides a good deal of psychotherapy today; this is the value system in which self-enhancement is an ultimate goal, as opposed to self-sacrifice in the interests of enhancing others or society in general. Hare-Mustin et al. question what should be done when the therapist has personal or moral problems with the client's goals. The reverse can also become a problem, namely when the therapist's goals and values, which arise out of his theoretical orientation, come into conflict with those of the patient and/or those of the significant others in that patient's life. This latter problem becomes acute with adolescents in therapy and in family therapy situations. The personal and therapeutic philosophy of the therapist can also conflict with a particular patient's religious values. The basic ethical principle (which is recognized in all the ethics codes) of respect for human dignity demands that in such situations the therapist explore the potential conflict areas early in the process and establish, together with the patient, some agreed-upon ground rules for dealing with this sensitive area.

Perhaps the most difficult obstacle to overcome in commiting oneself to the best interest of the patient lies in the area of therapist self-gratification at patient expense. The problem with this issue is that the process is exceedingly subtle. The goal of all therapy training is, of course, to sensitize the therapist to this kind of process in such a way that he is in a position to use himself as an appropriate therapeutic instrument. In the psychoanalytic framework, this involves dealing with the issue of counter-transference. The problem is particularly acute in therapeutic relationships between males and females. Chesler (1972) argues that male therapists inevitably relate to female clients in an exploitative way. When such problems are not subject to resolution in a reasonable amount of time, the appropriateness of the particular therapist for a particular client becomes questionable. The American Psychological Association's *Standards for Providers of Clinical Psychological Services* states that psychologists have the right and responsibility to withhold services where differences with the clients might impair the effectiveness of the relationship.

Conflict of interest comes into play when therapists allow themselves to become involved in dual relationships with patients. This means that in addition to their therapist-patient relationship, there is some other relationship between them. Frequently, therapists find themselves in this situation because they enter into the therapy relationship assuming that the other relationship is remote or insignificant, only to find that the dual relationship creates an acute problem later in the therapy process. In reporting on the adjudication of ethics complaints, the American Psychological Association's committee on scientific and professional ethics and conduct describes a situation in which a psychologist employed at an agency undertook to do therapy with another employee of the same agency, and this ultimately led to a breach of confidentiality (Sanders and Keith-Spiegal, 1980).

The dual-relationship conflict of interest problem finds it most serious expression in the sexual involvement between patient and therapist. The nature of the therapeutic relationship is such that the possibility of sexual involvement between patient and therapist is ever present. All the ethics codes specify the unethical nature of such contact and professional conduct regulations of the state licensing authorities usually contain some reference to prohibit this kind of activity. The New York State professional conduct regulations specifically refer to sexual contact between psychologist and patient or between physician and patient as unprofessional conduct. Carriers of malpractice insurance will not pay claims involving sexual contact between patient and therapist.

Sanders and Keith-Spiegal (1980) describe several instances of such behavior which usually proved destructive to all concerned and led to the dropping of the individual from membership in the Association, as well as to loss of license in one instance. Reports of sexual involvements between therapist and client tend predominantly to specify a male therapist and female client. One ethics action (Sanders, 1979), however, described a situation in which a female therapist conducted marital counseling with a couple, after which the couple separated and divorced. Soon after that, the female therapist married the male member of the couple. The first wife filed the complaint.

Still another kind of conflict of interest arises when therapists see patients as employees of institutions. The standards for providers of clinical psychological services deal at great length with the problems which arise when there are dual loyalties to institutions and clients. The medical ethics principle which applies to the psychiatrist in this situation states that "a physician should not dispose of his services under terms or conditions which tend to interfere with, or impair the free and complete exercise of his medical judgment and skill."

Where employment conditions are such that the dual-allegiance problem cannot be avoided, the *Standards for Providers* suggests that the psychologist should be actively involved in working to modify the system (i.e., in the institution or agency) in such a way that the problem is ameliorated.

5. *The patient has a right to be informed of the plan of treatment and to have his consent obtained in advance.*

The responsibilities of the therapist in this instance include the following:

    a. To develop a written plan of treatment;
    b. To present this plan to the patient, making certain the patient understands its essential aspects and to obtain his or her concurrence;
    c. To review and update that plan periodically in consultation with the patient.

This right of the patient is implicit in a number of the other rights and has been already discussed to some extent in other sections. It is presented here for purposes of emphasis and is elaborated in the American Psychological Association's *Standards for Providers.*

As has already been pointed out, the use of a plan of treatment lays the foundation for informed consent on the part of the patient. The right to be informed in advance is particularly important in those instances in which the therapist contemplates employing therapeutic devices which the client may find unpleasant, anxiety-provoking or noxious in any way. It is felt that if this kind of information is presented in the context of the ultimate benefits to be hoped for, it should not have the effect of persuading patients against entering therapy. Hare-Mustin et al. (1979) suggest that the presentation of a plan should include presentation of alternatives to therapy. They recognize that such behavior may have the effect of driving away potential clients: They argue, however, that it could have the opposite effect of persuading some clients who might otherwise have dropped out of therapy, to continue. The problem with this is that examination of the list of alternatives that they offer reveals that these are not alternatives at all for a person who is really seeking a psychotherapy experience. Any treatment plan should be based on, or include as part of the process, an assessment of the client's need for psychotherapy and his ability to benefit from it. If such an assessment yields a negative conclusion, appropriate measures must be taken and discussed.

6. *The patient has a right to consultation and a right to referral.*

The responsibilities which are associated with these rights are as follows:

   a. To respect the patient's request for consultation with another professional;
   b. To initiate the suggestion of outside consultation when it is called for, but the patient is reluctant to initiate it for fear of angering the therapist;
   c. To make appropriate recommendations of consultants from among members of the therapist's own profession or related professions;
   d. To be aware of one's own limitations, both professional and psychological, which may require referral of this case to another professional;
   e. To be aware of potential or emergent problems confronting the patient which may transcend the therapist's area of competence (e.g., medical, legal, or financial);
   f. To be aware of the network of available resources for referral of the patient;
   g. To build working relationships with other professionals and with agencies that will facilitate the consultation and referral process.

Sources for these rights and responsibilities are to be found in the ethics codes of the three mental health professions. In addition, the American Psychological Association's *Standards for Providers* provides direction in this regard. The ethics code for physicians states, "A physician should seek consultation upon request; in doubtful or difficult cases; or whenever it appears that the quality of medical service may be enhanced thereby." The American Psychiatric Association's annotations to this principle state that while the psychiatrist may suggest possible consultants, it is the patient or his family who should be given free choice of consultant. The *Standards for Providers* emphasizes that the practitioner should inform himself about and use the network of human services in his or her community to the benefit of the client. The problems that may occur in implementing these principles often revolve around the question of recognition of qualifications and competencies of other professionals both within and without one's own profession. The professions tend to differ with regard to their preoccupation with or concern over the qualifications and competencies of members of other professions. Thus, for example, the American Psychiatric Association's ethics code devotes a great deal of attention to assuring that the psychiatrist does not delegate to a psychologist or other nonmedical person any matter requiring the exercise of "professional medical judgment," and emphasizes that in referring patients for treatment to any other practitioner, the psychiatrist should ensure that the allied professional "is a recognized member of his/her own discipline and is competent to carry out the therapeutic task required." The code goes on to state that "the psychiatrist should have the same attitude toward members of the medical profession to whom he/she refers patients." The implicit or explicit request for outside consultation represents a source of tension in the therapeutic relationship because of the close personal nature of that relationship. It may be seen by the therapist as a manipulative device or as a manifestation of transference. It may represent an implied questioning of the competence of the therapist which may in turn arouse defensiveness on the part of the therapist. Any of these concerns may be valid or appropriate or may serve to obscure the question of what is in the best interest of the patient (see Hare-Mustin et al., 1979 on this). In psychotherapy, however, consultation plays still another and, in fact, a more important role—that is, therapist-initiated consultation with other professionals. Consultation with colleagues and/or ongoing supervision are necessary in the maintainence of therapeutic perspective even for the most seasoned and experienced professionals.

7. *The patient has a right to have an accurate record kept of the therapeutic process, to have access to that record, and to have copies made available to other practitioners or appropriate individuals at his or her direction.*

The therapist's responsibilities associated with this patient's right are the following:

a. To maintain an accurate record of the therapeutic process;
b. To keep that record current;
c. To keep that record for an appropriate length of time subsequent to the termination of treatment;

    d. To maintain a system to protect the confidentiality of such records;

    e. To maintain the record in such a form so as to allow the patient access to his or her record without harming his or her best interests;

    f. To provide copies or summaries of the records at the patient's request to other professionals.

The major issues relevant to this principle concern what information should or should not be included in such a record; to whom and under what circumstances shall such information be released; and for what length of time shall the record be kept. The *Standards for Providers of Clinical Psychological Services* examines these issues, as do the regulations governing professional conduct in New York State. The *Standards* states that the records should include identifying data, dates of services, types of services, significant actions taken, and outcome at termination. The professional conduct standards state that the record should reflect the evaluation and treatment of the patient accurately. The regulations also require the health professional to make copies of that record available to the patient upon his or her written request, or to another licensed health practitioner, consistent with that practitioner's authorized scope of practice. The regulations do, on the other hand, state that the practitioner may withhold information from a patient if, "in the reasonable exercise of his or her professional judgment, he or she believes that release of such information would adversely affect the patient's health." This qualification, even in an atmosphere which generally calls for full disclosure of any records, reflects the Board of Regents' recognition of the need for the health practitioner to be judicious in implementing this principle. This writer vividly recalls a relevant incident which he experienced many years ago. A patient at a Veterans Administration hospital happened to see his chart on a desk in an office when the ward clerk stepped out for a moment. He took the opportunity to glance through the chart and subsequently at a group therapy session expressed his dismay at the diagnostic and prognostic statements made by his doctors. (His diagnosis was schizophrenic reaction, chronic, severe.) A short time later he was permitted to leave the hospital on a weekend pass, and committed suicide.

The New York State professional conduct regulations require retention of records for at least six years and at least one year after the minor patient reaches the age of twenty-one years. The *Standards for Providers of Clinical Psychological Services* recommends retention of a full record for three years after the completion of the planned services or after the date of last contact and a full record or summary of the record to be maintained for an additional twelve years. The conventional record contains the presenting problem, the therapist's assessment or evaluation of the individual, the treatment plan, progress notes, and termination note. More recently, many institutions have introduced the so-called problem-oriented record system. According to this system, the record is built around a list of problems presented by the patient and a treatment plan, written so as to provide an approach for each of the problems. Subsequent notes or comments are all related to one or more of the initial problems on the problem list. At termination, the treatment that was offered for each of the problems is noted, as is the response to such treatment and the current status of each problem. Records are, of course, exceedingly important for the professional discipline process, as well as being a source of information from which documentation may be provided to third party payers. In New York State, all practitioners are required to make available to the office of professional conduct any relevant records with respect to an inquiry or complaint about the licensee's unprofessional conduct.

There is a particular type of record which is unique to the therapy process and that is the process recording. Many therapists regularly make process recordings of sessions; some make taped records of sessions and then use the tapes to make notes. Many therapists believe that such process recordings should not be considered part of the patient record since there is no particular benefit to be derived from keeping them there and they most often contain specific quotes which might, at some point, be used in a manner which is harmful to the patient. Those therapists feel that the process recording constitutes the therapist's personal notes and are used mainly for the purpose of helping to further the therapeutic process.

There is reason to suspect that in many instances, given the time pressures under which psychotherapists work, record keeping suffers; and yet, adequate, accurate records represent the most potent factor in protecting the therapist from later difficulties of a legal nature in connection with his professional activity.

8. *The patient has a right to privacy and confidentiality in connection with psychotherapy.*

The therapist's responsibilities associated with this principle include the following:

a. Not to reveal information about a patient without that patient's prior written consent;

b. To be judicious in determining just what information it is appropriate to reveal and to whom, once consent has been obtained;

c. To make the patient aware of possible harmful effects to his best interests should certain information be released;

   d. To release information concerning a patient without his consent only when required to do so by law, and to inform the patient of this;

   e. To consider confidentiality issues in deciding what information regarding a patient should or should not go into a patient's record;

   f. To make final disposition of the patient's record in a manner which does not compromise confidentiality.

The principle of confidentiality has been emphasized as a primary obligation of the psychologist and is treated with equal seriousness in the ethics codes of the other mental health professions. It is also to be found in the *Standards for Providers* and in the regulations governing professional conduct in most states. Much has been written about this issue over the years; most recently a comprehensive review of the issues and problems appeared in *American Psychologist* (Everstine et al., 1980). In that article, the authors discuss the conflict between the individual's constitutional right to privacy and society's need to be informed about certain acts or intentions of individual citizens. They also discuss the concern about violence in our society, which led to the famous Tarasoff decision in which the court "presumably wished to enlist the aid of psychotherapists as early warning detectors of violent tendencies in their clients." They make it quite clear that the increasing reliance on third party payers has resulted in a tremendous erosion of confidentiality. In regard to this, they ask whether it is ethical for psychologists to attach confidential evaluations to their payment claims and even more broadly, they ask whether "he who pays the piper, calls the tune." It has been pointed out in regard to third party payers that the information submitted to them is stored in computers and that this computerized information is certainly not immune to scrutiny in a way which clearly violates the principle of confidentiality. This fact must certainly be made very clear to the patient. An even more imminent concern regarding confidentiality is that insurance forms often pass through the personnel offices of many large companies on their way to the third party payer. It is clear that these departments do not respect the confidentiality of these documents and very often information of a diagnostic nature may be contained therein, which might be very harmful to the patient in regard to his or her career. In connection with this, it has been suggested that therapists should routinely send such forms directly to the carrier and never to the personnel office of the employer.

   The Tarasoff decision, which was settled out of court, said in effect that the parents of a murder victim were entitled to damages because a psychologist who saw the murderer in therapy failed to warn the victim of the danger. Everstine et al. conclude that this decision results in a narrow interpretation of therapist-client privilege and reflects a belief that the privilege should be sharply restricted. They also review the issue of psychotherapist-client privilege as it exists in California law and found that such confidentiality must be breached under six conditions:

1. When criminal action is involved;
2. When information is made an issue in a court action;
3. When information is obtained for the purpose of rendering an expert's report to a lawyer;
4. When the psychotherapist is acting in a court-appointed capacity;
5. When the psychotherapist believes that the client is a danger to him or herself, or to others;
6. When a client is under the age of sixteen and the therapist believes that the client has been the victim of a crime and judges such disclosure would be in the client's best interest.

In New York, there is a clear-cut mandate requiring the breach of confidentiality when an issue of child abuse is involved. Everstine et al. note that under California law there are various kinds of privilege and the psychotherapist-client privilege is most vulnerable to breach. By contrast, there is no psychotherapist privilege in New York; privilege, however, exists independently for each of the licensed mental health professions. As far as psychologists are concerned, the law states that the confidential relations between a psychologist and his client are placed on the same basis as those provided by law between attorney and client. This is considered a fairly strong statement of confidentiality that is not easily broken. Psychiatrists in New York State, on the other hand, are covered by the patient-physician confidentiality rule, which is considered somewhat weaker. The California group concluded that in respect to psychotherapy, little confidentiality exists. They also conclude, therefore, that the duty to warn not only refers to potential victims, as in the Tarasoff case, but also to the psychotherapy patient who must be warned with regard to the vulnerability of confidentiality. The lesson that must be learned from all of this is that it is incumbent upon the therapist to become completely familiar with the legal status of confidentiality in the particular locale in which he practices, and must then use that information to protect the best interests of his or her client.

9. *The patient has a right to redress of his or her grievances.*

The therapist's responsibilities related to this principle include the following:

a. To participate in various systems of accountability;
b. To deal with patient grievances in a spirit of objectivity;

    c. To make the client aware of the various avenues open to him or her for the expression of grievances that are not resolved in the context of therapist-client discussion;

    d. To make appropriate records and information available to duly constituted peer review groups and to statutorily constituted professional conduct authorities.

All the various ethics codes recognize an ethical practitioner's responsibility to respond in a cooperative manner to inquiries on the part of the various accountability systems that operate in the profession. The general attitude of the codes is that the practitioner has the responsibility to treat these in other than an adversary manner. Yet the various groups recognize that since the ultimate outcome of a particular investigative procedure can be a decision which may be quite harmful to the practitioner, it is understandable that his response may initially have a significant self-protective element to it. The generally accepted notion of presumption of innocence is accepted in most accountability procedures. There are, generally speaking, four accountability systems in the licensed mental health professions, each of which somewhat overlaps with the others, and has some unique aspects as well. The state and national ethics committees overlap with one another a good deal. In some instances, the National Ethics Committee serves as a court of appeal. There is generally a single ethics code for a profession though there may be some particular principles enacted on a local level, and these govern the actions and procedures of the local ethics committee. The only punitive action open to the Ethics Committee is denial of membership in the organization, and the publication of that fact. Statutorily mandated systems of professional conduct or professional discipline at the state level parallel those of the Ethics Committees. The basis on which a determination of professional misconduct is made may be identical with those of ethics committees if the particular statute references the ethics code. In other instances there is a code of professional conduct either in statute or in administrative regulations. The issues raised in professional conduct cases are usually adjudicated by the state boards for the professions; in New York State, final adjudication is performed by the Board of Regents. In other states there may be overarching consumer affairs boards or commissions. Most statutes contain language which provides the practitioner, who has been disciplined, the option of appealing to the courts by instituting a civil action. This right is constitutionally guaranteed in relation to any kind of decision by any group. The patient, of course, also has the right to institute a civil action for malpractice. The peer review process tends to deal with issues of appropriateness of techniques, approaches, and fees often involving third party payers; the approach used most often is that of mediation between the practitioner and either the client or the third party payer. It should be noted that ethics committees and state boards performing professional conduct functions also use the approach of mediation where this seems most appropriate. The issues associated with redress of patient grievances are varied and complex. As mentioned earlier in connection with consultation and referral, Hare-Mustin et al. (1979) provide a comprehensive discussion of the various avenues open to the client and analyze the pros and cons of each. The requirement of making records available for peer review and ethics committees may be found in all the ethics codes and is often found also in professional conduct codes of the states. The New York State code of professional conduct stipulates that it is unprofessional conduct not to make one's records available to the state investigating body when a complaint of professional misconduct has been raised. The need for the therapist to monitor his or her own defensiveness in situations where challenges have been raised to the therapist's competence is self-evident.

10. *The patient has a right to a terminable experience.*

In regard to this right, the responsibilities of the therapist include the following:

a. To set a tentative termination date with the patient;
b. To review that termination date periodically, and revise it when necessary;
c. To raise with the client the issue of termination at an appropriate time if no termination date has been previously set;
d. To engage in periodic review, preferably in consultation with another practitioner of a long-term treatment case in order to assess the need for termination and strategies for termination.

There has been a good deal written about the anxiety associated with the issue of termination both for patient and therapist. The discussion has often centered on separation anxiety on the part of both parties. There is recognition that therapy is a process which tends to foster dependency of the patient upon the therapist for emotional support and dependency by the therapist on the patient for both financial support and ego gratification. With such powerful motives at work, the recognition of the need for a terminable experience on the part of the patient must be constantly brought to the fore in discussions of psychotherapy and in the mind of the therapist. It is too easy for a therapist to rationalize extending the process on the grounds that progress continues to be made and it is therefore in the patient's best interests. Dr. Bernard Kalinkawitz of N.Y.U. (emeritus), one of the most respected trainers of clinical psychologists in the country, once said, during a discussion of seduction of patients by therapists, that the most prevalent kind of seduction of patients is not sexual seduction, but rather manipulation of the patient's dependency needs by the therapist either consciously or unconsciously in order to keep him or her in therapy. The fact that the neurotic needs of both patient and therapist operate in the attempt to ignore the need for a terminable experience makes this a problem which tends not to surface readily. There tends instead to be an unconscious conspiracy on the part of both to ignore the calendar. As both patient and therapist come to rely more and more on third party payments, the influence of limitations of the reimbursement contract are playing an ever-increasing role in forcing a confrontation with the issue. In any case, as much as the responsibility of the therapist to enter into an initial agreement with a specific time limit has been recognized, it must also be recognized that this is a responsibility which many therapists will not completely fulfill. After the initial period of therapy has been concluded and the contract is either explicitly or implicitly renewed, it is all too often that this occurs on an open-ended basis because of the needs of both the therapist and the client. With this phenomenon in mind, we must examine strategies for developing a process which will lead to termination, in those situations in which no clear-cut termination date exists. As is true for many ethical issues, consciousness-raising experiences are required for patients and therapists alike. Both must ask themselves, "Are we becoming too dependent on one another?

The foregoing "bill of rights" for psychotherapy patients may be seen by some as overly burdensome upon the therapist and the therapeutic process. The emphasis currently being placed on consumerism would seem to dictate, however, that we who practice in this field had better take the initiative, and do so vigorously, lest the initiative be taken from us and placed into the hands of those who view psychotherapy with antagonism, and who seek change for the sake of appearances rather than substance.

REFERENCES

AMERICAN MEDICAL ASSOCIATION. *Principles of medical ethics,* with annotations approved by the American Psychiatric Association, 1978.
AMERICAN PSYCHOLOGICAL ASSOCIATION. *Characteristics and criteria for a specialty: Task force on specialty criteria,* final report, April 1980.
AMERICAN PSYCHOLOGICAL ASSOCIATION. *Ethical standards of psychologists, APA Monitor,* March 1977.
AMERICAN PSYCHOLOGICAL ASSOCIATION. *Standards for providers of clinical psychological services,* Draft #6, April 22, 1979.

BUCK, J. A., and HIRSCHMAN, R. Economics and mental health services: Enhancing the power of the consumer. *American Psychologist,* July 1980, **35**(7).

CHESLER, P. *Women and madness.* Garden City, N.Y.: Doubleday, 1972.

DÖRKEN, H., and WEBB, J. T. 1976 third party reimbursement experience: An interstate comparison by insurance carrier. *American Psychologist,* April 1980, **35**(4).

EVERSTINE, L.; EVERSTINE, D. S.; HEYMANN, G. M.; TRUE, R. H.; FREY, D. H.; JOHNSON, H. G.; and SEIDEN, R. H. Privacy and confidentiality in psychotherapy. *American Psychologist,* September 1980, **35**(9).

HARE-MUSTIN, R. T.; MARECEK, J.; KAPLAN, A. G.; and LISS-LEVENSON, N. Rights of clients, responsibilities of therapists. *American Psychologist,* January 1979, **34**(1).

HOGAN, D. B. A position statement on licensing counselors and psychotherapists. *Division of Community Psychology Newsletter,* 1979, **12**(3).

LONDON, P. *The modes and morals of psychotherapy.* New York: Holt, Rinehart, & Winston, 1964.

MESSICK, S. Test validity and the ethics of assessment. *American Psychologist,* November 1980, **35**(11).

NATIONAL ASSOCIATION OF SOCIAL WORKERS, INC. *Code of ethics of the National Association of Social Workers,* Washington, D.C., July 1, 1980.

NEW YORK STATE. *Laws of New York.* Chapter 987, 1971.

NEW YORK STATE. *Regulations of the Commission of Education,* Part 29, October 31, 1978.

SANDERS, J. R. Complaints against psychologists adjudicated informally by APA's Committee on Scientific and Professional Ethics and Conduct. *American Psychologist,* December 1979, **34**(12).

SANDERS, J. R., and KEITH-SPIEGEL, P. Formal and informal adjudication of ethics complaints against psychologists. *American Psychologist,* December 1980, **35**(12).

SZASZ, T. *Law, liberty, and psychiatry.* New York: Macmillan, 1963.

TYMCHUK, A. J.; DRAPKIN, R. S.; ACKERMAN, A. B.; MAJOR, S.; COFFMAN, E. W.; and BAUM, M. S. Psychology in action: Survey of training in ethics in APA-approved clinical psychology programs. *American Psychologist,* December 1979. **34**(12).

The Ethics of Psychodiagnostic Assessment

4

Fred Brown

In this chapter I present an explication of those ethical principles that must operate in the dyadic relationship between a patient who has been referred for a comprehensive psychological evaluation and a clinical psychologist who is skilled in the use of a battery of tests. It will be assumed that these skills are coordinated with a sound knowledge of psychodynamics and nosology and that the resulting psychological report will help the patient by helping the referring source to formulate the most effective interventional therapeutic procedures.

The test battery will be composed of those core techniques that have stood the test of time—tests such as the Wechsler Scales, Rorschach, T.A.T., Human Figure Drawings, and the Bender Gestalt Test, in addition to others suitable for evaluating brain damage, memory deficiencies, learning disabilities, and whatever falls into areas of the tester's competence. It is to be understood that a psychologist's acceptance of a referral outside his sphere of competence is unethical.

The climate surrounding psychological assessment has been rather stormy over the past few years, although a slight trend toward moderation has been noted more recently, Intemperate attacks have been directed at claims made for the validity and reliability of many psychological tests; it has been charged that findings derived from them are misleading or useless, and there is the more or less overt implication that those engaged in the practice of psychodiagnostics are marginal characters who have failed to attain the sublime heights occupied by therapists. Criticisms levelled at testing may be divided into those that are justified and constructive, which alert the examiner to the need for an ongoing scrutiny of his techniques, and those that are sweepingly nihilistic.

Holt (1970) decried the series of retreats by practitioners of personality assessment and of diagnostic testing with projective techniques in particular, writing that "Interest in the diagnostic function of the clinical psychologist has lagged; the general level of university training in clinical assessment has gone steadily down, and along with it probably the average level of competence in assessing personalities." Based upon my own observations, I question whether this lamentable situation has changed much in the ensuing decade.

After a cogent refutation of charges against psychodiagnosis, he writes:

> I am sure I do not surprise anyone by concluding, finally, that clinical psychology in general and the assessment of personality and psychopathology in particular *are* very much worthwhile. Indeed, I believe that psychology as a whole would be much poorer without psychodiagnosis and clinical assessment. There are powerful forces within psychology working to bring about this impoverishment in the name of science. The final irony comes when the enemies of clinical psychology try to use published successes and failures of what *they* call clinical and statistical predictions as evidence from which to generalize about the inadequacies of clinical methods. For in doing so, they forsake scientific standards of evaluating evidence and generalizing results, and let their prejudices blind them to the irrelevancy of the published surveys to the judgments they wish to make. [Pp. 348–349]

Throughout this chapter I shall be referring to private patients referred by psychologists, psychiatrists, psychoanalysts, social workers, neurologists, law firms, schools, and general practitioners.

A comprehensive test battery in the hands of a competent psychodiagnostician (Brown, 1960) can elucidate the patient's cognitive and perceptual style and functioning; the psychodynamic structure and its psychoeconomics; the strengths and weaknesses of defenses pertaining to interpersonal relations, sexuality, and personality integration. It provides data for the formulation of a dynamically oriented differential diagnosis and prognosis followed by relevant recommendations (Brown, 1952).

Those who attack psychological assessment should be aiming not at the tests but at those who abuse assessment by pretending to be competent in areas in which they are ignorant, owing to poor training under inferior and uncommitted teachers who never achieved a concert pitch level of efficiency attainable only by constant coping with a wide variety of cases referred for evaluation. Personal inadequacies are also frequently involved, but no trainee who has been exposed to lackadaisical supervision and half-hearted teaching and who has not enjoyed the benefits of constant clinical feedback during the internship and as often as possible in his daily practice, can do justice to the wealth of information available from test data. Furthermore, inferior integrative skills, compensatory pretentiousness that confuses "wild analysis" with profundity, excessive hedging that leaves a reader with a sense of vaguity, and diagnostic formulations that do not emerge logically from formal, stylistic, and psychodynamic components of the tests all combine to diminish the value of psychological assessment in a manner comparable to the operation of Gresham's law in economics. The admitted erosion of psychodiagnostic competence and the second-class status to which it has been assigned calls for a radical improvement in the caliber of teaching and training personnel if a valuable specialty in the field of clinical psychology is to be preserved.

Before coming to grips with ethical and moral problems, I would like to call attention to two other areas in which psychological test data can play an important role—teaching and research (Brown, 1971). Over many years spent teaching psychology trainees and psychiatric residents, I have found the psychodiagnostic test battery invaluable as a vehicle for transmitting an operational understanding of the psychodynamic process as it is reflected in documented data derived from scores and qualitative test data. Demonstration of the step-by-step inferential process comprises explication of a cross-scanning technique and the interlacing of test data with psychoanalytic personality theory directed toward the goal of fashioning a personality picture that will be specific for the patient. The teaching exercise is conducted without prior knowledge of the patient, and after the presentation the trainee or resident submits anamnestic and treatment data which are then correlated with psychological findings that permit the structuring of a composite three-dimensional portrait. These data serve as a basis for formulating treatment targets and strategies.

The accumulation of test data from a wide variety of patients, whether in an institutional setting or in private practice, creates an inexhaustible reservoir of raw material which can be used in ways limited only by the psychologist's research ingenuity. The alert clinician is of necessity constantly formulating hypotheses, confirming or rejecting them in conformity with synthetic principles that govern the organization of test findings, converging such findings upon meaningful conclusions, and generally adhering to the concept of an experimental design with an N of 1 as he prepares his report. By maintaining contact with the literature and sharpening his awareness of significant issues in the broad areas of personality and psychopathology, he is in a unique position to contribute to an understanding of human beings by utilizing material not so readily available from other sources.

It may be instructive to consider some facets of moral and ethical imperatives from a more general standpoint. It is taken for granted that the dictum of Hippocrates and of Maimonides, that nothing must be done that might injure the patient, applies rigorously to all who are engaged in the diagnosing and healing enterprises. Ethical principles are based upon humanitarian value judgments that follow unambiguously from the aforementioned central principle and are promulgated by the discipline and imprinted upon its adherents. Apart from unarguable dicta, there are certain components of the ethical spectrum that may not be stated explicitly but which nevertheless enter into ethical practice. These comprise what might be considered unwise or inappropriate procedures that may not specifically violate stated prohibitions but represent marginal and often overlooked infractions just within the borders of acceptability. For example, a psychological report might present I.Q. figures which give the impression that they were derived from a complete test without explaining that they were prorated; that the test battery might have been administered by an assistant might not be divulged in this report; or data obtained from a close questioning of the patient might be presented as if they had been deduced from the tests. There is certainly no prohibition against synthesizing interview and test data in a report—the procedure is even commendable—but the referring psychotherapist is under the impression that what he receives from an independent source utilizes materials and techniques different from his own, and in view of this implicit assumption, the examiner is obligated to distinguish between what is obtained from the tests and what is obtained through interrogation.

Some psychologists are inclined to omit a diagnostic formulation with the rationalization that this is only a "label" of little or no importance. Granted that diagnostic terms have tended to be imprecise in the past, recent advances (APA, 1979) appear to have sharpened diagnostic nomenclature and leave little warranty for omitting a diagnosis. Treating a patient without making a diagnosis is the worst kind of blind treatment, unlikely to be beneficial to the patient, and in my opinion constitutes a breach of ethical and professional responsibility when the patient's diagnostic status is left in limbo by the psycho*diagnostician*.

Another hidden aspect of the ethical spectrum that rarely surfaces pertains to what Schafer (1954) has so cogently delineated in his description of types of testers. I shall concentrate only upon those that have indirect but nonetheless significant relevance to ethical considerations by beginning with what he describes as the sadistic tester. This refers to an orientation that makes testing "a means of ferreting out the 'weak,' 'debasing,' 'humiliating'" aspects of the lives of hated others, leads to the assumption of a chief inquisitor's role, and results in an insensitivity to or ignoring of "signs of strength, adaptability and appeal in the patient." This is not an uncommon fault, but its commonness does not exonerate the tester from the charge of harming the patient. In addition, by stressing the negative, he presents a distorted picture of the patient that can prove misleading, discouraging to the therapist, and detrimental to the patient's welfare. The other extreme of an attitudinal polarity comprises testers who are masochistic, rigidly intellectualistic, and who have their own rigid defenses against hostility. Such attitudinal sets may result in test reports that are Pollyanish, filled with lacunae, or evasively meandering.

Two other types of testers comprise those with an uncertain sense of personal identity and those who are socially withdrawn or inhibited personalities. It can be predicted that reports emanating from such individuals will, in one way or another, contaminate the depiction of the patient's personality. One would hope and expect that supervising psychologists will detect such personality flaws and take measures to correct them during the internship year and to eliminate those who are unresponsive to rectifying measures from the training program. These personality deficiencies can lead to a violation of the patient's right to a just and humane evaluation and the referrer's right to a maximally helpful statement of the patient's assets and liabilities.

The problem of confidentiality is a recurring one that raises questions, especially for those clinicians who examine children and adolescents. A report sent to a school must of necessity differ from one sent to a therapist, and if the parent requests that the school be given a copy of the report, it is highly advisable to ascertain that such a report will be submitted to a specific and responsible person and that it will contain psychometric findings and inclusion of other data relevant to the clarification of a learning problem and its amelioration. There is little point in submitting psychodynamic interpretations that may becloud the issue and prove counterproductive.

Other ethical problems arise when the examiner is asked by parents to discuss the results of a child's or adolescent's tests. Parents frequently complain that when the therapist has agreed to discuss the report with them they have left his office with more anxiety and confusion than understanding. The therapist's guardedness in such cases, considering the detail that a good report should contain at all levels, is quite understandable in view of his loyalty to the patient, his awareness that "leaks" to the patient—intentional or inadvertent—may jeopardize the transference, and his unwillingness to become involved with parents who in some instances are being treated by other therapists and are part of the problem. The patient's therapist may occasionally request that the report be submitted to the parents' therapist in order to give him a better understanding of the family's psychodynamic configuration, but in my experience it is rare for a therapist to object to a conference between the examiner and the parents after such a plan is cleared with him.

Over the years I have found that approximately two hours should be set aside for such a conference. The utmost sensitivity to parental feelings and attitudes and a meticulous regard for the patient's welfare within the confines of confidentiality and ethics must be observed so that neither the patient nor the parents shall suffer harm from what is divulged. The session may be regarded as a compressed therapeutic one in which processes that are slowly paced in a treatment relationship are accelerated.

An inexperienced psychodiagnostician or one who has not resolved conflicts with his own parents may unconsciously identify with the child or adolescent and assume a partisan, accusatory attitude. He may be tempted to exhibit his expertise and profundity by dazzling the parents with his subtle insights, and thereby runs the risk of overwhelming his auditors and laying the ground for a disastrous backlash. Ethical considerations mandate a need to listen carefully prior to discussing test findings in order to gain some insight into the relationship between the parents, their feelings for the patient, attributive factors that enter into the situation, and avoidance of the possibility of scapegoating the child. The process demands careful preparation and constant self-monitoring, with emphasis upon the *phenomenology* of the patient's difficulties and a meaningful explanation of the patient's motivations and needs. The examiner has fulfilled his ethical and professional obligations when he has left the parents with a sympathetic understanding of the patient and with some notions of how to deal with negative aspects of his behavior as these interact with their own. Courtesy requires that the therapist be given a resume of the highlights of the session.

Other ethical problems arise when reports are requested by a law firm or by a court. In matters pertaining to divorce or custody cases, I prefer to work through a psychiatrist as the referral source and to submit the report to him with the understanding that it will be incorporated into his report. The same holds true for accident compensation cases, although quite often the psychologist may be called upon to present his findings in the role of expert witness. The psychologist has the option in all such instances to refuse the case for evaluation if he feels uneasy about testifying, and he should not hesitate to do so. Once he has understood the nature of the case and has accepted the client, whether the latter is a plaintiff or defendant, he preserves his ethical integrity by preparing a report that can stand up under intense cross-examination, and is free of arcane subtleties and conjectures. Under no circumstances should he allow himself to fall into the trap of a partisan posture. The foregoing are general comments that would be treated in greater detail by a forensic psychologist.

Under no circumstance will a report be sent to other than the referring source unless written permission is given for doing so by the testee, or, in the case of minors, by parents.

I have used the terms "moral" and "ethical" interchangeably but, while these terms surely converge and overlap, I would suggest that each carries a different connotation that has an important bearing upon professional practice. A moral orientation implies the ability to distinguish between right and wrong and has its roots in precepts and examples available to the child in his developmental period within the family and is reinforced by religious instruction, schooling, and role models. These contribute to the formation of a superego that will generate dissonance when there is a danger that a moral imperative is being violated. Practical judgment and common sense serve as reinforcers of a conformist orientation that is perceived by others as evidences of rectitude and reliability. In the professional context, codes of ethics are infused with morality and are imposed upon the practitioner by a body of peers so that a knowledge of right and wrong will merge with dictates pertaining to professional conduct. The essential ingredient of morality is thereby embedded within the concept of ethics, and the weakness of one or the other can impair professional integrity. In addition, standards (APA, 1977) are also formulated by professional bodies for the purpose of maintaining quality and consistency: "All psychologists in professional practice should be guilded by a uniform set of standards just as they are guided by a common code of ethics."

The practioner is consequently bound by moral imperatives, a code of ethics, and professional standards that converge upon the maintenance of a professional image that will inspire confidence and respect and to which all psychologists, regardless of their specialization, are obliged to conform.

Although codes of ethics are devised with these goals in mind, their implementation in certain settings may create problems. I refer specifically to *Principle 8: Assessment Techniques* (APA, 1979), which states:

> In using psychological tests psychologists respect the rights of clients to have a full explanation of the nature and purpose of the tests in language that the client can understand, unless explicit exception has been agreed upon in advance.
>
> They respect the client's right to know the results, the interpretations made for the conclusions and recommendations.

The psychodiagnostician is immediately confronted by difficult choices in his day-by-day practice if he wishes to adhere strictly to these principles. The projective techniques were developed for the purpose of investigating the patient's inner life as expeditiously and as painlessly as possible and to do so by circumventing resistance and other obstructive defenses encountered by the therapist. The need to maintain secrecy concerning psychological tests and their nature is implicit in the prohibition against publishing Rorschach plates in newspapers and magazines or describing what constitutes acceptable and unacceptable responses to them. These restrictions also apply to other psychological tests.

The therapist who refers a patient for psychological evaluation does so for a variety of reasons. These include the need for a differential diagnosis; presence or absence of organicity; the nature of a stubborn resistance and the reason for its persistence; a need to know "what is going on"; the dimensions and facets of the psychodynamic process and structure; suitability for a particular type of therapy and contraindications; prognostic indications; and help in formulating therapeutic strategies. The referral is based on the belief that the psychologist is competent to meet these needs by means of his expertise in the use of tests and his knowledge of human personality and its intricacies. It would indeed be rare for a therapist to send a "fully informed" patient for assessment, as any preparation of this kind, assuming it can be done, can arouse anxiety, apprehension, and perhaps a reinforced guardedness.

Likewise, if the psychodiagnostician were to follow this prescription to the letter, he would be in danger of violating the basic function of the tests: to by-pass resistances and to expose the intrinsic conflicts of the patient that are unclear or unknown to the therapist and presumably to the patient. There is an unavoidable element of deception in the diagnostic enterprise, and if we ask *"qui bono?"* the answer is and must be obvious.

A concrete example is afforded by the familiar testing situation in which a patient is requested to copy the Bender Gestalt designs. As each card is presented, and if the patient is at all anxious or suspicious, he may ask "What do these tell you?" At this point it would presumably be ethical for the examiner to explain that the circle of design "A" has feminine connotations and that the diamond has masculine ones. He would further explain that gross enlargement of the circle and diminishment of the diamond may indicate a pronounced feminine identification or orientation and feelings of inferiority and inadequacy concerning masculinity if the patient is a male. If a female, it would indicate the probability of marked narcissism and disparagement of the male, and for both patients elements of imbalance and/or distortions in the heterosexual relationship. If there is marked overlining on any of the designs, he would be told that these indicate paranoid trends (Pascal and Suttell, 1951). He might also be given to understand that certain deviations indicate weak or impaired reality testing and that scoring of the designs involves cutoff points that differentiate between malignant and benign conditions. The same would have to be done for each design, at which point the testing situation would surely be disrupted.

Or let us consider the Rorschach and the impact upon the procedure if the patient were to be given a *full* explanation of the nature and purpose of the test. One might conceivably begin the session with the warning that, "anything you say may be used against you," although in practice the patient is usually assured that the examiner will do his utmost to seek out the patient's strengths and positive resources. But let us assume that the ethical practitioner then explains that the test uncovers basic defenses and themes (Schafer, 1954) and proceeds to illustrate some of them. He further explains that Rorschach percepts may bring out latent homosexuality, homicidal or suicidal impulses, incestuousness, infantile parental fixations, and assorted psychopathologies. To enter into such "honest" disclosures about the Rorschach, T.A.T., and other tests of the battery would defeat the purpose of the tests by stripping away a necessary veil of innocence communicated by open-ended test instructions to "Just copy each design" of the Bender; to "Do as you please" in response to bids for structuring; simply to draw a whole person; to "Tell me, please, what could this be? What might it be?" on the Rorschach, and similar innocuous open-ended instructions for other tests. It is precisely the patient's ignorance of the test's power to penetrate defenses and to expose hidden needs, fears, wishes, and conflicts that makes it such a valuable resource to the helping professions.

The obligation to respect the client's right to know the results of the test and the interpretations that led to conclusions and recommendations cannot be fulfilled either by handing him a completed report or discussing the results with him in depth. As a rule, the therapist may have explained prior to referral that the report will not be made available to the patient but will be used for the therapist's guidance. Depending upon the circumstances, therapists will sometimes discuss some of the results with the patient in conformity with the exigencies of the therapeutic course.

The nature of an explicit exception to a rule that cannot be adhered to from the standpoint of professional realities also raises questions. The psychologist who would like to honor this principle is immediately confronted by the question of what to exclude, especially as he has no way of being sure of what the tests will reveal. Should it be agreed upon in advance that nothing pertaining to sexuality will be discussed? That unconscious motivations will be excluded from the discussion? That only descriptive material will be communicated without touching upon explanatory data? While at first glance an advance agreement on explicit exceptions seems reasonable, the explicitness of the exception can raise doubts in the patient's mind and can make him anxious about the information that is being withheld.

These considerations are germane to practical aspects of psychodiagnostic practice and are presented within the context of a referral from one professional to another. In instances where it is not the psychologist's policy to restrict referrals to professional personnel only and where there is an agreement to discuss the test results with the examinee, the psychologist must rely upon his judgment to present a balanced account of his findings and to keep his own counsel with respect to a *full* explanation of the nature and purpose of the tests.

When I have been asked what tests will show, I have explained that they are useful to the therapist and to the patient as well for clarifying the organization of the total personality, bringing the nature and content of conflict areas into sharper relief, and for the purpose of facilitating the therapeutic process in general. In most instances such preliminary questions may reflect anxiety and I have found that if the patient is told to withhold questions until the end of the examination he will very rarely bring them up once the session is ended.

Provision E 4.4.2.(APA, 1974) states that the validity of a psychological appraisal should involve an agreement with the psychiatric diagnosis and that "diagnostic terms should be defined specifically and described clearly." There is no argument over the latter, but it is doubtful that the former is always possible or even necessarily desirable. In some instances the therapist may discuss his diagnostic impression with the psychologist prior to the latter's appointment with the patient, but the test data may warrant an entirely different diagnosis. The therapist may require the reassurance of the psychologist's confirmatory findings, but if test results point in a different direction and if supporting evidence is presented cogently, then the therapist's need for an independent evaluation has been met and ethical proprieties have been preserved. Agreement with the psychiatrist's impressions and conclusions is not a crucial criterion by which the validity of test findings can be judged.

It might be helpful to summarize those ethical obligations that should govern psychodiagnostic practice and to bear in mind that the concept of ethics encompasses proprieties, commitments, and responsibilities:

> In using tests the psychologist will provide a comprehensive diagnostic formulation that evolves from his data and which will take into account differential factors. He will do this with the knowledge that a diagnosis is relevant to the planning of therapeutic strategies.
>
> He will clearly indicate in his report which data derive from interviewing and which are based upon test findings.
>
> He will be cognizant of his responsibility to reconcile contradictory findings (Brown, 1958) upon the assumption that these emerged from the patient and are likely to be crucial to an understanding of his defenses.
>
> He will strive to weigh and to balance positive and negative findings in an effort to aid in the mobilization of reconstructive resources within the patient by showing how they may be used in therapy.
>
> He will not report prorated data as if they were obtained from complete testing.
>
> If he offers an explanation of the tests, he will do so in a manner that will not diminish their usefulness nor arouse the patient's anxiety.
>
> He will, to the best of his ability, orient psychodynamic formulations toward meaningful behavioral referents rather than constructing fanciful theoretical structures of dubious value.

The psychodiagnostician is generally bound by the ethical principles that govern the practice of clinical psychology, the essence of which is to shield the patient from harm and to further his well-being. Ethical standards must of necessity be declarative and unambiguous, but in actual practice and from the standpoint of the active psychodiagnostic practitioner, there are certain exceptions and qualifications that must be taken into consideration and which neither impair the integrity of the psychologist nor violate the ethical principles to which he adheres.

REFERENCES

AMERICAN PSYCHOLOGICAL ASSOCIATION. *Standards for educational and psychological tests,* 1974.

AMERICAN PSYCHOLOGICAL ASSOCIATION. *Standards for providers of psychological services,* January 1977.

AMERICAN PSYCHOLOGICAL ASSOCIATION. Latest changes in the ethics code. *The Monitor,* November 1979, 16–17.

AMERICAN PSYCHIATRIC ASSOCIATION. *Diagnostic and statistical manual of mental disorders,* 3rd ed., 1979.

BROWN, F. Contribution of the psychologist to psychiatric problems of diagnosis and therapy. *Psychiatric Quarterly Supplements,* 1952, **26,** 8–21.

BROWN, F. The psychological test battery: Use of the test battery for psychodiagnostic appraisal. In D. Brower and L. E. Abt (eds.), *Progress in clinical psychology,* vol. 3. New York: Grune & Stratton, 1958.

BROWN, F. Contribution of the psychologist to problems of therapy. *American Journal of Orthopsychiatry,* 1960, **30,** 811.

BROWN, F. Roles and functions of the clinical psychologist in the department of psychiatry of a general hospital. *Mount Sinai Journal of Medicine,* 1971, **38,** 101–109.

HOLT, R. R. Yet another look at clinical and statistical prediction: Or is clinical psychology worthwhile? *American Psychologist,* April 1970, **25,** 337–349.

PASCAL, G. R., and SUTTELL, B. J. *The Bender-Gestalt test.* New York: Grune & Stratton, 1951.

SCHAFER, R. *Psychoanalytic interpretation in Rorschach testing: Theory and application.* New York: Grune & Stratton, 1954.

Ethical Issues in the Treatment of Psychotics and Borderline Psychotics

Hyman Spotnitz

Destructive physical and emotional interchange has characterized the experience of the severely disturbed throughout recorded history. Acting upon the negative emotions their deviant behavior induced, their contemporaries responded in ways that conformed to the mores of their epoch but that are now regarded as damaging. In the last few centuries, however, the idea that these people were sick took hold, initiating a shift away from restraints, isolation, and punitive handling toward humane management and treatment.

The healing professions have not as yet demonstrated great competence in resolving the deep-seated problems of patients suffering from psychotic conditions. Although it has been repeatedly demonstrated that many cases of psychotic illness are psychodynamically reversible, these patients do not respond adequately to the neutral stance and insight-oriented interventions that Freud recommended for patients with more readily reversible conditions.

In applying the more therapeutically effective approaches that began to evolve in the last few decades, the therapist needs to remain aware of the patient's values and of the prevailing social values. These diverge to some extent from the therapeutic values that primarily govern his interventions. Rather than imposing demands with which the patient cannot comply, the therapist may temporarily operate in terms of the patient's values to the extent necessary to help the patient achieve a therapeutic goal. If this maneuver does not appear to be leading in that direction, however, the therapist is justified in terminating the relationship. Concern for the patient cannot be so overriding that it gets one into personally and socially unacceptable difficulties.

Distinctions between ethical and unethical conduct in the outpatient treatment of individuals who are vulnerable to psychotic breakdown are unclear today. New treatment contracts that differ from the clear-cut and fixed contract in classical psychoanalysis are evolving to facilitate the ethical practice of psychotherapy.

Review of the Literature

Dawning Ethical Concerns

Before the terms "psychosis" and "neurosis" came into currency little more than a century ago, the distinction between these groups of emotional disorders was murky if not nonexistent. Such words as "frenzy," "lunacy," "mania," "madness," and "insanity" designated an abnormal state that was generally attributed to supernatural forces or sinfulness before it came to be regarded as illness. Among the afflicted, psychotic individuals were the first to command attention because they were recognized as a threat to society.

Gripped by the theory of demoniac possession, the ancient world entrusted psychotics to witch doctors and sorcerers. The Middle Ages injected doses of religious fanaticism into the treatment of the seriously deranged. They were branded as sinners in Satan's clutches; theologians and priestly healers applied "therapy" with torture racks, branding irons, and bonfires.

An exceptional few spoke out against the accepted practices of their times and implanted the notion that there might be other methods of dealing with deviants. With the suggestion that alternative courses of action were possible, the relative effectiveness of each course could be weighed. When the element of choice came into view, prescientific healing acquired an ethical dimension.

Hippocrates, for example, in the fifth century B.C., attributed the belief that epilepsy was sacred or divine to ignorance or wonder. The conjurors and purificators resorted to incantations to the gods, he added, because of their own inability to cure the disease.

Celsus, known as the Latin Hippocrates, apparently introduced the word "insania" (insanity) into medical literature in the first century A.D. The treatment of the psychoses that he reports in *De Medicina* "showed a practicality, a naturalism and a directness that ... made it a model for treatment of the insane for centuries" (Bromberg, 1954, p. 30).

To counteract depression, Celsus recommended, in addition to massage, vomiting, and exercise, simple methods of suggestion and logical persuasion, such as "causes of fright excluded, good hope rather put forward; entertainment ... sought by story-telling, and by games ... depression should be gently reproved as being without cause." But fetters were advocated to restrain the violent from harming themselves or others. The recommended responses to delusional states and chronicity also encompassed less gentle procedures:

> If however, it is the mind that deceives the madman, he is best treated by certain tortures. When he says or does anything wrong, he is to be coerced by starvation, fetters, and flogging. ... It also makes a difference whether from

time to time without cause the patient laughs, or is sad and dejected; for the hilarity of madness is better treated by those terrors I have mentioned. [Celsus, 1935, Book 3, p. 289]

Celsus and others who advocated punishment and torture, in our time, would certainly be charged with unethical conduct. But these were accepted practices in their day and were not recognized as harmful. Nor did they recognize that the recalcitrant patients were inducing in them the desire to inflict pain. They experienced no conflict about resorting to these measures. As Semelaigne, a French psychiatrist and grand-nephew of Pinel, remarked in 1931:

It is difficult to judge people of past ages by the ideas of today. Those who tried to master the violent and dangerous patients with irons and blows were not inhuman people; the majority of them were inspired with benevolent intentions and by their goal of bringing these people to health. The manners of our ancestors were rude in a way different from ours. It was a time when corporeal torture was of current usage. [Zilboorg and Henry, 1941, p. 517]

The sixteenth century set the stage for a secular therapy. Men imbued with the humanistic ideals of the Renaissance spoke out against superstitious beliefs and cruelties. Paracelsus and Weyer, German physicians, published works denouncing the excesses of the Inquisition. Weyer also attacked the notion that demons could inhabit the body or be driven out of it by violence. As the tide slowly turned during the next 200 years, the treatment of emotional disorders became a medical responsibility.

First to receive attention were the "lunaticks," herded together like criminals in the contemporary madhouses. They were all regarded as suffering from the same kind of illness. The general physicians who administered the treatment favored letting blood, cold baths, salves, emetics, and purgatives.

The first need was for humane reforms and the abolition of restraints. In 1793, at the Asylum de Bicêtre in Paris, inmates who had been chained to dungeon posts, some for several decades, were liberated from their iron anklets and handcuffs. (This most dramatic expression of a reform movement then under way in many countries was associated for more than two centuries with the name of Philippe Pinel; but the introduction of *traitement moral* at the Bicêtre is now attributed to Pinel's forerunner and mentor there, Jean-Baptiste Pussin, superintendent of the asylum [Weiner, 1979].) The dungeons were superseded by workshops and promenades.

Traitement moral transcended compassion and elementary medical remedies and synthesized social and therapeutic values. In his treatise on insanity, published in 1801, Pinel introduced the idea that something could be done to help these people. He outlined an approach to psychological therapy. Pinel stressed the need for physicians who would project themselves into the situation of these unfortunates and manage them through persuasion. Pinel and his associates initiated the practice of taking a detailed history of each patient. Direct knowledge of the individual and his problem made it possible to select the best treatment for him.

The crusade for asylum reform and humane treatment was pursued in the United States during the nineteenth century. Dorothea Dix, a retired school teacher who has been referred to as the American Pinel, campaigned for many years for humane care of the indigent insane in public institutions. In a "memorial" submitted to Congress in 1848, she reported witnessing

> more than 9000 idiots, epileptics and insane . . . destitute of appropriate care and protection . . . bound with galling chains, bowed beneath fetters and heavy iron balls attached to drag-chains, lacerated with ropes, scourged with rods and terrified beneath storms of execration and cruel blows; now subject to jibes and scorn and torturing tricks; now abandoned to the most outrageous violations. [Zilboorg and Henry, 1941, pp. 583–584]

Although isolation of the severely disturbed from the community was the primary function of the mental institutions, over the years the concept of exclusion was superseded by other approaches (Rosen, 1969). The gospel of moral treatment gave way to early institutionalization based on the "cult of curability," as Albert Deutsch (1949, ch. 8) referred to the high percentages of cures erroneously reported by the superintendents of mental hospitals during the nineteenth century. A pessimistic prognosis for psychotic patients followed the collapse of the curability boom. Bromberg, however, pointed to a significant psychological gain: "the slow dissolution of congealed hostility toward madmen, which had been bound into a prejudice that insanity was irreversible, and its replacement by an equally intense, though opposing, feeling of benevolence and optimism" (Bromberg, 1954, pp. 107–108).

In a sense, even semantic changes in the conceptualization of severe psychopathology helped improve the treatment climate for the severely disturbed, much as the recognition that they were not possessed but sick had improved it in an earlier era. D. J. Holmes has pointed out that the coining of the term *dementia praecox* had "helped save the afflicted from the witch-burner's torch, imprisonment, and worse" (1972). Later, when that diagnosis yielded to the "less damning concept" of the group of schizophrenias (Bleuler, 1950), it "also became conceivable that spontaneous remissions could occur and that certain types of 'schizophrenia,' might even be amenable to one form of treatment or another" (Holmes, 1972, pp. 934–935).

Freud's Views

Breuer's report of his treatment of Anna O., conducted in her home from 1880–1882, and reported in *Studies on Hysteria* (1893–1895), signaled the advent of scientific psychotherapy. Although her disturbance was diagnosed as hysteria, Breuer identified the manifest illness as "a psychosis of a peculiar kind" (p. 22) with hallucinations, paraphasia, and alternating states of consciousness accompanying the hysterical mechanisms. Some contemporary investigators have "rediagnosed" Anna O.'s condition as schizophrenia, others as a mourning reaction to the death of her father. Whatever the label, she was considered to be a seriously disturbed young woman.

Breuer employed hypnosis to help Anna O. recover her memories and talk about them; as she did so, her symptoms subsided. She called the treatment her "talking cure."

Freud tested the "talking cure" for several years on his own patients and confirmed its effectiveness. Abandoning other methods of therapy, he devoted himself exclusively thenceforth to psychotherapy. Hypnosis, which had been employed only to help the patient verbalize and discharge emotion spontaneously—the cathartic method—was dispensed with when Freud found that helping the patient talk freely was more efficient. The practice of analyzing and interpreting the patient's free associations came to be recognized as the therapy of choice for psychoneurotic patients. He reported, however, that psychoanalysis was less effective in the more severe conditions, especially schizophrenia.

Freud's numerous strictures against the treatment of psychotic patients were based on ethical concerns as well as considerations of technique and practicality. One who undertakes to treat a schizophrenic patient, he warned, "has committed a practical error; he has been responsible for wasted expenditure and has discredited his method of treatment. He cannot fulfil his promise of cure" (1913, p. 124). Convinced as he was of the "radical inaccessibility of the psychoses to analytic treatment," Freud maintained that it was "entirely legitimate to guard against failures by carefully excluding such cases" (1933, pp. 154–155). In short, "Psychotics are a nuisance to psychoanalysis" (Federn, 1952, p. 136).

Finally, in "An Outline of Psychoanalysis," Freud identified the primary problem underlying the treatment of psychotic patients, that is, the difficulty of securing their cooperation:

> If the patient's ego is to be a useful ally in our common work, it must . . . have retained a certain amount of coherence and some fragment of understanding for the demands of reality. But this is not to be expected of the ego of a

psychotic; it cannot observe a pact of this kind, indeed it can scarcely enter into one. . . . Thus we discover that we must renounce the idea of trying our plan of cure upon psychotics—renounce it perhaps for ever or perhaps only for the time being, till we have found some other plan better adapted for them. [1940, p. 173]

As Freud maintained, if you are convinced that you cannot cure a particular group of patients through your method of therapy, you are not unethical in withholding it from them.

Despite the continuing existence of a "cult of incurability," many psychoanalysts pursued the solution of the theoretical and technical problems that Freud had encountered. For example, the "no transference in psychosis" dogma (Federn, 1952, p. 142) gave way to the recognition of narcissistic transference and the finding that it could be exploited for therapeutic purposes. Increased emphasis was placed on the interpersonal character of the treatment relationship, the influence of counter-transference phenomena, and the scope of the practitioner's emotional commitment to a seriously disturbed patient. Any difficulties in establishing a therapeutically useful relationship with a schizophrenic individual were attributed by Fromm-Reichmann to the personality problems of the therapist rather than to the patient (1952).

R. P. Knight reported to the American Psychoanalytic Association that:

> The psychoanalytic technique has been modified in numerous ways in the last decade and a half in an attempt to treat successfully the psychoses, the borderline conditions, the character disorders, and various psychosomatic conditions which now present themselves in increasing numbers for therapy. [1953, p. 217]

Commenting on these efforts, Waelder reported that they were "therapeutically highly promising" with the group of borderline patients "who are, on the whole, successfully fighting off a psychosis of a schizophrenic type." He had not handled any "real psychotics," but as an "outside observer," he was "impressed by the fact that they all seem to require . . . great personal investment in terms of time, availability and effort" (1960, pp. 233–234).

Among some practitioners, demonstrations of the widening scope of psychoanalysis gave rise to a new ethical concern: if psychotic patients can be helped through psychotherapy, is it ethical to withhold it from them?

The Therapist's Values

Discussions of ethics and moral values per se have been relatively scarce in the psychoanalytic literature, but this ought not be attributed to lack of interest. References to these subjects are scattered throughout the literature on technique and counter-transference.

The traditional opinion on the place of moral values in the analytic situation is clearly expressed by Hartmann: the therapist's moral evaluations of the patient's material are "best kept in the background in contacts with the patient." In conducting the treatment, the therapist, while he keeps other values in abeyance, will "concentrate on the realization of one category of values only: health values." Their realization in his patients is the therapist's "immediate and overriding concern" (1960, p. 55).

Federn, reporting on his work with psychotic patients, cautioned against telling white lies or exposing patients to indignities. He advocated giving "full recognition of the patient's right to have his personality respected. . . . Our courting of the patient's confidence must be sincere" (1952, pp. 141–142).

Fromm-Reichmann viewed respect for the patient as a primary requisite for his treatment and advocated meeting patients "on the basis of mutual human equality" (1950, p. 17). Any inclination of a patient to put the therapist on an "authoritarian pedestal" ought not to be taken advantage of; she favored conducting the treatment as a collaborative enterprise to promote "the patient's tendency toward growth and maturation" (1950, p. 17).

According to Fromm-Reichmann, the view that the therapist "should be free from any evaluational goals while dealing with his patients" should apply only to personal values, such as religion, politics, and philosophy, that "one would not expect to be or become the patient's evaluational goals." She envisioned self-realization as the ideal goal of treatment, defining the term as the use of one's talents, skills, and powers to one's own satisfaction within the realm of a "freely established realistic set of values" (1950, pp. 33–34).

Sullivan observed that psychotic individuals engage in interpersonal processes that are "exactly of a piece with processes which we manifest some time every twenty-four hours. . . . In most general terms, we are all much more simply human than otherwise" (1953, p. 16).

Respect for the patient's right to self-determination and autonomy has been generally expressed. But Wolberg points to a need to blend this attitude with a "realistic appraisal of social disciplines to which the patient will have to make an adjustment" (1977, p. 971.)

The view that the psychotherapist can or ought to maintain an attitude of true neutrality finds few adherents today. It is indisputable, Holmes remarks, that psychotherapists "teach ethics, not as a rigid catechism to be memorized and held like a magical holy stone, but as an attitude toward self and other people that will increase the pleasure of all. . . . We also teach tactics . . . [and] about the importance of personal growth" (1972, pp. 1029–1030).

The widespread agreement that no psychotherapist can avoid imparting his own values to patients indicates an important change in the principles of treatment, according to Menninger and Holzman (1973). In a review of the theory that the analyst should not advise, sympathize with, make decisions for, or try to make a patient happy, they state that some analysts who recognize that they might occlude the treatment by conveying a moral attitude, "lean over a little bit the other way" (p. 99). Menninger and Holzman continue:

> In some psychoanalysts this attitude of nonjudgment becomes almost a religion. Some individuals get themselves into absurd and illogical predicaments in their zeal to supplant social vengeance with social understanding. But it is just as absurd to scold society and punish it for its stupidity as it is to scold a patient and punish him, and this attitude leads some analysts to espouse a *laissez faire* philosophy. ... The most free-thinking and modern young mother would probably not leave a two-year-old child to do as it likes in an ammunition factory, and for some patients the everyday social community is more dangerous than an ammunition factory. [pp. 99–100]

Conflicts in Values

Half a century ago, A. A. Brill attributed acceptance of a schizophrenic patient for analytic psychotherapy solely to the hope that an "unknown something" might change the patient into a normal human being. We have moved beyond therapeutic futility; the prevailing attitude today is one of therapeutic uncertainty.

It has been amply demonstrated that the functional psychoses and borderline psychotic states are psychodynamically reversible conditions. The degree of reversibility achieved, however, varies widely. Some practitioners are very successful in treating these conditions; others are not. Successful results are reported with increasing frequency; a psychotherapy that is more consistently effective with these patients appears to be evolving. Until it is accepted, however, it will continue to rank as an innovative procedure. To employ it may therefore be regarded as unethical; not to employ it may also be regarded as unethical.

To be more specific, the accepted methods of treating psychotics today—hospitalization, chemotherapy, and electroshock therapy supplemented by psychotherapy oriented to limited goals—are based on the belief that these severe disorders are incurable. To those who share that belief, it appears unethical to expose a patient to the risk of an innovative procedure. On the other hand, those who believe that its use entails no serious risk and is likely to be of substantial benefit will consider failure to employ the procedure—assuming that the patient wishes to undergo it—unethical.

In this area of psychotherapeutic practice, one is confronted with serious conflicts in values and other dilemmas. Some can be resolved on the basis of clinical experience and personal judgment. There are, however, common discrepancies between psychotherapeutic values and social values that appear to be irreconcilable. Activity that the practitioner regards as eminently ethical, immediately beneficial to the patient, and ultimately beneficial to many others in the future, may be frowned on by society.

Society favors short-term treatment, preferably instant cure. It tends to question the usefulness of a course of treatment that spans five or more years, especially if its success cannot be guaranteed. The long-term nature and cost of analytic psychotherapy in severe disturbances become ethical considerations.

Many years ago, as consulting psychiatrist to a child guidance agency, I directed a research project on the treatment of borderline psychotic children and their parents (Feldman, 1978). The project was inaugurated because, although these children were untreatable by the agency's standards, some social workers on the staff were greatly interested in treating them. I still recall being asked by the agency administrator, "Why should we treat a psychotic child when we can cure ten neurotic children in less time?" I replied, "You may feel no qualms about turning away a psychotic child, but you might insist on curing the illness if it were your own child."

Commitment to this long-range treatment has thus far been motivated primarily by parental concern about a seriously disturbed child and the adult patient's concern about his personal well-being. Most of the psychotic patients whom I have successfully treated had insisted on undergoing it after they or their parents were told by others that the patients suffered from an incurable disorder.

The great majority of private practitioners ministering to the treatment needs of the severely disturbed are very much aware of the vast numbers of patients who are deprived of their services. Among them are those chronically disabled inmates of the state hospitals for whom "the burden of poverty has been added to the burden of mental illness, resulting in multiple episodes of decompensation, reinstitutionalization, and discharge" (Okin, 1978, p. 1356). Because of the community's great need for expanded psychotherapeutic services, research-oriented practitioners are under strong pressure to demonstrate how much can be accomplished at minimal cost. But this is putting the cart before the horse. The best method of treating a particular category of patients *regardless of expense* has to be determined first; deciding how to apply that method in the least costly way is the second step.

At the present time we are still intent upon developing a more consistently effective approach to people suffering from the psychodynamically reversible psychoses. Until this approach becomes a reality, it will be the responsibility of the psychotherapist to help these patients decide between an accepted procedure that is not curative and an innovative procedure that is potentially curative.

From Rudimentary to Cooperative Relationship

Sufficient headway has been made in psychotherapy to put to rest Freud's idea that one has to possess a cooperative ego to be cured of a psychologically reversible psychosis. The lack of such an ego does mean, however, that treating such patients is in some respects like raising children. Children are not cooperative from birth; they must be trained to cooperate. Psychologically infantile patients are provided with such training as part of the treatment process.

This is, of course, a radical departure from the classical viewpoint that the possession of a "reasonable" ego to ally with the therapist's "analyzing" ego (Greenson, 1965) is a prerequisite for analytic treatment. To qualify for partnership in the working alliance, the patient is expected to be capable of functioning purposefully in his own interests and respecting the routines of treatment. Otherwise, the patient is "screened out" in the initial interview or discharged as unsuitable or unanalyzable at the end of the trial period.

In an intermediate position are the analysts who try to adapt themselves to the limitations of severely disturbed patients. These practitioners, operating intuitively, go as far as they can in making concessions to these patients. But the standard treatment contract is usually adhered to as much as possible.

A fundamentally different type of treatment contract is negotiated in the specific method of treatment that my associates and I refer to as modern psychoanalysis. This system of therapeutic analysis was formulated on the basis of clinical experience with preoedipal patients, and its implementation in the office treatment of schizophrenic patients has been reported (Spotnitz, 1969). The first meeting with the patient, the establishment of the contract, and the general conduct of the treatment are conceptualized in terms of dealing with resistance, as much as possible by helping the patient outgrow it. A wide range of therapeutic techniques, from emotional communication to interpretation, are employed for this purpose.

Initial Interview

It often takes an inordinately long time for a psychotic patient to commit himself to working for real change. What he primarily wants is to "feel better" now. And he is likely to convey the attitude that investing time and money in treatment would just prove that he is incurable. During the initial interview, as well as during the preliminary phase of the relationship, he is continually provided with an opportunity to resist direction.

On entering the office for the first time, the patient is usually steeled against the anticipation of wounding inspection and insistent probing. Rather than being put under pressure to disprove his unworthiness for time and assistance, the interviewer tries to convert the exploratory discussion into a therapeutic experience.

The candidate for treatment is not exposed to pressure to give information that he has withheld. He is not bombarded with questions. It is appropriate to ask what problems he wants help with. The answers given permit the therapist to study the candidate's attitude about treatment and to evaluate his willingness and ability to work with the therapist under mutually agreeable terms.

Acceptance of the characteristically irresolute attitudes that are communicated, verbally and nonverbally, during the initial interview helps the prospective patient express himself comfortably. Based on his voluntary disclosures, the interviewer formulates a tentative diagnosis, assembles a brief family history, and tries to anticipate the various obstacles to change that might arise in the course of the therapy. Slight pressure for disclosure may be exerted if the interviewer finds it difficult to decide whether he would be willing and able to deal with these obstacles effectively.

The prospective patient's requests for information about the nature of his illness require judicious handling in order to prevent severe narcissistic injury. A straightforward explanation of pathology is contraindicated; it may be experienced as an attack on his ego by someone who neither likes nor understands him. Such requests are often countered by questions that will stimulate the prospective patient to give his own impression of his problems, or the interviewer may characterize the illness in nontechnical terms. I have told many persons, for example, that their main problem was that they weren't trained properly; what I had to decide was whether I was competent to retrain them.

Professional or personal disclosures, even those made simply for reassurance, are inadvisable. The provision of such information, even when solicited, is almost invariably regarded as evidence of professional ineptitude. Rather than alleviating the candidate's own feelings of insecurity, such communications tend to intensify his reluctance to enter treatment.

Assurances of a successful outcome, whether explicit or implicit, are definitely contraindicated from a legal as well as a therapeutic point of view. A promise of cure on the therapist's part would constitute a clear breach of contract should the treatment be unsuccessful (Perri and Perri,

1978). Promises or even the suggestion of recovery are also out of order for another reason because they may strengthen the resolve of a negatively suggestible person laboring under an unconscious determination to outmaneuver the therapist, whatever the cost to himself. What motivates a question about outcome has to be determined before it is answered. It is preferable not to volunteer information on the length of the treatment and its emotional impact, both of which are uncertain at the initial meeting because of the factor of negative suggestibility.

The prospective patient meets with the attitude that he is acceptable, assuming the therapist is disposed to treat him. The therapist who for any reason does not want to undertake the treatment therapeutically communicates this rejection by attributing the decision to his own inadequacy.

Treatment Contract

When the relationship is formed, minimal demands for cooperation are imposed on the patient. Initially the therapist "accepts whatever contribution the patient is able to make and works systematically to transform an essentially rudimentary relationship into a cooperative one—a full-fledged working alliance" (Spotnitz, 1969, p. 72). The traditional criteria for analyzability thus fall by the wayside.

The treatment contract defines the degree of purposeful participation that can be reasonably expected of someone functioning at the patient's emotional level. Assuming that he agrees (verbally) to participate to that extent, the therapist initially assumes full responsibility for the treatment process. (Subsequently, the patient shares this responsibility, and does so in growing measure as the treatment progresses.)

The baseline requirements for ambulatory treatment are that the patient agree to come to the office at the appointed hours, to lie on the couch, to talk, and to pay for the treatment at the end of the month. The contract thus keys the rudimentary relationship to the mutual recognition and investigation of the difficulties that cluster around these requirements. By intervening to resolve the different patterns of resistances to performance that operate at each stage of the relationship, the therapist helps the patient achieve fuller cooperation and personality maturation.

The treatment is inaugurated on a nonintensive basis (usually one or two sessions a week). The therapist tests his ability to work with the patient during a trial period, which usually lasts about six weeks. The patient may leave treatment at any time but is helped to continue for two years—the minimum time required for significant change to occur. This is a general policy, but it is particularly important that it be observed with psychotics and borderline psychotics, who tend to equate the persistence of their troublesome feelings with lack of therapeutic progress.

If the treatment is terminated then or later by mutual agreement, the patient is given the option to return later if he wishes to achieve further progress. Successful results in the treatment of preoedipal conditions usually require at least five years, but the ultimate duration of the treatment is determined by the willingness of both partners to continue to work together.

The schema outlined above reflects the gradual progression of a seriously disturbed patient from a rudimentary to a cooperative relationship. This long-range therapeutic endeavor is governed by an evolving contract.

> It evolves in the patient's understanding of what is expected of him and it evolves in terms of what the analyst expects of him. This refers not only to such clear-cut modifications of the treatment as mutually agreed upon changes in fees or changes in the frequency of sessions . . . but also the evolution which is the result of progress in the treatment. [Perri and Perri, 1978]

The terms that the patient agrees to are criteria for cooperative behavior that he cannot meet at his current level of functioning. Rather than being penalized for nonperformance, he is helped to perform. And as long as he makes a conscious effort to operate in the spirit of the agreement, the therapist himself continues to perform. In other words, by structuring the contract so that performance by the patient at his current level of functioning is impossible, the therapist incurs the burden of resolving the patient's resistance to performing his contractual duties.

Participation of third party.   If, when the treatment is arranged for, the prospective patient's ego is so defective that he cannot make decisions regarding his own welfare, a substitute ego draws up the contract with the therapist. A relative or other responsible adult would officiate for a person who is so out of contact with reality, for example, that he has to be escorted to the office by a hospital attendant or by relatives. Other prospective patients, though not actively psychotic, may demonstrate incompetence by erratic behavior, gross inability to keep appointments, and the like.

In these cases, as in the treatment of minors, it is desirable that the third party and therapist maintain some form of regular contact until the patient is competent to negotiate on his own behalf. At that time, the original agreement is either confirmed or revised so that it eventually becomes a contract between the patient and the therapist.

Control of behavior.   The ability of patients to control their behavior sufficiently to be treated on an ambulatory basis is investigated during the trial period. An overexcitable person who begins by throwing books on the floor or banging at furniture may not qualify for office treatment.

After being told that he may belong in a hospital, however, the patient often makes a special effort to conduct himself so that the office treatment may continue.

The Treatment Situation

Use of the Couch

When the treatment gets under way, the patient is not asked to verbalize whatever comes to his mind. He may be instructed to tell his life story in any way he wants to, or simply to talk. Usually it is indicated that while he is free to withhold information, he is supposed eventually to say everything that occurs to him in the sessions. By resolving the patient's resistances to communicating freely, the therapist gradually educates him to free-associate.

The patient is also instructed at the outset of treatment to lie on the couch. Someone who objects to using it may be informed that it is better for the treatment if he verbalizes his immediate intrapsychic experience lying flat on his back with legs uncrossed, arms at his side, and palms up (Stern, 1978). The patient is permitted at times to sit up when he wishes. Early in treatment, a psychotic woman occasionally used to get off the couch to walk around the consulting room and bang at the walls. By resolving whatever resistances arise to reclining on the couch, the therapist gradually trains the patient to assume that position.

Of course, the use of the couch is not compulsory, and some schools of psychotherapy favor treating patients face to face. Indeed, it has been suggested that the couch, rather than serving a therapeutic purpose, has become an institutional symbol; Szasz refers to it as a pseudoinstrument (1974). I do not insist on its use, but it is usually better from the standpoint of treatment that the patient lie flat on his back during the sessions. In general, the use of the couch enables a patient to communicate with relative freedom from environmental and bodily stimulation; it also discourages destructive motor acitivity—a safety factor that needs to be considered when one is working with a psychotic patient (Spotnitz, 1969, 1976). Once the patient is in control of his behavior, the treatment can be conducted face to face if he so wishes.

Frequency of Sessions

The treatment schedule is governed primarily by the amount of time and effort the patient wishes to devote to the treatment and what the therapist judges to be the optimal intensity of contact. The spacing of the sessions does not appreciably influence the duration of treatment; as indicated above, a minimum of five years is required for the maturation of the preoedipal personality.

When the treatment is contracted for, the patient is asked how frequently he wants to come to the office and what he wants to pay for the sessions. As long as he is primarily concerned about alleviating suffering and handicapping symptoms, little else would be gained from working with the therapist more than once or twice a week. After the suffering begins to abate, however, the patient often develops a genuine desire to work more intensively on his problems. For that reason, the treatment may become more intensive in the later phases.

Fees and Financial Transactions

It is desirable that a fee be established that does not entail undue hardship for the patient or significant sacrifice for the therapist. The ideal fee, from the patient's point of view, is one that can be paid out of current income. It is borne in mind that the preservation of his capital resources is extremely important; if these are exhausted and the treatment fails, the patient may have to spend his remaining years as a public charge. The same considerations govern the fixing of the fee when family members or others assume the costs of the treatment.

If the amount that the patient wants to pay is substantially below the therapist's regular fee, the patient may be referred to a therapist who will treat him at a fee the patient can afford. Many therapists embarking on practice are extremely interested in working with psychotic and borderline patients. Because of this interest, these therapists may achieve better results in such cases than more experienced practitioners who are not as interested in handling them.

The patient is expected to keep track of the number of sessions he has during the month and to present properly executed checks for the amount due at the end of the month. Various difficulties in the management of money are observed. Some patients want to pay in advance or overpay; others miscalculate the number of sessions, underpay, or offer postdated or worthless checks. The normal range of variations in these matters is respected, but the same deviation month after month is dealt with as resistance. For example, with a patient who tends to overpay, it is appropriate to review the number of sessions held during the month; the patient may be trying, consciously or unconsciously, to find out whether the error will be overlooked or called to his attention.

Permitting a patient to go heavily in arrears is inadvisable. He may then be tempted to abandon the relationship and repeat the pattern with other analysts, leaving a train of debts in his wake. Resistance to paying on a monthly basis is therefore handled rather firmly in the early stage of treatment. How such a repetitive pattern is dealt with later depends on what is going on in the relationship.

Cancellations

Sessions that are cancelled by the patient because of physical illness are usually not charged for; those cancelled for nonmedical reasons at less than twenty-four hours' notice are charged for unless the therapist is able to allocate the time to someone else. (The latter policy applies even to acute personal emergencies and acts of God, but the patient may be offered an extra session without charge after verbalizing his resentment about being charged for the one he missed.) If the time was filled, the patient whose attitude is apologetic may be so informed during the next session. The vituperative patient may not know until the end of the month that he will not be charged for the missed session; that pleasant surprise is deferred to help him go on venting his resentment. The verbalization of anger is not interrupted unless the patient is deriving pleasure from being abusive.

To a physically ill patient, the idea would be communicated that the therapist is more interested in his general well-being than in adherence at that time to the treatment schedule. Thus, the patient is instructed to remain in bed rather than to keep an appointment if he has a temperature of 100° or higher. At times of serious physical illness, the patient is encouraged to follow the advice of his physician.

Vacation Breaks

The patient is notified of any planned interruption of treatment, notably the period when the therapist will be on vacation, several weeks in advance. Substantial interruptions are difficult for a seriously disturbed person to tolerate, especially during the first year of treatment. The patient is therefore helped to verbalize his feelings about an approaching break in treatment and asked how he would feel about keeping in touch with the therapist by phone or mail. The patient is also given the name of another therapist he might talk with during that period if he so wishes.

In general, patients are not encouraged to take their vacation at the same time as the therapist, nor are they charged for sessions missed when they take it at another time. Early in the relationship, however, those who have a choice of vacation periods may be asked why they do not arrange to do so. At a later stage, a compulsively compliant or defiant person may be asked why he does not take his vacation at another time.

Other Practices

Phone calls. When the treatment begins, a seriously disturbed patient needs to know that he can get in touch with the therapist between sessions. When the patient inquires about phoning, he is asked, "Why not?" Knowledge that one may phone at any time reinforces the ego; it also diminishes a negatively suggestible person's urge to do so. The relatively few persons who abuse the privilege are educated to exercise it more reasonably.

Letters. Patients are encouraged to write letters. These are answered, either verbally during the next session or in writing. A letter may be no more than a few thoughts and feelings that occurred to the patient following a treatment session. When given the opportunity to pursue a train of associations in this way, some patients derive considerable therapeutic benefit (Spunt, 1979).

Irreversible decisions. The therapist does *not* suggest when the treatment begins that the patient refrain from making any irreversible decisions about his life affairs. A caveat of this nature introduces potentially troublesome ideas before the patient is confronted with the necessity of committing himself to a course of action. If such a decision confronts the patient later, the therapist explores the situation with him. The patient is helped to balance pros and cons that occur to him and to decide for himself how to proceed.

Behavior outside the office. The therapist conveys the attitude that the patient is free to do anything he really wishes to do outside the office as long as it will not interfere with the therapeutic process. Any setting of limits on his behavior in the intervals between sessions is imposed as a matter of therapeutic strategy.

By and large, rules are issued simply to help patients function cooperatively in the relationship. To penalize someone for failing to obey them is an error in technique. Although a ritualistic approach to rules and arrangements is avoided, the therapist may at times demonstrate an unyielding attitude to help the patient verbalize a sense of self-control.

Contacts with the Family

Freud was seriously opposed to communicating with members of the patient's family. He referred to the intervention of relatives as a "positive danger . . . one does not know how to meet" (1917, p. 459). But Federn, in a report on the treatment of schizophrenic and manic-depressive patients, some of whom were referred to him by Freud, stated: "In no single case have I succeeded without the steady cooperation of the family or someone in their place" (1952, p. 120). Among others who have reported on the treatment of psychotic patients, the views of Fromm-Reichmann and Rosenfeld are representative.

Fromm-Reichmann stressed that the interviewing of a relative "without the patient's knowing it" (1950, p. 216) was contraindicated, but she favored seeing relatives with the patient's knowledge and consent. She found that collateral information thus secured, and used with discretion, accelerated progress at times. With an inarticulate or acutely disturbed patient, joint conferences with the patient and relatives were recommended.

Rosenfeld (1965) reported that the "complete cooperation" of the parents of a patient in an acute state of psychosis was extremely important. When relatives of a chronic paranoid schizophrenic requested Rosenfeld's help and advice, rather than see them himself, he advised them to "discuss their problems regularly" (p.125) with a colleague with whom he was working in close cooperation. Many therapists prefer to refer relatives to an associate.

Involvement of the family has now deepened, particularly stimulated by the studies of family transactions in schizophrenia. Family therapy is now conducted, both as a sole approach and, more characteristically, as an adjunct to the patient's individual psychotherapy. As Lidz points out, "The patient finds it easier to cope with the actual parent with a therapist present than with the parent as a malignant introject" (1972, p. 628). Parents may also be seen regularly, apart from the patient, as members of open-ended parent groups.

I have reported an experimental procedure in which the patient's family and the patient meet with the patient's therapist in a series of interviews. As I stated in an illustration of the use of this procedure with a severely disturbed adolescent and his parents, "the therapist so manages the interviews that the adolescent takes the initiative in helping his parents deal with their feelings" (Spotnitz, 1976, p. 230).

The governing principles in one's contacts with members of the patient's family are that they be made with the patient's permission, and that information disclosed by the patient in treatment sessions is not communicated without his knowledge and consent. By and large, the patient's participation in a discussion of family problems is desirable, provided that the therapist protects him from emotional confrontations that would have an undesirable impact on him at that stage of treatment.

Early in my practice I found it difficult at times to handle the complaints of parents who objected to a change in the patient's behavior. "I want you to influence my son (or daughter) not to talk back to me," was a characteristic communication from the parent of an adolescent emerging from a state of severe withdrawal and beginning to assert himself forcefully at home. The therapeutic significance of such a transformation is not always appreciated or welcomed by the family. One enraged father insisted that his son bury his anger, as he had in the past, and be respectful, whatever the psychic cost might be.

One way of handling such complaints is to get the family member to describe the situation and discuss it objectively with him, while maintaining a sympathetic attitude toward the patient. But I do not attempt to obtain confirmation of the situation or express approval of the patient's behavior in a family interview. An alternative approach, which I recommend, is to endeavor in the patient's treatment sessions to redirect his hostility, away from the parent to the therapist. The patient is thus helped to behave appropriately at home and in social situations.

Management of Psychotic Episodes

To maintain a therapeutic relationship, one needs to operate primarily in terms of what the patient agrees to and what one judges to be socially constructive. It may be difficult to reconcile these terms in the treatment of a patient who is vulnerable to psychotic reactions. Despite the safeguards built into the therapeutic process against further regression and breakdown (Spotnitz, 1969), from time to time a patient impresses one as being on the verge of a full-blown psychosis, suicidal, or homicidal.

Hospitalization.   Should the responsible relative be informed that the patient ought to be hospitalized? This is an extremely sensitive issue. A therapist who notifies the relative without the patient's express permission is probably foreclosing the possibility of resuming the treatment on the patient's discharge from the hospital. If the patient is opposed to hospitalization, for the therapist to recommend it is to violate the patient's confidence and thwart his wishes in the matter. Either eventuality makes it very difficult to treat the patient successfully, especially a borderline patient who was hospitalized without his consent.

On the other hand, the therapist may discuss the patient's currently dangerous state of mind with him and express the opinion that the patient needs to enter a hospital. If the patient agrees to this and either enters a hospital with the family's cooperation or signs himself into one voluntarily, the psychotherapeutic relationship may be resumed later.

Some patients are educated to the idea of entering a hospital when they need its protection. It is a sign of improvement when they do this unaccompanied and on their own initiative.

In general, the psychotherapist himself does not hospitalize the patient and does not prevent the patient from entering a hospital. The therapist takes the attitude that he does not want the patient to enter a hospital except for his own protection or for that of society.

Unquestionably, however, if a patient constitutes a danger to himself and others and is unable to take care of himself, provision for his care has to be made by others. Members of the patient's family usually make whatever arrangements are necessary in such an emergency, and they may call on a psychiatrist if the patient's commitment to an institution is necessary. It is preferable that the psychotherapist have nothing to do with the commitment.

If the patient enters a hospital that provides psychotherapy, the nature of his treatment there is determined by the practitioner assigned to the case. In a state hospital or other mental institution that provides only custodial care and chemotherapy, it may be possible to make special arrangements for the patient to receive psychotherapy during his confinement. If permission to visit him for this purpose is not granted to an outside therapist, the members of the family may devote their visits to helping him verbalize freely.

Psychotropic drugs. The use of one or more of the recently introduced psychotropic drugs, which help to control psychotic reactions, may serve as an alternative to hospitalization. Drugs may also be utilized to alleviate discomfort during periods when a patient is exposed to special environmental pressures.

The medical psychotherapist may prescribe the drugs himself but it is preferable that they be administered by someone else. I refer patients to a colleague who specializes in chemotherapy. The nonmedical practitioner who believes that a patient's functioning in psychotherapy would be facilitated by supplementary drug therapy may refer the patient to someone who is licensed to administer it. If, in the therapist's judgment, chemotherapy might facilitate the patient's recovery, failure to discuss that possibility with the patient might, in certain situations, be regarded as unethical conduct.

Some psychiatrists administer chemotherapy exclusively to psychotic patients and insist that they take the drugs prescribed regularly. I educate my patients to have drugs available for use when they cannot function without them, but to dispense with their use when they serve no important purpose.

Socially Destructive Situations

Patients who have sustained severe emotional damage in the course of their lives often feel like getting even with those they hold responsible.

Their communications are typically weighted with more aggression than those of neurotics and the psychotic patients demonstrate poorer judgment. (Borderline patients also talk at times about violent action, but they have periods of better judgment.) Early in treatment, if not in the initial interview, they may call on the therapist to help them engage in socially or personally destructive behavior. Their requests for approval and assistance in such activities give rise to moral conflicts that the therapist has to resolve on the basis of personal judgment. After being invited to be an accomplice in one or another crime that the patient contemplates, the therapist may seriously question his ability to direct the treatment into constructive channels.

Eissler's assertion that the therapist has a moral obligation not to "accept for mental treatment a subject whose moral conduct is offensive to him," is an accepted principle. He also states that the therapist should find out in advance "if he can"—key words—whether he would be able to tolerate the would-be patient's moral conduct (1971, p. 83).

In my view, it is unethical to continue working with a person who discloses his intention of engaging in socially destructive conduct unless there is a likelihood that it will not be engaged in—in other words, that the treatment will prevent its occurence. A patient who requests the therapist's assistance in perpetrating a crime or other socially destructive behavior has to be informed, sooner or later, that the therapist cannot be a party to it. But the immediate task confronting the therapist is to investigate the patient's request and, in the process, to try to help him abandon the contemplated act.

Many years ago, a successful business man who appeared to be an upright individual told me that he had left his wife and three children and wanted to marry his mistress. Inasmuch as his wife refused to give him a divorce, he planned to kill her. "I'd like you to help me do it," he added, "because I don't want to be caught in the crime."

My answer was that I could not be a party to murder. But instead of ending the interview forthwith, I listened to what he had to say and then made a counter-proposal: to help him extricate himself from his present situation, effect a reconciliation with his wife, and make a success of his marriage. The man said that he did not think that could be accomplished, but if I would accept him for treatment, he expressed willingness to explore the possibility. Two years later, after parting with his mistress—he said that he had "married her off" to somebody else—he and his wife were reunited and enjoying a cooperative relationship.

Another illustration of the type of requests that severely disturbed individuals may make was drawn from the case of a borderline psychotic in his early twenties. He was the only child and sole heir of a wealthy widow who opposed his every effort to live a life of his own. Shortly after he entered treatment, he said that he planned to kill his mother. It was his intention to push her down a flight of stairs. Would I advise him how to do it so that her death would appear accidental?

Why would I get implicated in such a crime? And if he actually committed it, what would be the effect on our treatment relationship? Did he think I would continue to work with him? And to what purpose, if he was going to end up in prison? We discussed these questions for several sessions. Eventually he decided that it would be better to give up the whole idea. Had he not dismissed it, I would have had to discharge him as a patient.

This rarely proves necessary, however. In most cases, the threat of being discharged from treatment eventually proves an effective—and sobering—deterrent.

It is my impression that when a patient threatens to become danger-ous, his hostility needs to be deflected from the environment and "tamed" in the treatment situation. In other words, instead of being dangerous to other people, it is better that he be threatening—verbally—to the therapist. The therapist who cannot help the patient direct his aggression toward the transference object cannot, in my view, be really helpful to a potentially violent patient.

If the treatment is discontinued for that reason, the therapist may have to notify the patient's family or the police of the patient's threats, preferably with the patient's consent. When he is informed that the therapist is required by law to report the situation, in my experience the patient usually agrees to verbalize his hostilities in the sessions without action.

But working to resolve the resistances of a patient—especially of a schizophrenic patient—to the verbalization of frustration-aggression is not a generally accepted procedure. It is the ultimate expression of the principle that the patient has the freedom to verbalize all his feelings and, in my experience, is the key to the cure of the schizophrenic patient. But it is an approach that almost inevitably creates conflicts between therapeutic values and the therapist's personal values.

In teaching the patient that he does not have to sacrifice his ego to preserve the object, as I stated in an earlier publication:

> The therapist must, so to speak, throw himself in the direct line of fire. He may expose himself to injurious action even as his self-preservative instincts are warning him that he would be better off if his treatment partner were shut up or locked up. ... But if carrying buried hostility is what made the patient ill, helping him to go on carrying it won't make him well. [Spotnitz, 1976, p. 116]

Admittedly, some element of risk is involved and many analytic therapists understandably object to risking their lives for the sake of curing a patient. Some object even to verbal attack, complaining that it causes unendurable pain and suffering beyond the call of duty.

The solution to this predicament is to teach the patient to *feel* like killing you, to *tell* you about it, and *not* to do it. Extensive training, however, is required to operate in this way. In the treatment of the severely disturbed, there are few absolute mandates. Much that was ethical in the past has ceased to be ethical in the present, and what will be ethical in the future will be determined by our greater skill in handling these patients. As we become able to treat them in a consistently effective way, the distinctions between ethical and unethical conduct will become increasingly clear.

REFERENCES

BLEULER, E. *Dementia praecox or the group of schizophrenias.* New York: International Universities Press, 1950.

BREUER, J., and FREUD, S. Studies on hysteria. In S. Freud, *Standard edition,* Vol. 2. London: Hogarth Press, 1955. (Originally published 1893-1895.)

BROMBERG, W. *Man above humanity.* Philadelphia: Lippincott, 1954.

CELSUS, A. C. *De medicina.* Trans. W. G. Spencer. Cambridge, Mass.: Loeb Classical Library, Harvard, 1935.

DEUTSCH, A. *The mentally ill in America,* 2nd ed. New York: Columbia, 1949.

EISSLER, K. *Talent and genius.* New York: Quadrangle Books, 1971.

FEDERN, P. *Ego psychology and the psychoses.* New York: Basic Books, 1952.

FELDMAN, Y. The early history of modern psychoanalysis. *Modern Psychoanalysis,* 1978, **3**, 15-27.

FREUD, S. On beginning the treatment. *Standard edition,* Vol. 12. London: Hogarth Press, 1964. (Originally published 1913.)

FREUD, S. Introductory lectures on psychoanalysis. *Standard edition,* Vol. 16. London: Hogarth Press, 1964. (Originally published 1917.)

FREUD, S. New introductory lectures on psychoanalysis. *Standard edition,* Vol. 22. London: Hogarth Press, 1964. (Originally published 1933.)

FREUD, S. An outline of psychoanalysis. *Standard edition,* Vol. 23. London: Hogarth Press, 1964. (Originally published 1940.)

FROMM-REICHMANN, F. *Principles of intensive psychotherapy.* Chicago: University of Chicago Press, 1950.

FROMM-REICHMANN, F. Some aspects of psychoanalytic psychotherapy with schizophrenics. In E. B. Brody and F. C. Redlich (eds.), *Psychotherapy with schizophrenics.* New York: International Universities Press, 1952.

GREENSON, R. S. The working alliance and the transference neurosis. *Psychoanalytic Quarterly,* 1965, **34**, 155-181.

HARTMANN, H. *Psychoanalysis and moral values.* New York: International Universities Press, 1960.

HOLMES, D. J. *Psychotherapy.* Boston: Little Brown, 1972.

KNIGHT, R. P. The present status of organized psychoanalysis in the United States. *Journal of the American Psychoanalytic Association,* 1953, **1**, 197-221.

LIDZ, T. The influence of family studies on the treatment of schizophrenia. In

C. J. Sager and H. S. Kaplan (eds.), *Progress in group and family therapy*. New York: Brunner/Mazel, 1972.

MENNINGER, K. A., and HOLZMAN, P. S. *Theory of psychoanalytic technique*, 2nd ed. New York: Basic Books, 1973.

OKIN, R. L. The future of state mental health programs for the chronic psychiatric patients in the community. *American Journal of Psychiatry*, 1978, **135,** 1355–1358.

PERRI, M. E., and PERRI, B. M. The therapeutic and legal aspects of the contract for psychoanalytic treatment. 1978. Unpublished paper. Available from Benito M. Perri, 22 Crosby Place, Huntington, N.Y., 11743.

ROSEN, G. *Madness in society*. New York: Harper & Row, 1969.

ROSENFELD, H. A. *Psychotic states*. New York: International Universities Press, 1965.

SPOTNITZ, H. *Modern psychoanalysis of the schizophrenic patient*. New York: Grune & Stratton, 1969.

SPOTNITZ, H. *Psychotherapy of preoedipal conditions*. New York: Jason Aronson, 1976.

SPUNT, A. R. Written communications in modern psychoanalytic treatment; Their use and psychotherapeutic value, 1979. Unpublished paper. Available from Arlene R. Spunt, 410 East 81st Street, New York, N.Y. 10028.

STERN, H. R. *The couch*. New York: Human Sciences Press, 1978.

SULLIVAN, H. S. *Conceptions of modern psychiatry*. New York: Norton, 1953.

SZASZ, T. S. *The ethics of psychoanalysis*. New York: Basic Books, 1974.

WAELDER, R. *Basic theory of psychoanalysis*. New York: International Universities Press, 1960.

WEINER, D. B. The apprenticeship of Philippe Pinel: A new document, observations of citizen Pussin on the insane. *American Journal of Psychiatry*, 1979, **136,** 1128–1134.

WOLBERG, L. R. *The technique of psychotherapy*, 3rd ed. New York: Grune & Stratton, 1977.

ZILBOORG, G., and HENRY, G. W. *A history of medical psychology*. New York: Norton, 1941.

Ethical Issues in the Treatment of Religious Persons

Joseph A. Braun

Humility before the flower at the timber line is the gate which gives access to the path up the open fell.

Dag Hammarskjöld

The subject—ethical issues in the psychotherapeutic treatment of religious persons—includes definitions of two terms which are by their very nature exceedingly broad: the definition of psychotherapy and the definition of religion. Psychotherapy will be defined inclusively as all psychological treatment methods in which a professional relationship is established. As psychoanalysis has historically been the prime catalyst for the psychotherapy-religion polemic, and since the ethical issues generated by this intensive form of treatment are applicable to other forms of psychotherapy, a psychoanalytic framework will surround this discussion. Religion will be considered broadly as the Judeo-Christian heritage within which psychoanalysis evolved. This religious tradition came under attack by psychoanalysis and is still the prime religious force with which the psychotherapeutic profession lives.

A close examination of the dialectic between psychotherapy and religion will disclose ethical issues raised by profound thinkers on both sides. Within this historical perspective ethical issues will then be considered to revolve around the monitoring of various countertransference feelings in the therapist. There will be additional reflections regarding the treatment of vowed persons in religious vocations.

The Dialectic Between Psychotherapy and Religion

The Posture of Freud

Freud (1907) viewed religion as a universal neurosis. He affirmed that religion was based on a longing for a father's protection in the face

131

of childish helplessness before the world (1927, 1930). Religion was judged a substitute for rationality and for the primacy of the intellect and of science.

The extent of kinship among Freud's writings on religion, his metapsychology, and his clinical, technical treatises changes according to the needs of the interpreter. Some analysts, loyal to an antireligious stance and with a great need to identify with a psychoanalytic *weltanschauung*, readily and uncritically incorporated Freud's writings on religion into their personal and professional belief systems as if it would be heretical not to take such a position. Freud, however, is very specific. In correspondence to his lifelong friend, the Protestant minister, Oskar Pfister, Freud tells Pfister that "psycho-analysis is neither religious nor nonreligious, but an impartial tool" (Meng and Freud, 1964, p. 17). While candidly admitting to Pfister his totally negative outlook on religion that lay behind *The Future of an Illusion*, Freud adds in a 1927 letter:

> Let us be quite clear on the point that the views expressed in my book form no part of analytic theory. They are my personal views, which coincide with those of many non-analysts and pre-analysts, but there are certainly many excellent analysts who do not share them. . . The analyst can of course make a bad technical mistake if he creates the impression of belittling this emotional demand [for religion]. [Pp. 117–118]

Pfister predicted that Freud's writings on religion would create undue animosity toward psychoanalysis as a clinical method. This prediciton was largely verified, aided, and abetted by the propensity of some of Freud's followers to overgeneralize and fail to distinguish between Freud the scientific clinician and Freud the personal philosopher.

Extensions of Freud's Theory

In contrast to Freud's emphasis on God as a father substitute, Kinkel (1922) explored the identification of the church with the mother of infantile experience. In a totally reductionistic stance, Moxon (1926) concluded that the psychoanalyst holds that religious beliefs are produced by unused, displaced, and projected libido; the person who satisfies libidinal needs directly in love and indirectly by work and play would have no energy for religious beliefs and mystical experiences. Jones (1928) asserted that the "Christian myth" was perhaps the most powerful and successful revolutionary fantasy in history because it was based on the oedipal themes of ongoing submission to the will of the father and simultaneous glorification of the power of the son. Further contributions to the psychological understanding of religious dogma and practice, religious ritual, and mankind's sense of guilt were made by Reik (1923,

1927, 1946, 1957, 1959). In writings that span two decades, the psychoanalyst Zilboorg (1967) strove to synthesize psychoanalysis and religion. Tarachow's (1976) study of St. Paul and early Christianity, and Dolto and Severin's (1979) interpretation of the Gospels are examples of continued psychoanalytic investigations of religion with no reductionistic philosophical polemic attached.

The Response from Protestant Christianity

The publication of Freud's *The Future of an Illusion* evoked an immediate response from the minister-analyst, Oskar Pfister. Pfister (1928a, 1928b)—convinced that there was no more genuine reality than a Christianity freed of infantilism and harmonious with reason—argued against Freud's total reduction of religion to neurotic and cultural forces. Certain that philosophy and psychoanalysis had common grounds for a relationship, Pfister nonetheless doubted whether any ethical system could be based solely on psychoanalytic positivism. Another minister, Müller-Braunschweig (1927) also integrated clinical psychoanalysis with ethics and pastoral care. He judged clinical psychoanalysis stripped of its philosophy as neither materialistic, utilitarian, nor hedonistic.

Within Protestantism, however, the psychotherapeutic movement did have unintegrative critics. Bonhoeffer (1972), for instance, who was executed by the Nazis in 1945, declared that there was far more at stake in life than the self-knowledge provided by psychology and psychoanalysis. Niebuhr (1941), considered one of the most important American theologians of this century, criticized Freud for an excessively superficial view of man. Niebuhr dismissed psychoanalysis as a pessimistic solutionless palliative against the disillusionment, cynicism, and pretense in modern culture. Adams' (1976) stance against any compromise with "the pagan system of psychiatry" as "the sin of accommodationism" is illustrative of currently continuing unblanketed criticism. From Adams' evangelical, Christian perspective, biblical counseling which uses the scriptures to espouse human ideals and values is the only effective and permissible mode of help for personal problems.

A central core of Protestant thinkers, however, continuing in the spirit of Pfister and Müller-Braunschweig, have been highly integrative of the theories of psychotherapy, albeit with profound questions, incisive criticisms, and augmentations. Caution was always advanced that the validity of a religious belief is not purely a psychological question and that the theologian has valid areas of inquiry regardless of any relevant psychological question (Goodenough, 1955; Homans, 1968; Lee, 1949; Roberts, 1950; Tillich, 1963; Wise, 1956; Ziegler, 1962). Some Protestant thinkers even organized a theology of psychotherapy around the theme of atonement and used insights about man derived from clinical work to make theological statements (Browning, 1966; Oden, 1966).

In a very thorough investigation, Outler (1954) saw both secular humanism and reductive materialism in the therapeutic subcultural milieu as standing against Judeo-Christian tradition. Good psychotherapy and healthy religion were seen as potential allies, however, in their respect for the individual, their emphasis on healthy wholeness, the granting of meaning to human behavior, their aim of a true morality based on genuine inner value judgments, and the sovereignty granted to love. Outler offered the guideline that:

> Christianity exceeds its rights when it seeks to direct or coerce a process of inquiry which respects its own proper limits. But it is entirely justified in demanding that the examination of first principles be conducted in the temple court of faith and commitment, and not be misrepresented as having been settled in the laboratory and the clinic. [P. 54]

Obviously the psychotherapy revolution was felt in theological camps within Protestantism where it was genuinely confronted and honestly integrated in many ways. Thus could Cox observe in 1973 that theology had so evolved over the past several decades that the Freudian charges that religion was only the means of individual repression and of social oppression were now antiquated.

The Response within Catholicism

Two antithetical responses to psychoanalysis and psychotherapy illustrate the evolution of Catholic thought. The first is a scholarly treatise on psychoanalysis prepared already in 1919 by a Swiss Benedictine, P. J. B. Egger. He viewed psychoanalysis as intrinsically fruitless and destructive because its shallow rationalism attempted to influence education, ethics, and pastoral care—fields that were considered nourishable only by Christian idealism. Psychoanalysis was seen as justification for both the traditional spiritual teaching against such "new psychological heresies" and for the practice of confession, which psychoanalysis would never in the least way replace.

The second significant response came from Pope Pius XII in September 1952. The papacy had long been silent regarding psychoanalysis and psychotherapy, but Pius XII was motivated to support therapy publicly by a short article published in the official clerical bulletin of the Rome diocese by a Monsignor Fellici. Fellici stated that it was impossible for a Catholic to use psychoanalysis actively as a therapist or passively as a patient without committing serious sin. Fellici's article was exaggerated by major newspapers into stories that the Catholic Church had condemned psychoanalysis. The pope took advantage of a scheduled address before a medical congress to try to counter Fellici's influence.[1]

In his talk, Pius XII expressed concern only about the "pansexual method of a certain school of psychoanalysis" (1952, p. 8) that appeared to countenance the arousing and acting on any sexual instinct and fantasy that might arise in treatment; a person was forbidden "to plunge so deeply into the world of sexual suggestions and tendencies" (p. 8). The Vatican newspaper, *L'osservatore Romano,* interpreted the Papal address, clarified that the speech did not reject psychoanalysis in general, and further stated:

> All the systems of psychoanalysis have in common certain principles, methods, and psychic experiments which are in no way contrary to natural ethics and Christian morality and therefore, are not in any way touched or reproved by the Sovereign Pontiff ["With Reference to Psychoanalysis," 1952, p. 17]

One year later, Pius XII addressed the International Congress on Psychotherapy and Clinical Psychology. In extending his discussion to ethical ramifications of the psychodynamic study of religion, he added a highly significant invitation to synthesis:

> We should certainly not find fault with depth psychology if it deals with the psychic aspect of religious phenomena and endeavors to analyze and reduce it to a scientific system, even if this research is new and if its terminology is not found in the past. . . . Prudence and reserve are needed on both sides in order to avoid false interpretations and to make it possible to reach a reciprocal understanding. [1953, pp. 10–11]

Considering the conservative nature of the Pius XII papacy, the previous anti-Christian trends in psychoanalytic philosophy, and some papal misconceptions of the process of psychoanalysis and psychotherapy, the papal documents were highly supportive of psychotherapy and expressed ethical concerns similar to those advanced by professional groups themselves.

A selectively critical, largely synthesizing approach characterized mainstream Catholic thought in the decade following the initial papal statements (Braceland and Stock, 1963; Donceel, 1961; Hagmaier and Gleason, 1959; Stern, 1954; VanderVeldt and Odenwald, 1952) to the point where the discoveries of psychoanalysis were included among the release of nuclear energy and the manipulation of genes and chromosomes as one scientist-theologian's signs of the evolution of man's mind (Teilhard de Chardin, 1964).

Modern statements about Christian beliefs from within Catholicism such as Küng's (1976) and Rahner's (1978) seem to reflect some of the previous criticisms against theology from rational science. Küng included a section in his work on the need for a nonreductionist demythologizing of dogma, noting that for a long time religious myths, legends, images, and symbols were cultivated in parts of Europe often at the expense of the essential religious messages.

The Response from Judaism

Although Freud's attacks on religion were primarily against Christianity in general, responses from Judaism were as diverse as those within Christianity. In a treatise advocating prayer as a cure in all nervous ailments, Rabbi Morris Lichtenstein (1936) dismissed psychoanalysis as erroneous and detrimental. Rosmarin (1939) excoriated Freud for his "many calamitous blunders" of scholarship in *Moses and Monotheism*. Totally different in content and spirit was Rabbi Liebman's (1946) popular work that welcomed and discussed the insights of Freudian psychology for all religions.

Spero (1976b, 1976c) has provided a comprehensive overview of writings specific to the relationship between psychotherapy and Judaism. Generally there has been an evolution toward integration, synthesis, and rapprochement. The ethical systems of the Talmud and Jewish tradition, with their concern for physical and mental health and their values of self-respect and respect for others, were seen as augmentations of psychological theories. The rituals, ceremonials, and festivals of Jewish life were similarly viewed as psychologically healthy in their provision of significant personal roles, social contacts, and mutual love. A rabbinical work such as Bleich's (1977) conveys an appreciation for the human wisdom, philosophy, and heritage behind traditional Jewish law.

Spero (1976d, 1978) further delineated the commonalities between Judaism and psychotherapy although Judaic belief was seen as adding qualitatively to each dimension of similarity. The ethical relativeness of psychotherapy was viewed as a moral position at odds with Judaic belief in intrinsic values.

The noted theologian and philosopher, Abraham Heschel, strove to imbue psychotherapy with Judaic wisdom. Religion has eluded objective psychological and sociological study, Heschel wrote, because "the *holy dimension* of all existence" and not a state of mind is what gives rise to faith (Heschel, 1951). He emphasized that being fully human requires not only instinctual satisfaction but also appreciation, wonder, and reverence for the mystery of living as well as a person's reciprocating response to the existential indebtedness for being alive (Heschel, 1965).

An overview of Judaism's dialogue with psychotherapy would be incomplete without mention of the religious philosopher, Martin Buber.

Buber (1958) originated the familar "I-Thou" as a paradigm of the ideal human relationship entered into mutually by both persons in the fullness of their being without reducing the other to a mere object of some need or aim. Buber has had a profound impact within all religions and his thought has been extended to the philosophy and nature of psychotherapy and psychopathology (Arieti, 1974; Friedman, 1960).

Concern within the Psychotherapy Profession: The Nature of Religion

The rally against a psychological reductionism of religion continued in psychological and philosophical circles generally along the same lines taken by theologians (Cupitt, 1976; De Luca, 1977; Fingarette, 1963; Maclaren, 1976; Neu, 1977). The religious symbol or myth may not just be a disguise or a decoration but a person's only way of apprehending reality (Bellah, 1974; Ricoeur, 1970).

Within the mental health field, then, religion has been opened to integrative study and discussion. In a committee report based on clinical observation, for example, religious ideas and actions were found to express not only the entire range of neurotic symptoms and to function as an organizing point for psychosis but also to play a healthy role in identification and character formation by providing "an integrated system for meeting and for expressing human needs at all levels of psychic organization" (GAP, 1968, p. 722). Mysticism was similarly associated in some persons with antisocial and pathological tendencies, while in other individuals it was linked to profound creativity and worthwhile productivity (GAP, 1976). Man, thus, knows and responds to the same fundamental premise of God's existence in very diverse ways, a phenomenon that the theologian might simply refer to as "the religious use of psychic function" (GAP, 1968, p. 722).

Loewald (1978), a psychoanalyst, believed that religious or mystical experiences are more than defensive sanctuaries; such experiences, he wrote,

> bring us in touch with levels of our being, forms of experiencing and of reality that themselves may be deeply disturbing, anxiety provoking to the common-sense rationality of everyday life. . . . They go against our penchant for objectifying and distancing our experience and our world in order to make and keep it manageable and tolerable. [P. 69]

In a manner reminiscent of Frankl's (1975) "unconscious God," Loewald argued that forms of religious experience are today repressed more deeply than sexuality beneath the guise of scientific rationality.

In Meissner's (1978) cogent presentation of a psychoanalytic viewpoint on religious experience, five stages of religious faith were presented as a developmental line based on levels of narcissism, self- and object-representation, and cognitive and affective individuation. Freud's theory and observations on religion, Meissner felt, were based on the second and third phases of religious development noted, leaving psychoanalysis with only a partial account of religious experience. Psychoanalysis was now felt to have conceptual resources to deal far more profoundly and less simplistically with man's religious experience.

Rizzuto's (1979) clinical investigation showed that the developmental process of forming a God representation extends beyond the projected father image to include the mother, siblings, grandparents, and early transitional object representations. Following Erikson's epigenetic stages, successive transformations of self- and object-representations were related throughout life to alterations in the God representation.

Admitting that psychiatry has added little to what the great religions have learned about human nature, Frank (1978) demanded a respect for transcendental belief systems and mysticism as enrichers of the human experience. The foregoing are examples of the productive inquiries made possible when religion is accepted as a coelucidator of the human predicament.

Concern within the Psychotherapy Profession: Morality

Erikson (1958) gave therapy the needed historical perspective when he summarized:

> We [psychoanalysts] were dismayed when we saw our purpose of enlightenment perverted into a widespread fatalism, according to which man is nothing but a multiplication of his parents' faults and an accumulation of his own earlier selves. We must grudgingly admit that even as we were trying to devise, with scientific determinism, a therapy for the few, we were led to promote an ethical disease among the many. [P. 19]

On the positive side, however, Hartmann (1960) noted that psychoanalysis may often make a person aware of genuine moral values and grant the autonomy needed to live and pursue them. He observed that a view of the psychological processes that have led to an individual's moral values did not mean that the values were arbitrary. The emphasis in psychoanalysis on the active acceptance of outer and inner reality, intellectual integrity, self-knowledge, and avoidance of easy rationalizations converges with the goal of many spiritual systems. Hartmann maintained that analysis does not aim at eliminating all guilt reactions from the human experience but rather at integrating guilt with a personal, authentic moral code.

A strong caution was issued against confusing psychological health values with moral values (Cohen, 1977; Hartmann, 1960). Conversely, evil cannot be reduced to illness with the sequitur that healthier child raising and education will eliminate evil. Psychotherapy increases man's capacity for free choice and hence his freedom in opting for moral evil (Grisez and Shaw, 1974). Man as a moral being, then, and the promotion of man as a responsible agent must become a prominent concern of the therapy practitioner as well as the theologian (Loewald, 1978; Menninger, 1973; Wheelis, 1973).

Bergin[2] is concerned that the profession of psychotherapy is still too alienated from many sound values present in healthy religion. From within the mental health professions come the two ideologies of "clinical pragmatism" that implements the values of the middle-class social system and "humanistic idealism." Both often criticize traditional religious values related to family life, child rearing, and social standards while themselves providing ambiguous tenets with moral and cultural relativism. Although some religious values are destructive, others such as humility, personal identity, emphasis on "self-control and free-agency," love for others, stability of marriage, realistic guilt with interpersonal responsibility, the growth that can come out of suffering, and the source of knowledge in mystical intuition or spiritual experiencing are viewed as naturally human and highly constructive. Bergin feels that a viable belief structure that contains these healthy values is a source of emotional stability, physical well-being, a stable identity, and the strengthening of the human personality and of society.

The Psychodynamics of Atheism

In a mirroring of the posture that God arises from a wish fulfillment, the observation was advanced that disbelief in God aften arises from the unconscious desire that God or father not be (Lee, 1949; Outler, 1954; Sanders, 1949). Atheism was felt to betray its infantile origin if father crept back in some way, as

> in the unquestioning acceptance of some human authority. . . . And atheism will also tend to betray its infantile origin by its pre-occupation in a negative way with the idea of God. . . . They [atheistic rationalists] seem to spend more time arguing about the non-existence of God than most believers give to thoughts of His existence. [Lee, 1949, p. 138]

One research study concluded that religious doubt was occasioned psychodynamically by a wish for and a dread of fusion with primal mother and by conflicting parental identifications (Helfaer, 1972). Other clinical studies explored cultural and individual dynamics related to atheism (Lepp, 1963; GAP, 1968). A noteworthy vignette was provided by Freud (1928) who posited oedipal dynamics to explain the sudden doubt in the existence of God felt by a young physician.

Some of the profoundest thinkers in both fields have enriched this multifaceted dialectic between psychotherapy and religion. The result has obviously not been a mutual elimination but rather a continuing synthesis whose motto could well be:

> Those who adopt the spiritual explanation are right when they defend so vehemently a certain transcendence of man over the rest of nature; but neither are the materialists wrong when they maintain that man is just one further term in a series of animal forms. [Teilhard de Chardin, 1959, p. 169]

The ethical issues relevant to the treatment of religious persons, then, do not just center in a few specific treatment problems, but encompass the deepest notions about the nature and meaning of man and of human life.

Countertransference:
The Arena for the Therapist's Ethic

Presuming that the therapist already possesses a genuine ethical core, the integrated personality needed to follow his or her ethical sensitivities, and a commitment to uphold the ethical code of his or her profession, then the foundation for working ethically with religious persons rests in the exploration and monitoring of the therapist's own emotional reactions. This principle applies to therapists of all persuasions. Patients create feelings in therapists, no matter what their clinical and theoretical stance. Within the psychoanalytic framework such emotional forces and reactions arising within the therapist in relation to persons in treatment are referred to as countertransference (using the totalistic definition offered by Kernberg in 1975). The countertransference can operate within any therapist so that the therapist dislikes religious patients, ignores the individuality of religious persons in treatment, stays blissfully ignorant of the complex dialectic between psychotherapy and religion, or remains unable to appreciate and to help the persons within their religious frame of reference because the therapist cannot deal with that frame. The countertransference forces may keep a therapist further embedded in barren, inaccurate theological notions and a sterile fund of knowledge from which to draw interpretations and understanding.

Whence these countertransferences? It will be illustrative at this point to explore briefly the dynamics at work in Freud's posture toward religion.

Freud had a Catholic nanny who took him to church services and taught him about the meanings of heaven and hell. His experiences were absorbed because Freud's mother remembered him giving speeches to the family about God. When Freud was two and one-half years old this nanny was discharged for stealing from the family and for encouraging Freud to steal for her. Freud's contacts with the hypocrisy of his culturally predominant religion started early (Roazen, 1976). Freud's later experiences within his anti-Semitic culture certainly further shaped his feelings toward religion. To his confidant, Pfister, he admitted in 1928: "I have found little that is 'good' about human beings on the whole; in my experience most of them are trash" (Meng and Freud, 1964, p. 61). Five years later, he was more specific: "There has been little occasion for me to change my opinion of human nature, particularly the Christian Aryan variety" (Meng and Freud, p. 140). There were thus powerful *cultural* forces at work in Freud's attitude toward religion.

According to a careful study by Wallace (1978b), Freud displayed embarrassment and intense conflict about his own strong mystical interests and his own belief in certain paranormal experiences such as telepathy. Apparently Freud felt these interests were bad for his scientific respectability. So great was his conflict that Freud later had no recall of a letter in which he stated that if he were again at the start of his career, he would perhaps select no other area to work in but parapsychology.

> Freud's failure to come to grips with this side of himself not only robbed him of considerable self insight (and probably creativity) but biased his treatment of certain subjects (religion, and even art and philosophy), caused his evaluation of the unconscious to be an overly pessimistic one, and forced him to retain more of the physicalist notions of his teachers than was beneficial to psychoanalysis. [Wallace, 1978b, p. 221]

Freud's *professional environment,* therefore, played a role in his stance against religion and in the suppression of his interest in mysticism and psychic phenomena.

On the level of *intrapsychic conflict,* Zilboorg (1967) was unconvinced that Freud's unconscious conflict regarding religion first arose from the simultaneity of Freud's religious and separation experiences with his Catholic nurse and the death of Freud's little brother, toward whom he had harbored strong death wishes. A series of scholarly explorations (Wallace, 1977, 1978a, 1978b) has shown how Freud's father conflict, the most central dynamic in his life, influenced the writings and the themes of *Totem and Taboo, Civilization and Its Discontents,* and *Moses and Monotheism.*

From the objective vantage point of history, therefore, within Freud the prototypical psychotherapist can be seen operating cultural, professional, and intrapsychic forces influencing his feelings and ideas about religion. A therapist of *any* orientation lives amidst the same triad of forces instilling various emotional reactions or countertransferences toward religion. These cultural, professional, and intrapsychic countertransferences will now be explored in greater depth.

Cultural Countertransference

A therapist is a product and a mirror of a specific cultural background that often leaves with the individual a legacy of attitudes for or against specific religious groups. Although the cultural influence may rest on a certain amorphous set of attitudes gained osmotically from family and environment, specific experiences in the individual therapist's life will shape, often quite sharply and definitively, his or her stance vis-à-vis religion in general, specific religious groups, and religious persons in psychotherapy. These learned attitudes and experiences will constitute cultural aspects of the countertransference (Spiegel, 1976).

One dramatic incident can illustrate the potential force of a cultural countertransference. Several years ago I was doing research on psychotherapists' empathy. I was using as one parameter a test of perceptual flexibility that required the therapist to find within a complex, multicolored design the hidden outline of a simple geometric form that was previously shown. A senior therapist was doing extraordinarily well on this test when suddenly he ran the full time limit on a figure, totally unable to find the hidden design. Perplexed and quite disappointed in himself, he asked to see once again the simple pattern he had been trying to locate. It was a symmetrical, double-lined cross. "You know," he said, in unforgettable words, "for *me* to have found that figure would have been to acknowledge *the* cross and I could never do that!" He then shared with me stories about his childhood in eastern Europe where his Jewish family had been brutally victimized in several pogroms fostered by the local Christian clergy. The bitter memories were still there.

The feelings demonstrated by this therapist are not a matter of intrafamilial conflict nor do they stem from psychosexual developmental problems. They are vivid, affect-laden memories of real cultural forces that are suppressed but close to awareness. If this therapist were facing a person in treatment who happened to be a nun with a cross around her neck, these feelings would shape a cultural countertransference that would prohibit treatment unless monitored and honestly explored. Perhaps an honest decision would have to be made that psychotherapy movement would be unlikely.

Cultural forces of this nature move in many directions. A therapist is ethically mandated to make sure they do not interfere with the course of treatment or with the understanding of the patient.

Subcultural Countertransference: The Mental Health Field

The psychotherapist works in a professional subculture distinctly at odds with the greater society on the issue of religion. Within the population at large, 68 percent are members of a church or synagogue, 56 percent are *active* members, and 42 percent attend services during an average week. Only 6 percent express no religious preference. At the level of inner experience rather than formal affiliation, 58 percent of the population respond that their religious beliefs are very important to them, and another 28 percent say their beliefs are fairly important—a total of 86 percent. Religious or mystical experiences, defined as moments of sudden religious insight, are reported by 31 percent of the population (American Institute of Public Opinion, 1978). Even among the "unchurched"—those with no church or synagogue membership and with no appreciable attendance—68 percent answer that religion is still very or fairly important in their lives and 84 percent respond that they prayed privately in the past month (Princeton Religious Research Center and The Gallup Organization, Inc., 1978).

Some available studies within the mental health profession underscore its fringe quality. Psychologists are less religious than both the general population and the general academic population. An atheistic orientation was reported by 34 percent of the psychologists. Psychology was not uniformly antireligious, however, as 43 percent believed in a transcendental diety and 47 percent were members of some church. There was no significant difference among the varied subspecialties within psychology. The researchers (Ragan, Malony, and Beit-Hallahmi[3]) raised the countertransferential issue of whether many psychologists by virtue of their professional milieu do not inappropriately and without awareness consider themselves the standards for others' conduct and judge the religious experiences of clients as atypical or pathological. Steinberg's (1977) study showed that among academic disciplines, the social sciences had the highest rate of apostasy: 44 percent of the Protestants, 35 percent of the Catholics, and 77 percent of the Jews in the social sciences at the academic level reported indifference or opposition to religion. These figures for the social sciences were in contrast to the faculty sample as a whole, of which 78 percent continued at least a nominal religious identity and 64 percent were deeply or moderately religious.

Nix (1978) studied the religious values of psychotherapists. Atheism was reported by 17.7 percent, and 9.7 percent stated they were agnostic. Some degree of religiosity was acknowledged by 60 percent of the psychotherapists, with 10.5 percent being very religious and 32.3 percent moderately religious. Only 16.8 percent felt that their religious beliefs were an important part of their philosophy of life. The therapist population was appreciably less religious than the general population and than others with about equal levels of education. There was no significant difference among the various theoretical orientations except for less personal religiosity and more negativism toward religion in the behaviorist group.

Nix also found that the less religious a therapist personally felt, the more negative was the therapist's attitude toward religion. Thus, 5 percent of the antireligious therapists reported that they actively discourage religious beliefs, a practice that would have to be termed an unethical bias. The religious and the antireligious therapists, evidently because of their comfort and acceptance of their own position and values, tended not to be silent but to deal themselves with religious issues arising in treatment. The less religious and the nonreligious therapists were less clear on how to handle religious issues in treatment and tended more to avoid the issues or defer to a clergyman, thereby confirming the maxim that the therapist who is sure of his values on any issue is able to face the same issue more solidly with a patient.

For the most part, Nix's respondents expected their colleagues to be negative and antagonistic toward religion. Only 10 percent of the respondents thought that their colleagues were in some way religious or held positive attitudes toward religion. The percentage of religious believers in the therapist sample was certainly higher than this stereotype, indicating that much silence from fear and conflict surrounds discussion of religion among therapists. The therapists as a group were more favorably inclined toward religion than academic psychologists who had provided the earliest professional training but who were often cited as generating an atmosphere in which religion was regarded as disreputable and hence suppressed as an interest.

There are forces at work, then, within the psychotherapy subculture based on attitudes toward religion felt during training years within academia and on fantasies about the reactions of colleagues that inhibit the investigation of religion and the appreciation of religious phenomena within the psychotherapeutic encounter.

Individual Countertransference

Although countertransference in the broadest sense has roots in the therapist's cultural and professional environment, the most potent source of the countertransference is generally each individual therapist's personality and inner conflicts. This is countertransference in its more traditional restricted definition wherein the therapist is gratifying personal needs based on past relationships rather than contributing to the endeavors of the therapeutic alliance. Owing to the uniqueness of each therapist and each patient, the variations of such countertransferences are almost limitless in number. But the religious person or a member of the clergy is more likely to stimulate an individual countertransference centered on the therapist's need for omnipotence, narcissism, and materialism. Sexuality is another area in which countertransference difficulties may arise. This area will be discussed later.

Omnipotence. Freud's analytic society was noted as having some of the characteristics of a religious sect with mutual beliefs, rituals, and members who may have been motivated by the same religious impulses that others direct more conventionally (Roazen, 1976). A minister-psychotherapist, expressing concern at the "amorality and immorality of some of the modern Messiahs" (DeYoung, 1976, p. 92), declared that psychoanalysis, behaviorism, and humanistic psychology were quasi-religions with their own cult, messiah, gospel, and scripture. In speaking of the transgression of arrogance at times committed in his profession, a psychiatrist has humorously referred to "religio psychiatri" (Menninger, 1954). All three observations bear witness to the potential counter-transference stance of omnipotence wherein the individual therapist needs to make his or her system of therapy or practice a quasi-religion rather than a treatment method.

The comparison between schools of psychotherapy and religion is not an accidental metaphor. The unconscious motivations underlying a vocation to the clerical life may be quite parallel to those leading persons to the psychotherapeutic profession. Analytic work with priests, for example, has found that the unconscious drives behind the religious vocation may include the need to be different and socially superior in a seemingly infinite way; neurotic drives for authority, power, and control; an "affiliation motivation" to belong to a group or family; and the need to be an idealized parental figure as an oedipal resolution (Ancona, 1976). The analyst Wheelis (1956) has compared the choice of work as a clergyman to that of a psychoanalyst, particularly in the ongoing conflict and interplay present within each vocation between a defensive retreat into orthodox dogma on the one hand and humanness and "mobile interaction" on the other. Among the motivations mentioned for work as an analyst, Wheelis included the achievement of vicarious intimacy by hearing secrets that not even a priest can hear and the use of intellectual insight in the struggle for self-mastery. The therapist's vocational hazard of grandiosity and omnipotence was also noted by Robertiello (1978), particularly as these qualities relate to the choice of spouse and the general tenor of the practitioner's marriage.

Marmor (1974) wrote that a prime occupational danger of psychotherapists is the unrealistic feeling of superiority that may be fostered by the unremitting exercise of authority over patients' lives and the seductive isolationism that keeps the therapist in the bubble of transference admiration from his or her patients and that prevents the therapist from directly observing others' equally fruitful work. Marmor is courageously observant of how so many leaders in the profession of psychotherapy surround themselves by fawning disciples rather than independently thinking colleagues, lending a cultlike atmosphere to schools of thought or training institutions. This "hubris factor in psychotherapy" (Smith, 1978), the lust for greatness and significance, is what causes a therapist to fall in love with his or her own image as it exists in the positive transference of his or her patients (Siegman, 1955). A more pathological form of the hubris factor is what makes a therapist vie aggressively with other persons in the private or professional life of a patient to become the ego ideal of the patient (Rosenman and Handlesman, 1978).

Personal therapy or a training analysis is no guarantee that grandiosity and needs for omnipotence will be resolved. These qualities may often linger, especially when an omnipotent therapist is chosen for unconscious reasons, which therapist's own idealized self-image coincides with the patient's transferential idealization. Left unexplored are all the personal and dynamic material behind the idealization, such as competitive aggression, power needs, and fear of authenticity and autonomy. The theoretical factionalism and politic power struggles within the psychotherapeutic profession appear to be bred at least in part by the lack of personal exploration of idealizations that remain as lingering loyalties to the idealized training figures and therapist, all of whom remain as essential components of the self-system and of ego defenses as well.

In working with religious patients, the therapist may find that personal needs for omnipotence are frustrated by the patient's continued adherence to a creed and involvement in religion, or by the dedication of a person in a religious vocation. The therapist whose personal identity is defined very much in terms of his profession and his school of thought may well be threatened by the breadth of a person's religious heritage. No school of psychotherapy can come close to the equivalent of the year 5740 on the Hebrew calendar. If we remember Freud's fantasy about being pope (Roazen, 1976), psychoanalysis has never even had its second pope, let alone its two hundred and sixty-fourth. No school of psychotherapy has been able to gather as many loyal disciples and believers around the world as any major religious denomination.

A defensive reaction in the omnipotent countertransference, then, may take the form of an unconscious formulation of treatment goals aimed at altering or eliminating the person's religious affiliation by sadistically shattering defenses or by making intellectually sweeping, reductionistic interpretations of the individual's belief system that are totally uncalled for by the evolutionary nature and current state of theology and by the very limitations of psychological knowledge. This countertransference tension may reach its height with clergy in treatment who may well address more willing listeners at a single religious service than the therapist could hope to face in numerous workshops. If the person with the religious vocation is in training as a therapist or analyst, the omnipotent therapist may well be out to convert and may unconsciously see loyalty to two worlds as an act of rejecting infidelity toward the therapist's own edifice.

Narcissism. An affective struggle between therapist and religious patient may well arise over the personal balance between concern for self-satisfaction, self-fulfillment, and self-development on the one hand, and concern for the other, altruism, and fulfillment by involvement on the other. Religious values have generally revolved around an equality between the two poles. Often religious persons who come to treatment neglect the self side of the equation, but it is equally true that many schools of personality and many therapists of different persuasions hold to the self side of the balance in theory and in their personal and professional lives. This self-preoccupation, endemic to our age, is subject to increased scrutiny and critique (Hakimi, 1970; Lasch, 1978) as typified by Bronfenbrenner's (1977) phrase: "doing your own thing—our undoing."

A further extension of this value issue is raised by the stance of religion's authentic social commitment. The philosophy of some psychotherapies is seen as stressing individualism and individual well-being as primary goals so that societal concern is deemphasized. With so many rights granted to the individual, the resultant problems in social ethics appear insoluble and the eventual outcome may be a chaotic society in which the individuals actually perish (Sherrill, 1957). The extent of the therapist's proselytizing of a philosophy concerned primarily with the self may be more a matter of the therapist's need to offer himself or herself omnipotently as a model of man and the therapist's not uncommon, uninvolved existence at the fringe of society than of any genuine theoretical persuasion.

Materialism. The therapist may experience countertransferential tension from a religious person's different orientation toward money, earnings, and accretion of material goods. In many positive ways we live in an age in which the materials of this planet are put to great practical use, transformed into objects desirable for the ease, comfort, and enjoyment of their owners. The rush to secure material goods, however, often becomes insatiable depending on the self-enhancement to the person of their visible accretion. A religious person and a member of the clergy often, though not necessarily, downplay the importance of material goods verbally or in actual behavior. A therapist can be justified in labeling such a stance masochistic, if enough is indeed known to support the conclusion that the person is inflicting self-punishment for unconscious guilt feelings and perpetuating intrapsychically a sadomasochistic relation with parents. But a therapist cannot deny that culture is often dangerously materialistic at the expense of human values and human well-being. Psychotherapists are not shielded from the materialistic culture. Greenson (1978) and Schmideberg (1974) have forcefully made note of a disturbing and growing materialistic stance among therapists with a noticeably stifling effect on both their humanity and their sensitivity toward human suffering.

Certainly the invidiousness that often accompanies such therapist proclamations as "I'm all booked up" is more often than not due to the underlying experience of accumulated people-objects that are symbols of success and the facilitators of credit card payments. When a therapist's parapraxis refers to his or her caseload as "papers" rather than the intended "patients," it is not an endogenous fancy to conclude that for this particular therapist patients are at a deepest level objects to advancement in fame, fortune, and workshops. If one listens one can easily feel the materialism at the expense of humanism that can corrode any therapeutic endeavor from its inception. Therapists sometimes discuss their fees not with an aim toward resolving practical problems but with an aggressive, self-aggrandizing competitiveness that is reminiscent of unsure adolescents in the locker room boasting either of physical endowments or conquests or clumsily compensating for the lack thereof. In some circles it is now considered acceptable to charge even for sessions missed owing to severe weather conditions. This extension of the concept of leased time appears devoid of reality and is solipsistically grounded in the therapist's need to accrue goods or to remain above the financial anxieties that beset the rest of mankind.

In the area of materialism, therefore, a religious person may not just confront a therapist with different values. The patient may offer a challenge to the therapist's very existential and moral posture vis-à-vis his practice and his patients. Freud and Pfister constitute an archetype of such an encounter. Only after his minister friend's admonition that he renounce the "impracticable proposition of getting rich honourably" (Meng and Freud, 1964, p. 24) was Freud able to follow his own genuine wish to work fewer hours by not replacing a terminated patient. Pfister's exposition of values enabled Freud to realize that his own father complex would not have permitted this decrease in income. Freud would have symbolically failed to correct his father's financial difficulties if he would not have earned as much money as possible.

Regardless of a therapist's call to recognize and value the uniqueness of each individual (Martin, 1978) countertransference problems related to omnipotence, narcissism, and materialism may block the therapist from fulfilling this call when working with a religious patient. The model for psychotherapy with such noncongruence in values is courageous honesty in self-exploration within the therapist so that the therapist can respect and deal with value systems other than his or her own. Also called for is a "participatory model of psychotherapy" (Coyne and Widiger, 1978), rather than one in which the professional therapist is the wielder of power regarding value dilemmas, ethical issues, goals, and decisions within treatment. Even within a specific school of psychotherapy a certain eclecticism can be maintained so that theoretical constructs are not reified to the point where individuals are material objects to fit into the theory (Pound, 1978).

Added Ethical Perspectives on the Treatment of Religious Persons

Overview of Treatment

French (1970) has conceived of psychoanalytic treatment as a resumption of a previously interrupted process of discriminatory learning. In treatment the patient learns to distinguish between the past and the present, between the transference projections and the present reality of the therapist, and between persons in the present environment who are different from parents or key figures and persons who may well be replicas of early figures. In the latter case, the patient is helped to distinguish between maladaptive, defensive ways of relating and reacting to these persons and constructive, alloplastic, nondefensive ways of relating or reacting.

The therapist must experience the same growth in discriminatory learning with regard to the persons he works with so that global impressions and sterotypes from his or her culture, the psychotherapeutic subculture, and the past as it now exists intrapsychically do not lead the therapist to potentially dangerous and damaging biases. There exist some bases for stereotypes of various religious groups and at times religious beliefs can be understood primarily in terms of mass psychology and group identity, as in the mass murders and suicides in Guyana in 1978. Nonetheless, at a level of experience with even moderately differentiated humans, there are almost as many varieties of Judaism as there are Jews, as many forms of Protestantism as there are Protestants, and as many breeds of Catholicism as there are Catholics. Research shows that although some denominational differences appear, different forms of personal religion exist within each denomination (Spilka and Mullin, 1977).

The therapist is in a position to help the person with a religious belief system make some needed discriminations between the essence of the belief system and historical and social accretions. The patient can be helped to discriminate between what early, perhaps misinformed teachers or clergy might have prohibited and what were in fact projections of the intrapsychic superego already crystallized from the family system. Outler (1954), citing the Swiss neo-Freudian, Charles Odier, noted that even in persons with severe anxiety about sin and damnation, "the self-condemning superego *precedes* and *exploits* such religious teaching, rather than is formed by them" (p. 210). The full answer when psychopathology and psychodynamics meld with religion lies not with the church or the temple but with the person's development, his unique oedipal constellation, his preverbal experience, and with his system of identifications, ego ideals, memories, dreams, and fantasies. The treatment goal is to separate the inner conflicts from the defense system that is uttering religious beliefs while not aiming omnipotently to destroy religion or to encourage a patient to become alienated from his or her sociocultural roots and identity. Both therapeutic goals and healthy religion are served by this stance (Spero, 1976a).

Autonomy in Morality

There has been a sociological change in American religion away from ritualistic function toward more privatization of religious belief (Newman, 1974). More autonomy is being exercised in moral decisions, the most noteworthy example occurring in the Catholic Church regarding contraception even in the face of the stability of the so-called official position. In a 1970 poll in Zurich, 78 percent of married Catholic couples felt that the choice of birth control was up to the couple (Kriech, 1976). A 1975 survey in the United States reported that 94 percent of couples using contraception were using methods forbidden by the church; the rejection of the teaching against artifical birth control occurred among religious and nominal Catholics who apparently viewed the issue as a matter of individual conscience (Westoff and Jones, 1977), a stance supported by many priests and theologians.

The autonomous approach to individual moral decisions based on mature assessment rather than on fear and guilt may be viewed as a healthy advance and highlights by contrast a particular ego deficit that may be therapeutically treated by its distinctness from healthy moral sensitivity. There are persons who at a frequency greater than the norm must get a *heksher* from their rabbi or must consult their minister or priest before any major or minor moral decision. Without any attack on the religion, the therapist can work with the historical, familial components of the guilt connected with independence, the dependence needed to gain love, and any other intrapsychic dynamic made available in therapy. A therapist not swayed by countertransference can explore and study the issues within the particular religion and accept the patient's personal religious framework as a valid one for that individual though subject to revision if found to be distorted by psychological factors. With such a stance a therapist will not do an injustice to the person.

Sexuality

The place of sexuality in religion is still subject to unfortunate stereotypes that will not be altered in a rigid cultural, subcultural, or psychodynamically determined countertransference posture. One stereotype based to some extent on actual past reality sees Catholicism as having a furiously and primarily antimasturbation moral theology. Brockman (1972), however, shows that there are four different theological stances toward masturbation that exist within Catholicism ranging from the stereotypical traditional position that masturbation is intrinsically evil to the position that there are far more vital issues of moral concern, that masturbation is a matter of sexual maturity and integrated sexuality, and that the greatest evil attached to masturbation is the guilt from early training and negative sexual attitudes. Another recent treatise (Kosnick et al., 1977) delineates three positions regarding masturbation: the traditional stance of objectively grave evil, the stance in which masturbation is objectively neutral, and an approach in which the human and moral meaning of masturbation is nonmoralistically individualized according to its many determinants. Issues of sexuality within Catholicism are thus in foment and transition (Böckle and Pohier, 1976) so that one theologian concludes regarding sexuality "that theologians are more certain about the insufficiencies of the past than the approaches of the present" (Curran, 1977, p. 185). Clearly, there is no unified Catholic sexual ethic. What is left for the therapist once again is the awareness of the role played by the individual's psychodynamics in the selection of a particular moral stance.

Two other studies deserve notice as they help to dispel stereotypes and an unproductive antireligious countertransference. First, in a popular survey of one hundred thousand women, religious females tended to be the most sexually satisfied, most sexually active, and most orgasmic. Explanations centered on the more liberal attitude toward sexuality now present within all major religions that coexists, however, with the traditional value system emphasizing commitment, mutual respect, intimacy, and fidelity (Safran, 1976).

In a study of happy marriages in which nearly 90 percent of the spouses said they would marry the same person again and in which none of the spouses was involved in extramarital relationships, there were nonetheless wide ranges of coital frequency and some sexual dysfunction, dispelling the myth that a near perfect sexual life is essential for a good marriage. Job pressures, fatigue, social demands, and children often limited sexual activity but most of the couples did not make the sacrifices in the rest of their life arenas that would have been needed for constant sexual acitvity. The authors cautioned that a "new tyranny of sexual freedom and activity should not replace an old one of sexual inhibition" (Frank and Anderson, 1979, p. 13).

This latter dictum is important because although Freud abandoned his theory of the actual neuroses caused by a current lack of sexual satisfaction, there are still therapists who, without any consideration of a patient's religious beliefs, value system, ego strength, and ongoing reality, espouse sexual activity as a life solution. The most determined suicide attempt I have ever encountered was made by an extremely depressed married woman mired down by a sadomasochistic marriage, problem children, and financial worries. Her therapist kept telling her that she needed more sex and should have an affair. Both her personal value system and her reality made that therapeutic goal quite impossible but her therapist continued to espouse a sexual affair as the antidepressant. She had placed hope in psychotherapy but had grown to feel that she had now failed her therapist just as she had failed her husband and children. Only the accidental discovery of her comatose body and a week in intensive care saved her life. In a countertransference framework that supersedes theoretical orientation, the hypothesis may be offered that the less a therapist has been able to integrate his or her sexuality within a mutually satisfactory relationship, the more investment the therapist will have in maintaining orgastic activity per se as a therapeutic goal without regard for individual value systems.

Genuine Moral Issues

The therapist needs to distinguish between the use of religious language and practice as the disguise for neurotic conflicts and occasions when patients are struggling with genuine moral or spiritual issues (Fingarette, 1963). In the latter instance, the therapeutic aim would be to help the patient experience the greatest amount of emotional and intellectual freedom in exploring the personal or societal moral dilemma along with as wide an awareness as possible of relevant issues and consequences pragmatically and psychologically.

Treatment of Vowed Persons in Religious Vocations

Persons who have made solemn promises or vows to own few or no personal possessions, to abstain from a sexual relationship and marriage, and to obey their superiors in a religious community or institution to which they affirm their loyalty present unique issues and questions for the psychotherapist. There are three aspects of such psychotherapeutic work that are particularly noteworthy from the standpoint of ethical practice: the area of sexuality, the person's transference to the religious institution, and the matter of vocational decisions during treatment.

Sexuality

There is probably no more highly charged arena in the treatment of the celibate then the issue of sexuality, its role in the transference and in reality. Probably no area is more prone either to challenge a therapist's personal metapsychological and psychopathological theories or to test the therapist's supposed freedom of inquiry and therapeutic neutrality. With a religious person with emotional problems who has chosen to live a life without a genital love relationship one can run the gamut from projecting Freud's earliest theories of actual neuroses to elaborate Jungian and existential postures. The aim, however, is always to advance a personalized theory for each patient by listening.

The therapist does well, first of all, to ponder Loewald's (1978) belief that sublimation may be a defense but may also be "a genuine appropriation" of a sexuality that is "not defensively or artificially insulated and drained of the fullness of our mental life" (p. 76). By not assuming that orgastic discharge per se would be the solution to the psychological problems of a celibate, a stance which would be a theoretical projection and more related to a countertransference problem, one can move rather easily within the celibate's frame of reference and help the person living within the same frame. Assuming that the person is adequately sublimating libidinal drives, is involved in some meaningful work with satisfying friendships, and is not romantically involved, the realm of sexuality is experientially quite akin to that of a sexually involved person on a convention trip who opts for temporary abstinence out of loyalty to a loved one. Certainly there is enough therapeutic evidence that, although convention coitus in a strange city may be sought after for sexual needs, it is just as likely to express separation anxiety, an inability to be alone with oneself, a defense against homosexual fears, a defense against the oedipal meaning of facing authorities or of acting as one, or a need for elemental narcissistic reassurance in the face of self-doubts. The sexual fantasies and feelings of individuals in religious vocations are often similarly understandable and analyzable from the same vantage points in addition to the instinctual one. An experiential analogue can also be made to the sexual fantasies and feelings experienced by a therapist during the course of his or her work. These are, one hopes, easily tolerated and utilized to understand the patient and the therapist's own stance. The sexual feelings may collect multiple meanings and no one expects them to be acted on.

Most helpful in ethically making sexuality an easier issue for therapeutic exploration is to help the religious patient appreciate the differences between a sexual fantasy, a dream with hidden sexual content, a dream with manifest sexual content but referring to other life areas, a certain sensuous feeling, a sexual feeling, a strong sexual urge, and full genital arousal from direct tactile stimulation of erogenous zones. A less repressive openness to sexuality is often a celibate's as well as a therapist's goal (Goergen, 1974). Of course, if the person vowed to celibacy comes to treatment in the midst of an active sexual life or relationship, the person automatically provides the active conflicts and affects needed to explore fully the sexual area and its concomitant vocational issue.

In the face of masturbation as a clinical issue, it is beneficial to employ Fried's (1967) observations on the nonlibidinal aspects of masturbation, particularly when masturbation occurs not just after passively induced endogenous or exogenous sexual tension but when the individual actively introduces the sexual tension by self-stimulation. Masturbation may be employed to gain a sense of self-mastery and control after frustrations, to counter disappointments and depression following anger-inducing situations, and to enhance self-awareness by reaffirming a sense of the boundaries of oneself when being alone creates intense anxiety and a sense of self-dissolution. If masturbation is dealt with as a purely sexual issue, unnecessary and erroneous conflict may be introduced into treatment. If masturbation is treated nonmoralistically under these additional rubrics it loses much of its exaggerated emphasis. Moreover, as the person gains more competence in dealing with anger and assertiveness and grows into a more stable identity as a person, the person will not have to struggle so vehemently against self-stimulated masturbation within the context of his or her existential commitment and current value system.

Institutional Transference

The uniqueness of therapeutic work with persons in religious vocations includes their vowed attachment, loyalty, and dependency to the particular religious community or institution. The nature of this relationship between the individual and the religious community is such that a variety of maladaptive patterns can easily develop. Owing to their propensity to be seen as parental figures in a large family, the religious authorities are easily the target for a full gamut of transferences from the individual. On the other hand, a position of authority over other adults that includes subjects with such vowed attachment and obedience is also open to abuse by the authorities. Thus must the therapist stay switched to two tracks of inquiry: first and foremost, the person's transference to the religious institution, and second, the qualities that are in reality possessed by the persons in parental or sibling positions to the patient. It is imperative to explore how the religious individual distorts, misinterprets, and overreacts to the religious institution in terms of the personal historical material accessible through behavior patterns, dreams and memories, and the transference. But there must also be an awareness on the part of the therapist of how idealization and masochism can blind the individual to the sadistic, power components of some religious authorities' personalities and manners of functioning. In this area, the person's sense of reality often needs to be affirmed and strengthened. This latter aim can be achieved most economically by dealing with those superego pressures and ego deficiencies that will not give credence and validity to interpersonal perceptions and affects. To interpret all difficulties within the religious institution only under the rubric of institutional transference or the like would be to destroy the individual's blossoming sense of reality.

Ethical Issues in a Vocational Decision during Treatment

The task with persons in a religious vocation is to help them discriminate among their own transferences, self-fulfilling prophecies, masochism, libidinal needs, and the like, and the reality that is constituted by their religious institution and its authorities. It is too facile a solution for the therapist (unethically) to externalize all problems on the religious institution or on religion. If the person comes to grips with inner and outer realities and opts to leave the religious vocation, he or she has faced the issues maturely and realistically. This is not the case if, in a blaze of glory, the person leaves "bad mother" or "bad father" without any ounce of compassion or ambivalence aided and abetted by the acting out of the therapist's countertransference. The therapist can perpetuate a maladaptive form of splitting where the religious community is seen and reacted to as the bad parent with the outer world or the therapist's institution, school of thought, or accompanying philosophy idealized. The secrets of a religious institution—sadistic power struggles, sexual misfits, alcoholics, megalomaniacs, psychopaths, and character assassins—are generally no less human and no more stunning than the secrets of any city hall, board of education, or of any professional group, including the mental health profession. If individuals feel that a vocational issue is raised as they proceed in treatment, they will make sound decisions if they realize that difficult people within the religion will have their counterparts outside.

With institutional transferences more or less resolved and understood, however, the person's vocational decision can rest on personal needs that are now presumably not subject to harsh superego pressure and have been allowed to blossom and crystallize through the therapeutic process. One woman experienced her religious community as a frustrating hindrance to personal development; she desired greater freedom in pursuing career goals and needed and very much wanted a heterosexual love life. She has resolved many transferences to persons both within and outside of the convent, including of course the therapist, and opted to leave the convent. Her choice proved to be a happy one for she made it on sound ground. Another woman in a religious vocation grew immensely in treatment, finding profound satisfaction in some deep friendships and meaningful work. She felt her new self would not fit in her community, that she had become too colorful a figure. As she explored her fears, she found they were quite groundless as others welcomed these changes. The thrust to leave in this case rested primarily on a transference to the institution. A priest felt tremendous guilt living in a monastery that was modern and comfortable but not extravagantly appointed. He was raised in a ghetto home where his psychotic parents terrorized their children. This priest tried to extricate all his siblings but they stayed enmeshed in the family pathology; the priest was the only one to redefine himself and lead a separate existence. His survivor guilt was as strong and as real as that of a survivor of a Nazi concentration camp. The monastery was a place he felt he did not deserve and so he would often provoke anger upon himself out of self-hate. In a final example, another woman's wish to leave the convent was at the moment it arose clearly a destructive maneuver to terminate treatment, as it would have to end owing to financial reasons and to her unreadiness at that point for any drastic change in life style. In these four cases, the thrust to leave the religious vocation was respectively based on sound reality, the institutional transference primarily, intrapsychic conflict primarily, and the force of resistance to psychotherapeutic change and progress. As the person in treatment must increasingly discriminate, the therapist must increase his own power of discriminatory learning so as not to oversimplify an issue.

The principles of multiple function and overdetermination (Wälder, 1936) and the roles of autonomous ego functions and existential reality are always to be considered when exploring each person's commitment and life work. Even with oedipal-level difficulties and deep family psychopathology as major vocational thrusts in the past, the present life work of these persons may nonetheless have acquired or have the potential to acquire full meaning and be comprised of adequate satisfactions in the work and friendship spheres. "If a person assumes a responsibility and then behaves irresponsibly with respect to it, one is entitled to suspect abnormality. But the choice of a role primarily on the basis of intrapsychic needs does not in itself invalidate the role nor does it render it pathological" (GAP, 1968, p. 675). Openness must also be allowed for such a life of dedication as a genuine adaptive and existential response that makes sense *within* the individual's frame of reference and identity, undistorted by a particular theory of psychopathology. This viewpoint is especially relevant when working with older persons in a religious community who may not have marketable skills or who may lack a formal college degree.

The ethical therapist is in a perfect position to appreciate this stance regarding vocational choice. It would probably be a rare psychotherapist who could truly state that inner conflicts, a need for personal therapy, or a variety of other psychodynamic motivations were not behind the journey into the profession of psychotherapy. Regardless of the fact that so-called healthier psychosexual development and identifications might well have created far different career goals, the present one of helping people as a psychotherapist does not in any way lose its meaningfulness or its deep satisfaction. With a certain humility, then, the same perception can be applied to the question of religious vocational decisions during treatment. It is not unreasonable to hypothesize that a therapist who would view separation from the religion or the religious institution as a sine qua non of a cure, and who would even introduce the issue as a goal in treatment would be seeking a "countertransference cure" (Barchilon, 1958) in which the patient would be achieving the separation-individuation and sense of autonomy from key figures that the therapist had yet to achieve from his own training figures or training institutions.

Destination

The future will see most psychotherapists continuing to refine their work within the boundaries of their art and science; not a few will play god, developing more quasi-religious systems and quasi-cults with small bands of loyal followers. Most theologians will develop and extend their work; some will cherish their documents as the final word in all matters including the inner psyche. But an ever-growing number of persons in each field will continue to appreciate the collective wisdom at the heart of *both* realms. They will be able humbly but accurately to help separate the wheat from the chaff in each other's fields, increasing the quality of the wheat and the very fertility of each field's soil.

NOTES

1. W. J. Bier, personal communication, 1968.
2. Lecture delivered in symposium sponsored by Albert Einstein College of

Medicine and The Institute for the Study of Human Knowledge, New York City, April 21, 1979.
3. Paper presented at the meeting of the American Psychological Association, Washington, D.C., 1976.

REFERENCES

ADAMS, J. E. *Your place in the counseling revolution.* Grand Rapids, Mich.: Baker Book House, 1976.

AMERICAN INSTITUTE OF PUBLIC OPINION. *Religion in America* (Gallup Opinion Index No. 145). Princeton, N.J.: The Institute, 1978.

ANCONA, L. Considerations on Christian vocations seen from the point of view of psychoanalysis. In B. B. Wolman (ed.), *Psychoanalysis and Catholicism.* New York: Gardner Press, 1976.

ARIETI, S. *Interpretation of schizophrenia.* New York: Basic Books, 1974.

BARCHILON, J. On countertransference cures. *Journal of the American Psychoanalytic Association,* 1958, **6,** 222–236.

BELLAH, R. N. Christianity and symbolic realism. In W. M. Newman (ed.), *The social meanings of religion.* Chicago: Rand McNally, 1974.

BLEICH, J. D. *Contemporary Halakhic problems.* New York: Ktav, 1977.

BÖCKLE, F., and POHIER, J-M. *Sexuality in contemporary Catholicism.* New York: Seabury, 1976.

BONHOEFFER, D. *Letters and papers from prison.* New York: Macmillan, 1972.

BRACELAND, F. J., and STOCK, M. *Modern psychiatry.* New York: Doubleday, 1963.

BROCKMAN, N. Contemporary attitudes on the morality of masturbation. *The American Ecclesiastical Review,* 1972, **166,** 597–614.

BRONFENBRENNER, V. Doing your own thing—our undoing. *MD,* 1977, **16,** 13–15.

BROWNING, D. S. *Atonement and psychotherapy.* Philadelphia: Westminster, 1966.

BUBER, M. *I and thou.* New York: Scribner's, 1958.

COHEN, E. Holiness and health: an examination of the relationship between Christian holiness and mental health. *Journal of Psychology and Theology,* 1977, **5** (4), 285–291.

COYNE, J. C., and WIDIGER, T. A. Toward a participatory model of psychotherapy. *Professional Psychology,* 1978, **9** (4), 700–710.

COX, H. *The seduction of the spirit.* New York: Simon & Schuster, 1973.

CUPITT, D. *The worlds of science and religion.* New York: Hawthorn, 1976.

CURRAN, C. E. *Themes in fundamental moral theology.* Notre Dame, Ind.: University of Notre Dame Press, 1977.

DE LUCA, A. J. *Freud and future religious experience.* Totowa, N.J.: Littlefield Adams, 1977.

DEYOUNG, Q. R. An unknown God made known (The religion of psychology). *Journal of Psychology and Theology,* 1976, **4** (2), 87–93.

DOLTO, F., and SEVERIN, G. *The Jesus of psychoanalysis.* New York: Doubleday, 1979.

DONCEEL, J. F. *Philosophical psychology.* New York: Sheed & Ward, 1961.

EGGER, P. J. B. *Die Psychoanalyse als Seelenproblem und Lebensrichtung.* Sarnen, Switzerland: Louis Ehrli, 1919.

ERIKSON, E. H. *Young man Luther.* New York: Norton, 1958.

FINGARETTE, H. *The self in transformation.* New York: Basic Books, 1963.

FRANK, E., and ANDERSON, C. Sex and the happily married. *The Sciences,* 1979, **19** (6), 10–13.

FRANK, J. D. *Psychotherapy and the human predicament.* New York: Schocken, 1978.

FRANKL, V. E. *The unconscious God.* New York: Simon & Schuster, 1975.

FRENCH, T. M. *Psychoanalytic interpretations.* Chicago: Quadrangle, 1970.

FREUD, S. Obsessive actions and religious practices. *The complete psychological works of Sigmund Freud,* Vol. IX. London: Hogarth, 1975. (Originally published 1907).

FREUD, S. The future of an illusion. *The complete psychological works of Sigmund Freud,* Vol. XXI. London: Hogarth, 1975. (Originally published 1927).

FREUD, S. A religious experience. *The complete psychological works of Sigmund Freud,* Vol. XXI. London: Hogarth, 1975. (Originally published 1928).

FREUD, S. Civilization and its discontents. *The complete psychological works of Sigmund Freud,* Vol. XXI. London: Hogarth, 1975. (Originally published 1930).

FRIED, E. Masturbation in adults. In R. F. L. Masters (ed.), *Sexual self-stimulation.* Los Angeles: Sherbourne, 1967.

FRIEDMAN, M. Dialogue and the "essential we." *American Journal of Psychoanalysis,* 1960, **20** (1), 26–34.

GOERGEN, D. *The sexual celibate.* New York: Seabury, 1974.

GOODENOUGH, E. R. *Toward a mature faith.* New Haven: Yale University Press, 1955.

GREENSON, R. R. *Explorations in psychoanalysis.* New York: International Universities Press, 1978.

GRISEZ, G., and SHAW, R. *Beyond the new morality.* Notre Dame, Ind.: University of Notre Dame Press, 1974.

GROUP FOR THE ADVANCEMENT OF PSYCHIATRY. *The psychic function of religion in mental illness and health,* Vol. VI, Report No. 67. New York: Author, 1968.

GROUP FOR THE ADVANCEMENT OF PSYCHIATRY. *Mysticism: Spiritual quest or psychic disorder?,* Vol. IX, Report No. 97. New York: Author, 1976.

HAGMAIER, G., and GLEASON, R. *Counseling the Catholic.* New York: Sheed & Ward, 1959.

HAKIMI, Y. A foreign psychiatrist looks at American psychopathology. *Resident and Staff Physician,* 1970, **46**, 131–139.

HARTMANN, H. *Psychoanalysis and moral values.* New York: International Universities Press, 1960.

HELFAER, P. M. *The psychology of religious doubt.* Boston: Beacon, 1972.

HESCHEL, A. J. *Man is not alone.* New York: Farrar, Straus & Giroux, 1951.

HESCHEL, A. J. *Who is man?* Stanford, Calif.: Stanford University Press, 1965.

HOMANS, P. (ed.). *The dialogue between theology and psychology.* Chicago: University of Chicago Press, 1968.

JONES, E. *Zur Psychoanalyse der Christliche Religion.* Leipzig: Internationaler Psychoanalytischer Verlag, 1928.

KERNBERG, O. *Borderline conditions and pathological narcissism.* New York: Jason Aronson, 1975.

KINKEL, J. *Zur Frage der psychologischen Grundlagen und des Ursprungs der Religion.* Leipzig: Internationaler Psychoanalytischer Verlag, 1922.

KOSNIK, A.; CARROLL, W.; CUNNINGHAM, A.; MODRAS, R.; and SCHULTE, J. *Human sexuality: New directions in American Catholic thought.* New York: Paulist Press, 1977.

KRIECH, K. A firsthand report on the current crisis in Catholic sexual morality. In F. Böckle and J-M. Pohier (eds.), *Sexuality in contemporary Catholicism.* New York: Seabury, 1976.

KÜNG, H. *On being a Christian.* Garden City, N.Y.: Doubleday, 1976.

LASCH, C. *The culture of narcissism.* New York: Norton, 1978.

LEE, R. S. *Freud and Christianity.* New York: Wyn, 1949.

LEPP, I. *Atheism in our time.* New York: Macmillan, 1963.

LICHTENSTEIN, M. *Cures for minds in distress.* New York: Jewish Science Publishing Co., 1936.

LIEBMAN, J. L. *Peace of mind.* New York: Simon & Schuster, 1946.

LOEWALD, H. W. *Psychoanalysis and the history of the individual.* New Haven: Yale University Press, 1978.

MACLAREN, E. *The nature of belief.* New York: Hawthorn, 1976.

MARMOR, J. *Psychiatry in transition.* New York: Brunner/Mazel, 1974.

MARTIN, A. R. Adapting psychoanalytic procedure to the uniqueness of the individual. *American Journal of Psychoanalysis,* 1978, **38,** 99–110.

MEISSNER, W. W. Psychoanalytic aspects of religious experience. In Chicago Institute for Psychoanalysis (ed.), *The annual of psychoanalysis,* Vol. 6. New York: International Universities Press, 1978.

MENG, H., and FREUD, E. L. *Psychoanalysis and faith.* New York: Basic Books, 1964.

MENNINGER, K. Religio psychiatri. In S. Doniger (ed.), *Religion and human behavior.* New York: Association Press, 1954.

MENNINGER, K. *Whatever became of sin?* New York: Hawthorn, 1973.

MOXON, C. *Freudian essays on religion and science.* Boston: Richard G. Badger, 1926.

MÜLLER-BRAUNSCHWEIG, C. *Das Verhältnis der Psychoanalyse zu Ethik, Religion und Seelsorge.* Schwerin i. Mecklb, Germany: Verlag Friedrich Bahn, 1927.

NEU, J. Genetic explanation in *Totem and Taboo.* In R. Wollheim (ed.), *Philosophers on Freud.* New York: Jason Aronson, 1977.

NEWMAN, W. M. *The social meanings of religion.* Chicago: Rand McNally, 1974.

NIEBUHR, R. *The nature and destiny of man,* Vol. 1. *Human nature.* New York: Scribner's, 1941.

NIX, V. C. *A study of the religious values of psychotherapists.* Doctoral dissertation, New York University, 1978. University Microfilms No. 7818443.

ODEN, T. C. *Kerygma and counseling.* Philadelphia: Westminster, 1966.

OUTLER, A. C. *Psychotherapy and the Christian message.* New York: Harper, 1954.

PFISTER, O. *Die Illusion einer Zukunft.* Leipzig: Internationaler Psychoanalytischer Verlag, 1928. (a)

PFISTER, O. *Psychoanalyse und Weltanschauung.* Leipzig: Internationaler Psychoanalytisher Verlag, 1928. (b)

PIUS XIII, Pope. *The moral limits of medical research and treatment.* Address to the First International Congress on the Histopathology of the Nervous System,

September 14, 1952. Washington, D.C.: National Catholic Welfare Conference.

Pius XII, Pope. *On psychotherapy and religion.* Address to the Fifth International Congress on Psychotherapy and Clinical Psychology, April 13, 1953. Washington, D.C.: National Catholic Welfare Conference.

Pound, A. In defence of eclecticism: A clinical psychologist's view of psychological theories. *Bulletin of the British Psychological Society,* 1978, **31,** 360–361.

Princeton Religious Research Center and the Gallup Organization. *The unchurched American.* Princeton, N.J.: The Center, 1978.

Rahner, K. *Foundations of Christian faith.* New York: Seabury, 1978.

Reik, T. *Der eigene und der fremde Gott.* Leipzig: Internationaler Psychoanalytischer Verlag, 1923.

Reik, T. *Dogma und Zwangsidee.* Leipzig: Internationaler Psychoanalytischer Verlag, 1927.

Reik, T. *The psychological problems of religion,* I. *Ritual.* New York: Farrar, Straus & Co., 1946.

Reik, T. *Myth and guilt.* New York: Braziller, 1957.

Reik, T. *Mystery on the mountain.* New York: Harper, 1959.

Ricoeur, P. *Freud and philosophy.* New Haven: Yale University Press, 1970.

Rizzuto, A-M. *The birth of the living God.* Chicago: University of Chicago Press, 1979.

Roazen, P. *Freud and his followers.* New York: New American Library, 1976.

Robertiello, R. C. The occupational disease of psychotherapists. *Journal of Contemporary Psychotherapy,* 1978, **9** (2), 123–129.

Roberts, D. E. *Psychotherapy and a Christian view of man.* New York: Scribner's, 1950.

Rosenman, S., and Handelsman, I. Narcissistic vulnerability, hypochondriacal rumination and invidiousness. *The American Journal of Psychoanalysis,* 1978, **38,** 57–66.

Rosmarin, T. W. *The Hebrew Moses.* New York: Jewish Book Club, 1939.

Safran, C. Why religious women are good lovers. *Redbook* (April 1976), pp. 103, 155–156, 158–159.

Sanders, B. G. *Christianity after Freud.* London: Geoffrey Bles, 1949.

Schmideberg, M. My experience of psychotherapy. *Journal of Contemporary Psychotherapy,* 1974, **6** (2), 121–127.

Sherrill, L. J. *Guilt and redemption.* Richmond, Va.,: John Knox Press, 1957.

Siegman, A. J. *Hybris*—a reaction to positive transference. *The Psychoanalytic Review,* 1955, **42,** 172–179.

Smith, A. H., Jr. Notes on the hubris factor in psychotherapy. *Voices,* 1978, **14** (3), 83–87.

Spero, M. H. Clinical aspects of religion as neurosis. *The American Journal of Psychoanalysis,* 1976, **36,** 361–365. (a)

Spero, M. H. The critical review in psychology and Judaism. *Journal of Psychology and Judaism,* 1976, 1(1), 79–97. (b)

Spero, M. H. The critical review in psychology and Judaism. *Journal of Psychology and Judaism,* 1976, **1** (2), 83–102. (c)

Spero, M. H. On the relationship between psychotherapy and Judaism. *Journal of Psychology and Judaism,* 1976, **1** (1), 15–33. (d)

SPERO, M. H. Psychological determination and the Judaic concept of free will. *Journal of Psychology and Judaism*, 1978, **2**(2), 5–18.

SPIEGEL, J. P. Cultural aspects of transference and countertransference revisited. *Journal of the American Academy of Psychoanalysis*, 1976, **4** (4), 447–467.

SPILKA, B., and MULLIN, M. Personal religion and psychological schemata: A research approach to a theological psychology of religion. *Character Potential*, 1977, **8** (2), 57–66.

STEINBERG, S. *The academic melting pot.* New Brunswick, N.J.: Transaction Books, 1977.

STERN, K. *The third revolution.* New York: Harcourt, Brace & Co., 1954.

TARACHOW, S. St. Paul and early Christianity. In B. B. Wolman (ed.), *Psychoanalysis and Catholicism.* New York: Gardner Press, 1976.

TEILHARD DE CHARDIN, P. *The phenomenon of man.* New York: Harper & Row, 1959.

TEILHARD DE CHARDIN, P. *The future of man.* New York: Harper & Row, 1964.

TILLICH, P. *The courage to be.* New Haven: Yale University Press, 1963.

VANDERVELDT, J. H., and ODENWALD, R. P. *Psychiatry and Catholicism.* New York: McGraw-Hill, 1952.

WÄLDER, R. The principle of multiple function: Observations on over-determination. *Psychoanalytic Quarterly*, 1936, **5**, 45–62.

WALLACE, E. R. The psychodynamic determinants of *Moses and Monotheism. Psychiatry*, 1977, **40**(1), 79–87.

WALLACE, E. R. Freud's father conflict: The history of a dynamic. *Psychiatry*, 1978, **41**(1), 33–56. (a)

WALLACE, E. R. Freud's mysticism and its psychodynamic determinants. *Bulletin of the Menninger Clinic*, 1978, **42** (3), 203–222. (b)

WESTOFF, C. F., and JONES, E. F. The secularization of U.S. Catholic birth-control practices. *Family Planning Perspectives*, 1977, **9**(5), 203–207.

WHEELIS, A. The vocational hazards of psycho-analysis. *International Journal of Psycho-analysis*, 1956, **37**, 171–184.

WHEELIS, A. *The moralist.* New York: Basic Books, 1973.

WISE, C. A. *Mental health and the Bible.* New York: Harper & Row, 1956.

WITH REFERENCE TO PSYCHOANALYSIS. *L'Osservatore Romano*, September 21, 1952. Trans. and reprinted by National Catholic Welfare Conference, Washington, D.C.

ZIEGLER, J. H. *Psychology and the teaching church.* New York: Abingdon Press, 1962.

ZILBOORG, G. *Psychoanalysis and religion.* London: Allen & Unwin, 1967.

Ethical Issues in the Institutionalization of Patients

Jerome Steiner

The term "ethics" refers to the system of values and rules of conduct by which people attempt to live together, to the "correctness" of motives and behaviors. In a "moral" society it is necessary to understand the ethical issues involved in those rules and practices by which some people are segregated from the rest of society by members of particular groups within that society. In this chapter, the complexities of forced institutionalization (involuntary commitment into a hospital) brought about by physicians, judges, attorneys and other social groups are examined.

Insofar as there is regulation, issues of power and control are fundamental and a priori to all social relationships. This is not the world of 1755, when it was assumed that self-control guided by reason was possible. Nor is it the world of Rousseau's "innocent savage"; in his "Discourses on the Origin and Foundations of Inequalities Among Men," Rousseau described a world in which inequalities arose from differences in personal merit, a world in which such merit was recognized by others. The twentieth century is a world popularly defined by the neurotic symptoms which arise from the conflicts between inborn instincts and the demands of social control (Freud, 1968). Such control is given over to others both to gratify the need to be cared for and as a protection against internal forces which seem potentially overwhelming. There have always been persons whose delegated task was to ensure comfortable survival. These persons had knowledge (truth) and methods (technology) and power over others granted by their fellows. In order to perpetuate himself, man had been willing to subject himself to the power of others within a complicated network of relationships. He had given up some of the freedom to do as he alone chooses (Rank, 1958). The feeling of protection which comes from dependence on those who are considered powerful finds its roots in the dependence on parental figures in childhood, within the family; the hierarchical relationships and rituals which form the bases for the inevitable inequalities in the state itself are taught and perpetuated. The earliest descriptions of the hierarchical relationships between people were in the sagas and epics. When traditions changed into rules concerning behaviors which guarantee survival, one might say a systematic code determining ethical behavior came into being.

When their survival is threatened, animals undergo a complex psychobiological "stress" reaction which results in "fight or flight" behaviors after an initial period of tension signals and prepares the neuroendocrine system. Among human beings, when fight or flight is not possible, tension increases and early signal anxiety gives rise to greater fear, often to panic. Such a response often interferes with the capacity to function. Automatic, unconscious mechanisms of defense reduce this tension, making survival possible. Despite the innate physical and psychological protections against death, and in addition to a state of tension when death threatens, human beings have the burden of self-conscious realization of danger and a learned concept of death. The thought itself comes to provoke anxiety. Death is feared in the abstract; man wishes to persevere. For Ernest Becker (1973) man's cognitive capacity is used to transcend his time-bound self through identification with an enduring culture. In its preservation, he places himself within a larger scheme, one which holds implications of eternity, and so he avoids the anticipation of a final and meaningless end. He has devised rituals— those culturally directed behaviors which are meant to control the material and animal world and thus transcend it (Reik, 1946).

In this scientific era, man has developed a physical technology and an economic system with which he can control his entire world. He gains power through technology and through economic success (Becker, 1975). All cultures in all times have given legitimacy to some of those who exercise power; the "source" of power itself shifts with the passing of time. According to Thomas Szasz (1974), after the fall of Rome, when society was theocratic, legitimization of the rules was given by God through the "revealed" Church. Deviation from the rules was either criminal or heretical. From the eighteenth century to the present, the source of legitimate power has been reason. Appropriate conduct has been determined by an elite, which acquired knowledge through scientific methods, and deviation is considered to be motivated either by criminal tendencies or by *loss of reason*, defined as "mental illness."

We must attempt to examine that process through which a patient (subject) and a physician (power figure) may be caught up in a system more concerned with the interplay of power than with the science and reason which assert that the primary ethical goal of society is the preservation of the individual's freedom to survive, in "good health," in the social and physical environment. Man has desired not mere survival, however, but painless survival. Technology which dealt with longevity was applied to the reduction of pain. The person in pain was defined as abnormal, as "sick." The ethical premises of that physician group responsible for defining the individual considered objectively as disobedient and subjectively as suffering, as "sick," must be carefully scrutinized.

Animals lower than man on the evolutionary scale exist in the here and now. The gratification of their needs is not delayed. So it is with babies and children. It is a sign of maturation that the human organism can delay these gratifications, or, when such fulfullment conflicts with other needs or goals, that it can permit gratification to remain unfulfilled. Of course, a sense of time and an ability to control impulses must develop before this is possible. The behavior of an animal is controlled by instinct and is a result of learning from experience. The human organism develops imaginative capacities. He is able to take "trial actions" which are purely mental functions. He can learn in an "as if" fashion, building on past experience and a sense of the present and future time. For man to live with others, he must exist as an historical animal, able to conceptualize himself within a temporal framework wherein gratifications are delayed, impulses are controlled, and consequences of behavior are imagined. The human being learns, by verbal communication and by viewing the behavior of others, the experiences of others in their past history, and can integrate them into his own system of behavior. The personal history of any one individual need not repeat the history of the entire social group, or of the family. He learns from the criticism of others, the imagined criticisms derived from his "historical" sense and from a series of rewards and punishments throughout his life. Man is a social animal; perpetuation of the species requires an ability to learn from the experience of others, both past and present. In order that all might live together, man must restrict the scope and timing of his actions. All impulses may not be gratified; those impulses which may be gratified may not be gratified at the present moment. Ethics are always restrictive. In ethical systems which most value the freedom and decision-making capacity of individuals, restrictive codes are needed when the behavior of one person impinges upon the behavior of others. Systems of ethics become translated into systems of law. At the point where public control of behavior is addressed by the law, obedience to the law becomes part of the survival system and, as a consequence, part of the ethical system from which the law has sprung.

The decision of which regulations could be appropriately applied to unreasonable, suffering persons who refuse treatments intended to cure remains with these in power. The physician both prescribes and requires treatment when he deems it necessary, even when the patient does not. In those societies which do not accept death as a right of the individual, forced treatment is deemed necessary to prevent a patient's self-inflicted pain or death or to decrease the threat of violence.

History

One phenomenon found in all religions is the requirement of various "purification" rituals and avoidance of that which is felt to be repugnant in behavior or environment before approach to the godhead might be attempted. The god becomes associated with concepts of "clean" and "pure." For example, the vestal virgin in Rome had to avoid particular sexual contacts scrupulously if they were to remain adequate servants for their god; or, the Roman Catholic must undergo the "cleansing ritual" of confession before he can participate in the miracle of the Sacrament, wherein wine and wafer are transubstantiated into the flesh and blood of Christ. The priestly class in Judaism must avoid all contact with the dead, hence cemeteries, if they are to be qualified to offer sacrifices in a future temple which might be built in Jerusalem. The concepts of uncleanliness or unworthiness referred also to social activities. In Judaism, the civil law which mandated cancellation of financial debts (after adequate repayment) each year in order for members of society to live harmoniously, became transformed into the necessity to come to terms with one's fellow men for all actions which might require punishment or blame or thanks before one might approach God in order to ask His forgiveness for sins committed (i.e., debts) on the Day of Atonement. Occasionally, there is a differentiation between man in his capacity to perform priestly functions and man as a social (and sinning) being, where the latter does not necessarily obviate the efficacy of the former. This might pose a problem for the man/priest, as in James Joyce's *Portrait of the Artist as a Young Man*. Despite purification rituals, avoidance of the unclean, etc., however, man's nature is to follow his impulses, to break rules, and often to err. Every religion allows deviation to a limited extent from that which is permissible, with methods whereby such deviation and contamination may be overcome. Deviation may be seen as a breakthrough of some essential sinfulness, whereby some new uncleanness is acquired by possession by dark, demonic forces. Contamination by repressed human forces or by demons is prevented by other ritual and avoidance behaviors. In fact, it was felt that the breakthrough of innate and sinful impulses after adequate purification was also caused by the influence of external evil forces. The demonic must be avoided in interpersonal relationships and priestly magic must be used to cope with it. The concept of contamination, held by the priestly class as it related to the moral effects of interpersonal relations, was studied in a special theological field— demonology. Daily observation of the behavior of people confirmed the belief of the priests and healers that humans could contaminate one another. The concept of contamination antedated scientific methods and the discovery of germs. Disease could be caused by physical influences such as the miasma in the swamps around the city of Rome. Particular environmental phenomena were constantly associated with physical illness. The world was populated by demons and harmful physical factors. As the physicians studied contamination and related it to physical factors, the science of epidemiology came into being. Physicians directed quarantine and officers of the state enforced the order as a law. When there was danger of contagion, the healer's task was to prevent further infliction of pain (illness) or threat to the survival of others brought about by his patient.

In the early eighteenth century, such dangerous and deviant persons were incarcerated under the most appalling conditions. By the late part of the century, the spirit of the French Revolution took hold. It was felt that Reason would guide behavior and that insanity was caused by a deficiency in reasoning capacity. Contamination by the behavior of other persons might be prevented through the light of reasonable thinking. In the past, kings and emperors enslaved people. Reasonable humans do not or should not enslave. In 1793, Pinel, the director of two mental hospitals in Paris, the Bicêtre and the Salpêtrière, removed the shackles from the limbs of mental patients (Zilboorg, 1941). English institutions underwent reform under the influence of Tuke and Muray; similar reforms took place in North America under the leadership of Benjamin Rush, Band and Kirkbride (Ackerknecht, 1959). As the social climate slowly changed, so treatment became somewhat more humane. These changes were instituted not for scientific but for philosophic reasons. In the "age of enlightenment," it was felt that while criminals and the mentally ill should be deprived of liberty because they were dangerous to society, their lives should be comfortable and their masters fair, not cruel. Through "moral" treatment, characterized by control, discipline and employment, the purpose of the segregation of those in mental distress was to restore reason which had been lost because of their exposure to severe and environmental stresses (Alexander, 1966).

In 1830, John Percival, the son of a British prime minister, wrote of his own hospitalization,

> First the suspicion and the fact of my being incapable of reasoning correctly . . . justified apparently every person . . . in dealing with me also in a manner contrary to reason . . . secondly, my being likely to attack the rights of others gave these individuals license, in every respect, to trample upon mine.

In his "Treatise on Insanity," Pinel described the discipline as necessarily frightening, coercive, and intimidating. Benjamin Rush, the "Father of American Psychiatry," interpreted it as "force applied by trickery" (Bateson, 1974).

Before the reforms of Pinel and Tuke came to public attention, persons judged insane whose families would not care for them and who were without means were likely to be banished to the colonies or jailed or put in the poor house. After these reforms, the insane were more likely to be removed from their families and sent to asylums in rural areas. There, while kept under strict control, they were made to do gainful work. Employment of patients not only defrayed the costs of asylum custody but was also a source of profit (Bickford, 1963). Patients might, however, have had considerable contact with the physician. In the United States, the asylums grew overcrowded as the century of expansion and immigration progressed. Control and employment continued, but contact with the physician diminished. Custodial treatment replaced moral treatment.

Thus matters stood well into the twentieth century. In 1955, the Congressional Joint Commission on Mental Illness and Health recommended community-based care and attacked the philosophy of the large state hospital. Legislators and courts acknowledged that, as asylums were custodial institutions, they might infringe on patients' rights as citizens and that due process, guaranteed under the Constitution, must be instituted.

In 1961, Jack Ewalt and Frances Braceland, representing the American Psychiatric Association, testified before the Senate Subcommittee on Constitutional Rights. They maintained that those same procedures necessary to protect rights "criminalized" the mentally ill by considering hospitals as institutions of incarceration and subjected patients to "embarrassment, indignity, publicity and exposure . . . of private affairs" (Braceland and Ewalt, 1962).

The Social Role of the Physician in Enforcing Treatment

It appeared that court procedures in which the psychiatrist and professional staff of the hospital defined the problems and made decisions that were routinely accepted by the judge, used the patients more as pawns than as examples of due process under the law.

During the past twenty years, however, the role of the psychiatrist has begun to change. He is no longer viewed as the priest-expert by the highest courts; he is recognized as a trained professional limited by human frailties and social climate. According to Judge Bazelon (Bazelon, 1978), this new social attitude may be the result of excessive recourse to commitment. It may also be the result of that change in social philosophy which puts less faith in a *pater familias* who judges social obedience as "goodness" and the display of unconscious forces as "evil." With the diminution of faith in the family, other personal relationships, and the government to ensure survival, the role of the psychiatrist as father has also diminished.

In medicine, generally, the physician cannot force treatment, (e.g., require blood transfusions of a Jehovah's Witness) without appeal to courts and law enforcement agencies in order to abrogate a person's right to protect himself from interference with his own person. Special injunctions and writs must be obtained by doctors in order to administer care (other than what may be required in an emergency). The situation is different for the psychiatric patient. Often, he must obtain legal relief in order to prevent or discontinue treatment; he cannot simply refuse it. Called "possessed" for centuries, the mentally ill were treated as outcasts or venerated as saints by priests who placed them in isolation to prevent contagion. When the principle of moral contagion was discredited, protective incarceration was redefined as asylum. The psychiatrist accepted from the priests the responsibility of forcing care and treatment on those unreasonable enough to refuse it. A problem once seen as theological was transformed into one seen as medical. The definition of what behavior is symptomatic, however, is usually dependent on social rather than medical considerations (Goffman, 1961).

The difficulties of involuntary commitment are complicated by the lack of a body of scientific evidence about mental illness itself (Goffman, 1963). Thus, the psychiatric standards for commitments are vague. Simply because he defines the patient as ill, a physician may commit a patient to a hospital in New York State for a maximum of seventy-two hours. When two physicians, however, detect a danger either to the life of the patient or the life of others, they may enforce sixty days of hospitalization. Although in either case patients have the right of appeal to court, 63 percent of patients in one study did not clearly meet the statutory requirements for any confinement (Scheff, 1973). The legal rulings by higher courts are quite clear that there should be a *presumption of sanity*, that the burden of proof of insanity is on the petitioners, and that there must be a preponderance of clear and unexceptional evidence. A *presumption of illness* by mental health officials, however, usually appears to be the determining factor.

On April 30, 1979, the Supreme Court ruled unanimously that a person cannot be unwillingly committed to a mental institution without

clear and convincing evidence of being both mentally ill and likely to be dangerous . . . the decision imposes a higher standard of proof than is currently required by New York, New Jersey and other States where a "preponderance of evidence" has been regarded as sufficient grounds for committing a person. The Court, in an opinion written by Chief Justice Warren E. Burger, concluded that the "preponderance standard" which applies to most private civil lawsuits, did not adequately protect the constitutional due process rights of a person facing institutionalization. At the same time, the Justices rejected arguments that the Constitution requires evidence that is "beyond a reasonable doubt," a standard that is applied in criminal cases. The decision, Addington V. Texas (No. 77-5992), sends back to the Texas Courts the case of a man whose mother filed a petition to have him involuntarily committed to a state mental hospital. . . . Justice Burger called the "beyond a reasonable doubt" standard inappropriate because, "given the lack of certainty and the fallibility of psychiatric diagnosis, there is a serious question as to whether a state could ever prove beyond a reasonable doubt that an individual is both mentally ill and likely to be dangerous." [*New York Times*, 1979]

The very procedures which are typically used to determine whether patients meet statutory requirements are open to question. They rarely screen *out* anyone. The procedures determining whether a patient meets these requirements for involuntary commitment to a hospital usually include the following:

1. Application by a concerned party (family member, physician, social agency, police, fire department, etc.) for such action to take place.
2. An examination by a physician licensed in the particular state; he need not be a psychiatrist.
3. An examination by a psychiatrist, licensed in the state; he need not necessary have passed his specialty board examinations.
4. The patient spends a mandated length of time in the hospital with a maximum stay dictated under the law. He is observed during this period by nursing staff and hospital physicians. By and large, the observing staff members are nonprofessionals, nurses' aides, and some nursing personnel having completed two years of a nursing school. Rarely have the nursing personnel at public institutions completed four-year degree requirements and rarely do they possess specific training in psychiatric nursing. The physicians responsible for observation are foreign-born and trained for the most part, working under special license in order to assure adequate distribution of needed medical services in unpopular areas in the country.
5. The patient is reexamined by a psychiatrist toward the end of his mandated stay, rarely if ever less than the maximum allowed under the legal statutes.
6. The patient is represented by a lawyer assigned by the court system in some jurisdictions in the United States.
7. The patient appears before a judge in a court, most often set up within the confines of the mental hospital.

These are the procedures I have personally observed in New York, Connecticut, Florida, and California. In order for a patient to arrive at a last step in this procedure, the patient has not been discharged at many points at which this might have been possible. Admission might have been denied upon application, the initial physician might have found the patient not suitable for involuntary commitment; the first psychiatrist, the hospital psychiatrists, or the reexamining psychiatrists may have found him ready for discharge. In my own experience, this rarely if ever happens. It would appear that the professionals involved in each step hesitate to disagree with their colleagues in the preceding examining steps. It is almost as if the intraprofessional relationships take precedence over the "responsibility" toward the patient's civil rights. I have never seen or heard of a judge moving beyond these examining circumstances, moving beyond routine questions and failing to follow the advice of the physicians and psychiatrists who have examined the patient before that time. I have never seen a discharge affected without a recommendation to that effect. Unfortunately, the original applicants for involuntary hospitalization have a bias in that direction; the examining physicians are biased to support one another and to support the mental hospital system of which they are a part; the lawyers and judges do not presume to take issue with the mental health "experts" and are more concerned with fulfilling statutory requirements. Despite behavioral appropriateness, appropriate speech, understanding of the situation, and good orientation, these patients, in my experience, are rarely presumed to be sane. Such presumption remains for the highest courts, those in various Courts of Appeal (viz., the Alabama jurisdiction under Judge Johnson, the District of Columbia jurisdiction under Bazelon) and the Supreme Court itself. Judges at the highest level are evidently able to opeate independently and with an ear toward the "expert" opinion but with some degree of reasonable doubt because of their presumption of sanity. In fact, psychiatrists may be found at this level who are not part of the mental hospital system in which the patients find themselves, who are not appointed from the same socioeconomic and geographic community as the other psychiatrists, but who are called in as independent consultants with recognized expertise because of their position in the medical community and their national specialty examining boards. On occasion this is possible should a patient find an interested advocate. My own experience has shown, however, that this is a rare phenomenon. Most courts retain patients in the hospital virtually automatically. Without court intervention, retention is certainly automatic. Examinations required for judicial opinion rarely support the patient's position when he denies that of the psychiatrist (Scheff, 1973). One study of the psychiatric examination (Steadman, 1973) described the two lines of questioning followed, one to determine the circumstance leading to hospitalization and the other to test orientation and capacity for abstract thinking. Questions were asked rapidly and the patient was given only a brief time to answer. Undue weight was given to patients' records, which were often condensed and confused. The authors of this study, who themselves interviewed all patients interviewed by the psychiatrist, were convinced that "even giving the examiners the benefit of the doubt . . . the examination failed to establish that the statutory criteria were met." In an average *nine* minutes spent with the patient, it was impossible for examiners to probe beyond standard orientation questions, questionable in themselves, since they have never been asked of the community as a whole. In any case, the conclusion that decisions were largely based on presumption of illness was unavoidable to these authors. An "incorrect" answer may have been caused by anything—an improperly formed question, a misunderstood reply, a problem of vocabulary, or something as subjective as attitude or tone. There was no real standard of abnormality beyond the impression formed by the physician from his own clinical experience:

> "The omissions and almost flippant brevity of these forms, together with the arbitrariness, lack of evidence, and prejudicial character of the examination . . . all support the observer's conclusion that, except in very unusual cases, the psychiatric examiner's recommendation to retain the patient is virtually automatic." Commitment was invariably recommended in borderline cases. [Steadman, 1973]

How wide and varied are physicians in linguistic skills and in clinical experience! Does the physician use the same idiomatic speech as another physician, the judge, the patient advocate, the patient himself? Indeed, in a process where language is so important, where descriptions, questions and answers are for the most part the behavioral evidence, particular attention should be paid to the skill in its use. In the commitment process, an application is made, describing behavior. It is likely that the applicants, the initial physician, the initially examining psychiatrist, and the hospital personnel have observed both verbal and nonverbal behavior of the patient. It is less likely, however, that nonverbal behavior has been observed by patient advocates, lawyers, judges, or reexamining psychiatrists, because of the period of treatment already taking place. In the last steps of the commitment process, the behavioral aberrations, most likely the stimuli of the entire commitment process are least observed. These aberrations are described. The bulk of these processes are instituted in public agencies, such as the community mental health center, the mental hospital, or the emergency room of a public general hospital. Furthermore, the greatest number of commitments are to public mental hospitals and the "observers" are public employees, as are the lawyers, advocates, etc.

Because of the faulty distribution of medical personnel in the United States, the foreign-born and foreign-trained physician may be granted temporary licenses (later to be granted permanent licensure after passing special examinations which are different from those given to American-trained physicians) provided that their work be done in a specialty relatively unpopular among American physicians (as is psychiatry in a public health facility) and in areas "needing" physicians, those most distant from university centers, in bad neighborhoods in the large cities, or far from the major medical centers of the large cities (as are most of the state mental hospitals). The command of the English language of these physicians is questionable, in my experience. I might go so far as to maintain that, as a group, they have no command of idiomatic speech at all. Nuance, tone, nonverbal accompaniments of speech, the meaning of words, semantics, constructions—these elements so important in accurate description and examination—are most often unlearned or misunderstood. One must ask other questions. Who are the foreign-born and foreign-trained physicians working in our public facilities? What are the social and governmental principles under which they were raised? Do they share the same concepts of patients' rights? Do they share the same concepts of the physician-patient relationship as their American-born and American-trained colleagues? One might assume that the American-born and trained physician shares more of the folkways, mores, and social principles of members of the legal profession and jurists involved in the commitment procedure than do those physicians most responsible for commitment. Were these issues unimportant and the examiners strictly to report "behavior" as it is seen, their evidence might yet be valuable for the court. In my own experience, in ten years in various public institutions, I have noted that these physicians do not do this. Rather, many of them keep the patient locked up for "examination" of his behavior, to make assumptions concerning that behavior under unlocked conditions and to present later to the court to show why their behavior has been correct, why the patient should be locked up, and how they have obeyed the law of their new country. When in doubt the groups fall back on their own concept of themselves as physicians. The greater the social discomfort, the more medical terminology, jargon, official-sounding diagnoses, and symptom lists are presented. Their clinical experience, however, has been garnered in the same public mental hospital facilities (and, possibly, in their homelands). Even before their particular examinations for foreign-trained physicians are passed, they are considered "expert" and are recognized as such by their colleagues who wrote the exam and who refuse to do service at the institutions for which this group is responsible. Such is the public posture of the medical profession. Privately, the American-born and trained physician has little respect for their expertise. The group employed at these institutions feels that they are second-class citizens. I am well aware that I speak from my own experience, which may be limited. I editorialize because there is little hard data to support my assertions concerning the discrepancy between public posture and private position. It is unfortunate that in commitment procedures, which often amount to incarceration, expertise is assumed. One might wonder whether that assumption might not change where a presumption of sanity is made for the patient. In criminal cases, a person is presumed innocent until proven guilty. In medical cases, a person is presumed ill until proven healthy. It would appear that human health is measured from zero sickness to very sick rather than on a scale of relative health. The rules derived for psychiatrists gave them, more than other physicians, authority to enforce treatment.

Physicians, like other humans, use a number of psychological methods to defend themselves against anxiety. It is difficult for the physician to say "I do not know" or "I cannot help" and feel comfortable. His training, his social task, dictates that he must have answers, he must produce "cures," and that he must be able to cope with all problems. Unfortunately, the physicians in mental health centers and mental hospitals are responsible for the most deviant segment of the mentally ill patient population. These are persons most difficult to treat—the chronically ill, the social and familial rejects—and these physicians are the least secure in their own social position in this country and have the lowest self-esteem because of the areas in which they feel forced to work. Yet, this committing group makes judgment concerning patients' social aptitudes, social judgments, and attitudes. One might wonder if the maverick might not be eliminated rather than facing the issue of "untreatableness" since facing this head-on reminds the physician of his own fallibility, a reminder which increases anxiety and discomfort.

Assumptions Underlying Commitment

1. Some assumptions regarding illness have been codified in laws as if they were self-evident truths. Until recently, the same language was used to describe both physical and mental illness (Szasz, 1957). Physical illness is usually diagnosed on the basis of measured biological changes, mental illness on the basis of behavior. Behavior deemed symptomatic of mental illness might be radically affected merely by altering the patient's social environment. Few physical illnesses can be effectively dealt with in such a manner. Furthermore, psychiatric methods of treatment have little in common with other medical treatments, since the focus is far less on bodily functions than on traits of character, styles of communication, and attitudes toward life, all of which are generally ignored in medical practice. In psychiatry, one rarely talks of cure. The mental hospital itself might be a place of retreat, away from the pressures of everyday life, not an institution devoted to active intervention. Frequently, such interventions take place in order to define the place as a hospital and to satisfy the court.

Methods of diagnosis and treatment in psychiatry are more frequently reflections of particular social philosophies than of scientific observation. Let us oversimplify the Marxian logic concerning some mental illnesses. Persons are social units contributing to a social whole. Those who will not contribute to the common good must therefore be mentally ill since their welfare is completely dependent on the welfare of the group as a whole. The social misfit, the maverick, is defined as ill by virtue of his deviation from permissible behavior. The Marxist feels that the individualistic, socioeconomic philosophy of capitalism is the cause of such illness. Should social deviation beyond that which is normative (since all societies permit some degree of difference) occur, it should be treated in the mental hospital, the clinic, or the dispensary as are other diseases related to faulty training and thinking. In these institutions, the patient remains a member of a social group; he works productively as soon as he is able to and he returns to his regular social group and work unit as quickly as possible, that is, as soon as he can control his deviant behavior and thinking. This system seems to have the advantage of speedy return to the community rather than suffering the disadvantage of long-term, involuntary hospitalization. Because of a definition of mental illness, however, which includes improper thinking or social agitation, the mental hospital may become a jail for those who disagree with the government (those who make the rules which define the common good). Political enemies may be defined as mentally ill and hospitalized until they cease being enemies by changing their ideas and activities or by a change in the attitude of the government itself. At a meeting of the World Congress of Psychiatry in Hawaii in 1979, the majority of members felt this issue to be of sufficient importance to pass a resolution condemming this practice. Are political enemies incarcerated because their views are dangerous or are they hospitalized because their views define them as mentally ill? Is the honesty of the physician who makes this judgment less than the honesty of a psychiatrist evaluating social behavior and language of an American citizen after an application is made by interested parties for him to do so? No culture is governed by the Platonic philosopher-king who will observe the observers, judge the judges, and grade the "correctness" of their various opinions and attitudes. Where there is dependence on the medical model in the definition of mental illness, whether in the Soviet Union or the United States, and an illness is defined as "organic," (as are dementia or delerium), then "it is a perversion and travesty to deprive needy and suffering people treatment in order to preserve a liberty which is in actuality so destructive as to constitute another form of imprisonment" (Chodoff and Taub, 1974). Should a mental disturbance, however, be manifested by symbolic language, as is hysteria, then it may not be illness at all but may be seen as "decision" or as "social deviation." Certainly, our democratic American philosophy does not consider social deviation or independent decision making as mental illness per se.

The assumption that there is no risk in psychiatric treatment without the consent of the patient has likewise been demonstrated to be false. Certainly involuntary hospitalization causes social isolation and may even prolong what might otherwise have been a transitory episode. Upon commitment, the patient enters a system that reinforces his position as a deviant (Goffman, 1959). In 1839, John Conolly notes, "Once confined, the very confinement is admitted as the strongest of all proofs that a man must be mad" (Szasz, 1970). When a person is evaluated retrospectively, any present bias in viewing personal history justifies the hospitalization and is used to convince the patient of its necessity. While involuntary hospitalization at the discretion of a physician might protect a patient from the potentially damaging stress and the unnecessary stigma of trial-like procedures, the same damage might be done by deception and forced treatment. Finally, the assumption that, in most mental illnesses, the patient is dangerous to himself or others has been enormously exaggerated. There is a difference between the assumption of dangerousness and a patient's statement that he *is* dangerous. In the Tarassoff decision (Annas, 1976), the psychiatrists were held responsible for informing the appropriate legal authorities where the patient stated his intent to do physical harm to another person. Even such statements, however, must be evaluated. A statement such as "I am going to kill the kid when he gets home; he took my keys and locked me out," is a casual figure of speech and does not denote murderous intent which will be carried out. Another statement might be seriously intended but impossibly implemented. The intended victim may be in another part of the country, in jail; the patient may have no history of any kind of effective action in any sphere; the patient may seriously intend such an action but have sufficient ethical scruples and self-control to control himself. On the other hand, a person might well intend to commit such an act, and be able to implement it. Judgment is required in all cases. Judgments concerning "dangerousness," however, without any statement on the part of the patient are made with the greatest difficulty and possibly with no greater accuracy than that due in chance alone (Guttmacher, 1965). In one state's survey of new patients in its mental hospitals, the issue of danger to self or others was mentioned in only 25 percent of cases, and even in those, it was not always clear that the risks were greater than those encountered in ordinary social life. Sadoff (1978) has questioned whether psychiatrists can predict violent behavior more accurately than it can be predicted on the basis of chance alone.

2. There are assumptions that invest the physician with curative ability. He is assumed to have knowledge that the patient does not have or would not understand. More importantly, in the performance of

various rituals which are understood only by him and his colleagues, he functions as a guru or priest, using a secret language (often nothing more than translations of symptoms into Latin or Greek). Once a patient is placed in his care, the psychiatrist and the mental institution are responsible for treatment. Clinical experience is the foundation of medical responsibility, the source of each physician's personal and indivdiualistic response to his cases (Friedson, 1976). His actions are supported by his will to believe in the value of his own first-hand experiences in the face of the inadequacy of general knowledge in his field. He feels that his work is unique and concrete, that no set rules apply since no two persons can share his experience. The power in the relationship between psychiatrist and patient is an illusion shared by both. The patient gives power to the psychiatrist who is then validated in it. The psychiatrist assumes that his education and experience enable him to judge whether a patient's accounting of his own actions is satisfactory. Should he be dissatisfied, the patient is considered "ill," perhaps a danger to himself and to society.

3. There are legal assumptions. If we examine the issue of social philosophy in terms of attitudes toward informed consent, it is clear that there is a conflict between an individual's right to freedom, autonomy, and personal choice, and the physician's duty to heal and to cure (Foster, 1978). Because of the gulf between the knowledge and experience of professionals and that of lay persons, these two groups cannot be equal partners in any discussion or contract. There can be no give and take as there is in business. Furthermore, a patient in trouble, overwhelmed by the problems of his illness and by medical controls, is in no position to exercise independent judgment. In some more enlightened states, a system of patient advocacy exists. I wonder whether patients know of its existence and how to use it. Who will help him to his ombudsman? In many jurisdictions, lawyers are appointed by the judiciary, independent of the mental hygiene system in each case. In my experience, however, these lawyers' tasks are to protect the legal rights of the patients and not to advise particular courses of action. Family, which in most cases applied for commitment, has biases in the direction of hospitalization and extrusion of the deviant member. In institutions where a "case manager" exists, this person coordinates the programs in the mental hospital and the communities. The physician cannot be called upon to help the patient exercise independent judgment, since he is part of a process from which the patient feels alienated.

The concern of Anglo-American law is to protect the rights of individual citizens. Thus, in the 1905 decision of *Mohr* v. *Williams, Minnesota*, the concept was established that the patient, and not the physician, had the right to make choices concerning physical interference with his own person. Nonetheless, in a study by Olin and Olin (Olin and Olin, 1975) 92 out of 100 patients did not understand the terms of the consent which they had signed. The social trend appears to be toward the increase of the participation of patients in making decisions about their own treatments.

The Fourteenth Amendment says that a person cannot be deprived of life or liberty without due process of law. Treatment, however, takes priority over issues of due process which may be suspended in emergencies. It is felt by some that involuntary hospitalization has led to the criminalization of the mentally ill. Commitment proceedings are cumbersome and time consuming. "Civil commitment statutes ... are weighted so heavily in favor of protecting ... civil rights ... that ... they often interfere with quick access to treatment on an involuntary basis" (Lebensohn, 1977).

The Eighth Amendment guarantees freedom from cruel and unusual punishment and implies a right to life and health as defined by the physician, not by the law. In *Donaldson* v. *O'Connor,* it was established that a mental patient in a hospital must receive more treatment than custodial care, otherwise his hospitalization must be considered as incarceration.

The assumptions made by the judiciary about due process and freedom from cruel and inhuman punishment as they relate to forced confinement have led to difficulties. In *Landau* v. *Werner,* the courts held psychiatrists culpable of malpractice for the destructive behavior of their patients. And yet appreciable change in a patient's behavior might be brought about only by drastic control of his environment, often amounting to custodial care in incarcerating institutions, or even changes in his body chemistry. The psychiatrist is not a godlike guru or a magician at all. He is simply a human being, caught in the conflict between his liability for damage and the imposition of cruel and unusual punishment in order to prevent such liability. It is clear, however, that deprivation of liberty, civil rights, and privacy (implied in custodial care and chemical control) cannot be considered a humane course unless one defines current social standards for behavior as the greatest good and conversion of the patient to these standards as humane.

The Dilemma of Psychiatric Ethics

So confused are the definitions of mental illness and so multitudinous the treatments, all of which have approximately the same chance of success, that the psychiatrist must base his decision to hospitalize on his personal definition of illness and his personal philosophy of what constitutes treatment and cure. There are some restraints to his action: the threat of a malpractice suit, the legal procedures to which the patient may resort to prevent confinement, or perhaps some pressures from his psychiatric colleagues. Principles of enforced hospitalization varying from physician to physician could hardly be defined as a systematic and rational code. It is amazing that under these circumstances the psychiatrist has such great power to limit a person's freedom. The use of this power appears to be materially affected by his financial, ideological, and political positions.

> One extremely important contingency influencing the severity of the societal reaction may be whether or not the original deviance comes to official notice. This paper suggests that in the area of mental disorder, perhaps in contrast to other areas of deviant behavior, if the official societal reaction is invoked, for whatever reason, social differentiation of the deviant and nondeviant population will usually occur. [Goffman, 1973]

At some times a physician may be an unwitting tool of his education, at other times a willing tool of the state, at still others he may even be a deliberate maker of mischief.

Goffman (1959), viewing commitment from a social perspective, describes the conditions affecting the individual's career as a patient, factors such as socioeconomic status, visibility of offense, proximity to a hospital, community tolerance, the action of a complainant. When a "pre-patient's" kin no longer identifies with him but with "authority," that person consigns him to a circuit of health agents and agencies that thrust him into the "betrayal funnel" wherein the very person to whom he appeals for protection becomes the source of his removal from regular social intercourse. The patient's rights would be better protected by curbing the power of the physician to incarcerate than by providing him with advocates after his incarceration. It might be thought that psychiatrists would prefer a clearly medical standard of enforced treatment (e.g., again, the blood transfusion for the Jehovah's Witness) to the sociological standard of the jailer. Yet, they generally defend their right to force treatment on the basis of a purely social rather than a purely medical model.

The physician's function is to reduce pain and promote longevity upon the request of persons who become his patients only at that time, unless they are unconscious, in which case such a request is implied and the physician may perform emergency treatment. Treatment is generally allowed to proceed until the person regains consciousness and gives permission, or until other persons in that patient's life give permission. This is a contractual model. In mental illness, symptoms of disorientation are equated with unconsciousness and call for emergency treatment. It is hard to understand how the concept of emergency can be so extended for the psychiatrist without knowing the historical context. In the fact of its ignorance with regard to cause and treatment of illness, the law has abdicated the power to enforce hospitalization to the psychiatrists who are assumed to be capable of shedding light on that ignorance. It appears that the psychiatrist has unconsciously and unwittingly acted as a social power-broker. He has used the pathology of the "patient" segment of society in order to control its deviant behavior. In so doing, he has transformed a theoretically contractual relationship between client and doctor into an "institutional" relationship, in which the doctor functions to remove control from the client's hands.

As Beigel has said (Beigel, Hegland, and Wexler, 1978), persons with mental illnesses are considered incapacitated, hence unable to gain respect for decisions concerning their own treatment. Yet these same persons are considered to have legal capacity. The individual who makes a "bad" decision is assumed to lack capacity, which means he has no right to make a bad decision. Legal capacity refers to understanding of functions, not to the weight a person chooses to give to them.

How can enforced hospitalization, simply on the basis of a doctor's experience in psychiatric practice, ever be ethical? If the physician is seen as an authority figure trusted by the patient because of the phenomenon of transference and owing to social compliance, it becomes apparent that their relationship is concerned with magic and with dependence similar to submission to a guru and not with contracts. This is not to say that one cannot endorse enforced hospitalization under any circumstances, but perhaps the psychiatrist must turn elsewhere for the power to treat as he sees fit, including the power to commit if he is convinced that this would ensure the success of his treatment, whether the patient wants it or not.

Psychiatrists too often take responsibility for assessing facts and making judgments in areas where they have no real competence. They are encouraged in this by a society that is deluded in the belief that science has the answers and that psychiatry is a science. Influenced by the institutions which they serve, by the social, political, and cultural concepts of their time, it is difficult for psychiatrists to isolate the necessary scientific data from the institutional interests and to make correct psychiatric judgments. ·

In 1973, Rosenhan (1973) reported an experiment with eight "sane" individuals who feigned symptoms of mental instability and were admitted to hospitals where they were labeled "schizophrenic." Despite changes in their behaviors, they were unable to convince the doctors that they were sane. Their diagnoses were clearly influenced by the environment, by the context in which the psychiatrists performed the examinations. Rosenhan verified that the sane could be diagnosed as insane in a second experiment at a research and teaching hospital where the staff, having heard the results of the first experiment, were told that at some time one or more pseudo-patients would seek admission. Each staff member was on guard to detect this. One hundred and ninety-three patients were admitted during a trial period of whom forty-one were said to be pseudo-patients by one doctor and twenty-three by another. In fact, Rosenhan had sent no pseudo-patients to this hospital.

A Polemic

Is it ethical for the physician to act in *loco juris?* Even as the natural descendants of the priestly class, would it not be more ethical for the psychiatric community to root out the unspoken prejudice toward persons who do not harm others, even though their behavior may be unpleasant, or unaesthetic (rather than immoral)? Can it be ethical for the physician, who has not reached consensus with his fellows concerning diagnosis, treatment, and desired outcome, to act as if such consensus has indeed already occurred?

The ethical basis for enforced commitment would be better served is psychiatrists made a great effort to improve the legal procedures, in view of the uncertainties of medical knowledge, rather than assuming the power of the judge and jury over the rights of their patients.

REFERENCES

ACKERKNECHT, E. H. *A short history of psychiatry.* New York: Hafner, 1959.

ALEXANDER, A., and SELESNICK, S. T. The enlightenment. In *The history of psychiatry.* New York: Mentor, 1966.

ANNAS, G. J. Confidentiality and the duty to warn. *Hastings Center Report 6,* 1976.

BATESON, G. (ed.). Percival's narrative. In T. Szasz (ed.), *The age of madness.* New York: Jason Aronson, 1974.

BAZELON, D. The psychiatrist in court. In J. P. Brady and H. K. Brodie (eds.), "The role of the psychiatrist in the criminal justice system," *Controversy in psychiatry.* Philadelphia: W. B. Saunders, 1978.

BECKER, E. *The denial of death.* New York: Free Press, 1973.

BECKER, E. *Escape from evil.* New York: Free Press, 1975.

BEIGEL, A., HEGLAND, K., and WEXLER, D. Implementing a new commitment law in the community: Practical problems for professionals. In W. E. Barton and C. J. Sanborn (eds.), *Law and the mental health professions: Friction at the interface.* New York: International University Press, 1978.

BICKFORD, J. A. R. Economic value of the psychiatric patient. *Lancet,* 1963, **1,** 714–715.

BRACELAND, F. J., and EWALT, J. R. Psychiatric points of view regarding laws and procedures governing the medical treatment of the mentally ill. *Special Information Bulletin,* American Psychiatric Association and National Association of Mental Health, No. 1 (1962), pp. 1–8.

CHODOFF, R., and TAUB, N. Involuntary hospitalization and treatability: Observations from the District of Columbia experience. *Catholic University Law Review*, 1974, **23**, 744–753.

FOSTER, H. H. Informed consent of mental patients. In W. E. Barton and C. J. Sanborn (eds.), *Law and the mental health professions: Friction at the interface.* New York: International University Press, 1978.

FREUD, S. Civilization and its discontents. In *Standard edition, Complete works*, Vol. XXI, trans. James Strachey. London: Hogarth, 1968.

FRIEDSON, R. *The profession of medicine: A study of the sociology of applied knowledge.* New York: Dodd, Mead, 1976.

GOFFMAN, E. The moral career of the mental patient. *Psychiatry*, 1959, **22**, 112–142.

GOFFMAN, E. The medical model and mental hospitalization: Some notes on the vicissitudes of the tinkering trades. In *Asylums*. New York: Anchor Books, 1961.

GOFFMAN, E. Types of error and their consequences in medical diagnoses. *Behavioral Science*, 1963, **8**, 97–107.

GOFFMAN, E. The effect of inmate status. In E. Rubington and M. S. Weinberg (eds.), *Deviance: The interactionist perspective.* New York: Macmillan, 1973.

GUTTMACHER, M. Personal communication, 1965.

LEBENSOHN, Z. M. Defensive psychiatry or how to treat the mentally ill without being a lawyer. In C. Goldberg (ed.), *Therapeutic partnership: Ethical concerns in psychotherapy.* New York: Springer, 1977.

New York Times. Supreme court roundup: Stiffer proof of mental illness demanded for commitment. May 1, 1979.

OLIN, G. B., and OLIN, H. S. Informed consent and voluntary hospital admission. *American Journal of Psychiatry*, 1975, **132**, 938.

RANK, O. *Beyond psychology.* New York: Dover Books, 1958.

REIK, T. *Ritual: Psychoanalytic studies.* New York: Farrar, Straus, 1946.

ROSENHAN, D. L. On being sane in insane places. *Science*, 1973, **179**, 250–258; **180**, 364–365.

SADOFF, R. L. Indications for involuntary hospitalization: Dangerousness of mental illness? In W. E. Barton and C. J. Sanborn (eds.), *Law and the mental health professions: Friction at the interface.* New York: International University Press, 1978.

SCHEFF, T. J. Screening mental patients. In E. Rubington and M. S. Weinberg (eds.), *Deviance: The interactionist perspective.* New York: Macmillan, 1973.

STEADMAN, H. Some evidence on the inadequacy of the concept and determination of dangerousness in law and psychiatry. *Journal of Psychiatric Law*, 1973, **1**, 409–426.

SZASZ, T. *Pain and pleasure.* New York: Basic Books, 1957.

SZASZ, T. *The manufacture of madness: A comparative study of the inquisition and the mental health movement.* New York: Harper & Row, 1970.

SZASZ, T. *The age of madness.* New York: Jason Aronson, 1974.

ZILBOORG, G. *A history of medical psychology.* New York: W. W. Norton, 1941.

Ethical Problems in Termination of Psychotherapy

Benjamin B. Wolman

The problems to be discussed in the present chapter hinge upon two thorny and controversial issues, namely, (1) the definition of ethical behavior, and (2) the criteria for termination of psychotherapy. At the September 1980 Montreal meeting, the Council of Representatives, the governing body of the American Psychological Association, could not agree on the changes in the code of ethics proposed by CSPEC, the Committee on Scientific and Professional Ethics and Conduct (APA, 1967, 1980; Gurel, 1977; Simon, 1977). The perennial question of what is right or wrong has apparently remained undecided, and one may question whether the Council of Representatives of the APA, which certainly has the right to set rules and regulations for its members, could ever become the final judge in moral issues. Moreover, one may doubt whether such a judge does exist, and if he or she does, why so many different moral systems are advocated and often imposed by religious, governmental, and political groups.

No less complex is the issue of terminating psychotherapy. A review of individual psychotherapy and behavior psychotherapy (Gomes-Schwartz, Hadley, and Strupp, 1978) assigns the numerous definitions of improvement in psychotherapy to three different categories, namely social functioning, sense of personal satisfaction or well-being, and personality integration. The disagreements are numerous and profound, and some of the authors mentioned in the above review maintain that the therapists are the least objective evaluators.

With these two caveat remarks, I shall introduce a proposal concerning ethical problems in termination of psychotherapy. I do not pretend to be infallible, but I hope I am reasonable.

Moral Judgment and Moral Behavior

Imagine an individual living on an isolated and uninhabited island; such an individual could be neither ethical nor unethical. Whatever he or she would do could be wise or silly, ingenious or mechanical, productive or counterproductive, but could not be moral nor immoral. Morality starts with a relationship to another person. There must be at least two parties to morality.

One may discuss the meaning of morality ad infinitum, but morality is always related to the manner one relates to another person or persons (Margenau, 1964). Ethical or moral principles (these two terms are used interchangeably) have been a priori determined by Immanuel Kant, logically deduced by Baruch Spinoza, related to religious principles by Martin Buber, and explained in hundreds of different ways by philosophers of all creeds at all times. Apparently there is no universal agreement concerning what is right and what is wrong.

I believe that the most objective, succinct, and simple definition of morality was given by the ancient Jewish sage, Hillel. When a pagan asked him to describe Judaism briefly, Hillel said, "Thou shalt love thy neighbor as thyself. That's all. Everything else is a commentary."

The term "love" might be somewhat ambiguous in this context; probably the following phrase could be safely substituted for the above one: "Treat your neighbor the way you want him to treat you." The shift is from the emotionally loaded term "love" to overt behavior, that is, to observable interaction. It is impossible to love everyone but it is possible to interact in a fair and just manner. Moral principles are rather vague as long as they are stated in terms of feelings, thoughts, and theories, but they can be clearly stated, objectively observed, experimentally tested and measured in overt behavior (Berkowitz, 1972; Colby et al., 1980; Kohlberg, 1979; Rest, 1979). In other words, *it is counterproductive to define ethics in abstract terms dealing with unobservables, but a scientific analysis of ethics can successfully scrutinize moral behavior* (Durkheim, 1961; Margenau, 1964; Piaget, 1932). *The relevance of moral judgment depends on its application in overt behavior, for what's good in convictions that are not practiced?*

Daily life and historical evidence bring numerous instances of lofty moral judgments and, at the same time, passive condoning or approval of or even active participation in immoral behavior. Several years ago I supervised a few psychologists who worked in a prison. I asked them to apply a brief oral questionnaire to burglars, muggers, and killers. The imprisoned sociopaths maintained that they had the right to do what they have done; in *Call No Man Normal* (1973), I called the sociopaths "innocent criminals." Some sociopaths and practically all other prison inmates passed the brief moral questionnaire with flying colors. All of them clearly distinguished between minor transgression and violent assault, and all of them verbally condemned stealing, cheating, robbing, and other criminal practices. Some of them pointed to the low moral standards of high public officials, such as President Nixon and Vice

President Agnew, and their "moral judgment" did not substantially disagree with the slogans and catchwords of some public officials.

The famous or rather infamous murder of Catherine Genovese is a case in point. Her neighbors heard her cries and saw her being murderously assaulted but no one came to her rescue. Of course, all these neighbors condemned murder, but no one helped and no one acted in accordance with his or her "moral convictions." The behavior of the so-called "innocent bystanders" has little in common with their morality, and a verbal condemnation of activities hardly proves one's allegedly high moral convictions (Latané and Darley, 1970).

It is rather unfortunate that "our current ways of assessing basic moral perspectives are heavily tied to the ability (and willingness) of a subject to express his thinking through language" (Carroll and Rest, 1981). It is my firm belief that such an assessment is not worth the paper on which it is printed; *morality is not a matter of words but of deeds.*

Moral Development

There have been several theories concerning moral development (Berkowitz, 1972; Carroll and Rest, 1981; Damon, 1978; Hoffman, 1970, 1979; Durkheim, 1961; Kohlberg, 1969, 1979; MacIver, 1966; Piaget 1932; Rest, 1979; Wolman, 1976, 1981), some of which are described below.

Durkheim (1961) traced the origins of morality to social pressure. No society can tolerate license, and every social system has built-in restrictions that limit the freedom of individuals. Society sets a system of rules that protect the rights of their members. There are indeed far-reaching differences in the moral rules and regulations set by different societies, but all of them reflect the need for preservation of the society as a whole. Eventually the members of a given society accept these rules, internalize them, convey them to the children, and act in accordance with them. The willing acceptance of group discipline is the core of moral behavior.

Piaget (1932) stressed the cognitive aspects of moral development. The early acceptance of parental authority leads to the development of the "heteronomous morality." As the child grows and interacts with peers and begins to understand the rules of reciprocity and cooperation, his behavior is guided by his own "autonomous morality." Moral development is a product of reorganization of the child's awareness and his thought processes.

Kohlberg (1969, 1979) elaborated Piaget's theory further and suggested six developmental phases related to the concept of justice. At the first stage, there is inequality between the two parties and little if any reciprocity. At the second stage, there is more cooperation and some degree of equality. At stage three, mutual affection and care are the key elements in friendship relationship. At the fourth stage, the cooperation and reciprocity becomes society-wide; all participants accept their social role according to the prevailing social and legal system. At the fifth stage of moral development, every person has equal voice in determining the social order; social consensus is the basic rule at the fifth stage. The sixth phase represents the absolute and impartial equal justice, irrespective of social consensus.

I have proposed a theory of moral development that goes through five phases, namely: (1) anomy; (2) phobonomy; (3) heteronomy; (4) socionomy; and (5) autonomy. According to this theory (Wolman 1976c), people are born *anomous*. They know of no restraint, no concern, and no consideration for anyone. The intrauterine life is clearly parasitic; the zygote-embryo-fetus is all out for itself and grabs whatever it can. Mother's body is self-sacrificing: it gives whatever it possesses to feed and to protect the unborn child.

Birth changes little in the parasitic attitude. Although the newborn must use his or her own respiratory system, the parasitic-dependent attitude continues even after cutting the umbilical cord. The infant wants what he wants and follows his instant stimuli and impulses. He operates on the principle of immediate gratification of needs called *Lustprinzip* (erroneously translated as pleasure principle) by Freud. Infants are anomous—that is, amoral and limitlessly selfish.

Morality means concern for fellow men, but it starts with restraints imposed from without. Fear of retaliation and punishment is the first though preciously small step toward behavior. The earliest restraints and rules are based on fear, thus the earliest phase of primitive morality is called *phobonomous*. With the development of rudimentary awareness of potential consequences, which Freud called "archaic ego," the child's selfishness faces restraints. He learns to obey because he fears. Fear is not morality, but primitive people and toddlers must be restrained from without. This restraint prepares the ground for more advanced phases or morality.

As the child becomes aware of parental love and care, he appreciates what he gets and begins to reciprocate. His "love" is quite selfish, for he loves only those who love him. He wishes to protect them, for he needs their protection. The child needs parental love and fears he may lose it, thus his attitude toward the parents is a combination of love and fear. The child willingly and fearfully accepts parental rules and prohibitions, and gradually absorbs these rules and perceives them as if they were his own. He may identify with the parents or parental substitutes and incorporate their prohibitions and norms. He may blame himself for occasional disobedience and develop *guilt feeling* whenever he violates parental rules. His behavior is *heteronomous*, for he wilingly obeys norms instituted by others whom he perceives as loving and powerful authority figures. In Freud's personality model, this self-regulatory agency is called *superego*.

Moral development does not reach its full development with a childhood acceptance of parental rules and the formation of superego. Preadolescents and adolescents develop close interpersonal relations with their peers and form groups, cliques, and gangs: Quite often these new social relations displace the child-parent attachments, and the rules of peer society become the ultimate source of moral or antimoral behavior. The individual's willful identification with the peer group to which he chose to belong becomes the guiding principle in his life for years to come, and often his loyalty persists until the end of his life. This willing acceptance of social norms, be it of a certain religious denomination, racial or ethnic group, or political party, leads to the formation of a new part of one's personality, which I would call the *we-ego*, and this group-identification period, I call *socionomous*.

Most people never transcend the socionomy and acceptance of the norms prevailing in their particular group, clan, subculture, or of some larger social segments. Most people follow certain rather limited moral rules that are binding in their particular group. They are "brothers" and "sisters" who abide by moral principles within their brotherhood and sisterhood.

The ultimate moral development goes beyond socionomy. It is related to the idea of power. Imagine an omnipotent being. An omnipotent being does not fear and does not need anything, thus he cannot hate or hurt anyone. The only thing he can do is to give what he has. He *must* build and create, love and protect. Those who reached this divine point, as Christ, Prometheus, Antigone, and some genuinely moral individuals, have developed a *vector-ego*, an ego that goes out of the self and reaches toward others. They have the *courage to give*. They do not need any restraint, for their life is devoted to helping others. *Summa ethica* is nothing else but *summus amor*. They are *autonomous* (Wolman, 1976a).

Autonomy, the highest level of morality, is exemplified in Ibsen's drama *An Enemy of the People*, in which one man stands up against the selfish and unfair practices of an entire town. Perhaps the APA Council of Representatives should be reminded that obedience to the prevailing laws has nothing to do with morality (APA, 1980). Soviet psychiatrists who commit political dissidents to mental hospitals act in accordance with the laws of their country; are their actions morally justified? (Fireside, 1979.) The infamous Senator Joe McCarthy had the law on his side; was it ethical to cooperate with his witchhunt? (Hellman, 1976). And what about Hitler's legal system? Didn't Hitler's henchmen follow their Nürenberg laws?

Morality and Interactional Patterns

The following pages are based on the assumption that morally autonomous individuals act in a fair and just manner irrespective of the prevailing sociopolitical or religious climate. Their morality does not depend on
others—it is autonomous.

Moral interaction with other people is guided by Hillel's prescription
of relating to others the way one wishes that they will relate to oneself.
Human interaction, however, takes place on several distinct levels. An
elucidation of the levels of interaction might be useful in analysis of the
therapist-patient relationship in the terminal phase of psychotherapy.

I have distinguished four types of interaction, namely hostile (H),
instrumental (I), Mutual (M), and Vectorial (V), according to the aims of
the participants (Wolman, 1974).

I have suggested a division of groups into classes or types based on
the principles of *power* and *acceptance*—power defined as the ability to
satisfy needs and acceptance as the willingness to do so. Undoubtedly,
the interpersonal relations are more related to the power factor than to
anything else. People seek help, people look for social contacts with those
considered powerful, influential, and competent, that is, able to satisfy
their needs. Although hardly any interpersonal relation can be devoid of
acceptance factors, there are many groups for which the satisfaction of
needs is the primary factor and acceptance is secondary. A student reg-
isters for a course in order to satisfy his own needs and cares little at the
beginning about the social relationship. Only a minimum of acceptance
is required, while the power of the instructor to satisfy the needs of the
student is the decisive factor. No one would listen to a friendly but
incompetent instructor.

A business association represents this type even more than a college
class. People join an association with the satisfaction of their own needs
primarily in mind ("to take"). This sort of group is instrumental in attaining individual goals, we therefore call it an "Instrumental Relationship."

Sometimes people join others on a "give and take" basis, not only for
the satisfaction of their own needs but also for the satisfaction of the
needs of friendly persons. The need to give and take originates from the
desire to have our needs satisfied, but it develops into a separate, independent urge. Even when we do not need people, we need to be with
them. The need to be accepted is a derived need, but it is nevertheless a
powerful need that determines the nature of friendship relations, sexual
relations, marriage, and so on. In the type of group based on "give and
take," the mutual acceptance counts most, and these are called "Mutual
Relationships."

Sometimes people's main objective is the satisfying of the needs of
others. They do not relate to other people for personal gain, nor are
they interested in being accepted by the others. People may join a charit-

able organization for the purpose of helping others, or they may join an idealistic group ready to work for the good of mankind. Their efforts represent a sublimated social need. The group they join is called a "Vectorial Group."

My theory of social development stresses the child's increasing ability to relate to other people within the framework of the four possible interactional patterns, namely hostility (H), instrumentalism (I), mutualism (M) and vectorialism (V). I assume that well-adjusted, mature individuals act *rationally* in all four directions. They can display hostile behavior in self-defense, they are instrumental (takers) in the pursuit of livelihood, they are mutual (givers and takers) with friends, sex partners, and spouses, and vectorial (givers) toward children and in charitable and idealistic activities. An ethical individual can interact in all four types of relationships, always following Hillel's principle (Wolman, 1981).

The Dual Nature of the Therapeutic Process

Treatment of mentally disturbed people is a giving, *vectorial* process. People come to the therapist seeking help, and it is the therapist's obligation to deliver it. Usually psychiatrists, psychologists, and other mental health workers are paid for their services by the patients themselves or by society at large through hospitals, clinics, and other institutions; thus the instrumental elements need not be overlooked. Not to deliver the expected and agreed upon goods and/or services, however, is unethical even in instrumental relationships, and ethical therapists do not violate their therapeutic commitment. *They treat their patients the way they expect to be treated when they seek medical, dental, or mental help.* In other words, *responsibility* is the chief aspect of psychotherapeutic ethics, and psythotherapists must deliver the agreed-upon services.

The nature of the services to be delivered depends on the therapist's scientific convictions. Every psychotherapist is allowed to set the goals in accordance with his or her beliefs. Setting therapeutic goals is an intrinsic part of therapeutic strategy, based on (1) a self-assessment of the therapist; (2) an assessment of the patient and his or her problems; and (3) an assessment of the ongoing therapeutic interaction.

The Therapist

In "Analysis Terminable and Interminable," Freud (1937) compared the psychoanalyst to other healing professionals:

> So long as he is capable of practising at all, a physician suffering from lung or heart trouble is not handicapped in diagnosing or treating internal disease. The analyst, on the other hand, because of the peculiar conditions of his

work, is really impeded by his own defects in his task of discerning his patient's situation correctly and reacting to it in a manner conducive to cure. So there is some reason in the demand for a comparatively high degree of psychical normality and correct adjustment in the analyst as one of his qualifications for his work. And there is another point: he must be in a superior position in some sense if he is to serve as a model for his patient in certain analytic situations and, in others, to act as his teacher. Finally, we must not forget that the relationship between analyst and patient is based on a love of truth, that is, on the acknowledgment of reality, and that it precludes any kind of sham or deception.

Here let us pause for a moment to assure the analyst that he has our sincere sympathy in the very exacting requirements he is expected to fulfill. It almost looks as if analysis were the third of those "impossible" professions in which one can be quite sure of unsatisfying results. The other two, much older-established, are the bringing-up of children and the government of nations. Obviously we cannot demand that the prospective analyst should be a perfect human being before he takes up analysis, and that only persons of this rare and exalted perfection should enter the profession. [Pp. 351–352]

Of course, this would be an exaggerated demand but a definite level of maturity must be a prerequisite for anyone entering the healing professions that deal with disturbed individuals. A physician who suffers from heart troubles can be quite an efficient heart specialist, but it is doubtful whether a neurotic psychotherapist could help people overcome irrational modes of behavior and become rational (Horwitz, 1974). Psychotherapy of all kinds and brands is *more being than doing*, and an alcoholic or depressive individual or one suffering any other mental disorder is unable to cope with emotionally disturbed patients. The requirement for a thorough therapy for future therapists is more than justified.

Ethical Requirements

What level of morality should be expected from people in the healing professions? What should one expect from clinical psychologists, psychiatrists, and psychiatric social workers who assume responsibility for the mental health of people who need help?

The answer is obvious: *helping others is implicitly an act of supreme morality. Men and women who enter the healing profession must act in an impeccably moral manner, and a strict code of ethics must be obeyed by people who take care of mentally disturbed individuals.*

It is therefore shocking that "surveys of graduate departments show that a distressingly small percentage of courses are devoted to ethics or to issues of scientific and professional conduct and practice" (Gurel, 1977, p. 380).

To be ethical implies to be truthful. Psychotherapists must not undertake the treatment of cases that they are not prepared to undertake. They must not promise things they cannot deliver. They must terminate treatment when it does not serve the best interest of the patient.

Therapists are neither angels nor saints and must not represent themselves as such. As mentioned above, psychotherapy is a vectorial process of giving help, but at the same time it is an instrumental process of earning a living. To be moral does not mean to love; one must act in a moral manner toward everyone, not only toward the beloved ones.

On several occasions patients have asked me, "Do you love me?" My answer was unequivocal: "I care for your well-being. It is my moral responsibility to do the best I can, but I am not a magician or an angel. Helping people is my profession: it is the way I earn my living. It is my job to help people, and I will conscientiously discharge my responsibility. I am not your father or your lover. I am your doctor, and I will do everything I can to help you."

In forty years of clinical practice, research, and teaching, I have trained and supervised scores of younger colleagues. Whether it was in the Postdoctoral Program in Psychiatry at the Albert Einstein College of Medicine, or in the Postdoctoral Program in Psychoanalysis and Psychotherapy at Adelphi University, or in the last thirteen years at the Doctoral Program in Clinical Psychology at Long Island University, or in many years of private supervision, the essence of my teachings and guidance could be presented in one short phrase: *A good psychotherapist gets involved with the patient's case without getting involved with the patient's personality.*

Personal involvement is a gross violation of therapeutic ethics. Patients come to us for treatment of mental disorders, not for a personal relationship. In 1973, at the International Congress of Group Psychotherapy, I chaired a session in which a young psychiatrist maintained that sexual relations with his patients represent breaking down the old-fashioned barriers and are therapeutically beneficial. I asked him whether his penis were endowed with some magic therapeutic powers while all other penises were just humble sexual organs?

Violation of the professional distance is tantamount to taking advantage of minors. Successful therapy, whether it is Freudian, behavioral, or of any other orientation, is always associated with some transference elements. Seeking help from someone is associated with looking up to the person who is expected to give the requested help. It puts the patient into a dependent attitude toward the therapist; such an attitude somewhat resembles the child-parent interaction.

The therapist must never violate the professional distance and must not take his or her responsibility lightly. I believe the psychotherapist's level of responsibility is second only to that of a surgeon. In surgery it might be a matter of life or death; in psychotherapy it is a matter of living well or living hell.

The therapist must become involved with the patients' cases, for their well-being is the therapist's utmost responsibility (Bordin, 1974; Geller and Berzins, 1976; Lazarus, 1974; Lazarus and Wilson, 1976; Luborsky, 1976; Strupp, 1972; Wilman, 1972, 1976b).

Emotional Problems in Terminating Psychotherapy

Some clinical psychologists, psychiatrists, and other healing professionals who are impressed by their own true or imaginary therapeutic achievements, develop megalomaniacal feelings, as if their clinical experience qualifies them for the titles of supermen or superwomen. A rather poorly equipped and/or inexperienced psychotherapist may develop an irrational feeling that the patient needs him or her far beyond the objectively expected therapeutic gains.

Helping people is emotionally rewarding, for, as a rule, those who give enjoy more than those who receive. Those who give feel strong, for it is within their power to give. They feel rich and powerful, whether they offer emotional, physical, or financial support. Those on the receiving end are glad to receive what they need, but they feel that they depend on the good will of others who have the power to give.

It is enjoyable to have the power to help, but it is not pleasant to give it up and to realize that one's help is no longer needed. Small wonder that psychotherapists might err in their estimation of the usefulness of their work and might be unconsciously motivated to postpone the termination of psychotherapy. An error in judgment is not a crime, but it may lead to unfair behavior that must be avoided. For all practical purposes, the termination of psychotherapy of every type resembles the termination of parental care. The aim of parental care is to help the child become a mature adult thus making further care superfluous. In a way, the terminating phase in the treatment of mental disorders resembles the weaning process of growing-up children who are ready to leave the parents and should be allowed to live their own lives. Even rational parents who know that their child must leave the nest might experience emotional difficulties. Taking care of someone is tantamount to investing one's emotions in the person one takes care of, and the more one cares, the more attached one becomes to the person whom one takes care of.

The therapist-patient interaction is a two-way process. Freud has coined the concept of transference (1915). Transference could be defined as libido (or destrudo, in the case of negative transference)—

cathexis. The infantile investment of positive or negative emotions onto the parents is reenacted in the emotions the patient invests onto the therapist. Freud also noticed the phenomenon of counter-transference, that is reverse cathexis from the therapist onto the patient.

The patient versus therapist attitude can be presented on two levels. On one level is the here-and-now relationship; the patient is aware that he goes to a doctor whom he pays or who is paid by society, and who is supposed to help him relieve his tensions and resolve his inner conflicts. But on the other level, a great deal of irrational feelings are directed against the therapist who serves as a target for the patient's emotional onslaughts.

Serving as a target for a continuous onslaught of human emotions is a great mental health hazard. Small wonder that psychiatrists have a high incidence of suicide, and some of Freud's early associates who were inadequately psychoanalyzed suffered mental breakdowns. It is self-evident that whoever intends to deal with the emotional problems of other people must put his own house in order and undergo his own analysis. In order to save drowning lives, one must be a good swimmer, well prepared for the job of lifesaving.

A good therapist must get involved with his patients without getting involved with them. The psychotherapist must get involved with the patient's case; he is determined to help his patients. His mind is set on helping people who are in trouble and he is ready to do so. But on the other side, he must not become personally involved with patients, or get caught in the murky waters of morbid counter-transference feelings. To be dependable and yet not involved is the task of the therapist. The therapist's attitude toward patients is a giving attitude; he or she must enable them to go through corrective emotional experiences to remedy their past bad experiences and to correct their personality deficiencies.

In order to do that, however, he must be emotionally independent and able to serve the needs of the patient and not his own narcissistic needs. If one tries to take a shortcut in defining psychotherapy and asks what its aim is, the answer is: *the aim of psychotherapy is to make it superfluous.* A good pyschotherapist works in such a way that his work becomes unnecessary. He helps the patients to grow up and at the end of his work, they don't need him anymore. Their dependence on him is terminated as they become independent in their lives and begin making their own rational decisions (Wolman, 1976b).

The termination of psychotherapy often presents considerable emotional difficulties for both the therapist and the patient:

> A therapist may resist termination initiated by the patient for a good reason such as transfer of job or going away to college. The therapist shows his resistance by labeling the termination "premature" and suggesting treatment is not "finished." Implicit here is the therapist's anxiety about separation, his

notion that therapy has a definite time limit, and that less time means lesser results, as if to say that the efforts and accomplishments of a short time have no merit unless one gets a diploma for the course. By maintaining a neutral attitude and accepting the reality of the external exigencies (let's see what we can do in this period of time), the therapist can avail himself of the opportunity to see that patients can be exceedingly productive under externally set time limits. The therapist has to learn to cope with the anxiety of letting someone grow up at his own rate, as well as handling his own anxiety about separation from the patient.

A number of patients announce their readiness to leave by reviving their original symptoms, long since gone. This revival is a disguise for separation anxiety and it is, covertly, a test of the therapist's willingness to let them go. Making explicit the separation anxiety as well as the fear of leaving resolves this issue. No patient should leave treatment without a mutual recounting of the issues covered, the goals achieved or failed, the delineation of the varying nature of the relationship, both real and unreal. The discoveries of positives as well as the uncovering of negatives have to be spelled out. [Witenberg, 1972, pp. 189–190]

The awareness of the emotional difficulties does not remove the difficulties, just as the awareness of a problem does not solve it. It is, however, rather difficult to solve a problem of which one is unaware. A clear understanding of the emotional difficulties in termination of psychotherapy is the first step in the right direction and enables the therapist to cope with them. A therapist who is unaware of the emotional pitfalls may fall prey to his or her lack of understanding, and postpone the termination of psychotherapy and thus act unwillingly and unwittingly against the best interest of the patient.

When to Terminate

The crucial questions are when and how therapy should be terminated. When is related to what the goals of treatment are and what are the objective criteria of attainment of the goals.

The universal, intrinsic goal of all psychotherapeutic method is to render itself superfluous. Psychotherapy, by its very nature, must be a self-terminating process (Glover, 1972; Strupp et al., 1969; Wolman, 1976b) The goal of therapy, however, and the point beyond which therapy becomes superfluous, is still a controversial issue.

Psychiatric and psychological literature is full of diverse views concerning the concept of mental health and cure (Bordin, 1974; Eysenck, 1961; Gomes-Schwartz et al., 1978; Horwitz, 1974; Simon, 1977; Strupp, 1972; Strupp et al., 1969; Strupp et al., 1977; Wolman, 1972, 1976a).

In "Analysis Terminable and Unterminable," Freud (1937) has

pointed out several important issues related to terminating treatment. Freud asked the question, "Is there such a thing as a natural end to an analysis or is it really possible to conduct it to such an end?" Freud wrote:

> We must first decide what is meant by the ambiguous term, "the end of an analysis." From the practical standpoint it is easily defined. An analysis is ended when analyst and patient cease to meet for the analytic session. This happens when two conditions have been approximately fulfilled. First, the patient must no longer be suffering from his former symptoms and must have overcome his various anxieties and inhibitions and, secondly, the analyst must have formed the opinion that so much repressed material has been brought into consciousness, so much that was inexplicable elucidated, and so much inner resistance overcome that no repetition of the patient's specific pathological processes is to be feared. If for external reasons one is prevented from reaching this goal, it is more correct to say that an analysis is imperfect than to say that it has not been completed.
>
> The second definition of the "end" of an analysis is much more ambitious. According to it we have to answer the question whether the effect upon the patient has been so profound that no further change would take place in him if his analysis were continued. The implication is that by means of analysis it is possible to attain to absolute psychical normality and to be sure that it will be maintained, the supposition being that all the patient's repressions have been lifted and every gap in his memory filled. Let us first consult our experience and see whether such things do in fact happen, and then examine our theory and learn whether there is any *possibility* of their happening. [P. 320]

> Our object will be not to rub off all the corners of the human character so as to produce "normality" according to schedule, nor yet to demand that the person who has been "thoroughly analysed" shall never again feel the stirrings of passions in himself or become involved in any internal conflict. The business of analysis is to secure the best possible psychological conditions for the functioning of the ego; when this has been done analysis has accomplished its task. [P. 354]

One must, at this point, make a definite and binding statement. Although there are no generally accepted criteria of "cure," *every therapist has the moral obligation to terminate his or her work as soon as further work will not bring additional and significant therapeutic gains.*

Professional Competence

It is apparently rather difficult to set one norm for all patients, thus the following caveat is advisable: there are limits of what any therapy can do, whether it follows the pattern set by Freud, Jung, Sullivan, or Wolpe.

In supervising younger colleagues, clinical psychologists, and psychiatrists, I have kept reminding them that *no one can turn an apple into an orange,* and there is no reason for trying to "overhaul" one's personality. The task of therapy is to make the apple a better apple, that is, to enable the patient to make the best possible use of his or her potentialities.

But what are these potentialities?

Termination of any type of healing procedure, including psychotherapy, is largely a matter of professional ethics. A physician must not keep a patient in a hospital or in out-patient practice beyond the point of being helpful to the patient. Being helpful is to a great extent a matter of judgment, both an objective and a value judgment. A competent physician should know what he or she can do for the patient. A correct assessment of one's own potentialities is one of the main prerequisites of ethical conduct in psychotherapy. All seasoned psychotherapists strictly adhere to this principle of not accepting a patient they cannot help and of telling the patient what they can and cannot do for him or her.

Professional ethics hinges on professional competence. An incompetent therapist is unethical for he promises services he cannot deliver. Competence means power to do things one is supposed to do. Professional ethics means not to promise to do what one cannot do and to terminate psychotherapy at the point when the therapist cannot do more for the patient.

One needs little power to hurt someone; a lone terrorist can wreck a skyscraper, but it takes a crew of competent builders to build a house. I defined power as the ability to satisfy needs, and acceptance as the willingness to do so (Wolman, 1974). An ethical psychotherapist is *strong* and *friendly,* that is, able and determined to satisfy the patient's need for professional help.

Competent healing professionals should know when to terminate their services. They do not discharge hospitalized patients prematurely nor do they discontinue their ambulatory services before the patient is ready. By the same token, they do not continue their services beyond the necessary point.

The objective judgment must be backed up by the moral value judgment. "Thou shalt not do to anyone anything you don't wish to be done to you," is the chief ethical principle. In my supervisory work with younger colleagues, I have repeatedly posed the same question to them: "Would you like your doctor or dentist to keep you or your spouse or your child in treatment beyond the point of necessary professional help? Keep this well in mind, and terminate psychotherapy as soon as the *patient* does not need it or as soon as *you* are unable to do more for the patient. In the latter case, refer the patient to a more competent colleague."

Termination of a Successful Psychotherapy

In many cases psychotherapists feel that their treatment goals have been attained. A patient who was continuously acting in a self-defeating manner has finally become a rational individual and acts in a positive, constructive manner. An impulsive, irresponsible adult whose behavior resembled infantile temper tantrums has "grown up" and begun to reflect upon his behavior and to exercise realistic judgment and self-control.

The nature of the terminating phase of psychotherapy depends on the nature of the treatment, whether it follows in the footsteps of Freud, Sullivan, Wolpe, or of any other school. The common denominator of the terminal phase is the awareness of both the therapist and the patient that the task has been more or less accomplished and further therapeutic interaction would be superfluous. Very rarely any of the colleagues with whom I worked or whom I supervised went beyond this point and tried unnecessarily to continue the therapeutic process. Certainly it is not too much to expect from a clinical psychologist, a psychiatrist, and a psychiatric social worker what one expects from an honest repairman, handyman, electrician, or plumber. In practically all cases I know of the psychotherapists were happy to see the successful completion of their work.

But even the most competent and most ethical psychotherapist cannot avoid some thorny questions. How successful was the therapeutic success? How adequate was the psychotherapeutic process? And, finally, can psychotherapy guard a patient against future conflicts and relapses?

Perhaps it is my own shortcoming as a psychotherapist, but I do not believe that psychotherapy of any type can ever be perfectly finished. Suppose the aim of psychotherapy was the removal of certain symptoms, such as bed wetting, insomnia, anorexia, or a phobia—could one criticize the therapist for not preventing recurrence of the same or similar symptoms or their substitution for other symptoms? Is the same expected from any other healing profession as dentistry or surgery or internal medicine? A dentist can fill a cavity; can he prevent, once and for all, further tooth decay or another cavity? Can a surgeon prevent future bone fractures? Does a cure of a disease prevent future diseases?

I explain to my patients that psychotherapy does not have a clear-cut ending, but there is no need to continue in (and pay for) a patient-therapist setting beyond its clear-cut usefulness. Freud called psychoanalysis an after-education and Alexander (1948) called it "emotional reeducation." I explain to my patients that as long as they will live, they will have problems and hardships. Our work has served its purpose if it has brought about (1) resolution of the problems the patient came with, and (2) strengthening of his personality.

The second task is of utmost importance for future behavior. Problems and hardships, frustrations and setbacks occur in life, but the terminal phase of psychotherapy must be directed toward enabling the patient to solve problems and cope with hardships. The psychotherapeutic process should teach the patient how to face the ups and downs of life. Psychotherapy should foster the courage to live and the ability to act in a rational way.

My own therapeutic technique is a far-reaching modification of Freud's method (Wolman, 1975). I distinguish three therapeutic phases, namely, (1) the analytic phase, (2) search for identity, and (3) becoming, self-realization. The aim of the analytic phase is the resolution of past conflicts that prevent the individual from attaining psychological maturity. The second phase is devoted to increasing one's self-awareness and discovery of one's desires, wishes, aptitudes, and options. In the third phase, the individual should be able to choose his or her pattern of life and have the courage to be oneself and the wisdom to cope realistically with whatever goes on in his or her life (Wolman, in press). As soon as the patient is capable of making his or her own decision and does not need therapeutic help, the therapy should be terminated.

Toward the end of treatment I usually explain my "theory of the Broken Knee Syndrome" to the patient. I say, "Let us imagine that someone broke a knee and underwent surgery. Let us assume that the surgery was successful and the knee is no longer broken, although it may remain quite sensitive for years to come. Of course, the patient should walk around and go about his or her business as usual, but it is not advisable to take unnecessary risks and/or overexert oneself. It is quite possible that on a rainy day or in case of exertion or fatigue the knee will react with pain. The patient will not need a new surgery, but it would be advisable to call on the surgeon for a checkup. Of course, should someone hit the cured knee with a sledge-hammer, the knee will require new medical care."

Limited Improvement

The task of the therapist is to be of service to people who come seeking help. When Freud was asked what is the best way to terminate psychoanalytic treatment, he said "to carry it out correctly" (Glover, 1972, p. 152).

Not every therapist is able to treat every patient as the other chapters of this volume explain. When a therapist feels that the task to be performed is not within his or her area of competence, the best way is tactfully to transfer the patient to a colleague who is equipped to deal with that particular case. This does not mean termination of therapy in general, but termination of a therapeutic interaction with a certain therapist.

For instance, I have been quite unsuccessful with certain patients (Wolman, 1972). Some of my quite successful colleagues have told me about their own therapeutic limitations. On a few occasions, severely deteriorated patients who spent years in mental hospitals have been referred to me and, after initial consultations, I have refused to work with them. I assume that other more gifted and/or more experienced therapists could have helped these unfortunate individuals, but I did not believe I was capable of successfully treating some of the badly deteriorated cases. It was my moral obligation to terminate my work after a few sessions and to refer the patients to a more competent colleague.

Some limitations are related to the nature of a particular type of disorder and a particular effect the said disorder has had on a particular patient. Obviously, whatever exists exists in a certain quantity, and there are apparently different levels and degrees of physical and mental health. Even the most competent therapist cannot attain the same level of improvement with different people. Some patients can make fantastic progress, while others may only show a rather limited improvement. A correct diagnosis is one of the main prerequisites of successful treatment, and a therapeutic strategy must be linked to a precise diagnostic evaluation of every single case (Wolman, 1978). Moreover, it is not enough to determine that a patient's case belongs to a certain clinical category; it is imperative to view the patient's personality, and his past and present environment, and to determine how far one can go in therapeutic work and what level of improvement presents the best possible outcome for the particular patient.

In my own work with schizophrenic patients, and supervision of younger colleagues who treated schizophrenics, I have developed a rather cautious and perhaps a timid attitude. I do not believe that one can always attain the same level of improvement. It is my feeling (I am using the word "feeling," owing to a lack of objective evidence) that therapists must not press their luck and try to eradicate whatever problems schizophrenics might have. My attitude is by no means universally accepted, and it might reflect both my theoretical views as well as my own shortcomings. Ultimately, as emphasized above, psychotherapy is more being that doing, and every psychotherapist uses his or her own personality no less than the skills he or she has acquired.

I do believe that I have been quite successful treating schizophrenic patients. In the numerous cases of schizophrenics I worked with (described in two books and several chapters and journal articles in the last thirty years), I have avoided setting absolute goals. Every new patient in a hospital or private practice has presented a challenge to what I hoped to be able to achieve. On a few occasions I refused to treat patients I doubted I could help. In most cases I was quite cautious not to go beyond an improvement that could be reasonably expected. I called this rule, "One step up" (Wolman, 1966); it implies cautious support of neurotic defense mechanisms and acceptance of milder symptoms in order to prevent a total collapse of personality structure. I was afraid that going beyond that point might cause severe regression. Trying to repair a damaged structure one must keep in mind how far one can go and how strong are one's foundations. When the foundations are not very strong, it might not be safe to be hasty. On many occasions I terminated my work with schizophrenics and settled for limited improvement.

Patients Have the Right to Know

Glover (1972, pp. 136ff) has noticed that "practitioners who advance in seniority tend to find their case lists loaded with disorders of intractable nature many of which have gone from pillar to post under the care of a variety of therapists of every description." Even cases that seem to be exceedingly difficult, however, and capable at best only of slight improvement, need not be denied treatment. Glover continued: "Organic physicians do not countenance for a moment such high-handed, arbitrary and rather cowardly policies." Thus, "the onus should lie on the diagnostic and prognostic skill of the consultant, who should of course forewarn or advise the prospective patient of the possible outcome of his treatment, whether favorable or unfavorable."

Patients have the right to know. Whenever my own disciples or supervisees have questioned this rule, I reminded them unequivocally of their own rights as patients in didactic psychotherapy or in any other healing situation. Psychotherapists are not supermen and must avoid megalomania and conceited, self-righteous attitudes. Every human being has the right to know what kind of service he or she receives or is about to receive, and psychotherapists must abide by this universal rule.

Glover (1972, p. 145) recommended that "the obvious course for the analyst to follow in difficult cases is to warn the patient beforehand that, whether after treatment he is better or not, he cannot expect more from this obviously promising form of therapy."

When Therapy Fails

Defeat is indeed a bitter and difficult pill to swallow and even more difficult to concede. It takes a great deal of strength to admit one's weakness. It is impossible always to be successful with all patients, and every therapist can tell many unpleasant and even embarrassing stories of his or her failures. Small wonder that psychiatric and psychological literature is full of descriptions of successful treatment and rather poor in accounting for frustrating cases and embarassing defeats (Eysenck, 1961; Claghorn, 1976; Horwitz, 1974; Simon, 1977; Strupp, 1969; Strupp et al., 1977; Wolman, 1972, 1976a).

In 1972, I published a collective volume, *Success and Failure in Psychoanalysis and Psychotherapy* (Wolman, 1972), for which I had asked several leading clinicians, among them E. Glover, L. S. Kubie and others to write on the subject, "When and Why I failed my patients."

Aaron Stein (1972) listed the following causes of failure (pp. 44–45): The general factors leading to failures in all forms of psychotherapy are:

1. Incorrect diagnosis and, therefore, selecting the wrong form of treatment; this stems from errors in estimating the amount of psychopathology. Treatment is begun with patients who present mild symptoms which later are found to mask very severe disorders often inaccessible to exploratory psychotherapy.
2. Untoward external conditions
   a. Where external conditions are so unfavorable that actual gain through remaining sick seems of greater value than the advantages of good health.
   b. Where the attitude of the family supports neurotic (or psychotic) manifestations in the patient.
   c. Reality factors—education, class, economic status, and the effect of trauma such as illness and loss.
3. Constitutional factors—strength of instincts and of conflicts centering around penis envy in women and passive attitudes in men.
4. Unfavorable modifications of the ego—severe characterological disturbances, and so on.
5. Transference and countertransference.

There are a great many reasons why a particular well-qualified therapist fails in a particular case, but it is the therapist's moral obligation to admit such failure, and in a most tactful way explain it to the patient and terminate the work that does not serve the patient's well-being.

How to Terminate

So far I have described what I consider the ethical ways of termination of psychotherapy, with the emphasis on *when* it should be terminated. But *how* to terminate must also be asked, and it is not an easy question to answer.

In fact, there is no way one could suggest a uniform, good-for-all way *how* to terminate psychotherapy. The therapist must take into account several variables, among them:

1. Was it, in his or her opinion, a successful treatment?
2. If yes, how successful was it?
3. What could be expected in the future?
4. Was it a failure?
5. How sensitive is the patient?

And there are several other variables, such as the patient's age, occupation, friends and relatives, family obligations, cultural environment, and so on and on.

The therapist's explanations must take all possible factors into consideration and weigh his or her words carefully. There is, however, one common denominator of all manners of terminating the psychotherapy: the *well-being of the patient*.

REFERENCES

ALEXANDER, F. *Fundamentals of psychoanalysis.* New York: Norton, 1948.

AMERICAN PSYCHOLOGICAL ASSOCIATION. *Ethical standards for psychologists.* Washington, D.C.: APA, 1967.

AMERICAN PSYCHOLOGICAL ASSOCIATION. *Ethics, money matters, main focus at Council. APA Monitor*, 1980, **11**, 1–11.

BERKOWITZ, L. (ed.). *Advances in experimental social psychology*, Vol. 6. New York: Academic Press, 1972.

BORDIN, E. S. *Research strategies in psychotherapy.* New York: Wiley, 1974.

CARROLL, J. L., and REST, J. R. Moral development. In B. B. Wolman (ed.), *Handbook of developmental psychology.* Englewood Cliffs, N.J.: Prentice Hall, 1981.

CLAGHORN, J. L. (ed.). *Successful therapy.* New York: Bruner-Mazel, 1976.

COLBY, A., GIBBS, J., and KOHLBERG, L. *Standard form scoring manual.* Cambridge, Mass.: Center for Moral Education, 1980.

DAMON, W. (ed.). *Moral development: New directions for child development.* San Francisco: Jossey-Bass, 1978.

DURKHEIM, E. *Moral education.* New York: Free Press, 1961.

EYSENCK, H. J. The effects of psychotherapy. In H. J. Eysenck (ed.), *Handbook of abnormal psychology.* New York: Basic Books, 1961.

FIRESIDE, H. *Soviet psychoprisons.* New York: Norton, 1979.

FREUD, S. Observation on transference-love. In *Collected papers*, Vol. 2. New York: Basic Books, 1959. (Originally published 1915.)

FREUD, S. Analysis terminable and interminable. In *Collected papers*, Vol. 5. New York: Basic Books, 1959. (Originally published 1937.)

GELLER, J. D., and BERZINS, J. I. A-B distinction in a sample of prominent psychotherapists. *Journal of Consulting and Clinical Psychology*, 1976, **44**, 77–82.

GLOVER, E. Remarks on success and failure in psychoanalysis and psychotherapy. In B. B. Wolman (ed.), *Success and failure in psychoanalysis and psychotherapy*. New York: Macmillan, 1972.

GOMES-SCHWARTZ, D., HADLEY, S. W., and STRUPP, H. S. Individual psychotherapy and behavior therapy. *Annual Review of Psychology*, 1978, **29**, 435–471.

GUREL, B. D. Ethical problems in psychology. In B. B. Wolman (ed.), *International Encyclopedia of Psychiatry, Psychology, Psychoanalysis, and Neurology*, Vol. 4. New York: Aesculapius Publishers, 1977.

HELLMAN, L. *Scoundrel time*. Boston: Little Brown, 1976.

HOFFMAN, M. L. Moral development. In P. H. Mussen (ed.), *Carmichael's manual of child development*. New York: Wiley, 1970.

HOFFMAN, M. L. Development of moral thought, feeling, and behavior. *American Psychologist*, 1979, **34**, 958–966.

HORWITZ, L. *Clinical prediction in psychotherapy*. New York: Aronson, 1974.

IBSEN, H. *An enemy of the people*. New York: Random House, 1950.

KOHLBERG, L. Stage and sequence: The cognitive-developmental approach to socialization. In D. Goslin (ed.), *Handbook of socialization*. Chicago: Rand McNally, 1969.

KOHLBERG, L. *The meaning and measurement of moral development*. Worcester, Mass.: Clark University Press, 1979.

LATANÉ, B., and DARLEY, J. *The unresponsive bystander: Why doesn't he help?* New York: Appleton, 1970.

LAZARUS, A. A. Multimodal behavioral treatment of depression. *Behavior Therapy*, 1974, **5**, 549–554.

LAZARUS, A. A., and WILSON, G. T. Behavior modification: Clinical and experimental perspectives. In B. B. Wolman (ed.), *The therapist's handbook*. New York: Van Nostrand Reinhold, 1976.

LESSE, S. (ed.). *An evaluation of the results of psychotherapies*. Springfield, Ill.: Thomas, 1968.

LUBORSKY, L. Helping alliances in psychotherapy. In J. L. Claghorn (ed.), *Successful therapy*. New York: Brunner-Mazel, 1976.

MACIVER, R. M. *The prevention and control of delinquency*. New York: Atherton, 1966.

MARGENAU, H. *Science and ethics*. Princeton, N.J.: Van Nostrand, 1964.

PIAGET, J. *The moral judgment of the child*. New York: Harcourt, 1932.

REST, J. R. *Development in judging moral issues*. Minneapolis: Minnesota University Press, 1979.

SIMON, G. C. Ethical and social issues in professional psychology. In B. B. Wolman (ed.), *International encyclopedia of psychiatry, psychology, psychoanalysis and neurology*, Vol. 4. New York: Aesculapius Publishers, 1977.

STEIN, A. Causes of failure in psychoanalytic psychotherapy. In B. B. Wolman (ed.), *Success and failure in psychoanalysis and psychotherapy*. New York: Macmillan, 1972.

STRUPP, H. H. Ferment in psychoanalysis and psychotherapy. In B. B. Wolman (ed.), *Success and failure in psychoanalysis and psychotherapy.* New York: Macmillan, 1972.

STRUPP, H. H., FOX, R. E., and LESSLER, K. *Patients view their psychotherapists.* Baltimore: Johns Hopkins University Press, 1969.

STRUPP, H. H., HADLEY, S. W., and GOMES-SCHWARTZ, B. *Psychotherapy for better or worse: An analysis of the problem of negative effects.* New York: Aronson, 1977.

WITENBERG, E. G. How not to success in psychotherapy. In B. B. Wolman (ed.), *Success and failure in psychoanalysis and psychotherapy.* New York: Macmillan, 1972.

WOLMAN, B. B. Interactional psychotherapy with schizophrenics. *Psychotherapy: Theory, Research and Practice,* 1966, **3**, 61–70.

WOLMAN, B. B. (ed.). *Success and failure in psychoanalysis and psychotherapy.* New York: Macmillan, 1972.

WOLMAN, B. B. *Call no man normal.* New York: International Universities Press, 1973.

WOLMAN, B. B. Power and acceptance as determinants of social relations. *International Journal of Group Tensions,* 1974, **4**, 151–183.

WOLMAN, B. B. Principles of interactional psychotherapy. *Psychotherapy: Theory, Research and Practice,* 1975, **12**, 149–159.

WOLMAN, B. B. (ed.). *The therapist's handbook: Treatment methods of mental disorders.* New York: Van Nostrand Reinhold, 1976. (a)

WOLMAN, B. B. *The process of treatment.* In *The therapist's handbook: Treatment methods of mental disorders.* New York: Van Nostrand Reinhold, 1976. (b)

WOLMAN, B. B. Moral principles. *International Journal of Group Tensions,* 1976, **6**, 1–4. (c)

WOLMAN, B. B. (ed.). *Clinical diagnosis of mental disorders.* New York: Plenum, 1978.

WOLMAN, B. B. Interactional theory. In B. B. Wolman (ed.), *Handbook of developmental psychology.* Englewood Cliffs, N.J.: Prentice Hall, 1981.

WOLMAN, B. B. International psychotherapy. In B. B. Wolman (ed.), *The therapist's handbook,* rev. ed. New York: Van Nostrand Reinhold, in press.

PART III

ETHICS AND TREATMENT APPROACHES

Ethical Issues in the Practice of Behavior Therapy

Stephen G. Flanagan
Robert Paul Liberman

Behavior therapy has its roots in the experimental analysis of behavior as developed by B. F. Skinner and his associates, and in a broader definition of experimental psychology.[1] From the early experimental work of Watson and Rayner (1920) and Jones (1924) on the acquisition and extinction of fear responses in children until the early 1960s, behavior therapy was tied to a narrow stimulus-response paradigm. Behavior therapists of the 1960s struggled for identity and recognition from a mental health establishment which was predominantly biological and psychodynamic in its orientations.

With increasing clinical success, experimental replications, and broader applications, came a phenomenal expansion in the behavioral literature and in the number of clinicians identifying themselves as behavior therapists. Expansion also occurred in conceptual models to encompass cognition and private events (Mahoney, 1974; Cautela, 1970), and self-directed as well as externally controlled behavior modification (Thoreson and Mahoney, 1974). Behavior therapy developed a broader base in experimental psychology, social learning, and empiricism (Bandura, 1969, 1974). Not all behavior therapists would subscribe to or celebrate a liberalized and expanded conceptual model for behavior therapy, but it is generally accepted that behavioral approaches to treatment have entered the mainstream in mental health, in services for the developmentally disabled, in medicine, and in education. The emerging field of behavioral medicine has involved behavior therapists and behavior analysts in the delivery of services to new patient populations and promises even wider dissemination and application of behavioral technology.

A suitable definition of behavior therapy, which reflects its broad base in contemporary practice, is provided by Linehan et al. (1978) for the Association for Advancement of Behavior Therapy:

> Behavior Therapy is a particular kind of therapy that involves the application of findings from behavioral science research to help individuals change in ways they would like to change. There is an emphasis in behavior therapy on checking up on how effective the therapy is by monitoring and evaluating the individual's progress. Most behaviorally-oriented therapists believe that the current environment is most important in affecting the person's present behavior. Early life experiences, long time intrapsychic conflicts, or the individual's personality structure are considered to be of less importance than what is happening in the person's life at the present time. The procedures used in behavior therapy are generally intended to improve the individual's self-control by expanding the person's skills, abilities, and independence. [p.18]

The primary defining features of contemporary behavior therapy are: (1) objectivity in the selection of target behaviors for intervention; (2) specification of the intervention procedures; and (3) insistence on data-based assessment and treatment evaluation.

Because of its striking success and overt specification of procedures and techniques, behavior therapy has been singled out for special concern in the protection of individuals receiving this mode of treatment. One difficulty in establishing ethical standards for behavior modification is the myriad types of settings and people dealt with by behavior modifiers. Informed consent, for example, is readily achievable and meaningful when an adult voluntarily goes to a therapist for treatment and relief of a self-defined problem. When involuntarily committed patients, or prisoners, or persons with mental retardation, however, are given the chance to participate in an institutional token economy, it is by no means clear that they can give truly voluntary consent. Prisons and institutions are closed societies that control and restrict human contact and flow of information, and consequently restrict a person's ability to evaluate the advantages and hazards of offered treatment (Bach-y-Rita, 1974).

Ethical problems facing the behavior therapist may stem in part from the restrictiveness of some settings in which behavior therapy is practiced. An equal challenge to ethical practice is posed by the nature of the clients who are served by behavioral clinicians, such as people with chronic psychoses or schizophrenia, or persons with severe and profound levels of mental retardation. These clients are often legally or functionally incapable of advocacy in their own best interests.

Behavior therapists are very sensitive to ethical practice, partially in light of the vulnerability of the field to "bad press" and public misinformation; but more to the point, a highly effective technology of behavior change may be used for inappropriate ends, abused, or misapplied, with serious consequences for the victim. This concern is consonant with general trends in society for greater accountability of service providers, as well as growing recognition and protection of the rights of prisoners, mental patients, children, and persons with handicaps. The Association for Advancement of Behavior Therapy (AABT) has published a set of guidelines for ethical behavioral treatment (Azrin et al., 1977). AABT has also established a Special Interest Group on Ethical and Legal Issues (Finesmith, 1979a), and provided expert consultation on guidelines for behavioral interventions by various states and treatment agencies (Stolz, 1977; Finesmith, 1979b).

The AABT ethical guidelines depicted in Table 1 are of particular note because they highlight questions relevant for all types of treatment modalities, not just for behavior therapy. The guidelines focus on eight areas of concern which are common to all psychosocial and somatic therapies: (1) consideration of the goals of treatment; (2) choice of treatment methods; (3) voluntary client participation; (4) protection of the interests of subordinated clients; (5) adequacy of treatment; (6) confidentiality of the treatment relationship; (7) referral of clients; and (8) therapist qualifications. The AABT guidelines in Table 1 are supplemented by additional guidelines, inserted by the present authors in italics, which apply to institutional settings. The AABT Committee noted that "the questions related to each issue have been cast in a general manner that applies to all types of interventions, and not solely and

TABLE 1.   Ethical Issues for Human Services

The following set of guidelines for ethical treatment has been prepared by a committee of the AABT and was adopted by the board of directors in 1977. The present authors have inserted, in italics, some additional guidelines. The committee noted that "rather than recommending a list of prescriptions and proscriptions, the committee agreed to focus on critical ethical issues of central importance to human services," and "the questions related to each issue have deliberately been cast in a general manner that applies to all types of interventions, and not solely or specifically to behavior therapy. The committee felt strongly that issues directed specifically to behavior therapists might imply erroneously that behavior therapy was in some way more in need of ethical concern than non-behaviorally-oriented therapies" (Azrin et al., 1977).

A. Have the goals of treatment been adequately considered?
  1. To insure that goals are explicit, are they written?
  2. Has the client's understanding of the goals been assured by having the client restate them orally or in writing?
  3. Have the therapist and client agreed on the goals of therapy?
  4. Will serving the client's interests be contrary to the interests of other persons?
  5. Will serving the client's immediate interests be contrary to the client's long-term interests?

(continued)

TABLE 1.   Ethical Issues for Human Services (*continued*)

6. *Have advisory boards or human rights committees been consulted in the case of pursuing novel treatment goals in an institutional setting?*
7. *Have the "mediators" of treatment (e.g., nurses, technicians, aides) been involved in the process of goal setting?*
8. *Do the goals of treatment include plans to restore the client to a less restrictive environment where feasible?*
9. *Do the goals of treatment include positive, constructive, and fuctional behavioral elements as contrasted with only suppressing undesirable behavior or instigating behaviors which are of convenience to the therapist or institution?*

B. Has the choice of treatment methods been adequately considered?
1. Does the published literature show the procedure to be the best one available for that problem?
2. If no literature exists regarding the treatment method, is the method consistent with generally accepted practice?
3. Has the client been told of alternative procedures that might be preferred by the client on the basis of significant differences in discomfort, treatment time, cost, or degree of demonstrated effectiveness?
4. If a treatment procedure is publicly, legally, or professionally controversial, has formal professional consultation been obtained, has the reaction of the affected segment of the public been adequately considered, and have the alternative treatment methods been more closely reexamined and reconsidered?
5. *Has the setting in which treatment is to occur been evaluated so that interfering conditions can be corrected and facilitative conditions be implemented? Does the implementation of the treatment produce a net increase or enrichment of rewards and behavioral options for the client?*
6. *Has the transfer of treatment effects to non-treatment situations been adequately considered?*

C. Is the client's participation voluntary?
1. Have possible sources of coercion on the client's participation been considered?
2. If treatment is legally mandated, has the available range of treatments and therapists been offered?
3. Can the client withdraw from treatment without a penalty or financial loss that exceeds actual clinical costs?
4. *If the treatment occurs in an institution, has the client been permitted access to sources of information and advice about the treatment in addition to the treating agent? Has access to relatives or professional consultants of the client's own choosing been made available to the client before and during treatment?*

D. When another person or an agency is empowered to arrange for therapy, have the interests of the subordinated client been sufficiently considered?
1. Has the subordinated client been informed of the treatment objectives and participated in the choice of treatment procedures?

   2. Where the subordinated client's competence to decide is limited, have the client as well as the guardian participated in the treatment discussions to the extent that the client's abilities permit?

   3. If the interests of the subordinated person and the superordinated persons or agency conflict, have attempts been made to reduce the conflict by dealing with both interests?

   4. *Does the subordinated client have access to an advocate or ombudsman, and lawyer?*

   5. *In the case of novel, experimental, or aversive treatment, has the client's guardian or a human rights advocate been consulted and their participation obtained?*

E. Has the adequacy of treatment been evaluated?

   1. Have quantitative measures of the problem and its progress been obtained?

   2. Have the measures of the problem and its progress been made available to the client during treatment?

   3. *Is there evidence that the program was carried out consistently and as planned when "mediators" of treatment are involved?*

   4. *Is there evidence of no unintended harmful consequences or side effects of the program?*

F. Has the confidentiality of the treatment relationship been protected?

   1. Has the client been told who has access to the records?

   2. Are records available only to authorized persons?

   3. *Is written permission obtained from the client before information about treatment is provided to others?*

G. Does the therapist refer the clients to other therapists when necessary?

   1. If treatment is unsuccessful, is the client referred to other therapists?

   2. Has the client been told that if dissatisfied with the treatment, referral will be made?

   3. *Are institutional resources made available to provide specialized services which are not "routinely" available, for otherwise refractory clients who require them?*

H. Is the therapist qualified to provide treatment?

   1. Has the therapist had training or experience in treating problems like the client's?

   2. If deficits exist in the therapist's qualifications, has the client been informed?

   3. If the therapist is not adequately qualified, is the client referred to other therapists, or has supervision by a qualified therapist been provided? Is the client informed of the supervisory relation?

   4. If the treatment is administered by mediators, have the mediators been adequately supervised by a qualified therapist?

   5. *Does the therapist obtain the latest information on treatment methods for the client's problem, such as attending workshops and institutes, reading journals and books, and participating in other continuing education activities?*

specifically to the practice of behavior therapy. The committee felt strongly that issues directed specifically to behavior therapists might erroneously imply that behavior therapy was in some way more in need of ethical concern than non-behaviorally-oriented therapies" (Azrin et al., 1977). We shall refer to the guidelines, by designating their letter and number from the table, as we review illustrative treatment programs that either subvert or sustain good ethical practice.

In this chapter, the authors present several cases of abusive control of others done in the guise or name of behavior therapy by persons inadequately trained or experienced to conduct behavioral treatment. These infrequent incidents provide dramatic evidence of unethical practices which are contrasted with the usually high ethical principles and practices of behavior therapy. The remainder of the chapter focuses on four major areas: (1) the selection of goals, planning, and delivery of services; (2) consent and protection of individual rights; (3) the professional therapist's responsibilities and qualifications, and control of service delivery; and (4) guidelines and regulations as ethical supports. One model of excellent ethical practice in behavior therapy, the Teaching Family, is reviewed from the ethical point of view.

Patient Abuse in the Guise of Behavior Therapy

Among the earliest examples of behavior therapy were studies using aversive conditioning methods to change sexual preferences of homosexuals, exhibitionists, and pedophiles. Most of these programs were carried out ethically with the greatest consideration given to informed consent, careful evaluation and screening, and the voluntary nature of the treatment contract. With the exception of a few studies, however, the early examples of behavioral treatment of homosexuality aimed only at the reduction or elimination of homosexual attraction and arousal and did not employ means for establishing or strengthening heterosocial and heterosexual atraction and skills. This unimodal approach to treatment disregards one of the tenets of ethical behavior therapy; namely, to strengthen adaptive behavior when weakening or eliminating maladaptive behavior (guideline A-9). More recently, clinicians and researchers have adhered to this tenet in their work with sexual deviations and gender identity problems (Rekers, 1977; Barlow, Reynolds, and Agras, 1973; Birk, Huddleston, Miller, and Cohler, 1971).

When carried out in total institutions with involuntary patients, treatment of homosexuality has sometimes been a travesty of behavior therapy. In the past, without currently operating constraints and safeguards provided by human subjects and human rights committees and administrative regulations on aversive conditioning, some professionals used callous and inhumane punishment procedures under the guise of "behavior modification" of homosexuality.

At one maximum security institution, the medical director, aided by psychologists (who did not have training in behavior therapy), carried out aversive treatment of men caught in homosexual activities, even mutually consenting relations. These inmates were brought, days later, to a treatment room in a dark corner of the hospital, where they were injected with anectine, a drug that produces muscle paralysis. Anectine is used in surgical procedures to relax muscles. It is also beneficially used in electroconvulsive therapy, so that the resulting convulsions don't produce bone fractures or muscle bruises. In this case, the anectine was used to paralyze the inmates for up to a minute while they were fully conscious. During this time, they were in a frightening state of suspended animation, unable to breathe or move, because their muscles were paralyzed. During the time they were under the influence of the anectine, they were harangued by the doctor about the evils of homosexuality and how bad they were. They were warned that future homosexual activity would lead to additional anectine "treatments." This was what they called "aversive conditioning" and "behavior modification." This blatant use of punishment was even published in a professional journal. In light of the ethical practice guidelines, this approach failed to gain clients' agreement to the goals (A-3); advisory review was not obtained (A-6); and positive, constructive goals were omitted (A-9). Safeguards were not observed for a treatment which was new and could be expected to be controversial (section B); and clients' participation was involuntary without alternatives (section C). Finally, the glib labeling of the procedures as "behavior modification" was done despite the lack of training or experience in behavior modification by the practitioners (H-1,5).

When a behaviorally trained psychiatrist, the late Michael Serber, came to this institution to work, he was aghast at this subversion of psychiatric treatment, and misinterpretation of behavior therapy. Serber protested so vigorously within the institution that the anectine procedure was stopped. When he protested to the American Psychiatric Association and requested that their ethics committee investigate this procedure, the result was only a perfunctory committee visit followed by a whitewash. The professionals involved suffered no penalties, not even a censure of their activities. It seemed that the American Psychiatric Association was more concerned with a scandal that might hurt the prestige of psychiatry than with enforcing ethical practice.

Serber took the ethical imperatives seriously in his own work with homosexuals. For example, two years before the American Psychiatric Association deleted homosexuality from its diagnostic manual as a category of mental illness, Serber was bringing gay liberation members to his institution to work with the homosexual, pedophilic inmates. Under Serber's supervision, and with their voluntary agreement, the inmates learned more mature social skills and age-appropriate ways of getting their sexual needs satisfied without approaching minors and engaging in child molestation (guidelines A-3,4,8,9; B-4,5,C). In his private therapy for couples with sexual dysfunctions, he pioneered in the ethical use of videotapes. With their consent, he made videotapes of their lovemaking and then used the tapes for feedback and instruction aimed at improving their sexual interactions. To safeguard the couple's privacy and confidentiality, he erased the tapes at the end of treatment in their presence (principle F-1,2).

Rivaling the anectine horror for breach of ethical principles was an "operant conditioning" program in a Vietnamese mental hospital, implemented during the American intervention in Indochina in 1966 (Cotter, 1967). During the war in Vietnam, the American Medical Association had an exchange program whereby physicians from the United States could donate three months of their time to provide medical services to the people of South Vietnam. Cotter, a California psychiatrist, volunteered for this AMA program. Prior to his departure, he decided to learn something about behavior therapy which was then in its infancy, and which he felt might be relevant to the large-scale psychiatric problems of an underdeveloped country. He visited the Neuropsychiatric Institute at UCLA where he observed the careful, systematic, and ethical use of operant conditioning with autistic children for teaching speech and self-care skills through the use of food and social reinforcement. He was impressed with demonstrations of the effects of food on motivating children to improve their behavior. He also paid a one-day visit to one of the earliest token economy wards at Patton State Hospital. This was the extent of his preparation for using behavior therapy with hospitalized patients in Vietnam. Since adequate training for competence in behavior therapy is of ethical importance (H-1,5), Cotter can be criticized for premature and unskilled entry into a new field.

He went to Bien Hoa Hospital in South Vietnam and found the medical conditions there overcrowded and atrocious. Patients were dying at the rate of one or two a day, which was ten or twenty times the usual rate for this hospital in previous years. Dysentery, tuberculosis, and malaria were rampant, and people were dying of malnutrition because food supplies were very low. Cotter also discovered that the tranquilizers which had been previously donated by an American drug firm had also been used up; thus, the patients were without food, without tranquilizers, and with a lot of physical disease.

After only a few days of casual observation and discussion with Vietnamese colleagues, Cotter decided on goals of treatment for the patients on the wards at Bien Hoa. The decision was to use a mass approach to "operant conditioning," with the long-term goal of getting patients out of the hospital and reducing the census. The short-term goal was to involve the patients in a three-month work program in the hospital as a way of preparing them for discharge. From an ethical perspective of informed consent, it is doubtful that the patients *understood* the goals; they certainly did not participate in choosing them (A-1, 2, 3).

Dr. Cotter went to each ward with a translator and asked, "Who wants to go home?" About one-third of the patients raised their hands. Then he said, "Well, you're going to have to work in order to support yourself when you go home, so you might as well start now. We can't let you go home and live off your relatives." Here is where Cotter made another ethical error—not realizing, when he set treatment goals, that support of an ill relative by the family is much more culturally accepted in Vietnam than it is in the United States (D-2, 3). When Cotter asked for patients to volunteer for in-hospital work details, he got about 10 percent of the patients to volunteer. With that as a "baseline," he decided to employ so-called behavior therapy that would be effective in motivating more of these patients to work. He came to the ward the next day, and through his Vietnamese interpreter, said "People who are too sick to work need treatment. Treatment starts tomorrow. Treatment is electroconvulsive therapy. It is not painful and there if nothing to be afraid of. When you are well enough to start work after receiving this treatment, let us know and we will stop treatment." The next day, 120 unmodified electroconvulsive therapies (ECI) were given to patients at the hospital.

Unmodified ECT is given without anesthesia or muscle relaxants, so the patients are conscious up to the time they go into a convulsion. In an article that was audaciously printed in the *American Journal of Psychiatry* (Cotter, 1966), Cotter defended his use of unmodified ECT, stating that because of the small size of muscles in the Vietnamese, none of them complained of symptoms of fracture or compression of the vertebrae which are common side effects when ECT is administered without anesthesia or muscle relaxants. These pejorative and erroneous anatomical references were similar to the ethnocentric views of the American military, which pronounced that the Vietnamese don't value life as much as Westerners.

ECT was given three times a week to all the patients who refused to go to work. Gradually, "improvement" in their behavior was noted, and more and more volunteered for work. Cotter acknowledged that, in many cases, patients began working because of their dislike or fear of the ECT and not because of any therapeutic benefit of ECT. Using behavior therapy jargon to legitimize the approach, he called his ECT-torture an example of "negative reinforcement" treatment (C-1,2;E-1,2).

Flushed with the success of his first venture into "operant condition-ing," Cotter went next to a female ward of 130 patients where he showed himself to be not only an unethical psychiatrist, but also a male chauvinist. He wrote in the *American Journal of Psychiatry,* "I expected the women to be more pliable. I hoped for quicker and better results with ECT from them. But instead, they didn't respond very well. Maybe it was because of their greater passivity or the women's attitude that success in life is achieved when they can be idle, when they don't have to move out of their chairs. At the end of 20 days of ECT therapy, only 15 out of 130 women were working." Cotter stopped the ECT and he said to the re-maining women at one of his grim ward rounds, "Look, we doctors, nurses, and technicians all have to work for our food, our clothes and our rent money. Why should you have it better? Your muscles are just as good as ours. After today, if you don't work, you don't eat. Who's ready to start work immediately, rather than missing any meals?"

Thus, his second so-called operant conditioning procedure was to deprive the female patients of meals, unless they worked. On the first day, twelve chose to work. The next day, after twenty-four hours without food, ten other women volunteered to work. After two days of missing meals, another ten volunteered. After three days of starvation, the re-maining women all agreed to work. This is a striking demonstration of the short-term effectiveness of ruthless and inhumane hospital man-agement under the guise of behavior therapy.

Cotter kept very busy during his two-month stint, giving ECT to men and making sure that the idle women didn't get the little food that was available. But toward the end of his stay, he was faced with the problem of making good on his promise to allow the patients to return home if they had worked in the hospital. He knew that it was going to be impos-sible to find their relatives and to resettle them in a country that was in turmoil with warfare. Cotter's dilemma over fulfilling his commitment to the patients was settled one afternoon over cocktails at the officer's club. He fell into conversation with a colonel who commanded the American Special Forces (Green Beret) troops in that area. The Green Berets were having difficulty recruiting Viet Cong prisoners and local inhabitants to work in agricultural fields being used as pacification projects. They needed Vietnamese people to serve as farm laborers to grow crops. Cotter and the colonel readily agreed that the "recovered" mental pa-tients could be hired by the U.S. Special Forces to form ten-person teams to go out and work in the American-supervised fields. This work as-signment was to be the community reentry and resettlement looked forward to by the patients. The patients were sent to eight agricultural camps in the middle of Viet Cong territory, really paramilitary forts each manned by fourteen American troops and Vietnamese "volunteers." The main purpose of these camps was to reduce the cost of flying in food for the Green Berets, and also to provide a better diet for the soldiers while they were in enemy territory.

Returning to the ethical questions—for whose benefit was this agricultural resettlement? Was it for the benefit of the Vietnamese patients or of the United States Army? What were the ethical implications of the horrible prospects that lay in store for these expatients when they left these forts and had to reintegrate with their Viet Cong countrymen? (A-4; C-1, 2, 3; D-2; E-3).

These examples of unethical practices in the name of behavior therapy serve to dramatize critical ethical issues which are of concern to us as human service professionals and as behavior therapists. What ethical standards should we employ in selecting goals and treatment procedures? How can we balance means and ends, as for example, when an aversive treatment procedure is considered for a harmful or life-threatening behavior? What safeguards can be implemented to protect the rights and welfare of patients, especially those with diminished capacity to give consent or who are treated involuntarily, which will also permit innovation, respect for the right to effective treatment, and cost-effective service delivery? How can we best assure that behavioral services are provided by well-trained, ethical, competent therapists? These challenges, and our steadily evolving solutions to them, are among the most important issues facing behavior therapy.

Goals and Treatment Planning

Agreement between therapist and patient in choosing the goals of treatment constitute a norm in behavior therapy (A-1 to 5). Verbalizing or writing the goals can help to clarify them, and should be done in plain language comprehensible to the client. In considered client-initiated goals, it is incumbent upon the therapist to consider the likely effects that meeting these goals would have on others, as well as the implications of short-term goals for the client's long-range best interest. In some instances, the client and therapist may reach an impasse, calling for an outside consultation, referral of the client to another therapist, or termination. Because of the objectivity and specificity of goals in behavior therapy, goal setting is rarely problematic in working with voluntary clients.

Ethical issues in goal selection become more critical when the therapist is consulting or providing services in settings where clients are unable, owing to involuntary treatment status or severe cognitive limitations, to participate fully in goal setting. Winett and Winkler (1972) have criticized behavioral programs in schools for focusing on maintenance of order, obedience to authority, and quietness as goals, rather than questioning traditional educational methods and actively working to develop more effective, child-preferred, learning environments. Institutional programs sometimes exploit token economy programs to foster submissiveness and compliance to caregivers' routines, rather than serving individual clients' specific needs for treatment, rehabilitation, and training (Martin, 1975). A prudent consultant or program manager might consider involving students or patients, their families, and other advocates external to the system as well as teachers or staff, in the choosing of appropriate goals.

Goals of treatment should include positive, functional, and constructive behavioral elements and should not be aimed only at suppressing undesirable behavior or instigating behaviors which are of convenience to others. For example, the first author was involved as a consultant to a residential program serving adolescents with behavior problems in which the staff, among other treatment modalities, were using relatively restrictive methods such as point fines and time out to decrease undesirable behaviors such as yelling, fighting, cursing, and vandalism. These restrictive procedures were not very effective in changing behavior, and program administrators were concerned that a punitive climate might be developing. The staff were anxious for the consultants to teach them more effective means for suppressing undesirable behavior. In working with the staff, the consultants helped them to see that the clients' social skills deficiencies were one factor underlying their inappropriate social behaviors. Suppressive goals were replaced or supplemented by skill-enhancement goals aimed at helping the clients maximize positive social reinforcement in their interactions with others, and a training program was implemented to help the staff learn the clinical skills necessary to conduct social skills training groups, and to use teaching interactions (Fixsen, Phillips, Phillips, and Wolf, 1976) in dealing with problem behaviors (A-7,8,9; H-1,4,5).

Selection of Treatment Methods

The ethical responsibility of the behavior therapist in selecting treatment procedures is to use methods which are maximally effective, efficient in time and costs, and pleasant for the client. As an experimentally oriented and data-based treatment approach, behavior therapy builds on the published literature as a resource in the selection of intervention strategies (B-1,3). Careful assessment of the client's behavioral repertoire, history, current situation and social conditions, and other relevant information is used to arrive at a prescription for change (E-1). Of equal importance to published sources is the caveat, "know thyself," given that therapist skills and characteristics are important determinants of therapeutic outcome

(Goldstein and Stein, 1976). Systematic evaluation of one's own successes and failures, as well as a realistic appraisal of one's clinical skills and deficiencies, are essential to responsible choice of treatment or to the decision to seek consultation or to refer (H-1,2,3,4,5).

When two or more procedures are possible, the client should be consulted in weighing the relative importance of differences between the methods (B-3). For example, a client may be presented a choice between *flooding* as a treatment for fears and phobias (Leitenberg, 1976), which is rapid and thus less costly but highly stressful, or *desensitization* (Wolpe, 1969), which is relatively more pleasant and comfortable, but which may require more time and may therefore be more expensive.

The use of restrictive and aversive treatment procedures, especially when applied to involuntarily confined patients or prisoners, or to people who have limited ability to consent or to represent their own interests—such as children, psychotic patients, and the mentally retarded—presents a serious ethical dilemma and justifies considerable deliberation and application of safeguards. The therapist or treatment team must be prepared to defend the decision to undertake such treatment to professional peers, parents and family members, and the public. The behavior therapist should also have the courage to pursue controversial treatments when such treatment is indicated and when the risks and hazards can be demonstrably outweighed by the benefits to the client.

Self-injurious behavior in a retarded person may serve to illustrate the ethical and clinical decision process:

1. What aspects of the current environment may contribute to the problems (B-5)? A humane and reinforcing environment which provides materials and structured activities, social interactions, and stimulation is a precondition for effective and ethical treatment. For example, in an unstimulating and socially deprived environment, self-injury may be strengthened by the attention the client receives as a consequence of the behavior.

2. How severe is the self-injury? Dangerous or life-threatening behavior justifies and demands effective treatment, and in the absence of less restrictive or aversive effective methods, may justify starting with a moderately or highly aversive or restrictive program. With less severe behaviors, less restrictive procedures, even if they may be somewhat less effective, should be attempted prior to implementing a more aversive procedure (A-5; B-1, 2, 3, 4).

3. What positive behaviors, if strengthened, might interfere with or compete with self-injury? Restrictive programming should rarely be used in isolation as treatment of self-injury. It is also necessary to combine positive reinforcement programs for nonoccurrence of the self-injurious behavior (differential reinforcement of other behavior) or for

occurrence of incompatible behavior (differential reinforcement of competing behavior) (A-9; B-5).

4. What are the current consequences of the behavior, and what methods are being used to control the behavior? In cases of severe self-injurious behavior, clients are often given high doses of psychotropic drugs for long periods of time, which may have the effect of severely limiting functional and adaptive behavior as well as reducing the maladaptive behavior. Alternatively, physical restraints are often used, such as tying the client's hands or totally immobilizing the client for long periods of time. A highly restrictive or aversive program, such as over-correction or response-contingent restraint, applied for a brief time in conjunction with positive reinforcement procedures for adaptive behavior, may have the effect of freeing the person from even more restrictive conditions. In the absence of treatment, drugging or restraint may persist for years or for a lifetime (A-9; B-5).

A behavior therapist who decides to intervene in a highly intrusive or restrictive way should carefully weigh the risks and benefits (B-1, 2, 6), conduct a thorough assessment (B-1, 2; E-1), and always consider less restrictive alternatives which may be equally effective (B-4). In such cases, the therapist should also consider professional peer review and consultation (B-4), and if treatment is being conducted in an institution, should consult advisory or human rights committees for their review and approval (A-6; B-4). If the client has been placed in a specialized treatment setting because of the behavior, an ethical therapist will also consider the degree of generalization associated with different procedures, and plan a program to return the client to his or her less restrictive "natural environment" when the behavior is under control in the special treatment setting (B-6).

Informed Consent

Some difficulties in setting ethical guidelines for behavior therapy come from the myriad settings and types of patients with which the therapists must deal. Consider the issue of informed consent. This is not usually a major problem when dealing with a patient suffering from neurotic anxiety or depression, who walks into a private office or into a community mental health center and says, "I'm hurting, please help me." The issue of informed consent is generally clear, particularly if the therapist describes the treatment methods and program in advance. Informed consent becomes blurred, however, in the case of involuntarily committed patients who are being recruited into a token economy program in an institution.

Informed consent requires that the patient: (1) has information about the prospective program or treatment being offered; (2) understands the information and the nature of the program; (3) understands if a risk exists; and (4) is able to evaluate whether the potential benefits of participating in the treatment outweigh the risks or possible hazards (DHEW, 1971). Adequate information on the program may be given by a project director, or by staff members, but an inpatient's judgment on balancing risks with benefits usually cannot be made satisfactorily without sources of advice from outside the institution (D-4). Unfortunately, prisons and hospitals are closed institutions which tend to restrict the flow of information and human contact between those who are inside and those who are outside.

Inpatients frequently lack access to information from outside, as well as advice from relatives who aren't always available for talk and counseling. There is no "physician friend" or professional to serve as a consultant to the patient, hired or contracted directly by the patient or inmate. All the institution's therapists and physicians are generally hired by the state and may therefore inadvertently or consciously be primarily serving the interest of the institution.

In closed institutions, there is also a lack of access to legal counsel. There is often censorship of mail and limitations on making phone calls. Even when the phone is available, calls may be permitted only at designated times. Thus, a total institution insulates and isolates the patient or inmate from the changing mores and values of the outside society, which are important in making judgments about treatment. People inside institutions don't often have easy opportunities to read newspapers, watch television, or listen to the radio. These constraints greatly restrict the prisoner's or institutionalized patient's ability to evaluate the relative advantages or disadvantages of an innovative behavioral program and make it difficult for them to make an informed decision about entering such a program.

Legal considerations also play a role in the procedures used to obtain informed consent for a particular intervention. When designing a treatment program for a voluntarily institutionalized patient, the most important legal consideration is obtaining informed consent. The basic elements of informed consent (DHEW, 1971) are:

1. Fair explanation of the procedure to be followed, including an explanation of those which are experimental;
2. Description of the attendant discomforts and risks;
3. Description of the benefits to be expected;
4. Disclosure of appropriate alternative procedures that would be advantageous to the subject;
5. Offer to answer any inquiries concerning the procedure;
6. Instruction that the subject is free to withdraw his consent and to discontinue participation in the project or activity at any time. [P. 7]

**TABLE 2.   Elements of the Behavior Approach Affected by _Wyatt_
v. _Stickney_ Decision**

Element	_Decision_
REINFORCERS	
1. Primary reinforcers	Patients must recieve, at the minimum, a diet meeting the recommended daily dietary allowance.
2. Activity reinforcers	The opportunity for religious worship shall be accorded to each resident who desires worship.
	Residents shall have a right to regular physical exercise several times a week.
	Residents shall have a right to be outdoors daily.
3. Material reinforcers	Each resident shall have an adequate allowance of his own clothing, or clothing supplied by the institution.
	Residents shall sleep in single rooms or rooms of no more than six persons; screens or curtains shall be provided to ensure privacy. Each resident shall be furnished with a comfortable bed, a closet or locker, and appropriate furniture.
4. Social reinforcers	Patients have the right to telephone communication and to send and receive mail.
	Patients shall be given suitable opportunities for interactions with members of the opposite sex.
PUNISHMENTS	
1. Corporal punishment	Corporal punishment shall not be permitted.
2. Restraint	Physical restraint shall not be employed as a punishment.
3. Seclusion, time out	Seclusion, defined as the placement of a resident alone in a locked room, shall not be employed.
	Legitimate "time out" procedures may be used if systematically applied in a behavior-shaping program under direct professional supervision.
TARGET BEHAVIORS	
1. Jobs within the institution	No resident shall be required to perform labor which involves the operation and maintenance of the institution. Residents may engage in such labor voluntarily if they are compensated in accordance with the minimum wage laws.

Element	Decision
	No resident shall be subjected to a behavior modification program which attempts to extinguish socially appropriate behavior or to develop new behavior patterns when such behavior modifications serve only institutional convenience.
THERAPY PROCEDURES	
1. Physician approval	No resident shall be subjected to a behavior modification program without prior certification by a physician that he has examined the resident and finds that such behavior is not caused by a physical condition which could be corrected by appropriate medical procedures.
2. Individualized treatment	Patients have the right to individualized treatment programs. These programs should be formulated by the institution and will include: a statement of specific needs and limitations of the patient, long- and intermediate-range goals; a statement of the least restrictive alternative for treatment with a projected timetable for their attainment. Programs will be continuously monitored using objective indicators. Each resident shall have an individualized posthospitalization plan.
3. Institutional review of therapy programs having aversive elements	Behavior modification programs involving the use noxious or aversive stimuli shall be reviewed and approved by the institution's human rights committee and shall be conducted only with the express and informed consent of the affected resident if able to give such consent, and of his guardian or next of kin, after opportunities for consultation with independent specialists and with legal counsel.

When working with involuntary, institutionalized patients, the legal issues are even more complex. This complexity is illustrated in the decision made in the case of *Wyatt* v. *Stickney* (Wexler, 1973) on the right to high-quality treatment. The court's decision in this case places restrictions on many of the basic techniques that can be used in therapy. Table 2 reveals the scope of this ruling on the practice of behavior therapy. None of the rights and reinforcers enumerated under the *Wyatt* v. *Stickney* decision can be made contingent for involuntary patients. Punishments are similarly restricted. Target behaviors for involuntary patients cannot include tasks that primarily subserve the maintenance of the institution. Similar rulings have placed restrictions on the behavioral treatment techniques which can be used with institutionalized juveniles and violent prisoners.

State and federal mental health agencies are concerned about legal rulings regarding the use of behavioral techniques in institutions. Many of these agencies have developed directives intended to safeguard the rights of involuntarily institutionalized patients. These directives match, and in some cases go beyond, those outlined in *Wyatt* v. *Stickney*. The practicing clinician needs to keep abreast of legal developments relevant to the practice of behavior therapy in institutions. We highly recommend a review of recent articles (Begelman, 1975; Wexler, 1973) and books (Martin, 1975) in this area. In certain cases, the clinician may need to consult with legal counsel or with representatives from legal and ethics committees of professional organizations such as the American Psychological Association, the American Psychiatric Association, and the Association for Advancement of Behavior Therapy.

Therapist Qualifications and Quality Control

As can be seen in section H of the AABT guidelines, the professional qualifications of the therapist are intrinsic to ethical practice. Many behavior therapists are critical of current approaches to quality control in the helping professions that are based upon licensing and certification for education, amount of supervised practice, and the ability to pass written and oral examinations. Such assessment methods seem far removed from the performance demands of clinical work with clients, and only peripherally sample the clinical skills necessary for successful, ethical practice. From a behavioral perspective, the central issue in therapist qualification is competence and skill, objectively defined and measured. Successful therapy is not viewed as an "art" accessible only to uniquely talented or gifted individuals. Therapeutic skill is viewed as an extensive, complex, integrated repertoire of therapist behaviors which is in principle, if not currently in fact, observable, measurable, and teachable.

A competency base for behavior therapy was outlined, for example, by Sulzer-Azaroff, Thaw, and Thomas (1975), whose questionnaire survey of prominent behavior therapists led to the development of a list of about seventy specific skills considered important to the practice of behavior therapy. Specification and reliable assessment of clinical skills can only be a first step in establishing a competency base for behavior therapy, especially when the only justification for inclusion of the skill is expert opinion.

Brockway has outlined methods for evaluating competence which encompass: (1) identification of skills necessary to a given area of practice; (2) specification of criteria by which the skills are deemed necessary for adequate service delivery (for example, client satisfaction, clinical outcomes); and (3) validation of the skills through demonstration that if the skills are exhibited, better patient outcome or service delivery results (Brockway, 1978a). The above model has been used to develop and evaluate skills in training programs for family care physicians (Brockway, 1978a) and for behavior therapists (Brockway, 1978b). The training program for behavior therapists defined skills in four broad areas:

1. Clinical interviewing and communication skills (e.g., reflective listening, communication of empathy);
2. Assessment and treatment skills (behavioral observation, technical therapeutic procedures);
3. Knowledge of human growth and development (analysis of behavioral information within a developmental perspective);
4. Analytical and ethical thinking (focusing questions in interviewing, ethical implications of treatment procedures).

While these preliminary efforts have been interesting, much work remains to be done if we are to establish a valid and useful competency base for clinical behavior therapy, and for other therapeutic and service modalities.

Accompanying recent developments in competency specification and assessment has been progress in the educational technology for teaching skills to therapists. In a review of six of the most widely used and thoroughly researched training programs, Ford (1978) reported that, while they emphasized different content areas, each program incorporated the following procedures:

1. Detailed instructions;
2. Modeling with discriminative cueing;
3. Behavioral rehearsal;
4. Detailed and immediate performance feedback;
5. Detailed and delayed performance feedback;
6. *In vivo* practice.

Such active/directive approaches to skills training have been demonstrated to be superior to traditional lecture-discussion methods of training. Despite conceptual advances and improved technology relevant to the teaching of clinical skills, many training programs still rely on traditional formats (Matarazzo, 1978). This discrepancy exists also in continuing education in behavior therapy. Data collected at preconvention Institutes of the Association for the Advancement of Behavior Therapy indicated that behavioral clinicians rely largely on lecture-discussion formats for continuing education, even though a major purpose of the

Institutes is to teach clinical skills to participants (Kuehnel, Marholin, Heinrich, and Liberman, 1978). In this study, trainee satisfaction was positively related to the occurrence of active/directive teaching formats.

Continuing education beyond the terminal professional degree is increasingly recognized as essential to maintaining clinical skills, and as an ethical responsibility of the professional (H-5). Organizations such as the American Medical Association and the National Association of Social Workers sponsor continuing education programs for their membership, and provide credit for participation. The American Psychiatric Association requires evidence of continuing education for renewal of membership. States are adding continuing education requirements for renewal of professional licenses and certificates. By engaging in a process of self-evaluation, taking a hard, honest look at one's strengths and weaknesses, successes and failures, and identifying current or future new professional roles and responsibilities, clinicians in the field of mental health can continue their education throughout their careers.

Guidelines and Regulations—Help or Hindrance?

Behavior modification has been singled out in recent years as particularly in need of regulation and close public scrutiny. This has been, in part, a response to highly publicized abuses in the name of behavior modification, such as those outlined earlier in this chapter; and is also partially due to public misinformation about behavior modification, which has been erroneously equated in the popular press with such practices as brainwashing, torture, psychosurgery, and drug treatment (Turkat and Feuerstein, 1978). Adding to the impetus for regulation of behavioral procedures has been isolated incidents of abuse by professionals who were ostensibly qualified as behavioral clinicians (Risley, 1975).

Although the promulgation of guidelines and regulations for the conduct of behavioral interventions seems to have potential for clarifying acceptable procedures, providing safeguards for ethical practice, and protecting clients' rights, critics have pointed to potential undesirable effects or side effects of such regulations:

1. Singling out behavior modification for regulation, rather than regulating all forms of intervention, may lead "gun shy" clinicians away from behavioral interventions in favor of less costly or strenuous (and often less effective) treatment alternatives, denying clients access to effective treatment (Goldiamond, 1975; Stolz, 1977).

2. In the absence of empirically derived facts, guidelines may be

heavily weighted with opinions of recognized experts which are presented as facts. Less sophisticated readers may fail to discriminate facts from opinions, leading to a rigid behavioral mythology not unlike existing mythologies in psychodynamic approaches (Sajwaj, 1977).

3. Guidelines may become seriously outdated in the light of new research findings. Unless measures are taken to overcome administrative and bureaucratic inertia and provide for periodic revision, guidelines will mandate outmoded practices (Sajwaj, 1977; Stolz, 1977).

4. It is likely that guidelines will be incorporated into legislation and judicial decisions as well as government regulations. This would compound the problem of bureaucratic inertia by making changes more laborious, time-consuming, and expensive (Sajwaj, 1977).

5. In addition to helping eliminate undesirable variations in practice, guidelines would also have the effect of discouraging innovation (Stolz, 1977).

6. Guidelines can produce an effect opposite to that intended: procedures which meet the letter, but not the spirit, of the guidelines may be protected from justified criticism and attack (Stolz, 1977).

7. Guidelines may carry the expansion of the regulatory bureaucracy beyond existing administrative structures, increasing the cost of service delivery without materially improving implementation of programs. This carries with it the imposition of further time constraints and effort required of professionals operating in systems with limited resources, leading to a net reduction in services provided to clients (Sajwaj, 1977).

Sajwaj outlines a scenario for a bureaucratic nightmare in which a professional, in order to introduce a novel and untried procedure in a residential program must go through eleven different levels of review by client, staff, supervisors, and administrators, obtaining signatures of physician and superintendent, approval by a research committee, a human rights committee, an advisory board, and review health and safety codes. Any change in the program at any level would necessitate recycling through all previous levels, and disapproval at any level would lead to rejection of the program regardless of the number of prior approvals (Sajwaj, 1977).

Paul and Lentz (1977) provided data from an example of the deleterious effects of guidelines on an ongoing behavioral program. Midway through a six-year project comparing milieu and social learning inpatient programs for chronic mental patients, the state of Illinois adopted regulations limiting time-out procedures to a maximum of one hour. Data from the research unit showed marked deterioration of patients' progress in a number of areas, declining staff morale, and an increase in the frequency of severe assaultive incidents which had been controlled by longer-duration time out. Renegotiation of policies, a time-consuming process, was necessary to allow for longer time-out durations under well-controlled conditions, before the gains of these clients could be partially reestablished.

It has been argued that the dangers of guidelines for behavioral treatment far outweigh the advantages, and that we should look rather to the professional organizations, and their ethical codes for self-regulatory practices to deal with inappropriate and unethical practices (Stolz, 1977). The AABT has adopted a compromise approach to the issue of guidelines for behavioral practice. Rather than issuing specific "dos" and "don'ts," a checklist of questions regarding ethical practice was provided. The AABT ethics committee noted that the guidelines were reminders to the therapist without the coercive tone implicit in a series of mandates, and that the guidelines were couched in general terms to apply to all psychological, psychiatric, and counseling practices (Azrin et al., 1977; see Table 1).

Is there any justification for promulgating *specific* guidelines, given the dangers and disadvantages outlined? In the case of involuntarily committed/treated clients and in the case of clients who are not competent, owing to severe mental retardation or psychosis to advocate their own best interests, a case can be made for specific, procedural safeguards. Clients have been abused for decades by a mental health establishment which, until recently, took a paternalistic stance in relation to client consent to treatment, participation in goal planning, and civil rights (Stolz, 1977). After the anectine horrors at Atascadero State Hospital in California, the American Psychiatric Association, as the relevant professional organization, declined to self-regulate and whitewashed the situation (Serber et al., 1975). Procedural safeguards are especially salient if restrictive or aversive interventions, behavioral or nonbehavioral, are to be employed. Guidelines cannot substitute for clinical and ethical judgment of the professional, but guidelines can require that the clinician be explicit and accountable about the rationale for using restrictive methods, systematic in his or her assessment and data collection, and conscientious in staff training, supervision, and evaluation of the procedures.

The pros and cons of guidelines may soon be a moot question, because while behavior therapists are busy criticizing guidelines, a number of public and private agencies are busy developing and implementing them. It seems inevitable that regulation will come, at least with respect to procedures which involve deprivation, restriction, and aversive events. Florida, Arizona, Minnesota, Wisconsin, California, and other states have already instituted guidelines in these areas. Behavior therapists now have the choice of participating in the development of guidelines and influencing the adoption of well-reasoned, technically accurate, flexible policies, or allowing bureaucrats to perform the task as they see fit. Several criteria for developing guidelines may be derived from the issues discussed here:

1. The language of guidelines should be sufficiently broad to encompass any treatment approach which involves a potential threat to the rights or welfare of clients, and not refer only to behavior therapy or behavior modification.
2. Opinions should be identified as such, and not presented as established facts.
3. Guidelines should incorporate a specific "review and revision" clause, specifying an interval of not more than five years between revisions.
4. Authors of guidelines should explicitly caution against adoption of the guidelines as government regulations or incorporation into laws, which cannot readily be changed.
5. Guidelines should be specific about the process of review and safeguards, but flexible with respect to variations in clinical implementation and allow for innovative approaches.
6. Guidelines should be implemented through existing administrative structures. New regulatory committees or bureaucracies should be avoided.
7. Staff qualifications should be referenced to specific competencies rather than to a particular professional discipline or vaguely defined "experience in the field."

Model of Treatment Quality and Ethics—The Teaching Family

The Teaching Family model developed at the University of Kansas (Phillips, 1968; Phillips, Phillips, Fixsen, and Wolf, 1971) serves as an affirmative example of ethical sensitivity in the design, staff training and certification, implementation, and evaluation of a behavioral treatment program. The Teaching Family was developed as an alternative to juvenile detention and state reformatories for youths convicted of crimes. Six to eight youths lives in a home in the community with a teaching-parent couple who served as counselors, trainers, and friends to the boys. Components of the Teaching Family model include family-style living, a self-government system, emphasis on counseling and personal relationships, systematic skill building, and the use of a token economy or point system for motivation.

In diverting clients from institutional to community-based programming, the Teaching Family met a first ethical criterion: providing services in the least restrictive environment (guidelines A-8;B-5). The youths were able to continue their education in community schools, maintain family contacts under some controls, and participate in normal community recreational and leisure-time activities as well as living in a family-type situation.

Since placement in the program was involuntary, typically referrals coming from juvenile courts, informed consent was compromised. One method of compensating for this was systematically to evaluate the youths' preferences for alternative effective treatment and training procedures, and to elicit their participation in goal setting via self-government (A-3;D-1,2,3). For example, several systems of arranging youths' accountability for household tasks were compared: individual versus group responsibility and consequences, and elected peer managership versus managership purchased with points by the highest bidder. In a series of experimental studies, it was determined that purchased and elected manager systems with individual assignments and consequences were equally effective, and superior to other systems. The elected managership was adopted because it was preferred by the youths in studies giving them the opportunity to choose one system or the other.

> When working with clients in a treatment setting it is often easy to be so concerned with "doing a good job" that we overlook an extremely important variable: the client's satisfaction with the treatment procedures. This is probably less of a problem in treatment settings that deal with clients who voluntarily submit to the procedures and who can leave any time they are dissatisfied. In these voluntary programs, the clients thus maintain some (at least implicit) consequences for staff behavior that makes them unhappy. However, in treatment settings where the client is not a voluntary participant, the staff must develop other means of evaluating the clients' preferences because the client cannot simply drop out of the program or vigorously register their dissatisfaction with the treatment procedures. [Phillips, Phillips, Wolf, and Fixsen, 1973]

Each major component of the Teaching Family model was installed only after carefully controlled research supported its effectiveness (B-1,3,5,6; E-1,2,4). Examples include the token reinforcement system (Phillips, 1968; Phillips, Phillips, Fixsen, and Wolf, 1971); home-based reinforcement for classroom behavior (Bailey, Wolf, and Phillips, 1970); and development of the self-government system (Fixsen, Phillips, Phillips, and Wolf, 1976).

The goals of the Teaching Family program were stated in positive terms. Rather than targeting objectives which merely suppressed maladaptive behaviors such as lying, fighting, stealing, and truancy, the program was organized to provide skill training in areas relevant to successful community and family living. Independent self-care, social skills, academic and vocational skills, problem solving, and recreational and leisure-time skills were specified, taught, and reinforced (A-9). In the choice of treatment goals, Teaching Family personnel relied on the principle of social validation (Fixsen, Phillips, Phillips, and Wolf, 1976). Arbitrary goal setting was avoided. Instead, the clinician submitted proposed goals or target behaviors to a variety of people, including youths, their parents or family, and community members, and selected as treatment objectives only those behavioral outcomes which were widely endorsed as desirable, appropriate, and adaptive for the clients.

With the documented and widely publicized successes of the Teaching Family approach came projects to expand and disseminate the model (Braukman, Fixsen, Kirigin, Phillips, Phillips, and Wolf, 1975). Early failure with teaching parents trained by traditional educational methods, including one year of coursework in applied behavior analysis and observation of clinical procedures, led to establishment of a competency-based training program to teach specific skills and to evaluate on-the-job performance of new teaching parents and the results they achieved. Only after evaluation proved the teaching-parent couple had the skills, were they certified (Braukman et al., 1975; Fixsen et al., 1976). In this manner, they successfully met the ethical criteria for therapist qualifications (section H).

Operating a Teaching Family group home places the clinician in a situation of accountability to a number of persons and agencies: the youths receiving services, parents and family, the juvenile courts, teachers, and myriad social agencies. The Teaching Family approach deals explicitly with these reponsibilities through systematic, scheduled feedback to the teaching parents. For example, satisfaction ratings are completed by youths on the teaching parents' fairness, effectiveness, relationship, and program quality, and school, court, and social agencies periodically rate their satisfaction with various aspects of their dealings with the teaching parents. Regular feedback is also provided by the teaching home's board of directors. Such consumer evaluation not only serves as part of the feedback to teaching parents in training, but occurs on an ongoing basis at regular intervals for all Teaching Family group homes. Consumer evaluation serves to keep teaching parents abreast of the status of their relationships to key social agencies and individuals. Such data may also serve a protective function in the event of negative comments or charges leveled against a Teaching Family program (A-4; B-5; D-3; E-1).

The Teaching Family approach demonstrates a high quality and ethical approach that extends to therapist qualifications, selection of goals and methods, client involvement, and evaluation of treatment efficacy. Balance is maintained among the interests of diverse parties concerned with the treatment program. The solid linkages among clinical practice, training, data-based research, and program evaluation which characterize the Teaching Family model exemplifies applied behavior analysis at its best, in terms of efficacy of the treatment program and adherence to ethical standards.

Summary

Ethical problems and issues that behavior therapists confront are identical to those of other mental health and human service professionals. These issues center on selection of appropriate treatment objectives and intervention strategies, respect for the well-being and rights of clients, and sensitivity to the sometimes conflicting interests of individual clients, their families and close associates, and society and society's agents. Behavioral clinicians have been sensitized to ethical issues by abusive practices in the name of behavior therapy, misinterpretation of behavioral treatment in the popular literature, and the potential for misuse inherent in a powerful technology for behavior change.

The AABT list of guidelines, *Ethical Issues for Human Services,* provides a comprehensive set of standards for weighing the ethical implications of clinical interventions. This chapter reviewed treatment programs that violated standards as well as a "model" program, the Teaching Family, in light of the AABT guidelines.

Behavior therapists practice in a wide range of settings with diverse client groups. In providing services to involuntary and severely disabled people, ethical dilemmas are significant. Therapists working in institutions can resolve some of these dilemmas if they:

1. Maximize client involvement in goal setting and treatment planning to the extent possible given the client's disability and legal status.
2. Enrich environments and use positive programming whenever possible, avoiding exclusive reliance on deprivation and negative or aversive control.
3. Use the least intrusive possible methods to promote the greatest possible level of enhanced social function.
4. Extend the "freedom" of the client by making more explicit and manageable the natural social contingencies of reinforcement of their environment, and give primary emphasis to constructive and functional behavior.
5. Analyze the institutional system and its contingencies which can be used to shape adaptive rather than maladaptive behavior.
6. Go beyond and outside the institution into the natural environments and reinforcement contingencies which will control the clients' behavior when they leave the hospital or prison.

7. Have the courage to pursue controversial treatments when they are in the client's interest. Balance the right to effective treatment with the other rights of the client for safeguarding their liberty and integrity.
8. Resist use of "behavior therapy" to legitimize either no treatment, the "token" token economies that reinforce behaviors convenient to institutions and caregivers, or retributive punishment and inhumane treatment as exemplified in the anectine and Vietnamese hospital situations summarized above.

Another ethical issue of concern to behavioral clinicians includes the procedures used for training and certifying therapists. Training needs to focus on skill acquisition through active/directive teaching methods, and certification should be based on assessment of competencies proven to be necessary for adequate service delivery. Guidelines or regulations for treatment should not erroneously convey the impression that only behavioral methods are in need of oversight. Promulgation of guidelines entails risks, including concretizing opinions into "facts," restrictions on innovation, and addition of levels of bureaucracy and costlier, less effective services. Guidelines are, however, justifiable in controlling clinical services for involuntary and severely disabled clients, especially when aversive or restrictive interventions are used. Behavior therapists participating in the development of guidelines can work toward developing standards that are technically accurate, flexible, easy to administer, and subject to revision in the light of new developments in the field.

NOTE

1. Portions of this chapter were presented in a workshop entitled "Ethical Principles in the Use of Behavior Therapy in Institutions," Western Regional Conference on Humanistic Approaches in Behavior Modification, Las Vegas, March, 1977. The workshop and this paper are dedicated to the memory of Michael Serber, M.D. The preparation of this chapter was supported in part by NIMH Research Grant MH30911. The authors appreciate the encouragement and high standards of ethical and quality treatment provided by Clint Rust, Executive Director, Doug Van Meter, Clinical Director, and Samuel Rapport, M.D., Medical Director, at Carmarillo State Hospital.

REFERENCES

Azrin, N. H.; Stuart, R. B.; Risley, T. R.; and Stolz, S. Ethical issues for human services (AABT Ethical Guidelines). *AABT Newsletter,* 1977, **4,** 11.

BACH-Y-RITA, G. The prisoner as an experimental subject. *Journal of the American Medical Association*, 1974, **229**, 45-46.

BAILEY, J. S., WOLF, M. M., and PHILLIPS, E. L. Home-based reinforcement and the modification of pre-delinquents' classroom behavior. *Journal of Applied Behavior Analysis*, 1970, **3**, 223-233.

BANDURA, A. *Principles of behavior modification*. New York: Holt, Rinehart, & Winston, 1969.

BANDURA, A. Behavior theory and the models of man. *American Psychologist*, 1974, **29**, 859-909.

BARLOW, D. H., REYNOLDS, E. J., and AGRAS, W. S. Gender identity change in a transsexual. *Archives of General Psychiatry*, 1973, **28**, 569-576.

BEGELMAN, D. A. Ethical and legal issues in behavior modification. In M. Hersen, R. M. Eisler, and P. H. Miller (eds.), *Progress in behavior modification*, Vol. 1. New York: Academic Press, 1975.

BIRK, L.; HUDDLESTON, W.; MILLER, E.; and COHLER, B. Avoidance conditioning for homosexuality. *Archives of General Psychiatry*, 1971, **25**, 314-323.

BRAUKMAN, C. J.; FIXSEN, D. L.; KIRIGIN, K. A.; PHILLIPS, E. A.; PHILLIPS, E. L.; and WOLF, M. M. Achievement place: The training and certification of teaching parents. In W. S. Wood (ed.), *Issues of evaluating behavior modification*. Champaign, Ill.: Research Press, 1975.

BROCKWAY, B. S. Evaluating physician competency: What difference does it make? *Evaluation and Program Planning*, 1978, **1**, 221-220. (a)

BROCKWAY, B. S. Evaluating the competency of behavior therapists. Methods and issues. Paper presented at the 86th annual meeting of the American Psychological Association, Toronto, Canada, August 29, 1978. (b)

BROWN, B. S., WIENCKOWSKI, L. A., and STOLZ, S. B. *Behavior modification: Perspectives on a current issue*. Rockville, Md.: U.S. Dept. of H.E.W. and N.I.M.H., 1975. (DHEW Publication No. (ADM) 75-202.)

CAUTELA, J. Covert reinforcement. *Behavior Therapy*, 1970, **1**, 33-50.

COTTER, L. H. Operant conditioning in a Vietnamese mental hospital. *American Journal of Psychiatry*, 1967, **124**, 61-66.

DEPARTMENT OF HEALTH, EDUCATION AND WELFARE. *Guidelines for research involving human subjects*, 1971.

FINESMITH, B. K. Ethical and legal issues special interest group. *Behavior Therapist*, 1979a, **2**(3), 11.

FINESMITH, B. K. An historic and systematic overview of Wisconsin's behavior management guidelines. *Behavior Therapist*, 1979b, **2**(2), 3-6.

FIXSEN, D. L.; PHILLIPS, E. L.; PHILLIPS, E. A.; and WOLF, M. M. Training teaching-parents to operate group home treatment programs. In M. E. Bernal (ed.), *Training in behavior modification*. New York: Brooks/Cole, 1976.

FIXSEN, D. L., PHILLIPS, E. L., and WOLF, M. M. Achievement place: Experiments in self-government with pre-delinquents. *Journal of Applied Behavior Analysis*, 1973, **6**, 31-47.

FORD, J. Training in environmental design. In L. Krasner (ed.), *Handbook of environmental design*. New York: Pergamon Press, 1978.

FRANKS, C. M., and WILSON, G. T. Ethical and related issues in behavior therapy. In C. M. Franks and G. T. Wilson (eds.), *Annual review of behavior therapy: Theory and practice*. New York: Brunner/Mazel, 1975.

GOLDIAMOND, I. Singling out behavior modification for legal regulation. *Arizona Law Review*, 1975, **17**, 105-126.

GOLDSTEIN, A. P., and STEIN, N. H. *Prescriptive psychotherapies.* New York: Pergamon Press, 1976.

JONES, M. C. A laboratory study of fear: The case of Peter. *Journal of Genetic Psychology*, 1924, **31**, 308-315.

KUEHNEL, T. G.; MARHOLIN, D.; HEINRICH, R.; and LIBERMAN, R. Evaluating behavior therapists' continuing education activities: The AABT institutes. *Behavior Therapist*, 1978, **1**,(4), 5-8.

LEITENBERG, H. Behavioral approaches to treatment of neuroses. In H. Leitenberg (ed.), *Handbook of behavior modification and behavior therapy.* Englewood Cliffs, N.J.: Prentice-Hall, 1976.

LINEHAN, M.; BOOTZIN, R.; CAUTELA, J.; LONDON, P.; PERLOFF, M.; STUART, R.; and RISLEY, T. Guidelines for choosing a behavior therapist. *Behavior Therapist*, 1978, **1**(4), 18-20.

MAHONEY, M. *Cognition and behavior modification.* Cambridge, Mass.: Ballinger, 1974.

MARTIN, R. *Legal challenges to behavior modification.* Champaign, Ill.: Research Press, 1975.

MATARAZZO, R. G. Reserach on the teaching and learning of psychotherapeutic skills. In S. Garfield and A. E. Bergin (eds.), *Handbook of psychotherapy and behavior change: An empirical analysis*, 2nd ed. New York: Wiley, 1978.

O'Leary, K. D. Behavior modification in the classroom: A rejoinder to Winett and Winkler. *Journal of Applied Behavior Analysis*, 1972, **5**, 505-511.

PAUL, G. L., and LENTZ, R. J. *Psychosocial treatment of chronic mental patients.* Cambridge, Mass.: Harvard University Press, 1977.

PHILLIPS, E. L. Achievement place: Token reinforcement procedures in a home-style rehabilitation setting for "pre-delinquent" boys. *Journal of Applied Behavior Analysis*, 1968, **1**, 213-223.

PHILLIPS, E. L.; PHILLIPS, E. A.; FIXSEN, D. L.; and WOLF, M. M. Achievement place: Modification of the behaviors of pre-delinquent boys within a token economy. *Journal of Applied Behavior Analysis*, 1971, **4**, 45-59.

PHILLIPS, E. L.; PHILLIPS, E. A.; WOLF, M. M.; and FIXSEN, D. L. Achievement place: Development of the elected manager system. *Journal of Applied Behavior Analysis*, 1973, **6**, 541-461.

REKERS, G. A. Atypical gender development and psychosocial adjustment. *Journal of applied Behavior Analysis*, 1977, **10**, 559-571.

RISLEY, T. R. Certify procedures, not people. In W. S. Wood (ed.), *Issues in evaluating behavior modification.* Champaign, Ill.: Research Press, 1975.

SAJWAJ, T. Issues and implications of establishing guidelines for the use of behavioral techniques. *Journal of Applied Behavior Analysis*, 1977, **10**, 531-430.

SERBER, M.; HILLER, C.; KEITH, C.; and TAYLOR, J. Behavior modification in maximum security settings: One hospital's experience. *American Criminal Law Review*, 1975, **13**, 85-99.

STOLZ, S. B. Why no guidelines for behavior modification? *Journal of Applied Behavior Analysis*, 1977, **10**, 541-547.

SULZER-AZAROFF, B., THAW, J., and THOMAS, C. Behavioral competencies for the evaluation of behavior modifiers. In W. S. Wood (ed.), *Issues in evaluating behavior modification.* Champaign, Ill.: Research Press, 1975.

THORESON, C., and MAHONEY, M. J. *Behavioral self-control.* New York: Holt, Rinehart, & Winston, 1974.

TURKAT, I. D., and FEUERSTEIN, M. Behavior modification and the public misconception. *American Psychologist,* 1978, **37,** 194.

WATSON, J. B., and RAYNOR, R. Conditioned emotional reactions. *Journal of Experimental Psychology,* 1920, **3,** 1–14.

WEXLER, D. B. Token and taboo: Behavior modification, token economies, and the law. *California Law Review,* 1973, **7,** 151–165.

WINETT, R. A., and WINKLER, R. C. Current behavior modification in the classroom: Be still, be quiet, be docile. *Journal of Applied Behavior Analysis,* 1972, **5,** 499–504.

WOLPE, J. *The practice of behavior therapy.* New York: Pergamon Press, 1969.

Ethical Problems of Group Psychotherapy

Max Rosenbaum

If you don't know where you are going, any road will take you there.
Chatterjee, an Indian philosopher

There is little attention paid to ethics in the field of group psychotherapy. The majority of group psychotherapy practitioners confuse ethics with the standards of practice. In earlier writings, I have touched upon the problem. The current concern is that professionals are adequately prepared for the work they do in group psychotherapy. The former chairman of the standards and ethics committee of the American Group Psychotherapy Association told this writer that 95 percent of his committee work concerned standards (Horwitz, 1979).

Group psychotherapy is generally practiced by professionals from three disciplines—social work, psychology, and psychiatry. Each discipline in turn sets up standards of training and attempts to formulate some code of ethics. The ethics code, however, is a relatively new concept and it is assumed that in some magical way, professionals should know what is ethical. There is a vast difference between setting up standards and defining a code of ethics. There is a constant muddying of the waters as group psychotherapy techniques are used by people from other disciplines, nurses, pastoral counselors, and many paraprofessionals. There is diminishing attention paid to ethics and growing concern expressed about standards and training. The avoidance of formulating a code of ethics perhaps masks a deeper anxiety. Professionals appear to be concerned that they will have to define good and bad professional conduct and face the anger of bad or corrupt practitioners.

We are currently experiencing in America an unraveling of the social fabric. Traditional mechanisms for getting people to work together for the common good are not working. Government officials and legislators act unscrupulously. Ethnic parochialism and favoritism is the order of the day. Mass circulation magazines profit from the theme of sexual exploitation and dehumanization appears widespread. The practicing psychotherapist is hard put to withstand the tide. More than ever, the psychotherapist must clarify his guidelines for professional behavior. Some years ago, Jacob L. Moreno stated what he believed to be a *Code of Ethics for Group Psychotherapy in Psychodrama: Relationship to the Hippocratic Oath* (1962). Moreno stated the following code for each group member:

> This is the group oath to therapeutic science and its disciples.
>
> Just as we trust the physician in individual treatment, we should trust each other. Whatever happens in the course of a session of group therapy and psychodrama, we should not keep anything secret. We should divulge freely whatever we think, perceive or feel for each other; we should act out the fears and hopes we have in common and purge ourselves of them. But like the physician who is bound by the Hippocratic oath, we are bound as participants in this group, not to reveal to outsiders the confidences of other patients.
>
> Like the physician, each of us is entrusted to protect the welfare of every other patient in the group. [p. 5]

The statement that Moreno asked his patients to accept was probably unnecessary since clinical experience indicates that patients learn to trust one another, care for one another, and come to realize that if any patient exposes another outside of the group, the same act may in turn be visited upon him.

Certainly the loneliness of contemporary society, and its constant mobility, leads people to search for settings where they can affiliate and have a sense of relatedness. More than ever we need principles to guide us in our work with patients. After Moreno's death, his widow, Zerka Moreno, formulated a proposed code of ethics (1978). While her goal was admirable, her proposed code seems to jumble ethical principles together with clinical practices. I shall list her code of ethics in a summary form:

1. The principle objective of group psychotherapy is to render service to every member of therapeutic groups and to the groups as a whole.

2. A group psychotherapist should practice methods of healing founded on a scientific basis, approved by official professional boards.

3. The designation *group psychotherapist* or *psychodramatist* should be used only by psychotherapists who have obtained training in recognized institutes of learning. As the field is new and expanding, the therapists should continuously improve their knowledge and skill; they should make available to other therapists and their patients the benefits of their attainments.

4. The principal objective of the group psychotherapist is to protect the patient against abuse and to render service to groups of patients with full respect for the dignity of every patient.

5. Therapeutic groups should be so organized that they represent a model of democratic behavior. Regardless of the economic, racial, and religious differences of the patients, they should be given "equality of status" inside the therapeutic group.

6. Should patients of the same therapeutic group pay the same fee or not? Could charging different fees to members of the same therapeutic group produce feelings of inequality and thwart the therapeutic aims?

7. The patients should be free to choose the therapeutic groups in which they participate as members. The therapist, in turn, is free to accept or refuse to serve in behalf of a therapeutic group. Indications or contraindications for "coercive" placement in the groups should be carefully weighed in exceptional cases, as in the treatment of deteriorated mental patients.

8. ... In group psychotherapy the Hippocratic oath is extended to all patients and binds each with equal strength not to reveal to outsiders the confidences of other patients entrusted to them. ...

9. Every patient is expected to divulge freely whatever he thinks, perceives or feels, to every other in the course of treatment sessions. ...

10. The timing of the "pledge" has to be carefully considered by the therapist responsible for the group. In order that it may not frighten the participants or produce the effect of an unnecessary restraint upon their freedom, it should not be discussed prematurely; the therapist should wait until the group is ripe and well formed and until the meaning of the pledge is clear to all members. [pp. 162–163]

While Zerka Moreno's intent is admirable, the central ethical issues are really masked by a statement of clinical practices. For example, should patients be free to choose what therapy groups they believe best for them? What about the professional judgment of the group therapist? It could be a popularity contest. Is the most popular teacher the best teacher? Is the most attractive group the most therapeutic? What does "scientific basis" mean? There are different paradigms of science. Humanists may find the tenets of logical positivism constraining and logical positivists may find existentialism mystical in nature.

I prefer to ask more critical questions. Do we have the right to impose discomfort or pain on other people to alter their behavior? Do we have the right to impose such procedures on people who are too young or intellectually and emotionally damaged to give informed consent to what they believe to be therapeutic procedures? (Miron, 1968; Senate report, 1974.)

It would seem helpful to start with what I believe to be basic. Therapy should not be harmful to the patient. What does harmful mean? An advocate of behavior modification may feel that the ultimate benefits of punishment or electric shock with an unruly, brain-damaged child, far outweigh the arguments of those who oppose corporal punishment. The brain-damaged child who is unruly may injure himself by banging his head against the wall. The same type of arguments may ensue when psychosurgery is proposed. But let us track back to an earlier time for a larger perspective.

Psychotherapists, as indeed most students of human behavior, work with *cause* and *reason* explanations. Aristotle differentiated between *four* different types of *cause* in order to explain behavior (Taylor, 1964, 1967).

1. *Efficient cause* which brings about some change.
2. *Final cause*—also called *telos*, end or purpose—why or what change is all about.
3. *Material cause*—the setting or material in which the change occurs.
4. *Formal cause*—the shape or pattern of what is changed.

Contemporary society, largely technological, stresses efficient cause. Psychotherapists are not free from the cultural pressure which stresses efficiency—the bottom line. What we should all be concerned about is final cause—what is the purpose of change? The tradition of the physical sciences, however, exists in human behavior to the extent that psychotherapists will engage in something that works without wondering about the ultimate, final cause. Most of the paradigms of psychological treatment are derived from eighteenth-century physics. They also appear to ignore Racan's poem: Nothing in the world lasts save eternal change (Racan, 1857).

My point is that Newton's laws of physics were helpful until Einstein established his theory of relativity. Newton's laws could function within a closed system. The most dramatic thing about the human experience, however, is the openness of the system. It is possible that psychotherapists are still reacting to the early constraints of the medieval Catholic church. Merton carefully analyzed the impact of seventeenth-century English Protestant theology on science (Merton, 1957).

When, after the Middle Ages, science began to flourish, there was a great concern that individual inquiry *not* be imprisoned by the earlier autocratic rule of the Church. Science became skeptical and questioning in its attitude. Protestantism stressed reason and the cognitive approach, as opposed to the emotional aspects of Catholicism. Scientists adopted the posture of neutrality and reason. The Protestant church emphasized the importance of utility and good works on earth as a way of entering heaven. The Protestant belief rejected theology as the pathway to God and stressed individualism. Nature was described as God's handiwork.

As the values of the Protestant Reformation became translated into the growth of the capitalist society and the middle class, many beliefs about individual freedom, private property, free enterprise, and Protestant goals and values began to be taken for granted. The behavioral scientist, part of the modern industrial society, often supported the values and interests of the culture and gave little thought to Aristotle's final cause. Psychotherapists, part of behavioral science, gave little or no thought to final cause.

Now the very fabric of our society appears to be unraveling. We can make no serious statements about the family because the concept of the family is questioned. Our generation has lived through the Vietnam War, a war which is considered wasteful of human life and resources and young people constantly question the verities of the Protestant ethic.

Some professionals assume that licensing or certification will take care of the ethical issue involved in the practice of psychotherapy. The thinking generally runs as follows: license competent people and exclude charlatans and incompetents. But the most recent survey of licensing describes it as a myth "that promises protection of the public but that actually institutionalizes a lack of accountability to the public. The collusion between the state and the professions is maintained by myth" (Gross, 1978).

There are no sweeping statements that will account for ethical standards. While confidentiality is crucial to effective psychotherapy whether group, family, or individual, the American Psychological Association's *Ethical Standards of Psychologists* (1963, 1967) have specifically allowed for exceptions to confidentiality "when there is clear and imminent danger to an individual or to society" (Principle 6, p. 4). Indeed, recent court cases have found psychotherapists liable if a criminal act was committed where the therapist knew the violent quality of the act that a patient was planning. It takes considerable clinical maturity to differentiate between the threats of a patient and the judgment that the patient may, for example, be seriously planning to murder an innocent person or to blow up an atomic reactor. An additional complication arises when the psychotherapist is beseiged by the therapeutic trends of this decade, what one author has described as "Psychobabble; fast talk and quick cure in the era of feeling" (Rosen, 1977). The therapist becomes fearful that he or she may be perceived as lacking in skills or awareness of the latest techniques.

Another possible problem is the use of techniques which mask the problems of the therapist. An example is placing a patient in a group when there is discomfort in the one-to-one relationship. It may also be an effort to avoid the anger that the patient stimulates in the psychotherapist. It may be a maneuver where the patient is placed in a group and becomes the focus of the group's anger. The patient is then set up as a scapegoat. Research indicates that psychotic patients are reacted to negatively by psychotherapists, people in the community, and by other psychiatric patients (Rabkin, 1972).

Patients who act in a bizarre and frightening manner often stimulate angry or negative responses from psychotherapists of all theoretic persuasions (Schwartz et al., 1974).

Professionals in all fields are rarely if ever value free. In a study of psychiatric hospitals, Rosenhan noted the abusive and contemptuous behavior exhibited toward the hospital patients by staff members (1973). Since patients in psychiatric hospitals have been badly hurt in their previous life experiences, rejecting them again doesn't seem to make much sense. It is poor psychotherapy. Every comprehensive survey of psychotherapists and their response to patients indicates that the dependent and compliant patient is more liked and stimulates very little anger on the part of the professional helper (Wills, 1978).

A cultural set exists in which people view another person's difficulty as evidence or a moral defect. According to Goffman's (1963) findings, people with physical defects are believed to have this defect visited upon them because of something that the family or parents had done. This goes back to medieval religious belief that the disadvantaged peoples of the earth simply deserve their fate (Ryan, 1971).

A "blaming the victim" approach ignores the observations of Comte, generally recognized as the intellectual father of social psychology. He viewed man as both the creature and the creator of the social world in which he lives. He identified the central problem of social psychology as follows: *how can the individual be both the cause and the consequence of society?*

Lest we become discouraged, we can take heart from the latest summary by Williams (1977). He collated evidence to support the conviction that behavior among the higher mammals is motivated more by altruism than it is by self-seeking action and unrestrained violence. His report is a critique of the reductionist doctrine that animal behavior is a conditioned response to stimuli. Williams presents evidence that the central factor of our instinctual heritage is the kinship of mutual aid. This should be reassuring to group therapists.

The famous Gestalt prayer of Fritz Perls is:

> I do my thing and you do your thing
> I am not in this world to live up to your expectations,
> And you are not in this world to live up to mine.
> You are you and I am I,
> If by chance we find each other, it's beautiful.
> If not, it can't be helped.

Greening, a humanist psychologist, gives a final version of the Gestalt prayer:

I do my laundry, and you do yours.
I am not in this world to listen to your ceaseless yammering,
And you are not in this world for any discernible reason at all.
You are you, and I am I, and I got the better deal.
And if by chance we find each other, it will be unspeakably tedious.
Fuck off. [Greening, 1977, p. 77]

Greening's summary of Perls' prayer appears to satirize the "new narcissism" that Perls espouses, which relates to ethics (Lasch, 1976, 1979).

Once again, the central issues are the criteria for mental health or the nature of what we mean by the good life. I believe that when an individual postulates values, there is a process of creation and reflection. We move beyond what is immediate and are constantly in dialogue with the world outside of ourselves and the world inside ourselves. Girvetz, the philosopher who is concerned with ethics, notes that the truly ethical comes to the fore when there are no existing guidelines to give us support. It is at this point that our morality becomes reflective and we reach a new level of becoming, where the self moves beyond current interests (1973). Group interaction moves group members to the reflective.

In the early work of Jean Piaget, he ascertained how children go about accepting the rules of the games they play. He questioned children carefully and in 1932 published *The Moral Judgment of the Child*. In the years that followed Piaget's original work, others have elaborated upon his analysis of moral judgment. As students of psychodynamics, we know the importance of language, linguistics, semantics, the impact of the questioner, and other myriad factors that are at work.

Jacques Lacan, the French psychoanalyst, stresses that the explication and integration of the unconscious material elicited from the patient must first be worked out within the therapist. Lacan believes that the unconscious is structured as a "natural language." According to Lacan, the basic philosophical problem of psychoanalytic inquiry relates to the problem of language. The science of linguistics is the model that psychodynamic therapists should use. Lacan states that Freud strayed from his fundamental findings when he adopted the models of physics and biology (1977).

The utility of simple models doesn't seem to work. In 1917, Albert Einstein wrote a letter to Felix Klein, one of his colleagues. He stated that no theory that he or any one else had arrived at was to be considered final. "No matter how we may single out a complex from nature . . . its theoretical treatment will never prove to be ultimately conclusive. . . . I believe that the process of deepening of theory has no limits."

When Einstein revolutionized the field of theoretical physics by the development of his general theory of relativity, he also experienced a profound personal change. This change was gradual. From his position as a young man with a logical positivist approach, he came to realize that our theories and concepts could never be arrived at by mere induction from experience but were *free* creations of the human mind. He searched for a unified field theory, a general-relativistic approach, and he became increasingly skeptical that quantum mechanics could be *the* complete theory of the physical world.

Piaget's efforts are worthy since they help us evaluate the moral dilemma. A readiness to accept responsibility for moral judgment is tied in with stages of personality development and the willingness to give up instant gratification. Loevinger (1976), in her work on ego development, has set forth stages of personality development. She is concerned, however, with "broader" personality issues than moral judgment.

The *is* and *ought to* is once more apparent. Perhaps Freud, an unusual man, had reconciled the *is* and *ought to*. In June 1938, he wrote, "You no doubt know that I gladly and proudly acknowledge my Jewishness though my attitude toward any religion, including ours, is critically negative." Yet later that year he wrote, "We Jews have always known how to respect spiritual values. We preserved our unity through ideas, and because of them we have survived to this day." The spiritual values that Freud wrote about are the system of ethics that Judiasm espouses—the *ought to*. Because Freud saw organized religion as the opponent of science, to which he subscribed, he took for granted that science in and of itself would be ethical. We know today that science, under the guise of neutrality, can visit barbarism upon the human race. The physicians who worked with Adolph Hitler called their experiments "works of science."

The psychotherapist, more than any other student of behavior, presents values to his patients by his very commitment to the affirmation of life. Some hold that psychotherapy is merely a subtle way of presenting value systems to patients through the benign influence of the psychotherapist. Perhaps this is so in the one-to-one dyadic psychotherapy. Once we enter into the group, the value systems of all present in the group become very clear. It is absurd to hold that psychoanalysis can dispense with value systems and concern itself only with the neutrality of scientific methods. There are many systems of science. What paradigm of science shall we use to be truly value free? It is very evident in the group when people of different religions, cultures, and life experiences come to meet with the professional psychotherapist.

The full-time student of ethics helps us define the principles involved in the *is* and *ought to*. Although we are not professional ethicists, we do have certain responsibilities as psychotherapists and group psychotherapists. The group psychotherapist cannot avoid the dilemma of what *is* and what *ought to be*. No amount of rational inquiry or statistical artifice relieves us of our concern for what *ought to be*. When we decide what is appropriate behavior, we *are* in the area of moral judgment (see Piaget) since we are out to motivate patients to act in a self-actualizing manner. We opt for productivity as opposed to self-destructiveness. We opt for life as opposed to suicide and yet we hold our clinical judgment in abeyance when terminally ill patients decide to die in a time and place of their own choosing. Freud, wracked with pain, finally prevailed upon Max Schur, his physician, and obtained medicine—a third of a grain of morphia. This is a small dose but it was enough to help a totally exhausted Freud, who rarely took anything stronger than an aspirin, finally to obtain the peaceful death of eternal sleep. Moreno, terminally ill, decided that he would die. He refused all food and made his own decision.

In Freud's correspondence with Putnam on the subject of ethics, two lines from his letters are especially relevant: "Ich betrachte das Moralische als etwas Selbstverstaendliches. . . . Ich habe eigentlich nie etwas Gemeines getan." This means, "I consider ethics to be taken for granted. Actually I have never done a mean thing." (Das Moralische also means that which is moral.) When I first read these lines I thought, how noble a man. I'm sure that Freud believed what he wrote but would Adler and Jung have agreed that Freud was ethical?

The current dilemma for psychotherapists is the emphasis in psychotherapy on what "is" as the ideal and avoidance of "what ought to be." The emphasis upon "is" may be a misreading of Freud's concern for the "reality principle." Freud spent most of his professional life avoiding the forthright expression of ethics, although his own life indicates that he was a very principled man with strong moral convictions. Early in his career he had translated the writings of John Stuart Mill and was aware of the British philosophical tradition. He seemed aware of the current ethical dilemma—that "*is*" expresses neither truth nor falsity nor moral judgment. "*Ought*" expresses moral judgment. This follows the ideas of David Hume, a Scotsman of the eighteenth century, who could find no argument for the existence of God. Hume believed that only those things exist which are perceived. We are all shut up in our minds and the outer world does not exist in substance. The chair in the room I am in exists because I see it. When I leave the room the chair no longer exists because I am not there to see it. If one follows Hume, one comes to a dead end—the ultimate in skepticism. It may be that Hume's ideas are the ultimate absurdity. We know that the real world exists because of what we perceive and our ideas and sensations about what we preceive. The chair does exist in the room after we leave the room. This is where psychotherapists become uneasy. How do we correlate what *ought to be* with what *is*. We return to the foundations of ethics and how to reconcile the three theories—virtue, duty, and the common good.

The study of ethics is a subspecialty in the field of philosophy. The study of philosophy is not to be viewed casually. Rather, it requires rigor and discipline. Perhaps this is why so many professionals avoid or ignore the problems of ethics in the field of psychotherapy and are quite content to view ethics as a body of rules governing professional behavior. This is a limited view. The rules of professional conduct may simply be another way of spelling out professional etiquette. In 1956, Zilboorg wrote:

> A psychoanalyst, like any human being, must have a philosophy of life or else he cannot function well as far as he himself or his patients are concerned. More than that: a psychoanalyst, more than any other professional man, must cultivate a philosophy of values, because the field that he is working in is always on the borderline of ontological and moral issues. [pp. 709-710]

Ontology is the science of being or reality, and some would say that the group psychotherapist, whatever his theoretic persuasion, deals with ontology. This volume contains codes of ethics of different professional organizations. Careful reading of these codes reveals that ethical problems are rarely covered, but rather, they describe rules of conduct. It is important for each therapist to establish a personal definition of ethics. In medical literature, ethics are presented as standards of behavior. In common usage, the words ethics and morals are used interchangeably. Most psychotherapists shy away from morals as a term, since they attach religious meaning to the word. Ethics seems more comfortable since it covers conduct. Professionals present ethics as a series of prohibitions: what the professional should and should not do. Ethics, however, means much more to the philosopher who is a professional student of ethics. For these ethicists, "ethics is a critical assessment of such bodies in the context of a comprehensive theory of human morality" (Jonsen and Hellegers, 1976). These ethicists define morality as the "actual behavior of human beings, involving judgments, actions, and attitudes constructed around rationally conceived and effectively based norms whereby that behavior can be judged right or wrong and around values whereby states affected by that behavior are judged good or bad."

The ostensible interest in ethics is both minimal and often an avoidance of more profound issues. It seems to reflect an enchantment with pragmatism, a belief that when people of good will meet together, good things will result. I am disenchanted with this approach, since it ignores the problem of evil—the one person who is not of good will and who can serve as a catalyst for destructiveness. It also avoids the historic meaning of ethics and stresses an optimistic view, or the "goodness" of the professional therapist.

Professional ethics are based on three foundations. The first is the theory of virtue; the good character of the professional is stressed. This may seem rather surprising since psychodynamic theory teaches us not to take anything for granted about the person, so why should we exclude group psychotherapists? Freud's great contribution was his hypotheses concerning the unconscious and psychic determinism.

The second foundation of professional ethics is the theory of duty. This may be found in Judaism and Roman Catholicism. This approach analyzes intentions, motivations, the circumstance, and the consequence. This results in judgments as to right and wrong, and ultimately innocence or guilt. Catholic theologians speak of "natural law" when they define good and evil. Contemporary students of ethics consider values as part of the theory of duty. Such values may include respect for life and compassion, values that were discussed in detail by Spinoza in his seminal work, *Ethics of Our Fathers*. Spinoza was absolutely deterministic. He believed that everything in the universe follows from something else. There is a definite chain with something preceding and something following. Spinoza denies free will; intellect and will are the same and will is the soul which knows and affirms what is true and what is false. Spinoza believed that man deceived himself by believing that he is free. He does this by avoidance of the causal chain of preceding and following events. The theory of duty founders on the concept of what is the nature of man so that it cannot stand by itself.

The third foundation of professional ethics is the theory of the common good. This is the theory of social justice. What is good for the society as well as good for the individual? This is another theory which cannot stand by itself since enormous atrocities have been committed under the "theory of common good or social justice." The American Indian, for example, was decimated, as the white settlers defined the common good. "The Nixon administration admired people who could be cold and dispassionate in making personnel decisions. To make concessions to people's feelings, to recognize that a particular objective was not worth destroying people in the process was not something that elicited any admiration. Such concern was viewed as a fatal flaw" (Jaffe, 1976). It appears that all three foundations are integral to a theory of ethics.

Confusion arises in psychotherapy and ethics when professionals do not agree on common principles. To illustrate, the code of ethics of the American Psychiatric Association explicitly prohibits psychiatrists from making public pronouncements about people who are in the public eye unless such people have given their approval for such a statement *after* they have been evaluated by a psychiatrist. Yet newspapers often publish statements made by psychiatrists who have never personally examined a person or persons in the public spotlight. These psychiatrists may feel that they subscribe to the theory of the common good. It is good for the society for citizens to be aware of the behavior of a certain individual.

But does the theory of the common good lead to premature judgment of innocence or guilt?

All too often the professional group psychotherapist advocates psychotherapy because it makes the therapist or patient feel better, yet the ethical issue remains untouched. The psychotherapist, out of fear that he is perceived as a moral arbiter, avoids setting forth his own value system. Consequently, he often avoids confronting the patient with ethical decisions that have to be faced. As I perceive this, when confronted, the patient becomes a responsible member of a culture because he is required to take a stand. The therapist should be reasonably clear that the patient does not accept the therapist's value system as a way of avoiding his own struggle and out of a need to please the therapist.

In a very profound way, the commitment of the therapist to work with a patient is a problem of ethics. It is a statement that he values someone enough to spend time with him. He may, of course, value himself so little that he needs to spend time with patients to justify his own existence. These are unconscious needs of the therapist which, it is hoped, will be brought to conscious awareness without burdening the patient. Each system of psychotherapy will be related to ethics as a discipline inasmuch as it stresses a rational approach, an emotive approach or a utilitarian approach. For example, Jay Haley, in his latest book, *Leaving Home: The Therapy of Disturbed Young People* (1980), states that his therapy and its premises are not related to a therapy based on the theory of repression where the individual is the problem. Therefore, he is not concerned with insight or awareness. People are not encouraged to express their feelings with the idea that change will occur. In describing the stages of his therapy, he states: "No blame should be placed on the parents. Instead, the parents (or mother and grandmother, or whoever it might be) should be put in charge of solving the young person's problem" (p. 44). Later he states that "the past, and past causes of the problem, are ignored and not explored. The focus is on what to do now" (p. 45). Yet earlier, the same therapist had written that his goal is to move the young person to more independence, either alone or with a wife. Haley is a family therapist who is radically opposed to a psychoanalytic psychodynamic approach and yet he apparently values the same ends as the psychoanalyst—the independence of the individual. He describes his patients as "mad" and states: "the term is not meant as demeaning. Another term which might be used is "eccentric." (p. 27). He is very specific when he states: "If one wishes to do effective therapy with mad people, it is best simply to abandon psychodynamic therapy. The therapist who attempts to be broadminded, trying to bring together psychodynamic theory and an approach based on restructuring a family, will be the most handicapped" (p. 24). Again we are faced with ethics, since Haley clearly deals with power in which he views the ends as justifying the means. The emphasis in Haley's approach is utilitarian: he stresses *what is*.

I have mentioned the problems of power as part of ethical problems because many people are concerned about counter-transference as a major problem for the novice or even for experienced therapists. Counter-transference is often defined as the therapist's feelings, largely unconscious, which are elicited by the patient's behavior. These feelings affect the objectivity of the therapist's clinical interventions so that psychotherapy becomes distorted, often ineffectual, and possibly destructive for the patient. I have discussed counter-transference in detail (Mullan and Rosenbaum, 1978), but the phase of counter-transference that is relevant here is the therapist's response to the patient's transference neurosis, namely the development of feelings of omniscience and omnipotence, as well as fantasies and strivings. In the group, it is relatively easy for the therapist to observe the reciprocal ties that bind two patients to one another and to objectify the distortions at work. But it is not easy to do so when there is a therapist-patient transaction at work. If the therapist is "well"—by which I mean open to self-examination—he will explore the patient's perception of the therapist's behavior. Because there are many perceptions at work in the group, the therapist cannot dismiss the patient's perceptions, as he might so easily do in the one-to-one relationship in individual psychotherapy. We again deal with power because the group therapist, by admitting to himself the wisdom and feasibility of the group approach, states to the patient, "I need others and you need others to help you with your problem. Either I cannot do it alone or I cannot do it as well." This is the expression of a value system on the part of the therapist who works with groups. The therapist opts for the group experience and argues against interpersonal isolation and intrapsychic alienation. This point of view is summarized by Simone Weil:

> A human being has roots by virtue of his real, active, and natural participation in the life of the community, which preserves in living shape certain particular treasures of the past and certain particular expectations of the future. [Weil, 1955, p. 43]

In the individual therapy experience, the therapist usually remains value free. His function is not to tell the patient what is right or wrong but to explore psychodynamics. As soon as the patient enters the group, other group members may react to behavior that is believed repugnant. There is no way in which the group therapist can forbid the expression of value systems on the part of other group members unless it is a completely controlled group with no free interaction. The risk at this point is that the group will establish social norms and that new group members will be forced to adopt these norms in order to be part of the group. The line is very thin. Should the pimp in the group be told that what he is doing is morally wrong, the exploitation of another human being? Sternberg (1965) was concerned with this type of problem. He wondered whether psychotherapy would work in prison settings. Would the practice of psychotherapy and especially of group psychotherapy violate the constitutional rights of inmates? Is this a legal or an ethical problem for the group leader? Are prisoners better off not disclosing information in the group? What assurance can be given that information disclosed in the group will not be used by other prisoners or by the prison custodial staff? Historically, rapists and child molesters are considered reprehensible by other prisoners and are subjected to a great deal of abuse. Should such prisoners be kept in a homogeneous group?

The issue of confidentiality must be fully and clearly explained to group participants. Each state has different legislation with respect to privileged communication. At the time of this writing, Florida has abandoned licensing of psychologists since "psychology" is seen as open to anyone who wants to psychologize. How does this affect confidences in therapy?

In New York, the issue of confidentiality between psychologist and client is clear. It is part of the Civil Practice Law and Rules, S405, Psychologist:

> The confidential relations and communications between a psychologist registered under the provisions of article one hundred fifty three of the Education Law (S7601 et sequence) and his client are placed on the same basis as those provided by law between attorney and client, and nothing in such article shall be construed to require any such privileged communication to be disclosed.

What this means legally is that a judge can order a physician to break confidentiality, as has been done in California with a physician going to jail as a consequence of his refusal to obey the order. The court cannot order an attorney to break confidentiality. Since psychologists are in the same category as attorneys, confidentiality is protected in the one-to-one relationship. Some of the implications of the confidentiality statutes are intriguing. In one case in New Jersey, when a psychiatrist was ordered to testify in a case and refused on the basis of confidentiality, he argued that he was a psychiatrist but actually using psychological methods and therefore a psychologist. This was done so that he could enjoy the protection of New Jersey's psychologist's law, which gives more protection to psychologists in the area of confidentiality than the medical law gives psychiatrists. The court insisted, however, that the physician-psychiatrist was medically trained and had to testify since the medical practices law gave him limited confidentiality.

The issue of confidentiality and privileged communication should be clear to all professionals. Confidentiality is the ethic that protects the client or patient. The client or patient must authorize any disclosure of information. There are unusual circumstances under which this principle may be abridged. The patient gives the therapist permission to release information. "In the patient's best interest" is the term used to justify divulging confidences. This covers significant danger to the patient. The patient may not agree that there is a significant danger. Many therapists believe that confidentiality should be absolute and that *no* circumstances justify the breach of confidentiality. In this instance, the psychotherapist should be prepared to be cited for contempt.

Confidentiality is considered on an individual basis, between therapist and patient. If there is a group of patients with a single therapist, the confidentiality applies only to the therapist. The patients who are present at the group meeting have no privilege of confidentiality. They may be called upon to testify. In my opinion, the recent decisions of the United States Supreme Court point to increasing erosion of the privilege of confidentiality. One attorney has suggested to me that the problem of privilege is overblown. All that the therapist or any patient has to answer when questioned is the stock "I don't remember." But this avoids the problem and merely teaches people to lie.

When there is joint counseling of a husband and wife by a psychotherapist, there is no *privilege* of confidentiality, according to a circuit court judge in Virginia (1979), who ruled that since statements were made to the psychiatrist in front of the spouse, there was no confidentiality. The implications of this ruling are disastrous for any type of marriage counseling. A sophisticated couple might avoid counseling since their joint sessions could conceivably end up in a court testimony if they should decide to divorce.

The areas of confusion become cloudier. In North Carolina, a psychotherapist can be sued if confidentiality is breached. At the same time, the law requires that the therapist report parents who engage in child abuse to the authorities. This issue will be discussed further on.

Privileged communication concerns itself with evidence law. The litigant has the right in any legal proceeding to withhold evidence that was originally communicated in confidence. The patient has the privilege, but the therapist has not. The patient may waive this privilege but the therapist has no decision to make in this regard. The patient may decide to waive the privilege or in some cases the judge may waive the privilege for the client if the evidence is believed to be crucial to the case. There are cases where the therapist may refuse to testify even though the patient has waived the privilege. The therapist may believe that it is a self-destructive act on the part of the patient.

Privileged communication is much narrower in its ramifications than confidentiality. There are law statutes that provide exceptions to privilege. This may in turn hamper the effectiveness of therapy. The *American Medical News* reported, in its January 12, 1979, issue, that the state of Pennsylvania's highest court, the Pennsylvania Supreme Court, reversed a lower court decision which held a psychiatrist in criminal contempt for refusing to reveal the information in a patient's records. In this case the court was attempting to determine the placement of the child of a patient being treated by the psychiatrist. Here the lower court judged the child's interests paramount and the highest court did not agree. The psychiatrist in question had treated the mother of the child. The thirteen-year-old child had a long history of delinquency and the court had to decide whether it was advisable to return the child to the mother. The psychiatrist claimed that medical ethics and the Pennsylvania physician-patient privilege statute precluded his sharing the contents of the patient's psychiatric record. The lower court fined the psychiatrist but the higher court did not agree. The opinion expressed, while reassuring to psychotherapists, does not grant professional status to fellow patients of someone in a group. These patients might conceivably be subpoenaed to testify. The Pennsylvania Supreme Court noted that the right of privacy, "has deeper roots than the Pennsylvania doctor-patient privilege statute, and the patient's right to prevent disclosure of information is constitutionally based." Further, the court noted, "the right to privacy derived from these constitutional underpinnings protects the privacy of intimate relationships like those existing in the family, marriage, motherhood, procreation and child rearing... the protection extends not only to the home... but also to the doctor's office, the hospital, the hotel room or as is otherwise required to safeguard the right to privacy involved in such intimate relationships." Lest the group psychotherapist take too much comfort from the Pennsylvania decision, I want to note that there are complex issues involved.

If there is psychotherapy of adults who abuse children, the issue of confidentiality becomes critical. The label "abusive parent" invites tremendous public criticism. Parents who fear such criticism may reject psychotherapy (Gelles, 1975). There are plans to identify and set up a registry of child abusers. This deals with confidentiality and includes the invasion of civil rights (Paulson, 1975; Whiting, 1977). Gabarino (1977) justifies the establishment of "intrusive monitoring networks" since he views the right to privacy as a mechanism by which individuals and families who need treatment are in fact isolated by privacy safeguards. But doesn't this lead to charges of coercion or that "Big Brother" is watching? Those who advocate group therapy programs for parents who are child abusers have emphasized that therapists should serve as "parent surrogates" (Paulson and Chaleff, 1973). The emphasis here is upon social skills training (Colman 1975) since it is believed that many biological parents have little or no awareness of what it takes psychologically to be a parent. The group becomes a social support structure and group membership gives the child-abuser parent some support in a highly critical culture.

For many years there has been intense criticism of both the theory and the technique of psychotherapy. Most of the criticisms center on the effectiveness of psychotherapy. The counter-arguments are that the psychodynamics of therapy do *not* invite the methods of the physical sciences as far as measurement of results. A theoretical physicist noted:

> The model of explanation in terms of cause, universal law, and movement, does not hold when we describe human actions. Communication—the transfer of pattern or meaning—is the principal relationship between men, while causality—the transmission of energy—suffices to relate things to each other. Human beings respond to meaning, not only to cause. Meanings are established by experience. . . . In any psychological or social theory we describe an organism, not a simple, relatively unorganized object like an atom: we have self-movement and evolution. Therefore, the explanation has a different aim from that in physics. [Hutton, 1974, p. 77]

The psychotherapist who engages in research in psychotherapy faces critical ethical problems. May we withhold psychotherapy as we compare control and therapy groups in order to evaluate treatment effectiveness, since we are called upon to validate the effectiveness or ineffectiveness of therapy? How will we monitor psychotherapy research so that the identity of group participants is disguised? There is an increasing use of one-way screens in training and research, as well as videotape recording. Patients often consent to procedures out of their own anxiety and the need to please the doctor. Is it ethical to exploit such a need? Of course the researcher can justify interventions in the cause of science and the welfare of man, but is the intervention fair? Is it right? Is it morally justified? I shall quote from one researcher to illustrate how the problem of ethics is ignored. Yalom et al. (1978) attempted to develop methods

> that would enable the alcoholic patient to work effectively in long term, interactionally based group therapy. . . . Our first step was to form an experimental group, using no selection criteria, in which we would try out various technical modifications we hoped might facilitate therapy. . . . The length of the alcoholic groups was predetermined by the research grant." [Pp. 419–420]

Nowhere in the article is there a discussion of the ethics of the approach used. It is not my intent to be captious but it would appear fair to patients to inform them of the research that is part of the psychotherapy process.

If research is being conducted to evaluate the effectiveness of psychotherapy, it may confuse the goals of treatment, both for the group psychotherapist and for the group patient. While there has been some coverage in psychotherapy literature which compares the effectiveness of treatment with different control groups, there has been almost no attention given to efficiency as the goal of treatment. By efficiency I refer to the costs of group psychotherapy, and indeed of all forms of pschotherapy. Costs cover both financial and emotional considerations. It would appear to be ethical for the therapist to make a clear statement to the patient as to what the joint goals are to be. Some people describe this as a contract but it is really much more than that. What is the group therapist looking for and what is the patient looking for? Many of the controversies surrounding psychotherapy relate to the goals of treatment. Is the effort of therapy to ameliorate problems that the patient presents? Is the effort made to effect a major change in life functioning? Should withdrawn children be placed in activity group therapy or a "modeling" form of group treatment so that they become less withdrawn? In this case, the assumed normative behavior is social interaction.

Kazdin and Wilson (1978) have described the problem of measuring therapy effectiveness as the "magnitude of therapeutic change." We now face the problems of adequate or acceptable change and the question of what adequate or acceptable means. What is *important* in therapeutic change? If change is defined as becoming something different, the definition is not applicable to symptom improvement or symptom relief. Each school of therapy reinterprets the patient's problems. Is it ethical to confront the patient with the broad panorama of life's difficulties if the patient's desire is simply to be relieved of job difficulties? Should the patient be told specifically that the focus is to be upon certain *problems* of living and that the group therapy will not ensure the capacity to handle subsequent problems? Does this stimulate increased anxiety?

In the early history of group psychotherapy, expediency was the important issue. An attempt was made to capitalize on time and effort, especially since there were few psychotherapists and many patients who needed treatment. Now we know that the group process itself is important and often indicated when there is a choice available of either individual or group treatment. While efficiency is admirable in terms of cost accounting and the use of minimally trained paraprofessionals, it may be very unfair to the patient. While there is evidence that untrained or marginally trained individuals perform adequately when asked to lead groups of patients, it may be related to the fact that neither patients nor group leaders are particularly aware of the deeper problems and will merely settle for a speedy solution. Again, we return to objectives of therapy.

The issue of efficiency and speedy results is also related to the encounter-group approach to psychotherapy. Encounter groups are discussed and evaluated as new techniques of group therapy. It is my belief that encounter groups are much more than new techniques. Back (1978) has discussed this in great detail. Encounter groups appear to be related to religious viewpoints. In the group psychotherapy model, there is a clear reciprocal relationship between the group leader and the group patients. The encounter group leader denies his responsibility to the "sick" patient. He avoids ethical problems since the *responsibility* of the physician is avoided but the *authority* of the physician is assumed. In the same way, the *authority* of the religious leader is accepted by the encounter-group leader but the *responsibility* is denied. The leader of the encounter group proclaims certain verities of life and most people enter encounter groups looking for that which they believe to be missing from their lives. Back (1978) has speculated that many people who join encounter groups are looking for a substitute or alternative to psychotherapy. There are group therapists who combine psychotherapy with some of the confrontational methods which they observe to be effective in encounter groups.

I have attempted to stimulate group therapists to be on guard. There are many problems that will arise in a society that is increasingly technological. It is important that the group therapist be at least a little clearer in topography than the group patient. An effort has been made to set forth some of the ethical problems the group psychotherapist will confront. If this stimulates further inquiry, this is all to the good. And good, is an ethical objective.

REFERENCES

AMERICAN PSYCHOLOGICAL ASSOCIATION. *Ethical standards of psychologists.* Washington, D.C., 1963, 1967, 1981.

BACK, K. W. An ethical critique of encounter groups. In G. Bermant, H. Kelman, and D. Warrick (eds.), *Ethics of social intervention.* New York: Halsted, 1978.

COLMAN, W. Occupational therapy and child abuse. *American Journal Occupational Therapy,* 1975, **29,** 412–417.

GABARINO, J. The price of privacy in the social dynamics of child abuse. *Child Welfare,* 1977, **56,** 565–675.

GELLES, R. J. The social construction of child abuse. *American Journal of Orthopsychiatry,* 1975, **45,** 363–371.

GIRVETZ, H. K. *Beyond right and wrong: A study in moral theory.* New York: Free Press, 1973.

GOFFMAN, E. *Stigma: Notes on the management of spoiled identity.* Englewood Cliffs, N.J.: Prentice-Hall, 1963.

GREENING, T. C. The Gestalt prayer: Final version? *Journal of Humanistic Psychology,* 1977, **17**(3), 77–79.

GROSS, S. J. The myth of professional licensing. *American Psychologist,* 1978, **33,** 1009–1016.

HALEY, J. *Leaving home: The therapy of disturbed young people.* New York: McGraw-Hill, 1980.

HORWITZ, L. Personal communication, 1979.

HUTTON, E. H. Letter. *Group Analysis,* July 1974, **7**(2), 77.

JAFFE, J. White House Staff Psychiatrist, 1971–1973; *San Francisco Chronicle,* Jan. 18, 1976.

JONSEN, A. R., and HELLEGERS, A. E. Conceptual foundations for an ethics of medical care. In R. M. Veatch and R. Branson (ed.), *Ethics and health policy.* Cambridge, Mass.: Ballinger, 1976.

KAZDIN, A. E., and WILSON, G. T. Criteria for evaluating psychotherapy. *Archives of General Psychiatry,* 1978, **35**, 407–416.

LACAN, J. *Ecrits.* New York: Norton, 1977.

LASCH, C. The narcissistic society. *New York Review of Books,* 1976, **23**(15), 5–13.

LASCH, C. *The culture of narcissism.* New York: Norton, 1979.

LOEVINGER, J. *Ego development: Conceptions and theories.* San Francisco: Jossey-Bass, 1976.

MERTON, R. K. *Social theory and social structure.* New York: Free Press, 1957.

MIRON, N. B. The primary ethical consideration. *Hospital and Community Psychiatry,* 1968, **19**, 226–228.

MORENO, J. L. Code of ethics for group psychotherapy in psychodrama: Relationship to the Hippocratic oath. *Psychodrama and Group Psychotherapy Monograph,* No. 31. Beacon, New York: Beacon House, 1962.

MORENO, Z. T. Psychodrama. In H. Mullan and M. Rosenbaum, *Group psychotherapy: Theory and practice,* 2nd ed. New York: Free Press, 1978.

MULLAN, H., and ROSENBAUM, M. *Group psychotherapy: Theory and practice,* rev. ed. New York: Free Press, 1978.

PAULSON, M. J., and CHALEFF, A. Parent surrogates roles: A dynamic concept in understanding and treating abusive parents. *Journal of Clinical Child Psychology,* 1973, **2**, 38–40.

PAULSON, M. J. Child trauma intervention: A community response to family violence. *Journal of Clinical Child Psychology,* 1975, **4**, 26–29.

PIAGET, J. *The moral judgment of the child.* New York: Harcourt Brace, 1932.

RACAN, J. DE BUEIL. *Oeuvres completes de Racan,* Nouvelle Edition. Paris: Chez P. Janet, 1857.

RABKIN, J. G. Opinions about mental illness: A review of the literature. *Psychological Bulletin,* 1972, 77, 153–171.

ROSEN, R. D. *Psychobabble: Fast talk and quick cure in the era of feeling.* New York: Atheneum, 1977.

ROSENHAN, D. L. On being sane in insane places. *Science,* 1973, **179**, 250–258.

RYAN, W. *Blaming the victim.* New York: Pantheon Books, 1971.

SCHWARTZ, C. C., MYERS, J. K., and ASTRACHAN, B. M. Psychiatric labeling and the rehabilitation of the mental patient: Implications of research findings for mental health policy. *Archives of General Psychiatry,* 1974, **31**, 329–334.

SENATE SUBCOMMITTEE ON CONSTITUTIONAL RIGHTS. *Individual rights and the federal role in behavior modification.* Washington, D.C.: U.S. Government Printing Office, 1974.

STERNBERG, D. Legal functions in prison group psychotherapy. *Journal of Criminal Law, Criminology and Police Science,* 1965, **56**, 446–449.

TAYLOR, C. *The explanation of behavior.* London: Routledge & Kegan Paul, 1964.

TAYLOR, R. Causation. *Encyclopedia of Philosophy,* 1967, **2,** 56–66.

WEIL, S. *The need for roots.* Boston: Beacon Press, 1955.

WHITING, L. The central registry for child abuse cases: Rethinking basic assumptions. *Child Welfare,* 1977, **56,** 761–767.

WILLIAMS, L. *Challenge to survival,* rev. ed. New York: New York University Press, 1977.

WILLS, T. A. Perceptions of clients by professional helpers. *Psychological Bulletin,* 1978, **85,** 968–1000.

YALOM, I. D.; BLOCH, S.; BOND, G.; ZIMMERMAN, E.; and QUALLS, B. Alcoholics in interactional group therapy—An outcome study. *Archives of General Psychiatry,* **35,** 1978, 419–425.

ZILBOORG, G. Psychoanalytic borderlines. *American Journal of Psychiatry,* 1956, **112,** 706–710.

Ethical Issues in Family Therapy

11

Nina D. Fieldsteel

The increasing interest in ethical issues and moral values in psychotherapy is in part related to the profound social crises of the past two decades. It is related to our concern with man's development as an ethical being and the interest in the psychological processes which affect the formation of moral values. Erikson's (1964) concepts relating "virtues" to the resolution of development crises and our reexamination of the superego and its protective and mastery functions have also led us to a new perception of the role of ethics and values in our work.

Ethics may be defined as the study of actions in the light of moral principles which have developed as we understand the intentions and consequences of those actions. Moral principles are composed of the codes of behavior which the individual develops and those which the society sets forth for its members.

Psychotherapists have had to reexamine the value systems implicit in their assumptions about the process of human development, about what constitutes normality and pathology, and about their professional function as agents of change. The initial effort was to define their function as scientific, to minimize the effect of subjectivity, and to see themselves as detached from value judgments. As our knowledge has expanded, this stance has become less tenable. We have had to examine our professional behavior and acknowledge that our value judgments, ethical beliefs, and moral values are reflected in our work. It has become increasingly important to make the implicit value systems explicit in the theoretical constructs and clinical procedures we use.

Family therapy immediately comes face to face with longstanding social, cultural, and religious assumptions. All human societies have had some rules for limiting the expression of sexual and aggressive behavior within the family group. The Judeo-Christian tradition has very strong limits on behavior within the family and profound assumptions about the importance of the family in the organization of society. From the commandment, "Honor thy father and thy mother," to the powerful symbol of the "Holy Family," the importance of family bonds for the security of the individual and the preservation of the social order is implicit in many of our beliefs. The concept of the patriarchial family is directly related to the economic organization of society. Psychoanalytic theory has, from yet another aspect, served to emphasize the importance of the family for individual growth and development. When one proposes to see the family unit as the focus for therapy and to effect change, one must consider how many deep-seated beliefs one may be proposing to change.

All therapy is concerned with change. Therapists vary in the ways in which they describe themselves and their role in producing change. Implicit in any discussion of change and the role of the therapist in the change process is the importance of the therapist's value system in determining the direction of changes as they occur. By its very nature therapy implies a concern with such concepts as health and pathology, reality and fantasy, social adaptation and affective functioning, and standards of acceptable interpersonal interactions.

In considering the ethical issues in family therapy it will be necessary to look at the different definitions of family therapy. Each has a different set of assumptions as to what is the focus for family change and how the therapist should function as an agent of change.

Definitions of Family Therapy

Family therapy is a treatment modality which focuses on the family as a whole as an effective way to produce change. Family therapy may focus on the family as a system, on the communications and interactions within the system, on the structures which maintain the symptom, or on the intrapsychic determinants of behaviors which are expressed in terms of interpersonal conflicts. In working with the individual patient, the therapist is not directly involved with the impact of the changes in the individual on the social context within which he or she functions. In family therapy, it is the concern with the individual as part of a system, the acknowledgment of the importance of the context within which behavior occurs, that makes it unique from the point of view of change and where change occurs.

Family therapy developed from a number of different sources. Three major areas of interest which led to the its development were the study of the schizophrenic patient, the experience with the serious limitations of treating the child patient independently of the family, and the study of communication patterns and language. Systems theory, which developed independently in several fields, supplied the theoretical constructs which allowed for the ordering of the multiplicity of phenomena observed in a family interaction.

In selecting several different definitions of family therapy, my aim is not to be comprehensive but representative, choosing those definitions which allow us to illustrate the implicit ethical issues more clearly.

From his background as a psychoanalyst and from his experience with working in a family group, Nathan Ackerman (1961) saw family therapy as a treatment modality which was concerned with the ways in which intrapsychic conflicts of individual family members and the conflicts expressed in family interactions were related. His language implied psychoanalytic formulations to define the origins of behavior, though he came to talk of the operations of observed behavior in terms of the family as a system. He was concerned with the relationship between intrapsychic conflict and interpersonal behaviors. To study this, he examined the relationship between conscious and unconscious motivations of behavior and the transferences both to the therapist and between family members. He stated that the aim of family therapy was:

1. to help the family achieve a clearer and sharper definition of the real content of the conflict. This is done by dissolving the disguises of conflict and the resulting confusion in family relationships. A greater accuracy of perception of family conflict is the goal.
2. to energize dormant interpersonal conflicts, bringing them overtly on the level of processes of family interaction, thus making them accessible to solution.
3. to lift concealed intrapsychic conflict to the level of interpersonal relations, where it may be coped with more effectively. [P. 65]

This view of family therapy, accepting as it does the psychoanalytic view of the primacy of the importance of intrapsychic conflict, and setting as its goal the examination of the effect of intrapsychic conflict on the family interactions, challenged several of the assumptions of individual psychoanalytic treatment. At the time that Ackerman began working with families these notions were considered quite radical. Family therapy, as it was defined, also raised several questions related to ethical issues.

The first question was that of the definition of confidentiality. This question has two sources, one practical, the other theoretical. The practical issues of confidentiality would emerge when the therapy started with an individual patient and then added the family. The theoretical question was concerned with whether an individual would be able to explore and expose the workings and origins of intrapsychic conflicts in any treatment situation other than in the intense dyadic patient-therapist relationship. Related to this was the question of whether the sharing of intrapsychic conflicts through fantasies, dreams, and transferences within the family would not threaten the family stability. By questioning whether this was ultimately "good" for the family, the critics of family therapy were indeed asking whether this was ethical behavior.

The process of family therapy appeared to pose a threat to long-held beliefs about the expression of sexual and aggressive feelings in the family. It seemed to suggest that the family organization, particularly the role of the parents, might be threatened.

It is interesting that Ackerman (1967) was one of the few family therapists who wrote about contraindications for family therapy. Among the contraindications he listed was the existence of legitimate family secrets which should be kept in order to maintain the integrity of the family.

Family therapy also developed from the study of schizophrenic patients and their families. Research focused on the family system, the organization of the family, and particularly on the communication patterns which set the structure of the family system. The focus of family therapy on the family system aims to understand the ways in which the system functions, maintains itself, and affects the development of its members. The analysis and understanding of the communication patterns are stressed, since the communications transmit the rules which maintain the system. "The symptom of any family member at a given time is a comment on a dysfunctional family system" (Satir, 1971). Satir talks of the person "wearing" the symptom as though it were a cloak which can be handed around to family members. The focus of therapy is to bring about changes in the system. The fundamental assumption is that changes in any part of the system affect the entire system. Systems theorists do not focus on history or on the intrapsychic, unconscious nature of the conflicts. They appear to have more clearly stated ideas of what is good and right in family functioning and are more direct about their role as facilitators of change. One of the ethical issues which this approach raised is whether what is "good" for one member of the family is necessarily "good" for all the family members.

Minuchin (1974) and his co-workers work with the structural aspects of the family system. Their primary focus is to "change the system so that it will no longer support the symptom" (Aponte and Hoffman, 1973). Structural family therapy has three axioms:

1. The individual's psychic life is not entirely an internal process. The individual influences his context and is influenced by it.
2. Changes in family structure contribute to changes in behavior and the inner psychic processes in the members of that system.
3. When the therapist works with a patient or with a patient family, his behavior becomes part of the context. [Minuchin, 1974]

In this definition of family therapy, the family therapist is required to take a more active role in the therapy. "Structural family therapy is a therapy of action" (Minuchin, p. 14).

The ethical issues which the structural approach raises are related to the importance of recognizing the possible differences in the value systems of the therapist and the family. There is the danger that the role of the therapist as a more active agent for change may shift the responsibility for the direction of change from the patient to the therapist.

In an effort to integrate the concepts of psychoanalysis and systems theory and to develop an integrative approach to family therapy, it is necessary to see the family as existing within a framework of complex systems. It is also the nexus of a complex of interacting systems. Each individual is a unique gestalt of biological, genetic, and intrapsychic dynamics. Such a broader conceptual framework makes the therapist's task more complex.

> An integrative approach to family therapy works with the operations of the family system, but also considers it important to deal with the intrapsychic determinants of the behavior of the individuals within the system. Interactions between family members are not only expressions of the family system, they are also expressions of intrapsychic conflict. The observable transactions of the family and the particular organization of the family as a system are related to and determined by both the conscious and the unconscious dynamics of the individuals within the family. [Fieldsteel, 1978, p. 130]

In this approach to family therapy the ways in which observable transactions and communications (verbal and nonverbal) make the unconscious conflicts explicit become important. The unconscious communications, the transferences within the family system, the individual's intrapsychic dynamics are all an integral part of the operations within the family system and must be considered if the therapist is to effect meaningful therapeutic change.

The ethical issues in this approach are related to those raised by Ackerman's theoretical approach. Issues of confidentiality, the importance of family structure, and the concepts of what is healthy family development determine how one works for change. The value systems of the family and the therapist must be examined. In this approach to family therapy the goal is to have the primary direction of change initiated by the family. The impact of the therapist's value system, however, must also be fully acknowledged.

Ethical Issues as Manifested in Clinical Practice

1. The Definition of the Problem and the Establishment of the Working Alliance

The usual experience for the family therapist is that a family presents an "identified patient" or an individual comes alone as the one needing help. The family therapist who redefines the problem as a family problem has made an assumption which presents an immediate ethical issue.

The therapist has assumed that he or she has the right, because of theoretical understanding and expert knowledge, to impose a new set of beliefs and values on the individual patient or family. The family or the individual comes requesting one kind of help: the therapist, using both the professional expertise and the power implicit in his position, is able to say to them that they must suspend their perceptions and trust his, that they must accept the therapist's definition of the problem. Because of the extreme inequality of the relationship between the patient and the professional, patients accept the therapist's perceptions as the truth. It occurs not only in family therapy, but in almost all therapy situations. It is more dramatic in family therapy, but it is not limited to family therapy.

Almost all therapists assume the right to redefine the presenting problem in terms of their own belief systems. How often have we heard ourselves say "the real problem is—"; "the presenting symptom means—"; or "what this patient really needs is—." We assume that it is within our rights to make recommendations and that this is not a violation of the patient's needs because of our knowledge and professional qualifications.

There is no doubt that the patient/family comes to us because of a sense of distress and a wish for relief. They come because we have knowledge, clinical skills, and professional expertise. But they also initially accept our statements because of the power they attribute to us and which we use. It is important for the therapist to recognize the difference between his professional skill and personal power. The patient may endow the therapist with power because of transference projections and infantile wishes for a powerful, good, and omniscient parent. The crucial issue is whether or not the therapist is seduced by the transference. The way in which it is used determines the nature of the therapeutic alliance. The goal of the therapeutic alliance should include the patient's understanding of both the problem and the process of therapy and the way in which the process helps in the resolution of the problem.

By redefining who is the patient—the family rather than the individual—we are also asking family members to sacrifice, at least temporarily, their autonomy and to accept our conviction that we know what they need and what will be best for them better than they do. If the therapist works from the position of the "superauthority," he poses an implicit threat to the parental authority. This forces the therapist to consider what value he places on the traditional family structure and the role of the parents in the family system.

It has been my experience that very few families come for family therapy with an understanding of what it implies. Those who do are usually families in which one or more of the family members have had a number of years of individual therapy, families who have plenty of insight but still "can't make it work."

Though we know that these impositions can occur only with the cooperation of the family, there is a serious question as to whether this cooperation is attained under circumstances which would be defined as "informed consent." It has seemed to me that the family therapist is under an ethical obligation to help the family understand what is involved in family therapy, why the therapist recommends family therapy, and what it will demand of the family members. In this way it becomes a cooperative venture rather than an exercise in power. A therapeutic working alliance is achieved when there is both the willingness to trust and an understanding of the goals which have been mutually established.

The ethical issue is not the fact that the therapist has a value system and a definition of what is conducive to optimal individual growth in a well-functioning family, but rather that the therapist can acknowledge what are his professional views and what are personal preferences arising from his own need systems.

2. Confidentiality

Other ethical issues arise in examining the problems of confidentiality as they develop in family therapy. When the family is seen as a unit from the onset of therapy, the guidelines for confidentiality may be established at the outset. But, as was stated before, the therapist often sees an individual (child or adult) and then sees this individual conjointly with the family. How then are the limits of confidentiality worked out for the therapist, the individual patient, and the family?

The procedure which satisfies my own commitment to the patients' rights is to help my patients try to define the limits of sharing before the family session. We discuss what they want to share. Where I have a different view, I may express what I would consider useful for the patient and the family and explore with them why the limits on sharing have been set where they are. Though we will explore the differences, I consider it my obligation to defer to the patient's boundary. This kind of limitation may also occur in the family session. Each family member has something he does not want to share. It is accepted as part of the structure of the family system. The boundaries may be redefined, at any time in the course of the family therapy sessions. The fact of what is shared may become a useful variable in the therapeutic process as changing individual needs reflect the way in which each individual defines himself or herself in relation to the family structure. One of my implicit goals for family therapy is to help family members individuate and redefine their relationships within the family system.

Generational boundaries also limit sharing. I assume that the preservation of generational boundaries enhances individual growth. I may work to help subgroups in the family preserve their secrets, keep their own confidences, and define their own roles within the family. Parents need not share everything with their children; adolescents need to define their own territory.

It is interesting that Ackerman (1967), early in his writing on family therapy, spoke of the contraindications to family therapy. One of the important contraindications was where there is a legitimate family secret to be maintained. The family, and sometimes the therapist, decides what is a legitimate family secret. After some exploration, the family, may decide to change what they define as secret, but they have an important voice in taking responsibility for establishing the constraints necessary to maintain those aspects of family structure which are necessary for improved family functioning.

3. Change

Family therapists who come from the discipline of individual therapy seem to experience less conflict with the definition of their role in family therapy when it is concerned with helping family members explore their intrapsychic conflicts and understand their impact on family interactions. They assume that they are working within the same guidelines that determined their role as the individual therapist. I do not believe this is so. The multiple transference between family members, as well as the multiplicity of transferences to the therapist, create a totally different field in which therapy is conducted. Related to this is the increaesed impact of the therapist's counter-transference reactions. The therapist must be constantly aware of these responses and of the ways in which they may affect what he sees as the necessary direction of change for the family.

Systems theorists seem to be more direct about their role as agents of change. Jay Haley's book is titled *Changing Families*. They do not assume, however, that the therapist's unconscious is a variable to be taken into account when considering how they affect the definition of aims and goals for family change. The ethical question centers on who defines the change: is it what the patient wants or what the therapist thinks it should be?

In describing the treatment of a family with an anorectic child, the therapist instructs the child, saying: "Tell your mother she does not love you and that's why you look like a scarecrow" (Minuchin, 1974). The crucial determining issue is whether that statement is based on what the patient has come to know or whether it is based on what the therapist believes to be true. Is a technique's effectivness enough justification to permit its use? Does the therapist's conviction that he knows what changes should take place entitle him to do whatever is necessary to make them come about? Many of us characterize such interventions as manipulative and see them as an exercise of the therapist's power.

Wachtel (1977), in *Psychoanalysis and Behavior Therapy*, suggests that as the therapist's role is demystified the patient is able to become more active. In talking of therapists' behavior, he says, "Communicating one's preferences openly and explicitly leaves the patient knowing more clearly where he stands and what is going on. He may still feel pressure and anxiety in response to the therapist's expectations, but he is potentially in a better position to sort out where his own preferences may differ from those of the therapist" (p. 282).

The action-oriented family therapists force us to recognize and accept the power of the therapist in the therapeutic relationship. They do not delude themselves that therapy is an egalitarian, democratic relationship. It would seem to me that it may not be at the outset, but that that is the goal toward which one works, in much the same way that that becomes one of the goals in child rearing.

The Therapist's Tasks in Developing Self-Awareness and an Awareness of Ethical Values

In all of the preceding discussion of ethics and therapy, we have made some assumptions about the therapist. At a symposium of the American Association for the Advancement of Science on "Ethics, Moral Values and Psychological Interventions," Wallerstein (1976) quoted Fletcher in his introduction and stated:

> The essential difference between science and ethics is that science is descriptive and ethics is prescriptive.... Scientific theories and statements depend for their validity upon verification; ethical theories and statements depend upon justification (do they do good?). [P. 369]

Erikson (1976), in a paper at that same conference, pointed out that psychotherapy exists in a unique area between the two.

In dealing with all of the general ethical issues, it becomes important also to consider the questions of professional ethics. Wallerstein (1976) states that "we are only ethical when we are constantly worrying about what is right; that is the burden of being a professional" (p. 372). Among the issues he suggests that the therapist must "worry" about are "the right to privacy," "professional and societal responsibility for the quality . . . of help offered," and the social impact of psychotherapy. He further states that "any interpersonal enterprise that deals with the values and the rights and the needs and the sensitivities of people is liable to, and often guilty of, improper coercive pressures upon the individual seeking help, some of the pressures deliberate and avowed, some of them unrecognized and unavowed, some unrecognizable because buried within the framework of the very assumptions upon which the whole endeavor rests" (p. 371).

Erikson (1976) continues this thought by adding that the task of the therapist is to "avow or disavow what ethics may be hidden in our work before we can indeed help clarify what ethics is and what we and ethics might yet do together" (p. 409).

I would expand this list of what is part of "the burden of being a professional" to include a consideration of the impact of the therapist's personal psychological organization on what is done in treatment and the importance of both the patient's and the therapist's unconscious in the interpersonal interaction. This latter effect is vividly amplified in family therapy.

In order to "worry" about what is right, to be ethical, the therapist has to have a healthy superego. There has long been an emphasis on the hostile, punitive aspects of the superego. This does not account for those aspects of the superego conducive to growth and effective interpersonal functioning. Schafer (1960), writing on the loving and beloved superego, suggests that it is important to focus on the contents of the superego which derive from the loved parent who provided both protection and ideals. This identification makes it possible for the child, and later the adult, to love and protect others and his society. These superego functions enhance self-esteem and increase pride as the individual evaluates the self in relation to the ego ideal. The development of the healthy, loving superego enables the adult to express "an affirmative sense of what man owes to man" (Erikson, 1976, p. 414).

This aspect of the therapist's personal growth has an important impact on his functioning, Particularly in family therapy, there is a need for a high degree of sensitivity to ethical issues which is possible only with the development of a loving superego. The ability to be sensitive to the social context, to use insight responsibly, to be critical without being destructive, and to be respectful of the social institutions, the family, and the individual's need for growth, requires a high level of complex integration on the part of the therapist.

The training of the family therapist requires attention to ethical issues as well as to techniques. Self-awareness and social responsibility are an important part of the professional ethics of all therapists. By being demanding of ourselves in our professional role, we may be able to be more responsible toward our patients.

REFERENCES

ACKERMAN, N. A dynamic frame for the clinical approach to a family conflict. In N. W. Ackerman, F. L. Beatman, and S. N. Sherman (eds.), *Exploring the base for family therapy*. New York: Family Service Association of America, 1961.
ACKERMAN, N. The future of family psychotherapy. In N. W. Ackerman, F. L.

Beatman, and S. N. Sherman (eds.), *Expanding theory and practice in family therapy.* New York: Family Service Association of America, 1967.

APONTE, H., and HOFFMAN, L. The open door: A structural approach to a family with an anorectic child. *Family Process,* 1973, **12**(30), 1–44.

ERIKSON, E. H. *Insight and responsibility.* New York: W. W. Norton, 1964.

ERIKSON, E. H. Psychoanalysis and ethics—Avowed and unavowed. *International Review of Psycho-Analysis,* 1976, **3,** 409–415.

FIELDSTEEL, N. D. An integrative approach to family therapy. In H. H. Grayson and C. Loew (eds.) *Changing approaches to the psychotherapies.* New York: Spectrum Publications, 1978.

MINUCHIN, SALVADOR. *Families and family therapy.* Cambridge: Harvard University Press, 1974.

SATIR, V. M. The family as a treatment unit. In J. Haley (ed.), *Changing families: A family therapy reader.* New York: Grune & Stratton, 1971.

SCHAFER, R. The loving and beloved superego in Freud's structural theory. *The psychoanalytic study of the child.* 15. New York: International Universities Press, 1960.

WACHTEL, P. L. *Psychoanalysis and behavior therapy.* New York: Basic Books, 1977.

WALLERSTEIN, R. S. Introduction to symposium on "Ethics, Moral Values and Psychological Interventions." *International Review of Psycho-Analysis,* 1976, **3,** 369–372.

Ethical Problems in Sex Therapy

12

Harold I. Lief

In a single decade following the 1970 publication of Masters and Johnson's *Human Sexual Inadequacy*, sex therapy has expanded so rapidly that it is now a new subspecialty. Perhaps 5,000 "sex therapists" are in the marketplace (100 of whom Masters believes to be competent). The rapid expansion has created great confusion. What *is* sex therapy? What is the difference between sex therapy and sex counseling? Is sex therapy a form of psychotherapy, or is it education? What are the requirements for accreditation as a sex therapist? Who is entitled to be called a sex therapist? Which of the many techniques used by sex therapists, such as surrogate partners, sexological examinations, are efficacious; which potentially harmful? If sex therapy is a specialized form of psychotherapy, is it to be subsumed under the traditional mental health disciplines, namely psychiatry, psychology, psychiatric social work, and psychiatric nursing, or is it a new discipline or specialty? How does it relate to the field of marital and family therapy, another psychotherapy field experiencing growing pains? In brief, sex therapy is a field that has not been defined, let alone standardized.

Not only is sex therapy a field in extreme flux, but it deals with a subject about which most people have intense feelings, strongly held beliefs, and well-defined values. When seen against this background, the usual ethical considerations in any form of therapy take on heightened significance. In the absence of standards of treatment and with uncertain methods of accreditation, safeguarding the welfare of the patient through providing informed consent so that he knows and agrees in advance to the form of treatment, protecting his confidentiality and rights of privacy, ensuring the patient's freedom from exploitation and assuring the competence of the therapist are much more difficult than is the case in types of psychotherapy which have been practiced for generations.

It is clear that the reader cannot comprehend the ethical issues of sex therapy without a proper appreciation of the field itself. This chapter, then, will include a brief overview of the field of sex therapy followed by specific ethical issues. These are:

1. The assurance of at least minimally adequate care;
2. Protection of the patient from exploitation which can be sexual, financial, or by value imposition;
3. Informed consent;
4. Confidentiality and privacy;
5. Ethical problems in clinical research;
6. Ethical issues in the training of the sex therapist.

The Sex Therapy Field

Professional Roles and Tasks

A World Health Organization report (1975) differentiated the levels of intervention for practitioners:

> Education, counseling, and therapy may be regarded as inseparable parts of the total effort in sexual health care. First, the provision of sexual health *education* to the community, to the physician, and to other health workers has the highest priority because this can be done with the least amount of training and will affect the greatest number of people. While sex education should be a basic part of preventive medicine, it has also been shown to be effective in assisting individuals and couples to overcome sex problems. Second, there is a need for *counseling* of individuals and couples with slightly more complicated problems; this can be carried out by a nurse, midwife, the general practitioner, the gynecologist, and others. Third, there is a need for in-depth sex *therapy* by specially trained professionals who see the people with the most complicated problems. Health and other community workers require more specialized training to undertake sex counseling and sex therapy.

Table 1 indicates a hierarchical arrangement of tasks and roles required to treat sexual problems.

The therapist should be not only a competent sex educator and counselor, but must have attained competence as a marital therapist and individual psychotherapist. In addition, the therapist must be able to use effectively the specialized skills, such as the graded behavioral tasks called "sensate focus" (Masters and Johnson, 1970), used to reduce the demand for sexual performance, to overcome sexual inhibitions, and to facilitate effective sexual communication. He or she must be able to assess adequately the degree to which biogenic factors have to be understood and treated.

The ability to take a sexual history and to conduct a sexual interview competently is required at each of the levels of intervention. The interviewer often gives tacit or explicit permission for patients to experiment with sexual behaviors that heretofore have been inhibited or associated

TABLE 1. Classification of Professional Tasks and Roles in Response to Sexual Problems

Level of Diagnosis of Sexual Problem	Patient Need	Professional Task	Professional Role
Sexual ignorance	Need to know	To provide accurate information	Inquirer-educator
Situational discomfort/anxiety	Need to relax	To reduce or eliminate immediate causes of sexual dysfunction	Counselor
Interpersonal distance/conflict	Need to reorient the relationship	To reshape dyadic system	Marital therapist
Historical intrapsychic conflict	Need to explore tension between intrapsychic and interpersonal systems	To explore the interface between historical conflict and sexual discomfort/dysfunction	Psychotherapist
All of the above	Flexible use of new repertoire of sexual behaviors	Formulating hierarchy of patient needs and incorporating those into a sequence of treatment	Sex therapist

with anxiety. Certain value differences between patient and therapist often occur during this process. The ethical problems involved in value differences will be described elsewhere in this chapter.

Values are usually designated as preferences. These in turn are linked to beliefs. Many beliefs surrounding sexual behavior are firmly held and, when challenged, may produce strong emotional reactions. Hence, even at the level of sexual education, value conflicts between the therapist and the patient often arise. This is particularly apt to occur when the therapist attempts to correct certain sexual myths; for example, mistaken notions about the effects of aging, the importance of penis size, the need for simultaneous orgasm, the dangers of oral sex.

Above all else, the sex therapist must be flexible. Frequently the sexual problem demands conjoint couple therapy before specific sexual techniques can be employed effectively. Less frequently, individual psychotherapy is required first. The most commonly used technique in sex therapy is sensate focus, namely graduated steps in mutual pleasuring, starting with nongenital pleasuring, proceeding to genital pleasuring, and finally to intercourse. If conjoint therapy is not carried out before sensate focus, the couple interactions may provide enormous resistance to the behavioral techniques included in sensate focus. Timing is thus a critical factor in using specific behavioral techniques. Sex therapists who can respond flexibly with a variety of treatment methods must have more intensive and more prolonged training than sex educators and counselors. They need to have had much greater clinical experience than counselors ordinarily possess in order to be able to select appropriate methods or to initiate changes in strategy and technique, as the circumstances suggest. In keeping with their increased sophistication, they must be relatively free from counterproductive biases and blind spots.

If one accepts the above definition of sex therapy, it becomes clear that even skillful psychotherapists who can treat an individual patient competently must add to their skills marital therapy and the specific techniques (at least sensate focus) of sex therapy. Thus, clinicians who have completed training in clinical psychiatry or psychology are not equipped to call themselves "sex therapists" unless they take additional training in marital therapy and the specific techniques of sex therapy.

It is no wonder then that Masters estimates that only 100 of 5,000 clinicians who label themselves "sex therapists" are truly competent. Some, but not all, sex therapists are also equipped to practice group therapy with patients with sexual dysfunctions or other problems. Group therapy skills are very helpful, even if not absolutely essential. In the same category is the capacity to carry out therapy with a co-therapist, in the event that co-therapy is the treatment of choice.

Special Techniques of Sex Therapy

As has been said, the most significant and widely used technique in sex therapy is sensate focus (occasionally combined with muscle relaxation). Sensate focus is the least controversial of the sex therapy techniques. The couple practices effective sexual communication and stimulation in privacy, so this is hardly controversial unless there is some attempt by the therapist to coerce the patient or couple by threat or intimidation to modify their values. Sensate focus can become a technique opposed by conventional ethics in health care if the therapist insists on watching the couple practice. There are a few therapists who insist on watching the couple practice "live." A somewhat larger number, although still a tiny minority of therapists, recommend the use of videotapes of sexual behaviors including coitus, so that these can be evaluated and criticized. For all but a few sex therapists the obvious invasion of privacy is sufficiently blatant to render this an inappropriate form of therapy. While Masters and Johnson certainly observe their research subjects in various forms of sexual activity, they never have done so with treatment couples.

The use of erotic films and other sources of erotic stimulation such as pornography as adjuncts to therapy is widespread. Here again, the major issue is one of value imposition, which will be discussed elsewhere in this chapter. The "sexological" evaluation has a number of variations, some of which raise more ethical questions than do others. In one variant the wife is examined with her husband in the examining room. During the examination the therapist stimulates her erotically responsive tissues, including the clitoris and nipples, and points out the erotic responses to both the woman patient and her husband. In a less frequent variant, the wife and husband are stimulated in a similar fashion by the therapist of the opposite sex, in the presence of both co-therapists. The possibility for sexual exploitation is obvious. (This is particularly true, of course, if the husband is not present during the wife's stimulation.) The demystification of sex is unfortunately all too often accompanied by its dehumanization.

In another variant no such stimulation is carried out. Instead, the anatomical parts are observed by the patient with the use of a hand mirror. To avoid any implication of improper erotic interest on the part of the therapist, the clitoris, for example, is touched with a tongue blade rather than with the examiner's finger. This technique is used to educate the patient and her husband about sexual anatomy and responsivity and can be done effectively in the absence of specific sexual stimulation. Another variant of this approach is the use of the so-called "psychic-pelvic" examination in which not only are the anatomical parts pointed out in the manner described above, but the female patient is asked to verbalize her thoughts and fantasies about her external and internal genitalia. Some extraordinary fantasies, including a lot of misinformation, may be reported in this fashion, giving the therapist the opportunity to correct myths and misinformation.

In addition to the sexological examination, the "laying on of hands" may occur in a variety of other specialized methods of treatment. These methods are usually considered under the general rubric of "body work." In addition to individual and group massage, body work may refer to nude encounter groups, and hot tubs and saunas, the object of which is increased freedom and comfort with one's own body. These methods are not generally used; they form part of the treatment plan in a limited number of sex clinics. The possibility of sexual exploitation is so great that the Code of Ethics of the American Association of Sex Educators, Counselors, and Therapists (AASECT) precludes client nudity other than during a physical examination by a licensed physician, nurse, or physician's assistant. Since sexual problems often have a medical basis, physical examination may be a most important part of the evaluation. The usual medical physical examination, therefore, has to be sanctioned as part of the patient's work-up. AASECT restricts the physical examination to those practitioners in the health field whose privilege to examine the nude body has been approved by society for centuries.

The item about nudity from the AASECT Code of Ethics was roundly criticized by Wardell Pomeroy, Ph.D., Academic Dean of the Institute for Advanced Study of Human Sexuality at San Francisco (1979). Dr. Pomeroy feels that "the discipline of sexology is still in its infancy, and those of us in the field must be careful to promote actions which enhance it, rather than impede it. There is still much experimentation and research to be done, especially in sex therapy and sex education. To impede the development of objective inquiry is, in my estimation, a grievous error." Dr. Pomeroy goes on to say that

> perhaps the single most destructive movement within the sex field today is to move to "ethicize," for such a move signals the attempt by a particular school of thought to set a moral system which excludes other schools of thought which disagree with them. It is a power trip without integrity, the last refuge of an old guard whose time has passed. There is a move to capture a field, to limit the freedom to examine data, to stop persons guided by evidence, and to stifle questioning of assumptions. It censors persons from telling what they know and crushes the spirit of free inquiry so desperately needed in a new field, so lacking in research and development. In the worst sense, it is the attempt to set rules of conduct upon persons in the helping professions through unwarranted harassment and coercion through "loyalty oaths." [p. 1]

I do not see how one can disagree with the notion that to establish a code of ethics is in itself an ethical decision. Most senior researchers and clinicians in the sex therapy field believe, however, that a code of ethics is essential in order to prevent the all too easy sexual and financial exploitation of patients, especially since it is a field in which the virtual absence of credentialing opens the field to outright quacks and untrained or semitrained professionals, some of whom may enter the field not only because of the money to be made, but because of their desire to gratify their own sexual or power needs. Without a code of ethics the field is open to an "anything goes" perspective. Here, then, are two contrasting ethical polarized positions: establish a code of ethics with such latitude that it is essentially completely permissive, so broad and vague that there are no sanctions against exploitive behavior or, on the other hand, arrive at a code of ethics that may stifle the freedom of inquiry and of experimentation.

Perhaps it is because I am a physician and have therefore always practiced under an ancient code of ethics that I feel my own ethical choice is to promote a code of ethics which, if it errs, does so on the side of protecting the patient from exploitation. I am sure that in some instances body work such as group massage in a hot pool by skillful and dedicated therapists may be very effective. One example is the use of this technique for women who have had mastectomies. On the other hand, one can see that a similar nude encounter with an untrained, unethical, or exploitive person might have unfortunate consequences.

Another controversial issue in sex therapy is the use of surrogate partners. Few sex therapists use partner surrogates, and fewer still will admit to the practice. Many more, however, believe that the surrogate partner may have an important place in the treatment of men with sexual dysfunctions, particularly in men without available partners. The reasons for hesitancy in using surrogates are:

1. The possible moral and legal link between the "procurement" of a surrogate partner and "pimping" for a prostitute.
2. It may not violate the therapist's own personal ethical standards, but the therapist may fear the risk of condemnation from other professionals or from the community. A number of court decisions have warned professionals not to depart too far from community values and the public's concept of what is appropriate treatment. In addition to potential legal action by accrediting or professional associations, the therapist may fear a malpractice suit.
3. The fear that the surrogate partner may be incompetent; many of them refuse supervision by sex therapists, believing themselves to be better "therapists."
4. Even if the treatment by the surrogate is successful, the patient

may not be able to "transfer" his newly learned skills to another female partner.

Despite the fears of legal action, I am unaware of any criminal prosecution of a sex clinic. There is one unverified report that in one state a psychologist faced litigation for giving a client the name of a prostitute acting as a sex therapist (Perr, 1975). It is true that a civil action suit was brought against Masters and Johnson. In that case the plaintiff was the husband of a woman allegedly used as a surrogate partner. It is my belief that in that instance, without the knowledge of the clinic administrators, an appointments secretary substituted herself for the surrogate partner. There was no way that Masters and Johnson could allow the case to go to court, even though they had an excellent chance for complete vindication. The confidentiality of their patients would have been violated if the names of the patients had been revealed, so the case was settled out of court. Despite the absence of any criminal prosecution, many therapists are fearful of being charged with being panderers, or even as pimps. The latter allegation could be avoided if no money is exchanged between the therapist and the surrogate. The surrogate, however, could potentially face criminal charges of prostitution. Theoretically, even the customer-patient could face prosecution. If the patient were married, he could also be charged with adultery. It is clear that prosecuting attorneys are not eager to bring charges against sex therapists or people they employ as surrogates. A test case might clear the air, but as yet none has been arranged (Jacobs et al., 1975; Wolfe, 1978).

Specific Sex Therapies: Are They Dehumanizing?

A charge made by a number of prominent psychoanalysts including Leslie Farber and Natalie Shainess is that specific sex therapy, certainly sensate focus and other techniques such as the use of surrogate partners, are dehumanizing. They claim that sex in this fashion becomes mechanical, dehumanizing, and depersonalizing—push-button sex, as it has been called. It is claimed that the behavioral techniques employed in sensate focus rob the couple of the vitality and spontaneity, the mystery, even the joy of sex. In response to this, one must remember that the patients are troubled and sex is usually not joyful for them; in fact, it is often painful and anguishing. Sex behavior is a learned skill like dancing or tennis. There are innate factors in all these skills, but almost all of the components have to be learned. Once learned and mastered, the activity can become much more spontaneous and joyful. Not infrequently patients complain of the artificiality of sensate focus, the fact that it is planned, organized, rehearsed, and not very spontaneous. This calls into question one type of values, namely *telic,* referring to ultimate means and ends (Levitin, 1973). This is surely one case in which the therapist should be able to convince the patient that the ends justify the means.

Classification of Sexual Disorders

In this chapter various forms of sex therapy have been described without defining the types of diagnostic entities for which the therapy is relevant. The most common problems are either psychosexual dysfunctions or "concerns" ("difficulties"). The new Diagnostic and Statistical Manual III (DSM-III) of the American Psychiatric Association has these categories of psychosexual dysfunctions:

inhibited sexual desire;
inhibited sexual excitement, e.g., impotence in the male, "frigidity" in the female;
inhibited female orgasm ("preorgasmia");
inhibited male orgasm (retarded ejaculation);
premature ejaculation;
functional dyspareunia;
functional vaginismus.

Sexual concerns or difficulties are not classified in DSM-III, being regarded as either relatively unimportant or not sufficiently organized to be classified as a dysfunction. Yet, the difficulties or concerns may create more marital dissatisfaction than specific sexual dysfunctions (Frank et al., 1978). These difficulties include conflicts over frequency of sex, the timing of sex, the initiation of sex, the degree of passivity or activity of each partner, the feelings that accompany sex (e.g., "he doesn't express any feelings when we make love," or conversely, "I am turned off by her intense passion"), aspects of the sexual repertoire such as oral sex, and sexual skills and communication.

Ethical issues may be related to the specific nature of the patient's problems. This is particularly true of psychosexual disorders in DSM-III, which are as follows: gender identity disorders such as transsexualism, and the paraphilias, namely fetishism, transvestism, zoophilia, pedophilia, exhibitionism, voyeurism, sexual masochism, and sexual sadism. Finally, under "Other Psychosexual Disorders," DSM-III lists egodystonic homosexuality and an unclassified group of psychosexual disorders.

There are unique ethical problems in the treatment of homosexuals and of those individuals with paraphilias or disorders of gender identity. Although the therapy for these disorders involves a number of ethical issues such as confidentiality and privacy and informed consent, the most important ethical issue in the treatment of people whom society has often regarded as deviant is in the potential conflict of values either between the patient and his therapist, or between the therapist and society. Ethical issues of the treatment of gender disorders, paraphilias, and of homosexuality are described in the section on value imposition.

Professionalization of Sex Therapy

The basic question to be addressed here it whether sex therapy is a set of procedures that may be encompassed under psychotherapy, or whether we are indeed witnessing the development of a new profession (LoPiccolo, 1978). Bear in mind that this issue is relevant to ethics because it is relevant to the ethical dimension of competence. If the client does not get his "money's worth" owing to the therapist's incompetence, an ethical violation takes place.

In order to assess *competence* in sex therapy, it is necessary to understand the major elements of sex therapy. Some of these have already been described in this chapter, but LoPiccolo's summary is so concise that I wish to paraphrase it. He cites seven major elements in the therapy of sexually dysfunctional couples. Sex therapy is generally brief—not more than ten to fifteen sessions. The elements are as follows:

1. The sexual dysfunction is *couple related.* The husband-wife interaction is an essential ingredient in treating sexual dysfunction.
2. *Education* and *permission:* not only is information transmitted, but the couple is given permission by the therapist to try out new sexual techniques.
3. *Changing negative attitudes.*
4. *Reduction of anxiety.* Sensate focus or even specific behavioral psychotherapy techniques such as systematic desensitization are used to reduce performance anxiety (see also item 7 below, as an anxiety-reducing technique.
5. Emphasis on *effective communication* utilizing feedback during sexual activity.
6. Use of *marital therapy techniques* to diminish or eliminate the sabotaging elements of the relationship.
7. *Reducing the demand for performance.* Typically, sexual intercourse is forbidden until the couple goes through a series of nondemanding activities. This permits the buildup of confidence, increasing communication; when confidence is restored, intercourse is permitted.

The sex therapy field seems to be going in two directions simultaneously. On the one hand, it seems to be a subspecialty of psychotherapy;

on the other, a new profession seems to be emerging. Each perspective has obstacles. Students who graduate from doctorate clinical psychology programs or physicians finishing psychiatric residency are not qualified for sex therapy, since those programs do not usually include the required specialized training in sex or marital therapy. Only 7 percent of doctorate programs in clinical psychology have any formal training in sex and marital therapy. Similarly, nurses and social workers receive little or no training in sex and marital therapy. Continuing education efforts to upgrade the skills of current practitioners of psychotherapy are almost totally inadequate.

Problems in the development of a new profession revolve around two issues: inadequate training and the likelihood that National Health Insurance (NHI), when it comes, will not cover the clients of therapists who are not in the recognized mental health professions, and may not cover sex and marital therapy even when provided by the mental health professions any more than they are now being funded by third-party carriers, unless the therapist "cheats a little" on the insurance forms. In any case, most new professional sex therapists are people with minimal training in psychotherapy who rely on educational methods and standardized behavioral therapy techniques that may not be advisable for many of their clients. Somewhat fewer of the new professionals are well-trained psychotherapists with little or no training in the specialized field of sex therapy.

The issue may be decided by economic factors. It appears as if NHI, if it comes, will not pay for outpatient psychotherapy of any kind unless the services are "personally rendered" by a "qualified mental health professional," which a draft of an NHI plan by the Senate Finance Committee in February 1980 defines as a psychiatrist who is certified or has completed three years of residency training in the field, a licensed or certified Ph.D.-psychologist, a psychiatric nurse, or a psychiatric social worker with at least a master's degree. If this is what we can anticipate for psychotherapy, we certainly can expect the same or greater restrictions for sex and marital therapy; indeed, these areas may be excluded from coverage altogether. If almost every form of health care is covered by national health insurance, the issue will come down to the extent people will be willing to pay for these services privately. As suggested above, sex therapy is not now covered by third party carriers unless the mental health professional finds some biogenic cause for the sexual problem (in which case the therapist has to be a physician), or enters "anxiety" or "depression" as the diagnosis for one of the spouses, who is thus made the "patient." The argument that sex and marital therapy prevent physical and mental illness and save insurance dollars does not seem to be persuasive to the insurance carriers.

As was stated previously, the issue is one of *competence*. Will the vicissitudes of the marketplace attract, or will they drive out, unqualified people? Although it is difficult to predict the impact of NHI on the marketplace when most of health care will be financed by the government, it is likely that only traditional mental health practitioners will be in a position to qualify as caretakers. It will be the obligation, then, of mental health professionals who are also trained sex therapists to teach the specific skills of sex therapy to the next generation of psychiatrists, psychologists, social workers, and nurses. Since nonpsychiatric physicians will also be "covered" by NHI, they will also need to upgrade their psychotherapy as well as their sexual therapy skills.

Specific Ethical Issues

Competence

How can the consumer of sexual health care be assured of at least minimally adequate care? How can the field of sex therapy ensure a basic level of professional competence including standards of ethical behavior for its practitioners? To accomplish this requires some form of regulation. Regulation implies some form of accreditation. Hogan (1979) has reviewed the field of regulations in psychotherapy, and has related these to outcome research and the factors that are significantly related to positive outcome. For example, Luborsky and his associates (1971) found that the level of experience, particular skills, and interest patterns are all directly related to the effectiveness of psychotherapy. It is likely that what is true of psychotherapy is also true of sex therapy, although the outcome studies that have been carried out have not focused upon the variables Luborsky found to be significant.

Previously the dangers of ethical guidelines themselves were pointed out. Similar dangers are present for regulation. Regulation may limit freedom of innovation and may eliminate some methods before sufficient time has elapsed for adequate study. There are many questions about the training for sex therapy that are still unsettled; e.g., the extent of medical training. Premature closure imposed by regulation could jeopardize the satisfactory settlement of these issues. Other disadvantages of accreditation include the inevitable formation of regulatory bodies and consequent bureaucratic impediments. Accreditation can also lead to the monopolization of the field by some powerful groups. Regulation may mean the acceptance of a very low order of competence. Monopoly of the field may also interfere with the broad dissemination of health care to all levels and groups in the population.

On the other hand, the advantages of regulation are:

1. It establishes credibility in the eyes of other professionals and of consumers of sexual health services.

2. Satisfactory self-regulation by the field itself makes the field less subject to outside control.
3. Ensuring a basic level of professional competence assures the patient or client of at least minimally adequate care.
4. Regulation helps to ensure that the client will not be exploited or harmed by the practitioner.
5. Certification or licensing would make it more difficult for a practitioner to make false claims.
6. Accreditation may help to delineate levels of competence, helping inadequately trained professionals to recognize their own limitations and providing a process by which clients can select appropriate counselors or therapists.
7. Accreditation promotes consumer awareness and helps to educate the public about the services offered.
8. A professional organization or accrediting board makes it possible for consumer complaints to be lodged more effectively.

In short, there is a choice between increased order and more effective functioning based on accreditation versus increased freedom for experimentation with new methods or approaches, both in training and in therapy (Lief, Sarrel, and Sarrel, 1980).

If we define the field of sex therapy as a form of psychotherapy that involves "complexities of constitutional endowment, physical health, developmental history, intrapsychic conflicts" (Meyer, 1976), as well as interpersonal conflicts between partners and sexual ignorance, the implication is clear that a medical orientation is essential for many, if not most, problems. To what extent is personally rendered medical care, or at least supervision, a sine qua non of competence in the field? The frequent appearance of biogenic factors in the etiology of sexual dysfunction warrants close medical supervision. As one example, Spark and his colleagues (1980) found that 37 of 105 consecutive patients with impotence had had previously unsuspected disorders of the hypothalamic-pituitary-gonadal axis.

In evaluating the importance of competence as an ethical issue, one must clearly differentiate between the incompetent therapist and the exploitive one. One should not equate technical and moral objections, although both are ethical concerns. As Redlich (1977) puts it, "Would we consider a surgeon who treats the patient ineptly to be as reprehensible as a surgeon who deliberately hurts him?"

The types of accreditation are as follows:

1. Membership in professional organizations;
2. Specific accreditation by a professional organization;
3. Accreditation by a professional examining board;
4. Accreditation by a governmental agency—either certification or licensure.

Each of the above methods has its advantages and disadvantages, and each affects the issue of competence in different ways. For a fuller discussion of accreditation, see Lief, Sarrel, and Sarrel (1980).

Exploitation of the Patient

Exploitation may be financial, sexual, or through value imposition.

Financial.   In a television report on sex therapy, a commentator said, "There are millions of dollars in sex therapy; it's big business. Somebody will want to make these millions" (Redlich, 1977). The possibility of financial exploitation has brought irresponsible persons into the field—some are outright quacks; others are people with little professional training. The fairly widespread practice of asking that the patient pay the total cost of the treatment program in advance is questionable. For fifteen sessions, the fee charged by some private sex therapy clinics may be $4,000 or more. If regulating the field will assure the patient, as well as professional colleagues, of the credibility of the sex therapist, and if it will inhibit the therapist from making false claims, financial exploitation should be significantly reduced.

Sexual Exploitation.   Of all the ethical issues in sex therapy, sexual exploitation has received the most attention. Erotic contacts with patients are prohibited by the codes of ethics of all the major health professional organizations. These codes continue the tradition of the Hippocratic oath. Taboos against sexual relations between therapists and patients have been with us for thousands of years. The vast majority of mental health professionals strongly condemn therapist-patient erotic contact (Marmor, 1976; Hare-Mustin, 1974; Redlich, 1977). That erotic contact between therapist and patient was occurring more frequently than professionals realized, was brought to our attention by Masters and Johnson (1970). Many clinicians report that patients who have had sexual relations with their therapist have been psychologically scarred. Additional treatment by another therapist is often difficult (Barnhouse, 1978; Ulanov, 1979; Voth, 1972; Collins, Mebed, and Mortimer, 1978).

Only a few therapists have been overtly in favor of sex between therapist and patient. These include McCartney (1966) and Shepard (1971).

Despite the almost universal rejection of the therapeutic utility of erotic contact between therapist and patient, several surveys have demonstrated that a substantial minority of professionals conceptualize some substantial benefit from such contact. A survey of physicians' attitudes and practices regarding erotic and nonerotic contact with patients (Kardener, Fuller, and Mensh, 1973) revealed that about 15 percent of physicians had had erotic contact, approximately half of which was coital.

About 20 percent, however, believed that such contact might be beneficial. Nonpsychiatric physician-respondents in the survey had somewhat
higher figures than those for psychiatry. Of the physicians who had had
intercourse with their patients, 80 percent had had intercourse with
more than one patient. Similar figures for clinical psychologists were
reported in a study by Holroyd and Brodsky (1977). If these are the
percentages of erotic contact for those physicians and psychologists who
responded to the surveys, what about those physicians (54 percent) and
psychologists (30 percent) who did *not reply?* Still more astonishing is that
25 percent of freshmen medical students saw no objection to a sexual
relationship between doctor and patient, provided that the therapist was
"genuine and authentic" (Taylor and Wagner, 1976).

There is much greater approval of nonerotic physical contact with
patients and of partner surrogates on the part of health professionals
(Len and Fischer, 1978). Yet, the freer the physician is with nonerotic
contact (the "laying on of hands"), the more likely he will also be to
engage in erotic practices with his patients (Kardener, Fuller, and Mensh,
1976). The ethical conflict revolves around the fact that the physical
expression of caring, such as by touching and hugging, perhaps even
kissing, may be less understood, more misinterpreted, and may lead to
malpractice suits. The clinician often has to curb his natural tendency to
express himself in such a caring way because of the possibility of being
misunderstood, or because it may break the barrier to more definite
erotic contact. More female physicians than male physicians believe in
nonerotic touching, yet only one female therapist of 147 surveyed acknowledged erotic contact (Perry, 1976). Ingrid Bergman's behavior as
the psychoanalyst in Hitchcock's movie *Spellbound* is extremely atypical.
Her therapy is hardly orthodox, but then again, how many male patients
look like Gregory Peck?

Sexual exploitation of the patient occurs in all types of clinical practice. The frequency is somewhat greater among physicians practicing
family medicine or general practice than among psychiatrists or psychologists. We have no statistics about the prevalence among clinicians
who actually are or who at least claim to be sex therapists. Yet where
sexual matters are a primary subject of discussion between the therapist
and the patient, it is plausible that the temptation for erotic contact
would be greater in sex therapy than in other areas of practice. The
discussion of intimate and personal matters not ordinarily shared with
others tends to lead to a greater feeling of intimacy between the dis-
cussants; yet at this time to my knowledge there has been no attempt
either to confirm or to refute this hypothesis.

Despite the lower prevalence of erotic contact between therapist and
patient among psychiatrists and psychologists in comparison to family
physicians, for example, when one examines malpractice suits in the

United States for sexual abuse or disturbance of marital relationships because of sexual contact between therapist and patient occurring between 1957 and 1976, a span of almost twenty years, only twelve cases of this sort are on record (Hogan, 1979). Of these twelve, the therapists charged with abuses included seven psychiatrists, three psychologists, and two family physicians. The most notorious of these cases, popularized in Lucy Freeman's *Betrayal*, was that of *Roy* v. *Hartogs*. In Hogan's casebook, *Roy* v. *Hartogs* (*Case 234*) is described as follows:

> Julie Roy went to see Dr. Renatus Hartogs, a psychiatrist, in March of 1969 to try to cure her sexual problems. After about 6 months Dr. Hartogs prescribed sexual relations as part of her treatment; more specifically, the doctor convinced Julie to have sexual relations with him. This treatment lasted 13 months. Julie charged Dr. Hartogs with malpractice in prescribing an unorthodox, emotionally damaging form of treatment, while disregarding the standard forms of treatment that might have helped her. As part of his defense, Dr. Hartogs claimed that he had been impotent since 1965 because of a hydrocele, but the court found that he had indeed had sexual intercourse with Julie.

The trial court found for the plaintiff; this decision was affirmed in the Appellate Court in 1976, and $25,000 was the "relief granted."

Another case which illustrates the gradual change from nonerotic to erotic contact is that of *People* v. *Bernstein* (*Case 209*):

> Dr. William G. Bernstein was a psychiatrist and neurologist. Madaline was a 16-year-old unmarried high school student who had been suspended from school after having sexual intercourse with a few boys at a party. Her mother brought her to Dr. Bernstein for treatment. Initially, Bernstein simply asked about her past, but during one session Madeline began crying and he put his arm around her and kissed her on the forehead. In Madeline's subsequent visits, the sessions began normally enough, but about 45 minutes into the sessions he would draw the blinds and join her on the couch, where they kissed and fondled each other. Finally, one such encounter led to sexual intercourse. Dr. Bernstein was tried on criminal charges for statutory rape.

The verdict was against the psychiatrist, who received a criminal sentence.

In several instances therapists were charged with disturbing marital relations. A typical situation is where the therapist has sexual relations with a married woman and then advises her to divorce her husband. In one such case the psychologist-therapist lost his license; in another, the psychiatrist settled out of court for $50,000.

Power is an essential feature in erotic relationships between the doctor and the patient. While it is true that sexual gratification is a significant factor, in most instances it is less important than the unconscious desire to exert power and control over vulnerable and sometimes helpless patients. The patient's need for pseudo-love, for admiration, for being wanted and desired, to overcome loneliness, and even occasionally to find sexual gratification, plays into the power needs of these exploitive therapists. A substantial minority of female patients who get caught up in this exchange of erotic favors are seductive women who use sex to equalize the power in the relationship (a form of revenge against male dominance).

Kardener et al. (1973) stated that 50 percent of physicians they surveyed engaged in nonerotic hugging, kissing, and affectionate touching; 25 percent of the psychologists reported similar behavior. Since clear-cut erotic activity starts off with nonerotic contact, these figures indicate the potential magnitude of the problem.

Masters has termed sex between therapist and patient "rape." This is not far-fetched. Even in the absence of direct force or threat of force, the unequal power arrangements bewteen the two participants create a situation akin to rape. Much of the need to exert this sort of power and control over a woman by a man is generated by fear and hate. Germaine Greer (1970, p. 247), referring to rape, states:

> The act is one of murderous aggression, spawned in self-loathing and enacted upon the hated other. Men do not themselves know the depth of their hatred. . . . It is a vain delusion that rape is the expression of uncontrollable desire or some kind of compulsive response to overwhelming attraction.

Imposition of Values

Supervisors of sex therapy often impart a cliché to trainees: "Don't impose your own values on your patients." The issue is not so simple. Any psychotherapeutic process inevitably involves imparting values to the patient. One fairly obvious example involves resistance. To some extent, every patient consciously or unconsiously prefers to "let sleeping dogs lie." The resistance to uncovering thoughts or feelings is a value that requires challenge and change. Siding with the patient's desire for increased self-reliance and coping abilities pits the therapist against the patient's regressive values of dependency and neurotic self-sabotage. Psychoanalysis almost inevitably brings prejudices that have to be faced and mastered to the surface.

Similarly in sex therapy, as Marmor states in the discussion of Redlich's chapter "The Ethics of Sex Therapy" (Masters, Johnson, and Kolodny, 1977), "By its very nature the desensitization that is such an essential component of contemporary sex therapies involves altering or at least modifying long-held values with regard to sex. The question, then, is not whether such changes are appropriate, but rather to what degree" (p. 157). Certainly the reduction of the inhibiting effects of an archaic conscience is an essential ingredient of sex therapy. Modifying long-held attitudes that sex is not only sinful, but dirty and disgusting, is an accepted part of therapy.

Redlich points out that there are inherent values in sex therapy which may not coincide with those of the patient: "These values are: (1) sex is a natural function; (2) therapy consists less of learning procedures than of removing culturally and psychologically acquired obstacles; and (3) treatment is directed at the dysfunction of the *couple*, not of the individuals" (1977, p. 147). There is, at least in this value orientation, an implicit assumption of the equality of sexes. Frequently, sex therapy proceeds without explicit attention to the unspoken value position regarding equality of the sexes.

As in all of psychotherapy, the therapeutic task is not to push the patient too far or too fast in the direction of value change. Insisting that the patient change his life style or his sexual orientation or to experiment with practices which he still finds abhorrent is not good psychotherapy. As Redlich (1977) states, "Should sex therapists influence their patients to change their values beyond the prerequisites for therapy? I strongly believe they should not" (p. 147).

Assumptions about the values held by the patient are also dangerous. The recommendation to masturbate, without first finding out the patient's attitude toward this practice, is poor treatment. There are still many people who regard masturbation as reprehensible. Intervention to modify values at a pace consistent with the patient's ability to change should be the therapist's goal. Even showing films of explicit sex without first ascertaining how the patient feels about such graphic depiction, let alone forcefully recommending that the couple engage in oral sex or some other sexual activity that one spouse or both find repugnant, is unethical. The sine qua non of ethics is freedom of choice. While promoting this idea to the couple as an essential value position in sex and marital therapy, it hardly behooves the therapist to ignore it in his interactions with patients.

Value Imposition in Homosexuality

Homosexuality is no longer officially recognized as an illness. The American Psychiatric Association removed it from its list of mental illnesses, substituting the term "sexual orientation disorder" for those people troubled by homosexual impulses or behavior who come for treatment in order to rid themselves of undesirable feelings and behavior. In the current DSM-III, "sexual orientation disorder" was replaced by "ego-dystonic homosexuality." Despite the removal of homosexuality from its classification of mental illnesses, many psychiatrists still feel that homosexuality is pathological. Almost 70 percent of psychiatrists who responded to a survey by *Medical Aspects of Human Sexuality* believe that homosexuality is still pathological (Lief, 1977).

Some psychiatrists, responding to the need to restore "normalcy," still feel that they should try to persuade homosexual patients to change their sexual orientation to heterosexuality. Most homosexual patients come to psychiatrists for the treatment of depression, anxiety, and relationship problems, and have no desire to modify their homosexual behavior. Psychiatrists who attempt to persuade homosexuals to follow a heterosexual path are imposing their values on these patients. Today most psychiatrists, despite the medical imperative to remedy a "pathological state," believe that such an attempt at persuasion is unethical.

The psychosexual disorder termed "ego-dystonic homosexuality" is reserved for those patients who have "a desire to acquire or increase heterosexual arousal, so that heterosexual relationships can be initiated or maintained" (DSM-III). If a patient complains of overt homosexual arousal and feels that it is unwanted and a source of distress and wishes to change, there is no ethical conflict in initiating therapy aimed at changing the patient's sexual orientation. There may be a value conflict, however, between the therapist and the gay community, since it is the official policy of the gay community to dissuade active or potential homosexuals from changing their sexual orientation to heterosexuality. In practice, however, the individual clinician is rarely subjected to pressure from the gay community.

A frequent source of value conflict arises when parents bring an adolescent son or daughter to the therapist in order to change what the parents perceive as potential or actual homosexual behavior. When there is a sharp conflict between the parents and the homosexual adolescent who does not wish to change his or her behavior, the therapist ethically must side with the adolescent against the parents. The decision to take the side of the adolescent depends on an appropriate appraisal, because in many instances the adolescent is in conflict and in doubt about which orientation to pursue. A conflict in ethics arises if the therapist, in an authoritarian fashion, tries to persuade the adolescent to follow one path or the other; it is preferable to allow the natural process of psychotherapy to aid the adolescent in making his or her own ultimate decision. At times the therapist has to serve as a buffer between the adolescent and parents or other authority figures in the community. The general formulation of the ethical problem is that the therapist should avoid imposing his values on the patient struggling with homosexual impulses or behavior. At the same time, the therapist must be certain that he is not unduly influenced by parental or community pressure.

Value Imposition in Transsexualism

In the management of transsexualism, value conflicts between the therapist and the patient are common. Most patients attempt to pressure the clinician into providing psychotherapy and endocrine therapy for the two years usually required by the surgeon prior to surgical intervention. Many clinicians are in doubt about the effectiveness of sex-change surgery; in any case, the patient's desire for such a profound alteration in his or her body and body image often imposes a threat to the clinician's own concept of gender identity and of self. Clinicians' anxieties and doubts are often reflected in either an abrupt refusal to deal with patients requesting sex-change surgery, or in a vacillating approach to its management. These doubts have now been accentuated by the refusal of one of the pioneering clinics in the United States, Johns Hopkins Hospital, to continue providing the surgical procedure for changing a person's sex. This decision preceded, and apparently was not influenced by, the report by Meyer and Reter (1979) of Johns Hopkins. Their findings of a long-term followup study concluded that transsexuals who had had their sex organs altered surgically did not fare better than those who had not undergone surgery. The hospital's decision and Meyer's report have created a polarization of foes and adherents of sex-change surgery. John Money, also at Johns Hopkins, has attacked Meyer's report as statistically unsophisticated and believes that it should therefore be disregarded. Many clinicians, however, who had doubted the effectiveness of the procedure have nov had their doubts reinforced by Meyer's report. Since the diagnosis required in order to differentiate schizophrenics, homosexuals, and transvestites from transsexuals is often difficult to arrive at, many clinicians seem ready to abandon surgery as the recommended treatment. In doing so, they have to reject the values of their patients who request sex-change surgery. We see in this controversy a conjunction of values concerning the integrity of the body and values derived from technical-scientific data. It is often difficult to distinguish how much influence each value is having on the clinician.

Value Imposition in Paraphilias

In addition to feelings of disdain and contempt (conscious, partially conscious, or unconscious) toward people with sexual behaviors that deviate from commonly accepted community standards, the clinician often has to deal with patients who are in the office only because they have been remanded there by the legal system. The patient is usually reluctant to change his behavior, but agrees to do so only through legal coercion and the fear of punishment for failing to come for therapy.

This often increases the therapist's negative feelings. The sex therapist has to make certain that his counter-transference does not interfere with treatment, and at the same time has to ally himself with those forces within the patient that push the patient toward a healthier adaptation.

Since many of the patients come to clinicians because of court referral, there is an additional ethical issue of confidentiality. A report may be required by legal authorities in order to keep the patient out of jail. How to satisfy this need, while respecting the confidentiality of the patient, is sometimes a delicate matter.

Another issue arises if the paraphilial behavior, or even homosexual behavior, occurs in a married man who has kept this behavior hidden from his wife. (On occasion a lesbian wife keeps her homosexual behavior hidden from her husband.) The need to maintain confidentiality may be a source of stress for the therapist. The ethical conflict between honesty as a value and the need not to inflict pain or damage on the spouse or on the relationship is one with which both the patient and the therapist may have to struggle.

Informed Consent

When sex therapy follows the psychoanalytic-psychodynamic model of psychotherapy with individual patients or even with couples, the problems of informed consent are similar to those discussed elsewhere in this book. The therapist should explain to the patient or to the couple the content of the therapy, estimate the number of sessions, the approximate length of time it will take, state the fees, and should respond honestly to the patients' concerns about the nature of the treatment.

One difference between sex therapy and other forms of therapy concerns the nature of the material discussed. Sex involves highly charged feelings and strongly freighted values. These come into focus when the therapist assigns certain behavioral tasks. As noted in the section on imposition of values, however, when a form of sexual behavior is suggested as a way of increasing sexual excitement or expanding the couple's sexual repertoire, the suggestions may conflict with values held by the patient. In discussing the possible courses of action, the therapist is providing the basis for the patient's informed consent. It is not always possible to anticipate the patient's reactions to the therapist's instructions. Consent may be given grudgingly. The patient may not verbalize negative feelings and will react with hostility toward the therapist and the treatment, even though the therapist had made an honest attempt to explain the procedure. This reaction has been noted with the use of films of explicit sex, for example.

There is always some possibility of untoward reactions toward the sexological examination, unless that procedure is fully explained in advance. When it comes to the use of surrogate partners or even of studies of nocturnal penile tumescence (NPT) in the diagnosis of impotence, written informed consent provides the greatest assurance that the procedure will be carefully delineated and understood by the patient. It also protects the therapist against malpractice lawsuits.

Written informed consent should be obtained for sex-reassignment surgery. If the therapist is also responsible for hormonal treatment prior to surgery, written and signed informed consent should be obtained from the patient before the hormonal treatment is begun. Informed consent prior to the sex-reassignment surgery should clearly indicate that there are alternative forms of treatment. Up to now, no surgeon or associated therapist has been sued for "mayhem." Mayhem is defined by Webster's Third International Dictionary as "the malicious and permanent crippling or mutilation or disfiguring of another, usually a deprivation of a bodily part." The theoretical possibility of criminal action against a physician involved in sex-change surgery makes it mandatory that informed consent for this type of sex therapy be drawn up scrupulously, for the protection of the patient and for the professionals involved.

Informed consent of legal minors may create a difficult problem, particularly if the child opposes treatment but the therapist and the parents believe it will be helpful. In some states minors, upon reaching the age of majority, have been successful in suing physicians for allegedly injurious acts, even though these acts had been perpetrated with parental consent.

Confidentiality and Privacy

Since in our culture, at least, there is a connection between sexual activity and privacy, confidentiality plays a special role in sex therapy; it is even more important than in other types of psychotherapy. (When Captain Cook arrived in Tahiti, he and his men were astonished to find that the natives copulated in public, and ate in privacy. In that culture, there were practically no inhibitions about sex, except for some forms of incest, but there were many inhibitions about eating.) Although for most people the valence between sex and privacy is greatest, others regard certain dimensions of life such as financial information, criminal behavior, political beliefs, religious beliefs, racial prejudices, and in some instances even physical sensations, as matters of privacy and confidentiality. Yet, above all else, privacy and sexuality are associated in the socialization process in the United States. Privacy breeds shame; it also protects our self-esteem, yet seems to be a necessary part of intimacy. Sharing our thoughts and feeling is a dimension and expression of intimacy; sharing our bodies is another. If our feelings, thoughts, aspirations, hopes, and fears were shared with a multitude of people, or if we copulated in public, the special sense of sharing with a "significant other" that privacy makes possible would be gone. Privacy and intimacy are associated in our society.

Confidentiality in sex therapy, then, assumes unusual proportions: (1) because of the frequent association of shame with sexual impulses or behavior and the possible feeling of humiliation at the disclosure of sexual material; (2) because even in the absence of shame, our pride seems definitely to be connected with our sexual capacity, so that any disclosure of inadequacy may be a threat to our self-esteem; and (3) as indicated, owing to the specific relationshp of sexual behavior to intimacy. Thus, assurance of confidentiality is an essential safeguard of the intimacy required for effective sex therapy.

What are some of the specific problems that may arise in sex therapy? The most clear-cut instances of threat to confidentiality arise in couple therapy when the therapist learns that one of the spouses is having an extramarital relationship, or that one spouse is secretly bisexual, or that one spouse has venereal disease but has not disclosed it to his or her marital partner. These are often difficult matters for the therapist, particularly if disclosure is essential for the therapy's success. In such instances the therapist usually tried to persuade the "secret holder" to transmit this information to the spouse.

Sex therapy often involves couple therapy. If legal action is brought by one spouse against the other as in divorce or custody of children, records can be obtained by subpoena. Since the therapist had been dealing with the relationship rather than with either one of the spouses as the indicated patient, he is placed in a difficult situation. The therapist should try to persuade the attorney who arranged for the subpoena that the therapist's testimony as an expert witness will *not* benefit the attorney's client; usually this is persuasive. State laws vary; indeed, the attitudes of judges vary to such an extent that it is impossible to foretell whether the judge will insist on the therapist's disclosing confidential matters, threatening contempt of court if the clinician refuses, or whether the judge will be lenient toward the therapist who desires to maintain confidentiality. In most but not all instances, the therapist's firm resolve not to disclose potentially harmful information will work.

The guidelines of the conference on sexual ethics of January 25–27, 1978, in St. Louis include the following provisions:

When sex therapy involves one or more therapists working with a client couple, whether married or not, unusual circumstances pertaining to confidentiality may arise, In such instances, the following considerations apply: (a) Disclosure of information that one client has requested be kept confidential from his or her partner should not be made without the express consent of the person providing the confidential information. (b) When only one client of a client couple provides consent to the release of confidential records or information, the sex therapist is responsible for releasing only information about the consenting client and must protect the confidentiality of all information deriving from the nonconsenting client. . . . In treatment of a couple, when neither client has requested that any matters be held confidential or kept secret from the other, but when the therapist(s) judges that there is a significant risk to discussing jointly information not known to one client, it is the responsibility of the therapist to point out this fact to the relevant person and to obtain his or her consent before disclosure of such information. [Kolodny, 1978]

Group sex therapy must proceed with the same degree of caution found in other types of group therapy. Again, sexual material, however, generally carries a more intense feeling than other life issues; in other words, the implications of a breach of confidentiality in group sex therapy may be more serious than with other types of group therapy.

As in other forms of psychotherapy, when the therapist learns there may be potential harm to another—e.g., rape, pedophilia, severe sexual sadism, etc.—the therapist's ethical conflict involves the need to maintain confidentiality versus the protection of possible victims. Recent court decisions (see the Tarasoff decision) now push therapists toward protecting potential victims, even if it requires a breach of confidentiality. Ethical conflict is so serious that each case must be evaluated on its own merits.

The potentials for the breach of confidentiality in clinical sex research are great. Information must be obtained on all patients in a particular cohort and the information must be retained for analysis. The possibility of the material being shared by clerks and secretaries potentiates the chances of breaches in confidentiality. Strict maintenance of coding devices, limiting access to data kept under lock and key, permitting only the research professionals to have access to them, are essential items in maintaining confidentiality.

Clinical Research

The ethics of other forms of sex research such as questionnaires, field surveys, observational studies including participant observation, e.g., group sex, are not under the rubric of "clinical research." Studies of the process of therapy, e.g., the personality of the therapist compared with the technique employed, and outcome studies are two of the major types of clinical research. Others include the case history method, frequency counts, correlational studies of variables, and the like. The value conflicts possible in behavior therapy techniques have been referred to in a previous section, as well as the issues with regard to breaches in confidentiality in clinical research.

One form of outcome research involves the staging of spurious types of intervention unknown to the subject. This could be a breach of informed consent. It should be carried out only if it is the only way to conduct the research (which is unlikely) and if there is absolutely no danger of harm to the subjects.

Placebo research should carry with it the same safeguards found in other forms of blind or double-blind studies. Putting patient-subjects on waiting lists or giving them what is in the therapist's judgment a less useful form of treatment in order to carry out a research design, may be unethical if it carries with it any real danger to the patient—for example, dissolution of a shaky marriage.

Audiorecording and videotaping of sessions for research purposes carry the danger of breach of confidentiality, as noted in a previous section of this chapter. While this issue holds true for all data collection, it has special relevance to videotaping, a technique used much more freely in marital and family therapy than in individual psychotherapy.

In the United States, the treatment of institutionalized sex offenders by anti-androgens has come to a halt because of governmental injunctions. The same is true of psychosurgery, a technique now used in West Germany. In that country sex offenders have been treated with stereotaxic brain surgery of the ventro-medial nucleus of the hypothalamus. The ethical issue is to what extent incarcerated persons or persons under threat of incarceration can give a noncoercive consent, even in the face of a future that is potentially more destructive than the therapy.

When research or training is carried out in the context of providing therapeutic services, the potential exists for conflict of interests. If there is danger of damage to the patient or patients, it is necessary to modify or terminate the research or training, even in the face of the client's consent to participate in the research or training-related therapy.

Ethical Problems in the Training of Sex Therapists

At the very center of the ethical concerns about training is the major dimension of competence. This has been addressed in the section on competence. For a more extended discussion of this, see Lief, Sarrel, and Sarrel (1980).

An extremely significant ethical issue is the relevance of the trainee-applicants' personal sex history. How important is this in affecting their competence as sex therapists or in their future handling of ethical issues? If an applicant's personal sex life is relevant, to what extent and in what manner may inquiry be made, while protecting that individual's right to privacy? One of the guidelines drawn up at the Second Congress on Ethical Issues in Sex Therapy and Research reads as follows:

> Persons seeking or pursuing training in the field of human sexuality may be queried about their private personal sexual histories and attitudes, since these may materially affect the competence, integrity, judgment, and objectivity of professional performance. Such persons should be informed in advance of the relevant limits of confidentiality pertaining to this material. [Kolodny, 1978]

Summing Up

In sex therapy, a field of enormous flux where new techniques and changes in professionalization take place more rapidly than in older, more settled types of psychotherapy, ethical issues are also more volatile. In combination with the special place of sexuality in our lives (are the ethical issues in the treatment of respiratory illness as freighted?), ethical concerns assume great importance in the practice of sex therapy. These concerns are not "academic"; they require the active attention of the therapist in every session of sex therapy.

REFERENCES

BARNHOUSE, R. T. Sex between patient and therapist. *Journal of the American Academy of Psychoanalysis*, 1978, **6**(4), 533–546.

Behavior Today, January 7, 1980, **10**(52), 4. (Relations of doctor-patient sex to malpractice insurance).

COLLINS, D. T., MEBED, A. A. K., and MORTIMER, R. L. Patient-therapist sex: Consequences for subsequent treatment. *McLean Hospital Journal, Illinois*, Winter 1978, **1**, 24–36.

DAHLBERG, C. C. Sexual contact between patient and therapist. *Contemporary Psychoanalysis*. Spring 1970, **6**, 107–124.

DAVISON, G. C. Homosexuality: The ethical challenge. *Journal of Consulting and Clinical Psychology*, 1976, **44**(2), 157–162.

FRANK, E., ANDERSON, C., and RUBINSTEIN, D. Frequency of sexual dysfunction in "normal" couples. *New England Journal of Medicine*, July 20, 1978, **299**(3), 111–115.

GORDIS, L., and GOLD, E. Privacy, confidentiality, and the use of medical records in research. *Science*, January 11, 1980, **207**, 153–156.

GREER, G. *The female eunuch*. New York: McGraw-Hill, 1970.

HARE-MUSTIN, R. I. Ethical considerations in the use of sexual contact in psychotherapy. *Psychotherapy: Theory, Research and Practice*, Winter 1974, **11**(4), 308–310.

HOGAN, D. B. *The regulation of psychotherapists*, Vol. 1. Cambridge: Ballinger, 1979.

HOGAN, D. B. *A review of malpractice suits in the United States*, Vol. 3. Cambridge: Ballinger, 1979.

HOLDEN, C. Ethics in social science research. *Science*, November 2, 1979, **206**, 537–540.

HOLROYD, J. C., and BRODSKY, A. M. Physical contact with patients. *American Psychologist*, October 1977, 843–849.

JACOBS, M., THOMPSON, L. A., and TRUXAW, P. The use of sexual surrogates in counseling. *Counseling Psychologist*, 1975, **5**, 73–76.

KARDENER, S. H. Sex and the physician-patient relationship. *American Journal of Psychiatry*, October 1974, **131**(10), 1134–1136.

KARDENER, S. H., FULLER, M., and MENSH, I. N. A survey of physicians' attitudes and practices regarding erotic and nonerotic contact with patients. *American Journal of Psychiatry*, October 1973, **130**(10), 1077–1081.

KARDENER, S. H., FULLER, M., and MENSH, I. N. Characteristics of "erotic" practitioners. *American Journal of Psychiatry*, November 1976, *133*(11), 1324–1325.

KOLODNY, R. C. Conference report: Ethical guidelines for research and clinical perspectives on human sexuality. *Newsletter on Science, Technology, and Human Values*, June 1978, No. 24. Harvard University Program on Science Technology and Human Values.

LEN, M., and FISCHER, J. Clinicians' attitudes toward and use of full body contact or sexual techniques with clients. *Journal of Sex Research*, February 1978, **14**(1), 40–49.

LEVITIN, T. Values (Allport-Vernon-Lindzey Study of Values). In J. P. Robinson and P. R. Shaver (eds.), *Measures of Social Psychological Attitudes* (rev. ed.). Ann Arbor: Institute for Social Research, University of Michigan, 1973.

LIEF, H. I. Commentary on sexual survey #4: Current thinking on homosexuality. *Aspects of Medical Sexuality*, November 1977, **11**(11), 110–111.

LIEF, H. I., SARREL, P., and SARREL, L. Accreditation and training in sex therapy. In W. H. Masters, V. E. Johnson, R. C. Kolodny, and S. Weems (eds.), *Ethical issues in sex therapy and research*, Vol. 2. Boston: Little, Brown, 1980.

LOPICCOLO, J. From psychotherapy to sex therapy. *Society*, 1977, **14**(5), 60–68.

LOPICCOLO, J. The professionalization of sex therapy: Issues and problems. In J. LoPiccolo and L. LoPiccolo (eds.), *Handbook of sex therapy*. New York: Plenum Press, 1978.

LUBORSKY, L.; CHANDLER, M.; AUERBACH, A. H.; ET AL. Factors influencing the outcome of psychotherapy: A review of the quantitative research. *Psychological Bulletin*, 1971, **75**, 145–185.

MACKLIN, R. Ethics, sex research, and sex therapy. *Hastings Center Report*, April 1976, **6**(2), 5–7.

MARMOR, J. Sexual acting-out in psychotherapy. *American Journal of Psychoanalysis*, 1972, **22**, 3–8.

MARMOR, J. Some psychodynamic aspects of the seduction of patients in psychotherapy. *American Journal of Psychoanalysis*, 1976, **36**, 319–323.

MARMOR, J. Discussion of paper by F. Redlich. In W. H. Masters, V. E. Johnson, and R. C. Kolodny (eds.), *Ethical issues in sex therapy and research*, Vol. 1. Boston: Little, Brown, 1977.

MASTERS, W. H., and JOHNSON, V. E. *Human sexual inadequacy.* Boston: Little, Brown, 1970.

MASTERS, W. H., JOHNSON, V. E., and KOLODNY, R. C. (eds.). *Ethical issues in sex therapy and research,* Vol. 1. Boston: Little, Brown, 1977.

MASTERS, W. H.; JOHNSON, V. E.; KOLODNY, R. C.; and WEEMS, S. (eds.). *Ethical issues in sex therapy and research,* Vol. 2. Boston: Little, Brown, 1980.

McCARTNERY, J. Overt transference. *Journal of Sex Research,* 1966, **2**, 227–237.

MEYER, J. K. Training and accreditation of the treatment of sexual disorders. *American Journal of Psychiatry,* April 1976, **133**(4), 389–394.

MEYER, J. K., and RETER, D. J. Sex reassignment. *Archives of General Psychiatry,* August 1979, **36**, 1010–1015.

NOLL, J. O. The psychotherapist and informed consent. *American Journal of Psychiatry,* December 1976, **133**(12), 1451–1453.

PERR, I. Legal aspects of sexual therapies. *Journal of Legal Medicine,* January 1975, 33–38.

PERRY, J. A. Physicians' erotic and nonerotic physical involvement with patients. *American Journal of Psychiatry,* July 1976, **111**(7), 838–840.

POMEROY, W. B. A Critique of AASECT's Code of Ethics, quoted in *Sexuality Today,* July 2, 1979, **2** (36).

REDLICH, F. Ethics of sex therapy. In W. H. Masters, V. E. Johnson, and R. C. Kolodny (eds.), *Ethical issues in sex therapy and research,* Vol. 1. Boston: Little, Brown, 1980.

SCHULTZ, L. C. A survey of social workers' attitudes and use of body and sex psychotherapies. *Clinical Social Work Journal,* 1975, **2**(2), 90–99.

SCHULTZ, L. G. Ethical issues in treating sexual dysfunction. *Social Work,* March 1975, 126–128.

SHEPARD, M. *The love treatment: Sexual intimacy between patients and psychotherapists.* New York: Peter H. Wyden, 1971.

SIASSI, I., and THOMAS, M. Physicians and the new sexual freedom. *American Journal of Psychiatry,* November 1973, **130**(11), 1256–1257.

SPARK, R. F., WHITE, R. A., and CONNALLY, P. B. Impotence is not always psychogenic. *Journal of the American Medical Association,* Feb. 22/29, 1980, **243**(8), 755–755.

STONE, A. A. The legal implications of sexual activity between psychiatrist and patient. *American Journal of Psychiatry,* October 1976, **137**(10), 1138–1141.

TAYLOR, B. J., and WAGNER, N. N. Sex between therapists and clients: A review and analysis. *Professional Psychologist,* 1976, **7**, 593–601.

ULANOV, A. B. Follow-up treatment in cases of patient-therapist sex. *Journal of the American Academy of Psychoanalysis,* 1979, **7**(1), 101–110.

VOTH, H. M. Love affair between doctor and patient. *American Journal of Psychotherapy,* 1972, **26**, 394–400.

WOLFE, L. A question of surrogates in sex therapy. In J. LoPiccolo and L. LoPiccolo (eds.), *Handbook of sex therapy.* New York: Plenum Press, 1978.

WORLD HEALTH ORGANIZATION. Education and treatment in human sexuality: The training of health professionals. *Technical Report Series 572,* Geneva, Switzerland, 1975.

Ethical Considerations in the Professional Applications of Hypnosis

Melvin A. Gravitz
Joseph E. Mallet
Paul Munyon
Manuel I. Gerton

In use for more than two centuries, the modality of hypnosis has been in a state of rapid growth in recent years. Increasing numbers of people are obtaining benefits from this form of treatment through modern psychotherapy, medicine, dentistry, and other areas. In 1957, the American Society of Clinical Hypnosis was organized with twenty members. Today, that society has more than 4,100 members who are either physicians (52 percent), psychologists (31 percent), or dentists (17 percent). In addition, numerous law enforcement agencies in the United States are using forensic or investigative hypnosis, and it has been estimated that every major police force in the country will employ such techniques within the next decade. The number of medical and dental schools and graduate programs in clinical psychology offering courses in hypnosis for health professionals has doubled in the last five years, and some observers have predicted that by the end of the 1980s most large hospitals in this country will have an expert in hypnosis on their staffs (D'Aulaire & D'Aulaire, 1980). Moreover, an increasing number of continuing education programs on hypnosis may be found throughout the country. Equally telling, perhaps, is the fact that it is no longer uncommon to hear a successful athlete give the credit for his or her improved performance to a hypnotist rather than to a dedicated coach. Given our society's current preoccupation with self and self-improvement, the trend for the future appears to be one of accelerating growth in the public demand for hypnosis.

The clear prospect for the rapid increase in the use of hypnosis and in the number of individuals with various backgrounds and training practicing the method highlights the need for a critical examination of the ethical considerations involved. The examination of such ethical issues in hypnosis assumes added significance because at the present time only a few jurisdictions have laws that relate directly to the use of hypnosis. In nearly all jurisdictions, poorly trained and even totally unqualified individuals are able to represent themselves as professionals qualified in hypnosis, and an increasing number appear to be doing so. Moreover, health professionals with training in hypnosis may extend their practice beyond their areas of specialization and competence, often without an adequate appreciation of the responsibilities which ought to attend such actions.

Little has been written in the professional literature about the ethical or professional considerations associated with the use of hypnosis (see Gormley, 1961; London, 1964). While most health care professions whose members might employ the modality have promulgated general ethical standards or guidelines for their members, no standards have been established to deal directly with the use of the method itself. Indeed, the largest national organization, the American Society of Clinical Hypnosis, instead of establishing an independent code of ethics, simply mandates its members to observe the standards of their primary professions. A similar position prevails in the smaller Society for Clinical and Experimental Hypnosis. The International Society of Hypnosis, however, has recently published a comprehensive set of ethical practice standards, with particular attention given to forensic hypnosis.

The purpose of this chapter is to consider some of the basic ethical issues that may be encountered in the professional use of hypnosis and to provide stimulation for further consideration of these important matters. The focus is on the ethical considerations in the professional use of hypnosis in three different settings: clinical or therapeutic, forensic and investigative, and laboratory research. This paper also presents a brief discussion of considerations associated with the commercial use of hypnosis for entertainment purposes. Ethical principles associated with a therapist incorporating hypnosis into self-help, self-improvement programs are considered as part of the discussion of clinical applications of hypnosis.

Hypnosis in Clinical Settings

Four general ethical considerations associated with the use of hypnosis in various clinical or therapeutic settings are noted. First, under what circumstances might the use of hypnosis pose genuine risks for the patient or client, and what are the ethical responsibilities of the therapist in those situations? Second, what ethical considerations are encountered when practicing hypnosis outside one's area of competence and training? Third, what are the responsibilities, if any, of the hypnotherapist to explain the dynamics of hypnotic interaction to the subject? Fourth, what are the basic ethical issues associated with using hypnosis as part of a self-help, self-improvement program?

Numerous reports in the literature have addressed the question of possible risks inherent in clinical applications of hypnosis. In one of the earliest reports on the subject, Schultz (1922) cited one hundred cases of apparent adverse reactions, which included headaches, tremors, and the development of neurotic and psychotic symptoms. In a later study, Levitt and Hershman (1961) contacted 301 practitioners who used hypnosis in a clinical setting. Forty-three percent of the psychologists and 27 percent of the other therapists who responded reported that they had observed undesirable consequences such as fainting, dizziness, headache, vomiting, anxiety, depression, panic states, excessive dependency, sexual difficulties, and overt psychosis. Other investigators have reported similar undesirable effects that were attributed to the use of hypnosis (e.g., Meares, 1961; West and Deckert, 1965; Arieti and Chrzanowski, 1975; Estabrooks, 1943; Heyer, 1931; Williams, 1953; Wolberg, 1948; Orne, 1965; Rosen, 1953, 1960).

Most investigators, however, have found that hypnosis posed no inherent risk for the subject (e.g., Brenman and Gill, 1947; Janet, 1925; Le Cron, 1961; Neustatter, 1940). Kroger (1963) also includes Freud in this latter group.

Some researchers of this question have specifically commented on the proposition that the alleged undue effects should not be attributed directly to the use of the hypnotic modality. Conn (1972) held that some apparent adverse effects could be accounted for by the hypnotist's lack of skill and experience or by the inadequate screening, diagnosis, and management of psychotic patients. Weitzenhoffer (1957) noted that the possibility of adverse effects in treatment is not specific to hypnosis and that their reported occurrence depends not on the use of the method itself, but on the competence and integrity of the practitioner employing hypnosis. Furthermore, it is generally recognized that clinical intervention in an emotionally charged situation (which psychotherapy represents) may have the potential for the development of some adverse effects. It does appear that the act of intervention, rather than the method (hypnosis), may be sufficient to explain most incidents not accounted for by either the practitioner's lack of skill or the improper use of hypnosis.

While clear consensus on the inherent risks of hypnosis may be unobtainable, there should be general agreement that the hypnotist must meet the basic ethical and professional requirements of appropriate competence and integrity. An examination of issues associated with two alleged dangers of hypnotic intervention—symptom substitution and coercion—will serve to illustrate the importance of these requirements.

One of the potential hazards cited in connection with hypnosis is the substitution of symptoms, perhaps more debilitating, for problems treated by direct hypnotic symptom removal or suppression. Reports of symptom substitution are not easily evaluated because of the lack of specificity with regard to the type, severity, and duration of the difficulties treated or about the treatment techniques actually employed. Both Meares (1961) and Conn (1972), among others, reported that they had never observed substitute symptom formation in their practices, while other therapists have reported on adverse sequelae to hypnotic symptom removal, some of which were more severe than the symptom removed (e.g., Joseph et al., 1949; Seitz, 1953; Rosen, 1953; Meldman, 1960; Rosen and Bartemeier 1961; Teitel, 1961). Interestingly, Spiegel (1967) has suggested that if the therapist believes in symptom substitution, then that belief might be communicated to the patient and might therefore influence the patient's subsequent behavior.

Despite the lack of agreement about the occurrence of or explanation for symptom substitution, clear agreement exists on the important role the therapist plays in limiting the possibility of undue consequences. For example, Hilgard and her colleagues (1961) noted that symptom removal in psychotic patients is ill advised. Moreover, they found that cases where adverse consequences were observed in conjunction with hypnotic therapy were typically being handled by inadequately prepared therapists. Others concur in this emphasis on the critical importance of adequate training and experience for hypnotherapists and have highlighted the therapist's need for awareness of the complexities of psychological symptoms, for proper selection of subjects, and for judicious and skillful treatment planning and implementation (e.g., Weitzenhoffer, 1957; Brenman and Gill, 1947; Spiegel, 1978; Hartland, 1965; Kroger, 1963).

The competent treatment of physical symptoms in medical and dental settings demands additional considerations. Careful screening and preliminary examination of potential hypnosis patients is important. Without those steps, the application of hypnotic techniques could mask the organic cause of a symptom, thus possibly permitting the disorder to progress too far for effective treatment (Weitzenhoffer, 1957). Furthermore, it is recognized that the longer a physical symptom has been part of an individual's daily experience, the more likely it is that the symptom has taken on psychological meaning (e.g., secondary gain) as well. Sudden direct removal of such a symptom could create negative consequences, such as the emergence of underlying anxiety. The frequent overlapping of physical disorders and psychological dynamics clearly places significant responsibility on the hypnotherapist. Unless therapists have both adequate medical and psychological training, they clearly have an ethical responsibility in cases which go beyond their competence to arrange for referral to or consultation with specialists who are properly trained.

In sum, the hypnotic therapist has the ethical responsibility to be properly trained and competent. This means not only that such therapists should be well trained in the techniques of hypnosis, but that they must possess a thorough knowledge and understanding of psychological and psychodynamic phenomena and must be able to recognize when any given situation requires training or skill beyond that which they possess. Moreover, it may be concluded that hypnotherapists have an ethical responsibility not to allow their practice to be drawn beyond the limits of their competence. Accordingly, a hypnotist should consider it unethical to employ hypnosis in areas outside his or her fields of training and specialization.

A second suggested danger associated with hypnosis is coercion. Laboratory investigations and clinical reports on alleged coercion have focused on antisocial or criminal acts such as invasion of a subject's privacy or inducing the subject to inflict bodily harm on another. Three major literature reviews (Barber, 1961; Orne, 1972; Conn, 1972) and numerous specific studies have addressed this topic; nevertheless, no definitive conclusions have been reached. Obviously, fundamental ethical and legal considerations proscribe direct testing of the possibility of hypnotic coercion to serious antisocial behavior, while laboratory studies have been too artificial to render valid or definitive results.

Regardless of one's position on the question of the theoretical possibility of coercion, the ethical issues involved are clear: the hypnotic practitioner must respect the client's moral code and right of free will. If the therapist respects the subject's fundamental integrity, coercion— deliberate or inadvertant—should not be possible. It should be understood clearly that such an ethical stricture requires not only competence and integrity on the part of the therapist as hypnotist, but that the practitioner must be adequately trained in the fundamentals of human psychology and psychodynamics.

A variation on the issue of antisocial coercion is the possibility of sexual coercion or seduction by the use of hypnosis. Such a possibility has been of concern to investigators of hypnosis since the time of the French Commission of Inquiry into Animal Magnetism (1784). In a secret addendum to its report, the commission expressed concern about the possibility of hypnotic seduction. Since that time, however, numerous writers have pointed out that the hypnotic context is not unique among therapeutic settings with regard to the hypothetical potential for sexual abuse (Meares, 1961; Orne, 1972). Indeed, whenever a therapist is in a position to dispense or withhold approval or acceptance from a client or patient, a possibility of sexual coercion may exist. Clearly, such a situation does not depend solely or even primarily on the use of hypnosis. Whether hypnosis by itself is sufficient for seduction is still being debated professionally and in the courts; regardless of the eventual outcome of this debate, there is obviously an ethical standard to be observed. If the hypnotherapist respects the personal integrity of the client, there should be no possibility for coercion or abuse, sexual or otherwise.

Does the hypnotist have an ethical or professional responsibility to explain the dynamics of hypnotic interaction to the subject? Certainly a misconception exists among many laypersons that all self-control is surrendered to the hypnotist. Some observers believe that serious consequences can result for both the client and the therapist if this misconception is not dispelled. Perry (1977) has asserted that a belief in the inability to resist is itself sufficient to create a self-fulfilling prophecy. Such a belief, moreover, could lead to subsequent accusations of coercion or seduction. On the other hand, there are those who believe that hypnosis may be more effective in certain settings if it is not demystified; that is, the hypnotic situation (in a Sullivanian sense) might itself possess therapeutic value. The therapist may be able to use the client's lack of sophistication about the extent of his or her self-control; however, the resultant behavior is then likely to be at least partially a function of demand characteristics. In such a situation, the likelihood of resistance to treatment may be increased. Furthermore, under such circumstances the subject may be deprived of the opportunity to participate fully and freely in the hypnotic experience and, thus, may be denied an occasion to acquire a feeling of personal mastery and self-control.

On balance, it would appear that both the patient and the therapist would benefit more if the freedom of the client were clearly recognized by both parties. Moreover, if hypnotherapists have an ethical responsibility to respect the integrity of their clients, they may have a responsibility to explain to those clients their "rights" in hypnosis by explaining the dynamics of the hypnotic process.

Finally, what ethical considerations are associated with the therapist's incorporation of hypnosis into a self-help program? Those considerations are essentially the same as the ethical issues for any other clinical application of hypnosis; the diligence, however, that ought to be exercised in order to assure that ethical and professional responsibilities are met in this context may be much greater than that required in the standard clinical setting. Obviously, in the self-help program the therapist in a sense trains the client to be a hypnotist. Thus, the therapist has the responsibility to ensure that the client clearly understands such dynamics of the hypnotic process as are appropriate and fully appreciates the definite limits of his or her opportunity to use that understanding. The therapist, moreover, has the responsibility to determine with as much certainty as possible that the client can properly handle the responsibilities associated with making oneself at the same time both hypnotherapist and client.

Hypnosis in the Forensic Setting

Hypnosis is today being used with increasing frequency in the United States and elsewhere to enhance or refresh the recall of witnesses for both criminal and civil cases. This is considered to be a nontherapeutic application of hypnosis in that the primary objective of using the modality in this context is not the improvement of the mental or physical well-being of the subject. Three broad ethical or professional issues must be considered when discussing the forensic application of hypnosis. First, who is qualified to serve as a forensic or investigative hypnotist? Second, what is ethical behavior for a forensic or investigative hypnotist attempting to gather information from a subject? Third, what ethical obligations exist with respect to making the information obtained using hypnosis available to others?

The Society for Clinical and Experimental Hypnosis has recently promulgated strong objections to the training of police officers as hypnotechnicians or to the use of hypnosis by police officers. Several reasons may be cited in support of the society's position. First, police officers typically have limited training in and understanding of scientific psychology, psychodynamics, psychopathology, and human behavior. In addition, they are basically oriented toward solving a crime or gathering evidence rather than toward the protection of the health or psychosomatic integrity of the subject. Thus, they may be likely inadvertently to distort the information received from the subject by unconsciously biasing the subjects' memory. Finally, there exists the question of unavoidable conflict of interest, which in the final analysis will have to be settled by the courts.

Who, then, is qualified to serve as a forensic or investigative hypnotist? The requirements of competence and integrity are the same in the forensic setting as in the clinical situation. A qualified forensic hypnotist is someone who first of all is fully competent to be a good clinical or forensic hypnotist. Fundamentally, the basic requirement of competence for a hypnotist transcends the narrow limits of whatever discipline or specialty the practitioner may represent.

There are additional ethical or professional considerations that may be encountered when using hypnosis for a forensic purpose. First, the hypnotist must take care to enhance the validity of memories elicited. The practitioner must be especially sensitive to the fact that the mere wording of a question can significantly distort memories (Hilgard and Loftus, 1979, p. 342) and that hypnotised individuals tend to make more errors answering leading questions than they do ordinarily (Putnam, 1979, p. 444). Further, they must understand that the possibility of subtle and unintentional communication of information to the witness by verbal or nonverbal cues from others in the room is a definite possibility

(Worthington, 1979, p. 414; Orne, 1979, p. 311). Finally, the forensic or investigative hypnotist must be aware that the subject matter in question frequently involves traumatic past experiences of the subject (Kroger and Douce, 1979, pp. 362, 370). Consequently, the "need to know" must be carefully balanced against the needs of the subject with respect to the events under investigation. The hypnotist obviously should be adequately prepared by training and experience to deal with the emergence of any unexpected emotional behavior on the part of the subject.

The forensic hypnotist also has certain responsibilities associated with making the information obtained available to others. First and foremost, the practitioner has an obligation to explain the limitations of information obtained under hypnosis to all concerned in advance of the interview. Moreover, prior arrangements should be made for whatever corroboration is necessary. Guidelines for this and other safeguards are available from a number of sources (Schafer and Rubio, 1978; Orne, 1979; Ault, 1979). Finally, the forensic hypnotist has the responsibility of full honesty and integrity in transmitting to others what has been learned from the interview under hypnosis. The ethical responsibility to guard against subjectivity in reporting the results of an interview is as great if not more so as the responsibility to conduct the actual questioning properly.

On the basis of recent clinical experience and evolving legal decisions, the following set of procedures and safeguards is recommended for use whenever hypnosis is employed as an aid in forensic investigation. First, the hypnotic session should be conducted by a clinically competent psychologist or psychiatrist who is specially trained in the use of hypnosis. Second, the qualified professional conducting the session should be independent of any of the interested parties, including prosecutor, investigator, or defense. In addition, any information given to the hypnotist by law enforcement personnel prior to the hypnotic session should be in written form, so that the extent of the information the subject could have received from hypnosis can be verified. Furthermore, the hypnotist should obtain from the subject a detailed description of the facts as remembered prior to induction. The hypnotist should of course exercise due diligence to avoid adding new elements to witnesses' reports. Fifth, all contacts between the hypnotist and the subject should be recorded, preferably by videotape, but certainly by audiotape. Finally, only the hypnotist and the subject should be present during any phase of the hypnosis session, including the pre- and posthypnotic briefings.

Hypnosis in the Experimental Setting

The use of hypnosis in human experimentation or the direct experimentation with hypnosis may be the consummate nonclinical application of hypnotic intervention. In experimentation, the primary objective is to gather information about hypnosis or about certain psychological characteristics of a sample population by the use of hypnosis. An improvement in the psychological or physical well-being of an individual subject for the sake of the subject is a secondary objective at best. What then are the ethical considerations associated with hypnosis used in an experimental setting? Certainly, the ethical and professional responsibilities of the practitioner who uses hypnosis in or for experimentation are no less important than those of the therapist. The relevant question, then, is whether there are special considerations for the experimenter that go beyond those of therapist?

Orne (1965) has suggested that a clear distinction should be made between the episodic and often impersonal nature of the experimental setting and the more enduring and personal aspects of therapy. Moreover, the greater the length of time the therapist and client spend together, the intensity of the relationship that develops, and the emotional aspects of the material covered combine to make therapy a highly affect-laden environment in which reactions to hypnosis may be strong.

Nevertheless, several aspects of the typical hypnosis experiment may contribute to making it an emotionally charged setting and, thus, may influence the validity of the results obtained and even pose a threat to the welfare of the subject. First, experiments frequently involve some type of perceptual distortion, which can be stressful and unsettling for some subjects. Second, experiments may require subjects to attempt to relinquish some amount of self-control. This can also make the situation trying for certain subjects. Finally, most beginning subjects possess numerous misconceptions about hypnosis, which are difficult to correct entirely beforehand and which may contribute to bias in the experiment (Sakata, 1968).

The extent to which these and other aspects of the use of hypnosis in an experimental setting can lead to adverse after-effects has been examined in general studies. In an early study (Hilgard, Hilgard, and Newman, 1961), approximately 8 percent of the 220 volunteers who were administered the Stanford Hypnotic Susceptibility Scale reported undesirable after-effects. While these were mainly short term, for five of the subjects the effects lasted for at least a few hours. The undue effects reported included a feeling of being "in a fog, numbness in arms and legs, and acute anxiety over continuing the experiment." Interestingly, the experimenters noted a positive relationship between after-effects and unpleasant childhood experiences with chemical anesthesia. Overall, these experimenters concluded that "a routine experience of hypnosis is generally harmless in a student population," (p. 477) but investigators should be alert to the possibility of after-effects.

J. Hilgard (1974) replicated the general experiment thirteen years later. In the second study, student volunteers were administered a more difficult form of the Stanford Scale (Form C), which contains items such as age regression and hypnotic dream that are considered likely to evoke emotional response. Predictably, the percentage of subjects reporting adverse effects increased from 7.7 to 31 percent, with the undue behavior including headache, dizziness, nausea, stiff neck, drowsiness, cognitive distortion, anxiety, and night dreams about hypnosis. Hilgard noted that many of the effects actually began during the hypnotic session, and she interpreted these effects as a change in state within hypnosis which took the nature of a "restructuring" from which some subjects require time to recover (p. 287). While neither this nor the earlier study employed a control group, one may still conclude that precautions should be taken to avoid the premature departure of a subject after hypnosis.

Faw, Sellers, and Wilcox (1968), in a study which did incorporate a control group, compared the after-effects of hypnosis for a sample which had been administered a group hypnotizability scale with a control group which had merely attended discussion groups. It was concluded that hypnosis may actually be beneficial: the hypnotized subjects had improved MMPI scores, fewer self-referrals to the counseling center, and less need of medical attention within ninety days than had the control group.

In a recent study, Coe and Ryken (1979) compared the after-effects from the Stanford Hypnotic Susceptibility Scale (Forms A and C) with those from four other activities: (1) participating in a brief verbal learning experiment; (2) taking a college exam; (3) attending a college class; and (4) experiencing college life in general. The authors found that "in no case did hypnosis have any more negative effects than at least some of the other samples, and for the more serious negative sequelae, it had fewer adverse effects than the exam, class, or college life samples" (p. 677).

The studies cited above were concerned primarily with undesirable after-effects, but adverse reactions to experimental hypnosis may also occur during the hypnotic session. Turner (1960) reported such an occurrence in the case of a female participant in an experiment involving hypnotic suggestions of hypothermia. She developed spontaneous age regression to a traumatic childhood experience with decidely adverse consequences. Age regressions suggested by hypnosis may also pose a potential for undesired effects; in fact, Weitzenhoffer (1957) has held that such regressions are potentially the most risky hypnotic phenomena. There is the possibility of inadvertently regressing a subject to a traumatic experience (p. 355), with the accompanying likelihood of a strong undue emotional reaction.

In sum, although there are nearly always minimal negative effects connected with episodic induction procedures (Orne, 1965), even an experimental setting where no psychotherapy is intended may turn spontaneously into a highly charged emotional experience. Furthermore, residual effects may persist for some time, even after the hypnotic state has apparently been terminated; for example, there is the possibility of uncancelled suggestions later spontaneously manifesting themselves (see, for example, Lindemann, 1973; Bowers, 1956; Jolowicz, 1947) or of delayed response to suggested age regression (Hilgard, 1965).

In considering the special circumstances that may be associated with experimental hypnosis, an experimenter must appreciate the potential for a subject to convert a research experience into one embodying the emotional charge of a therapeutic experience. Accordingly, rigorous control of subject selection and subject care are essential, and, of course, the experimenter must never put the desire for results ahead of the welfare of the subject. Thus, the experimenter may have an even greater obligation than the therapist to ensure that the subject gives informed consent before the onset of the experiment. The experimenter must also take steps to ensure that those who learn hypnotic techniques in the course of the study do not misuse what they might have acquired by practicing on themselves or others. Clearly, where the ongoing transference ties of the clinical therapeutic relationship are not present, the professional has a fundamental ethical responsibility clearly to communicate concern about the abuse of hypnosis by the nonprofessional and to avoid or limit the chance that his or her efforts will be misused by others as much as possible.

Hypnosis in Entertainment Settings

Historically, the greatest public exposure to hypnosis in a nontherapeutic context has come from stage hypnosis—hypnosis used for entertainment. Indeed, it may be that stage hypnosis accounts for the majority of public experience with any or all applications of hypnosis. While one might properly exclude this use of hypnosis from a discussion of professionally responsible applications of hypnosis, the preeminent role that this commercial application may play in shaping public understanding or misunderstanding of hypnosis requires that at least brief consideration be given to the "ethics" of stage hypnosis.

Stage hypnosis is clearly not therapeutic, since the primary objective of that commercial enterprise is the audience's entertainment, not the improvement of the physical or emotional welfare of the subject. There already exists a significant body of literature containing reports of actual physical or emotional harm to the subject as a result of stage hypnosis (Schultz, 1922; Weitzenhoffer, 1957; Wolberg, 1948; Crasilneck and

Hall, 1975; Bryan, 1962; Starker, 1974; Harding, 1978; Kleinhauz et al., 1979; Van Pelt, 1952; West, 1965; Erickson, 1962; Rosen, 1957, 1960; Marcuse, 1964).

Clearly, the important question is whether stage hypnosis can ever be considered an ethically responsible use of hypnosis. The answer to that question must be an emphatic negative; there are too many factors inherent in stage hypnosis that are by their very nature antithetical to responsible ethical and professional behavior to allow any other answer. For example, the stage hypnotist's desire both to impress and to amuse the audience means that the interests of the subject must be subordinated to those of the hypnotist. Moreover, stage hypnosis does not allow for the preliminary psychological and medical screening necessary to guard against complications developing with inappropriate subjects. The stage hypnotist is also unlikely to be professionally qualified to handle possible crises such as hysterical reactions and spontaneous abreactions or to detect and treat serious residual effects. Indeed, if the hypnotist is an itinerant entertainer, no personal followup with subjects is possible.

In addition, a number of other features of stage hypnosis may render it detrimental to the general welfare of the audience. First, members of the audience are in effect exposed to a brief "how to" course without any training in the dynamics of hypnotic intervention, and subsequent experimentation by audience members on themselves or friends could create significant complications. Second, highly suggestible members of the audience become hypnotized inadvertently while observing the proceedings, which could clearly lead to complications developing without the availability of professional help.

Finally, because the stage hypnotist may consistently mislead or misinform the audience about the true nature and value of hypnotic intervention, stage hypnosis can deprive the public of the understanding and appreciation of hypnosis necessary for effective use of hypnosis in the therapeutic context. Harding (1978) has compiled a list of common misconceptions perpetuated by the typical stage hypnotist. They include: (1) the hypnotist has total control; (2) hypnosis is instantaneous; (3) those who do not respond properly are stupid; (4) the subject is unaware of any unsuggested perceptions; (5) amnesia is the rule; and (6) the subject can be manipulated to violate his or her basic moral code.

A subsidiary consideration concerns whether or not a professional may responsibly train those who might intend to use hypnosis in an entertainment setting. The Society for Clinical and Experimental Hypnosis (ISH, 1979, p. 455) considers the training of laypeople to use hypnosis with others to be unethical. A survey undertaken in late 1980 with the members of the American Society of Clinical Hypnosis clearly showed that an overwhelming majority were in favor of continuing stringent controls over training and membership in the Society. *Ethical Standards of Psychologists* (1979), a publication of the American Psychological Association, states that a psychologist must not knowingly allow his services to be used by others for purposes inconsistent with the values of individual dignity and worth. That could clearly be understood as a prohibition on training professionally unqualified individuals to use hypnosis or those who intend to use hypnosis in an irresponsible manner, such as for entertainment purposes. Moreover, since stage hypnosis inevitably involves the casual teaching of hypnotic technique to laypersons, these standards also serve as an indirect though firm sanction of stage hypnosis.

Conclusions

The fundamental ethical considerations in professional applications of hypnosis are those relevant to clinical or therapeutic applications. Foremost, the hypnotherapist must be competent as a hypnotist and well trained in psychodynamics and psychopathology. Furthermore, the practitioner must respect the personal integrity and free will of the client or patient. The therapist, moreover, must be aware of his or her own professional limitations and must not extend the use of hypnosis beyond the limits of his or her training and experience. Finally, when the therapist intends to incorporate hypnosis into a client's self-help program, due diligence must be exercised to ensure that the client is capable of assuming the responsibility of being both hypnotherapist and client simultaneously.

The basic ethical responsibilities of the forensic or investigative hypnotist are those of the hypnotherapist. In addition, however, the forensic hypnotist must be aware of the requirement to balance the "need to know" against the needs of the subject with respect to the event under investigation. Finally, the forensic hypnotist must be aware of the limitations as well as the advantages of investigative hypnosis, must ensure that all reasonable precautions are taken to enhance the validity of the information obtained, and must communicate a realistic appraisal of the limitations on information so obtained to all concerned.

The basic ethical responsibilities of the experimental hypnotist are also those of the hypnotherapist. In addition, the experimenter must recognize the potential for adverse effects that exists because of the episodic nature of the experimental setting. Specifically, the experimenter must be aware of the possibility that a strong emotional charge may be introduced into the experimental setting, of the possible occurrence of random effects, and of the need to provide for followup to ensure that any after-effects do not go untreated.

The commercial use of hypnosis for entertainment purposes is antithetical to the ethical responsibilities of the professional hypnotist. The rights and needs of the subject must never be neglected or willfully subordinated to other objectives. Furthermore, it should be considered unethical behavior knowingly to train anyone who intends to use hypnosis in an irresponsible manner.

REFERENCES

AMERICAN PSYCHOLOGICAL ASSOCIATION. *Ethical standards of psychologists.* Washington, D.C.: American Psychological Association, 1979.

ARIETI, S., and CHRZANOWSKI, G. (eds.). *New dimensions in psychiatry: A world view.* New York: Wiley, 1975.

AULT, R. L., JR. FBI guidelines for use of hypnosis. *International Journal of Clinical and Experimental Hypnosis,* 1979, **27,** 449-451.

BARBER, T. X. Antisocial and criminal acts induced by hypnosis: A review of the experimental and clinical findings. *Archives of General Psychiatry,* 1961, **5,** 301-312.

BOWERS, M. K. Understanding the relationship between the hypnotist and his subject. In M. V. Kline (ed.), *A scientific report on "The search for Bridey Murphy."* New York: Julian Press, 1956.

BRENMAN, M., and GILL, M. M. *Hypnotherapy: A survey of the literature.* New York: International Universities Press, 1947.

BRYAN, W. J., JR. *Religious aspects of hypnosis.* Springfield, Ill.: Thomas, 1962.

COE, W. C., and RYKEN, K. Hypnosis and risk to human subjects. *American Psychologist,* 1979, **34,** 673-681.

CONN, J. H. Is hypnosis really dangerous? *International Journal of Clinical and Experimental Hypnosis,* 1972, **20,** 61-79.

CRASILNECK, H. B., and HALL, J. A. *Clinical hypnosis: Principles and applications.* New York: Grune & Stratton, 1975.

D'AULAIRE, E., and D'AULAIRE, P. O. When hypnosis casts its spell. *Reader's Digest,* January 1980, 102-106.

ERICKSON, M. H. Stage hypnotist back syndrome. *American Journal of Clinical Hypnosis,* 1962, **5,** 141-142.

ESTABROOKS, G. H. *Hypnotism.* New York: Dutton, 1943.

FAW, V., SELLERS, D. J., and WILCOX, W. W. Psychopathological effects of hypnosis. *International Journal of Clinical and Experimental Hypnosis,* 1968, **16,** 26-37.

GORMLEY, W. J. *Medical hypnosis: Historical introduction to its morality in the light of papal, theological and medical teaching.* Washington, D.C.: Catholic University Press, 1961.

HARDING, H. C. Complications arising from hypnosis for entertainment. In F. H. Frankel and H. S. Zamansky (eds.), *Hypnosis at its bicentennial.* New York: Plenum Press, 1978.

HARTLAND, J. The value of "ego-strengthening" procedures prior to direct symptom-removal under hypnosis. *American Journal of Clinical Hypnosis,* 1965, **8,** 89-93.

HEYER, G. P. *Hypnosis and hypnotherapy.* London: C. W. Daniel, 1931.

HILGARD, E. R. *Hypnotic susceptibility.* New York: Harcourt, Brace, & World, 1965.

HILGARD, E. R., and LOFTUS, E. R. Effective interrogation of the eyewitness. *International Journal of Clinical and Experimental Hypnosis,* 1979, **27,** 342–357.

HILGARD, J. R. Sequelae to hypnosis. *International Journal of Clinical and Experimental Hypnosis,* 1974, **22,** 281–296.

HILGARD, J. R., HILGARD, E. R., and NEWMAN, M. R. Sequelae to hypnotic induction with special reference to earlier chemical anesthesia. *Journal of Nervous and Mental Disorders,* 1961, **133,** 461–478.

INTERNATIONAL SOCIETY OF HYPNOSIS. Resolution adopted August, 1979. *International Journal of Clinical and Experimental Hypnosis,* 1979, **27,** 453.

JANET, P. *Psychological healing: A historical and clinical study,* Vol. 1. London: Allen & Unwin, 1925.

JOLOWICZ, E. Consciousness in dream and in hypnotic state. *American Journal of Psychotherapy,* 1947, **1,** 2–24.

JOSEPH, E. D., PECK, S. M., and KAUFMAN, R. A psychological study of neurodermatitis with a case report. *Journal of Mount Sinai Hospital, New York,* 1949, **15,** 360–366.

KLEINHAUZ, M.; DREYFUSS, D. A.; BERAN, B.; GOLDBERG, T.; and AZIRI, D. Some aftereffects of stage hypnosis: A case study of psychopathological manifestations. *International Journal of Clinical and Experimental Hypnosis,* 1979, **27,** 219–226.

KROGER, W. S. An analysis of valid and invalid objections to hypnotherapy. *American Journal of Clinical Hypnosis,* 1963, **6,** 120–131.

KROGER, W. S., and DOUCE, R. G. Hypnosis in criminal investigation. *International Journal of Clinical and Experimental Hypnosis,* 1979, **27,** 358–374.

LE CRON, L. M. *Techniques of hypnotherapy.* New York: Julian Press, 1961.

LEVITT, E. E., and HERSHMAN, S. The clinical practice of hypnosis in the United States: A preliminary survey. *International Journal of Clinical and Experimental Hypnosis,* 1961, **11,** 55–65.

LINDEMANN, H. *Relieve tension the autogenic way.* New York: Peter C. Wyden, 1973.

LONDON, P. *The modes and morals of psychotherapy.* New York: Holt, Rinehart & Winston, 1964.

MARCUSE, F. L. *Hypnosis throughout the world.* Springfield, Ill.: Thomas, 1964.

MEARES, A. An evaluation of the dangers of medical hypnosis. *American Journal of Clinical Hypnosis,* 1961, **4,** 90–97.

MELDMAN, M. J. Personality decompensation after hypnotic symptom suppression. *Journal of the American Medical Association,* 1960, **173,** 359–361.

NEUSTATTER, W. L. *The early treatment of nervous and mental disorders.* London: Churchill, 1940.

ORNE, M. T. Undesirable effects of hypnosis: The determinants and management. *International Journal of Clinical and Experimental Hypnosis,* 1965, **13,** 226–237.

ORNE, M. T. Can a hypnotized subject be compelled to carry out otherwise unacceptable behavior: A discussion. *International Journal of Clinical and Experimental Hypnosis,* 1972, **20,** 101–117.

ORNE, M. T. The use and misuse of hypnosis in court. *International Journal of Clinical and Experimental Hypnosis,* 1979, **27,** 311–341.

PERRY, C. Uncancelled hypnotic suggestions: The effects of hypnotic depth and hypnotic skill on the posthypnotic persistence. *Journal of Abnormal Psychology*, 1977, **86**, 570–574.

PUTNAM, W. H. Hypnosis and distortions in eyewitness memory. *International Journal of Clinical and Experimental Hypnosis*, 1979, **27**, 437–448.

ROSEN, H. *Hypnotherapy in clinical psychiatry*. New York: Julian Press, 1953.

ROSEN, H. Hypnosis and self-hypnosis in medical practice. *Maryland Medical Journal*, 1957, **6**, 297–299.

ROSEN, H. Hypnosis: Applications and misapplications. *Journal of the American Medical Association*, 1960, **172**, 683–687.

ROSEN, H., and BARTEMEIER, L. H. Hypnosis in medical practice. *Journal of the American Medical Association*, 1961, **175**, 967–979.

SAKATA, K. I. Report on a case failure to dehypnotize and subsequent reputed aftereffects. *International Journal of Clinical and Experimental Hypnosis*, 1968, **16**, 221–228.

SCHAFER, D. W., and RUBIO, R. Hypnosis to aid the recall of witnesses. *International Journal of Clinical and Experimental Hypnosis*, 1978, **26**, 81–91.

SCHULTZ, J. *Gesundheitsschaedigungen nach Hypnose.* (*Health damage after hypnosis*). Halle: C. Marhold, 1922.

SEITZ, P. F. D. Experiments in the substitution of symptoms by hypnosis: II. *Psychosomatic Medicine*, 1953, **15**, 405–424.

SPIEGEL, H. Is symptom removal dangerous? *American Journal of Psychiatry*, 1967, **123**, 1297–1283.

SPIEGEL, H., and SPIEGEL, D. *Trance and treatment: Clinical uses of hypnosis*. New York: Basic Books, 1978.

STARKER, S. Persistence of a hypnotic dissociative reaction. *International Journal of Clinical and Experimental Hypnosis*, 1974, **22**, 131–137.

TEITEL, B. Post-hypnotic psychosis and the law. In the *Scientific Papers of the One Hundred and Seventeenth Annual Meeting of the American Psychiatric Association in Summary Form*, pp. 108–110. Washington, D.C.: American Psychiatric Association, 1961.

TURNER, J. A. Hypnosis in medical practice and research. *Bulletin of the Menninger Clinic*, 1960, **24**, 18–25.

VAN PELT, S. J. Some dangers of stage hypnotism. *British Journal of Medical Hypnotism*, Spring 1952.

WEITZENHOFFER, A. M. *General techniques of hypnotism*. New York: Grune & Stratton, 1957.

WEST, L. J., and DECKERT, G. H. Dangers of hypnosis. *Journal of the American Medical Association*, 1965, **192**, 9–12.

WILLIAMS, G. W. Difficulty in dehypnotizing. *Journal of Clinical and Experimental Hypnosis*, 1953, **1**, 3–12.

WOLBERG, L. R. *Medical hypnosis*, 2 vols. New York: Grune & Stratton, 1948.

WORTHINGTON, T. S. The use in court of hypnotically enhanced testimony. *Journal of Clinical and Experimental Hypnosis*, 1979, **27**, 402–416.

The Ethical Practice of Biofeedback

14

Gordon F. Derner

Biofeedback in its simplest definition is a technique which allows the person to improve his or her control over physiological activities by supplying the person with information about the activity. The mirror serves as a biofeedback instrument. When a person parts his or her hair, the person ordinarily will look into a mirror in order to be sure the part is straight. The knowledge of the position of the arm as obtained from the image in the mirror supplies the physiological information to control the arm movement. A more mechanical example of feedback is the information supplied by a gyroscope on a ship. As the ship begins to tilt to the port side, the gyroscope supplies the information of the tilt which is used by its centering procedures to cause the ship to begin to tilt in the opposite direction toward the starboard. If the gyroscope did not supply information about the starboard tilt, the ship would continue tilting to the starboard until it rolled onto its side, but the gyroscope will give information as the ship tilts too far to the starboard and the centering device will begin to tilt the ship to the port side. When this feedback is done on a sensitive enough level, the appearance of the ship is to be perfectly stable in its movement through the sea.

Our body has many built-in feedback systems, such as the semicircular canals of the ear which function to maintain the stability of our bodies. When we do the remarkable feat of standing on two points, our feet, we are able to maintain the position of our body in its perpendicular relationship to the earth because the semicircular canals give us information that tells us whether we are tilting so much in any direction that we would fall. Chemicals or even trauma can interfere with this apparatus. The effects of alcohol is a good example of how that feedback system can be made inoperative so that the person will stagger instead of walking straight.

In recent years the supply to a person of exquisite information about bodily functions has become part of the basis for the treatment modality called biofeedback. Through work with electroencephalography, Kamiya (1969) discovered that subjects could be made aware of when their occipital brainwaves were being generated in a range of eight to

313

thirteen cycles per second (alpha waves) in contrast to the generation of a faster frequency. That is, the patient with electrodes attached to the outside of the skull was able to identify these very low amplitude waves which would ordinarily be outside of any conscious awareness. What allowed the brain wave information to come within conscious awareness was the observation of the actual movement of the waves through the electronic measurement which was being conducted. The patient could see a pattern of his or her brainwaves and then within bodily awareness, be able to differentiate the slower from the faster rate. What seemed even more remarkable was that a person could produce the internal bodily state that would bring about the slower waves. When the alpha waves occurred, the patient was often feeling languid, relaxed, and calm. This discovery of brainwave control led to the excitement about alpha-wave conditioning. In some circles it was viewed as an approach to Nirvana and received much attention in the popular press. As a treatment modality with biofeedback, it has limited application, at least at present.

An impressive research which identified the refined level of discrimination which could be accomplished when information systems were made available to the subject was conducted by Basmajian (1963). Basmajian inserted a hair-thin needle into a muscle fibre so that only a single motor neuron was measured. The subject was able to activate the single muscle neuron while preventing all the other neurons in the same bundle from being activated. This refined behavior was possible because the subject had the electrical output of the neuron shown on an oscilloscope available to him or her.

A third area of research which led to the expansion of the use of biofeedback was done by Miller (1969) and his colleagues at Rockefeller University. The scope of their investigations was to determine whether the autonomic nervous system was truly involuntary, that is, that it could not be controlled by deliberate direction of the subject. Miller devised an experiment in which a rat's skeletal muscles were paralyzed by the use of curare, allowing only the smooth muscles or involuntary muscles to function. The rat was trained to dilate or constrict the blood vessels of its ear to avoid an electric shock to its tail. The rat learned to accomplish this task so that the ear would become pink with vasodilation and white with vasoconstriction. Although there has been difficulty replicating the early Miller experiments, the leadership they supplied in demonstrating that the autonomic nervous system is as susceptible to training as is the central nervous system has led to a wide variety of biofeedback procedures in the treatment of stress or psychosomatic disorders.

One important element of biofeedback as a treatment modality as compared with many medical procedures is that it is an active rather than a passive treatment modality. The patient him or herself must bring about the changes, not the surgery or medication or the self-limiting quality of the disorders under investigation. Diseases such as the common cold do not require treatment because they are self-limiting. In some instances diseases which are self-limiting have a shortened course by the use of medication or other external interventions. By contrast, biofeedback requires the person to make the internal changes by the cognitive awareness of what is happening in a particular part of the body which is mediated by the central nervous system or the autonomic system and then internally to bring about the bodily changes to assist the person in regaining function or health.

It is important to note the several levels of consciousness involved in biofeedback. The first level is when a person is fully aware of what is happening; this is called full consciousness. At this point reading the material in this book is a conscious act. If the reader allowed his or her eyes simply to scan the page, the information would be of little consequence unless conscious attention was paid to the content. When we are aware of what is going on either internally or externally, we call that conscious. A second level is unconscious. Unconscious is the residue of prior experience to which the person is presently not attending or of which the person is presently unaware. Some experience can be out of awareness and never again recalled. An example would be an attempt to recall what one had for breakfast six years ago as of the present date. Forgetting occurs in a very rapid drop, particularly after routine experiences. Other information may be out of awareness momentarily or for long periods and may still be recoverable to awareness upon search for it. An example would be a remembrance of a third-grade teacher. Some of the material that is unconscious may be related to unhappy or traumatic life experiences and therefore kept out of awareness. In techniques like hypnosis, psychoanalysis, and other types of psychotherapy, there is often an attempt to help patients regain the remembrance of such unconscious material. A third level is subconscious. Subconscious is that bodily activity which can never be brought into verbal awareness because there is no direct connection between the verbal areas of the brain and the particular function. Examples are the beat of the heart, the production of digestive juices in the stomach and intestine, the filtering of liquid into the bladder and other internal bodily functions which are mediated by the autonomic nervous system. It is the area of the subconscious which is crucial in much of biofeedback therapy.

Biofeedback has as a principle of psychological behavior the application of a learning paradigm. The potentiation of the learning in the treatment of tension-related disorders is best accomplished by dealing with situational factors or personality issues which bring about the tension or psychosomatic disorder in conjunction with biofeedback. Biofeedback, therefore, is more than a mechanical technique of information sharing. It is part of a total treatment modality which includes not only literal biofeedback information supplied by the various biofeedback electronics devices, but also the working with the patient's psychological condition, that is, his or her thoughts, feelings, cognitions, and interpersonal relations. To make maximum use of the biofeedback modality, therefore, a concurrent involvement in psychotherapy is a crucial aspect of patient care. The effective application of biofeedback also requires the person to develop the psychophysiological style which keeps tension at a low level. The treatment, therefore, includes not only the use of the biofeedback device and psychotherapy, but also home exercises which help the person develop increased control over his or her total body.

Some of the home procedures are identified by various methods of induction. The most simple of these is relaxation exercise which is not unlike the meditation procedures of some Eastern religions. While the exercise is similar to these religious practices, its use as a modality is not related to religious or mystical purposes; it is used to affect the autonomic nervous system.

The autonomic nervous system mediates the activity of the visceral organs. When there is high sympathetic arousal, the body needs more oxygen, increases blood pressure, increases heart rate, produces peripheral vasoconstriction, increases respiration rate, decreases digestion, and in every way acts as if to prepare the person to protect against danger. The preparation is a remnant from our most primitive past in Oldouvi Gorge where it was necessary to be constantly on the alert for danger and to be prepared for attack by fellow humans, humanoids, animals, natural forces, or whatever. The sympathetic system arousal is the response of the person to the danger which prepares the body for "fight or flight," as identified by Cannon (1929). Such a biological system was helpful when true danger occurred, but in modern living the sympathetic nervous system is aroused to high levels by activities and events which cannot be met by either flight or fight. As a consequence, the body is prepared for emergencies without any outlet for the emergency and the body begins to be more and more tense. The blood pressure which has been elevated by the sympathetic arousal to prepare the individual to deal with the danger now begins to stabilize at a higher level and the person develops essential hypertension or other psychosomatic disorders. The organs of the viscera become battered by high sympathetic arousal when the arousal does little if anything to help the person in his or her daily living. Counter to high arousal of the sympathetic system is the arousal of the parasympathetic or simply the reduction of the sympathetic. When the parasympathetic system is aroused, the body reaches a state of relaxation. Relaxation is used here not in the sense of a vacation or recreation as a contrast to work, but rather as a bodily state in which there is reduced or lower sympathetic arousal. When these sympathetic/parasympathetic arousal levels develop, the body is put in a position of less strain. The heartbeat and the respiration rates are slower, the blood pressure is lower, the digestive activities can go on, the peripheral blood vessels can vasodilate so that there is peripheral warming and the sense of both physiological and psychological tension is reduced. It is to activate this level of bodily response to which the relaxation exercises and other home exercises are directed. They are usually nonspecific, but more generalized in the reduction of the flight or fight response and the activation of the relaxation response. All depend on a series of procedures which narrow the focus of attention.

The narrowing of the focus of attention can be accomplished by the concentration on a single word or phrase which is repeated by the person sitting or lying in a comfortable, quiet place. The passive volition in the repetition brings about the narrowing of attention with concomitant physiological changes. An adaptation of a Hindu technique, transcental meditation, was widely publicized in part because of the interest in it of prominent public figures, including the Beatles. Research on the technique of repeating a phrase or mantra demonstrated that it does produce low arousal (Wallace, 1970). The mantra used is a Hindu phrase, but similar results are obtainable with even the simpler technique described by Benson (1975) to bring about the "relaxation response." The Benson technique has the person seated with eyes closed repeat the word "one" mentally to him or herself in conjunction with each exhalation. A more elaborate program, Clinically Standardized Meditation, has been developed by Patricia Carrington (1977). The person has a choice of phrases for repetition, but thoughts are allowed to occur freely while the Benson technique requires that extraneous thoughts be disregarded.

A system of cognitive focusing with a psychophysiological shift somewhat similar to the meditative procedures, but much more sharply defined as Autogenic Training (AT), was developed by Schultz, and further developed by Luthe (1969). AT requires a person to focus his or her attention in a fixed routine fashion on a part of the body and it requires an awareness of the sensation in that part of the body. The procedure first focuses on the right arm feeling heavy, then other limbs feeling heavy, then limbs warm, attention to the heart beat as calm and regular, attention to the breath, visceral sensation, and cooling of the forehead. There are specific statements to be used for specific conditions so that the patient will focus upon the functioning of some part of his or her body through cognitive input.

An earlier technique, Progressive Relaxation was developed by Jacobson (1929) which only recently has had a resurgence in becoming part of the regimen of treatment of psychosomatic disorders. Although Jacobson developed his procedures in the 1920s, there has been considerable delay in its widespread use. In part, the delay in acceptance was probably due to the fact that Progressive Relaxation as practiced by Jacobson is excruciatingly detailed and time-consuming. The essential characteristic of the method is to tense a muscle or group of muscles deliberately so that the person is very aware of the tension and then slowly to allow the tension to diminish until the muscle is in a relaxed state. This sharpening of the difference between the tense and relaxed muscle is particularly useful in helping the person become acutely aware of tension when it exists in the body.

A variety of tension reduction methods are used in modern work with biofeedback, but imagery and hypnosis, particularly for the purpose of teaching self-hypnosis, are also used. Each method in turn focuses the attention in a narrow fashion so that the person may allow his or her body to reach a state of very low arousal. These several relaxation procedures used in home practice in conjunction with instrumentation and psychotherapy are the program of biofeedback treatment.

The practitioner of biofeedback will need knowledge of anatomy, particularly of muscle groups, psychophysiological functioning, and psychosomatic disorders. Some knowledge of electronics and the use of sensing devices is also needed. In psychology content, the person must know learning theory, psychodynamics, and psychopathology which would be particularly necessary for the treatment of emotional and behavioral disorders. The basic psychological processes of psychodynamics, cognition, perception, and learning are crucial areas of scientific knowledge which are used in treatment. Any one phase of the biofeedback treatment may be done by a person who is particularly knowledgeable in that area but who is not necessarily able to supply the full treatment. For example, a biofeedback technician may learn the techniques for using the instrumentation which will be used in conjunction with the psychotherapy being conducted by the psychologist or his or her counterpart in mental health.

The major use of biofeedback is in the treatment of tension-related or psychosomatic disorders. Some of the psychosomatic conditions which have been helped by biofeedback are hypertension, cardiac arrythmias, migraine headache, tension headache, Raynaud's Disorder, tinnitus, and anxiety state. Since the treatment modality is so new, considerable experimentation has been conducted on its application to a variety of other disorders including epilepsy, diabetes, anal incontinence, and asthma. A particularly noteworthy feature of biofeedback is its noninvasive character. There are no side effects of a deleterious nature such as can occur with the use of medication. It has neither the traumatic effect nor the finality of surgery. In a number of instances biofeedback therapy has been shown to be as effective as, or more effective than, chemical and surgical intervention. In many instances, therefore, it can be the treatment of choice or at least a modality worth trying.

Another use of biofeedback is to help persons regain muscle control after it has been lost through cerebral vascular accident or some other cause. The person still may have some small muscle contraction ability, but it is on such a low amount of discharge that he or she is not aware that it is occurring. By the use of the highly sensitive recording techniques of biofeedback electronics, the person can learn that he or she does have that control and can gradually, through exercise with the biological information being fed back to him or her, obtain a greater amount of control. The work of Basmajian (1978) in this area is particularly noteworthy.

The major biofeedback devices are the electromyograph, temperature monitoring units, the psychogalvanometer, and the electroencephalograph.

The most frequently used biofeedback instrument is the electromyograph or EMG. The EMG measures the electrical discharge of the muscle potential. Contraction of the muscle produces an electrical current of low voltage which is amplified to inform the patient of the tension level. Three surface electrodes are applied to the muscle. The electrodes are usually silver-silver chloride and are attached with electrode collars. In some instances needle electrodes may be used.

The surface on which the electrodes are to be placed is thoroughly scrubbed to remove the debris of sloughed-off skin, makeup, skin oil, and dirt. The electrodes are prepared with electrode jelly and adhesive collars. One of the electrodes serves as a ground while the other two serve as active electrodes. The EMG analyzes the current flow of the muscle potential between each active electrode and the ground, and reports the level in microvolts. Contractions of the muscle are accompanied by the electrical current which activates a signal to the subject. The signal can be given in several ways. Sound patterns can be given which increase or decrease as analogs of the activity. The information can be given in a binary or off-on fashion in relation to a predetermined threshold of output. Exceeding or dropping below the threshold gives feedback. The EMG can be prepared to play music when below or above threshold, give colored light patterns, or turn sound off and on. Analog feedback is used more frequently because it reflects not only changes but also the magnitude of the change. In practice, the biofeedback specialist sets a goal for each session so that the subject will need to manifest increased control from the level of the beginning base rate but not so difficult that no change is observable to the patient during the session. It is the clinical judgment of these parameters which is important in the biofeedback treatment modality. When the clinician is working with the patient to increase the movement, as for example in footdrop after a cerebral vascular accident, the goal would be to increase the motor output with concomitant greater ability to manipulate the affected parts. If general relaxation is the therapeutic goal, then the patient would be taught to reduce output.

EMG biofeedback is used in most clinical applications of biofeedback because of its general relaxation value. The concept of relaxation, or low arousal level, is part of the psychiological countering of the stress which can lead to the psychosomatic disorders as well as to anxiety states.

The most usual placement for tension reduction is on the forehead or the frontalis muscle. This placement is chosen for several reasons. First, it is easily accessible for the application of surface electrodes. Second, the tension level of the frontalis tends to correlate highly with the state of tension in other muscles throughout the body. Third, its level of relaxation or of tension may easily be demonstrated simply by asking the person to tighten his or her jaw or to wrinkle his or her forehead.

It is particularly important that the electrodes be properly placed on the muscle. If the electrodes are spaced too far apart, several muscle groups will be measured simultaneously and make it difficult to control any one set. Further, if placement is on muscles such as those of the throat, very small electrodes are used and placement is quite delicate. On the forehead, the placement is usually between two and three centimeters apart. Often one or two centimeters between electrodes is a more satisfactory placement. It is therefore necessary for the practitioner to have a thorough knowledge of the muscle systems and to keep a muscle atlas at hand for referral.

The second most widely used biofeedback instrument is the temperature control unit. It is very much like an ordinary household thermometer except that it is more highly sensitized and calibrated so that it can measure units as small as one-hundreth of a degree change. This small degree change, however, is less frequently used than is the one-tenth of a degree change. In use the person has a thermistor attached to his or her finger. As the blood flow in the finger changes, the temperature also changes. With vasodilation there is a greater amount of blood flowing through the blood vessels since the lumen of the blood vessels widens and temperature is higher. In vasoconstriction, there is a more restricted blood flow because the lumen of the blood vessels narrows and the temperature is lower. The temperature varies with the dilation or constriction. The blood vessel changes are mediated by the sympathetic nervous system. There is vasoconstriction with high arousal of the sympathetic system, while there is vasodilation with reduced sympathetic arousal. Sympathetic arousal is associated with internal tension. Training with the biofeedback equipment is directed toward lowering sympathetic arousal which will be shown to the patient as increased digital temperature as the vasodilation occurs. On a subconscious level, the patient is able to regulate the level of sympathetic arousal. The thermistor is usually attached to one of the fingers, as this is an easy for placement and permits easily ascertainable changes in the level of arousal. As with all the biofeedback instruments, the information on changes can be conveyed to the patient with a variety of outputs. The direct read-out of the temperature, auditory sounds that decrease or increase in frequency, tone, or in pitch as changes occur, or signal lights, are all possible feedback modalities. In the most usual treatment procedure, the patient is asked to increase his or her peripheral digital temperature while observing the feedback information. Sometimes the training includes decreasing as well as increasing the temperature to improve the level of control although it is more difficult for most patients to learn to decrease the temperature. Because the peripheral temperature is related to the level of sympathetic arousal, temperature feedback is particularly useful for autonomic nervous system conditioning.

The third type of instrument used is the psychogalvanometer. Emotional reactivity is manifest by palmar sweat-gland activity. By sending a low-level electrical current through electrodes across the palm, the conductivity or resistance level will indicate the amount of palmar sweating. This device has been used in human psychological research for nearly a century. It is useful as a reflection of immediate emotional response. While there is a slight delay of response after the stimulus is shown, the instrument can show the response to an expressed idea or only a thought. When emotion is activated, slight palm sweating occurs, while the sweating diminishes in a more relaxed state. If the person is emotionally aroused, the perspiring hand allows the electricity to flow more readily, giving a higher score on conductivity. If the person is in a relaxed state, the dry palms inhibit the electricity flow, resulting in a lower score. The response is called the galvanic skin response, or GSR. An alternate technique is to measure the muscle potential of the sweat glands of the palm in what is called the electrodermal response or EDR. One important problem is using a GSR is the susceptibility of the body to ambient temperature so that there will be more perspiration on a warm day than on a cool day. Further, the exact placement of the electrodes can become crucial. It is more difficult to have a session-to-session standard to be met than is the case for the other two modalities described. Again, as with the other two instruments, feedback can be a variety of sounds or visual signals.

A fourth instrument is the electroencephalograph or EEG. This device measures the electrical discharge of nerve impulses in the brain. In the beginning of the use of biofeedback, the EEG was seen as a primary tool but at present it is used with considerably less frequency. The exact nature of what is being measured is somewhat disputed. The measurement is probably of the action of hundreds of thousands of nerve cells primarily in the cerebral cortex. For ease in communication about these waves they are defined according to frequency in cycles per second.

These are labeled for communication as delta for less than four cycles per second and found when a person is asleep, theta from four to eight cycles per second when the person is in a drowsy state, alpha from eight to thirteen cycles per second when the person is in a relaxed state, and greater than thirteen is labeled beta, when the person is alert. Additional differentiation is also done where needed in research or treatment.

Heart rate is measured by the electrocardiograph, the ECG or EKG. The heart contraction is a very powerful electrical signal so it is easily monitored with skin electrodes placed over the heart. While the exact shape of the heart rate pattern is of particular interest in the diagnosis of cardiac disorders, the pulse rate is most frequently used for training in biofeedback. The nerve impulses that regulate the heart are both the sympathetic and parasympathetic, which counteract each other. With high arousal of the sympathetic system, the heartbeat is more rapid while increased parasympathetic activity reduces the heartbeat. The pulse rate is the interbeat interval from one ventricular contraction to the next counted for a one-minute period. By use of a direct pulse-rate counter or with an EKG device, the subject is informed as to his or her pulse rate. The feedback information can be beats per second averaged over four or more beats, or it can be given as binary information with green-light/red-light indicating when the person is above or below a predetermined training goal. The more elaborate use of EKG generally is not found in usual biofeedback clinical treatment but the pattern itself might be used in experimental treatment modalities.

Blood pressure control is another biofeedback treatment modality. The usual procedure to measure blood pressure is to apply an occlusion cuff to the upper arm, shutting off the blood supply in the artery extending to the lower arm. The pressure is then gradually reduced until blood again begins to flow through the blood vessels. The sound of the blood flow can be readily detected through a stethoscope applied to the brachial artery. When the pressure is reduced so that the blood is flowing through the artery in its normal fashion, the clicking sound of the blood flow will no longer be heard. These Karotkoff sounds identify the systolic and diastolic heart action. The first reading, the systolic, is of the heart contracting and is the more labile heart action. The lower reading, the diastolic, is the expansion of the heart muscle as blood flows into the heart and is less labile. The blood pressure is measured in terms of a mercury column with the millimeter of column height at systole and diastole as the blood pressure, for example 135/75. The use of the occlusion cuff presents a problem for biofeedback since the cuff cuts off the blood flow to the hand and lower arm. While such stoppage can be done on occasion, to do it on a continuous basis could create severe problems. One device, which uses the occlusion cuff, pumps the pressure to only one or two mercury points above the anticipated systolic level or one or two points below the diastolic level. In the former case, the blood flow is stopped for only a fraction of a second and the device can be used therefore as a continuous feedback device. An indirect way to measure blood pressure is from the pulse-wave velocity. Two sensors are applied, one on the radial artery at the wrist and the second at the crook of the arm at the brachial artery. The time of flow from the wrist to the elbow gives a measure of the pulse-wave velocity. This measure, while inversely correlated with the blood pressure, is used as a blood pressure signal to the subject.

Other biofeedback devices have been developed, such as a procedure for monitoring anal sphincter muscle control for treatment of fecal incontinence. Relaxation of the muscle permits fecal incontinence. In treatment the patient is made aware of his or her sphincter relaxation with an EMG device which relays information that the sphincter is inappropriately relaxing and so the patient can learn to maintain the tension necessary to prevent incontinence. Other devices have been used to measure gastric secretion output, asthmatic breathing, and other physiological signs directly.

The several devices used are only part of the total treatment modality and are generally used in conjunction with psychotherapy, albeit brief therapy. In addition, the patient's homework is crucial to the self-regulation of the physiological functions. The relaxation exercises required as homework assignments are used as a prophylactic measure even when the acute symptoms have diminished or disappeared.

Biofeedback as a comprehensive modality with biofeedback equipment, psychotherapy, and home exercises, is used for a number of psychological and psychosomatic disorders. Treatment of tension headache (Budzynski et al., 1970) has been particularly successful. Migraine headache has been successfully treated with temperature control techniques (Sargent et al., 1972, 1973; Wickramasekera, 1973). Raynaud's disease, in which there is rapid vasoconstriction of the peripheral blood vessels of the extremities causing painful vasospasms, has also been successfully treated with temperature control (Surwit, 1973). Patel and colleagues (1975) have been very successful in the treatment of hypertension with and without the use of biofeedback devices per se. Cardiac arrhythmias (Engel, 1973) and cardiac neurosis (Wickramasekera, 1974) have been successfully treated by heart-rate training. Anxiety states have been alleviated by using GSR in conjunction with more formal psychotherapy (Toomim and Toomim, 1975). Treatment of anorexia nervosa and of allergic reactions has also been successful (Derner, 1978). A particularly striking success has been in muscle rehabilitation (Basmajian, 1978). A partial list of disorders using biofeedback would include also insomnia, muscle spasms and tics, voice disorders, stress management, epilepsy, pain control, peptic ulcers, premature ventricular contractions, impotence, bruxism, and lower back pain. Olton and Noonberg (1980), in an excellent and comprehensive text, present biofeedback treatment and cover twenty-six relevant psychosomatic disorders. A comprehensive review of research prepared by Ray et al. (1979) covers twenty-one disorders with which biofeedback has been used. The exhaustive key-indexed reference of Butler (1978) has 2300 items. While it is not always successful, there is reason to be optimistic about the expansion of conditions for which biofeedback will be the primary or an adjunctive treatment.

Because of its rapid and recent development, the legal control over biofeedback treatment is unclear and even confused. Although there are no legal standards for licensure, the Biofeedback Society of America has established a national certification program. Some states such as California have included biofeedback among the licensed activities for psychologists in the state. The federal Medical Devices Act requires the user to be a licensed provider so that each state must determine whether to incorporate biofeedback as a permitted practice for its various licensed health professions.

The Biofeedback Society of California has established minimal training and experience in biofeedback as basic to ethical practice. The requirements include 120 hours of specific training in biofeedback. Since biofeedback is used in clinical conditions requiring patient-doctor interaction, the professional must be qualified in his or her profession as a psychologist, physician, nurse, or physical therapist, and must have the biofeedback training in addition. The training of technicians who work under the supervision of a professional person will not have to be as exhaustive.

The specific biofeedback training recommended includes forty hours of didactic instruction with usually twenty-five hours of lecture on basic information in feedback and control systems, learning and conditioning, biological bases of behavior including nerve function, the nervous system, muscle system, and the viscera, psychophysiology, and electronics. Fifteen hours are devoted to the specific use of instruments, recording equipment, and record keeping; these areas are often presented through audio and visual tapes and films and as well as through hands-on laboratory work. Ten hours are devoted to the careful study of case histories with emphasis on procedures, clinical decisions, the role of the practitioner, and transferential and countertransferential affects. After the fifty hours, or in tandem, twenty-five hours are devoted to personal experience with the instruments supervised by a specialist and a peer trainee. Thirty hours of clinical practice with patients and fifteen hours of supervision complete the specialty training. With such a limited amount of training, it must be clear that professional ethics and integrity demand due respect for one's limitations as well as one's skills. Specific ethical statements encompass the concept of professional integrity. Practitioners should be expected to keep up with the current literature including journals such as *Biofeedback and Self Regulation,* and the *American Journal of Clinical Biofeedback* and the Aldine yearbooks. Membership in a national or state biofeedback society such as the Biofeedback Society of America is highly desirable and attendance at scientific meetings should be a part of professional growth. Certification of the Biofeedback Society of America offers the practitioner an opportunity to have an intensive peer review of his or her work through a comprehensive written examination and an oral examination. Admission to the certification program requires the appropriate degree in the person's profession, demonstrated training and experience, and then evaluation through examination. Independent practice should be encouraged only by those who have met such a review and are appropriately certified.

A Biofeedback Code of Ethics

1. The practitioner shall follow the code of ethics of his or her profession, e.g., the American Psychological Association or the American Medical Association Code of Ethics.
2. The practitioner shall apply biofeedback only after adequate training and supervised experience and only within the practitioner's area of professional competence.
3. Consultation with health specialists for areas in which the practitioner is not competent should be available; e.g., psychologists have medical consultation available, physicians have psychological consultation available.
4. Care must be taken to avoid claims of effectiveness for biofeedback where the procedure is still experimental and a full description of procedures should be given to the patient prior to treatment.
5. The relationship between the patient and practitioner shall be maintained as confidential with appropriate steps taken for anonymity for subjects in research projects or publications.

REFERENCES

BASMAJIAN, J. V. Control and training of individual motor units. *Science,* 1963, **141,** 440–441.

BASMAJIAN, J. V. (ed.). *Muscles alive: their functions revealed by electromyography,* 4th ed. Baltimore: Williams & Wilkins, 1978.

BASMAJIAN, J. V. (ed.). *Biofeedback: Principles and practice for clinicians.* Baltimore: Williams & Wilkins, 1979.

BENSON, H. *The relaxation response.* New York: William Morrow, 1975.

BROWN, B. *Stress and the art of biofeedback.* New York: Harper & Row, 1977.

BUDZYNSKI, T. H., and STOYVA, J. M. An instrument for producing deep muscle relaxation by means of analog information feedback. *Journal of Applied Behavior Analysis,* 1969, **2,** 231–237.

BUDZYNSKI, T. H., STOYVA, J., and ADLER, C. Feedback-induced muscle relaxation: Application to tension headache. *Journal of Behavior Therapy and Experimental Psychiatry,* 1970, **1,** 205–211.

BUTLER, F. *Biofeedback: A survey of the literature.* New York: Plenum, 1978.

CANNON, W. B. *Bodily changes in pain, hunger, fear and rage,* rev. ed. New York: Appleton, 1929.

CARRINGTON, P. *Freedom in meditation.* Garden City, N.Y.: Anchor Press/ Doubleday, 1977.

DERNER, G. F. Biofeedback in psychodynamic psychotherapy. In J. L. Fosshage and P. Olsen (eds.), *Healing: Implications for psychotherapy.* New York: Human Sciences Press, 1978.

ENGEL, B. T. Clinical applications of operant conditioning techniques in the control of the cardiac arrhythmias. *Seminars in Psychiatry,* 1973, **5,** 433–438.

FULLER, G. D. *Biofeedback: Methods and procedures in clinical practice.* San Francisco: Biofeedback Press, 1977.

FULLER, G. D. Current status of biofeedback in clinical practice. *American Psychologist,* 1978, **33,** 39–48.

JACOBSON, E. *Progressive relaxation.* Chicago: University of Chicago Press, 1929, 1938.

KAMIYA, J. Operant control of the EEG alpha rhythm and some of its reported effects on consciousness. In C. T. Tart (ed.), *Altered states of consciousness.* New York: Wiley, 1969.

MILLER, N. E. Learning of visceral and glandular responses. *Science,* 1969, **163,** 434–445.

OLTON, D. S., and NOONBERG, A. R. *Biofeedback: Clinical applications in behavioral medicine.* Englewood Cliffs, N.J.: Prentice-Hall, 1980.

PATEL, C. H., and NORTH, W. R. S. Randomized controlled trial of yoga and biofeedback in management of hypertension. *Lancet,* 1975, **7925,** 93–95.

RASKIN, M., JOHNSON, G., and RODESTVEDT, J. W. Chronic anxiety treated by feedback-induced muscle relaxation. *Archives of General Psychiatry,* 1973, **23,** 263–267.

RAY, W. J.; RACZYNSKI, J. M.; ROGERS, T.; and KIMBALL, W. H. *Evaluation of clinical biofeedback.* New York: Plenum, 1979.

RUGH, J. D., PERLIS, D. B., and DISRAELI, R. I. *Biofeedback in dentistry: Research and clinical applications.* Phoenix: Semantodontics. 1976.

SARGENT, J. D., GREEN, E. E., and WALTERS, E. D. The use of autogenic feedback training in a pilot study of migraine and tension headaches. *Headache,* 1972, **12,** 120–124.

SARGENT, J. D., GREEN, E. E., and WALTERS, E. D. Preliminary report on the use of autogenic feedback training in the treatment of migraine and tension headaches. *Psychosomantic Medicine,* 1973, **35,** 129–135.

SCHULTZ, J. H., and LUTHE, W. *Autogenic therapy: Autogenic methods.* New York: Grune & Stratton, 1969.

STERMAN, M. B. Effects of sensorimotor EEG feedback training on sleep and clinical manifestations of epilepsy. In J. Beatty and H. Legewie (eds.), *Biofeedback and behavior.* New York: Plenum, 1977.

SURWIT, R. S. Biofeedback: A possible treatment for Raynaud's disease. *Seminars in Psychiatry,* 1973, **5,** 483–490.

TOOMIM, M., and TOOMIM, H. Psychodynamic correlates of the paradoxically invariant GSR. *Proceedings of the Biofeedback Research Society,* 1975, **6,** 31.

WALLACE, R. K. Physiological effects of transcendental meditation. *Science,* 1970, **167,** 1751–1754.

WICKRAMASEKERA, I. E. Temperature feedback for the control of migraine. *Journal of Behavior Therapy and Experimental Psychiatry,* 1973, **4,** 343–345.

WICKRAMASEKERA, I. E. Heart rate feedback and the management of cardiac neurosis. *Journal of Abnormal Psychology,* 1974, **83,** 578–580.

Ethics and Psychopharmacology: Revolution or War?

Joseph T. Martorano

We have the power to make this the best generatior. in the history of mankind—or to make it the last.

John F. Kennedy

It is slightly more than two decades since the psychopharmacological revolution began. During this time, the immense, heady, early promise of psychotropic agents has been blurred and limited by increasing factionalism among concerned sectors as to who shall provide the control and direction of the standards that form the basis for ethical drug use.

This was is no longer quiet. Reports of conflict between medicine, government, the judiciary, industry, and even the patients are seen almost daily in the media. The scope and power of psychopharmacology has broadened until its control has become a matter of national concern, not only in terms of the treatment of mental patients, but also in the consideration of the possible use of drugs as a means of achieving new forms of social control. Hence, each of the involved sectors is engaged in trying to establish a base with which to form guidelines that best achieve their goals. This type of conflict can be very useful in shaping a dynamically oriented ethic that allows growth of the health delivery system for psychopharmacology. It can, however, be so obstructionistic that it interferes with the proper establishment of the necessary vehicles to promote safe, effective drug use for the general population.

The development of modern psychopharmacology has greatly influenced the reshaping of ethical practices in medical and psychological treatment. Since 1789, when ethical conduct was described as conformity to accepted professional standards of behavior (Moore, 1978), the prevailing medical ethic has been largely an operationally based one. In the past, the determination of treatment has dealt solely with a simple dictum of a rapidly evaluated effectiveness. If the drug works, its use is ethical: conversely, the use of a drug that doesn't work is unethical.

The long-term nature of psychotropic drug use, however, was questioned as serious side effects cropped up after several years. Now the psychopharmacologist is faced with the increasingly delicate dilemma over establishing a balance between immediate efficacy and possible long-range problems. These evaluations are made even more difficult because psychotropic drugs differ from previous medicines. They create more differences in the ability of an individual to function in relation to his social environment. This alteration may obscure the originally intended effect of the drug, and thus establishes an imbalance that needs further correcting.

For example, an individual who is too anxious on his job may become even more anxious if treated with an anxiolytic agent that causes drowsiness and impairs ability to function at work.

The full measure of the social implications of the use of psychotropic agents came almost immediately after the initial introduction of chlorpromazine into medical practice, which resulted in the release of a large number of previously incarcerated inpatients. The return of these patients into society before they were completely prepared and while they still lacked adequate social skills, caused minor social revolutions in a number of large urban environments. The implications of psychopharmacological effects had to be more adequately studied in relationship to the environment in which the patient functions.

The Recent Emergence of Psychopharmacology

Psychotropic drug use has changed since ancient times when these drugs were used primarily by priests, shamans, and medicine men to seek an expansion of the conscious state (Caldwell, 1970). In antiquity, psychotropic drugs came chiefly from plants. Early Greek history, ranging from Pythia to Helen, is filled with references to the use of drugs to change perception and alter mood. Psychotropic drugs have appeared in plants ranging from the pink Rauwolifia in the distant Himalayas to the ubiquitous cannabis growing wild all over the world.

Nonetheless, the history of modern psychopharmacology is surprisingly limited and concise. Though various drugs, including amphetamines and antihistamines, had been used to treat psychiatric disorders in the 1930s, the dramatic starting point of the history of modern psychopharmacology can be dated directly to the introduction of the first drug to restore and maintain mental health—the use of chlorpromazine in 1952 at Val-de-Grace, the famous Parisian psychiatric hospital.

Chlorpromazine was the first nonhypnotic antipsychotic drug, which could decrease psychotic activity without inducing overwhelming sedation. It achieved therapeutic effect without altering the level of consciousness, and as much, represented a vast improvement over the previous "tranquilizers," which depended on the development of a state of near unconsciousness to maintain an element of control with the patient.

In the space of relatively few years, chlorpromazine and its related phenothiazine derivatives changed the face of psychiatric care. Mental hospitals were drastically reformed and wards reserved for the physical containment of disturbed and dangerous patients rapidly evolved into treatment-oriented facilities as the available therapeutic modalities became dramatically effective, almost overnight.

The use of chlorpromazine rapidly stimulated research and invoked the use of already existing drugs in terms of their capacity to alter the mind as in the case of reserpine, which was used as a tranquilizer. Shortly thereafter, in 1955, the first effective antidepressants were introduced by Jean Delay, and then meprobamate (Miltown) appeared as the first effective antianxiety agent.

With the rapid introduction and development of new drugs, including antidepressants and antianxiety agents, by the end of the 1950s, the psychiatrist had a formidable array of psychotropic drugs to treat schizophrenia, depression, and other mental disorders. Within another decade, the use of psychotropic drugs became so common that by 1970, one out of every ten Americans took an antianxiety agent over a six-month period (Shader, 1976).

The Development of the Sensitizing Stage

Psychopharmacology is such a newly developing field that its basic parameters are yet to be delineated. Consequently, the development of a code of ethics for the field is at a point described by K. D. Clouser (1975) as a sensitizing stage in which basic knowledge is still forthcoming. Despite the early promises of three decades ago, new discoveries about the full implications of the long-term use of psychotropic agents are emerging almost daily. Through the discovery of such unfortunate major side effects as tardive dyskinesia, it has become evident that not all of the effects of drugs are immediately apparent even when approved for use by the federal government. The social manifestations of drug therapy are, however, far more subtle. The effect of drug-induced drowsiness on job performance, or sedation affecting sexual performance and marital situations must be considered.

Because of the vastness of the possible social implications of psychotropic drug use, individual physicians have lacked positive direction as ethicists, and the government has instead stepped in with a staggering

else is necessarily a mystery to the average doctor. [Quoted in Peter, 1977, p. 333]

Since drug therapy lends itself so readily to statistical analysis, there has been well-developed quantification of how the therapy should be conducted, particularly in terms of dose levels. The embryonic nature of psychopharmacology, however, has necessitated the alteration of these standards. Physicians are frequently faced with the dilemma of balancing unusual treatment, like an exceedingly high dose of antidepressants, which may be effective, and facing the possibility of incurring legal and ethical sanctions by violating the existing prevailing standards of drug practice. The problem can be best understood by examining the separate aspects of the treatment situation.

Diagnosis

In drug therapy, the diagnosis usually leads to the choice of medication. Sophisticated computer techniques which allow treatment on the basis of symptom-clusters with favorable prognosis have recently been developed.

Since the diagnosis of a specific mental disorder can be ambiguous and difficult to ascertain, there are frequent disagreements among professionals over the choice of treatment and the application of a drug treatment program. Consider the patient who presents a depressive symptomatology. If there are clear-cut signs of an endogeneous depression, then the treatment can be handled with a trial of antidepressant agents. But often the disorder is not quite so clearly delineated and ethical problems may occur in decision-making processes.

It is of utmost importance to be as precise as possible in establishing a diagnosis. Since there is no present laboratory confirmation of mental disease, the establishment of a diagnosis is of particular significance to the psychiatric patient. Labeling a patient "schizophrenic" by treating with one of the major tranquilizers such as thorazine (chlorpromazine) inevitably leads to negative connotations regarding work and social adjustments based on the limited prognosis of the disease. Therefore, it becomes ethically imperative for the psychopharmacologist to work carefully with the referring and treating personnel to monitor the disclosure of intimate diagnostic details closely.

This need for precise diagnosis has created a trend to standardized nomenclature, which has been used to determine acceptable patterns of treatment and reimbursement by insurance companies, Medicare, and Medicaid programs. Thus, the choice implied in diagnosis is directly related to the establishment of specific standards for care.

Treatment and Treatment Effect—The Ethical Implications of Drug Choice

Once the diagnosis and etiology are as clear as possible, the relative merits of the different forms of treatment have to be assessed. At this point, if drug treatment is to be considered, the physician has several immediate ethical determinations. For example, a patient's mental status must be evaluated so that the physician can decide how he should be told about the anticipated effects of the drugs. Legal decisions have made it clear that the physician is responsible for informing the patient fully about the drug.

The operational difficulties associated with drug choice reside mainly in weighing the positive and negative effects and then responsibly communicating the possibilities of these effects to the patient. At this point, informed consent enters the clinical picture. The recent victories of the patient's rights movement imply certain ethical responsibilities that had not previously been clear:

Legally competent patients have the right to refuse drug treatment.

Incompetent patients cannot be treated with drugs as punitive or restrictive measures.

Patients should be advised on the expectation of the treatment course.

This can be a formidable task since few if any drugs have a capacity for total therapeutic effectiveness. In addition, most drugs have the potential for minor and/or severe side effects. To the extent that the physician is able to communicate the possibility of these occurrences, he is ethically responsible for doing so. Such information, however, may be detrimental to the patient who cannot weigh the many factors involved so as to arrive at a decision whether or not to consent to a particular drug regimen. Too often, overinvolvement of patients may prove undesirable because patients may develop a sense of disappointment if the anticipated goal is not reached immediately. It is therefore incumbent on the physician to work with each patient to monitor his drug treatment program closely and to maintain communication as to the state of the therapy. Failure to do so may leave the individual practitioner ethically and even legally vulnerable. As Irving Ladimer (1975) summarized:

> Drugs are no longer solely agents for medical service—if they ever were—but clearly stand for more confounding issues related to a patient's right to have them or get them, the physician's right and responsibility to refuse them and, most important, the subject of guidance and control.

The treating physician is certainly in a stronger position if he can inform the patient of all possible effects in advance. While this is often theoretically possible, it may be difficult to implement in actual clinical practice.

Almost all psychotropic agents alter the capacity of clear mentation and change the relationship between the patient and the environment. Specifically, psychiatric agents may have undesirable sedative effects that can adversely influence the level of alertness and related motor functions, such as driving or operating machinery.

The clinician is therefore ethically and legally bound to monitor closely not only a patient's symptoms, but also his interaction with the working environment.

Too Much Drug/Too Little Drug

The question of dosage level is frequently a practical ethical problem. Too much drug may yield an undesired side effect or an unexpected drug interaction, while too little drug may prevent the achievement of the desired therapeutic effect. The prevailing ethic is that the physician is responsible for keeping himself informed about relevant changes in the application and use of drugs. A great many effects of drugs, however, are not immediately apparent and the balance is often difficult to achieve with regard to proper dosage.

The issue of dosage illustrates the dynamic nature of drug therapy. As new knowledge is rapidly being incorporated by the integration of computer-based knowledge systems, it has become exceedingly difficult for the individual practitioner to remain *au courant* and proficient. Specifically, in dealing with the depressed patient, the psychopharmacologist is faced with the ethical judgment of how much and for how long. While guidelines were being established, the norms for blood levels proved far too low in many cases and the suggested levels had to be elevated. Unfortunately, for years many experts were functioning outside what would be regarded as the standard practices of their medical community. This leads to the thorny problem, which has cropped up quite frequently in psychopharmacology, of how to handle knowledge, which clearly anticipates and precedes the prevailing general treatment procedures. If the clinician believes he knows a better way, when is he ethically justified in instituting his own methodology?

Side Effects and Drug Interactions

This is yet another area that often poses subtle ethical problems for the practitioner. It can be very difficult to obtain the delicate balance between therapeutic and negative effects of drugs. The use of psychotropic agents is quite complex and even expert clinicians frequently encounter unanticipated and undesirable reactions. When this happens, according to established medical standards, the physician should have working criteria in terms of a flow chart to provide guidelines for treatment (Martorano, 1978). Since pharmacotherapy is easily quantified, there are discrete choices that must be made on the basis of well-tested criteria, which serve to alert the well-informed doctor of expectations regarding the hazards of a particular medicine.

How Long to Treat

This is a curiously vague area which has recently been attracting interest as the prophylactic properties of certain drugs such as lithium have been more clearly described. It certainly would be considered unethical to continue a patient on a drug which has known prophylactic properties for a lifetime without supervision. How much supervision and what levels of drugs should be maintained in the long term psychiatric patient remains a dilemma still to be solved. The primary ethical problem focuses on the question of whether it is appropriate to keep a patient on a drug which may have serious side effects when there are no positive indications that the disorder (mania depression) will recur. For instance, lithium has recently been reported occasionally to cause spontaneous, severe kidney damage (Gardos, 1979). The same question is even more serious in regard to neuroleptic agents used in the treatment of psychotic disorders, particularly schizophrenia, which may cause tardive dyskinesia after a period of time.

The advent of tranquilizers in the 1950s drastically reduced the number of institutionalized patients from 559,000 in 1955 to fewer than 170,000 today. But, while tranquilizers are allowing many patients to lead productive lives, it is apparent that the antipsychotic agents are creating a serious neurological disorder, tardive dyskinesia (Steinman, 1979). It is usually a severe disease characterized by incapacitating, involuntary neurological movements that are often irreversible. Such incapacitation has raised a number of important legal and ethical questions about the use of major tranquilizers and has forced a crucially needed reassessment about the patterns of tranquilizer use and its overall long-term value.

The principal clinical difficulty associated with the drug is that it does not develop until the patient has been taking it for many months or even for years. By that time permanent damage may have been done. And the incidence of tardive dyskinesia has increased until it now represents a major health problem. This disease has also forced an evaluation of exactly what informed consent means, and has resulted in judicial reevaluation of the patient's right to refuse treatment.

The ethical dilemma is awesome. The treating physician has to make a premature choice between instituting a necessary treatment and weighing against the possibility of causing a future severely disabling disease—presently untreatable—whose advent is impossible to predict. Consider the problem of the psychopharmacologist. He is treating a severely ill psychotic patient. Every time he reduces the drug level, either the patient relapses into a psychotic state or he increases the possibility of a relapse into a psychotic state. If he doesn't lower the blood level and/or discontinue the drug, he increases the chances of the patient eventually developing tardive dyskinesia. Clearly, the only recourse lies in developing more accurate knowledge to ascertain which patients are more susceptible to the disease or hot to detect the possibility of serious side effects earlier.

The clinician, however, still has to make forced clinical choices while awaiting the introduction of newer, more useful material. Again, the only acceptable ethical recourse is to follow the prevailing standard in the community. Yet, the question of who shall determine these standards is still in the process of resolution. Although an increasing amount of control is being usurped by the courts, who act as the legal arms of the federal government, the shift is to governmental implementation of standards by which medicine shall be practiced.

Abusive Potential of Psychotropic Agents

This is a controversial area which is still being studied. The ethical situation has been greatly complicated for doctors by the media's overemphasis on the potential for addictive drug abuse, which has confused patients and caused difficulty in correct drug compliance.

Drug Abuse Potential of Alcohol

The relationship between psychopharmacology and alcohol as an abusive substance has also recently come under scrutiny. For example, if taken daily, the drug antabuse will cause a severely uncomfortable experience if alcohol is also ingested. The ethical issues must be considered when the alocholic is asked to give informed consent prior to the ingestion of the drug. The physician has only experimental guidelines to allow him to inform the alcoholic of the physical risks involved in the consumption of alcohol while the patient may be on antabuse. Yet, the severity of the reaction varies greatly and is unpredictable. A dilemma therefore exists where a useful drug may cause a terrible effect.

Some of the above ethical clinical difficulties may be illustrated in the use of tricyclic antidepressant agents which have long been poorly understood by the general public. There has also been some failure on the part of many physicians to communicate the complexity of its clinical course. The main effect of these agents is often misperceived as similar to a stimulant (Hollister, 1978). Unfortunately, when the patient fails to experience immediate stimulation, and has instead to tolerate the frequently uncomfortable autonomic side effect and to endure a long period before the start of visible improvement in mood, he becomes discouraged and wants to discontinue the drug. Further, there may be inadequate compliance owing to the depressed mood, which is manifested in irritability, inattention, a failure of concentration, and possible uncooperativeness.

Thus, the physician has an extraordinary task in improving communication with a patient who may be slowed down in his verbal responses. Contributing to these difficulties have been actual changes in the understanding of how to use the drug. The initial recommended dose levels were too minimal and ineffective. The dose levels and the means of giving the drug have therefore been substantially raised. Consequently, there is a formidable task in adhering to continually evolving standards of drug use and effect.

In choosing a drug treatment program, the most important issue is balancing immediate therapeutic gains with the possibility of detrimental long-term effects. Physicians also have to face the reverse possibility—immediate negative effects as opposed to long-term therapeutic gains. Few if any drugs exist which do not present the patient with the possibility of serious, adverse side effects or drug interactions. It is the ethical duty of the physician to keep himself well informed to make the most propitious clinical choice possible.

The Role of Government in the Ethical Practice of Drug Therapy

I do not rule Russia: ten thousand clerks do.

Nicholas 1 (1776–1855)

As the importance of drug therapy in psychiatry has increased, the government has assumed an increasingly significant role in establishing ethical standards and guidelines for drug use. The courts and regulatory agencies are being used to assure that these ethical standards are maintained.

In examining the current relationship of the government to ethics in psychopharmacology, there is evidence of enlarged governmental control in all areas which leads to the issue: who must the government regulate in regard to drug therapy?

It would seem that the government has a popular mandate which might be interpreted to regulate the following sectors:

1. *The practice of medicine,* including the administrative, clinical, and research arms.

2. *The systems for delivering health care* (Medicare, Medicaid), and the settings in which health care is delivered (hospitals, outpatients, clinics).

3. *The rights of the people* for whom the health care systems function. In regard to drug therapy, these basic ethical rights include the right to safe, effective, and therapeutic drugs. To maintain this right, the government has instituted reasonable maximal allowable costs (M.A.C.) for the drugs. This has created a conflict between the government and the drug industry over what the reasonable allowable cost is.

4. *The pharmaceutical industry,* in the manufacturing, marketing, and distribution of the drugs, is regulated to assure the public of the maximal ethical performance of an industry vital to the maintenance of public welfare.

5. *The general public* to gather enough appropriate monies, for the maintenance of the vehicles to deliver health care. Certainly, rising health costs have become one of the dominant issues of this era.

This is an extraordinarily complex ethical issue. There has never been an adequate ethical formula which will equate human life with economic reality. We routinely expect the government, however, to determine the right equation to maintain fair allocation between the monies it takes from us and the services it delivers. Recently, this concern for cost-cutting has caused the government to set woefully inadequate standards for the financial reimbursement of the pharmaceutical treatment of mental illness. With the use of such devices as maximal allowable costs per drug, the government has reached out to develop standards in areas where government expertise is lacking. Currently, economic considerations have increasingly dictated moral choices in medicine particularly related to psychiatric treatment. The government's limitation on the length and amount of treatment could imply that the government has priority considerations that may override the health of the individual patient, especially with regard to the right to adequate long-term drug treatment.

Each of the intentions would appear to have a paradoxical counterpart. If drug costs are to be kept reasonable, then there also has to be a limitation on the standards for drug manufacture or else the costs will become prohibitively expensive. This is further complicated by an opposing need to maintain quality, assuring bioavailability and bioequivalence of the necessary drug. And the current trends to limit medications and to allow people the choice creates further ironies. While limiting drugs is a desirable position, it is often mistakenly perceived to imply that mental illness isn't real—causing a decrease in the effective application of the delivery of the drug.

6. *The usage and availability of illegal, abusive, and/or ineffective drugs.* With the legal distribution and use of alcohol, the widespread use of illegal psychostimulants, and the generalized prevalence of marijuana and other drugs, it appears that government regulations frequently oppose the desires of the governed population. In general, however, the courts assume that the government has the greater capacity for ascertaining moral standards. The courts have defended the right of the government to control drug usage by its citizenry.

The Current Trends in Regulation

In order to control these varying sectors more effectively, a number of bureaucratic organizations have been developed to provide several different tiers of regulations. These regulatory agencies fall into two major categories:

1. *Direct Government Organizations.* These include the Department of Health, Education, and Welfare (HEW), the Federal Drug Administration (FDA), and the Bureau of Narcotics and Dangerous Drugs (BNDD). As part of the federal government, these agencies rely on either legislative mandate and/or judicial intercession for establishing a legitimate basis for functioning. In addition to the delays caused by complex bureaucratic procedures, a major ethical stumbling block is that the agencies are dependent upon selecting appropriate medical experts whose knowledge they may draw upon in establishing ethical guidelines. Since expertise is a quality that is particularly difficult to discern, the agencies lean toward selecting professionals who are politically sympathetic. This may lead to a bias in developing a political rather than a knowledge-oriented base for an ethical code.

2. *Indirect Agencies.* There is a growing trend to use government supervision to force the medical profession toward self-regulation. Since the basis for the ethical practice of medicine still lies in the tenet that the physician is expected to practice medicine in accordance with the accepted medical standards of his professional community, the tendency has been to try to make medical therapy uniform by having physicians form organizations to determine correct local procedures.

Two major innovations which have been established recently to enforce standards, are the Continuing Medical Education requirements (C.M.E.) and the Professional Standards Review Organization (P.S.R.O.).

Continuing Medical Education

Licensure, the first step taken by the government to attempt to assure high quality care to the public, measures formal professional qualifications (credentials and test scores) early in the physician's career. Adequacy here is presumed to mean competence for life, unless overwhelming evidence to the contrary emerges.

The government has decided that to maintain quality in the delivery of medical services, practicing physicians ought to receive continuing medical education. Therefore, in a movement that is not yet finalized, physicians and other health professionals are being compelled either by specialty boards and/or local and state governments to meet additional educational requirements. Guidelines of what is acceptable are being developed for these educational requirements. While C.M.E. is not yet under federal control, it seems inevitable that the government will control the regulation of continuing medical education by making it a requirement for continued licensure.

Professional Standards Review Organizations

These organizations form the central core of what may eventually become future avenues of determining the basis of ethical standards in the practice of medicine. This is particularly important for drug therapy because the scope of drug therapy has spread immensely and its clinical operations are well suited to predetermined ethical guidelines.

There is some concern that the P.S.R.O.s are perhaps the last opportunity for medicine to regulate itself before the government takes over the task, while others feel that the crisis in the health care system is actually due to unprecented government intervention in the daily practice of medicine.

P.S.R.O.s originated in the Public Law 92-603, passed in late 1972. They were initially established to provide nationwide review of the quality and necessity of hospital care provided for beneficiaries of Medicare and Medicaid. The mandate and privileges, however, have been extended greatly and seem destined to provide a means of determining what is standard for medical practice on a local level (Dorsey, 1975). Since most peer review is concerned with how a procedure is done rather than with the outcome of treatment, psychopharmacology has certainly displayed exemplary standards when compared to the rest of psychiatry by its setting of increasingly specific indications for drug use as well as stringent criteria for dosage and duration in regard to psychopharmaceuticals.

Peer review can be seen as the determination of ethical standards by the majority. This dependency on operative standards functions to validate what Samuel Butler once said: "Morality is the custom of one's country and the current feeling of one's peers. Cannibalism is moral in a cannibal country" (quoted in Peter, 1977, p. 173).

In cases where substandard performance is observed, there are two principal recourses: education for those who lack knowledge, and the curtailment of privileges—either via professional practice privileges associated with the medical profession or more drastically, legal privileges extended by the state. The state is currently responsible for medical licensing—an archaic situation which greatly limits the effective distribution of medical care.

In using P.S.R.O.s, the government is essentially asking the physician to work within the framework of maximizing utilization of medical dollars while minimizing waste. The determination of what is "wasteful" medical practice is a difficult one. An illustration of such determination is seen in the treatment of patients who are on antipsychotic drug regimes. Because of the possibility of a blood dyscrasia, it is theoretically advisable that the patient routine receive periodic blood counts. The practitioner runs into a dilemma here. Too frequent blood counts will discourage the patient and increase the chance of poor compliance. Yet, infrequent counts may increase the possibility that a blood dyscrasia will go undetected and thus will not fulfill the criteria for established medical practice.

If P.S.R.O.s are used correctly, they can form the basis for the provision of statistical information which yields direct guidelines for determining good clinical practice (how to improve the quality of psychiatric care). P.S.R.O.s could ameliorate the hiatus in psychopharmacology where the outcome is too remote from action in contributing meaningful information that can be used to revise current practices (Dorsey, 1974).

Negative Concerns Regarding the P.S.R.O.s.   There are many critics of P.S.R.O.s, who point to the fact that there may be a "cookbook" type of approach which will substitute for good clinical judgment. These critics fail to acknowledge that the day of the spontaneous innovator is disappearing and is being replaced by a more effective methodology which will allow the majority to receive more rationally based treatment.

The concern over the establishment of P.S.R.O.s by the government is again a microcosm reflecting major conflicts in the battle for who shall establish the ethical standards for psychopharmacology.

There are certain grave problems in this battle. While the government can be of enormous value in supervising and monitoring medical practice, it is extraordinarily difficult for nonmedical personnel to gather enough expertise to make properly developed authoritative judgments about the more complicated psychopharmacological issues. How the government agencies seek to inform themselves and remain up to date about medical matters in an area where even recognized experts have difficulty keeping abreast with expanding knowledge becomes a matter of great importance.

There remain numerous difficulties in the proper choice of who shall serve as authorities in medicine. The politically oriented doctor is most often a physician who is inclined to administrative detail rather than to direct research and clinical skills. Further, the position of physicians in government is often ethically compromised by mixed allegiances. Thus, the proper choice of how to gather the necessary medical knowledge to allow the government to make informed choices in medical matters remains a major unresolved problem.

Legal Issues in Ethical Psychopharmacology

In psychopharmacology the basic problem with the legal aspects of ethical issues has been a jurisdictional one. Over the past two decades, there has been difficulty in ascertaining who is setting the guidelines. In earlier times, the physician had almost the sole responsibility for determining the guidelines for medical care. The government, however, has recently increased its power and control in this area broadly, especially via the federal courts which have tended to give the government increasing jurisdictional power.

There has also been a further severe dilution of the ability of the physician to ascertain ethical guidelines because of the increased desire of patients to participate in determining their treatment.

These two forces have created additional pressures which have limited the physician's authority to set ethical guidelines. This interface has been felt primarily in the malpractice issue. The evolution of major expensive litigation against individual physicians and institutions has resulted in the development of a "defensive" style of medicine where the physician's behavior may be shaped by a desire to protect himself rather than by an undiluted concern to act in the best interest of the patient. As René Descartes observed, "A state is better governed which has but few laws, and those laws strictly observed" (quoted in Peter, 1977, p. 225).

Today, the standards for exacting ethical practice have grown increasingly restrictive, particularly in the field of psychopharmacology. This can be clearly observed in the growing importance of the physi-

cian's package insert (*Biological Therapies in Psychiatry Newsletter,* 1978)—
the tissue-thin paper contained in the drug package—which provides
exacting standards for drug use and restrictions regarding dose levels.
Once the clinician uses the drug in a manner other than that described
on this small and frequently outdated paper, he is on the defensive. Such
an action can be legitimated legally and ethically only if he provides
sufficient medical expertise to justify his actions. Therefore, more and
more physicians are limiting their practice methods to the exact standards prescribed by the guidelines furnished by the federal government.

Another broad area which interacts with the jurisdictional difficulties
in establishing ethical guidelines has been the increased utilization of the
doctrine of informed consent. This doctrine has enjoyed broadened
application as it has been interpreted to increase the responsibility of the
physician in discussing the difficulties inherent in the treatment with the
patient. While the average patient is entitled to the truth, this particular
truth is almost impossible to deliver. In order to inform the average
patient of the difficulties in drug treatment, the physician would have to
be able to translate all the implications of the package insert into a
language that a layperson could understand, which could be a formidable and time-consuming task. Further, the doctrine of informed consent
is to allow the patient to make an informed choice as to his treatment
which the patient frequently may not be intellectually or emotionally
equipped to make. In psychiatry, this doctrine has particular difficulties
in working with psychotic populations. The issue of who *can* be informed if the individual isn't capable of being informed is particularly
vexing. The general tendency has been to acknowledge incompetence as
the criteria for the patient not being able to give informed consent. This
is still a very tricky problem and there are many dangerously violent
patients who are competent but who may not be capable of informed
consent.

All these problems have played against a larger canvas of legal responsibility. What is the doctor's obligation to the individual patient and
to the community in prescribing medication? With the release of large
numbers of patients from state hospital systems, it has become apparent
that the responsibilities to the individual patient and to the community
are often opposing considerations. For example, oversedation might not
be in the best interest of an individual patient, but if the patient has a
history of acting-out or violent behavior, it might be in the best interests
of the community-at-large to keep him sedated.

The psychiatrist has been walking a tightrope that seems to be getting
tighter with regard to the uncooperative patient. While the legal doc-
trines have clearly spelled out that each patient is entitled to the least
restricting form of treatment, there is a narrow road to be followed
regarding who is really able to cooperate. William McKinley put it so

well: "Our differences are politics. Our agreements, principles." What does one do with the uncooperative patient who is creating trouble for an entire family? How does one handle an adolescent child? At what age does the patient resume responsibility for his own treatment? In a narrower sense, what kind of psychotic patient is able to decide treatment courses for himself?

Unfortunately, there is limited medical input into the courts and because of a lack of available medical knowledge and expertise, many judicial decisions are fundamentally weakened. Further, the demands and concerns of the courts can be imperfect and self-serving since they are generally supportive of the governmental systems from which they derive these powers. At each turn in the road, various court decisions have increased government involvement. Consider the FDA. Initially, Congress did not intend the Food and Drug Administration to interfere with medical practice. But, while the use of a marketed drug for an indication not approved by the FDA is not necessarily improper and certainly not illegal, a drug's use in this fashion is termed "unapproved use," and thus opens the doors to ethical sanctions and claims of medical malpractice.

When it is necessary to give a drug in a manner not indicated by community use or FDA guidelines, current ethical mandates indicate that the physician should fully inform the patient and his family, obtain written clearances if possible, and acquire institutional sanctioning of the appropriateness of the procedure.

Legal Basis for the Patient's Rights Movement

In the context of the patient's rights movement, several important legal notions have been developed to ensure the patient's constitutional rights. The patient's rights movement has contributed to a clearer definition of the rights of patients, which include:

The right to be informed.
The right to have an available health delivery system that provides safe, maximally effective treatment.
The right to be free from abusive confinement and treatment.
The right to have the safest drug available.
The right to be assured ethical treatment which assumes dealing with a fully informed, competent, and moral clinician.

Thus, over the past two decades, the courts have slowly and progressively delineated constitutional bases for psychiatric patients to have a right of self-determination in their own treatment (Harvis, 1979).

Few would deny a right to some form of self-determination in treatment, but self-determination in drug therapy is particularly difficult when the mental limitations of the psychiatric patient often prevent development of the judgment necessary to ascertain the amount and direction of treatment. Legally, the severely incapacitated patient has fewer rights of self-determination. The right to determine the degree of incapacitation, however, is shifting away from the treating physician.

This is illustrated by a recent extraordinary decision in which the court not only decided that the treatment rendered was incorrect, but also then proceeded to suggest the appropriate direction of treatment (*Medical World News*, 1979). In this case (*Rennie* v. *Klein*), a U.S. District Court told doctors at a New Jersey mental hospital that they could not force fluphenazine on an unwilling psychotic inmate—at least not until the patient had been given a trial of lithium and an antidepressant.

Judge Stanley S. Brotman said that the mental patient has a constitutional right to control his body except in three circumstances:

When the patient is a danger to others in the institution and can't be kept away from others.

When the patient has been declared incompetent by the courts (not by the treating physician) and the medicine is a treatment, not a containment modality.

When less troublesome means of treatment do not exist.

In this far-reaching case, the judge felt that fluphenazine should never be allowed for use with this patient who possibly showed signs of tardive dyskinesia—a view that the hospital physicians opposed because they felt the patient was faking the symptoms in court. The judge concluded that tardive dyskinesia might well be worse for the patient than his present symptoms.

The Right to Treatment

Writing in *The Legal Aspects of Medical Practice*, Barbara D. Harvis, J. D. (1979) cites three landmark cases over the last decade that have formed a strong constitutional basis for the efforts to humanize the conditions of confinement in state mental institutions and to restore dignity to patients.

Because of these and other relevant cases, patients now have been assured minimum due process at civil commitment hearings, and a constitutional foundation for the right to treatment during confinement has been firmly established. Further, hospitals are required to obtain informed consent before instituting treatment.

The landmark case is *Wyatt* v. *Stickney* (1971) where the court actually ordered the setting of minimum constitutional standards. These include:

1. The right of the mental patient of privacy and dignity (based on the First, Fourth, Ninth, and Fourteenth Amendments).
2. The right to the "least" restrictive conditions necessary to achieve the purposes of commitment (*Shelton* v. *Tucker,* 1960).
3. The right to be free from unnecessary or excessive medication.

In this case, the courts decided that medication could not be used as a punishment. Further, the court ruled that medication could not be used for the convenience of the staff as a substitute for a treatment program, or in excessive amounts which would interfere with the treatment programs (*Wyatt* v. *Hardin,* 1975). Contained in this order was the implication of a growing realization that existing drug treatment programs in institutions were badly run and contained an inordinate and frequent number of instances of overmedication for the purpose of containment. It is well recognized that the minimally staffed state institution is a vehicle for containment rather than for treatment. Unfortunately, by defining the patient's indisputable rights, the court set forth the implication that it is possible to form and implement intensive treatment programs that could lead to improvement in all patients. The court, however, appears unaware of the frustration involved with the failure of existing drugs to live up to their early promise. This is particularly the case with chronic mental disease where drugs are often, somewhat ironically, best used as containment rather than treatment modalities.

The case of *Wyatt* v. *Hardin* (*Medical World News,* 1979) went one step further by setting procedural safeguards for certain treatment modalities such as lobotomy, psychosurgery, or other unusual, hazardous or surgical procedures. A clause in this case affects drug therapy because it sets limits for "aversive conditioning or other systematic attempts to alter behavior by means of a painful or noxious stimuli."

The Right of Equal Protection

This right is defined by the Equal Protection clause of the Fourteenth Amendment, which requires each state to treat similarly situated persons equally. This has focused primarily on the competence of the mentally ill patient to affect his own treatment. In the case of *Winters* v. *Miller* (1971), a civil rights action was brought by an involuntarily committed Christian Scientist who protested against "forced" medication. The court declared that in the absence of a determination of incompetence, a mentally ill person remains free to refuse treatment. Thus, the current interpretation of the Equal Protection clause is that compelled psychiatric treatment is allowed only where the patient is clearly mentally incompetent.

The incarcerated patient, who is treated by the forcible administration of drugs, would be a victim of the violation of the Eighth Amendment which prohibits cruel and unusual punishment as decreed by several court decisions. This presents difficulty in determining an ethical stance for physicians treating patients who are uncontrollably violent or dangerous. The doctor and other administrative personnel are often faced with a dilemma in balancing drug treatment. They are clearly violating the patient's rights with the use of excessively sedative drug treatment. Yet modern psychopharmacology is presently capable of controlling these parameters only within reasonable limits.

Treatment and Patient's Rights

A crucial point is currently being reached in dealing with patient care. The psychopharmacological revolution improved therapeutic possibilities so that the old system of care in which mental hospitals functioned almost as prisons no longer exists. The dramatic impact of neuroleptic therapy altered the focus and left an overlooked, not yet well, ex-hospital patient at a precarious plateau because no system was provided to teach him the social skills needed for reentry into society. Thus the mental health system has to change its shape to accommodate the changing needs of the patient.

This problem has been intensified because there has been a *dilution of the commitment procedures*. Further, the present commitment procedure is a legal rather than a medical matter. Thus, the ethical stance of the physician has been shifted by legal force until the present position is such that he has to seek active cooperation with a willing patient. If the patient's behavior exceeds certain ill-defined guidelines in terms of actual (not potential) violence, then the physician must seek a cumbersome course through the courts to confine the patient. While this seems to protect the rights of the individual patient more, it certainly seems to have led to an increased amount of violence by uncontrolled mental patients, who have self-regulated their drug regimes to the point of ineffectiveness so that their antisocial impulses are out of control. It is an urgent and compelling matter for the courts to define the terms of the future power of physicians in relation to confining mental patients.

Freedom of Thought

Freedom of thought is a mental quality which the state cannot control according to the mandate of the First Amendment of the Constitution. The courts have generally found in favor of a fundamental right.

In *Scott* v. *Plante* (1976), the court stated that the "involuntary administration of drugs could interfere with the First Amendment rights of the patient." The court also held that the patient has protection under the First Amendment to maintain the right to generate ideas. Any interference with such generation is a violation of the First Amendment.

Mind Control

In reality, freedom of thought is a right relegated to the individual by the state and political system. A television documentary on *Mind Control* described the illegal and immoral attempts of the CIA to perform mind control experimentation without the informed consent of the subject. This disastrous, ill-conceived experiment resulted in at least two known deaths. In this case, the ethical culprit was clearly the government. It behooves our beleaguered judiciary to protect the individual against government encroachment. The same ethical and legal standards that bind the individual practitioners should apply to governmental agencies. This is becoming an increasingly important issue. As the noted authority, Frank Ayd, writes in the *International Drug Therapy Newsletter*, "biochemical and pharmacological developments in the past twenty-five years have made it possible for man to discover, synthesize and study the direct and indirect effects of drugs on the brain and hence on all human behavior" (Ayd, 1969).

In a short time, drugs will be able to achieve increased mind control. It is imperative that an ethic be developed prior to the introduction of such drugs in order to limit their social use as weapons between nations and to allow them instead to improve the status of mankind. On the immediate horizon, Dr. Ayd (1969) sees new forms of drugs: drugs to combat boredom; drugs to raise intelligence; drugs to transport man to mystical heights; drugs to curb human reproduction; new chemical aphrodisiacs; drugs to induce hibernation and to ease hunger pains; drugs to incapacitate a population temporarily; and beyond these immediate developments lie drugs of far greater capacity—drugs with the potential to control entire civilizations. More than ever, some universal ethic is needed to control the drugs that could control people. For example, the law has yet to define the role of drugs for aggression clearly. Sidney Cohen (1979) has described conditions that lead to drug-induced violence but has pointed out that no legal standards exist for sorting out the implications of giving drugs in a violence-prone setting. Should the physician orient himself to diminishing violence at all times, and to what extent is that done at the expense of the rights of the individual patient?

Certainly, the recent legal trends have been to allow individual freedom. As drugs increase in their predictable capacities, however, it may well be that we will have drugs that can actually curb violence. In that case, the role of the treating facility will have to be both ethically and legally revised.

Finally, the psychotropic drug treatment also has created other significant social changes in family and community structure. It is becoming increasingly clear that it is the responsibility of the health care delivery system to provide an adequate support system to accompany the reentry of the patient into the community and to treat the needs of the community as they are altered by the changing individual patient.

In relation to drug therapy, a major issue that has been heightened by the patients' rights movement is compliance—the degree of reliability that the patient will actually take, or be given, a drug. In drug therapy, the primary failure has been in maintaining compliance. The mental patient is often uncooperative in taking a drug on his own. This is even more so when his awareness is heightened so that the physician can no longer take legal action to control him by such procedures as possible commitment for failure to take the drug.

Thus, the shape of the therapeutic relationship has changed. The new ethical mandate is one for improved communication between the patient and the doctor. It is necessary for the medical profession to acquire new skills in discussing treatment with the patient and in learning to work more effectively with support systems, such as family and friends, to maximize drug compliance and maintain the necessary therapeutic gains of the psychopharmacological revolution.

Drug Ethics and the Pharmaceutical Industry

The pharmaceutical industry is perhaps unique in American business because of the degree of responsibility and ethical self-enforcement that is required by legislative mandate and government regulations. Despite an excellent record of self-monitoring, governmental regulation by the Department of Health, Education, and Welfare, and the Federal Drug Administration has hindered the introduction of new drugs into this country by insisting on an extraordinarily expensive, and cumbersome, three-tiered preliminary testing program involving extensive animal studies and lengthy clinical trials.

The present governmentally determined criteria for the introduction of new drugs is far more rigorous than in other countries of equal medical capability, and has severely limited freedom and accessibility of drug choice in this country.

Research and Development

A vital part of the American pharmaceutical industry is its commitment to research and development capacities. Overly stringent Food and

Drug Administration regulations, however, are delaying the approval of new drugs and discouraging other aspects of drug research in both private industry and other medical research. A spokesman for the American Medical Council on Scientific Affairs, Dr. Raymond Gifford (1979), has declared that "the benefits derived from the FDA's current safeguards and efficacy procedures and conservatism exceed the detriments that are caused by the lack of availability of new drugs into the U.S.," while the FDA feels that there is a small but justifiable drug "lag" in this country because the American attitudes toward drug safety confer indisputable benefits that bear certain costs in terms of slower drug approvals. The approval of a drug requires twenty-five times as much paperwork in the United States as compared to Great Britain, and twice the time is involved to process a new drug application.

A vital number of needed drugs with proven safety and effectiveness, like the new tetracyclic antidepressant agents, have therefore had a delayed introduction into the United States. Because of the growing complexity of the interactions between government and industry, there has been a proliferation of interfaces where more easily usable ethical standards are needed.

An excellent illustration is the issue of bioequivalence. Because of the rising costs of health care, bioequivalence is becoming a prominent area of concern. There have been many problems because the nature of mental disease often requires long-term drug use, which makes the cost of drugs prohibitively expensive for the average patient. Thus, the government is pressing for the use of the more reasonably priced generic drugs in an effort to reduce medical costs. But this is not a simple issue since the major drug houses contend that it is more expensive for them to maintain exacting manufacturing standards that will assure bioequivalency (where the same amount of drug will yield the same amount of chemically active therapeutic substance).

The intricacy of this dilemma is well illustrated by amitriptyline (Elavil)—the most widely used antidepressant agent of the tricyclic family. Although eleven firms manufacture the drug, only five firms had submitted *in vivo* and *in vitro* bioequivalency data for FDA approval as of January 1979. Furthermore, a growing number of reports from practicing physicians had suggested that various marketed brands of amitriptyline may not have comparable therapeutic effects (Hoffman, 1979). The FDA therefore had to rule against the establishment of a maximum allowable cost for amitriptyline. This brief episode illustrates the extraordinary complexity that is becoming more prevalent as the government and industry strive to maintain a reasonable system of checks and balances to preserve an ethically based system of drug delivery.

The ethical problem, however, is a familiar one—the ambiguous balance between cost and quality control. Undoubtedly, the best possible quality of manufacturing in the production of a drug should be maintained. But in reality, it is necessary to offset the best production versus the affordable cost. The use of a well-produced drug is limited if prohibitive costs prevent its maximum utilization.

In pharmaceutical manufacturing, the trend has been toward overall increased control of the industry by government regulations which constantly redefine the standards for manufacturing and research. Unfortunately, these standards have become so stringent that they often pose a formidable ethical dilemma since they increase the internal production costs of manufacturing a drug and decrease the amounts of time and money available for research and development of newer drugs. Hence, a need for clearer communication channels between industry and government has become vital if more functional ethical standards are to be developed to preserve the delicate balance between need and availability.

Educational Responsibilities of the Pharmaceutical Industry

Drug companies have long maintained certain well-defined educational responsibilities regarding the use of their drugs. In the past two decades, increasing legal mandates and ethical concerns have shifted the tone of the educational programs from promotion-oriented vehicles into strictly regulated explanatory advertising that emphasizes the correct use of the drug and seeks to curb abuse of drugs.

Necessary drugs are often used before all their effects are fully understood. Unfortunately, certain drugs like amphetamines with a potential for abuse were frequently overused because of their short-term capabilities. It has therefore become increasingly important for industry, using its vast resources, to unite with the government and the medical profession to promote maximum early availability of information regarding psychotropic agents.

Research—The New Ethic

Ethical criteria for drug research have undergone considerable revision in the past decade. This is largely due to intensified scrutiny by government, medical, regulatory agencies, and to increased responsibility of the patients as legislated by the courts. Concern for ethical and legal considerations has limited the range of freedom that drug research formerly enjoyed. Gone are the days of "research overkill." As a result, new ethical criteria are evolving. These carry a clear mandate that the researcher is responsible for considering all possible effects of drug treatment, including the possibility of long-term harmful complications. Several years ago, the problems associated with thalidamide and its adverse teratogenic effects allowed the federal government to institute more guarded controls over research and the introduction of new drugs. These controls overcorrected the situation and caused a significant decrease in the number of new and necessary drugs that have been introduced in this country.

Drug development is a time-consuming, expensive, and complex process. Standards for drug safety and effectiveness are established by the FDA, and these must be met before a drug can become available for general use. Most new drugs are synthesized in pharmaceutical company laboratories. Each year, about 170,000 chemical substances are examined for potential medical use, but only about ten to twenty of these are developed to the point where they become prescription drugs. The total cost for drug research and development in the United States is more than $1.3 billion a year.

Despite the extravagant costs of new drug development, there is a clear demand in the new ethic for increased drug safety. In the United States, intensive animal studies must be completed before a drug can even be considered for experimental introduction with human subjects.

Today, the researcher has to explain all of the possibilities of drug actions to involved subjects. This directive comes from a landmark case which decreed that drug research can be carried on only in regard to specific disease state investigations.

Gone are the umbrella mandates to develop new drugs quickly. Instead, each drug can be investigated only for a specifically defined purpose and for a specific disease. The new ethic limits the double-blind study. The necessity of gaining completely informed consent makes it unlikely that a patient would willingly suffer the possibility of remaining untreated in order to accept a test research protocol. Concerning the traditional subjects for psychiatric research, there is the question of whether people of limited mental capacity can truly develop "informed consent." Drug research has traditionally relied on constructive use of institutional subjects. There is, however, increasing concern that the rights of these beleaguered populations should not be violated in drug testing.

The National Drug Research Act of 1974 established a National Commission for the Protection of Human Subjects of Biomedical and Behavioral Research which is responsible for the application of ethical principles to subjected populations. Prior to this commission, the Department of Health, Education, and Welfare had been responsible for ethical guidelines in the application of research with mentally disabled populations. Specifically, the guidelines deemed that the research can be done—only if it is related to the existing disease in regard to etiology, pathogenesis, pretention, diagnosis, or treatment. In addition, the research can be affected with institutionalized patients only if it cannot be obtained with subjects who are not institutionalized or mentally disabled (Curran, 1974).

Research must now be directly related to the needs of the subjects. A population can no longer be randomly chosen for new drug research simply on the basis of ready availability. This position is further strengthened by the judicially imposed limitations establishing the patient's right to treatment and a right to be free from unnecessary or excessive medication. Clearly, the intended direction is that research subjects are individuals with protected rights.

The costs of introducing a single drug through the three necessary stages for FDA approval are rising to the point that it is unprofitable to attempt to introduce a new drug unless approval is virtually certain.

The belated introduction of lithium into this country had a number of fascinating ethical implications. In the early 1950s, lithium was originally introduced as a chloride compound with the unfortunate result that several deaths were precipitated primarily in cardiac patients. The carbonate form, however, was used with a long history of safety for almost two decades in Europe before lithium was allowed reentry into the United States.

In the meantime, its efficacy in manic disease was well documented and was accepted by many leading psychopharmacologists. A black market was created in this country. Unless the patient was being treated by a physician who had an investigational license to use this drug, he was unable to obtain it. Patients who needed the drug were often advised to go to Europe to secure this vital medication.

The fascinating aspect of these cases was the ethical dilemma of the individual physician who either had to treat the patient inadequately or had to use illegal means to provide the best available treatment. In making such a moral choice, should the physician consider prevailing statutes or the needs of the patient? The delay was increased because no single drug company could do all the required research, which had already been done in excellent fashion in Europe, to qualify the lithium for introduction to the United States, and yet make a viable profit.

Research design now faces new highly specific problems and ethical considerations. By their nature, psychotropic agents are frequently long-term drugs. One of the more ambiguous questions the clinician has therefore to face is how to determine when a drug has been given long enough. Another difficult question is how to design specific research protocol that is ethically sensitive so that the patient is not exposed to unwarranted danger simply to demonstrate long-term safety. On the other hand, long-term safety through research is not established. Does the drug have long-range effects that are yet to be determined? Even relatively safe intermediate-acting drugs can sometimes run into immense complications over an extensive period of time.

Obviously, some type of accommodation has to be developed to satisfy the demands of research in terms of future population while not violating the rights of research populations. At the present time, this type of ethical surveillance is becoming well established in the form of judiciary review, peer and governmental supervision, as well as reform and citizen watchdog groups.

Summary of Current Problems in Ethics and Psychopharmacology

It is, of course, impossible to do more than briefly review and survey some models of the prevailing problems in this area. They include:

How to maintain an increasingly effective, operationally based ethic while incorporating some realistic considerations that provide a better overview for overall direction.

How to balance the treatment of the individual patient while considering the implications of such treatment for the social structure.

Recent reviews have revealed the stagnation of the community-based psychiatric programs. There is a major need to reevaluate what is being done for the changed condition of the patient after he has obtained the maximum benefits of drug therapy. The considerations include:

How to weigh the various factors in treatment to provide a more effective framework which weighs the therapeutic promise and expectation against the possibility of serious medical complications due to drug interactions or side effects.

How to provide a health delivery system that uses psychotropic drugs adequately, but that is not so expensive as to exclude patients from treatment.

How to provide legal safeguards against inappropriate treatment while maintaining an interface that encourages full treatment of the patient.

How to maintain a constant means of reeducation that ensures against inappropriate drug use, and promote integration of newer drugs into active medical practice as soon as possible.

How to design research protocols that provide extensive necessary information while not violating the rights and needs of research subjects.

How to simplify communications between existing concerned sectors to minimize factionalism and to improve communications and decision making.

How to diminish unnecessary bureaucratic red tape that delays new drug introduction and limits the usefulness of proven drugs.

This is related to the major problem of how to reorient the system to keep medical knowledge flowing and prevent administrative domination from hindering the delivery of necessary proven psychopharmacological programs. This is especially true with the need for the institution of systems of early detection and prophylactic treatment of mental disease.

How to create a new freedom for research in both the pharmaceutical companies that do the majority of research with psychotropic drugs and the medical community.

This new wave of research freedom should be accompanied by increased funding on a federal level that allows more basic scientific experimentation.

How to decrease the costs of introduction of new drugs in terms of both time and money while facilitating the availability of proven new drugs in a manner that is framed by clear safeguards.

Further exploration of the rights of patients in drug therapy that may serve in some way to obfuscate and sedate their minds.

The establishment of a balance between mental clarity and central nervous systems sedation is vitally needed in order to promote the general level of mental health. There is, however, only too often a lack of definitive guidelines in establishing exactly what effects such sedation has on an individual in such delicate areas as job, social, and sexual performances. There is a definite need for clearer guidelines.

How to make clear criteria available for ascertaining when a given drug is effective.

How long is it morally right to continue giving a drug for the sake of containment and for purposes other than direct therapy of the considered individual.

Finally, consideration as to how to incorporate the members of new psychiatry, the paraprofessionals, in a meaningful way that helps implement the useful delivery of pharmacologically oriented health services.

The Future

With the revolution in medical technology, the future of psychopharmacology is truly spectacular. The recent computer-based expansion of knowledge will make a number of new drugs available that can do astonishing things beyond the wildest speculations of fifty years ago.

Drugs are being developed that will control aggression, improve concentration and memory, combat aging, and even improve basic intelligence levels. Limitless possibilities seem to exist with chemicals that can be added to the drinking water to decrease aggression and hostility. Chemicals may be called upon to create a controlled hallucinatory environment; they may reach into the depths of the mind, neutralize, and even cure schizophrenia and other mental disease.

The future evolution of ethics in psychopharmacology is closely related to the development of newer, more effective drugs. With the continued acceleration of knowledge, mankind will undoubtedly intensify its elusive search for nirvana through drugs. The quest for mind control will be considered in the arena of psychopharmacology and the field will gain importance as a means of social control. Already, psychopharmacology has promulgated a massive social revolution by releasing thousands of patients from state hospitals into the streets of the community. As the growth of drugs continues, the social implications of psychopharmacology will make the development of clear ethical guidelines an important societal need.

The Trend toward Greater Specificity and Governmental Control

As the effectiveness and power of drugs increase, there will undoubtedly be controversy over who shall ultimately control the introduction and use of these drugs. Following current trends, it now seems inevitable that the federal government will rely on organizations and committees to regulate drugs more specifically. This trend will be aided by an integration of computer use, which seems well suited for the often linear nature of psychopharmacological material.

The growing number of organizations will lead to a bureaucratic proliferation of regulations and a centralization of control with a rise in the legal interventions based on judicial determinations by the government. Certainly the tightrope will be a narrow one of existence between the pressure of increased regulatory complexity and an increased clarity of treatment focus.

The Centralization of Standards

Within this framework, it is likely that there will be a trend toward the development of central standards, which will be determined by government-appointed committees and will set a basis for the ethical determinations of medical practice. Thus, the quality of psychopharmacology will be very much dependent upon the wisdom of those who are chosen to devise and maintain these centralized standards. These crucial positions will have to be a dynamic balance between research, clinical, and administrative personnel. A domination of any overprevailing bias will be sharply reflected in a decrease in the quality of health services. There will be a shift from the ethic of the individual burden into a diffused work ethic where the supervisory and monitoring organizations like the emerging P.S.R.O.s and the C.M.E. accreditation boards will provide the prevailing standards for ethical behavior.

Health as a Right: The Trend away from the Primary Physician

Medicine is moving away from the control of the individual medical doctor. In 1900, 67 percent of health treatment was directly applied by physicians. Today, the statistic is less than 10 percent (Herrington, 1979).

In the immediate future, the number of medical paraprofessionals will double in the next ten years as health care increasingly becomes a government-provided right and not a privilege. A great number of these paraprofessionals will be skilled computer technicians who use computer methodologies such as those that are already functioning in a limited capacity to take histories, make diagnoses, and suggest courses of treatment. While the ultimate control and decisions will still be made medically, more of the initial determinations will be provided by this computer-based science which is ideally suited to ready quantification from its target symptoms to well-delineated therapeutic endpoints that serve as vectors for psychopharmacologic treatment.

The Retention of the Operationally Based Ethic

It seems likely that this linear nature of psychopharmacology, combined with continuing therapeutic efficacy, will provide for the retention of an operationally based ethic which will prevail even more in its influence on the other forms of treatment of mental illness. This operational ethic will be further enforced by the use of centrally based, medically administered, government-appointed committees like the current Task Force on Psychopharmacologic Criteria Development (Dorsey, 1979) to establish well-delineated ethics based on a further refinement of symptom formation and drug treatment techniques which will elevate future psychopharmacology to an even greater pivotal position of preeminence in regard to both professional and governmental importance.

REFERENCES

AYD, F. J. Manipulating and controlling human behavior by drugs. *International Drug Therapy Newsletter,* January 1969, **5** (5).

Biological Therapies in Psychiatry Newsletter. What does FDA approval mean? September 1978, **1** (9).

CALDWELL, A. E. The history of psychopharmacology. In *Principles of psychopharmacology.* New York and London: Academic Press, 1970.

CLOUSER, K. D. Medical ethics—Some uses, abuses and limitations. *New England Journal of Medicine,* 1975, **283,** 382–387.

COHEN, S. Aggression: The role of drugs. *Drug Abuse and Alcoholism Newsletter,* February 1979, **8** (2).

CURRAN, W. J. Ethical issues in short term and long term psychiatric research. In *Medical, moral and legal issues in mental health care.* Baltimore: Williams & Wilkins, 1974.

DORSEY, R. PSRO's: Salvation or suicide for psychiatry? *Psychiatric Opinion,* 1974, **11,** 6–12.

DORSEY, R. Peer review of psychotropic drug use: Panacea or Pandora's box? In *Rational psychopharmacotherapy and the right to treatment.* Baltimore: Ayd Medical Communications Press, 1975.

DORSEY, R., AYD, F. J., and COLE, J. Psychopharmacological screening criteria development project. *American Medical Association News,* March 9, 1978, **241** (10), 1021–1029.

GARDOS, G. *Clinical Psychiatry News,* July 1979, **4.**

GIFFORD, R. Article—AMA says "drug lag" hampers care in U.S. *American Medical Association News,* July 6, 1979, **2.**

HARVIS, B. D. A review of the rights of psychiatric patients. *Legal Aspects of Medical Practice,* January 1979, **17** (1).

HERRINGTON, B. S. Computer technicians said to be supplanting psychiatry. *Psychiatric News,* July 6, 1979.

HOFFMAN, J., director, Professional Communications, Merck Sharp and Dohme. Personal communication, July 1979.

HOLLISTER, L. Treatment of depression with drugs. *Annals of Internal Medicine,* 1978, **89,** 78–84.

LADIMER, I. Rational psycho-pharmacotherapy and judicial interpretations of the right to treatment: An outline. In *Rational psychopharmacotherapy and the right to treatment.* Baltimore: Ayd Medical Communications, 1975.

MARTORANO, J. T. The use of tranquilizers in surgical patients; Part I: The analytic agents—An overview. *Journal of Surgical Practice,* February 1978, **7** (1), 43–48.

Medical World News. Overriding a patient's drug veto. February 19, 1979, 104.

MOORE, R. A. Ethics in the practice of psychiatry: Origins, functions, models and enforcement. *American Journal of Psychiatry,* February 1978, **135,** 2.

PETER, L. J. *Peter's quotations.* New York: Bantam, 1977.

Scott v. Plante. 532 F. 2d 939 3rd Circuit, 1976.

SHADER, R. *Progress in Psychiatric drug treatment,* vol. 2, chap. 45. New York: Brunner/Mazel, 1976.

Shelton v. Tucker. 364 U.S., 1960, 479, 4888.

STEINMANN, M. The catch 22 of antipsychotic drugs. *New York Times Magazine,* March 18, 1979.

Winters v. Miller. 446 F. 2d 65 2nd Circuit, 1971.

Wyatt v. Hardin. Civ. Act. No. 3195-N. M.D. Alabama, 1975.

Wyatt v. Stickney. 325 F. Supp. M.D. Alabama, 1971, 781, 785.

Ethical Problems in the Use of Videotape

Milton M. Berger

What is the reason for the creation, perpetuation, and demand for adherence to ethics by all those whose vocation involves a working relationship which calls for quality, dependability, reliability, trust, and humane sensitivity to the personhood and human rights of others? When these exist in the relationship between patients and psychotherapists, there is little or no likelihood of exploitation or misuse of the patient. A patient who is in treatment with a well-trained mental health professional can fairly reliably be assured that he will be protected and treated justly and ethically.

The history of man's evolution is unfortunately replete with evidence of man's inhumanity to man. And examples of man's inhumanity to man exist in our field as well as all others because our field is peopled with men and women who are mortal and human—not immortal or superhuman—who are frail and susceptible to marketplace urges of the flesh and pocketbook—not strong and invulnerable to the temptations foisted on us daily through the media and other environmental bombardments. The need for the creation and perpetuation through the years of "Hippocrates Oath" and its equivalent for other professions lies in the potential for unethical conduct by medical and other therapists.

An important but almost always overlooked area of concern to anyone who collects videotapes of patients in a private practice setting is the issue of "What happens to my tapes of patients if I die?" Because of my age, 62, and because I recently rewrote my will, I realized how important it was to arrange for the disposition of confidential office tapes in a will or in a codicil attached to the will. Despite our concern for posterity or residual narcissism or simply inability to discard things which relate to ourselves, it is vital that we consider what happens to the audiovisual materials which patients allowed us to have in good faith as confidential, and to provide for their disposal upon our death. Who, besides ourselves, is going to take the time to see what we conjecture to be so valuable that it should be preserved? Who would preserve it and in what form? And would respect for the patient's confidentiality be properly and professionally exercised?

My considered opinion is that we should state clearly that "Upon the event of my death I hereby direct my executors to destroy the contents of any audio or videotapes which are in my home or in my office and are my possession which contain the voice or picture of any patient currently seen in practice or who has been seen by me in the past." The destruction of the contents of these tapes can be accomplished by subjecting them to a strong electromagnetic field, thus preserving the tape stock itself for future use (you should seek consultation on this), or the entire tapes themselves may be incinerated.

You may wish to direct that any tapes which remain in your office after your death which have already been edited and for which patients have given written permission for use for medical educational purposes can be donated to a medical or psychiatric center with the stipulation that they would be appropriately treated with regard for privacy and confidentiality and used only for professional purposes with the rights of the patients respected in perpetuity.

Ethics is the study and evaluation of human conduct in the light of moral principles. It is based on theories which have developed over time as to man's conscience and responsibility for his actions. Intuitionists like Rousseau believed that conscience is innate and instigates moral action. Empiricists like Comte, Locke, and John Stuart Mill explained it as a by-product of experience. Idealists such as Plato and Kant found its basis in metaphysics. Hegel and Marx taught that the state is the arbiter of morals. Dewey and Felix Adler taught that the individual is in control of his morals.

At my present age of 62, I believe from my observation and knowledge of myself and others in the world we live in that the authorities of states and religions have made pronunciamentos on conscience, responsibility, morality, and ethics in the name of those institutions. And we as individual men and women were exposed over and over again during childhood to presentations repeating what sometimes sounded like platitudes coming from authorities communicating from actual and figurative podiums and pulpits. And, because these authorities, in the form of parents, teachers, clergymen, politicians, police, and others, could and did reinforce their messages, each of us has to some degree developed what is referred to in more orthodox psychoanalytic circles as a superego which houses our sense of conscience and responsibility. That is one view.

I believe we have incorporated a great deal related to conscience and responsibility but that for most of us there is a public life and a private life in which these are lived and expressed differently. In public most espouse the values most repeated as worthwhile by respected others in the past and present. But in private most individuals decide for themselves which values and customs they will live up to. And so we can only hope that the process of maturation allows people to comprehend the magnitude of paradox which offers such concepts as "being my brothers keeper" and yet believing that "God helps those who help themselves." Is the concept of "who is my brother?" narrowly limited to some of the world's population, e.g., my family, my professional colleagues, my co-religionists, members of my racial and my national group? Or is it a broad concept in which all people everywhere are my brothers and even all creatures, large and small, are also related to me and I am responsible for all and everyone.

Each sensitive person who is aware of how easily life is snuffed out at times and how very sensitively vulnerable each of us really is and how small and insignificant we are in a world which is so large and populated by many living things and creatures and plants and fish and birds, sooner or later then comes to a level of considering the impact of his or her conduct on others and controlling what properly is to be controlled in the relationship between man and man.

In the final analysis, harm will not be done to patients by psychotherapists because there are laws or codes or punishments for violators of laws or codes, but rather because psychotherapists are mature, concerned, sensitive individuals who respect the power of the relationship between therapists and patients. Knowledge of that power and of the capacity to control the self in using the many powers and tools available to psychotherapists is the major sine qua non the patient has to rely on.

The subject of ethical issues in film and video research recordings was addressed in 1978 by Lavender, Davis, and Graber, whose specific interest was the ethics of research in kinesics. They pointed to the growth of the biomedical research ethics "movement" which has taken clearer shape since its impetus from the Nuremberg trials of unethical practices by Nazi doctors. They emphasize that

> principles and procedures which have become accepted behavioral research practices include: (1) that subject participation is to be completely voluntary; (2) that subjects may withdraw at any time without prejudice; (3) that subjects must be informed in language they can understand, not only of the procedures and purposes but also of the risks and benefits of the research; (4) that there should be a designated individual or committee independent of the project to whom subjects can make complaints. The committees are to insure that the confidentiality and privacy of subjects are protected and that the potential or known risks to the subject are clearly outweighed by the general benefits of the research. In addition, attention is given to procedures for diminishing or alleviating any stress or risks incurred by the subjects. [p. 11]

These authors also commented on the special problems in protecting research subjects who are filmed in naturalistic encounters. Certainly the psychotherapeutic interview which is videotaped for treatment, training, and/or research is a naturalistic encounter in which the patient is seen with the least amount of social facade or cover-up. They expressed concern that "films and videotapes: (a) usually show the face; (b) may be easily copied, distributed and shown; (c) make possible the analysis of behaviors that is usually 'candid' and sometimes out of the normal awareness of the subjects in the naturally occurring situation; and (d) have a special impact and interest of their own" (p. 13).

From the principles and procedures ennumerated above, it should be clear to all involved in the use of video in psychotherapy or for training or research that ethical practice implies that no one should be videotaped without his or her knowledge. While it is true that knowledge that one is being videotaped does more or less alter how one is and what one expresses consciously, it is unethical, though rationalized as more pure and scientific, to videotape a patient through secret cameras and then to ask his or her permission to use the recorded data for psychotherapy, research, or for training purposes.

Rosenbaum (1978) wrote of Harry Stack Sullivan's stated concern with "the duplicities of the culture and the schizophrenic's observation of the artificiality of the hospital structure," which seems to be contradictory to his questionably unethical use of "a microphone on his desk, concealed by an ornamental device, so that his conversations with the patient could be recorded." The material was soundtracked down to another floor where recordings were made by Sullivan's secretary. Rosenbaum makes a point in this example with a pioneering psychotherapist of "the contradiction between what is professed and what is practiced." A major point in regard to the ethical use of videotape in psychotherapy is that the patient is never to be videotaped with concealed equipment without his or her knowledge.

As a young man in college, I was intrigued by the history of medicine and of the relationship between physicians and their patients. I was an habitué of the magnificent rare-book room of the general library at the University of Michigan where I studied the writings of Hippocrates, Celsus, Galen, and others. At age 18, I wrote a ninety-page treatise on "The Scientific Accuracy of Hippocrates Aphorisms." Throughout these early medical writings I found intermittent references to the ethics of the physician. And so, having been long-steeped in this subject, it was with no idle interest that I read in the *New York Times* on July 23, 1980 that the American Medical Association had just adopted a new ethics code for physicians. Examining portions of that code from the viewpoint of the theme of this chapter, "Ethical Problems in the Use of Videotape" may prove to be a worthwhile point of departure not only for me as a physician who is a psychotherapist healer, but for all healers who are psychotherapists.

The preamble for this 1980 ethics code states:

The medical profession has long subscribed to a body of ethical statements developed primarily for the benefit of the patient. As a member of this profession, a physician must recognize responsibility not only to patients, but also to society, to other health professionals, and to self. The following Principles adopted by the American Medical Association are not laws, but standards of conduct which define the essentials of honorable behavior for the physician. [AMA, 1980]

The code continues to enumerate seven principles. Let's look at some of these principles as stated and consider them in the light of the ethics of video in psychotherapy. Principle I states:

A physician [let me substitute the word psychotherapist for physician] shall be dedicated to providing competent medical service [let us substitute the word psychotherapeutic for medical] with compassion and respect for human dignity.

Unfortunately video has been used in psychotherapy at times without compassion or respect for human dignity. To be compassionate for and with another person, hereinafter called the patient or client engaged in psychotherapy with a psychotherapist, means that the psychotherapist knows the experiential meaning of compassion and possesses the capacity to be compassionate with this specific other person, patient, or client, with whom it is proposed that the electronic tool called video be used. Video is for the purpose of recording for instant and/or later feedback to the patient and/or others what the "eye" of the camera sees, which is usually more in some factual ways than what psychotherapists see during an actual psychotherapy session. But we should also note the fact that psychotherapists can see and sense some flesh and blood elements that video itself cannot perceive.

If, for counter-transference or other reasons in the relationship, the psychotherapist finds it difficult and perhaps even impossible to be compassionate with a particular patient with whom he is planning to use video, then he will unquestionably be violating the very first enunciated principle of ethics of the AMA, namely, to be compassionate. His counter-transference or annoyance or frustration with the patient may lead him to experience and see the patient as an object, as an "it" rather than as a "thou" in the sense of Martin Buber's "I-Thou" relatedness. To the degree he sees the patient-person as an "object," he is unable to have the kind of soft, warm, kindly, compassionate feeling for the pained and suffering patient which would enable him to identify with the patient. The need to identify pertains to identifying with the patient during the videotaping experience of having aspects of self being recorded without being aware of those very aspects of self for which permission has been given to record, as they are being recorded. A compassionate feeling for the patient, which is at the same time being sympathetic, is one which allows the psychotherapist to feel a kindly resonance toward and with the patient. This resonance cannot be present if the therapist is experiencing the patient more as object than as person. That quality of empathy which goes along with and is an aspect of a successful therapist-patient relationship will therefore be more or less missing or diminished with such a patient-person, and the outcome of the use of the electronic adjunct called video with that patient will be less likely to be salutory, i.e., for the benefit of the patient and will more likely lead to a negative result. In one clinical center the psychiatric residents tend to recommend videotape playbacks for patients they cannot seem to reach through their usual psychotherapeutic skills and it covers a layer of therapeutic pessimism with such patients. Such an attitude is not conducive to success.

Principle I also mentions respect for human dignity. When video is used in psychotherapy is must be clearly known to all concerned that the camera's eye can be merciless and does not by itself know the meaning of respect for the sensitivity and vulnerability of the patient, which, it is hoped, the skilled therapist does know or can quickly sense or intuit about a particular patient. So then, if the light conditions under which the videotaping is being done are such that shadows appear under the eyes and elsewhere on or around the patient's face which make the patient appear older or weary or less attractive than he or she is in reality, the patient will find it hard to believe the therapist is respectful of his or her human dignity. The patient may feel and think "It's awful enough to be here in therapy exposing myself to this other person who I believe probably can see right through me and knows what a failure I am in living up to others' standards of decency, goodness, and perfection, but oh, how awful it is for this person [the therapist] to train the camera on me in such a way as to show how physically ugly and weary and over-the-hill I am as well. It's crazy for me to come back for more of this and to pay for it in hard-earned dollars unless I'm really more of a masochist than I think I am." So, too, in the videorecording process, there can be distortions of presentations of the self which, because the lens is out of focus or not allowing appropriate light to come through, gives the patient a distorted view of self. Patients already have problems with those distortions in self-perceptions of who they believe they are and who they believe they should be in accordance with their inner idealized images of themselves which may be changing from moment to moment in the daily living of each patient. If the recorded picture shows distortions that are due to equipment dysfunction, the therapist should immediately acknowledge it to the patient so the patient doesn't unnecessarily add to his or her self-hate.

Patients are invariably burdened with self-hate and it is one of the stated or implicit goals of psychotherapy to reduce self-hate while heightening self-esteem, self-worth, and self-love. The use of video in psychotherapy while not to be in the service of artifice or falsification should be so sensitively integrated into the orchestration of the psychotherapeutic work and its many levels of confrontation that it does indeed constructively enhance insight into who one really is so that movement forward can occur in reality while self-esteem, self-love, and satisfaction in living are enhanced.

It is indeed paradoxically fortunate that those psychotherapists who use video in their work with patient/clients are more likely to become sensitized to and more expert in their capacity to comprehend metacommunications and nonverbal communications that carry messages which can tell you that the patient is not comfortable or pleased with inner reactions to the video self-image confrontation being experienced at the moment. A compassionate psychotherapist will perceive those minute nonverbalized clues that reveal that what is needed is to focus on what has been triggered off in the patient by the video confrontation just lived and that it might be prudent to turn off the recording and playback equipment while using the more traditional talking relationship to work through what has been enacted in the patient person-electronic equipment-therapist person, transaction. The equipment and its use must be in the service of the patient's work in psychotherapy and not in the service of the media.

Principle II of the aforementioned AMA code of ethics states:

A physician shall deal honestly with patients and colleagues, and strive to expose those physicians deficient in character or competence, or who engage in fraud or deception.

How does this principle apply in whole or in part to psychotherapists who use video in the conduct of their professional work as an art and science. There is a basic need for honesty in the development and nurturance of the patient-psychotherapist relationship. In times like ours in the 80s, when the use of electronic surveillance and videotaping for the purposes of entrapment are publicized in the media, the need for the patient to trust the psychotherapist is even greater than usual when the therapist suggests the use of an audiovisual adjunct to the curative process, inasmuch as audiovisual recordings are even closer to the revelation of one's private self than is a report of one's words or behaviors by a second party to a third party.

Robert Burns wrote:

> O wad some Power
> the giftie gie us
> To see oursels as
> others see us!

And with the advent of television, we can now see ourselves more or less as others do, when we are non-self-consciously interacting in verbal-nonverbal dialogue with therapist(s) and other family members or group members during a psychotherapy session. Video playback brings past moments of our functioning back from the past to the present moment, giving us a second chance, or a third, fourth, or fifth chance to witness, recall, experience, and reexperience ourselves as we were "there and then." The audiovisual data which truthfully presents us as we were at the moment that we were videotaped may be more or less harmonious with our recalled memory of ourselves on that occasion. Or it may be more or less discordant with our memory and reveal to us (a) expressions of our inner being then that we did not consciously intend to express though we were privately aware of them, or did not know we were revealing to others by our nonverbal behaviors, tones, attitudes, and metacommunications, or (b) expressions to others of our inner being at that time which we did not realize were occurring, let alone being revealed. Such moments of awareness and insight during video replay can be startling, shocking, or relieving at times.

The video picture made available for self-confrontation in psychotherapy can affect the patient by:

1. The multilevel impact of sense of immediacy of the past in the present which it presents.
2. The presentations of desirable or undesirable incorporated aspects of one or both parents, grandparents, or significant others.
3. The impact of magnification of a facial look, a shoulder shrug, a look of terror, a self-effacing smile, a demeaning or discounting attitude, or a hand movement expressing helplessness.
4. The repeated pattern of multilevel contradictory communications presented via simultaneous verbalized and nonverbalized messages as well as the impact of such communications on others.
5. The presentation of data indicating that the audiovisual presentation of self grossly violates and contradicts one's idealized self-image.

Video, then, is an invasive technique which penetrates and makes visible to self and others far more of what is going on in a person than what is visible on the skin or surface of self. And the same consideration of the rights of the patient are indicated in its use as are indicated with any other invasive technique.

It is truly a leap and expression of faith, or perhaps at times of desperation, which leads patients to consent to the use by their psychotherapist, in other places for other audiences, of audio and/or videotape recordings of them made during psychotherapy sessions. And the psychotherapist is ethically obligated to tell the patient honestly what will be done with such recordings. Most patients already trust that what they say to psychotherapists will be kept in confidence. But they need to hear the therapist state what he intends to do with the voice and picture recordings of them in interaction with him which he is seeking permission to make.

For me, the primary honest truth is to say that "I intend to use these to complement our work together and hope that you, too, will see them as an addition of something very valuable for you—and, by the way"— said smilingly—"at no extra charge to you. In fact, I hope before long you'll bring in your own audiotape recorder to tape our sessions and that you'll take the time and effort to listen to them over and over again at home. I'm sure you'll find so much more in what goes on here between us than you've realized up 'till now." And I say all that honestly because *I* know it is true!

What patients most want to hear is that they won't suddenly see these video pictures of themselves in a documentary program on commercial, cable, or educational TV. They also want to know that the therapist won't show these pictures to friends or colleagues for entertainment. And that is why it is so important in preparing the written videotape consent form that the specific limited uses for these tapes should be stated. And if the patient is asked for consent to show them to medical, psychiatric, or other professional audiences, the language of the consent form should be as clear as possible. We'll talk more about this under the specific topic of informed consent and written consent forms and statements to be made regarding confidential information on videotape programs released for showing to audiences in far-away places.

If the videotapes or audiotapes are to be used for supervision of work with this particular patient by a respected senior colleague, you may be surprised to find out how pleased the patient is that you will keep him or her in mind after they have left your office. It isn't just purely unhealthy narcissism but rather a healthy need for recognition and significance by significant others, feelings which were hardly known in childhood, which leads patients to be pleased that you are reviewing your work with them with some more experienced colleagues. And, of course, if you are a writer, then patients may be pleased to know you consider what they say or what has given them such pain in living significant enough to be noted, written about, and shared with others. That is, of course, unless they are a bit or very paranoid and have the grandiose idea that even though you say you will disguise their identity in writing about them, they are such significant persons that they will be recognized by the world at large. With such patients it is better to be very careful, very prudent, very proper, and very professional, and to maintain as positive a transferential relationship as possible. If you don't, a lawsuit may lie ahead! Or perhaps it would be better not to include their specifically personal remarks in your edited works.

If you intend to use edited segments of a taped psychotherapeutic session or a whole psychotherapy session for an edited program for distribution to the mental health profession, be clear about what you're asking the patient to sign on the release form. If you're asking for permission to show what was expressed during the psychotherapy session to a nonprofessional audience, you're asking the patient to give you the right to show to laymen what was originally expressed in a confidential setting and relationship without any notion that you might wish to show it to public audiences. Now you're beginning to walk where angels fear to tread and could get yourself into serious legal difficulties. It's better to obtain legal counsel and help in defining and stating the altered contract you are now arranging with your patient.

Let us now move to the increasingly important topic of informed consent. The newest decisions on this matter made by state and federal courts indicate a trend to include almost "all and everything" about the matter on a mandatory basis. In medicine as a whole, however, there is a reaction against giving the "all and everything" of information on side effects and consequences of surgery or medications which might lead to the patient becoming so apprehensive that he will not consent to the surgery or to taking the prescribed medicine. As for video, there is little likelihood that a properly informed and prepared patient will refuse to agree to its use during a psychotherapy session because he may have a strong reaction to it as long as he or she knows and trusts that the audiovisual record will be destroyed shortly thereafter or, if retained, will not be shown for any purpose whatsoever to other patients, colleagues, students, or friends of the therapist. The difficulties with the application of informed consent to the use of video in psychotherapy lie in two main areas. The patient is usually asked to sign a release or permission form for the videotaping and for its showing at later times to clearly designated types of audiences, prior to the taping of the actual interview session. He or she is therefore asked to give "blanket" permission in advance or perhaps, one might say blindly, to have audiovisual recordings of him shown to others while he is expressing and revealing himself or herself in ways which at the moment of signing he or she cannot really know will be revealed. It is done on the basis of trust and/or a positive transference relationship or for money or other favors or gifts or rewards.

I have in the past videotaped a family in crisis who gave permission to be videotaped and to have the tape shown to other mental health professionals and paraprofessionals in the psychiatric, medical, and allied health professions, in return for the promise of free psychotherapy for a limited period of time. This is the contract signed by each member of the family:

CONSENT FORM FOR VIDEOTAPES, SOUND MOTION PICTURE FILMS & AUDIOTAPES

I,   , the undersigned, hereby voluntarily consent to and knowingly authorize the taking of videotapes, films, photographs or audiotapes of me on   (Dates) and to the reproduction, publication, and transmission of the same in such edited or unedited form as Health and Education Multimedia, Inc. may decide in programs prepared and presented for free or paid rental and sales distribution by Health and Education Multimedia, Inc. of 50 East 72nd Street, Suite 4B, New York, New York 10021, or its representatives.

I do not expect any moneys, royalties or payments of any kind now or in the future from Health and Educational Multimedia, Inc. or from any other source.

I give this consent with the understanding that programs prepared from the videotapes of me are primarily intended for the purpose of continuing education and training of professionals and paraprofessionals in the psychiatric, medical, and allied health professions in order to promote: prevention of illness, maintenance of health, as well as improved care and treatment of the emotionally and mentally disabled.

I hereby waive, for the purposes of this consent, any privilege of confidentiality.

_____	_____
Date	Signature
	_____
	Address
_____	_____
Witness	Signature of Maker

When the videotaped material produced in family therapy sessions with this family was edited by Health and Education Multimedia, Inc. into a final videocassette program made available for purchase and rental to professionals, it carried the message "this program contains privileged information which must be respected," and the purchaser's order form for the program requires that this statement be signed: "I certify that I understand the legal and human implications of confidentiality and privileged information and that I will respect that right by showing HEM restricted audiovisual programs only to qualified viewers." It is the obligation of those who produce programs with patients for distribution to others for education and training to protect the rights of the patient as much as possible.

Now we come to a rather delicate aspect of this matter called informed consent. If you as a videotaper who has already received consent in writing to videotape patients, now record patients expressing themselves in ways and matters which you then or later believe as an ethical practitioner should not really be exposed to others, what should you do? If you as an experienced, ethical, concerned, humanistic psychotherapist think that the material you have videotaped could, if shown to others now or in the future, truly be harmful to the patient, you have two ethical choices. First, you can decide not to use those segments of the recorded material about which you are doubtful, and second, you can review the material in question with the patient to ask him or her to decide whether he or she wishes you to proceed with its showing. If he or she believes it will not be harmful now or in the future, then ask the patient to sign another permission form stating that he has been shown the previously recorded material and still wishes—as of this date—to give consent to your showing and/or distributing it to the specific audiences delineated in the initial agreement. Or the patient may wish to limit the audiences previously agreed to while still permitting the material to be shown. The psychotherapist should in no way coerce the patient to sign.

I have used the following technique for my own legal protection at times and to record evidence of my own ethical behavior when asking a patient to sign permission for me to use a videotaped psychotherapy session containing especially sensitive data with other persons. While the video equipment is still running, and therefore recording me in dialogue and interaction with the patient, I will ask the patient for permission to use the recorded videotape of our session. The videotape records the act, context, and attitudes of myself and my patient as I ask for permission, produce the prepared form if he or she verbally agrees, and as we both read and sign the written release form. While the videotape recording is still being made, I also say "Do you in any way feel coerced into signing this agreement for me to use this material concerning you in the education of others?" The patient usually states, "Of course not. If I didn't want to give you permission, I wouldn't give it to you." I then state, "Do you in any way fear that if you don't agree to sign the permission I will reject you or refuse to continue to treat you or will alter the quality of care and concern I have for you as a patient-person?" Again, the patient usually responds, "Of course not. If I thought that's the kind of person or therapist you are, I wouldn't return to you at all."

What is most important legally is that this recorded material presents evidence to anyone who sees it as to the attitudinal, behavioral, and contextual atmosphere of the signing and the voluntary trusting and trusted nature of our relationship. Any jury examining this videotaped recording would conclude no coercion or unethical pressure was being exerted to obtain the patient's permission. The language of metacommunication and nonverbal behavior of two people in intimate, interactional dialogue is known to all human beings who are called upon to examine and decide whether undue pressure or coercion is being exerted by either party in a human transaction in a professional relationship.

In 1970, Harry Wilmer—a major pioneer in the development of videotape techniques for psychotherapy and training—made a clear-cut statement for video users which is worth repeating because of its succinctness and continuing applicability:

> We never make a videotape without the patient's consent and without fully explaining to the patient beforehand what is being done and why. When minors are involved, consent is also obtained from parents or guardians. With informed consent, there is no intrusion of privacy. The only possible breach of confidence would be the misuse of tapes by showing them to persons other than select professional audiences, and no ethical person would permit this.

Much consideration should be given by each psychotherapist in consultation with legal counsel to the permission form he prepares for patients to sign to allow the videotaping and the showing, reproduction, or distribution of the videotaped material to others. The subject is covered in some detail in the chapter by David Noah Fields on "Legal Implications and Complications—Model Forms For Signed Releases" in Berger (1978).

In my experience, a patient who is videotaped in a private practice setting during psychotherapy is much more likely than a hospitalized patient to understand the nature of the process, to be informed as to what the purposes are for the videotaping, what hoped-for goals might be achieved and what will be done with the videorecorded data afterward. In these days when defensiveness against the possibility of suit for malpractice is the rule rather than the exception, it is more than likely that a privately practicing psychotherapist will inform the patient and obtain his consent before turning on audiovisual recording equipment. In my own private office, I keep all video equipment in the open at all times to acquaint new patients with the fact that I have such equipment. Most often patients will inquire about the presence of the equipment and if able to be assertive, may facetiously ask if I do studio photography or make movies in my spare time. This gives me an opportunity to inform them that I use the video equipment when I believe it is appropriate and when my patients voluntarily consent to my using it with them in order to expedite and enhance the psychotherapeutic work in which we are engaged. I point out that our goal is to expand their observing ego so that they can learn more about the truth of themselves intrapsychically and interpersonally in a shorter time with less pain and less expenditure of money.

When the patient expresses curiosity about the video equipment, it is an appropriate time to begin to prepare the patient for the future use of the equipment by asking such questions as, "What reactions are you having to the presence of the equipment?" You thus flush out what may otherwise remain unspoken and may elicit varying degrees of anxiety concerning you, your equipment, and your intent to maintain the confidentiality of what the patient tells you in this privileged relationship. Patients may express anxiety and even severe apprehension about finding out that their inner pictures and self-images may turn out to be quite different from the pictures that they will see on video playback. They may not feel ready for such a revelation or confrontation. It is most important for the ethical practitioner to face this evidence of resistance sensitively and to work it through before proceeding to use the equipment. This is a moment to sense and assess the degree and power of the patient's idealized image(s), narcissism, and fear of really finding out the truth about self.

Since my initial involvement with video for psychiatric training and treatment in 1966, I have never ceased to be impressed and at times startled by the initial reactions of patients to video self-image confrontation. Because video is such a powerful invasive tool which can reach into the heart of one's psyche, it must be used with the utmost of professionalism and caution and with exquisite respect for the implications of and attention to the patient's nonverbal as well as verbal reactions. From the beginning of the modern audiovisual era thirty years ago, there has been a concern with the possibilities of protherapeutic and antitherapeutic consequences of audiovisual self-image confrontation.

In my experience with video self-confrontation, most patients seeing the playback of themselves in the social interaction of the psychotherapy experience immediately see and react negatively to some aspect of themselves. This is referred to as social self-criticism. It is precisely because of this that I believe the ethical use of video in psychotherapy with patients requires that the psychotherapist should not only have been through one or more video self-image confrontations but should also be trained to prepare patients for their initial video self-image confrontation by spending as much time as necessary in eliciting responses to the following questions:

1. How do you react to the idea of our using video equipment to help you see yourself?
2. Do you have any advance anxiety about it?
3. What is your anxiety about?

4. What do you expect to find when you see and experience the
   video playback of yourself?

Asking these questions may bring forward for discussion and working
through many aspects of self-image and body concept which have not
previously emerged during psychotherapy with that person. I believe it is
unethical simply to videotape a patient and replay the videotape to the
patient instantly or at a later time without preparing the patient for the
experience in the fashion described. It is relatively impossible to predict
which patients will have a negative, "I can't believe it" reaction to their
abrupt video self-confrontation experience. In my experience, the more
ill patients are, the more negative is their initial reaction to their first
playback experience and the longer it takes until they can verbalize
something positive about what they see of themselves on the video
monitor. And patients who say they have no reaction to their video
self-image confrontation tend to have a very poor prognosis for working
in psychotherapy.

It behooves the therapist to be alert to all cues and knowledge which
have already come from or may come from the patient relating to his or
her actual self-image and idealized self-image (Berger, 1977).

Most often the question of informed consent is invoked concerning
the use of videotape with a hospitalized patient. Patricia Wald has stated
that if information given to a hospitalized, mentally ill patient about a
procedure or medication is only enough to be a gesture, then it is not
enough to be considered informed consent.[1] In my experience as director of education and training at South Beach Psychiatric Center on Staten Island, New York, a facility of the New York State Office of Mental
Hygiene, we have often asked hospitalized inpatients and/or members of
their families to sign permission forms for videotaping of interviews with
the patient. In my experience, it is best to allow ample time to explain the
reason for the videotaping, for the patient or patient's family to read and
understand the printed consent form, and to respond to any questions
they may have concerning the videotaping or the form they have been
asked to sign. The most common, anxiety-laden question asked by the
patient or concerned family member is, "How do I know this won't be
used on network television?" I respond truthfully and completely by
rereading the statement on the permission form which states that the
videotape is to be used only for medical and psychiatric education which
means we could not use it for public dissemination or broadcast. If the
patient or family appears to be hesitant after my verbal assurance and
explanation, I offer to write on the permission form the specific words
they would like to see in writing, which usually is "No part of this
videotape being made of (*patient's name*) on (*date*) can be used on commercial television broadcasts at any time." Most often the patient and

family are satisfied with that additional specific statement and then proceed to cooperate voluntarily with participation in the interview which
will be videotaped through cameras and by camera operators out in the
open in our hospital video studio. After the interview of the patient by a
member of our professional staff or by a distinguished visiting consultant, we offer to show all or part of the interview to the patient and
family. We also arrange for the patient to see a playback at a later time, if
he or she so wishes, with their therapist in order to obtain the potential
therapeutic benefits of video replay.

Other important issues related to informed consent with hospitalized
patients are those concerning competency and incompetency. Certainly,
most adult patients treated privately in their offices by psychotherapists
are considered competent. Being in treatment does not establish even a
presumptive incompetency. And that is also true of adult patients diagnosed within the context of the DSM-III, 1980 Axis II as Borderline
Personality. Such patients can consent to videotaping of their
psychotherapy sessions and it is recommended that the consents be
explicit and in writing because of the volatile and intermittently psychotic functioning of borderline patients.

In making videotapes of patients, it is advisable whenever possible to
caution patients against use of their own last name or the names of other
people who might be known to the unknown future viewers of this
videotape in its recorded or in an edited version. Hospitalized patients
are more likely to forget this injunction and will therefore mention the
names of others they are talking about inadvertently or out of hostility. It
behooves the videotape producer to remove such names if possible as a
potential protection against dissemination of confidential or libelous material. Try, whenever possible, to preclude exact identification of the
persons presented and avoid or consider deletion of patently humiliating or defamatory material. Such material may be dramatic, interesting,
or shocking, but it rarely adds to the scientific, medical, or
psychotherapeutic data being recorded for treatment, training, or research purposes.

Let us review some general trends in regard to competency and
incompetency of hospitalized patients. The adjudication of mental illness is not an adjudication of incompetency. When a hospitalized patient
is legally competent, he should not be prevented from executing legal
documents. And most hospitalized patients, especially those suffering
from an acute mental disorder, are considered mentally competent from
a legal point of view. When hospital officals believe that a patient is in
fact incompetent, they should notify those persons who may appropriately initiate guardianship or committee proceedings.[2] The 1968 *Report of Mental Competency* stated that "there should not be a single criterion of competency applicable to all legal functions, but rather that the

criteria should vary depending upon the function to be performed."
Even though adjudicated incompetent, a mentally ill person may make a
will or enter into a valid contract and may even enter into a valid marriage during a "lucid interval." There is no clear-cut decisional law on
the subject of whether a patient adjudicated incompetent can authorize
the use of videotapes showing him being interviewed or receiving other
treatment in a hospital setting. The general law on the right of incompetents to enter contracts varies from state to state.

David N. Fields, LL.B., is the most learned person I know on this
subject. He writes:

> Hence, one who deals with an adjudicated incompetent patient, irrespective
> of whether he is confined in a hospital, should proceed with the utmost
> caution. Even if a hospital director were to permit the making of films or
> videotapes of hospital patients, their subsequent exhibition might constitute
> the tort of invasion of privacy or defamation of character or illegal publica-
> tion of privileged communications or matters. If film or videotapes can be
> made in a manner which will not reveal the identity of the patient, the risks of
> exhibiting them may possibly be avoided.
>
> What should be done in dealing with 1) patients who have been legally
> found to be incompetent but who have not been legally restored to compe-
> tency even though they have recovered, and 2) patients who have never been
> adjudicated to be incompetent but who in fact are so mentally ill that they
> cannot be said to have the capacity to contract? With respect to the recovered
> patient it would be wise to defer taping their therapy sessions for showing to
> others until they have procured a judicial ruling that they have been restored
> to competency. To tape the sessions of nonadjudicated patients, whose illness
> raises a doubt as to their capacity to enter legally valid contracts, would be
> extremely risky and should not be undertaken.
>
> Of course there is a riskless method of dealing with adjudicated incompe-
> tents, patients who have not been adjudicated but who are too ill to have
> capacity to contract, hospitalized patients and others whose status is doubtful.
> The patient, or his committee, or the hospital director may seek prior court
> authorization of the taping of therapy sessions, hospital interviews or hospi-
> tal activities in which the patient is involved. If such court authorization is
> obtained, there should be no risk at all in making and exhibiting the
> videotapes. Obviously, however, it would be time consuming and expensive
> to even attempt to obtain judicial approval in numerous cases and there
> would be no guarantee that courts would approve in all or most of the cases
> presented. The concept of prior judicial approval, therefore, must be re-
> garded as theoretically possible but highly impractical.
>
> Minor patients, like adults, may be competent or incompetent. It is
> doubtful that competent minors can effectively authorize taping of psychiat-
> ric sessions or hospital activities. Minors may disavow their transactions in
> many situations, provided their attempts to disavow "are used as a shield and
> not a sword." Only subsequent litigation and court decision would determine
> whether a minor had properly disavowed a consent to the use of tapes or

films. Clearly there may be an element of risk in using such films. It goes without saying that the risk would be enormously increased if tapes of incompetent minors were used. In institutions, consent by the authorities may limit the risk if identification of the patients is avoided.

In summary, then, concerning the issues of hospitalized mental patients signing permission forms to be videotaped, it is my opinion that if a patient is hospitalized voluntarily and has not been declared incompetent, and if the patient understands the reasons he or she is being asked to have an interview with him or her videotaped and signs a permission form for this, and voluntarily walks without being carried or pushed to the video studio and shows that his or her participation in a videotaped interview is voluntary and not against his or her will, it will probably hold up in court as informed consent. It is most important to remember that the courts are interested in the patient's rights and what you have done to protect those rights and what use you have made of those videotapes in deciding on any case which comes before them. An ethical psychotherapist does not act in a way which will harm the patient.

Examples of Nonethical Use of Video

A couple troubled with major sexual and other marital dysfunctions recently informed my wife and myself (Berger and Berger, 1979) in their initial consultation session that the wife had sought help some months previously by going to a major university medical school sexual dysfunction clinic. At the conclusion of her first interview she was told she must bring her husband with her for the second session or they would not be able to help her. She pleaded with and successfully cajoled her embarrassed, resistive husband into coming to the clinic with her for the second appointment. Upon entry, he was given forms to complete related to his insurance coverage and then a resident physician came over and asked the couple, Jay and Mary, to follow him. On the way down the hall they noticed three younger medical students following them too at about the same moment that they heard the doctor tell them, "We're going down to the studio where we will be videotaping our session." Jay heard no more as he grabbed Mary by the arm, turned around, and stated, "Not me. You're not putting me on videotape. Let's get out of here." They hurriedly left and did not go back. It's a wonder they later came to us for help.

This report of what I clearly consider an instance of unethical use of video in clinical psychotherapeutic practice is a simple but eloquent example of a noncompassionate and nonrespectful attempted use of video in psychotherapy. In the most simple fashion, there is a clear-cut violation of the concept of informed consent; the patients were never told about the clinic's use of videotaping, the purposes and goals of videotaping, nor were they asked to participate voluntarily. There had been no attempt made to respond to any feelings or questions which the couple may have had about participating in such an experience. There was a complete lack of preparation which must include listening to any resistance and working it through as it occurs before going on.

It has come to my attention that some publicly funded, tax-exempt facilities which use video in their training programs refuse to treat patients who will not agree to being videotaped. In such instances, which clearly violate ethics, a form of coercion or arm-twisting is used to obtain agreement to participate from some individuals and families seeking desperately needed help. The need for relief of emotional and psychological intrapsychic or interpersonal suffering thus leads to individuals who are financially as well as emotionally and psychologically impoverished agreeing to videotape in order to gain access to psychotherapeutic help.

I witnessed another instance of the unethical use of video playback in dance therapy a few years ago. I was walking in the corridor outside of the media studio located in the main administration building at our psychiatric center when I noticed a dissheveled young woman in her early twenties writhing on the floor of the corridor while a dance therapist was entreating her to return with her to the nearby video studio. I called the therapist aside to inquire what was going on and learned that she had gotten one of our media staff to videotape her doing dance therapy with this acutely psychotic patient and then arranged to have the tape played back. When the patient saw herself on the television monitor, she became thoroughly agitated and ran out to the corridor where she was in great distress when I came upon the scene. Upon questioning, I learned that the young dance therapist had had no prior experience or training in the use of video replay self-confrontation with patients. She had embarked on her "experiment" with innocent good will and a lack of training or knowledge of the powerful impact of self-image confrontation upon anyone, especially a disturbed schizophrenic patient suffering from distorted perceptions of self and others.

I cannot overemphasize the powerful impact of the videotaped self-image confrontation experience and the importance of training in its use and in preparing patients for this powerful experience. In the process of experiencing a video playback of how one was a few minutes previously, there is the most unusual opportunity to see and hear how the camera recorded me as being then, in contrast to my own intensely personal memory or feeling recollection of my perception of myself, then. If and when these two pieces of data, one recorded electronically on the videotape and one recorded inside myself, are indeed harmonious, I am fortunate in feeling integrated and whole. If, however, there are gross discrepancies and disharmony between my inner recollection of myselves and what I perceive on the television monitor, I may be more than a little perturbed and may go into an acute crisis of discombobulation, confusion, self-doubt, despair, rage, or self-hate. If the video feedback brings to me through presentation of attitudes and nonverbal behaviors, data confirming what I have up until now been unable to or refused to admit about myself, I may become very distressed. It is at just such a moment that a competent, compassionate psychotherapist would know to turn the equipment off while working through with me what the playback has triggered in me. A compassionate psychotherapist with a respect for my limitations would sense my inner disturbance and, remembering that the equipment is to be used for the benefit of the patient and not vice versa, would turn it off.

An ethical psychotherapist would seek training in the use of a powerful new procedure before using it with patients; to learn its indications, contraindications, constructive, and nonconstructive potentials before adding the procedure to his or her therapeutic armamentarium. The psychotherapist who wishes to use video with patients in individual, couple, family, or group psychotherapy must seek training. There are individuals, organizations, books, articles, and videotapes which offer such training. In Seattle, Washington: Hugh James Lurie, M.D.; in Vancouver, B.C.: Lybba Tyhurst, M.D.; in Los Angeles: Marcia Kraft Goin, M.D.; in Lansing, Michigan: Norman Kagan, Ph.D.; in Madison, Wisconsin: Carl Whitaker, M.D.; in Huntsville, Alabama: Robert E. Froelich, M.D.; in San Antonio, Texas: Harry A. Wilmer, M.D.; and in New York City: Ian Alger, M.D., and myself, as well as many other experienced colleagues throughout the country, offer formal and informal training, guidance and supervision in the art as well as the science of the ethical use of video in psychotherapy. South Beach Psychiatric Center in Staten Island, New York, offers an ongoing 400-hour Media Training Fellowship Program. Health and Education Multimedia, Inc. in New York City, the American Psychiatric Association, and the American Group Psychotherapy Association offer annual courses, seminars, or workshops on video in treatment. There is an international *TV in Psychiatry Newsletter*, edited by L. Tyhurst in Vancouver, B.C., and my comprehensive text (Berger, 1978). Color videotape cassettes are also available for training, e.g., "Video Replay in Individual Psychotherapy," from the Media Department at South Beach Psychiatric Center, Staten Island, New York, and "Video Replay in Group Psychotherapy," from Health and Education Multimedia, Inc. in New York City.

I have decried as unethical the use of the terms *videotherapy* and *videotherapist* (see Berger, 1978, pp. 136–138) as they represent a direction leading to abuses and exploitation of patients. The development of video as a tool to aid us in researching, teaching, and practicing psychotherapy is comparable in its potential for shedding light on the work and process of psychotherapists and psychotherapy to the microscope's potential to shed light on organisms, cells, tissue, and human physiological structure.

What perturbs me so much about the potential for unethical conduct if *videotherapy* becomes acceptable and widespread as a term and process is the implication that the therapeutic potential resides in the videorecording and replay of data rather than in the skill and sensitivity of a trained psychotherapist who at appropriate times in the course and context of the psychotherapy sessions can apply the additional data and knowledge made available through video equipment in the working through process. I shudder to think of the possibility of untold, untrained entrepreneurs purchasing video equipment to record and replay people to themselves who will believe they are receiving the benefit of psychotherapy. It is not information or data or words or insights alone which lead patients to change in psychotherapy. Psychotherapy is an intimate, sensitive, mutually dependent process in which the therapist's empathetic qualities of relating, understanding, communicating, motivating, and inspiring the patient's will and capacity to risk changing call for sensing and timing of the nature and depth of what is communicated. The video machinery just doesn't do that. The hand that guides the camera allows a psychotherapeutic assistant to focus during or after video replay on the formed but unshed tear, the repeated, demeaning, discounting facial expression, shoulder shrug and hand movement, the perplexed brow which is worn like a fixed mask representing the incorporation of the patient's father who always looked this way, or the shit-eating grin which is the hallmark of the self-effacing person who needs to be liked by everyone at all times. Presentations on video playback of data which has either been previously unknown to the patient, although knowable or known to others, and data which the patient has until now believed was kept private and not expressed outwardly, stimulate reactions which require the supportive, interpretative, and compassionate help of a trained psychotherapist. This then is not videotherapy but psychotherapy with the use of video as an adjunctive tool!

The psychotherapists who, like myself, have given repeated support to the use of video as adjunct in psychotherapy advocate the integration of video usage with a multiplicity of simultaneous or alternating techniques and theoretical approaches used in eclectic psychotherapy with individuals, couples, families, and groups of patients. Only rarely is a single video self-confrontation replay used as the methodology, as is done in many academic research projects purporting to draw conclusions about the impact of self-image confrontation. Most often, patients are exposed to segments played repeatedly with the discussion guided by the therapist to enable the patient to comprehend more fully the impact of what is presented and experienced during the replay. The repetition of replays over time lead to a reinforcement of awareness and understanding while simultaneously heightening the patient's motivation to work toward change. As any experienced psychotherapist or patient knows, anything which can increase motivation to work toward change is worth consideration. And evidence through video replay that the patient has already changed to some degree in ways which are meaningful serve as a feedback loop to further motivation and capacity to risk new ways of being in interaction with others.

Conclusion

In this chapter I have presented the need for consideration and codification of what in terms of the professional conduct of psychotherapists might be considered as ethical concerns. Included are such issues as the necessity for an ethical code because of the nature of man in relationship with himself and others, the ethics of video in psychotherapy in the light of the 1980 AMA code of ethics—compassion, respect, honesty, integrity, and the principles of informed consent—the potential of unknown effects following the use of video as an invasive technique; legal aspects of competency and informed consent; preparation of the patient for the appropriate timing in the use of video self-confrontation; the motivating power of video replay; and the dictum that the video electronic equipment is to be used in the service of the patient.

NOTES

1. Patricia Wald was a key figure in the development of the Mental Health Law Project in 1972, with fellow attorneys Charles Halpern, Bruce Enneis, and Paul Friedman. This project grew out of the Center for Law and Social Policy, an organization supported by the American Civil Liberties Union. Her interest and competence as a lawyer in the field of mental health public interest law were established through her work as Director of Litigation of the Mental Health Law Project in Washington, D.C.
2. Many of these remarks are taken from the 1968 *Report of Mental Competency* of the George Washington University Institute of Law, Psychiatry and Criminology, and the chapter by attorney David Noah Fields, whose life has been devoted to protection of the rights of the mentally ill, "Legal Implications and complications," in M. M. Berger (1978).

REFERENCES

American Medical Association Code of Ethics. *New York Times,* July 23, 1980.

BERGER, M. M. The "I can't believe it" reaction to video self-confrontation. *Current Concepts in Psychiatry,* 1977, **3,** 2–6.

BERGER, M. M. (ed.). *Videotape techniques in psychiatric training and treatment.* New York: Brunner-Mazel, 1978.

BERGER, L. F., and BERGER, M. M. Couple therapy by a married couple, *Journal of the American Academy of Psychoanalysis,* 1979, **7,** 219–240.

FIELDS, D. N. Legal implications and complications—Model forms for signed releases. In M. M. Berger (ed.), *Videotape techniques in psychiatric training and treatment,* rev. ed. New York: Brunner-Mazel, 1978.

GEERTSMA, R., and REIVICH, R. Repetitive self-observation by videotape playback, *Journal of Mental Nervous Disorders,* 1965, **141,** 29–41.

LAVENDER, J., DAVIS, M., and GRABER, E. Film/video research recordings: Ethical issues. *Kinesics,* 1978, **1,** 9–20.

REIVICH, R., and GEERTSMA, R. Experiences with videotape self-observation by psychiatric in-patients., *Journal of the Kansas Medical Society,* 1968, **69,** 39–44.

ROSENBAUM, M. The issues of privacy and privileged communication. In M. M. Berger (ed.), *Videotape techniques in psychiatric training and treatment,* rev. ed. New York: Brunner-Mazel, 1978.

WILMER, H. A. Use of the television monologue with adolescent psychiatric patients. *American Journal of Psychiatry,* 1970, **126,** 1760–1766.

PART IV

ETHICS BEYOND PRIVATE PRACTICE

Ethical Problems of Therapists in Government and Industry

Peter G. Bourne

A few years ago a military policeman at the Walter Reed Army Medical Center was sent to see a psychiatrist because he gave a ticket on two separate occasions to the post commander for speeding on post. Although he was faithfully carrying out his job, it was felt that anyone who showed such poor judgment as to ticket the commanding general, even though he was breaking the law, must have some psychological problem. The psychiatrist to whom the military policeman was sent was also under the command of the same ticketed general, and it was to the latter that the report on the patient would ultimately go. The psychiatrist could determine no evidence of significant mental illness, and was impressed by the man's deeply held belief that no one should be above the law. To diagnose the patient as mentally ill would have conveniently saved face for everyone, and would have unfairly given the man a label he would have had to wear the rest of his life. Given the intricacies of military etiquette, to pronounce him free of any mental illness would mean opening a Pandora's box of problems for the military policeman, the general, and the psychiatrist himself. Such are the ethical dilemmas faced by psychiatrists and psychologists in the government which the private practitioner never has to face.

Surprisingly, the problems of medical ethics as they relate to mental health care, and particularly the dilemma posed by the conflict of interest between government and therapist, have only been seriously addressed in the last ten years. A number of books, dealing generally with ethical issues and mental health, were published in the last 100 years (Bain, 1869; Baldwin, 1906). It was, however, only in 1973 that the American Medical Association published its principles of medical ethics with annotations for psychiatry. After laboring for three years, the American Psychiatric Association did not produce its own code of ethics until 1975 (Moore, 1978).

Ethical considerations have been central to the general field of medicine for more than two thousand years. The Hippocratic oath, while of uncertain origin, is known to date from the fourth century B.C.

It contains two basic elements. The first is an admonition to the physician to honor his teacher as a parent and to teach his teacher's sons with the same dedication. The second component of the oath is a series of specific items concerning the physician's conduct in the practice of medicine, including protecting a patient's confidentiality, proscribing sexual contact with a patient, performing no surgery, and protecting the patient from harm. While this covenant for physicians is outdated in some respects by more recent scientific developments, including the development of relatively safe surgical procedures, it was of monumental consequence. Not only did it dominate the profession for two millenia but it gave medicine a degree of respect and prestige that no other profession has yet achieved. Certain modifications in the basic concepts of the Hippocratic oath were made in 1794 in Percival's "Medical Ethics, or A Code of Institutes and Precepts Adopted to the Professional Conduct of Physicians and Surgeons." Recognition was given to the role of surgeons, but the fundamental themes of secrecy, compassion, proper care of patients, and upholding the dignity of the profession were maintained. In addition, special concern for the dying was emphasized.

In 1847, the then recently created American Medical Association adopted a code of ethics that largely derived from Percival. It was revised in 1912, 1947, and 1957, but even in its present form, it still strongly reflects the persisting influence of Hippocrates (Konold, 1979).

Both with regard to general medical practice and mental health care, codes of conduct have almost exclusively focused upon the health care practitioner as an independent entrepreneur. Although most aspects of the code of ethics apply equally well to the physician working in an institutional setting, there have been relatively few efforts to address the ethical dilemmas that are created by working in such a situation (Breggin, 1971; Shore and Golann, 1973). Serious questions have been raised as to whether the physician can be expected to adhere to the traditional standards of medical ethics, particularly those relating to patient confidentiality. These questions have focused particularly on the military and college settings (Bourne, 1967; Halleck, 1971). What is striking, however, is how little serious attention has been given to the problems of the health care practitioner in a governmental or industrial setting, and how few solutions have been offered for solving them. This in large part reflects the complexity of the issues involved, the absence of easy solutions, and the powerful conflicting forces with vested interests that are at play.

The Third Party

When a patient voluntarily contracts for the services of a physician, the physician is solely the patient's agent. The patient is entitled to expect certain things from the physician including adherence to certain ethical standards. The physician has an obligation to the patient and to no one else, and is clearly in a position to put the patient's interests above all other interests. Particularly in dealing with mental health problems, an integral part of the benefit that the patients derive from the therapy is the assurance that the therapist has an undivided commitment to helping them with their problems.

All this changes once a third party enters the picture, whether it is as seemingly benign as an insurance company to pay the patient's bills, or as menacing as an employer who wants access to the confidential content of therapy sessions. The quality of the relationship between the patient and the therapist is irrevocably altered once that relationship is no longer encapsulated intact, as is inevitably the case in government or industry. It does not necessarily invalidate the relationship nor does it necessarily preclude the possibility of the patient receiving adequate and appropriate care, but the nature of the relationship is nonetheless different.

Although the problems faced by psychiatry in a governmental or other institutional context may take many forms, it inevitably derives from this fundamental issue.

Matthew said, "No man may serve two masters." Yet this is the heart of the dilemma faced by the psychotherapist who is both employee and healer. As an employee, the therapist has clear obligations to his employer which may well be consistent with the interests of his patient, but when they are not, he is faced with a serious conflict. The most extreme and best publicized example of this dilemma is the role of psychiatry in the Soviet Union, where considerable controversy has been created. Where all psychiatrists serve the state and the interests of the state are put above those of the individual, the therapists' obligations are clear-cut. What has happened in the USSR is that the Soviet psychiatrist, faced with the conflict between serving the interest of the state and that of the patient has simply resolved the issue in favor of the state (Shestack, 1976). From the standpoint of the state there is little or no distinction between political dissent and social deviancy, and the tools of psychiatry—including involuntary hospitalization—are viewed as legitimate means for inducing behavioral change, especially social conformity if it is deemed in the interest of society as a whole.

While it is easy to single out the Soviet Union for attention because the position there is extreme and relatively crystalized, and because of America's general antipathy toward their poltical system, there is evidence that psychiatry is used to varying degrees as an instrument of the state in many countries, including particularly South Africa and several countries in Latin America. Even in this country, during the Viet Nam War, political dissenters who were sent to federal prisons were frequently given psychiatric labels as a way of trying to discredit them with other prisoners, and to allow more restrictive control of their behavior.

In most instances in this country the problems faced by the psychiatrists are of far lesser consequence. Thomas Szasz (1963) has pointed
out, however, that if a psychiatrist tries to serve society and a patient
simultaneously, society's needs generally take precedence, and the patient's welfare is inevitably jeopardized. The pressure exerted on the
therapist in favor of the institution's needs, whether governmental or
other, may be subtle and often vigorously denied by both the therapist
and the institution. Yet, no psychiatrist who works for an institution,
whether it is a college, a governmental agency, or a corporation, is completely free from coercive influence, or truly able to give his undivided
commitment to his patients.

Reimbursement for Services

An important factor influencing the nature of the therapist-patient relationship is the manner in which the therapist is reimbursed for his services. In a one-to-one relationship where the patient is paying for the
treatment he receives, there is no question as to who has the therapist's
allegiance. Once, however, some entity other than the patient is paying
for those services, the obligations of the therapist are inevitably divided.
Even when the payment is from an insurance company the perspective
of the therapist changes. In 1950 insurance payments covered a little
more than 30 percent of all health care costs; now they cover nearly 70
percent of health care bills. Attitudes particularly change if, for instance,
the reimbursement rate for the individual patient is below the therapist's
customary fee. When the therapist is salaried, and his income is not
directly dependent upon the number of patients he sees, or on the
manner in which he treats them, but rather upon maintaining good
relations with his superiors, his allegiance to his patients will be in severe
jeopardy, even if there is no direct interference with the manner in
which he conducts the therapy. The extent of his independence will be
dependent upon the degree to which the traditional Hippocratic values
have been inculcated into his own value system. Some physicians retain a
remarkable degree of commitment to their patients and resist many of
the pressures to switch their allegiance. They can never, however, maintain complete independence. Over time, many just find it easier to suc-
cumb to the urge to protect their own vested interests, and end up seeing
their responsibility to their patients as only secondary to their role in
their institutions. The therapist employed by an institution, whether in
private industry or government, is going to be substantially influenced
by his own sense of self-preservation and his first concern will be to keep
his job, maintain his income, and avoid the wrath of his superiors.

    It is perhaps worth looking at what it is that most institutions require of their employee therapists that may create conflicts in the care of patients. Every agency, whether a university, a corporation, or a part of the government, wants to maintain stability. Neither corporations nor government agencies want to hire or promote an individual who might bring about drastic change within the organizations (Halleck, 1971). This is particularly true if the person appears to be sufficiently nonconformist as to ignore the established way of doing things, or the existing chain of command. They are willing to use psychiatrists to help maintain corporate or community stability, and to encourage the maximum degree of conformity.

Stigma and Employment

The stigma associated with mental illness makes the issue of hiring of particular significance in the governmental or corporate setting. While cancer, venereal disease, and in the past tuberculosis, have been physical conditions which carried with them a certain social opprobrium, they do not compare with mental illness in terms of the shame and pervasive prejudice that is engendered. Merely to have seen a psychiatrist would have been at one time and in some places still is enough to place a person's future career in severe jeopardy, to cause them to be ostracized by their fellow workers, and to put them in a position of feeling constantly on the defensive. In some instances for an employee to have a member of his family receive psychiatric care, especially his wife, could cause serious problems with his employer. What is different about mental illness is that it is the treatment rather than the disease that evokes the prejudice. The emotionally disturbed individual may be accepted as eccentric or strange, but once he has a clinical label, is seeing a psychiatrist or psychologist, or particularly if he is hospitalized, he is ostracized and may become the focus of fear and suspicion.

In recent years, owing to the vigorous education programs launched by the National Mental Health Association and other groups, and the willingness of various public figures, especially some people with drinking problems to discuss their experiences publicly, the stigmatization of mental illness has been significantly diminished. It does, however, remain a serious problem causing a difficult dilemma for professionals in the field. On principle we decry the stigma associated with mental illness, and urge that those with such problems should be completely open and not seek to hide their difficulties. At the same time we admonish employers to ignore a history of mental illness in making personnel decisions. Unfortunately, while it is easy to generalize, we are faced with a very different situation when dealing with the problems of one individual. However much we may decry the prejudice and stigma, it *is* very real, and we run the risk of making our patients the victims of our own social protest if we do not accept what they are up against. The reality is that an individaul applying for a job is likely to be at a distinct disadvantage if the employer knows that he or she has received professional care for mental illness. Patients frequently ask therapists whether they should disclose their history of emotional problems when applying for a job. The therapist may know that such a disclosure could well be the sole justification for denying the patient a job, yet can hardly recommend that they lie. While each case is different, most therapists tend to encourage their patients to be strictly accurate in filling out application forms or in interviews, but to keep the information they divulge to a minimum, volunteering no details for which they are not specifically asked. While an employer has the right to inquire about the general health status of an applicant, the potential employee enjoys a certain right to privacy as he or she would in not being obliged to volunteer the clinical details of a physical condition, for instance with a urological or gynecological condition. The problem faced by the potential employee who has a history of mental illness, or is currently in therapy, is that while employers can make a reasonably accurate assessment of the impact on job performance of an appendectomy or a broken leg, they tend, through ignorance, to overestimate the decrement in performance which may be caused by emotional problems. Exposure to unfamiliar diagnoses, clinical terminology, and particularly awareness that an individual has been hospitalized, are likely to cause a disproportionate adverse reaction in the employer who knows little about mental illness.

It is legitimate, some would argue, for an employer to take mental illness into account as part of the evaluation of a potential employee. Particularly in the private sector where the survival of a company can be dependent upon the ability to make profits, and to maintain the highest performance level of its staff, they have the right to hire only those people who appear to have no liabilities. No one, for instance, would argue against the right of a company to ask if a person they were considering hiring as a driver suffered from black-out spells. Similarly, it is clear that certain psychological conditions will reduce an individual's performance level, and in such cases as a history of manic depressive psychosis, alcoholism, or past suicide attempts, a certain risk factor realistically exists when such an individual is hired. The key issue is not whether past or present mental illness should be taken into account in evaluating a potential employee, but rather that it should be considered in the appropriate context, and given only the weight in the final decision that it realistically warrants. Having received professional help for an emotional problem should not in itself, for instance, be grounds for rejecting an applicant. In fact, such an individual may be more healthy than the person who lacks the insight to recognize he has problems and needs help.

The ideal situation would be one in which personnel officers and others involved in hiring are fully familiar with various mental health problems, and are able to place them in the proper perspective without prejudice as with most physical ailments. Although a certain amount can be achieved by specific education programs for corporate and governmental personnel officers, and by encouraging these institutions to hire mental health professionals to assist in the assessment of applicants, the major problem remains the need to change the attitudes of society in general. It is unrealistic to expect those involved in hiring, whether in government or the private sector, to move too far ahead of the rest of society. Tremendous progress has been made in the last ten years in changing public attitudes, and in reducing the stigma associated with mental illness. Interestingly this change has been significantly facilitated by concurrent movements to reduce prejudice in hiring minorities, women, and the physically handicapped. Efforts to educate the public, together with the passage of various antidiscrimination laws through the Congress, have had the effect of sensitizing the American people in general to the injustice of allowing bias against any one characteristic or feature to be the overriding factor in denying a person employment.

While the situation has improved, the prejudice against the mentally ill remains strong, and the education process is far from complete. Only through continuing efforts to reduce the stigma, especially in smaller cities and communities, will the person with a history of mental illness be guaranteed that it is not jeopardizing their employment opportunities.

Confidentiality

The maintenance of confidentiality is fundamental to the full range of ethical concerns in the treatment of the mentally ill. It takes on a special significance in the institutional setting of government or industry. Fear of losing their job, compromising promotion opportunities, or mere embarrassment among fellow workers may be a strong inhibiting factor for individuals seeking help for emotional problems.

Until relatively recently most health insurance programs did not provide coverage for mental illness, and while federal employees now have such coverage, many employees in the private sector do not. While the provision of coverage for mental illness has provided access to treatment for many people who could not otherwise afford it, it has at the same time created serious new difficulties with regard to confidentiality. There is normally no way that an employee can take advantage of that coverage without other people in the organization being aware of it. This may only involve people in the personnel department, or it may involve one's immediate supervisors. In many instances a diagnosis must be supplied in order for the therapist to be paid. The employee not only loses the right to his own privacy, he also loses control over who has access to this information, and the extent to which it may be used to his detriment. In general those dealing with such information are aware of its sensitivity and are extremely discrete about the manner in which it is handled. There is, however, no protection against those who do seek to misuse the information, or fail to protect its confidentiality. These are usually not health professionals but individuals who do not necessarily have any sense of ethical obligation to treat the information with discretion. There are also those employers who feel they have a legitimate right to know about the health problems, including the emotional difficulties, of their employees.

In recent years there has been steadily increasing concern about the handling of health records with insurance companies and quality assurance agents, researchers and statisticians, the government, the courts, employers, credit companies, banks, and life insurance companies having growing access to health records which they regarded as essential to make necessary administrative decisions. In 1976 the National Commission on the Confidentiality of Health Records was created to monitor and to advocate the confidentiality of health records and to develop guidelines that would protect the right of confidentiality while allowing the necessity of access.

For all the talk about protecting confidentiality, the evidence suggests that we are not being very successful, and that professionals in the field are not protecting records the way they should. In his testimony before the Senate Watergate Committee, John Erlichman referred to the break-in at the office of Dr. Louis Fielding, Daniel Ellsberg's psychiatrist, and said that "it was well known to all lawyers that it was very simple to get hold of any medical records by many other means, that it was unnecessary to be involved in any break-in of a doctor's office." A company called Factual Services Inc. was advertising its services in 1976 to obtain medical records without authorization for lawyers who had only to supply an individual's name. This firm was prosecuted by the State of California and in the course of the investigation it emerged that at least fifty-five insurance companies had been involved with this operation which was stealing records from psychiatrists, physicians, and hospitals all over America. With the potential for disclosure so great it is hardly surprising that there is such a great degree of concern.

In a government or corporate setting where the competition among ambitious young professionals may be intense, fear about disclosure that they are receiving treatment for mental health problems, whether justified or not, can be considerable. Concern centers particularly, not on holding their present positions, but how such disclosure is likely to affect their ability to compete in the future for promotions. The question of confidentiality can assume enormous importance both in their own minds and in reality. For some, the fear that awareness by peers or superiors that they were receiving professional help can be so great that they prefer not to use the insurance coverage to which they are entitled and choose instead to pay out of their own pockets. In most instances, these already highly successful individuals have relatively minor problems, and are seeking treatment to improve their performance still further, or to alleviate emotional discomfort that they feel as a result of their present adjustment. The fear is that the magnitude of their problems will be misinterpreted, and that questions may be raised, about either their judgment or their future ability to perform. Under such circumstances their fears are probably amply justified, especially in the corporate setting where substantially less justification is required for adverse personnel decisions that are influenced by access to confidential information than is the case in government.

Where treatment is received from a practitioner outside the government or corporate setting, the concerns of the employee are limited largely to a worry that others will find out that they are receiving professional help, or at most that a diagnosis will appear in their files to which an uncertain number of people might have access. For the person who receives professional care from a therapist employed by the organization for which he works the risk with regard to confidentiality is comparably greater.

Two different settings need to be considered. First, government-operated treatment facilities, either hospitals or outpatient programs, which serve the general public should be regarded as being in a special category. Although financed or run by the government, they differ relatively little from private institutions as far as ethics in practice are concerned, being in general self-contained medical entities that are protected from government intervention. A patient who seeks treatment in a community mental health center or a state hospital will generally be assured the same degree of confidentiality as if he or she went to a private clinic. Patients who are hospitalized under court commitment do not enjoy the same protection as far as the disclosure of necessary information to the court is concerned. The manner, however, in which they are handled and the extent to which information is disclosed is carefully prescribed by the courts creating little dilemma for the therapist whose role is relatively clear-cut. Although abuses and injustices have inevitably occurred, the procedure is designed primarily for the interests of the patient, and what is lost in terms of confidentiality one hopes balanced by a broader protection of the patient's rights, and those of society when an individual is to be forcibly detained.

The second circumstance is that in which a government or corporate employee is provided treatment within the organization by health professionals who are themselves employees of the same organization. The patient faces several potential problems:

1. Disclosure of the fact that he or she has a problem and is receiving professional care.
2. Inadvertent leakage of confidential information by those who have access to the clinical records, or even by the therapists themselves.
3. Deliberate sharing of confidential material by the therapist with others in the organization for them to use in making decisions with regard to the patient that may be in the patient's interest, but which are most likely to be first and foremost in the interest of the organization.

Apart from the dilemma the therapist faces with regard to his obligation to preserve the confidentiality of information about his patients, he may be subjected to other, more subtle pressures. Therapists will very frequently be asked to make what are basically administrative decisions that they should not have to make. Rather than ask the therapist merely to evaluate or treat a patient, administrators will ask him to determine whether the patient should be discharged or promoted, thereby relieving them of the responsibility for making the administrative decision themselves. Therapists who work for corporations or government must also guard against imposing an institutional value system on their patients in the course of therapy. The values of the institution can often be conveyed in an unconscious and unintentional way.

In the federal government the direct treatment of mental health problems by the therapists in the employ of the government is relatively unusual. The most significant situation of this type is in the armed services. This, however, is a special situation and military psychiatry should perhaps be looked at as completely distinct from any other therapeutic setting. There is no question in the military that the therapist is serving the interests of the organization. His mandate is "to conserve the fighting strength," and military needs clearly supersede individual rights in the traditional therapist-patient relationship. Most therapists in the military do adhere, to their best ability, to the same ethical standards with regard to confidentiality that they would observe in a civilian setting. At any time, however, when there is a conflict between the interests of the patient and that of the military, the latter takes precedent. Clinical records in the military are a part of the individual's total military records. There have been instances where clinicians have sought to deny non-medical personnel access to patients' files, but they have invariably failed. The result is that most military psychiatrists must act judiciously in determining what to commit to paper, and what to keep to themselves in their treatment of military personnel. Apart from the issue of confidentiality, they face other dilemmas they would not have to face as civilians. Military psychiatrists are routinely involved in personnel and administrative decisions, particularly in the decision to expel tens of thousands of individuals from the military who are determined to be unsuitable or unfit for military service each year. In a judicial proceeding, a military psychiatrist takes his career in his hands when testifying as an expert witness if he does not support the position of the military.

An argument can be made that because of the special nature of the military, and because of society's need for such an institution, the normal individual rights that are guaranteed to a civilian American cannot be provided for someone on active duty. In the absence of a military draft, it is argued that anyone who enlists voluntarily relinquishes certain of his rights. Freedom of speech, the right to confidentiality, and certain judicial protections cannot be guaranteed in the military. It is also claimed that the ethical standards that govern psychiatric practice cannot be the same if the military is to function effectively.

Whatever the merits of these arguments, the military is of special interest because, with the possible exception of the federal prison system, it represents the most extreme example of the conflict in American society between the right of the individual in treatment for psychological problems, and the interests of the institution to which he and his therapist belong. At the same time the military is also perhaps less hypocritical than other organizations for which psychiatrists work, in that the priority of the psychiatrist's responsibility to the military over that to his patient is explicit and clear-cut. In other government or corporate settings the question of dual allegiance is always there, but is frequently denied or obscured. If one looks at those institutional demands that are so evidently placed on the military psychiatrist, they become much easier to detect in other settings.

There are two other places worth mentioning where direct services are delivered in the federal government. The Central Intelligence Agency, while it uses private psychiatrists to treat some of its employees, also has a staff of psychiatrists who treat those who work for the Agency, particularly in emergency situations. Because of the unique nature of the organization's work, the psychiatrist who is treating an employee of the Central Intelligence agency is often put in the interesting situation of having to protect not only the confidentiality needs of the patient but also those of the institution. He is faced not merely with the usual situation where there is concern that the employer will violate the confidences of the patient, but also with the reverse where there is fear that the disturbed employee will betray the confidences of the organization.

The Central Intelligence Agency is such a unique setting, and involves so few mental health professionals, that it does not warrant extensive discussion, yet it does pose a most unusual set of ethical concerns for those who provide clinical services under its auspices. In addition, an even smaller number of psychiatrists and psychologists are actually involved in the Agency's program operations and research. While their role and the activities in which they are involved are classified, questions have been raised in the general press in recent years about the ethical aspects of their activities.

The State Department provides clinical care for its employees to a limited degree, especially on an emergency basis. A matter of major conflict in recent years has been the failure of the department to extend the same services to foreign service officers' dependents. It has provided an interesting dilemma because in many instances the foreign service officer's problems may involve his family more than him, and particularly if members of his family are dysfunctional overseas, his work may be affected as much as if the problem were his own.

Treatment of the Politician

Special problems exist for politicians who receive care for mental health problems. By far the most publicized event of this type in recent years was the disclosure that Senator Tom Eagleton had not only been hospitalized for mental illness but had received electroshock therapy; the disclosure forced Eagleton to withdraw as the Democratic Vice Presidential nominee with Senator George McGovern in 1972. Although Eagleton had been treated with great concern for confidentiality, with his records kept under a pseudonym, once he became the center of public attention, not only was the fact of his treatment leaked, but reporters even obtained unauthorized secret access to his hospital records.

Until relatively recently, there was a tradition among reporters, especially in Washington, never to report on the private lives of public figures in the areas of philandering, mental illness, or excessive alcohol use. This tacit policy has dramatically changed for many reasons. In part it has to do with the shifting emphasis in the media not merely to report the news, but to try to influence events. A relationship that was once regarded as like a "gentleman's club" between political reporters and politicians, has changed dramatically with the entrance into the profession of many women and young reporters who grew up in the 1960s with little reverence for institutions or for authority in general. An attitude of "no holds barred" has grown up. This changing attitude has been further accentuated most recently by the events surrounding Watergate. Not only was a new ethic emphasizing total exposure and openness created, but many reporters, particularly those who were young and ambitious, recognized that investigative reporting with the unearthing of even trivial facts about public figures, if they proved embarrassing, could give the reporter immediate recognition and success. For most reporters now, there are no areas that are "off limits," and any personal information about a public figure, even if it would be damaging to that person's political career, is considered fair game. The libel laws leave public figures effectively without recourse against reporters, or against publications which do not adhere to the truth or which distort the facts. While the major national publications express concern about the overall accuracy of stories they run, there are many less reputable, but still mass-circulation, publications which make little effort to conceal that the extent of their readership's gullibility rather than the accuracy of the material is the primary determinant of the content of their stories. These publications tend to emphasize, in particular, licit or illicit romantic liaisons, health problems including mental health, and other sensitive aspects of the lives of public figures, often basing their stories on rumor or speculation.

An interesting dilemma has been created in that one reason for the greater willingness of reporters to write about mental illness and alcoholism has to do with the relative success in destigmatizing these problems. Those of us in the mental health field cannot very well tell the press that mental illness and alcoholism should be treated no differently from any physical illness, and then be upset because they then report on these subjects in an open manner. Painful though it may be for the individuals involved, the press may in fact be performing an important service in the long run in desensitizing the general public to the shame previously associated with these human problems, even if their short-term motivations are much less benign.

The diminished reluctance of the press to publicize the personal problems of public figures seems to have had two effects. First, it has forced many prominent people to acknowledge their problems publicly. This has been far more true with alcoholism than with other forms of mental illness. Senator Harold Hughes, Congressman Wilbur Mills, Senator Herman Talmadge, Betty Ford, and Joan Kennedy have all been willing to talk about their difficulties with alcohol. For the American people, alcoholism is easier to accept than mental illness, in large part because of the moral element that is still associated in the public mind with this disease. The recovered alcoholic who is willing to admit his problems is accepted as a repentant sinner who has confessed his sins. The public admission is seen as part of the punishment they must undergo after which the American people will be willing to forgive them. Although we in the mental health profession like to think of this as reflecting increasing acceptance of alcoholism as a disease, it is probably still far from being accepted as such by the bulk of the population.

Although some individuals, most notably Betty Ford, have publicly acknowledged that they have been in psychotherapy, the public is not yet willing to accept mental illness, in general, in a public figure without penalizing that individual in some way. Considerably more time and education will be necessary before the public can accept that a person may have received treatment for an emotional problem and assess what effect that might have on his or her ability to perform their job as an elected, or appointed official in realistic terms. It is perhaps instructive to look at what has happened in the last thirty years with regard to divorced individuals seeking public office. At one time it was virtually impossible for a divorced man or woman to seek major public office. Attitudes have, however, changed so much that it is now not only no bar to holding office, but it is not even considered worthy of raising as an issue. Scarce mention was even made of Ronald Reagan's divorce in the 1980 presidential race. It may be expecting too much to think that the issue of treatment for mental illness could be so easily neutralized, but it is clear that the potential for considerably greater acceptance is there.

The second reaction to the changed behavior of the press has been one of even greater secretiveness, and even greater concern for the protection of confidentiality. While it is easy for those in public office to deplore the stigma associated with mental illness and to advocate total frankness, most individuals do not want to jeopardize their own careers by in any way being a test case. Careful concealment of hospitalization, the use of pseudonyms, and the seeking out of therapists whose record on confidentiality is untarnished are considered as important as ever. Even relatively routine health problems are kept by some individuals in the closest confidence. A physician who treats one member of the United States Senate told me, "You don't think the Senator or his family ever get prescriptions filled in their own name, do you?" adding that if I repeated his statement he would deny it. It becomes a vicious cycle in which those in the best position to take the leadership in reducing the stigma, and who in many instances have done so as a general principle, are the most responsive to the fact that the stigma persists when it comes to their own and their families' personal lives.

In small communities it may be virtually impossible for a therapist to conceal an emotional problem from which they or a member of their family are suffering. There are so many potential sources from which such information can become disseminated, ranging from pharmacists to members of the individual's own staff, among whom unexplained absences can lead to immediate speculation. Anonymity is much easier to obtain, even for public figures, in the large cities. There are therapists in most cities, and especially in Washington, whose practices are heavily comprised of individuals holding sensitive positions, and who are highly skilled at maintaining secrecy with regard to their patients. Separate exits and entranced to their offices are routine, so that arriving and departing patients never see each other. In addition, scrupulous care is used in making sure that their secretaries or anyone else who has to know the patient is there, guards the information assiduously. One danger the therapist who sees many such individuals must guard against is revealing to other patients the extent of their knowledge in a particular area, which by inference would suggest that they could only have obtained it from another patient.

When hospitalization is necessary, maintaining confidentiality is markedly more difficult merely because of the number of people who have to be given access to sensitive information. The urge to brag to friends or family about their contact with a hospitalized celebrity may be overwhelming, particularly for those who are not professionals. There are, however, many well-established hospitals which have had extensive experience handling public figures, where the entire staff is fully aware of the need for confidentiality, and where many individuals have been treated successfully without any public awareness, and without their careers being jeopardized in any appreciable way.

Security Clearance

A unique problem exists in the federal government—the need for security clearances. Security clearances provided at different levels allow individuals access to information with varying degrees of sensitivity. While this system is necessary to protect certain information, it is generally of questionable value in its present broad application, being largely an anachronism from the hysteria of the McCarthy era. Extensive background investigations are made routinely on individuals appointed to senior positions in the federal government. This includes attempts to determine various aspects of their personal life, including the details of any treatment they may have had for emotional problems. The background investigations have recently come under serious criticism, because the questions asked of acquaintances about the life styles of women were significantly different from those asked about male appointees, implying that a radically different set of standards was being applied to each sex as to what was considered acceptable by the civil service and F.B.I. investigators. In addition, there is very little evidence that there is any correlation between the information collected in these very expensive investigations, and the degree to which a person subsequently poses any real security risk. In fact the overwhelming majority of individuals who receive security clearances, even top-secret clearances, rarely see any information that could be considered of any truly sensitive nature from a security standpoint. In addition the system in many ways serves as an incumbrance, because so many documents which deal with the most routine matters are given top-secret classifications.

Once a security clearance is completed, it is passed to an individual's superior with attention being drawn to whatever areas the investigators feel are noteworthy from a security standpoint. These relate usually to issues of life style, legal problems, and treatment for mental illness. It is then up to the superior to decide whether or not the individual should be given a security clearance. The superior can approve the clearance, can specifically deny it, or can procrastinate and take no action. Both of the latter two courses effectively preclude the individual from being able to carry out his or her job because they will be denied access to even routine documents and will be barred from many meetings.

Now, under the Freedom of Information Act a person can obtain copies of the report the F.B.I. has prepared on them, and they have the right to try to refute any inaccuracies that appear. This is, however, a difficult and time-consuming activity. They have no recourse with regard to any negative decision their superior may make on their clearance, because there are no clear bases on which the decision is made, other than the superior's general subjective opinion. The problem is worsened by the fact that rather than flatly deny a clearance, the superior can claim for months that it is still under study, thereby making it impossible for the employee either to function effectively in the job, or to come to grips with why he has not received the security clearance.

Apart from the clearance itself, the nature of the background investigations can undo all other efforts to protect the confidentiality of the individual in therapy. The background investigators will ask the therapist for information on the nature of the individual's problems. Obviously the therapist will reveal only what the patient authorizes him or her to release. Too great a reluctance to reveal confidential information can, however, be reflected in a damaging way in the final background report.

For the most part background investigations are treated with the utmost sensitivity, and overwhelmingly security clearances are given regardless of what the investigations turn up. They still, however, pose problems on a number of scores. First, the whole process is of questionable value. That an individual has risen successfully in his career to a point where he is considered for appointment to a senior position where he will be dealing with sensitive material is in itself a far better guarantee than any screening that any background investigation can provide that he will treat it with the greatest discretion. Second, at a time when we are particularly concerned about an individual's right to privacy, to put a detailed account of the most sensitive issues concerning an individual's private life in writing, and then without necessarily guaranteeing its accuracy, to provide it to a person's superior so that potentially arbitrary and detrimental decisions can be based on it, makes little sense. Third, and in some ways most important, it has a chilling effect on the willing-

ness of individuals who need professional help for mental health problems to seek it.

The Future

If present trends continue, it can be anticipated that the coming years
will see a further reduction in the stigma associated with mental illness.
Both in government and in the corporate world this should lead to a
greater ability for those with mental health problems to be hired, and for
this issue to play a steadily diminishing role in determining whether an
individual is promoted in competition with other employees. It is hoped
that the role of the mental health professional will become less one in
which he is hired to protect the institutional interests of an organization,
but more one in which he can play an educational role in helping employers to recognize the effects of mental illness appropriately. The
ethical pressures now placed on the mental health professional working
in such a setting should decline correspondingly.

The relative lack of concern by professional organizations in the
mental health field with the question of ethics in practice remains a
problem. It is startling that, for instance, the American Psychiatric Association had not formulated a code of ethics until 1973. While this
organization even now pays lip service to the question of ethics and such
specific issues as the patients' right to privacy, it is inordinately cautious
about taking a definite position in any specific instance. This is in part
because psychiatry itself as a profession remains subjected to a degree of
bias, being neither fully accepted in society nor in the mainstream of
medicine. As a result there is considerable concern about further
jeopardizing the position of the organization by entering into any areas
of controversy. If, however, public attitudes toward the mentally ill are
to change, and if we are to protect patients from the increasing incur-
sions upon their records, then the mental health professionals must
speak up more forcefully, as for instance reporters do whenever they
feel the confidentiality of their sources is in jeopardy. In particular, the
professional organizations must come to grips with the issue of therapists
in institutional settings. A code of ethics that could guide both the
therapist and his employers in the organization would be an immense
asset.

Only a change in public attitudes will truly neutralize the difficulties
faced by the politician who has mental health problems. If anything, the
intensity of press inquiry is likely to increase, and anything about which a
politician can be made to feel embarrassed is likely to be used against
him. The only way this will change will be when, as with divorce, such
information is no longer considered newsworthy.

In any therapeutic session the responsibility ultimately lies not with any set of ethics or public attitude, but with the therapists themselves. It is what they regard as ethical practice, and their sense of responsibility to their patients, that truly make the difference.

REFERENCES

BAIN, A. *Moral science: A compendium of ethics.* New York: American Book Co., 1869.

BALDWIN, J. M. *Social and ethical interpretations in mental development: A study in social psychology.* London: Macmillan, 1906.

BOURNE, P. G. The Hippocratic revolt. *Ramparts,* 1967, **6,** 57–58.

BREGGIN, P. R. Psychotherapy as applied ethics. *Psychiatry,* 1971, **34,** 59–74.

HALLECK, S. *The politics of therapy.* New York: Science House, 1971.

KONOLD, D. E. History of the codes of medical ethics, in W. T. Reich (ed.), *Encyclopedia of bioethics.* New York: Free Press, 1979.

MOORE, R. A. Ethics in the practice of psychiatry—Origins, functions, models and enforcement. *American Journal of Psychiatry,* 1978, **135,** 2.

SHESTACK, J. J. Psychiatry and the dilemma of dual loyalties. In *Medical, moral and legal issues in mental health care.* Baltimore: Williams & Wilkins, 1976.

SHORE, M., and GOLANN, S. E. *Current ethical issues in mental health.* Washington, D.C.: Government Printing Office, 1973.

SZASZ, T. *Law, liberty and psychiatry.* New York: Macmillan, 1963.

Ethical Issues in Psychotherapy Research

George Stricker

Research in psychotherapy represents an intersection of the scientific enterprise with the helping professions, and this research is subject to ethical considerations from both areas. The treatment which is under scrutiny must itself conform to ethical principles, as embodied by one of a number of professional codes of ethics, such as that of the American Psychological Association, and the research methodology which determines the nature of the scrutiny must also conform to this code, as well as to a separate code of ethical principles for research.

The boundaries of this chapter will be set by a specific concern for the research activity. The ethics of the psychotherapy conducted in field studies will not be addressed, as this has been fully considered elsewhere in this volume. Issues that arise from the methodology of field and analogue studies, and any treatment offered in field studies which is not naturally existing but is offered in order to be studied, will be addressed.

One further area which will be excluded from extended consideration, but which is of great relevance to the research investigator, is the legal sanctions governing research activity. This is an ever-changing area which has generated volumes of literature in its own right and cannot be easily summarized since it varies from state to state. It should, however, be noted that ethics and law are distinctly different areas. A code of ethics represents a profession's internal attempt at self-regulation. It is educational in intent and describes what the professional should and should not do. Law represents the external imposition of constraints, and statutes and regulations contain a set of prescriptions and proscriptions which describe what the professional must and must not do.

The confluence of research and treatment activities and goals will often redound to the mutual benefit of each. Research can be stimulated by ideas which derive from treatment issues, while treatment can be informed by research findings. On the other hand, however, there are occasional conflicts which arise from the varying objectives of what Blumgart (1970) refers to as the therapeutic alliance and the scientific alliance. The relationship between the therapist and the patient results in a therapeutic alliance, the prime concern of which is the welfare of the

403

patient. The relationship between the experimenter and the subject results in a scientific alliance for which the primary objective is the discovery of new knowledge. While the primary aim of one alliance may be the
subsidiary objective of the other, priorities do differ. This conflict can be
most heightened in studies where the therapist is also the principal investigator, and the patient is also a research subject.

It is clear that the therapist-investigator and the patient-subject are
participants in the research enterprise. It is not always as clear that both
the profession and the state are also involved in shaping the nature of
the research investigation, and that they occasionally represent different
interests. This may have been illustrated most clearly when Chester M.
Southam was elected to the presidency of the American Association for
Cancer Research just three years after New York State had suspended
but stayed the suspension of his license to practice medicine because of
his role in the Jewish Chronic Disease Hospital Case (Katz, 1972).

A United States Senate Committee studying behavior modification
(1974) highlighted the discrepancy when they commented, "The problem of ethical experimentation is the product of the unresolved conflict
between two strongly held values: the dignity and integrity of the individual, and the freedom of scientific inquiry." This statement puts the
research enterprise in direct opposition to human dignity, an unfortunate polarization which has set the tone for many of the legal constraints
placed on researchers. The need for these constraints follows from some
gross abuses, often in the medical and pharmacological area, such as the
Tuskogee study and the thalidomide tragedy. It is not limited to this
area, however, as behavioral scientists who use research methods that
employ gratuitous deception are not free from culpability. Although the
impact of these procedures was not sufficiently gross to call down legal
action in and of itself, professional responsibility also was not well developed enough to institute appropriate safeguards.

Hershey and Miller (1976), in a discussion of the relationship of
ethics and law to research, noted that "all regulation of activity conducted by humans can be taken to denote doubt that ethical and legal
requirements will be met solely through the exercise of individual integrity, particularly when it involves contact with others, which has a potential for exploitation" (p. 10). It is clear that ethics and law both represent
constraints on the freedom of the investigator. One traditional approach
to ethics, unfortunately, has been what May (1975) has called philanthropic ethics. Under this arrogant system falls a relationship in which
physicians decide what their duties are, and patients are obliged to be
thankful for services received. This tradition no longer suffices. In this
area, as in other areas where a profession assumes the responsibility for
self-regulation, it is unlikely that law will be necessary if ethics are effec-

tive in protecting the public, and it is a certainty that if ethics fail, laws will be promulgated.

Historical Perspective

A historical perspective, which is most instructive in supplying an appropriate context for this chapter, must be concerned with the general issue of research procedures. There have not been any landmark cases involving psychotherapy research, but the establishment of ethical codes and procedural regulations which govern such research has arisen from a series of medical and pharmacological activities. Case law in this area is scattered and inconsistent and it is largely irrelevant, since the courts usually use the term "experimentation" to refer to a deviation from standard medical practice rather than to a systematic research investigation, and the remedy, therefore, usually lies in action for torts such as malpractice, negligence, or battery. It should be noted, however, that therapeutic experimentation, which supposedly pursues the welfare of patients, is held to a less strict standard of accountability than is nontherapeutic experimentation, which is primarily concerned with the generation of knowledge. The development of elaborate ethical codes and regulatory procedures followed from the publicity surrounding dramatic instances of gross abuse. For this reason, I will first review four landmark instances of such abuse, and follow the discussion with a brief review of some of the codes and procedures which were developed in response to these cases. This section will draw heavily on material presented by Katz (1972), Hershey and Miller (1976), and Annas, Glantz, and Katz (1977).

The watershed in this area is the case of the *United States* v. *Karl Brandt*, who was the principal defendant among twenty-three physicians placed on trial at Nuremberg for their role in Nazi experiments with concentration camp inmates. Some of the defendants were internationally prominent scientific investigators, some of the experiments were well designed by objective standards of scientific inquiry, and all were noteworthy for their brutality and atrocity, which resulted in the extreme suffering and often the death of the research subject. Among the topics of study were such matters as the limits of human endurance and existence at high altitudes, the most effective means of treating people who had been frozen, which required severe chilling of the subjects, the treatment of various diseases such as malaria, epidemic jaundice, typhus, and infected wounds, all of which involved infecting subjects, and experiments about the effects of different poisons. Sixteen of the twenty-three defendants were found guilty, and seven were sentenced to death. More importantly, however, the trial gave rise to the promulgation of the Nuremberg Code, the first extant comprehensive articulation of research ethics.

The next major exemplar was the thalidomide tragedy, which came to light in 1962. Unlike the other cases, this did not involve scientific investigation, but the ramifications following its uncovering have great import for research endeavors. Thalidomide is a drug which was used widely in Europe, and was introduced in this country on an experimental basis. After many years it was discovered that its use by pregnant women led to gross neonatal deformities, and the inadequacies of the procedure for determining safety and efficacy postponed the discovery of this consequence until after thousands of deformed children had been born. The courts have provided some financial recompense, but there is no remedy for the needless suffering that has been caused. As a result of this scandal, the Food and Drug Administration introduced far stricter and more well-defined procedures governing product experimentation than had existed previously, including a specification of a legal requirement for consent.

Shortly after the thalidomide scandal, in an atmosphere already sensitized to the abuses of research, widespread publicity was given to a program being conducted at the Jewish Chronic Disease Hospital in Brooklyn. Twenty-two chronically ill and debilitated patients were given a hypodermic injection of suspensions containing cells from cultures of human cancer tissue. The patients had not been informed that live cancer cells were being used, or that the purpose of the experiment was to study the body's capacity to reject foreign cells, an objective that was far removed from the patient's therapeutic regimen. The hearings that resulted from this case led to a suspension of the medical license of two physicians, a suspension which was stayed on conditions of probation. It also crystallized the issue of proper consent and led to the adoption of far clearer policies about the experimenter's obligations to the subject.

The research abuse of longest standing is also the one which gained public recognition most recently. The Tuskegee study began in the 1930s, but its procedures only came to light in the early 1970s. It was a study of the natural course of untreated syphilis and required that treatment be withheld, even though the efficacy of penicillin therapy was widely known. Some subjects were even prevented from obtaining treatment in order to study the disease better. The study was discontinued amidst much furor in 1973, and many of the subjects received some relatively small (no more than $37,500) financial settlements. The study further underlined the need for proper review of research activities and clear enforcement of existing regulations.

While it is unlikely that research in psychotherapy could ever reach these scandalous levels, it is entirely possible for other treatment procedures with mental patients, such as drugs, electroshock therapy, and especially psychosurgery, to do so. In any case, the web of codes of ethics and government regulation that arose from these cases give shape to the arena within which psychotherapy research must be conducted.

In attempting to reach a basis for decision in the trial of the German physicians, the court applied natural law reasoning, spelling out ten principles which define what it considered the appropriate bounds for medical experimentation. These principles have come to be known as the Nuremberg Code. Although the code may be considered part of international law, particularly since it was adopted by the United Nations in 1946, its status in the United States is unclear, and it is only rarely cited in court decisions. Its importance lies in its position as the first systematic statement of research ethics, and its role as the basis of many other formulations of codes of ethics which either adopt or react to its provisions. The first principle of the Nuremberg Code spells out the conditions for informed consent, indicating that it must be competent, voluntary, informed, and understanding, and it does not permit any exceptions to this doctrine. The remainder of the code describes some of the further bounds of research activity, addressing such issues as the value of the research, the precautions taken to assure the safety of the subjects, the risk-benefit balance, the training of the experimenter, and the patient's right to withdraw from the experiment. These issues recur in all subsequent research codes, reinforcing the importance of the Nuremberg Code as the precursor of all current formulations of ethical principles.

A second major document in international law is the Declaration of Helsinki, a statement initially prepared by the World Medical Association in 1964. It provides guidelines for the performance of research which agree in some part with the Nuremberg Code, but which also depart from it in some crucial ways. The basic principles of the Declaration of Helsinki are consistent with the Nuremberg Code and refer to the training of the experimenter and the risk-benefit balance, noting the special caution that is indicated where the personality of the subject is liable to be altered. The declaration goes on, however, to distinguish between therapeutic and nontherapeutic clinical research, and establishes far stricter requirements for consent in nontherapeutic research. The Nuremberg Code did not draw this distinction and did not allow any deviations from the principle of informed consent. The Declaration of Helsinki also provides for proxy consent, an issue not addressed by the Nuremberg Code.

A number of professional and scientific associations have promulgated codes of ethics which deal with research activity in whole or in part. Many of these maintain the distinction between therapeutic and nontherapeutic research and, when they do, they hold nontherapeutic research to more stringent standards of accountability. In relation to psychotherapy research, this would suggest that patients in treatment would be considered subjects in therapeutic research, while subjects in analogue studies or in control groups would be considered subjects in nontherapeutic research. The most elaborate association statement of research ethics was promulgated in 1973 by the American Psychological Association. It will not be discussed at this point, but will be cited frequently in the next section, which considers specific ethical issues.

Prior to the 1960s, there was little statutory or agency regulation of research (Curran, 1970). The tradition was that experimentation, broadly defined, was performed at the personal risk of the therapist, with the patient having access to legal recourse through charges of malpractice or battery. The first exception of consequence was the action of the Food and Drug Administration following the thalidomide incident. The FDA introduced a legal requirement for informed consent procedures, and also required a demonstration of efficacy rather than solely harmlessness. There was a proviso that control subjects should be told that they were involved in an experiment, but need not be told what drug they were receiving.

Lack of compliance with this regulation, however, combined with the Jewish Chronic Disease Hospital case, led to the patient consent regulations of 1966. These were based on the Declaration of Helsinki and the Nuremberg Code, defined key statutory terms, and spelled out conditions for obtaining informed consent. They distinguished between therapeutic and nontherapeutic studies, and did not permit any exceptions in the case of nontherapeutic research. The only exception allowed for therapeutic research that is relevant to psychotherapy is the proviso that informed consent need not be obtained when the therapeutic procedure is in the patient's best interest. These regulations allowed controlled studies if the subject was told of the possibility that he might be used as a control, and it required that subjects be told of alternate forms of treatment if any were available.

The National Institutes of Health (NIH) is not a regulatory agency, but it is involved in the support of a national research program. In 1966, the NIH required institutional guarantees of compliance with ethics and research standards. They sought to protect the rights and welfare of subjects through obtaining informed consent and assessing the risks and potential benefits of a study. While this is a decentralized approach which places the initial burden on the individual institution, the study sections of the NIH, which grant research awards, also consider and weigh ethical issues. Although these guarantees of compliance only pertain to NIH-funded research, it has become commonplace for institutions to establish research committees in order to provide guarantees, and these committees will often review nonfunded research.

Thus, we can see that self-regulation, decentralized regulation, statutory regulation, and international law have combined to form an elaborate network designed to provide an approximation of the bounds of research which had been sought by the Nuremberg Tribunal. Some principles are universally agreed upon, while others are more nebulous and are still the subject of vigorous debate. The next section will consider some specific issues, particularly as they relate to psychotherapy research.

Current Ethical Issues

A consideration of the application of a code of ethics to research in psychotherapy requires that we define both research and ethics. Although the word tends to be used loosely by practitioners, research is a formal procedure designed to elicit knowledge which may be generalized. Attempts to understand a specific patient are not research activities, unless done in a framework which would produce wider implications. Tinkering with specific techniques is also not a research activity, unless it is done in a way that will systematically evaluate the effects of the new techniques. Thus, research must be a carefully designed endeavor, subject to methodological evaluation, and it differs from the day-to-day experimentation that may occur in a practitioner's office, which is subject to evaluation on clinical grounds.

Judging the ethical propriety of any research activity involves a prior statement of an ethical position, and this can lead to wide disagreement, depending upon whether the ethical system is one of relativism or absolutism. Most organizational codes of ethics are relativistic in that they seek the solution of ethical dilemmas in a risk-benefit framework, within which the value of the research is weighed against the possible risk it might create for the subject. Opponents of this position often refer to a Kantian position, decrying the use of the end to justify the means and preferring categorical prohibitions of potentially risk-producing activities.

There are a number of different paradigms for psychotherapy research which differ in the types of ethical issues they are likely to produce. The goal of the research may be stated in terms of the outcome, the process, or a combination of the two. Outcome studies focus on an evaluation of psychotherapy, while process studies address contingencies within the therapeutic situation. A more sophisticated study might focus on both issues and attempt to discern the effect of certain process variables on outcome. These studies, regardless of goal, might be done in either a naturalistic or an analogue setting. A naturalistic study capitalizes on existing psychotherapeutic relationships, usually has reasonable external validity in that results are generalizable, and may have problems in the area of internal validity, since research design is imposed after the fact. An analogue study brings the psychotherapeutic situation under laboratory control and studies some approximation of treatment, increasing the internal validity at the expense of external validity. Naturalistic studies have ethical problems in areas such as invasion of privacy, while analogue studies are more likely to involve some deception, two areas which can both be considered within the scope of informed consent. Naturalistic studies are more likely to use subjects whose disability raises questions about the nature of the consent, while analogues avoid this problem by using healthy, rational subjects, creating a difficulty with generalizability.

The National Institutes of Health distinguish among four categories of clinical research (Bartholome, 1977). These include research studies which conform to established and accepted standards of practice, research which deviates from accepted practice but is specifically aimed at alleviating the patient's condition, research which is related to the condition but from which the patient will not receive any direct benefit, and nontherapeutic research in which there is no intent to treat the patient's illness. Psychotherapy research can fall readily into the first two categories, in that evaluations of existing approaches to practice and of modifications to those approaches can be performed. It is difficult to imagine psychotherapy research within the third category, for if treatment is related to the patient's condition, the patient should be receiving some benefit. There is, however, a good deal of related research in the area of personality theory in which research will attempt to understand the patient's condition, but the patient will not receive benefit. The fourth category, in which there is no intent of treating the patient's difficulty, is a description of a control group. The four types of research have increasing likelihood of ethical problems. There are few problems when the patient is receiving standard treatment and is likely to benefit, while there are many problems when the patient's problems are recognized but go untreated.

With this brief introduction as a means of establishing a context, we can go on to examine a number of specific ethical issues which are likely to arise, and relate each one to the overall area of psychotherapy research.

Justification of Research

Before any concern about how research is conducted can be raised, the issue of whether or not it should be conducted must be addressed. While there are no spokesmen for the position that research should not be done, there are many who would suggest that some specific studies, regardless of their methodological adequacy, should not be done. The Nuremberg trials were responsive to this very issue. The code of ethics of the American Psychological Association (1973) makes it clear that the ultimate responsibility for this decision rests with the experimenter. The first two principles of the research code state that the investigator has personal responsibility for the ethical acceptability of the study and for the conduct of all participants to whom some research activity is delegated. In cases where there is any question of deviance from accepted standards, the investigator must seek the counsel of colleagues but cannot avoid the final responsibility for research decisions.

The first decision that must be made in determining whether or not a study is justified concerns the nature of the question that is raised by the project. If the question itself is not ethical, then the study should not be performed. The research performed in concentration camps provides us with an example of methodologically sound approaches to unethical questions. Within the framework of psychotherapy, comparisons among existing methods appear to be well within the bounds of ethics, but a decision as to whether a treatment is better than no treatment at all does raise an ethical issue, since it implies allowing some patients to remain untreated. The use of a control group adds to the scientific validity of a project, although the extent to which this is achievable in psychotherapy research is a complicated question which will be addressed in a later section. The willful withholding of treatment from needy patients, however, is not an ethical act, and to do so in the supposed service of scientific principles is a questionable activity. The one exception to this principle is in the case of scarce resources, so that a large number of patients would have to go untreated regardless of the demands of the research protocol. In such a situation an untreated control is necessitated by the unavailability of psychotherapists, and random assignment to treatment control groups is not only scientifically sound, but it is possible to argue that it is also morally proper.

If we have determined that the research question falls within the bounds of ethics, the next issue concerns the methodology of the study. The most clear statement relevant to this point has been made by the National Commission for the Protection of Human Subjects of Biomedical and Behavioral Research (1977). The commission clearly states that "Respect for human subjects requires the use of sound methodology appropriate to the discipline. The time and inconvenience requested of subjects should be justified by the soundness of the research and its design, even if no more than minimal risk is involved" (p. 3). This statement is tantamount to indicating that a study which is scientifically unsound is, of necessity, unethical. The American Academy of Pediatrics Committee on Drugs (1977) is in agreement with this position, and also feels that poor scientific design or uncontrolled experimentation is unethical. There are two interesting implications of this position, occurring at different ends of the research activity continuum. The first implication occurs in the planning stage and suggests that institutional review committees, which are empowered to make decisions about the ethics of studies submitted to them, should also consider methodological questions. Such committees currently address a variety of procedural issues, but they typically will not comment about substandard research methodology. If, however, such methodology constitutes prima facie evidence of unethical conduct, a review committee should not approve a study which does not meet high scientific standards. The second implication occurs at the end of the research process when the results of the study are submitted for publication. There is a lively debate as to whether or not journals should publish studies which have employed unethical procedures. If journals instructed their editorial reviewers to comment about ethical issues specifically, and if they clearly stated that they would reject any article, regardless of its findings, if it was ethically questionable, this would create additional pressure on the investigator to assure that standards of ethics were met. Additionally, if journals adopted higher standards of scientific adequacy, the likelihood of proliferation of second-rate research activity would be reduced. There are pressures toward such proliferation from within the academic community, which functions in a publish or perish manner, and additional encouragement from the development of computer technology, which allows for the ready generation of trivial data analyses.

If we can assume that a study is addressing an ethical question in a sound manner, the next question, and perhaps the most difficult to answer, concerns the benefits and risks of the study. This involves a careful consideration of what is to be gained by the study, what risks to the participants are involved in the study, and what the relative weights of these two factors are. This is clearly a highly subjective decision, and one in which the investigator has a considerable vested interest. For this reason, it is recommended that the investigator seek the advice of colleagues in any situation where the decision is not readily apparent. There are a number of institutional and statutory jurisdictions where this recommendation is given the force of law, in that a study cannot be conducted without the specific approval of an institutional review board. It is the duty of this board to consider benefits and risks and to arrive at an ethical decision which will protect the rights of the subjects.

The question of weighing benefits and risks has a peculiar twist in the research enterprise. Generally, when we use benefit-risk language, we assume that an act will provide a certain number of benefits for an individual, but that that person will also incur a number of risks, and the relative strengths of these must be weighed. When this language is used in research, however, it should be clear that most of the benefit is for society, in the form of increased knowledge, and that most of the risk is the subject's.

A number of general principles can be stated, some of which have more controversy surrounding them than others. It seems clear that a study which does not show evidence of potentially producing some benefit should not be conducted, even if the attendant risks are minimal. This is a further extension of the principle that scientifically unsound studies should not be conducted, and is a recognition that a subject's time and energy should not be wasted for no purpose. There is more controversy surrounding an extreme formulation of this principle, which holds that a study should not be done if the subject himself does not directly benefit from the research, unless he gives consent. This creates difficulty when the subject is not a competent adult, and so cannot provide consent. The logic here is Kantian, and sees the subject as being used as a means to an end unless he benefits from the research procedure.

It should be clear that this formulation uses a very narrow conception of benefit. A variety of benefits have been suggested which go beyond the immediate self-interests of a subject. These include the stimulation derived from a break in the usual routine of the day, the opportunity to satisfy an exploratory drive, and, perhaps most important, the opportunity that is given to the subject to perform a prosocial act and contribute to the welfare of the larger society. When this argument is extended, it would follow that it is morally correct to be of service, and so it is the obligation of people to participate in research. While this argument usually appears in literature concerning the use of children as subjects, since they may not have the capacity to give informed consent, it is also consistent with an obviation of the need for adult consent, since adults, too, share the obligation to be of service. It would appear that the most reasonable point of view lies between the extreme which states that everyone is morally obligated to be a subject and the opposite extreme, which states that nobody should be a subject unless he chooses to or receives direct benefit from doing so. How one weighs the alternatives is quite subjective, and seems properly placed with a committee of colleagues and consumers whose interests transcend the immediate project.

Informed Consent

The issue of weighing risks and benefits can be mooted in the event of the informed consent of the subject. Informed consent can be defined as the subject's assent to participation in the research after having received an explanation and reached an understanding of the procedures of the experiment and their associated risks and benefits. Crucial to informed consent is the quality of the explanation which is provided to the subject.

In clinical situations it has been typical to compare the explanation to the standard of what the average provider would tell, but there has been movement in some jurisdictions toward adopting the standard of what a reasonable person would want to know. It would seem prudent in research situations to adopt this more conservative standard, and to be sure that the patient is told everything that a reasonable person would need to know in order to reach a decision as to whether or not to participate.

The primary elements in informed consent are knowledge, voluntariness, and competency. Not only must the subject have enough knowledge to be considered informed, the consent must be offered voluntarily by a person judged competent to offer it. The Nuremberg Code, which devoted much attention to informed consent, stated that the subject must have the legal capacity to give consent, must be able to exercise free power of choice, must have sufficient knowledge upon which to decide, and must have sufficient comprehension to make an enlightened decision.

The usual method of eliciting consent involves the presentation of a form containing all necessary information, often supplemented by an oral explanation, and always having the possibility of questions which may be raised by the subject. According to the Department of Health, Education, and Welfare regulations (45 CFR 46.103(c)), there are a number of elements that must be contained in the consent form. These include a statement of the purpose of the research, the procedures involved, the risks and the benefits, the right of the subject to withdraw at any time, and an invitation to ask questions. In a survey by Cooke and Tannenbaum (1977), it was found that about 15 percent of the actions taken by institutional review boards involved modifications of the consent procedures, and that the consent forms were generally difficult to read. If informed consent is considered a genuine part of the research enterprise rather than a hurdle to be surmounted, it is important that the forms are clear, accurate, and comprehensible, so that subjects can truly feel informed and give voluntary consent.

In some cases (discussed in detail in the next section) the subject is unable to give consent because of some factor which produces a deficiency in understanding, such as age or competency. In such cases, proxy consent is often elicited. The Declaration of Helsinki explicitly allowed this, and while the Nuremberg Code did not, it may have avoided it because it was not relevant to the case under consideration. Some critics (Ramsey, 1970) have branded proxy consent a contradiction in terms, since consent implies an autonomous decision which cannot be made by a surrogate. The absence of proxy consent would rule out all children and many mental patients from research, and this would be disastrous to the psychotherapy research endeavor. On the other hand, to give proxy consent for psychotherapy involves the assumption that the patient wants to change, and this often is not valid.

One issue which often arises in psychotherapy research concerns the use of existing records which have been collected for administrative or clinical purposes, but whose utility for research later becomes apparent. While consent may have been obtained for the initial purpose, the patient certainly was not informed about use for research purposes. Does such use constitute an invasion of the patient's privacy and, if so, is this a risk that requires the patient's permission to incur? Where the patient is still available, it is clear that permission should be sought. Many records, however, are dated and patient permission would be difficult if not impossible to obtain. In such cases, it is always essential to retain the anonymity of the patient. Permission should be sought from an agent acting as an ombudsman in the patient's behalf, such as the institutional review board or the institutional administrator. Clearly, data should not be used beyond the specific purposes for which permission was granted. Ferguson (1977) summarizes a position with regard to these records in an apt fashion when she says, "Where the records exist in any case, for *other purposes related* to education or health maintenance, and where adequate precautions are taken to *preserve confidentiality* in analyzing them for research purposes, no particular problems would seem to be involved" (p. 4–18).

A similar issue is raised by the collection of unobtrusive measures. These are measures collected in such a fashion that the subject is unaware, heightening their ecological validity because they are emitted in an entirely natural way. An example of an unobtrusive measure in psychotherapy research is the promptness of payment of bills, which may reflect important transferential elements. It is usually good practice, if an unobtrusive measure is to be employed, to seek the patient's permission after the fact, along with providing a debriefing about the meaning of the measure. The investigator must be prepared to discard the data if such permission cannot be obtained.

In some cases, it is possible to anticipate the possibility of the future usefulness of the data which is collected. If the initial informed consent procedure includes permission for future research uses, future difficulty can be avoided. Certainly, if sessions are being tape recorded, patient permission must be obtained, and this should include the possibility that the tapes will be used for research purposes at a later time. While it is not possible to spell out the details of the research if we are seeking blanket permission for future activities, it is possible to guarantee anonymity in all such future projects.

Informed consent is a means by which the patient is given the right to decide which activities to engage in, and to avoid being subjected to any risks, however mild and subtle they may be, without first choosing to do so. Stated in this way, it is clearly an important component of a research project. Additionally, a consent procedure will serve to demystify the relationship between the subject and the experimenter. Orne (1962) has shown the powerful impact that demand characteristics can have on the behavior of the subject, and a reduction in the potency attributed to the experimenter might add validity to the research data. We must also bear in mind that the concept of informed consent is based on the notion of rational decision making. In all research situations, but particularly in psychotherapy research, the likelihood of transferential distortions calls the rationality of the decision into question. Nevertheless, the only alternative to allowing the patient to decide for himself is a paternalistic stance which is not likely to be acceptable to any institutional review board, or to be constructive within the treatment situation.

Principles three and four of the Research Code of Ethics of the American Psychological Association are specifically concerned with the issue of informed consent. Principle three states:

> Ethical practice requires the investigator to inform the participant of all features of the research that reasonably might be expected to influence willingness to participate, and to explain all other aspects of the research about which the participant inquires. Failure to make full disclosure gives added emphasis to the investigator's responsibility to protect the welfare and dignity of the research participant. [P. 1]

This last sentence allows for the possibility of consent which is not fully informed. The fourth principle speaks to the possibility of concealment or deception, and the ensuing responsibility of the investigator to debrief the subject. Principles five, six, and seven are also relevant to informed consent. Principle five underlines the freedom of the subject to decline participation in research or to discontinue his participation. Principle six refers to the establishment of a clear and fair agreement between the investigator and the research participant, and this agreement seems similar to the consent contract. Principle seven reinforces the need for consent whenever the participant will experience any risk because of the research project.

Selection of Subjects

If truly informed consent were universally obtainable, there would be no ethical issues surrounding the selection of subjects, since all subjects would be acting as independent, autonomous agents. There are a number of subjects, however, thought of as being vulnerable, uncomprehending, or disadvantaged, from whom informed consent is either impossible or suspect. Children are not viewed as having sufficiently mature judgment to reach an independent decision, raising the question of proxy consent, which has already been discussed. Patients with severe mental or emotional problems, such as retardates or psychotics, may not have the competency to comprehend the information that is proffered. People in institutional settings, such as hospitals or prisons, may feel under some element of coercion, or may be offered unfair inducements to influence their decision. If we recall that the primary elements of informed consent are knowledge, voluntariness, and competency, it is clear that some patients cannot integrate the information, some are not competent to evaluate it, and others are in no position to act in a voluntary manner. In psychotherapy, where many patients may be considered to have impaired judgment, some are in institutional settings, and all are in a relationship which is a source of powerful influence, the issue of patient selection is particularly important.

There are a number of considerations which influence our decision as to who should be used as a research subject. A major problem is the possibility of the overuse of convenient subjects, which may be an appropriate or an exploitative strategy. There are those who subscribe to a principle of randomness, feeling that the benefits and opportunities of participation should be distributed equitably throughout society, with each individual offered an equal opportunity to participate. Others feel that it is appropriate to use any available subject, since the pursuit of knowledge is a critical value for society. Unfortunately, many investigators use all available subjects, not out of philosophical conviction about primacy of knowledge, but out of administrative convenience. It seems as though justice dictates that special groups should be used, with their informed consent, if the research pertains to their circumstances, in that information can only be obtained from them. In all other cases, they should have the random opportunity to participate, but they should not be used adventitiously. Interestingly, this ethical solution also has methodological consequences, in that it will promote generalizability and expand our base of knowledge. It is fortunate that the ethical and the methodological decisions coincide, but it is still common for the exploitative decision to govern the selection of subjects.

Many issues arise when we are interested in the study of children. At one extreme, Ramsey (1970) feels that "To experiment on children in ways that are not related to them as patients is already a sanitized form of barbarism" (p. 12). Most writers recommend that there must be increasingly stringent criteria if the children will not benefit directly from participation, or if there is any risk involved. As a rule of thumb, childhood is considered to include the years until thirteen, as adolescents are considered capable of making the decision required for informed consent. Below age thirteen parental permission is required, with the word "permission" chosen rather than "consent" in recognition of the autonomous nature of consent. Further, for children over seven, their assent is also sought, although it is not legally binding. In general, if the child objects to participation this should be determining, unless the refusal will entail a serious health risk. Thus, a child might refuse to participate in a psychotherapy research project and that refusal would be respected, but if he does not wish to be in psychotherapy at all, that wish might be overruled by a parent. The National Commission for the Protection of Human Subjects of Biomedical and Behavioral Research (1977) has approved of the participation of children as research subjects as long as a number of conditions are met. These involve a determination by an institutional review board that the research is scientifically sound and significant, that it has been done previously on adults and older children, that the risks have been minimized, that the privacy of the child is protected and the data are confidential, and that the subjects have been selected in an equitable manner without overusing easily available subjects.

Barber (1976) has conducted a survey concerning the use of research subjects. He found that poor patients are most likely to be used as subjects, and that their proportion increases as the risk-benefit ratio becomes more unfavorable. This economically disadvantaged group is least able to protect itself and to give genuinely informed consent, leading to their exploitation in research as in other areas of life. An informal survey of the specific samples of patients used in psychotherapy research found an overrepresentation of clinic, public hospital, and student patients, along with an underrepresentation of private patients. This not only constitutes an exploitation of the powerless, but also leads to a gap in our knowledge about a significant portion of our patient population.

It should also be noted that there are some possible benefits to the subject as a consequence of participation in a research project. Other than the indirect benefits that are derived from participation in prosocial activity, information may be gathered about the needs of the subject, and it is the responsibility of the investigator to communicate this information to the responsible party. This is less likely to occur in psychotherapy research since the patient's needs are the issue of treatment, but in personality research it is not unlikely that such a circumstance will prevail.

By definition, the patient in psychotherapy is a member of a special population, and the provision of services during the research provides the patient with a benefit for participation. To make psychotherapy contingent upon participation in research, however, constitutes an unfair inducement and would not be seen as consistent with informed consent. The major concerns that are relevant to the research, then, are to avoid making the service contingent on acquiescence to participate, and to avoid studying one segment of the population to the exclusion of a more privileged segment. In discussing the issue of subject selection, Jonas (1970) has stated that it is an inflexible principle that utter helplessness demands utter protection. This principle avoids exploitation, but the perception of helplessness rests with the investigator. It is important for both research and treatment that we recognize the need for protection where it exists, but that we do not overestimate the need and, by doing so, deprive the patient of the experience of autonomous choice.

Use of Control Groups

One of the basic premises of research design is that a treated group must be compared with an untreated group if we are to determine whether or not the treatment was effective. There are many ramifications in arriving at a decision about the meaning of treatment, and it is enormously complicated to define "untreated," but ordinary wisdom holds that such a comparison must be made. On the other hand, in order to have an untreated group, we must make the conscious decision to withhold psychotherapy from some patients who might benefit from therapeutic attention and this is not only of questionable ethics, but it also may create malpractice liability and even criminal culpability (Stone, 1978). We are thus faced with an apparent contradiction between the demands of sound methodology and the dictates of our ethical standards. On closer examination, however, it is possible to develop a research paradigm that satisfies the highest standards of research design without compromising our ethical principles.

In reaching a recommendation that only volunteer subjects be used, Freund (1970) states, "While experimental volunteers are probably motivated rather specially as a group, the question of motivation is so subtle and pervasive in so many aspects of life that it seems inappropriate to plumb this factor with special penetration in screening for medical experimentation" (p. xvi). While this may be true of medical experimentation in general, it is singularly untrue of psychotherapy research, since the crux of psychotherapy involves an exploration of the subtle and pervasive aspects of motivation. To ignore this factor is to lose sight of our prime activity. The primary argument that will be made is that any comparison among groups, if it is to be valid, must compare equivalent groups, and differences in motivation represent a striking source of inequality. Thus, traditional choices of control groups such as normal controls, waiting list controls, and placebo controls are fundamentally different in motivation from the psychotherapy group because if they were not, they would not allow themselves to remain untreated. A person who is assigned to a waiting list, particularly in a metropolitan area, who allows himself to remain without treatment for any appreciable length of time, is not motivationally equivalent to a person in treatment. The only exception to this principle occurs in a closed institutional setting where all treatment is under administrative control. In such a situation, psychotherapy can be systematically assigned and withheld on a random basis without jeopardizing the equivalence of the groups. To do so, however, is grossly unethical if treatment is available, and if it is not available, it probably is illegal to continue to incarcerate the untreated patient.

One of the prime problems faced by any control group procedure is differential attrition. Not only are more people likely to leave the control group, or to seek out alternative forms of help while remaining in a control procedure, they are also likely to be motivationally different. The control group is likely to contain the people who are healthier and feel less in need of help, or people who are quite passive and will not pursue the help they need. The promise of eventual treatment which occurs when a person is placed on a waiting list will temporarily mitigate some of these factors, but then the issue of time becomes a factor. If a person is on a waiting list for a long period of time, differential attrition will occur. If the time on the waiting list is short, it no longer represents an adequate control for a more lengthy treatment procedure. Finally, patients in a no-treatment condition will have different expectancy of improvement, and this may produce change in its own right.

No-treatment and waiting list controls also have difficulty with patients in great, apparent need of treatment. If such patients are assigned randomly, as the research protocol dictates, a great clinical disservice will be done to them. If they are all assigned to the treatment group, a major source of group inequality is built into the design. If they are all withdrawn from the program so that they can be treated, the generalizability of the study's findings is limited to less seriously needy patients.

For these reasons, as well as many others, it is unusual to see a no-treatment or waiting list psychotherapy control. Instead, there are placebo controls or groups given nonspecific factors common to psychotherapy, such as attention and regular service. After discussing the difficulty in creating a placebo that can arouse and retain credibility, O'Leary and Borkovec (1978) go on to list three potential sources of harm from the placebo methodology. The first of these is the deception that occurs when a patient is placed in a placebo condition, but given the impression that he is being helped. Secondly, the patient is deterred from seeking meaningful treatment while under the impression that he is being treated and, it must be added, may lose faith in psychotherapy, and thus the deterrent may extend beyond the research project. Finally, there is always the possibility that deterioration will occur in the absence of psychotherapy. Therefore, it does not seem either ethically or methodologically defensible to suggest that patients be assigned to any treatment procedure that we do not feel has promise of being helpful.

If we rule out no-treatment, waiting list, placebo, and nonspecific factor controls on both ethical and methodological grounds, we are left with the problem of demonstrating the efficacy of psychotherapy over and above naturally occurring change. In order to do this, we must have comparison groups, but the comparison can be between two or more active treatment procedures. As one possibility, Kazdin and Wilson (1978) recommend the comparison of component elements such as relaxation with and without accompanying hierarchies of anxiety-producing visualizations. This is a viable possibility for very specific techniques, such as systematic desensitization, but it is unlikely to be possible for dynamic psychotherapy, where relationship factors are critical and technique is less specific. A second possible comparison can hold the psychotherapy constant, but vary parameters such as treatment length, session frequency, fee structure, etc. This can produce answers to important questions about the relative efficacy of a number of treatment variations. It is also possible to vary patient and therapist characteristics, so that we can see the relative value of an approach with different types of patients, or as applied by different types of therapists, or with different patient-therapist combinations. The most grand comparison would involve the comparison of two or more treatment modalities, but this may be less successful since therapies have different parameters and goals, so that a fair comparison may not be feasible.

By replacing control groups with comparison groups, we avoid the ethical problem of leaving some patients without assistance, and all the attendant methodological complications of that strategy. We are still left with the need to decide how patients are to be assigend to the various treatment alternatives. Randomization seems the wisest course here, with each patient informed that he will be randomly assigned to one of a number of treatment alternatives, each of which is viewed as potentially capable of being helpful to him. At the conclusion of the research, if one method proves clearly superior, it would be appropriate to offer that treatment to members of the other groups if they are still in need of assistance. It is certainly most defensible methodologically, and it does not, with the present state of the art, produce ethical complications. If we should reach a point where it becomes clear that a certain treatment is best for a certain patient when delivered by a certain therapist with a certain goal in mind, we might hesitate to assign that patient to any other condition, but we will not reach that point until many of the comparison studies that are recommended have been successfully completed. Until that time, both ethics and methodology would be best served by random assignment of patients to a range of comparison groups.

Concluding Remarks

The research investigator and the public may find themselves subject to two syndromes of hypocrisy described by Cahn (1964). The first is called the Pharaoh Syndrome, and refers to the building of the pyramids at the cost of hundreds of thousands of lives. Egyptian accounting may have computed the cost of wages, food, animals, and supplies, but not of human lives, which were considered part of the social cost of a great achievement. If research findings are achieved at the expense of the dignity or welfare of the subject, there is a tendency for the investigator to consider this part of the necessary social cost of advancing knowledge.

The second syndrome is the Pompey Syndrome, a name derived from a character in Shakespeare's *Antony and Cleopatra*. One of Pompey's lieutenants asks permission to cut the throats of Pompey's great rivals. Pompey, bound by honor to reject the offer, regrets that he was asked and states: "Being done unknown I should have found it afterwards well done, but must condemn it now." Society is pleased to reap the fruits of research without asking about the methods, while retaining the right to berate the investigator who is caught using a questionable method.

Justice Brandeis told us that sunlight was the most effective of all disinfectants, and the research version of sunlight is informed consent. As long as the subject knows what the situation asks of him, and freely consents to participate, there is no problem. The less informed or free to choose the subject is, the more we begin to incur social costs which our society will only tolerate as long as it, too, can be kept out of the sunlight.

The investigator may feel caught in a *Catch 22* situation. Some investigators feel that their choice is to do a study in violation of the code of ethics by not seeking truly informed consent, or to do it poorly, which is itself an unethical act. One alternative to this dilemma is not to do research at all, but the use of untried or undemonstrated techniques without provision for evaluation is also unethical. The way out of this difficulty is to make ethics and methodology consistent; this chapter has attempted to suggest a number of alternatives toward this goal.

It should be mentioned that much of the research that has been performed derives from a model emphasizing the power of the experimenter and the helplessness of the subject. One function of informed consent is to realign this relationship so that research becomes a cooperative effort conducted in an atmosphere of trust and voluntary participation. Psychotherapy has moved more toward this model of collaboration between participants, rather than the model of the performance of a service by an omnipotent doctor upon his grateful patient. Research can also move in the direction of colleagiality, and informed consent is a vehicle that can help to accomplish this goal.

Ultimately, the issue may not be one of ethics, but rather of values. We do not have the easy choice between a good and an evil, an ethical and an unethical, alternative. The construction of a code of ethics presupposes a clearly defined system of values, and what is seen as ethical may not be absolute, but usually varies as a function of values. The person doing research in psychotherapy must think through the matter of values very clearly and then, within the constraints imposed by law and regulations, pursue a path which would best actualize these values. Finally, it must be observed that the existence of law and regulations in this area represents a societal statement that the value system of researchers has not been sufficiently well defined and constructive, so that external constraints are needed to fill a void created by the absence of internal ones.

REFERENCES

AMERICAN ACADEMY OF PEDIATRICS, COMMITTEE ON DRUGS. Guidelines for the ethical conduct of studies to evaluate drugs in pediatric populations. In National Commission for the Protection of Human Subjects of Biomedical and Behavioral Research, *Research involving children.* Washington, D.C.: DHEW publication no. (os) 77-0005, 1977 (Appendix).

AMERICAN PSYCHOLOGICAL ASSOCIATION, Committee on Ethical Standards in Psychological Research. *Ethical principles in the conduct of research with human participants.* Washington, D.C.: Author, 1973.

ANNAS, G. J., GLANTZ, L. H., and KATZ, B. F. *Informed consent to human experimentation: The subject's dilemma.* Cambridge: Lippincott, 1977.

BARBER, B. The ethics of experimentation with human subjects. *Scientific American,* 1976, **234** (2), 25-31.

BARTHOLOME, W. A. The ethics of non-therapeutic clinical research on children. In National Commission for the Protection of Human Subjects of Biomedical and Behavioral Research, *Research involving children.* Washington, D.C.: DHEW publication no. (os) 77-0005, 1977 (Appendix).

BLUMGART, H. L. The medical framework for viewing the problem of human experimentation. In P. A. Freund (ed.), *Experimentation with human subjects.* New York: George Braziller, 1970.

CAHN, E. Drug experiments and the public conscience. In P. Talalay (ed.), *Drugs in our society.* Baltimore: Johns Hopkins Press, 1964.

COOKE, R. A., and TANNENBAUM, A. S. *The performance of institutional review boards.* Ann Arbor: University of Michigan Press, 1977.

CURRAN, W. J. Governmental regulation of the use of human subjects in medical research: The approach of two federal agencies. In P. A. Freund (ed.), *Experimentation with human subjects*. New York: George Braziller, 1970.

FERGUSON, L. R. The competence and freedom of children to make choices regarding participation in biomedical and behavioral research. In National Commission for the Protection of Human Subjects of Biomedical and Behavioral Research, *Research involving children*. Washington, D.C.: DHEW publication no. (os) 77-0005, 1977 (Appendix).

FREUND, P. A. (ed.). *Experimentation with human subjects*. New York: George Braziller, 1970.

HERSHEY, N., and MILLER, R. D. *Human experimentation and the law*. Germantown, Md.: Aspen Systems, 1976.

JONAS, H. Philosophical reflections on experimenting with human subjects. In P. A. Freund (ed.), *Experimentation with human subjects*. New York: George Braziller, 1970.

KATZ, J. (ed.). *Experimentation with human beings*. New York: Russell Sage Foundation, 1972.

KAZDIN, A. E., and WILSON, G. T. *Evaluation of behavior therapy: Issues, evidence and research strategies*. Cambridge: Ballinger, 1978.

MAY, W. F. Code, covenant, contract or philanthropy. *Hastings Center Report*, 1975, **5**, 29-38.

NATIONAL COMMISSION FOR THE PROTECTION OF HUMAN SUBJECTS OF BIOMEDICAL and BEHAVIORAL RESEARCH. *Research involving children*. Washington, D.C.: DHEW publication no. (os)77-0005, 1977.

O'LEARY, K. D., and BORKOVEC, T. D. Conceptual, methodological and ethical problems of placebo groups in psychotherapy research. *American Psychologist*, 1978, **33**, 821-830.

ORNE, M. J. On the social psychology of the psychological experiment with particular reference to demand characteristics and their implications. *American Psychologist*, 1962, **17**, 776-783.

RAMSEY, P. *The patient as person*. New Haven: Yale University Press, 1970.

STONE, A. A. The history and future of litigation in psychopharmacologic research and treatment. In D. M. Gallant and R. Force (eds.), *Legal and ethical issues in human research and treatment*. New York: Spectrum, 1978.

UNITED STATES SENATE, Committee on the Judiciary, Subcommittee on Constitutional Rights. *Individual rights and the Federal role in behavior modification*. Washington, D.C.: Author, 1974.

APPENDIXES

The Principles of Medical Ethics with Annotations Especially Applicable to Psychiatry (APA)

In 1973, the American Psychiatric Association published the first edition of *The Principles of Medical Ethics with Annotations Especially Applicable to Psychiatry*. Subsequently, revisions were published as the board of trustees and the assembly approved additional annotations. In July 1980 the American Medical Association approved a new version of the *Principles of Medical Ethics* (the first revision since 1957) and the APA Ethics Committee incorporated many of its annotations into the new principles, which resulted in the 1981 edition.

Foreword

All physicians should practice in accordance with the medical code of ethics set forth in the Principles of Medical Ethics of the American Medical Association. An up-to-date expression and elaboration of these statements is found in the *Opinions and Reports of the Judicial Council* of the American Medical Association.[1] Psychiatrists are strongly advised to be familiar with these documents.[2]

However, these general guidelines have sometimes been difficult to interpret for psychiatry, so further annotations to the basic principles are offered in this document. While psychiatrists have the same goals as all physicians, there are special ethical problems in psychiatric practice that differ in coloring and degree from ethical problems in other branches of medical practice, even though the basic principles are the same. The annotations are not designed as absolutes and will be revised from time to time so as to be applicable to current practices and problems.

Following are the AMA Principles of Medical Ethics, printed in their entirety, and then each principle printed separately along with an annotation especially applicable to psychiatry.

Principles of Medical Ethics, American Medical Association

Preamble

The medical profession has long subscribed to a body of ethical statements developed primarily for the benefit of the patient. As a member of this profession, a physician must recognize responsibility not only to patients, but also to society, to other health professionals, and to self. The following Principles, adopted by the American Medical Association, are not laws, but standards of conduct which define the essentials of honorable behavior for the physician.

Section 1

A physician shall be dedicated to providing competent medical service with compassion and respect for human dignity.

Section 2

A physician shall deal honestly with patients and colleagues, and strive to expose those physicians deficient in character or competence, or who engage in fraud or deception.

Section 3

A physician shall respect the law and also recognize a responsibility to seek changes in those requirements which are contrary to the best interests of the patient.

Section 4

A physician shall respect the rights of patients, of colleagues, and of other health professionals, and shall safeguard patient confidences within the constraints of the law.

Section 5

A physician shall continue to study, apply, and advance scientific knowledge, make relevant information available to patients, colleagues, and the public, obtain consultation, and use the talents of other health professionals when indicated.

Section 6

A physician shall, in the provision of appropriate patient care, except in emergencies, be free to choose whom to serve, with whom to associate, and the environment in which to provide medical services.

Section 7

A physician shall recognize a responsibility to participate in activities contributing to an improved community.

Principles with Annotations

Following are each of the AMA Principles of Medical Ethics printed separately along with annotations especially applicable to psychiatry.

Preamble

The medical profession has long subscribed to a body of ethical statements developed primarily for the benefit of the patient. As a member of this profession, a physician must recognize responsibility not only to patients, but also to society, to other health professionals, and to self. The following Principles, adopted by the American Medical Association, are not laws, but standards of conduct which define the essentials of honorable behavior for the physician.[3]

Section 1

A physician shall be dedicated to providing competent medical service with compassion and respect for human dignity.

1. The patient may place his/her trust in his/her psychiatrist knowing that the psychiatrist's ethics and professional responsibilities preclude him/her gratifying his/her own needs by exploiting the patient. This becomes particularly important because of the essentially private, highly personal, and sometimes intensely emotional nature of the relationship established with the psychiatrist.

2. A psychiatrist should not be a party to any type of policy that excludes, segregates, or demeans the dignity of any patient because of

ethnic origin, race, sex, creed, age, socioeconomic status, or sexual orientation.

3. In accord with the requirements of law and accepted medical practice, it is ethical for a physician to submit his/her work to peer review and to the ultimate authority of the medical staff executive body and the hospital administration and its governing body. In case of dispute, the ethical psychiatrist has the following steps available:

   a. Seek appeal from the medical staff decision to a joint conference committee, including members of the medical staff executive committee and the executive committee of the governing board. At this appeal, the ethical psychiatrist could request that outside opinions be considered.
   b. Appeal to the governing body itself.
   c. Appeal to state agencies regulating licensure of hospitals if, in the particular state, they concern themselves with matters of professional competency and quality of care.
   d. Attempt to educate colleagues through development of research projects and data and presentations at professional meetings and in professional journals.
   e. Seek redress in local courts, perhaps through an enjoining injunction against the governing body.
   f. Public education as carried out by an ethical psychiatrist would not utilize appeals based solely upon emotion, but would be presented in a professional way and without any potential exploitation of patients through testimonials.

Section 2

A physician shall deal honestly with patients and colleagues, and strive to expose those physicians deficient in character or competence, or who engage in fraud or deception.

1. The requirement that the physician conduct himself with propriety in his/her profession and in all the actions of his/her life is especially important in the case of the psychiatrist because the patient tends to model his/her behavior after that of his/her therapist by identification. Further, the necessary intensity of the therapeutic relationship may tend to activate sexual and other needs and fantasies on the part of both patient and therapist, while weakening the objectivity necessary for control. Sexual activity with a patient is unethical.

2. The psychiatrist should diligently guard against exploiting information furnished by the patient and should not use the unique position of power afforded him/her by the psychotherapeutic situation to influence the patient in any way not directly relevant to the treatment goals.

3. A psychiatrist who regularly practices outside his/her area of professional competence should be considered unethical. Determination of professional competence should be made by peer review boards or other appropriate bodies.

4. Special consideration should be given to those psychiatrists who, because of mental illness, jeopardize the welfare of their patients and their own reputations and practices. It is ethical, even encouraged, for another psychiatrist to intercede in such situations.

5. Psychiatric services, like all medical services, are dispensed in the context of a contractual arrangement between the patient and the treating physician. The provisions of the contractual arrangement, which are binding on the physician as well as on the patient, should be explicitly established.

6. It is ethical for the psychiatrist to make a charge for a missed appointment when this falls within the terms of the specific contractual agreement with the patient. Charging for a missed appointment or for one not cancelled 24 hours in advance need not, in itself, be considered unethical if a patient is fully advised that the physician will make such a charge. The practice, however, should be resorted to infrequently and always with the utmost consideration of the patient and his/her circumstances.

7. An arrangement in which a psychiatrist provides supervision or administration to other physicians or nonmedical persons for a percentage of their fees or gross income is not acceptable; this would constitute fee-splitting. In a team of practitioners, or a multidisciplinary team, it is ethical for the psychiatrist to receive income for administration, research, education, or consultation. This should be based upon a mutually agreed upon and set fee or salary, open to renegotiation when a change in the time demand occurs. (See also Section 5, Annotations 2, 3, and 4.)

8. When a member has been found to have behaved unethically by the American Psychiatric Association or one of its constituent district branches, there should not be automatic reporting to the local authorities responsible for medical licensure, but the decision to report should be decided upon the merits of the case.

Section 3

A physician shall respect the law and also recognize a responsibility to seek changes in those requirements which are contrary to the best interests of the patient.

1. It would seem self-evident that a psychiatrist who is a lawbreaker might be ethically unsuited to practice his/her profession. When such

illegal activities bear directly upon his/her practice, this would obviously be the case. However, in other instances, illegal activities such as those concerning the right to protest social injustices might not bear on either the image of the psychiatrist or the ability of the specific psychiatrist to treat his/her patient ethically and well. While no committee or board could offer prior assurance that any illegal activity would not be considered unethical, it is conceivable that an individual could violate a law without being guilty of professionally unethical behavior. Physicians lose no right of citizenship on entry into the profession of medicine.

2. Where not specifically prohibited by local laws governing medical practice, the practice of acupuncture by a psychiatrist is not unethical per se. The psychiatrist should have professional competence in the use of acupuncture. Or, if he/she is supervising the use of acupuncture by nonmedical individuals, he/she should provide proper medical supervision. (See also Section 5, Annotations 3 and 4.)

Section 4

A physician shall respect the rights of patients, of colleagues, and of other health professionals, and shall safeguard patient confidences within the constraints of the law.

1. Psychiatric records, including even the identification of a person as a patient, must be protected with extreme care. Confidentiality is essential to psychiatric treatment. This is based in part on the special nature of psychiatric therapy as well as on the traditional ethical relationship between physician and patient. Growing concern regarding the civil rights of patients and the possible adverse effects of computerization, duplication equipment, and data banks makes the dissemination of confidential information an increasing hazard. Because of the sensitive and private nature of the information with which the psychiatrist deals, he/she must be circumspect in the information that he/she chooses to disclose to others about a patient. The welfare of the patient must be a continuing consideration.

2. A psychiatrist may release confidential information only with the authorization of the patient or under proper legal compulsion. The continuing duty of the psychiatrist to protect the patient includes fully apprising him/her of the connotations of waiving the privilege of privacy. This may become an issue when the patient is being investigated by a government agency, is applying for a position, or is involved in legal action. The same principles apply to the release of information concerning treatment to medical departments of government agencies; business organizations, labor unions, and insurance companies. Information

gained in confidence about patients seen in student health services should not be released without the student's explicit permission.

3. Clinical and other materials used in teaching and writing must be adequately disguised in order to preserve the anonymity of the individuals involved.

4. The ethical responsibility of maintaining confidentiality holds equally for the consultations in which the patient may not have been present and in which the consultee was not a physician. In such instances, the physician consultant should alert the consultee to his/her duty of confidentiality.

5. Ethically the psychiatrist may disclose only that information which is relevant to a given situation. He/she should avoid offering speculation as fact. Sensitive information such as an individual's sexual orientation or fantasy material is usually unnecessary.

6. Psychiatrists are often asked to examine individuals for security purposes, to determine suitability for various jobs, and to determine legal competence. The psychiatrist must fully describe the nature and purpose and lack of confidentiality of the examination to the examinee at the beginning of the examination.

7. Careful judgment must be exercised by the psychiatrist in order to include, when appropriate, the parents or guardian in the treatment of a minor. At the same time the psychiatrist must assure the minor proper confidentiality.

8. Psychiatrists at times may find it necessary, in order to protect the patient or the community from imminent danger, to reveal confidential information disclosed by the patient.

9. When the psychiatrist is ordered by the court to reveal the confidences entrusted to him/her by patients he/she may comply or he/she may ethically hold the right to dissent within the framework of the law. When the psychiatrist is in doubt, the right of the patient to confidentiality and, by extension, to unimpaired treatment, should be given priority. The psychiatrist should reserve the right to raise the question of adequate need for disclosure. In the event that the necessity for legal disclosure is demonstrated by the court, the psychiatrist may request the right to disclosure of only that information which is relevant to the legal question at hand.

10. With regard for the person's dignity and privacy and with truly informed consent, it is ethical to present a patient to a scientific gathering, if the confidentiality of the presentation is understood and accepted by the audience.

11. It is ethical to present a patient or former patient to a public gathering or to the news media only if that patient is fully informed of enduring loss of confidentiality, is competent, and consents in writing without coercion.

12. When involved in funded research, the ethical psychiatrist will advise human subjects of the funding source, retain his/her freedom to reveal data and results, and follow all appropriate and current guidelines relative to human subject protection.

13. Ethical considerations in medical practice preclude the psychiatric evaluation of any adult charged with criminal acts prior to access to, or availability of, legal counsel. The only exception is the rendering of care to the person for the sole purpose of medical treatment.

Section 5

A physician shall continue to study, apply, and advance scientific knowledge, make relevant information available to patients, colleagues, and the public, obtain consultation, and use the talents of other health professionals when indicated.

1. Psychiatrists are responsible for their own continuing education and should be mindful of the fact that theirs must be a lifetime of learning.

2. In the practice of his/her specialty, the psychiatrist consults, associates, collaborates, or integrates his/her work with that of many professionals, including psychologists, psychometricians, social workers, alcoholism counselors, marriage counselors, public health nurses, etc. Furthermore, the nature of modern psychiatric practice extends his/her contacts to such people as teachers, juvenile and adult probation officers, attorneys, welfare workers, agency volunteers, and neighborhood aides. In referring patients for treatment, counseling, or rehabilitation to any of these practitioners, the psychiatrist should ensure that the allied professional or paraprofessional with whom he/she is dealing is a recognized member of his/her own discipline and is competent to carry out the therapeutic task required. The psychiatrist should have the same attitude toward members of the medical profession to whom he/she refers patients. Whenever he/she has reason to doubt the training, skill, or ethical qualifications of the allied professional, the psychiatrist should not refer cases to him/her.

3. When the psychiatrist assumes a collaborative or supervisory role with another mental health worker, he/she must expend sufficient time to assure that proper care is given. It is contrary to the interests of the patient and to patient care if he/she allows himself/herself to be used as a figurehead.

4. In relationships between psychiatrists and practicing licensed psychologists, the physician should not delegate to the psychologist or, in fact, to any nonmedical person any matter requiring the exercise of professional medical judgment.

5. The psychiatrist should agree to the request of a patient for consultation or to such a request from the family of an incompetent or minor patient. The psychiatrist may suggest possible consultants, but the patient or family should be given free choice of the consultant. If the psychiatrist disapproves of the professional qualifications of the consultant or if there is a difference of opinion that the primary therapist cannot resolve, he/she may, after suitable notice, withdraw from the case. If this disagreement occurs within an institution or agency framework, the differences should be resolved by the mediation or arbitration of higher professional authority within the institution or agency.

Section 6

A physician shall, in the provision of appropriate patient care, except in emergencies, be free to choose whom to serve, with whom to associate, and the environment in which to provide medical services.

1. Physicians generally agree that the doctor-patient relationship is such a vital factor in effective treatment of the patient that preservation of optimal conditions for development of a sound working relationship between a doctor and his/her patient should take precedence over all other considerations. Professional courtesy may lead to poor psychiatric care for physicians and their families because of embarrassment over the lack of a complete give-and-take contract.

Section 7

A physician shall recognize a responsibility to participate in activities contributing to an improved community.

1. Psychiatrists should foster the cooperation of those legitimately concerned with the medical, psychological, social, and legal aspects of mental health and illness. Psychiatrists are encouraged to serve society by advising and consulting with the executive, legislative, and judiciary branches of the government. A psychiatrist should clarify whether he/she speaks as an individual or as a representative of an organization. Furthermore, psychiatrists should avoid cloaking their public statements with the authority of the profession (e.g., "Psychiatrists know that . . .").

2. Psychiatrists may interpret and share with the public their expertise in the various psychosocial issues that may affect mental health and illness. Psychiatrists should always be mindful of their separate roles as dedicated citizens and as experts in psychological medicine.

3. On occasion psychiatrists are asked for an opinion about an individual who is in the light of public attention, or who has disclosed information about himself/herself through public media. It is unethical for a psychiatrist to offer a professional opinion unless he/she has conducted an examination and has been granted proper authorization for such a statement.

4. The psychiatrist may permit his/her certification to be used for the involuntary treatment of any person only following his/her personal examination of that person. To do so, he/she must find that the person, because of mental illness, cannot form a judgment as to what is in his/her own best interests and without which treatment substantial impairment is likely to occur to the person or others.

NOTES

1. *Opinions and Reports of the Judicial Council* (Chicago: American Medical Association, 1981).
2. Chapter 8, Section 1 of the By-Laws of the American Psychiatric Association states, "All members of the American Psychiatric Association shall be bound by the ethical code of the medical profession, specifically defined in the *Principles of Medical Ethics* of the American Medical Association." In interpreting the APA Constitution and By-Laws, it is the opinion of the Board of Trustees that inactive status in no way removes a physician member from responsibility to abide by the *Principles of Medical Ethics*.
3. Statements in italics are taken directly from the American Medical Association's *Principles of Medical Ethics* or annotations thereto (Chicago: American Medical Association, 1981).

Code of Ethics (NASW)

Adopted by the Delegate Assembly of the National Association of Social Workers, October 13, 1960, and amended April 11, 1967:

Social work is based on humanitarian, democratic ideals. Professional social workers are dedicated to service for the welfare of mankind, to the disciplined use of a recognized body of knowledge about human beings and their interactions, and to the marshaling of community resources to promote the well-being of all without discrimination.

Social work practice is a public trust that requires of its practitioners integrity, compassion, belief in the dignity and worth of human beings, respect for individual differences, a commitment to service, and a dedication to truth. It requires mastery of a body of knowledge and skill gained through professional education and experience. It requires also recognition of the limitations of present knowledge and skill and of the services we are now equipped to give. The end sought is the performance of a service with integrity and competence.

Each member of the profession carries responsibility to maintain and improve social work service; constantly to examine, use, and increase the knowledge on which practice and social policy are based; and to develop further the philosophy and skills of the profession.

This Code of Ethics embodies certain standards of behavior for the social worker in his professional relationships with those he serves, with his colleagues, with his employing agency, with other professions, and with the community. In abiding by it, the social worker views his obligations in as wide a context as the situation requires, takes all the principles into consideration, and chooses a course of action consistent with the code's spirit and intent.

As a member of the National Association of Social Workers I commit myself to conduct my professional relationships in accord with the code and subscribe to the following statements:

> I regard as my primary obligation the welfare of the individual or group served, which includes action for improving social conditions.
>
> I will not discriminate because of race, color, religion, age, sex, or national ancestry and in my job capacity will work to prevent and

eliminate such discrimination in rendering service, in work assignments, and in employment practices.

I give precedence to my professional responsibility over my personal interests.

I hold myself responsible for the quality and extent of the service I perform.

I respect the privacy of the people I serve.

I use in a responsible manner information gained in professional relationships.

I treat with respect the findings, views, and actions of colleagues and use appropriate channels to express judgment on these matters.

I practice social work within the recognized knowledge and competence of the profession.

I recognize my professional responsibility to add my ideas and findings to the body of social work knowledge and practice.

I accept responsibility to help protect the community against unethical practice by any individuals or organizations engaged in social welfare activities.

I stand ready to give appropriate professional service in public emergencies.

I distinguish clearly, in public, between my statements and actions as an individual and as a representative of an organization.

I support the principle that professional practice requires professional education.

I accept responsibility for working toward the creation and maintenance of conditions within agencies that enable social workers to conduct themselves in keeping with this code.

I contribute my knowledge, skills, and support to programs of human welfare.

Ethical Principles of Psychologists (1981 Revision)

This version of the Ethical Principles of Psychologists[1] (formerly entitled: Ethical Standards of Psychologists) was adopted by the American Psychological Association's Council of Representatives on January 24, 1981. The Ethical Principles of Psychologists (1981 Revision) contains both substantive and grammatical changes in each of the nine ethical principles which comprised the Ethical Standards of Psychologists previously adopted by the Council of Representatives in 1979, plus a new tenth principle entitled: Care and Use of Animals. Inquiries concerning the Ethical Principles of Psychologists should be addressed to the Administrative Officer for Ethics; American Psychological Association; 1200 Seventeenth Street, N.W.; Washington, D.C. 20036.

Preamble

Psychologists respect the dignity and worth of the individual and strive for the preservation and protection of fundamental human rights. They are committed to increasing knowledge of human behavior and of people's understanding of themselves and others and to the utilization of such knowledge for the promotion of human welfare. While pursuing these objectives, they make every effort to protect the welfare of those who seek their services and of the research participants that may be the object of study. They use their skills only for purposes consistent with these values and do not knowingly permit their misuse by others. While demanding for themselves freedom of inquiry and communication, psychologists accept the responsibility this freedom requires: competence, objectivity in the application of skills, and concern for the best interests of clients, colleagues, students, research participants and society. In the pursuit of these ideals, psychologists subscribe to principles in the following areas:

1. Responsibility
2. Competence
3. Moral and Legal Standards

4. Public Statements
5. Confidentiality
6. Welfare of the Consumer
7. Professional Relationships
8. Assessment Techniques
9. Research with Human Participants
10. Care and Use of Animals

Acceptance of membership in the American Psychological Association commits the member to adherence to these principles.

Psychologists cooperate with duly constituted committees of the American Psychological Association, in particular, the Committee on Scientific and Professional Ethics and Conduct, by responding to inquiries promptly and completely. Members also respond promptly and completely to inquiries from duly constituted state association ethics committees and professional standards review committees.

Principle 1. Responsibility

In providing services, psychologists maintain the highest standards of their profession. They accept responsibility for the consequences of their acts and make every effort to insure that their services are used appropriately.

a. As scientists, psychologists accept responsibility for the selection of their research topics and the methods used in investigation, analysis, and reporting. They plan their research in ways to minimize the possibility that their findings will be misleading. They provide thorough discussion of the limitations of their data, especially where their work touches on social policy or might be construed to the detriment of persons in specific age, sex, ethnic, socioeconomic or other social groups. In publishing reports of their work, they never suppress disconfirming data, and they acknowledge the existence of alternative hypotheses and explanations of their findings. Psychologists take credit only for work they have actually done.

b. Psychologists clarify in advance with all appropriate persons and agencies the expectations for sharing and utilizing research data. They avoid relationships which may limit their objectivity or create a conflict of interest. Interference with the milieu in which the data are collected is kept to a minimum.

c. Psychologists have the responsibility to attempt to prevent distortion, misuse, or suppression of psychological findings by the institution or agency of which they are employees.

d. As members of governmental or other organizational bodies, psychologists remain accountable as individuals to the highest standards of their profession.

e. As teachers, psychologists recognize their primary obligation to help others acquire knowledge and skill. They maintain high standards of scholarship by presenting psychological information objectively, fully, and accurately.

f. As practitioners, psychologists know that they bear a heavy social responsibility because their recommendations and professional actions may alter the lives of others. They are alert to personal, social, organizational, financial, or political situations and pressures that might lead to misuse of their influence.

Principle 2. Competence

The maintenance of high standards of competence is a responsibility shared by all psychologists in the interest of the public and the profession as a whole. Psychologists recognize the boundaries of their competence and the limitations of their techniques. They only provide services and only use techniques for which they are qualified by training and experience. In those areas in which recognized standards do not yet exist, psychologists take whatever precautions are necessary to protect the welfare of their clients. They maintain knowledge of current scientific and professional information related to the services they render.

a. Psychologists accurately represent their competence, education, training, and experience. They claim as evidence of educational qualifications only those degrees obtained from institutions acceptable under the Bylaws and Rules of Council of the American Psychological Association.

b. As teachers, psychologists perform their duties on the basis of careful preparation so that their instruction is accurate, current, and scholarly.

c. Psychologists recognize the need for continuing education and are open to new procedures and changes in expectations and values over time.

d. Psychologists recognize differences among people, such as those that may be associated with age, sex, socioeconomic, and ethnic backgrounds. When necessary, they obtain training, experience, or counsel to assure competent service or research relating to such persons.

e. Psychologists responsible for decisions involving individuals or policies based on test results have an understanding of psychological or educational measurement, validation problems, and test research.

f. Psychologists recognize that personal problems and conflicts may interfere with professional effectiveness. Accordingly, they refrain from undertaking any activity in which their personal problems are likely to lead to inadequate performance or harm to a client, colleague, student, or research participant. If engaged in such activity when they become aware of their personal problems, they seek competent professional assistance to determine whether they should suspend, terminate, or limit the scope of their professional and/or scientific activities.

Principle 3. Moral and Legal Standards

Psychologists' moral and ethical standards of behavior are a personal matter to the same degree as they are for any other citizen, except as these may compromise the fulfillment of their professional responsibilities, or reduce the public trust in psychology and psychologists. Regarding their own behavior, psycholgists are sensitive to prevailing community standards and to the possible impact that conformity to or deviation from these standards may have upon the quality of their performance as psychologists. Psychologists are also aware of the possible impact of their public behavior upon the ability of colleagues to perform their professional duties.

a. As teachers, psychologists are aware of the fact that their personal values may affect the selection and presentation of instructional materials. When dealing with topics that may give offense, they recognize and respect the diverse attitudes that students may have toward such materials.

b. As employees or employers, psychologists do not engage in or condone practices that are inhumane or that result in illegal or unjustifiable actions. Such practices include but are not limited to those based on considerations of race, handicap, age, gender, sexual preference, religion, or national origin in hiring, promotion, or training.

c. In their professional roles, psychologists avoid any action that will violate or diminish the legal and civil rights of clients or of others who may be affected by their actions.

d. As practitioners and researchers, psychologists act in accord with Association standards and guidelines related to the practice and to the conduct of research with human beings and animals. In the ordinary course of events psychologists adhere to relevant governmental laws and institutional regulations. When federal, state, provincial, organizational, or institutional laws, regulations, or practices are in conflict with Association standards and guidelines, psychologists make known their commitment to Association standards and guidelines, and wherever possible work toward a resolution of the conflict. Both practitioners and researchers are concerned with the development of such legal and quasi-legal regulations as best serve the public interest, and they work toward changing existing regulations that are not beneficial to the public interest.

Principle 4. Public Statements

Public statements, announcements of services, advertising, and promotional activities of psychologists serve the purpose of helping the public make informed judgments and choices. Psychologists represent accurately and objectively their professional qualifications, affiliations, and functions, as well as those of the institutions or organizations with which they or the statements may be associated. In public statements providing psychological information or professional opinions or providing information about the availability of psychological products, publications, and services, psychologists base their statements on scientifically acceptable psychological findings and techniques with full recognition of the limits and uncertainties of such evidence.

a. When announcing or advertising professional service, psychologists may list the following information to describe the provider and services provided: name, highest relevant academic degree earned from a regionally accredited institution, date, type and level of certification or licensure, diplomate status, APA membership status, address, telephone number, office hours, a brief listing of the type of psychological services offered, an appropriate presentation of fee information, foreign languages spoken, and policy with regard to third-party payments. Additional relevant or important consumer information may be included if not prohibited by other sections of these Ethical Principles.

b. In announcing or advertising the availability of psychological products, publications, or services, psychologists do not present their affiliation with any organization in a manner that falsely implies sponsorship or certification by that organization. In particular and for example, psychologists do not state APA membership or fellow status in a way to suggest that such status implies specialized professional competence or qualifications. Public statements include, but are not limited to, communication by means of periodical, book, list, directory, television, radio, or motion picture. They do not contain: (i) a false, fraudulent, misleading, deceptive, or unfair statement; (ii) a misinterpretation of fact, or a statement likely to mislead or deceive because in context it makes only a partial disclosure of relevant facts; (iii) a testimonial from a patient regarding the quality of a psychologist's services or products; (iv) a statement intended or likely to create false or unjustified expectations of favorable results; (v) a statement implying unusual, unique, or one-of-a-kind abilities; (vi) a statement intended or likely to appeal to a client's fears, anxieties, or emotions concerning the possible results of a failure to obtain the offered services; (vii) a statement concerning the comparative desirability of offered service: (viii) a statement of direct solicitation of individual clients.

c. Psychologists do not compensate or give anything of value to a representative of the press, radio, television, or other communication medium in anticipation of or in return for professional publicity in a news item. A paid advertisement must be identified as such, unless it is apparent from the context that it is a paid advertisement. If communicated to the public by use of radio or television, an advertisement shall be prerecorded and approved for broadcast by the psychologists, and a recording of the actual transmission shall be retained by the psychologist.

d. Announcements or advertisements of "personal growth groups," clinics, and agencies give a clear statement of purpose and a clear description of the experiences to be provided. The education, training, and experience of the staff members are appropriately specified.

e. Psychologists associated with the development or promotion of psychological devices, books, or other products offered for commercial sale make reasonable efforts to insure that announcements and advertisements are presented in a professional, scientifically acceptable, and factually informative manner.

f. Psychologists do not participate for personal gain in commercial announcements or advertisements recommending to the public the purchase or use of proprietary or single-source products or services when that participation is based solely upon their identification as psychologists.

g. Psychologists present the science of psychology and offer their services, products, and publications fairly and accurately, avoiding misrepresentation through sensationalism, exaggeration, or superficiality. Psychologists are guided by the primary obligation to aid the public in developing informed judgments, opinions, and choices.

h. As teachers, psychologists insure that statements in catalogs and course outlines are accurate and not misleading, particularly in terms of subject matter to be covered, bases for evaluating progress, and the nature of course experiences. Announcements, brochures, or advertisements describing workshops, seminars, or other educational programs accurately describe the audience for which the program is intended as well as eligibility requirements, educational objectives, and nature of the materials to be covered. These announcements also accurately represent the education, training, and experience of the psychologists presenting the programs, and any fees involved.

i. Public announcements or advertisements soliciting research participants in which clinical services or other professional services are offered as an inducement, make clear the nature of the services as well as the costs and other obligations to be accepted by the participants of the research.

j. Psychologists accept the obligation to correct others who represent that psychologist's professional qualifications, or associations with products or services, in a manner incompatible with these guidelines.

k. Individual diagnostic and therapeutic services are provided only in the context of a professional psychological relationship. When personal advice is given by means of public lecture or demonstration, newspaper or magazine articles, radio or television programs, mail, or similar media, the psychologist utilizes the most current relevant data and exercises the highest level of professional judgment.

l. Products that are described or presented by means of public lectures or demonstrations, newspaper or magazine articles, radio or television programs, or similar media meet the same recognized standards as exist for use in the context of a professional relationship.

Principle 5. Confidentiality

Psychologists have a primary obligation to respect the confidentiality of information obtained from persons in the course of their work as psychologists. They reveal such information to others only with the consent of the person or the person's legal representative, except in those unusual circumstances in which not to do so would result in clear danger to the person or to others. Where appropriate, psychologists inform their clients of the legal limits of confidentiality.

a. Information obtained in clinical or consulting relationships, or evaluative data concerning children, students, employees, and others, are discussed only for professional purposes and only with persons clearly concerned with the case. Written and oral reports present only data germane to the purpose of the evaluation and every effort is made to avoid undue invasion of privacy.

b. Psychologists who present personal information obtained during the course of professional work in writings, lectures, or other public forums either obtain adequate prior consent to do so or adequately disguise all identifying information.

c. Psychologists make provisions for maintaining confidentiality in the storage and disposal of records.

d. When working with minors or other persons who are unable to give voluntary, informed consent, psychologists take special care to protect these persons' best interests.

Principle 6. Welfare of the Consumer

Psychologists respect the integrity and protect the welfare of the people and groups with whom they work. When there is a conflict of interest between a client and the psychologist's employing institution, psychologists clarify the nature and direction of their loyalties and responsibilities and keep all parties informed of their commitments. Psychologists fully inform consumers as to the purpose and nature of an evaluative, treatment, educational or training procedure, and they freely acknowledge that clients, students, or participants in research have freedom of choice with regard to participation.

a. Psychologists are continually cognizant of their own needs and of their potentially influential position vis-á-vis persons such as clients, students, and subordinates. They avoid exploiting the trust and dependency of such persons. Psychologists make every effort to avoid dual relationships which could impair their professional judgment or increase the risk of exploitation. Examples of such dual relationships include but are not limited to research with and treatment of employees, students, supervisees, close friends, or relatives. Sexual intimacies with clients are unethical.

b. When a psychologist agrees to provide services to a client at the request of a third party, the psychologist assumes the responsibility of clarifying the nature of the relationships to all parties concerned.

c. Where the demands of an organization require psychologists to violate these Ethical Principles, psychologists clarify the nature of the conflict between the demand and these principles. They inform all parties of psychologists' ethical responsibilities, and take appropriate action.

d. Psychologists make advance financial arrangements that safeguard the best interests of and are clearly understood by their clients. They neither give nor receive any remuneration for referring clients for professional services. They contribute a portion of their services to work for which they receive little or no financial return.

e. Psychologists terminate a clinical or consulting relationship when it is reasonably clear that the consumer is not benefiting from it. They offer to help the consumer locate alternative sources of assistance.

Principle 7. Professional Relationships

Psychologists act with due regard for the needs, special competencies, and obligations of their colleagues in psychology and other professions. They respect the prerogatives and obligations of the institutions or organizations with which these other colleagues are associated.

a. Psychologists understand the areas of competence of related professions. They make full use of all the professional, technical, and administrative resources that serve the best interests of consumers. The absence of formal relationships with other professional workers does not relieve psychologists of the responsibility of securing for their clients the best possible professional service nor does it relieve them of the obligation to exercise foresight, diligence, and tact in obtaining the complementary or alternative assistance needed by clients.

b. Psychologists know and take into account the traditions and practices of other professional groups with whom they work and cooperate fully with such groups. If a person is receiving similar services from another professional, psychologists do not offer their own services directly to such a person. If a psychologist is contacted by a person who is already receiving similar services from another professional, the psychologist carefully considers that professional relationship and proceeds with caution and sensitivity to the therapeutic issues as well as the client's welfare. The psychologist discusses these issues with the client so as to minimize the risk of confusion and conflict.

c. Psychologists who employ or supervise other professionals or professionals in training accept the obligation to facilitate the further professional development of these individuals. They provide appropriate working conditions, timely evaluations, constructive consultation and experience opportunities.

d. Psychologists do not exploit their professional relationships with clients, supervisees, students, employees, or research participants sexually or otherwise. Psychologists do not condone nor engage in sexual harrassment. Sexual harrassment is defined as deliberate or repeated comments, gestures, or physical contacts of a sexual nature that are unwanted by the recipient.

e. In conducting research in institutions or organizations, psychologists secure appropriate authorization to conduct such research. They are aware of their obligation to future research workers and insure that host institutions receive adequate information about the research and proper acknowledgement of their contributions.

f. Publication credit is assigned to those who have contributed to a publication in proportion to their professional contribution. Major contributions of a professional character made by several persons to a common project are recognized by joint authorship, with the individual who made the principal contribution listed first. Minor contributions of a professional character and extensive clerical or similar nonprofessional assistance may be acknowledged in footnotes or in an introductory statement. Acknowledgment through specific citations is made for unpublished as well as published material that has directly influenced the research or writing. A psychologist who compiles and edits material of others for publication publishes the material in the name of the originating group, if appropriate, with his/her own name appearing as chairperson or editor. All contributors are to be acknowledged and named.

g. When psychologists know of an ethical violation by another psychologist, and it seems appropriate, they informally attempt to resolve the issue by bringing the behavior to the attention of the psychologist. If the misconduct is of a minor nature and/or appears to be due to lack of sensitivity, knowledge, or experience, such an informal solution is usually appropriate. Such informal corrective efforts are sensitive to any rights to confidentiality involved. If the violation does not seem amenable to an informal solution, or is of a more serious nature, psychologists bring it to the attention of the appropriate local, state, and/or national committee on professional ethics and conduct.

Principle 8. Assessment Techniques

In the development, publication, and utilization of psychological assessment techniques, psychologists make every effort to promote the welfare and best interests of the client. They guard against the misuse of assessment results. They respect the client's right to know the results, the interpretations made and the bases for their conclusions and recommendations. Psychologists make every effort to maintain the security of tests and other assessment techniques within limits of legal mandates. They strive to assure the appropriate use of assessment techniques by others.

a. In using assessment techniques, psychologists respect the right of clients to have a full explanation of the nature and purpose of the techniques in language that the client can understand, unless an explicit exception to this right has been agreed upon in advance. When the explanations are to be provided by others, the psychologist establishes procedures for insuring the adequacy of these explanations.

b. Psychologists responsible for the development and standardization of psychological tests and other assessment techniques utilize established scientific procedures and observe the relevant APA standards.

c. In reporting assessment results, psychologists indicate any reservations that exist regarding validity or reliability because of the circumstances of the assessment or the inappropriateness of the norms for the person tested. Psychologists strive to insure that the results of assessments and their interpretations are not misused by others.

d. Psychologists recognize that assessment results may become obsolete. They make every effort to avoid and prevent the misuse of obsolete measures.

e. Psychologists offering scoring and interpretation services are able to produce appropriate evidence for the validity of the programs and procedures used in arriving at interpretations. The public offering of an automated interpretation service is considered as a professional-to-professional consultation. The psychologist makes every effort to avoid misuse of assessment reports.

f. Psychologists do not encourage or promote the use of psychological assessment techniques by inappropriately trained or otherwise unqualified persons through teaching, sponsorship, or supervision.

Principle 9. Research with Human Participants

The decision to undertake research rests upon a considered judgment by the individual psychologist about how best to contribute to psychological science and human welfare. Having made the decision to conduct research, the psychologist considers alternative directions in which research energies and resources might be invested. On the basis of this consideration, the psychologist carries out the investigation with respect and concern for the dignity and welfare of the people who participate, and with cognizance of federal and state regulations and professional standards governing the conduct of research with human participants.

a. In planning a study, the investigator has the responsibility to make a careful evaluation of its ethical acceptability. To the extent that the weighing of scientific and human values suggests a compromise of any principle, the investigator incurs a correspondingly serious obligation to seek ethical advice and to observe stringent safeguards to protect the rights of human participants.

b. Considering whether a participant in a planned study will be a "subject at risk" or a "subject at minimal risk," according to recognized standards, is of primary ethical concern to the investigator.

c. The investigator always retains the responsibility for insuring ethical practice in research. The investigator is also responsible for the ethical treatment of research participants by collaborators, assistants, students, and employees, all of whom, however, incur similar obligations.

d. Except for minimal risk research, the investigator establishes a clear and fair agreement with the research participants, prior to their participation, that clarifies the obligations and responsibilities of each. The investigator has the obligation to honor all promises and commitments included in that agreement. The investigator informs the participant of all aspects of the research that might reasonably be expected to influence willingness to participate, and explains all other aspects of the research about which the participant inquires. Failure to make full disclosure prior to obtaining informed consent requires additional safeguards to protect the welfare and dignity of the research participant. Research with children or participants who have impairments which would limit understanding and/or communication, requires special safeguard procedures.

e. Methodological requirements of a study may make the use of concealment or deception necessary. Before conducting such a study, the investigator has a special responsibility to: (i) determine whether the use of such techniques is justified by the study's prospective scientific, educational, or applied value; (ii) determine whether alternative procedures are available that do not utilize concealment or deception; and (iii) insure that the participants are provided with sufficient explanation as soon as possible.

f. The investigator respects the individual's freedom to decline to participate in or to withdraw from the research at any time. The obligation to protect this freedom requires careful thought and consideration when the investigator is in a position of authority or influence over the participant. Such positions of authority include but are not limited to situations when research participation is required as part of employment or when the participant is a student, client, or employee of the investigator.

g. The investigator protects the participants from physical and mental discomfort, harm, and danger that may arise from research procedures. If risks of such consequences exist, the investigator informs the participant of that fact. Research procedures likely to cause serious or lasting harm to a participant are not used unless the failure to use these procedures might expose the participant to risk of greater harm, or unless the research has great potential benefit and fully informed and voluntary consent is obtained from each participant. The participant should be informed of procedures for contacting the investigator within a reasonable time period following participation should stress, potential harm, or related questions or concerns arise.

h. After the data are collected, the investigator provides the participant with information about the nature of the study and attempts to remove any misconceptions that may have arisen. Where scientific or humane values justify delaying or withholding information, the investigator incurs a special responsibility to monitor the research and to assure that there are no damaging consequences for the participant.

i. Where research procedures result in undesirable consequences for the individual participant, the investigator has the responsibility to detect and remove or correct these consequences, including long-term effects.

j. Information obtained about the research participant during the courses of an investigation is confidential unless otherwise agreed upon in advance. When the possibility exists that others may obtain access to such information, this possibility, together with the plans for protecting confidentiality, is explained to the participant as part of the procedure for obtaining informed consent.

Principle 10. Care and Use of Animals

An investigator of animal behavior strives to advance our understanding of basic behavioral principles and/or to contribute to the improvement of human health and welfare. In seeking these ends, the investigator insures the welfare of the animals and treats them humanely. Laws and regulations notwithstanding, the animal's immediate protection depends upon the scientist's own conscience.

a. The acquisition, care, use, and disposal of all animals is in compliance with current federal, state or provincial, and local laws and regulations.

b. A psychologist trained in research methods and experienced in the care of laboratory animals closely supervises all procedures involving animals and is responsible for insuring appropriate consideration of their comfort, health, and humane treatment.

c. Psychologists insure that all individuals using animals under their supervision have received explicit instruction in experimental methods and in the care, maintenance, and handling of the species being used. Responsibilities and activities of individuals participating in a research project are consistent with their respective competencies.

d. Psychologists make every effort to minimize discomfort, illness, and pain to the animals. A procedure subjecting animals to pain, stress, or privation is used only when an alternative procedure is unavailable and the goal is justified by its prospective scientific, educational, or applied value. Surgical procedures are performed under appropriate anesthesia; techniques to avoid infection and minimize pain are followed during and after surgery.

e. When it is appropriate that the animal's life be terminated, it is done rapidly and painlessly.

NOTE

1. Approved by the Council of Representatives (January 1981). These Ethical Principles apply to psychologists, to students of psychology, and others who do work of a psychological nature under the supervision of a psychologist. They are also intended for the guidance of nonmembers of the Association who are engaged in psychological research or practice.

Index